THE MISSION BIBLE COMMENTARY
✝

The Gospel According to Luke
& The Acts of the Apostles

PAUL BRUNS

The Gospel According to Luke
&
The Acts of the Apostles

The Mission Bible Commentary

A Set of Mission-Focused Commentaries
The New Testament Series

by

Rev. Dr. Paul C. Bruns

Published by Mission Nation Publishing, Inc.
Book Series

All Biblical quotations are taken from the English Standard Version (ESV)
and are used by permission

2016

ISBN 978-0-9966779-5-0

In over 30 years of hard-earned overseas mission experience (overseeing church growth and development in a relatively remote area, working with a translation team to produce a complete Bible, and 10 years in a seminary classroom), Rev. Dr. Bruns has gained keen insights into how God's mission takes place in various contexts. Thanks to Dr. Bruns for combining those insights with Biblical scholarship to look at the Gospel of Luke from the frame of missions and for making those results available to students of the Bible around the world.

Rev. Charles Tessaro. Since finishing the Eleme New Testament in 2002 and assisting with the consultant checking of the Ikwerre New Testament in 2010, Chuck and Karen are principally responsible for mentoring LBT's International Associates in Nigeria and training and consulting with various Old Testament translation teams.

I have studied through Dr. Bruns' Luke/Acts Commentaries. I worked in Nigeria on Bible translation with Kukele speakers. I know these commentaries will be a wonderful tool for all third-world translators and Bible students.

Rev. David N. Boettcher, M.Div., M.A. in Linguistics.

Hundreds, even thousands, of faithful pastors who serve in the villages, towns and cities across Africa have little or no access to solid Biblical resources as they prepare to teach and preach. With this commentary, Dr. Bruns seeks to change this trend by making his commentary available in formats that are easily obtainable anywhere. He also keeps pastors who speak English as a second or third language in mind by presenting the reader with many technical points of Scripture in non-technical English. Most importantly, the commentary constantly points the reader to the cross and seeks to engage today's believer in God's action of reaching out to people who are living and dying without knowing Jesus! In light of these reasons and many more, this commentary has significant potential for making an impact on global Christendom!

Rev. David Erber, Lutheran Church Missouri Synod area director for

West and Central Africa, David is responsible for ministering to other LCMS personnel serving in these parts of Africa. He leads a team of seminary instructors and church planters who serve Lutheran churches in Benin, Burkina Faso, Gambia, Ghana, Guinea, Ivory Coast, Liberia, Nigeria, Sierra Leone and Togo.

In his commentary on Luke, Dr. Bruns has combined his scholarship and mission experience of forty years to faithfully present the Gospel in a fresh way that is flavored by a different culture and perspective. With different cultures coming our way, we have much to learn.
Rev. Tyrus Miles, Pastor Emeritus, Zion Lutheran Church, Portland, Oregon.

Table of Contents

**General Introduction to
 The Mission Bible Commentary**

Introduction to the Gospel According to Luke & to the Acts of the Apostles

The Gospel According to Luke
- Chapter 1
- Chapter 2
- Chapter 3
- Chapter 4
- Chapter 5
- Chapter 6
- Chapter 7
- Chapter 8
- Chapter 9
- Chapter 10
- Chapter 11
- Chapter 12
- Chapter 13
- Chapter 14
- Chapter 15
- Chapter 16
- Chapter 17
- Chapter 18
- Chapter 19
- Chapter 20
- Chapter 21
- Chapter 22
- Chapter 23
- Chapter 24

The Book of Acts
    Chapter 1
    Chapter 2
    Chapter 3
    Chapter 4
    Chapter 5
    Chapter 6
    Chapter 7
    Chapter 8
    Chapter 9
    Chapter 10
    Chapter 11
    Chapter 12
    Chapter 13
    Chapter 14
    Chapter 15
    Chapter 16
    Chapter 17
    Chapter 18
    Chapter 19
    Chapter 20
    Chapter 21
    Chapter 22
    Chapter 23
    Chapter 24
    Chapter 25
    Chapter 26
    Chapter 27
    Chapter 28

The Mission Bible Commentary

General Introduction

The level of language that I used in this set of Commentaries
The level of language that I have used is very deliberate. Based on more than 30 years of experience as a foreign missionary, I have seen that the need for this type of mission-based commentaries is truly enormous, because the need extends far beyond the native-English speaking world. I have observed four things: **a)** First, in many areas of the world where the Christian Church is still relatively young, the majority of the church leaders have received only minimal training. Therefore, they have limited Bible knowledge. **b)** Secondly, the majority of these church leaders also lack Bible helps that they can use to teach others. **c)** Thirdly, of course, the sad result is that the members of these churches also lack Bible knowledge. **d)** And finally, of course, the vast majority of these people are also non-native speakers of English.

Therefore, although, as a Bible scholar, I have made every attempt to be as technically correct as possible, I have also made a very serious attempt at consistently controlling the level of language that I used, so that everyone will be able to understand. I used short sentences. I always made all of the participants in a sentence (subject, object and indirect object) as clear as possible. And I also avoided using the passive voice as much as possible. (Such as: an active verb: "I hit John." rather than a passive verb: "John was hit (by me).") However, these are only some of the most important adjustments that I made to the level of language I used. I tried, at all times, to focus on what non-native speakers of English would understand.

I, of course, hope that many Christians around the world will be eager to use this set of Commentaries. Therefore, I want to begin by saying that even though my Commentaries may not "sound" scholarly, I trust that no Bible scholar will be put-off by the level of language that I have used; they are also meant for you! I hope that everyone can benefit.

The purpose of this Set of Mission-Focused Commentaries
The main *purpose* of this set of mission focused Commentaries is to fill a large gap. At least to my limited knowledge, a set of Bible Commentaries that has this same mission focus does not exist. It may be that I am uninformed since I served the Church as a foreign missionary in Nigeria my entire career from 1964-1997; and I had very little contact with developments in the field of Biblical studies during that period of time. Yet, this gap surprises me, since the entire Bible reveals, in many beautiful and carefully planned details, how God's mission-heart has always been busy carrying out his gracious mission-plan to lost mankind. I have, therefore, attempted to describe in my Commentaries some aspect of God's mission-plan in every verse of the New Testament, beginning with the Gospel of Luke. And in addition, in the paragraphs that follow, I have also attempted to very briefly describe God's mission-plan in order to prepare you, my readers, for what you will see in my Commentaries.

All of Scripture reveals the mission-heart of God and his mission-plan.
God *is* love (1 Jn 4:16), and therefore, he has a most gracious mission-heart. And mankind is the crown of his creation and the main object of his love; therefore, he has always longed to live together with all human beings in perfect relationships in a perfect world forever (Ezek 18:32; 1 Tim 2:4). That was and still is his eternal plan.

However, he also created mankind with the freedom to choose whether they would return his love or not, since it would not be true love if he forced anyone to love him. And sadly, the first two persons that he made, Adam and Eve did soon make the wrong choice and chose to sin (Gen 3:1-14), and thus they also passed their sin on to all of their children, to all of mankind (Ps 51:5).

But God had, of course, foreknown this tragedy; and even before creation, his mission-heart had already compelled him to graciously create a mission-plan; therefore, he quickly called Adam and Eve to repentance and faith and promised that he would send someone to destroy the power of sin and death (Gen 3:15). And since he graciously never forces anyone to return his love, he depended on them to tell others the message that he graciously loves all people. Therefore, they should repent of their rebellion against him and return his love (Mt 5:14).

Furthermore, since his mission-heart is full of grace and great patience, God likewise made three choices: that he would not send his rescue immediately, that his Gospel would remain <u>unwritten</u> for many generations, and that he would allow his mission-plan to develop very slowly over many, many years as he patiently waited for those who are lost to repent (2 Pt 3:9).

However, after Adam and Eve bore children, the question is: did they tell them and others about God's love for them? The Old Testament gives us only a few clues that they must have done so. In spite of the fact that the early chapters of Genesis record many, many years of human history, we read about only a <u>few</u> people, such as Enoch (Gen 5:24) and Noah (Gen 6:9) who loved and worshipped God—but very few indeed!

Then, after many years, God continued to develop his mission-plan by calling Abraham to be the father of a new nation, the nation of <u>Israel</u>, whom he chose to be his special people (Deu 7:7). He graciously gave Abraham <u>faith</u> in himself, and blessed him and his descendants, <u>so that</u> they would be able to be a blessing to all other nations by telling them about God's love for them (Gen 12:1-3).

But then God, once again, allowed much time to pass and several generations of Israelites were born before he sent one of their own sons, Moses to be his first <u>prophet</u>. From that point on, God graciously began to reveal his holy Word to the prophets of Israel, so that they would <u>write down</u> his message of Law and Gospel and <u>proclaim</u> it to their people, as well as to all other nations (Deu 18:15). Generation after generation, he inspired the prophets to reveal more and more about the coming Messiah/Savior; and these revelations eventually formed the Old Testament.

But of course, since God had given his chosen people mission-hearts he still depended on them to go to the lost people of all nations to proclaim his holy Word. Unfortunately, however, Scripture records that, over many years, very few Israelites obeyed this command. And furthermore, some of his own people were very stubborn and persistently chose to reject him (Acts 13:46); and therefore, after being extremely patient with those who were stubborn, he ultimately had to reject them and eternally condemn them (Mt 13:13; Rom 9:13).

Then, *"when the fullness of time had come"* (Gal 4:4), God revealed the very heart of his mission-plan by sending his own Son, Jesus to be born into the nation of Israel as the only true God/man, in order to rescue all of lost mankind from sin (Lk 1:31-33). And then, after Jesus' ascension, God began to carry out the final stages of his mission-plan in a new era by beginning to create a *new* nation of Israel, the Church. He did so by sending his Holy Spirit to empower the mission-hearts of the faithful believers on Pentecost Day (Acts 1:8). Thus, the new Israel includes both a remnant of his chosen people from the old Israel as well as Gentiles from every nation on earth who trust in Jesus as their Lord (Rom 11:25-26).

Furthermore, the Holy Spirit then also continued to inspire men to write down his holy Word in the New Testament, so that he can use both the Old and the New testaments to strengthen his Church, in order to prepare them to go and tell the Gospel to the lost people of all nations (Rom 10:17; Gen 12:1-3). And this last part of his mission-plan will not be complete until the Lord Jesus returns on the Last Day. And on that Last Day, God will finally fulfill his original plan by bringing together his new nation of Israel in order to live with them in a perfect new world forever (Rev 21:1-2).

The Bible also reveals many mission principles
This careful examination of the Bible with mission-focused eyes has also produced a list of mission principles in two categories: mission messages and mission imperatives. They are defined as follows: **a)** In numerous verses throughout the Bible, the Lord of the mission has given

us Christians very clear Law and Gospel <u>Mission Messages</u> for us to proclaim; and they are labelled (M. M.) in these Commentaries. **b)** And in many verses throughout the Bible, he has also given us Christians very clear <u>Mission Imperatives</u> for us to obey; and they are labelled (M. I.) in these Commentaries.

When formulating each new mission message or imperative, every effort was made to be faithful to the wording of the text at hand so that it is clear that this verse is the primary source of the new mission message or imperative. No wording is brought in from other passages of the Bible even though they may obviously be parallel passages.

The two categories:

Name	Label	Definition
Mission Messages	M. M.	<u>Mission Messages</u> that Christians proclaim
Mission Imperatives	M. I.	<u>Mission Imperatives</u> that Christians obey

The following examples illustrate how mission messages and imperatives are referenced in these commentaries:

First occurrences:
a) In the comments on (Lk 1:1), a new mission message appears thus: M. M. Lk 1:1: Jesus earned salvation for <u>all</u> lost people from <u>every</u> nation on earth.
b) Since one <u>part</u> of a single verse may reveal one mission message and another *part* of the same verse may reveal a second mission message, the first new mission message may appear thus: M. M. Ro 8:29a: God the Father…And the second new mission message may appear thus: M. M. Ro 8:29b: Because God…

Other references:
a) In the comments on all other verses in the Bible, the mission message from (Lk 1:1) is referenced thus: ([1]M. M. Lk 1:1). And the principle is

printed out fully as a footnote at the bottom of the page.
b) In the comments on one verse, <u>two</u> references, one to a mission message and one to a mission imperative may appear thus: ([2]M. M. Lk 1:1 & [3]M. I. Lk 4:35).
c) However, in the comments on <u>one</u> verse, if there are <u>two</u> references to two mission messages, the M. M. is not repeated thus: (M. M. Lk 1:1 & [4]Ac 13:46). Likewise, if there are <u>two</u> references to two mission imperatives, the M. I. is not repeated thus: (M. I. Lk 4:35 & [5]Ro 12:1).

(Note how the principles are listed in the footnotes below.)

(All Bible quotations are from the English Standard Version (ESV), published by Crossway.)

Rev. Dr. Paul C. Bruns
2016

---

[1] M. M. Lk 1:1: Jesus earned salvation for *all* lost people from *every* nation on earth.

[2] M. M. Lk 1:1: Jesus earned salvation for *all* lost people from *every* nation on earth.

[3] M. I. Lk 4:35: Christians should view every person as a whole person, and show him compassion by caring for *both* his physical and spiritual needs as they go on their mission.

[4] M. M. Ac 13:46: As he did with the old Israel, God *first of all* strengthens the faith of the new Israel, the Church with his Word and Sacraments, so that they can go and witness to the lost people of all nations.

[5] M. I. Ro 12:1: Christians should respond to God's mercy by offering their total bodies as living sacrifices to their Lord, which will please him only because they offer them with grateful hearts.

The Gospel According to Luke
&
The Acts of the Apostles

Introduction

Luke was probably the <u>author</u> of both the Gospel According to Luke and also the Acts of the Apostles:
The following evidence points to the most likely conclusion that a man named <u>Luke</u> was the <u>author</u> of <u>both</u> the Gospel that bears his name and also of the Acts of the Apostles.
1) While the author's name is mentioned nowhere in either book, much evidence points to a man named Luke.
2) The author says that he wrote both this Gospel (Lk 1:3) and also the Acts of the Apostles (Ac 1:1).
3) The language and structure of both books confirm this.
4) The two books are addressed to the same person, Theophilus.
5) The Acts of the Apostles refers to this Gospel (Ac 1:1).
6) The author of the Acts of the Apostles uses the plural pronoun *"we"* in several sections: (Ac 16:10-17; 20:5-21:18; 27:1-28:16), which clearly indicates that a man named Luke was Paul's companion when he described these events.
7) Both books have the same mission theme; and we see this theme in Jesus' own words in both books. In the Gospel According to Luke, Jesus said, *"The Son of Man came to seek and to save the lost"* (Lk 19:10). And in the Acts of the Apostles, Jesus commanded his disciples: *"You will be witnesses for me in Jerusalem, in all of Judea and Samaria, and to the ends of the earth"* (Ac 1:8). Furthermore, we see this mission theme fully developed throughout the Acts of the Apostles. In Acts chapters 1-12, Luke reports that Peter's main mission was to the <u>Jews</u>; and then in chapters 13-28, Luke dramatically shifts his focus to Paul's four missionary journeys to the <u>Gentiles</u> (Gal 2:7-8).
8) Luke began both books in a similar manner. He began his Gospel by saying, *"Dear Theophilus: Many people have done their best to write a report of the things that have taken place among us...And so, Your*

Excellency...I thought it would be good to write an orderly account for you" (Lk 1:1-3). Then in the Acts of the Apostles (Ac 1:1-2), he continues his narrative by saying, *"Dear Theophilus: In my first book I wrote about all the things that Jesus did and taught..."*

9) Luke connected his two books together in a close <u>time</u> sequence. He ends his Gospel by saying in (Lk 24:52-53), *"They worshiped him and went back into Jerusalem, filled with great joy, and spent all their time in the Temple giving thanks to God."* And he began his second book as if only a brief period of time had passed by saying in (Ac 1:1), *"Dear Theophilus: In my first book I wrote about all the things that Jesus did and taught from the time he began his work until the day he was taken up to heaven."* It may, indeed, be that there was only a short time that lapsed between the two books.

10) And finally, there is some evidence that, for a period of time, the two books were distributed together as <u>one</u> volume among the Christian churches in the Roman Empire. (And this is one of the main reasons why I am likewise joining the Commentary of the two books together yet today.)

<u>Who</u> was Luke?
Who then was Luke?

1) Luke was most probably a <u>Gentile</u> and <u>not</u> a Jew. While some scholars insist that he was a Jew, just like most (or all?) of the other Biblical authors, at least two pieces of evidence indicate that he was, in fact, a Gentile. First of all, the author addressed both his Gospel and the Acts of the Apostles to a <u>Gentile</u> named Theophilus (1:3; Ac 1:1). While this is certainly not conclusive evidence that Luke was also a Gentile, it does not seem reasonable that a Jewish author would have done so. The second piece of evidence is much clearer in (Col 4:10-11, 14), where Paul writes in verses 10-11, *"Mark the cousin of Barnabas...and Jesus who is called Justus. These are the only men of the circumcision [Jews] among my fellow workers for the kingdom of God."* And then, in verse 14, Paul mentions that Luke is one of his fellow workers. While this is not internal evidence in the Gospel According to Luke, it is very clear external Biblical evidence.

2) Luke clearly says that he was <u>not</u> an eyewitness of Jesus' life and

mission, since he wrote his Gospel after *"having followed all things closely for some time past"* (Lk 1:3) from *"those who from the beginning were eyewitnesses and ministers of the word have delivered them to us"* (Lk 1:2).
3) Luke was a physician or a doctor, who was well educated in Greek culture (Col 4:14).
4) As noted above, Luke was a loyal and frequent companion of Paul, *"the apostle to the Gentiles"* (Ac 9:15).
5) And finally, Luke was likewise a very diligent student of Paul's theology. Examples of this abound in both of his books; however, we perhaps see the clearest example in the manner in which Luke began his Gospel. He explains what the main focus of his Gospel was: *"it seemed good to me also…to write an orderly account for you, most excellent Theophilus"* (Lk 1:3), concerning *"the things that have been accomplished among us [by our Lord Jesus]"* (Lk 1:1). Luke focused on the person and work of Jesus, just as Paul likewise says very clearly in (1 Cor 2:2), *"I decided to know nothing among you except Jesus Christ and him crucified."*

The recipients of the Gospel According to Luke and the Acts of the Apostles:
Luke wrote his Gospel as well as the Acts of the Apostles to three different audiences: to a man named Theophilus, to his fellow Christians, and to all unbelievers.
1) Luke explicitly addressed his Gospel (Lk 1:3) and the Acts of the Apostles (Ac 1:1) to a man named Theophilus. Theophilus was: **a)** A Roman official (i.e., a Gentile) or at least of a person of high position and wealth. **b)** He was possibly also Luke's patron who was responsible for seeing that Luke's writings were copied and distributed.
2) Secondly however, it's likewise immediately apparent in both books that Luke also intended them to be read by a much wider audience. He was also writing to all Christians who were living at that time. When Luke said in (Lk 1:1) *"the things that have been accomplished among us,"* he was certainly including all Christians. He was not only talking about Theophilus and himself. Likewise, when Jesus said in (Ac 1:8), *"you will receive power when the Holy Spirit has come upon you, and*

you will be my witnesses," Luke obviously understood that Jesus was commanding all Christians to go. Luke was, no doubt, very well aware of the fact that very few Christians knew the true story of the life of Jesus and of the beginnings of the Christian Church. They were scattered in small churches all over the Roman Empire, and many of them were suffering persecution. Therefore, it would have been very encouraging for them to hear a reminder of what their dear Lord had accomplished for them, and also to learn that they were not alone in their mission to the world.

3) And finally, Luke certainly wanted all unbelievers, both Jews and Gentiles alike, to also read both books. Luke wanted all people of all nations to understand at least three things: **a)** They too are *"the lost"* people who need to be *"saved"* (Lk 19:10). **b)** In his rich grace, Jesus came to fulfill everything that is written in the Bible, in order to *"seek and save"* them (Lk 22:37; 24:44). **c)** And therefore, that Jesus also graciously commanded all Christians to go into the entire world to proclaim the Good News about him (Lk 24:47; Ac 1:8).

Luke's unique perspective:
The evidence that Luke was a Gentile therefore begs the question: Was any other book of Scripture written by a Gentile? And all of the evidence that we have to date indicates a clear, "No!" All other authors were almost certainly Jews. (While we may never be certain who wrote some of the books, such as the Epistle to the Hebrews, the internal evidence in all of these uncertain cases points overwhelmingly to a Jewish author.) Therefore, we should not be surprised to discover, on closer examination, that the Holy Spirit inspired the Gentile, Luke to write a very unique perspective in his Gospel about our Lord's mission to the world. And obviously, he had this same unique perspective in the Acts of the Apostles concerning the way in which the apostles and the entire early Christian Church obeyed their Lord's command to carry his Good News to all nations.

We see this in at least three different ways.
1) In his Gospel, Luke demonstrates a deep appreciation of the fact that Jesus had to be a Jew in order to fulfil the whole Law for *all* of his

fellow human beings, because it would have been completely impossible for him to do so as a Gentile. <u>Three</u> times he was careful to record Jesus' own words: *"Today this Scripture has been fulfilled in your hearing"* (Lk 4:21). *"I tell you that this Scripture must be <u>fulfilled in me</u>"* (Lk 22:37). And *"everything written about <u>me</u> in the Law of Moses and the Prophets and the Psalms must be <u>fulfilled</u>"* (Lk 24:44). Thus, Luke embraced the fact that, in his rich grace, his dear Lord Jesus chose to be a Jew for *his* sake and for the sake of the people from <u>all</u> nations on earth because all are lost. And therefore, Luke describes his Lord's human nature as a true *Jew* in far greater detail than any other Gospel writer, especially in chapters 1 and 2.

2) Luke also used a type of <u>central theme</u> that he took from a statement of Jesus in (Lk 19:10), *"For the Son of Man came to seek and to save the lost,"* in order to emphasize throughout his Gospel that this wonderful Good News about Jesus is a <u>universal</u> message. Therefore, he emphasizes from many different vantage points that *"the lost"* people who his Lord was (and still is) graciously *"seeking and saving"* are people from <u>every</u> nation on earth (Lk 4:24-27; 6:17; 7:10; 10:13-14; 10:33; 17:16-18; 19:9).

3) And finally, it is, of course, not surprising that Luke continues to use this same central theme in the Acts of the Apostles. He modified the form of his theme, but the <u>universal</u> meaning is the same. Luke first strikes the same theme by, once again, using Jesus' own Words in (Ac 1:8), *"You will be my witnesses in Jerusalem and in all Judea and Samaria, and to <u>the end of the earth</u>."* Furthermore, in Acts chapters 1-12, Luke wrote that Peter's main mission was to the <u>Jews</u>; and then in chapters 13-28, Luke dramatically shifts his focus to Paul's four missionary journeys to the <u>Gentiles</u> (Gal 2:7-8). Therefore, the evidence is very clear that <u>only</u> a Gentile author could have expressed such a <u>unique</u> universal view of the Good News about Jesus. No Jewish author could have done it. Inspired by the Holy Spirit, the Gentile Luke expressed this universal view very clearly and beautifully in his Gospel as well as in his Acts of the Apostles.

Rev. Dr. Paul C. Bruns
2016

The Gospel According to Luke

Chapter 1

Dedication to Theophilus 1:1-4

1:1　*Inasmuch as many have undertaken to compile a narrative of the things that have been accomplished among us,*
1:2　*just as those who from the beginning were eyewitnesses and ministers of the word have delivered them to us,*
1:3　*it seemed good to me also, having followed all things closely for some time past, to write an orderly account for you, most excellent Theophilus,*
1:4　*that you may have certainty concerning the things you have been taught.*

1:1 (1) The phrase, *"the things that have been accomplished"* in verse 1, refers to everything that Jesus did in his earthly life in order to *"accomplish"* or fulfill all of God's promises (18:31; 2 Cor 1:20), so that he could: **a)** *"save the lost"* people of all nations, **b)** and also fulfill his mission of *"seeking the lost"* (vs. 45, 55; 4:21; 19:10). Luke thus faithfully recorded these things that Jesus did in the following chapters. **2)** Since (as the best evidence indicates) Luke is writing to a fellow Gentile, Theophilus, the word *"us"* in the phrase *"among us"* strongly implies *"among us [Gentiles]."* Luke is here telling his fellow Gentiles the heart of the Gospel—that Jesus did everything to fulfill God's Laws *"among us"*—that is among all people of all nations, so that he could be the only person who could and did earn eternal life for all of his brothers and sisters (Lev 18:5; Ezek 20:11). Furthermore, he wanted all of his brothers and sisters of all nations, and not just Jesus' own nation, the Jews, to be witnesses to how he perfectly obeyed his Father's will. Jesus may have lived his life and carried out the vast majority of his mission in the land of Israel, apart from brief excursions into Samaria (Jn 4) and the region of the Gerasenes (8:26), but his life of perfect obedience was *not* hidden away where only one nation could see it (Mt 3:15; 5:17). What tremendous Gospel this is! Jesus earned salvation for everyone! He truly came to *"seek and to save [all] people who are lost"* (19:10)! Thus, already in verse 1 of chapter 1, Luke gave Theophilus and all of his readers a very clear hint that the tremendous Gospel of Jesus is a universal Gospel message. It's the first new mission message. M. M. Lk 1:1: Jesus earned salvation for all lost people from every nation on earth. **1:2 (1)** Those who followed Jesus and *"were [daily] eyewitnesses"* of his ministry were: the twelve disciples and some women (8:1-3). All of the people in this inner circle of his disciples were undoubtedly all Jews since (as we shall soon see) Jesus' mission was first to the Jews. The Holy Spirit used what they personally saw and heard to create faith in their hearts, and moved them, as faithful servants, to proclaim to others the Gospel that they themselves had heard ([6]M. M. Mt 5:14). **2)** Luke says that these people who witnessed God's saving action *"have delivered them [the narrative of his life] to us [Gentiles]."* Note two important things: **a)** First of all, in this way, Luke acknowledges that his faith depended on other Christians telling him about Jesus. God's gracious mission-heart has always compelled him to never force his love on anyone; therefore, he has always used Christians to proclaim the Gospel message, so that his Spirit can use his Word to create faith in repentant hearts (Rom 10:17). Thus, the Holy Spirit has always planned that the Gospel about Jesus should not remain hidden with those who were *"eyewitnesses"* (v 2) of Jesus' ministry. The Gospel is the only tool that the Spirit uses to continue to create faith in many who hear it (v 2; 24:48; [7]M. M. Ro 10:17a). **b)** Secondly, everything that Luke implied in verse 1 when he said, *"among us"* obviously applies here as well. A key element of God's call to Abraham in (Gen 12:1-3) was his promise to bless Abraham, so that he and his children would pass these blessings on to all other nations by telling them the Gospel message. God gave the nation of Israel this awesome responsibility; and he therefore, depended on them to share the Gospel message with other nations and to not keep it for themselves (20:9-19). **3)** What, then, were some of the ways that Jesus' disciples (his witnesses) passed on what they had witnessed? They did so: **a)** on two missionary journeys to Jewish towns (9:1-6; 10:1-16), **b)** to Gentiles on Pentecost (Ac 2:5-12; Ps 45:17), **c)** to Paul in

Jerusalem (Gal 1:18), **d)** in all four Gospels, **e)** and Paul passed it on to Luke (and other Jews and Gentiles) during their mission journeys. In this way Jesus continued to "seek...the lost" through his disciples ([8]M. M. Lk 1:1).

1:3 Why did Luke *"write an orderly account"* (v 3) for Theophilus about Jesus' mission? He was obeying his Lord's call to be his witness, the same call that he gives to everyone who trusts in him. As Jesus' twelve disciples faithfully witnessed to Jesus' life and mission, so likewise Luke in turn faithfully passed the Gospel on to Theophilus, a fellow Gentile and to other Gentiles through his account in this Gospel, and then also through the book of Acts ([9]M. M. Mt 5:14).

1:4 Jesus himself, his twelve disciples, and all of his disciples who followed him were witnessing to the truth about Jesus; nevertheless, there undoubtedly also were, at the same time, numerous false reports about Jesus that were being spread by unbelievers. Thus God's Word was standing in sharp contrast to Satan's lies as a witness to the Truth for all who heard it. It was *"profitable for teaching, for reproof, for correction, and for training in righteousness"* (2 Tim 3:16; Jn 20:30-31). What Jesus did was all "certain" (v 4) because it was all historical facts, God acting in history; and it was not myths or false stories that Satan had invented and passed on to human beings. Jesus' many disciples believed in him because they saw with their own eyes all of the things that he did; then they also witnessed the historical fact that God had raised him from the dead. Therefore, it's obvious that only a true message was, at that time and still is, worth passing on to others (19:10; [10]M. M. Lk 13:24).

Birth of John the Baptist Foretold 1:5-25

1:5 *In the days of Herod, king of Judea, there was a priest named Zechariah, of the division of Abijah. And he had a wife from the daughters of Aaron, and her name was Elizabeth.*

1:6 *And they were both righteous before God, walking blamelessly in all the commandments and statutes of the Lord.*

1:7 *But they had no child, because Elizabeth was barren, and both were advanced in years.*

1:8 *Now while he was serving as priest before God when his division was on duty,*

1:9 *according to the custom of the priesthood, he was chosen by lot to enter the temple of the Lord and burn incense.*

1:10 *And the whole multitude of the people were praying outside at the hour of incense.*

1:11 *And there appeared to him an angel of the Lord standing on the right side of the altar of incense.*

1:12 *And Zechariah was troubled when he saw him, and fear fell upon him.*

1:13 *But the angel said to him, "Do not be afraid, Zechariah, for your prayer has been heard, and your wife Elizabeth will bear you a son, and you shall call his name John.*

1:14 *And you will have joy and gladness, and many will rejoice at his birth,*

1:15 *for he will be great before the Lord. And he must not drink wine or strong drink, and he will be filled with the Holy Spirit, even from his mother's womb.*

1:16 *And he will turn many of the children of Israel to the Lord their God,*

1:17 *and he will go before him in the spirit and power of Elijah, to turn the hearts of the fathers to the children, and the disobedient to the wisdom of the just, to make ready for the Lord a people prepared."*

1:18 *And Zechariah said to the angel, "How shall I know this? For I am an old man, and my wife is advanced in years."*

1:19 *And the angel answered him, "I am Gabriel. I stand in the presence of God, and I was sent to speak to you and to bring you this good news.*

1:20 *And behold, you will be silent and unable to speak until the day that these things take place, because you did not believe my words, which will be fulfilled in their time."*

1:21 *And the people were waiting for Zechariah, and they were wondering at his delay in the temple.*

1:22 *And when he came out, he was unable to speak to them, and*

> 1:23 *they realized that he had seen a vision in the temple. And he kept making signs to them and remained mute.*
> 1:23 *And when his time of service was ended, he went to his home.*
> 1:24 *After these days his wife Elizabeth conceived, and for five months she kept herself hidden, saying,*
> 1:25 *"Thus the Lord has done for me in the days when he looked on me, to take away my reproach among people."*

1:5-25 In his own gracious timing, God began to carry out the central act of his plan of salvation by sending John, in order to baptize and prepare his chosen people to receive his own beloved Son (Gal 4:4-5). This preparation was essential in order to complete God's whole plan to rescue the lost from every nation on earth (19:10).

1:7 To clearly demonstrate that the birth of John was God's own <u>gracious</u> action in human history, he chose to give a child to a <u>barren</u> woman, Elizabeth and to parents who also were <u>too old</u> to conceive a child. If John had been born at a normal childbearing time in their lives no one would have seen God's gracious action in his birth. Yet it's obvious that many Jews still missed seeing these clear signs that God was beginning to carry out his plan of salvation (19:10).

1:14, 16 The many who will *"rejoice"* in verse 14 certainly includes both Jews and Gentiles in view of what verse 1 says, *"the things that have been accomplished among us [Gentiles]."* However, as a faithful son of Abraham, John's <u>first</u> duty was to call his fellow Jews to repentance and faith (v 80; Rom 1:16), but he also faithfully made the same call to any Gentiles whom he encountered (3:14). God did not modify this mission message until after Pentecost Day ([11]M. M. Ac 13:46). Many people of all generations have *"rejoiced"* that he was born and continue to *"rejoice"* that God has kept all of his promises. The Lord of the mission continues to carry out his mission through his Church yet today (19:10).

1:16-17 (1) In view of the fact that Luke was a disciple of Paul, it's very possible that, in verses 16-17, Luke was thinking of *"the <u>new</u> Israel,"* which now includes Christians of all nations. Paul later wrote in (Rom 11:25-26), *"I want you to understand this mystery, brothers: a partial* *hardening has come upon Israel, until the fullness of the Gentiles has come in. And in this way all Israel will be saved..."* **2)** Also note that verses 16-17 comprise Luke's first direct reference to the central theme of his Gospel (19:10), *"For the Son of Man came to seek and to save the lost."*

1:18 Zechariah's question in verse 18, *"How shall I know this?"* seems to be similar to Mary's question in verse 34, *"How will this be, since I am a virgin?"* However, Mary apparently asked in <u>faith</u>, but Zechariah was, for a time, doubting God (Mt 14:31), since he was asking for a sign. And the angel clarifies this by continuing in verse 20, *"But you have not believed my message."* His question was unfortunately typical of some of the Jews of his day who were seeking signs (Mt 12:38; 1 Cor 1:22). Asking for a sign or miracle is demanding that God prove who he is by showing that he can meet that person's needs when and how <u>he</u> wants God to do it; it is therefore a selfish and sinful attitude ([12]M. I. Lk 11:10).

Birth of Jesus Foretold 1:26-38

1:26 *In the sixth month the angel Gabriel was sent from God to a city of Galilee named Nazareth,*
1:27 *to a virgin betrothed to a man whose name was Joseph, of the house of David. And the virgin's name was Mary.*
1:28 *And he came to her and said, "Greetings, O favored one, the Lord is with you!"*
1:29 *But she was greatly troubled at the saying, and tried to discern what sort of greeting this might be.*
1:30 *And the angel said to her, "Do not be afraid, Mary, for you have found favor with God.*
1:31 *And behold, you will conceive in your womb and bear a son, and you shall call his name Jesus.*
1:32 *He will be great and will be called the Son of the Most High. And the Lord God will give to him the throne of his father David,*
1:33 *and he will reign over the house of Jacob forever, and of his*

> *kingdom there will be no end."*
> 1:34 *And Mary said to the angel, "How will this be, since I am a virgin?"*
> 1:35 *And the angel answered her, "The Holy Spirit will come upon you, and the power of the Most High will overshadow you; therefore the child to be born will be called holy--the Son of God.*
> 1:36 *And behold, your relative Elizabeth in her old age has also conceived a son, and this is the sixth month with her who was called barren.*
> 1:37 *For nothing will be impossible with God."*
> 1:38 *And Mary said, "Behold, I am the servant of the Lord; let it be to me according to your word." And the angel departed from her.*

1:26-27 We see in verses 26-27 that the heavenly Father graciously chose to send his Son, Jesus to be born in <u>humble</u> circumstances. Luke says that *"the angel Gabriel was sent from God to a city of Galilee named Nazareth to a <u>virgin</u> betrothed to a man whose name was Joseph."* Nazareth was certainly a humble town, and Mary was a humble virgin betrothed to a humble carpenter named Joseph. Even though Jesus was also the King of kings and he will, one day soon, *"reign over the house of Jacob forever"* (v 33), God graciously chose that he should be born in humble circumstances. He did not choose the capital city of Jerusalem where Jesus would be raised with honor as a prince; rather, he wanted people from every nation on earth to see his <u>grace</u>. It's another new mission message. M. M. Lk 1:26: The heavenly Father sent his Son, Jesus to be born as a true human being and live in <u>humble</u> circumstances, so that everyone from every nation on earth would see his <u>grace</u>.

1:27 (1) Note that Luke, a Gentile does not try to hide the fact that Jesus was a true *Jew* born into a Jewish family. Verse 27 says that *"a virgin betrothed to a man whose name was Joseph, of the <u>house of David</u>."* And verse 31 says very clearly, *"you will conceive in your womb and bear a son, and you shall call his name <u>Jesus</u>."* Some see evidence in verse 27 that, together with Joseph, Mary was <u>also</u> a descendant of King

David, but that is by no means conclusive. What is clear is that Jesus was from the royal line of King David because he was the legal, adopted son of Joseph and hence verse 32 says, *"The Lord God will give to him the throne of his father David"* (3:23). Luke is careful to make it clear that Jesus was indeed not only a Jew but also from the royal line of King David (v 32; 19:10). Jesus was not only a true human being, he was also a true Jew so that, he could become the King of kings in his heavenly kingdom forever. Verse 33 says that *"of his kingdom there will be no end."* It is a new mission message. M. M. Lk 1:27: Jesus had to be born as a true human being and as a true Jew in order to become the King of kings in his heavenly kingdom forever. **2)** Some Africans I have known have been openly offended that Jesus was a Jew; and they therefore wrongly assumed that they could dismiss Jesus as irrelevant since he was not an African. Likewise, some artists in past centuries have made Jesus appear to be Chinese or Indian or African in an apparent attempt to make him "their own Jesus." (As an example of this, I have a wooden crucifix in my office made by an African artist. He made the cross out of pale wood, but Jesus he carved out of ebony.) I have no doubt that Luke would say that, while these artists may be devout, they are wrong both historically and also theologically. He would say that "Jesus is "my Jesus" because he was a Jew; he had to be a Jew so that he could fulfill all righteousness for me and for all nations" (19:10; Lev 18:5). **3)** Although the name Jesus was a fairly common name at that time, Jesus' name had a very literal meaning here of, *"He saves"* (Mt 1:21; 19:10). As such, he was true God; and everything else that the angel Gabriel said about him in verses 31-38 emphasizes this same truth ([13]M. M. Lk 1:35 & [14]Ro 1:16b).

1:28 It was purely by his rich grace that God chose Mary and called her, *"O favored one"* (v 28) to be the mother of his Son. And in faith, she acknowledged her unworthiness, as she says in verse 38, *"Behold, I am the servant of the Lord."* And also, very significantly, she confessed that she was also sinful by saying that she needed her son to be her own Savior. She says in verse 47, *"my spirit rejoices in God my Savior."* By grace alone, God chose Mary for this unique task; just as, even before he created the world, he likewise chose a remnant of the nation of Israel together with some people from *every* nation on earth to be his own forever (Rom 9:23-24).

1:32-33, 35 (1) Verses 32-33, 35 emphasize again and again that Jesus was also true God. *"He will be great and will be called the Son of the Most High. And the Lord God will give to him the throne of his father David, and he will reign over the house of Jacob forever, and of his kingdom there will be no end"* (vs 32-33)...*the child to be born will be called holy—the Son of God"* (v 35). No other human being has ever been both true man and true God. (Note that the phrase, *"the Son of God"* is a technical term in the Hebrew language that does not mean "a descendant of God," but it conveys the deep mystery that Jesus has all the characteristics of God, yet he is also a true human being. It is beyond all human understanding.) Jesus had to be both God and man because his blood had to be our human blood and also God's own holy blood in order to be a worthy sacrifice for all of mankind (Heb 13:12, 20-21). God's plan to save all of mankind from sin was perfect in every aspect (19:10; [15]M. M. Ac 4:28). It's a new mission message. M. M. Lk 1:35: Jesus had to be born as true God, in order to rescue all of mankind from sin.

1:34 As was noted at verse 18, Mary's question in verse 34 seems to be similar to Zechariah's question; however, she did not demand a sign as he did. She asked in faith in verse 45 about something that was outside of her past experience. It was also important for God's plan that the mother of Jesus should have humble faith in her son because it would be tested repeatedly and most severely.

1:37 While both John's and Jesus' conceptions may seem impossible for feeble human beings to understand, both were, of course, not only very easy for God, but they fit perfectly into his plan of salvation (19:10). The plan he chose in both cases showed his rich grace and love to the entire human race. Since *"nothing will be impossible"* for him (v 37), he obviously could have solved the problem of sin in an entirely different way. Because mankind obviously deserved it, he could have, in his justice, destroyed the universe that he had made, and created an entirely new world. But that would have been contrary to his nature, since *"The LORD is good to all, and his mercy is over all that he has made"* (Ps

145:9; [16]M. M. Ro 1:19). Therefore, such a plan was actually from this point of view *"impossible"* for him to even consider ([17]M. M. Lk 1:26). **1:38, 47 (1)** Mary trusted in God's grace for her because she said in verse 38, *"Behold, I am the servant of the Lord; let it be to me according to your word."* And she also said in verse 47, *"My spirit rejoices in God my Savior."* She did not trust in her blood relationship to Jesus, even though no other person ever had such a close blood relationship to him. Instead, only a faith relationship with Jesus saves all people of all nations (8:21; [18]M. M. Ro 3:26). Therefore, Jews have no advantage over Gentiles; all are equal under God's rich grace by faith in the same Lord Jesus. In sharp contrast to Mary, many Jews of her day sinned by trusting in their blood relationship to Abraham (3:8), and not by trusting in God's grace ([19]M. M. Lk 13:24). **2)** Furthermore, the heavenly Father gave Mary (and Joseph) two very unique and extremely important assignments: **a)** to faithfully care for the physical needs their child, **b)** and also to faithfully obey all of God's Laws on his behalf, since, especially when he was a helpless baby, he was obviously unable to do so himself (2:23). It's equally obvious that they did nothing to earn any merit before God by their actions since they did them in faith. They would only have done these very vital tasks if they had had faith in God and trusted in him to carry out his plan of salvation by using them. God has never graciously given any other parents such a completely unique set of vocations so that they could carry out their mission to Jesus, to their whole family, and ultimately to the lost from every nation on earth. God's grace is so rich and amazing ([20]M. M. Mt 2:6)! And it's likewise amazing that Luke also recognized these truths, as we see so frequently and clearly in his account.

Mary Visits Elizabeth 1:39-45

1:39 *In those days Mary arose and went with haste into the hill country, to a town in Judah,*
1:40 *and she entered the house of Zechariah and greeted Elizabeth.*
1:41 *And when Elizabeth heard the greeting of Mary, the baby*

1:42   *leaped in her womb. And Elizabeth was filled with the Holy Spirit,*
1:42   *and she exclaimed with a loud cry, "Blessed are you among women, and blessed is the fruit of your womb!*
1:43   *And why is this granted to me that the mother of my Lord should come to me?*
1:44   *For behold, when the sound of your greeting came to my ears, the baby in my womb leaped for joy.*
1:45   *And blessed is she who believed that there would be a fulfillment of what was spoken to her from the Lord."*

Mary's Song of Praise: The Magnificat 1:46-56

1:46   *And Mary said, "My soul magnifies the Lord,*
1:47   *and my spirit rejoices in God my Savior,*
1:48   *for he has looked on the humble estate of his servant. For behold, from now on all generations will call me blessed;*
1:49   *for he who is mighty has done great things for me, and holy is his name.*
1:50   *And his mercy is for those who fear him from generation to generation.*
1:51   *He has shown strength with his arm; he has scattered the proud in the thoughts of their hearts;*
1:52   *he has brought down the mighty from their thrones and exalted those of humble estate;*
1:53   *he has filled the hungry with good things, and the rich he has sent away empty.*
1:54   *He has helped his servant Israel, in remembrance of his mercy,*
1:55   *as he spoke to our fathers, to Abraham and to his offspring forever."*
1:56   *And Mary remained with her about three months and returned to her home.*

1:50 God has made and continues to make every human being from our first parents, Adam and Eve. Who can even begin to count how many people he has made? Yet, as verse 50 says, *"his mercy is for those who fear him from generation to generation."* He made each and every one in his mercy and love, and he longs for each and every one from every nation to turn to him in faith and be his own forever (1 Tim 2:3-4, 19:10). However, since God creates all of mankind with a free will, Adam and Eve soon made the wrong choices by disobeying him. But God had, of course, foreknown this tragedy; and even before creation, his mission-heart had already compelled him to graciously create a mission-plan. Therefore, he graciously sent his own beloved Son Jesus as our Savior (1:47; Gen 3:6; [21]M. M. Lk 1:1).

1:51 In his grace, Jesus did not come to earth in order to punish any of his brothers and sisters, as (Jn 3:17) says so clearly, *"God did not send his Son into the world to be its judge, but to be its savior."* Nevertheless, in great sadness, and after great patience, God must eventually condemn to hell for all eternity some people *"the proud"* (v 51) who persist in their rebellion against him (Rom 9:22-23; [22]M. M. Ro 9:15).

1:51-53 God does not discriminate between any people he has made. He offers his grace to all; but unfortunately not all people cling to his grace in faith. Some people, either because of pride or because they love money and power, become blind to their need for his grace. But those who are poor and humble in heart (Mt 5:3) have only God's grace to cling to; and in his grace, Jesus came to make this possible (19:10; [23]M. M. Ro 3:24).

1:54 All other nations on earth may look at God's choice of the nation of Israel and very wrongly think that God discriminated against their nations. They may think that he must have been playing favorites! But why did he choose Israel, and not another nation, to be his special people? He, in fact, had only one reason: in order to display his rich grace to all mankind; and he displayed his grace (and continues to do so) in at least five different ways: **a)** He did not choose a powerful nation like Egypt, but a small, weak nation (Deut 7:6-8; Is 41:8-9). **b)** Obviously, only one woman could have been Jesus' mother, and she could only belong to one tribe and one nation. Therefore, in order for Jesus to be a true human being, God could do it no other way; and he chose a humble woman, not a princess. **c)** Jesus could only have fulfilled the whole Law of God if he were a Jew (Lev 18:5). **d)** And Jesus had to be a <u>Jewish</u> prophet, priest and king ([24]M. M. Lk 1:27). **e)** While it's true that God showed his mission-heart by blessing Abraham and the whole nation of Israel <u>first</u>; he did so with a very important <u>purpose</u>, so that they would not keep his blessings for themselves, but <u>so that</u> they would be his <u>missionaries</u> and pass his blessings on to other nations. And obviously this huge task carried with it many responsibilities (Gen 12:3, Is 19:23-25; [25]M. M. Ac 13:46). And then, after Jesus' ascension, God began to carry out the final stages of his eternal mission-plan in a <u>new</u> era by beginning to create a <u>new</u> nation of Israel, the Church. He did so by sending his Holy Spirit to empower the mission-hearts of the faithful believers on Pentecost Day (Acts 1:8). Thus, the new Israel includes both a remnant of his chosen people from the old Israel as well as Gentiles from every nation on earth who trust in Jesus as their Lord (Rom 11:25-26). And on Pentecost Day, he also began to strengthen the faith of the believers with his holy Word, so that they would be able to be his missionaries to all other nations (M. M. Ac 13:46).

1:55 It is clear from some of Paul's Epistles that he may have been the person who taught Luke that the <u>true</u> spiritual descendants of Abraham are all who <u>trust</u> in God's promises as Abraham did, whether they are Jews or Gentiles (3:8; Rom 4:11; 11:26; Gal 3:7). God's gracious plan was to create one new Israel of Christians from <u>all</u> nations on earth (19:10; [26]M. M. Mt 2:6).

1:56 Luke records these facts in verse 56 in order to emphasize that Jesus was <u>both</u> true man and true God; it makes it clear that Joseph could not have been his father since Mary had left Nazareth before they had any sexual relationships; God was his Father. He was conceived in Mary and delivered by her in a very normal way, as a <u>true</u> human being. (Obviously, it was also a <u>miraculous</u> conception, as verse 35 says!) But unfortunately, some years later, many people in Jesus' own "home" town of Nazareth did <u>not</u> believe that he was both true man and true God (4:22; [27]M. M. Lk 1:26 & [28]Lk 1:35). And sadly, anyone who doubts either part of his dual nature is <u>not</u> his <u>true</u> spiritual brother or sister, since they do not have a <u>faith</u> relationship with him (8:21). And a Jewish

<u>blood</u> relationship with him (not even Mary's) means nothing for their salvation ([29]M. M. Lk 1:27).

The Birth of John the Baptist 1:57-66

1:57 *Now the time came for Elizabeth to give birth, and she bore a son.*
1:58 *And her neighbors and relatives heard that the Lord had shown great mercy to her, and they rejoiced with her.*
1:59 *And on the eighth day they came to circumcise the child. And they would have called him Zechariah after his father,*
1:60 *but his mother answered, "No; he shall be called John."*
1:61 *And they said to her, "None of your relatives is called by this name."*
1:62 *And they made signs to his father, inquiring what he wanted him to be called.*
1:63 *And he asked for a writing tablet and wrote, "His name is John." And they all wondered.*
1:64 *And immediately his mouth was opened and his tongue loosed, and he spoke, blessing God.*
1:65 *And fear came on all their neighbors. And all these things were talked about through all the hill country of Judea,*
1:66 *and all who heard them laid them up in their hearts, saying, "What then will this child be?" For the hand of the Lord was with him.*

1:58 (1) God's mission-heart is full of grace and mercy for all of the people whom he has already made and ever will make. And furthermore, he longs for all people to see his grace and mercy for them in his plan of salvation; therefore, he has done so by showing his <u>grace</u> to at least three women by giving them children: Abraham's <u>barren</u> wife, Sarah, Zechariah's <u>barren</u> wife, Elizabeth, and Jesus' <u>virgin</u> mother, Mary. And he did so at crucial junctions in his plan of salvation in each case ([30]M. M. Ro 8:29b). **2)** Thus, it is significant to note in verse 58 that Elizabeth's *"neighbors and relatives <u>heard</u> that the Lord had shown* *great mercy to her, and they rejoiced with her."* At least these few Jews heard about God's grace, as he had hoped they would. Therefore, when Zechariah added his <u>verbal</u> witness in verses 63-65 to what they had seen, they too spread the good news far and wide that God' was finally beginning to fulfill his promises to them (v 65-66; [31]M. M. Mt 5:14). *"And all who heard them laid them [the Good News] up in their hearts"* (v 66; 2:19). They began to think about what they had seen and heard; and therefore, no doubt, they also began to watch for more gracious acts of God ([32]M. M. Lk 1:26).

1:63-65 Obviously, both Mary's song and also her long visit (vs 39-56) had made deep impressions on Zechariah. And then, he was unable to speak for nine months, which also gave him a long opportunity to think about what was happening. He therefore, began to realize that God was beginning to fulfill the many promises that he had made to his people, Israel to send the Messiah to them. Furthermore, it must have touched him deeply to realize that God was using his own family to carry out his plan of salvation. Therefore, when God restored his ability to speak, Zechariah's mission-heart moved him to eagerly <u>witness</u> to the people who came to the circumcision of his son, John about what God was doing [33]M. M. Mt 5:14).

Zechariah's Prophecy 1:67-80

1:67 *And his father Zechariah was filled with the Holy Spirit and prophesied, saying,*
1:68 *"Blessed be the Lord God of Israel, for he has visited and redeemed his people*
1:69 *and has raised up a horn of salvation for us in the house of his servant David,*
1:70 *as he spoke by the mouth of his holy prophets from of old,*
1:71 *that we should be saved from our enemies and from the hand of all who hate us;*
1:72 *to show the mercy promised to our fathers and to remember his holy covenant,*
1:73 *the oath that he swore to our father Abraham, to grant us*

1:74 *that we, being delivered from the hand of our enemies, might serve him without fear,*
1:75 *in holiness and righteousness before him all our days.*
1:76 *And you, child, will be called the prophet of the Most High; for you will go before the Lord to prepare his ways,*
1:77 *to give knowledge of salvation to his people in the forgiveness of their sins,*
1:78 *because of the tender mercy of our God, whereby the sunrise shall visit us from on high*
1:79 *to give light to those who sit in darkness and in the shadow of death, to guide our feet into the way of peace."*
1:80 *And the child grew and became strong in spirit, and he was in the wilderness until the day of his public appearance to Israel.*

1:68-79 Most people who were present that day and heard Zechariah sing his inspired song would, no doubt, have assumed that *"Israel"* in verses 68-69 referred to the physical descendants of Abraham; however, when Luke heard it years later he probably thought of Abraham's spiritual descendants—Christians from every nation on earth (3:8), since he had learned from Paul that Jesus came to create a new spiritual Israel (19:10; Rom 11:26).

1:71, 74 In verses 71 and 74, Zechariah was not singing about the Gentile enemies of Israel, such as the Roman Empire; rather Israel's true enemies were, and still are, their spiritual enemies, mainly the devil and his evil angels. Therefore, he was praying in his song that God would soon defeat the spiritual enemies of the new Israel, the Church on the cross (19:10); so that *"we, being delivered from the hand of our enemies, might serve him without fear in holiness and righteousness before him all our days"* (vs. 74-75). It was, and still is the Lord of the mission who is in full control of the situation and carrying out his wonderful plan of salvation ([34]M. M. Ac 4:28).

1:79 It is the Lord [Jesus] who will *"give light"* (v 79) through his glorious empty tomb (19:10). And it is not only the Gentile nations of the earth who live *"in the shadow of death;"* it is all unbelievers from all nations who, by their lost human nature, live in spiritual darkness because they are lost in sin (19:10). The sad truth is that all of mankind is born living in the darkness of the devil's power and of the fear of death; and therefore, Christians are always eager to share the grace that they have received, because only Christians can shine the light of Jesus' empty tomb in this terrible darkness ([35]M. M. 2 Cor 3:18 & [36]M. I. Mt 7:14).

1:80 When verse 80 says that John would make a *"public appearance to Israel,"* it means that God had called him, as an Old Testament prophet, in order to baptize people and proclaim the Law and Gospel message to his fellow Jews first (v 54; [37]M. M. Ac 13:46). But of course, that does not mean that John ignored all of the Gentiles he met, because we read that he also called some of them to repentance and faith (3:7-15; 7:30). Furthermore Jesus himself, no doubt, also first proclaimed the Law and Gospel message to his fellow Jews, although none of the Gospels explicitly say this (2:46-47; Mk 1:14-15).

---

[6] M. M. Mt 5:14: When the Holy Spirit creates faith in a person's heart, he also graciously gives him a new mission-heart that is eager to shine the light of the Gospel throughout the whole world.

[7] M. M. Ro 10:17a: The Holy Spirit *only* creates and preserves faith by using the message of God's grace in his holy Word.

[8] M. M. Lk 1:1: Jesus came to seek and save all lost people from every nation on earth.

[9] M. M. Mt 5:14: When the Holy Spirit creates faith in a person's heart, he also graciously gives him a new mission-heart that is eager to shine the light of the Gospel throughout the whole world.

[10] M. M. Lk 13:24: The only way to enter the Kingdom of God is to have faith in Jesus as one's Savior.

[11] M. M. Ac 13:46: As he did with the old Israel, God first of all strengthens the faith of the new Israel, the Church with his Word and Sacraments, so that they can go and witness to the lost people of all nations.

[12] M. I. Lk 11:10: Christians should continuously pray to their heavenly Father and always depend on his grace, and not on their own feeble strength, because he always loves them.

[13] M. M. Lk 1:35: Jesus had to be born as true God, in order to rescue all of mankind from sin.

[14] M. M. Ro 1:16b: The Gospel is so powerful because it contains the central truth that Jesus rose from the dead with a glorified body in order to save all of his brothers and sisters from sin and death.

[15] M. M. Ac 4:28: The heavenly Father is always in full control of his mission to all nations of the world.

[16] M. M. Ro 1:19: God clearly reveals <u>four</u> things in the universe: **a)** that he made it, **b)** that he exists, **c)** that he has almighty power and glory, **d)** and that he still controls it.

[17] M. M. Lk 1:26: The heavenly Father sent his Son, Jesus to be born and live in <u>humble</u> circumstances, so that everyone from every nation on earth would see his <u>grace</u>.

[18] M. M. Ro 3:26: God is just and fair to <u>everyone</u>, both when he condemns <u>all</u> people of all nations because all have sinned, and also when he <u>only</u> declares those people righteous who have faith in Jesus.

[19] M. M. Lk 13:24: The <u>only</u> way to enter the Kingdom of God is to have <u>faith</u> in Jesus as one's Savior.

[20] M. M. Mt 2:6: Jesus was born in Bethlehem, so that he could be the King of the new Israel and rule over them as their dear Shepherd.

[21] M. M. Lk 1:1: Jesus came to seek and save <u>all</u> lost people from <u>every</u> nation on earth.

[22] M. M. Ro 9:15: Before creation, God <u>foreknew</u> and graciously chose the people whom he would adopt as his children at their Baptisms; however, he did not predestine all of the other people to eternal condemnation, because he dearly loves <u>all</u> of the people he makes; and he therefore is <u>always</u> extremely patient with those who stubbornly persist in their sin, until in the end he reluctantly condemns them to eternal punishment.

[23] M. M. Ro 3:24: Jesus lived a life of perfect obedience and shed his precious blood on the cross, in order to graciously set all nations free from sin, which a person only receives by faith in him.

[24] M. M. Lk 1:27: Jesus had to be born as a true human being and as a true Jew in order to become the King of kings in his heavenly kingdom forever.

[25] M. M. Ac 13:46: As he did with the old Israel, God <u>first of all</u> strengthens the faith of the new Israel, the Church with his Word and Sacraments, so that they can go and witness to the lost people of all nations.

[26] M. M. Mt 2:6: Jesus was born in Bethlehem, so that he could be the King of the new Israel and rule over them as their dear Shepherd.

[27] M. M. Lk 1:26: The heavenly Father sent his Son, Jesus to be born and live in <u>humble</u> circumstances, so that everyone from every nation on earth would see his <u>grace</u>.

[28] M. M. Lk 1:35: Jesus had to be born as true God, in order to rescue all of mankind from sin.

[29] M. M. Lk 1:27: Jesus had to be born as a true human being and as a true Jew in order to become the King of kings in his heavenly kingdom forever.

[30] M. M. Ro 8:29b: Because God knew before he created the world that the people he would make in his perfect image would soon sin and tarnish his image, he therefore, already had a gracious predestination <u>plan</u> to send his Son Jesus to rescue them from sin, so that he could <u>recreate</u> the people he had chosen back into his perfect <u>image</u>.

[31] M. M. Mt 5:14: When the Holy Spirit creates faith in a person's heart, he also graciously gives him a new mission-heart that is eager to shine the light of the Gospel throughout the whole world.

[32] M. M. Lk 1:26: The heavenly Father sent his Son, Jesus to be born and live in <u>humble</u> circumstances, so that everyone from every nation on earth would see his <u>grace</u>.

[33] M. M. Mt 5:14: When the Holy Spirit creates faith in a person's heart, he also graciously gives him a new mission-heart that is eager to shine the light of the Gospel throughout the whole

world.

[34] M. M. Ac 4:28: The heavenly Father is always in full control of his mission to all nations of the world.

[35] M. M. 2 Cor 3:18: The Spirit of Jesus opens the eyes of all Christians so that they can see the glory of the Lord Jesus, and then he also daily transforms them in an ever greater degree of glory into the glorious image of Jesus.

[36] M. I. Mt 7:14: Christians should hurry on their mission to the world because people who are lost have many enemies who lure them away from Jesus; and therefore, few of them find faith in Jesus which is the only gate into his Kingdom of life.

[37] M. M. Ac 13:46: As he did with the old Israel, God _first of all_ strengthens the faith of the new Israel, the Church with his Word and Sacraments, so that they can go and witness to the lost people of all nations.

Chapter 2

The Birth of Jesus Christ 2:1-7

2:1 *In those days a decree went out from Caesar Augustus that all the world should be registered.*
2:2 *This was the first registration when Quirinius was governor of Syria.*
2:3 *And all went to be registered, each to his own town.*
2:4 *And Joseph also went up from Galilee, from the town of Nazareth, to Judea, to the city of David, which is called Bethlehem, because he was of the house and lineage of David,*
2:5 *to be registered with Mary, his betrothed, who was with child.*
2:6 *And while they were there, the time came for her to give birth.*
2:7 *And she gave birth to her firstborn son and wrapped him in swaddling cloths and laid him in a manger, because there was no place for them in the inn.*

2:1-2 In verses 1-2, Luke refers to people who are well known to historians; therefore we can be sure yet today that he is recounting real history and not a myth that he or someone else created by his imagination (Gal 1:11-12). Jesus was born as a true human being, so that he could destroy the power of sin that corrupted all of mankind and all that God has made. He came *"to save the lost,"* his fellow human beings (19:10). If he had remained separate from human history, he could not have done anything about the sin that infects us all like a cancer ([1]M. M. Lk 1:1).

2:4 (1) God made the universe and remains in control of all that he has made ([2]M. M. Ro 1:19), therefore, he was, of course, able to use a pagan Gentile ruler to move Joseph and Mary from Nazareth to Bethlehem at just the right time, so that his promise that Jesus would be born in that specific town would be fulfilled (Micah 5:1; Gal 4:4). He was fully in control in order to carry out his plan, even though the people involved did not always understand that (19:10; [3]M. M. Ac 4:28). **2)** Furthermore, we once again see that the heavenly Father chose little Bethlehem, and not the capital city of Jerusalem, to be the birthplace of his Son, so that people everywhere would see his grace. He wanted all to see that it was he who was graciously carrying out his divine plan; and it was not any human being who was doing it ([4]M. M. Lk 1:26 & [5]Lk 1:27). **3)** Luke continues to emphasize that Joseph and Mary were Jewish and that Jesus was a descendant of King David, as an adopted son of Joseph. This was absolutely essential in order to carry out God's plan (19:10; M. M. Lk 1:27).

2:5 Jesus had to be a descendant of King David; but was he his descendant through his stepfather Joseph, or through Mary, or through both? Matthew clearly says that Joseph was a descendant of King David (Mt 1:16). What about Mary? Some Bible scholars find evidence in this verse 5 and also at (3:23) that Mary was also required to go to Bethlehem because she was also a descendant of King David, but the evidence seems to be slim. Nevertheless, these historical facts are also vital points of theology since only a descendant of King David could have fulfilled God's promises to King David ([6]M. M. Lk 1:27).

2:7 (1) Luke makes it clear that, although he was true God, Jesus' birth was completely normal; he was also a normal human being and fully Jewish. But what a terrible risk he and his Father had to take in his normal birth! Since Adam's sin also corrupted the body of Mary, Jesus could have died in the womb or in the birth process, as it happens all too often. But God's mission-heart and deep love for all of the people he has made (and ever will make) compelled him to take this terrible risk that his whole plan could collapse in a dead baby. This clearly teaches us just how great his grace is for us, and also just how important it was to him that Jesus had to have a human body (19:10; Ps 22:9-10; Heb 10:5). 10:5). **2)** Also note that when they cut his umbilical cord he shed his first divine/human blood for us (Heb 2:17; [7]M. M. Heb 9:12). How easily that historical fact has been overlooked! **3)** The words in verse 7, *"there was no place for them in the inn"* echo John's statement in his Gospel about Jesus' incarnation (Jn 1:10-11), *"He was in the world, and the world was made through him, yet the world did not know him. He came to his own, and his own people did not receive him."* In these verses we see that the nature of mankind's sin is not just disobedience, but also open rebellion against God (Rom 5:10). For Jesus to set aside his divine power for a time to become a human being in a <u>welcoming</u> world would have been wonderful enough; but to do so for a <u>hostile</u> world clearly shows the incomprehensible depth of his love and grace for his world (Eph 3:18-19). And we also once again see the vast depth of God's <u>grace</u> for us in sending his Son, Jesus ([8]M. M. Lk 1:26 & [9]Lk 1:27).

The Shepherds and the Angels 2:8-20

2:8   *And in the same region there were shepherds out in the field, keeping watch over their flock by night.*
2:9   *And an angel of the Lord appeared to them, and the glory of the Lord shone around them, and they were filled with fear.*
2:10 *And the angel said to them, "Fear not, for behold, I bring you good news of great joy that will be for all the people.*
2:11 *For unto you is born this day in the city of David a Savior, who is Christ the Lord.*
2:12 *And this will be a sign for you: you will find a baby wrapped in swaddling cloths and lying in a manger."*
2:13 *And suddenly there was with the angel a multitude of the heavenly host praising God and saying,*
2:14 *"Glory to God in the highest, and on earth peace among those with whom he is pleased!"*
2:15 *When the angels went away from them into heaven, the shepherds said to one another, "Let us go over to Bethlehem and see this thing that has happened, which the Lord has made known to us."*
2:16 *And they went with haste and found Mary and Joseph, and the baby lying in a manger.*
2:17 *And when they saw it, they made known the saying that had been told them concerning this child.*
2:18 *And all who heard it wondered at what the shepherds told them.*
2:19 *But Mary treasured up all these things, pondering them in her heart.*

> 2:20 *And the shepherds returned, glorifying and praising God for all they had heard and seen, as it had been told them.*

2:9 (1) Why did God send his angel to shepherds whom people in that culture looked down upon as low-class people? From their response it's clear that they had been <u>faithfully</u> waiting for the Messiah whom God had promised to send in the Old Testament. God knew that they would therefore also faithfully spread this great Good News (19:10). **2)** However, in sharp contrast, the rich and powerful *"teachers of the Law"* (v 46), who claimed that they knew the Law (the Old Testament) so well, had not learned the <u>two</u> very different teachings that it contains: **a)** First of all, in it, God condemned them (and all people) as sinful (the Law) and showed them their <u>need</u> for a Savior (Gal 3:23). **b)** Secondly, in it, God also <u>promised</u> them (and all people) (the Gospel) that he would send his Messiah to save the world (24:27, 44; Gal 3:24). The Old Testament pointed them to this newborn baby in a manger (v 7) and to this boy in the Temple (v 46); and they totally missed it. They didn't get the message; and therefore, they also were not able to carry out their responsibility as *"teachers of the Law"* and as sons of Abraham to shout this Law and Gospel message far and wide to their own people or to the Gentiles (Gen 12:3; Lk 20:19). Yet, if they had understood it and believed, with their great power in their society, they could certainly have been more effective in spreading the message than poor shepherds were ([10]M. M. Lk 1:1).

2:10 In verse 10, we see God continuing to carry out his plan of giving the Jews his Gospel <u>first</u>, so that they would take the responsibility of sharing this *"message that will fill <u>everyone</u> with joy"* with <u>all</u> nations ([11]M. M. Ac 13:46).

2:11 (1) Both the Greek term, *"Christ"* (v 11) and the Hebrew term "the Messiah" mean "the Anointed One," the person whom God especially chose (1:31). This tiny baby was the one God himself had anointed to be the Prophet, the Priest and the King of Israel (Ps 45:7, Is 61:1). He was true God and true man, a true <u>Jew</u> because God's "Anointed One" obviously <u>had</u> to be a Jew (19:10; [12]M. M. Lk 1:27 & [13]Lk 1:35). How could he possibly have anointed a Gentile to be this one unique man?

Such a person could have done <u>nothing</u> to fulfill that role (24:44). **2)** While the shepherds may have initially thought of *"your Savior, Christ the Lord"* in very narrow terms as their own personal Messiah and Savior from sin or from sickness and physical hardship, they did <u>not</u> keep such a tremendous Gospel to themselves. Many other Jews, however, could only think in narrow <u>political</u> terms when they thought about God's promised Messiah. They hoped for their own King of Israel who would overthrow the oppressive Roman government. But since Luke was a Gentile, he certainly was thinking in the broadest possible terms, that Jesus was the Messiah and Savior from sin for the <u>whole</u> world (Mt 1:21; [14]M. M. Ro 3:24).

2:12 The mark of identification that the angel gave to the shepherds was normal clothing for a newborn baby of a <u>humble</u> family, so that the shepherds would not look for the child of a rich, royal family. Thus, we once again see that every aspect of God's plan of salvation emphasized his rich <u>grace</u> for all mankind. If Jesus had been born in a palace and dressed in royal clothing, few would have seen God's gracious hand in this birth. Nevertheless, this tiny child was both humble and also a mighty King of kings, *"a Savior, Christ the Lord"* (v 11). He was the Lord's humble, *"suffering servant"* and King (Is 42:1, 52:13, Mt 20:28) who came to serve all people, in order to show his grace to all who are lost (19:10; [15]M. M. Ro 9:15).

2:14 God sent his *"peace,"* his gift of grace in the form of this helpless baby, so that <u>all</u> the sons and daughters of Adam and Eve of all generations and all ethnic groups would have only <u>one</u> way to receive his grace, through <u>faith</u> in this God/man baby. Obviously, there is not one ounce of discrimination in God's plan of salvation. All are equal under his grace because *"he is pleased"* with <u>all</u> of them (v 14; 19:10, 1 Tim 2:3-4; [16]M. M. Ro 5:1). When the new Israel, the Church faithfully proclaims the Gospel message, as the angels in verse 14 did, the Holy Spirit creates faith in those who hear it (Rom 10:17). It has always been God's gracious plan to <u>only</u> create faith through his holy Word (including his spoken Word before Moses wrote down his first Words), in order to form his new, holy nation, Israel (Rom 11:26; M. M. Ro 9:15).

2:15-16 (1) The shepherds were obviously men of faith, but their fellow Jews had told the next generation about God's past deeds and his promises for so many generations without seeing their fulfillment that it was probably not easy for them to keep the faith. They had only <u>heard</u> all the stories of the Exodus—how God had invaded human history so dramatically; and how he had promised many times to do so again. Now suddenly, the angels told them that here was their Messiah! God was once again acting very dramatically in history, but in a totally different way from what they had expected (19:10). Of course, the shepherds were in a hurry to check it out! **2)** Luke's down-to-earth account throughout this section makes it very clear that this story is no myth. The baby who would soon be the focus of <u>all</u> human history had been born in a way that was plain for all to see; and the shepherds would be the <u>first</u> ones (after Joseph and Mary, of course) to actually see him with their own eyes ([17]M. M. Lk 1:27).

2:17 (1) Why did the shepherds believe so quickly? Even though the angels had just appeared to them so dramatically, when they were actually there kneeling before their King, all of the physical evidence told them that this was just a <u>normal</u> human baby. Therefore, it obviously was the Holy Spirit who used the witness of the angels to give them the eyes of <u>faith</u> to see <u>God</u> himself in this helpless baby, the God/man (19:10; [18]M. M. Ro 10:17a). Only the eyes of faith could see the truth that this baby was *"the hope of all the ends of the earth and of the farthest seas"* (Ps 65:5) and *"the hope of Israel"* (Ac 28:20). **2)** After seeing such an amazing miracle, who could keep such tremendous Gospel to himself? They *"made known"* (v 17) what the angels had told them about this baby to everyone. They did exactly what God knew that they would do (v 9) and quickly and <u>faithfully</u> shared the Gospel message (Mt 5:14).

2:18 In verse 18, we are left wondering if these people who heard the Gospel "wondered" in faith or unbelief. Were they waiting for the Messiah <u>in faith</u>; and when he actually finally came they were so full of wonder that they faithfully spread the story far and wide (19:10)? Or was their amazement a result of unbelief, and they dismissed it as impossible and kept silent about it (Mt 22:22)? Note a similar context in

(5:26) where Luke says quite clearly, *"And amazement seized them all, and they glorified God and were filled with awe, saying, 'We have seen extraordinary things today.'"* In this verse, Luke makes it clear that, in the midst of *"amazement"* and *"awe,"* they showed their <u>faith</u> by praising God ([19]M. M. Lk 13:24).

2:19 This verse clearly indicates that Mary also had seen with the eyes of <u>faith</u> that her baby, who appeared to be like any other baby, was in fact quite extraordinary indeed. However, since we know that the Holy Spirit only creates faith by means of <u>hearing</u> the Gospel about Jesus (M. M. Ro 10:17a), we are compelled to ask the questions: when and how did Mary hear the Gospel about Jesus' mission to the world that she would have in her heart to ponder? **1)** First of all, the angel told her the wonderful Gospel that her son would be the Son of God and her eternal King (1:31-33). And it also was the Holy Spirit who inspired her song in (1:46-55), in which she explicitly sang that her son was also her *"Savior"* (1:47). **2)** Secondly, how much had Mary learned from the Old Testament about God's promises to send a Savior/Messiah? **a)** In her culture, only <u>male</u> children went to the local synagogue daily in order to learn to read by memorizing the Old Testament; and the synagogues were the only places where copies of the Scripture were kept. **b)** Therefore, neither Mary nor any other woman knew how to read; they could only sit quietly in a separate part of the synagogue on the Sabbath, which was the day of worship and listen as the leader read parts of the Scripture and explained their meaning. **c)** Furthermore, most of the teachers of the Law at that time were hoping for a political Messiah who would rescue them from the oppressive Roman government and not a Savior from sin. No wonder most common people knew very little about what kind of Messiah they should hope for. Their unfaithful spiritual leaders had been almost totally irresponsible missionaries of the Gospel ([20]M. M. Ac 13:46). **3)** Some modern scholars speculate that it was Mary who, many years later, personally shared the details of Jesus' conception and early life with Luke. And if they are correct, then, Luke's statement in verse 19 that *"Mary treasured up all these things"* is very interesting indeed. It is very reasonable to assume that Luke did, indeed, make sure that he talked to Mary herself about exactly what happened, because he says in (1:3) that he carefully sought out all the details of how God carried out his plan of salvation so that he could be a faithful witness to the truth ([21]M. M. Ac 17:11).

2:20 Luke reports in this verse that *"the shepherds returned, glorifying and praising God for all they had heard and seen,"* which is another way of saying that they were faithfully spreading their joy over *"all they had heard and seen."* In verse 17, *"they made known"* what the angel had told them; and after they actually saw baby Jesus, they were filled with even more joy, *"glorifying and praising God."* The Holy Spirit had also graciously given them new mission-hearts ([22]M. M. Mt 5:14).

Jesus Presented at the Temple 2:21-38

2:21 *And at the end of eight days, when he was circumcised, he was called Jesus, the name given by the angel before he was conceived in the womb.*

2:22 *And when the time came for their purification according to the Law of Moses, they brought him up to Jerusalem to present him to the Lord*

2:23 *(as it is written in the Law of the Lord, "Every male who first opens the womb shall be called holy to the Lord")*

2:24 *and to offer a sacrifice according to what is said in the Law of the Lord, "a pair of turtledoves, or two young pigeons."*

2:25 *Now there was a man in Jerusalem, whose name was Simeon, and this man was righteous and devout, waiting for the consolation of Israel, and the Holy Spirit was upon him.*

2:26 *And it had been revealed to him by the Holy Spirit that he would not see death before he had seen the Lord's Christ.*

2:27 *And he came in the Spirit into the temple, and when the parents brought in the child Jesus, to do for him according to the custom of the Law,*

2:28 *he took him up in his arms and blessed God and said,*

2:29 *"Lord, now you are letting your servant depart in peace, according to your word;*

2:30 *for my eyes have seen your salvation*

2:31 *that you have prepared in the presence of all peoples,*
2:32 *a light for revelation to the Gentiles, and for glory to your people Israel."*
2:33 *And his father and his mother marveled at what was said about him.*
2:34 *And Simeon blessed them and said to Mary his mother, "Behold, this child is appointed for the fall and rising of many in Israel, and for a sign that is opposed*
2:35 *(and a sword will pierce through your own soul also), so that thoughts from many hearts may be revealed."*
2:36 *And there was a prophetess, Anna, the daughter of Phanuel, of the tribe of Asher. She was advanced in years, having lived with her husband seven years from when she was a virgin,*
2:37 *and then as a widow until she was eighty-four. She did not depart from the temple, worshiping with fasting and prayer night and day.*
2:38 *And coming up at that very hour she began to give thanks to God and to speak of him to all who were waiting for the redemption of Jerusalem.*

2:21 (1) Obviously Jesus had to be a Jewish baby since a Gentile father would never have circumcised him. As a faithful Jew, Joseph circumcised his adopted son (v 39); and in this way he obeyed the Law of Moses when Jesus, obviously, could not do so. Thus, Jesus fulfilled God's Law on behalf of all of his fellow human beings (1:1; Lev 18:5). This would have been utterly impossible if his parents had been Gentiles ([23]M. M. Lk 1:27)! **2)** It is also very significant to note that this is the second time that Jesus shed his blood for all of his brothers and sisters of all ethnic groups. The first time was when his umbilical cord was cut (2:7; [24]M. M. Ro 3:24).

2:23-39 No less than four times in verses 23-39 Luke continues to emphasize that Joseph and Mary faithfully obeyed all of the Laws of Moses that *"fulfilled all righteousness"* (Mt 3:15) on behalf of Jesus, which made him part of their culture and society (Lev 18:5). No doubt, because they were born and raised in pious families, both of them were pious and faithful Jews who were obedient to God. Therefore, once again, their obedience would have been utterly impossible if they had been Gentiles. If they had lived in any other culture in the history of mankind, their religious customs would have compelled them to make their new-born child a part of their culture in totally different ways. But because they were Jews they obeyed all of God's Laws. And in addition, they also did so for the benefit of all other nations. How wonderful and perfect was God's plan of salvation for all people ([25]M. M. Lk 1:1)!

2:25-26 A few pious believers like Simeon were still faithfully waiting for *"the Lord's Christ," "the consolation of Israel."* How could there have been so <u>few</u> Jews who were still faithful? Luke names a few: Zechariah, Elizabeth, Mary, Joseph, Simeon and Anna; and he also mentions a few shepherds without naming them. In addition, the other Gospel writers list only a few more faithful Jews. Yet, according God's perfect plan of salvation, he had chosen an entire <u>nation</u> to wait for his *"consolation"* in their Messiah (v 25). They <u>all</u> should have been eagerly waiting to see God fulfill all of his promises to send a savior, so that they could spread this great Gospel message to other nations. However, the vast majority of them were looking for a King who would restore their nation to its former glory. God was <u>depending on</u> this smallest of all nations to be faithful in this mission task for the sake of all other nations ([26]M. M. Ac 13:46). And they very nearly failed completely in their responsibility; if it had not been for the faithful few they would have!

2:30-31 (1) Astonishingly, what Simeon holds in his arms and <u>sees</u> with his <u>physical</u> eyes is a helpless newborn baby, but with his eyes of <u>faith</u> he sees something totally different. He sees *"the desired of <u>all</u> nations"* (Hag 2:7 (NIV); 1:1, 43). **2)** When verse 31 refers to *"all peoples"* it very clearly echoes what Luke said in (1:1), *"the things that have been accomplished among <u>us</u>,"* since the word *"us"* refers to *"all peoples"* from all nations on the earth. God has excluded no nation from his love and grace since he continues to seek all lost people through his faithful Church (19:10; M. M. Ac 13:46). It's completely impossible for us today to estimate just how many people God has made to live on the earth, but the number must be staggering. Nevertheless, God loves each and every one of us <u>equally</u>; and therefore, he *"prepared"* (v 31) a plan from eternity to save all of us (Is 11:10). And his <u>gracious</u> mission-heart will not rest until each lost sheep (Ch. 15) has a chance to *"see"* with Simeon's eyes of <u>faith</u> that this apparently helpless baby is the God/man. When those who have seen him faithfully share the Gospel with others, they too will *"see"* and believe. Our gracious Lord has no other people to depend on, because only those who have *"the light of the world"* can share it ([27]M. M. Mt 5:14 & Ac 13:46)!

2:32 This helpless baby is also *"a <u>light</u>…to the Gentiles"* and the *"<u>glory</u> to your people Israel,"* just as Jesus called himself *"the light of the world"* (Jn 8:12). In the Bible, light is a metaphor for life and salvation; and its opposite, darkness is a metaphor for sin and death. And in verse 32, *"light"* and *"glory"* mean the same thing; therefore, in this verse, the Holy Spirit promised through Simeon that *"the light of the world"* would shine <u>first</u> on *"your people Israel,"* and then shine from them on all other nations who *"sit in darkness."* This is the awesome mission task that our gracious Lord has given to his Church (1:79; Rom 15:8-9; Is 9:2; M. M. Ac 13:46).

2:33 Why did Jesus' parents *"<u>marvel</u> at what was said about him?"* Perhaps they were just shocked that Simeon had immediately recognized who their son truly was. Or perhaps they *"marveled"* because the enormous reality of who Jesus truly was had not yet begun to sink in. And in addition, they were, of course, just normal first-time parents who were struggling with some sleepless nights and all of the constant care that a newborn baby demands. What an awesome responsibility God had given them; and how extremely vital it was that they do the best job that they could, so that God could continue to carry out his mission plan to the world! He was clearly in control and empowering them ([28]M. M. Ac 4:28 & Ac 13:46).

2:34 When Simeon says that "this child is appointed for the fall and rising of many in Israel" he teaches two truths: **a)** first, that one of the tasks God had given Jesus was the mission to <u>first of all</u> proclaim the Law and the Gospel message to his own people Israel (4:20-21), **b)** and secondly that his message to them was a <u>two-edged</u> sword that cuts with both the Law and also the Gospel (Heb 4:12; Mk 1:14-15). As such,

Jesus was, of course, God's greatest prophet (Heb 1:1-2). Yet, while God's gracious mission plan is that all people would one day hear the Gospel edge of the sword and trust in this baby Jesus for their salvation (Jn 3:16-17), some stubbornly reject him until finally, after long patience, God must harden their hearts so that they are condemned by the Law edge of this sword to live in darkness forever (20:17-18; 1 Cor 1:23; 1Pt 2:6-8; [29]M. M. Ac 13:46).

2:35 (1) Verse 35 is the first indication in Luke's Gospel that baby Jesus was born to die. And of course, his mother would likewise suffer the pain that only a mother can feel when her child is suffering (Jn 19:25-27). The fact that the Holy Spirit predicts Jesus' suffering here makes it clear that God was in control; and his suffering and death would not be merely accidental or merely what some evil men decided to do to him. It was an essential part of God's plan of salvation (9:22; Is 53:3; [30]M. M. Ac 4:28). **2)** Why Simeon did not also address Joseph in verse 34 and why Joseph disappears from all of the accounts of Jesus' life after verse 51 will no doubt always remain a mystery to us. And we'll never know whether Joseph was still alive when Jesus suffered and died; and therefore Joseph also felt the pain. Nevertheless, there can be no doubt that, along with his mother, Jesus' true heavenly Father (v 49) was also pierced with pain at his Son's horrible death (23:46; Mt 27:46).

2:37 Why did both Simeon and Anna have such strong faith? The answer lies in their daily presence in the temple for two reasons: **a)** First of all, because the Holy Spirit has always used only hearing his Word to create and strengthen faith, as St. Paul says in (Rom 10:17), *"Faith comes from hearing, and hearing through the word of Christ."* They were hearing God's Word every day to strengthen their faith ([31]M. I. Ro 10:17c). **b)** And secondly, because in all of Israel, no one, not even the teachers of the Law, had personal copies of even a small portion of the Scriptures. The religious leaders of the Jews very carefully kept all of the copies of the Scriptures only in the temple in Jerusalem or in the synagogues in other towns. Thus, Simeon and Anna had nowhere else to go but the temple to hear God's Word quoted from the written Word. Clearly, they had such strong faith because they heard God's Word in the temple *"night and day"* ([32]M. I. Lk 12:40). It's possible that Anna even lived in a room within the temple complex.

2:38 (1) Anna the prophetess may never have had any children of her own, but, like Simeon, God blessed her by graciously allowing her to, not only hold this dear child in her arms, but also to see him as her dear Savior with the eyes of faith. (While the text does not say that she also took him in her arms, she, no doubt, would have done so.) She too was part of the faithful remnant in Israel who had been waiting for him for many, many generations (v 25; 1:68; 19:10; 24:21; Is 40:1-2; Is 52:9). **2)** And such tremendous Gospel was too good to keep to herself; so, in faith, *"she began to give thanks to God and speak of him to all who were waiting for the redemption of Jerusalem [all of Israel]"* (v 38). She immediately fulfilled her first responsibility to tell her fellow Jews (Rom 1:16; [33]M. M. Ac 13:46 & [34]Mt 5:14). **3)** Furthermore, it's possible that her witness and Simeon's witness also bore fruit in the heart of the priest who offered the doves that day. Luke says in (Ac 6:7), *"And the word of God continued to increase, and the number of the disciples multiplied greatly in Jerusalem, and a great many of the priests became obedient to the faith."* If this priest heard and believed, the witness of a fellow priest would have been very meaningful to his fellow priests ([35]M. M. Mt 5:14).

The Return to Nazareth 2:39-40

2:39   *And when they had performed everything according to the Law of the Lord, they returned into Galilee, to their own town of Nazareth.*
2:40   *And the child grew and became strong, filled with wisdom. And the favor of God was upon him.*

2:40 (1) In verse 40, Luke reemphasizes the truth that the child, Jesus was completely unique; he was both true man and true God. Many people have been offended by this truth and refused to believe in him in a large part because it is a great mystery that no person can fully understand; therefore, it is only by the hand of faith in God's promises that anyone can grasp it. But his unique nature was an absolutely vital element of God's perfect plan of salvation; and Luke did not miss its significance, and therefore, he recorded it for the sake of all mankind ([36]M. M. Lk 1:27 & [37]Lk 1:35). **2)** Verse 40 is also the only small bit of information that fills the long gap in the historical record in any of the four Gospels between Jesus' birth and his trip to Jerusalem when he was twelve years old (v 41). What a difficult task it must have been to raise a completely perfect child together with other children who were sinful! And the following events in Jerusalem do in fact illustrate some of the frustrations and misunderstandings that his parents must have gone through almost daily. Yet, on the other hand, they also faithfully gave Jesus a pious home environment that (humanly speaking) must have made it easier for Jesus to continue to obey all of God's Laws perfectly. Their pious Jewish home was thus <u>vital</u> in order for him to complete God's plan (M. M. Lk 1:27).

The Boy Jesus in the Temple 2:41-52

2:41 *Now his parents went to Jerusalem every year at the Feast of the Passover.*
2:42 *And when he was twelve years old, they went up according to custom.*
2:43 *And when the feast was ended, as they were returning, the boy Jesus stayed behind in Jerusalem. His parents did not know it,*
2:44 *but supposing him to be in the group they went a day's journey, but then they began to search for him among their relatives and acquaintances,*
2:45 *and when they did not find him, they returned to Jerusalem, searching for him.*
2:46 *After three days they found him in the temple, sitting among the teachers, listening to them and asking them questions.*
2:47 *And all who heard him were amazed at his understanding and his answers.*
2:48 *And when his parents saw him, they were astonished. And his mother said to him, "Son, why have you treated us so? Behold, your father and I have been searching for you in great distress."*

2:49 *And he said to them, "Why were you looking for me? Did you not know that I must be in my Father's house?"*
2:50 *And they did not understand the saying that he spoke to them.*
2:51 *And he went down with them and came to Nazareth and was submissive to them. And his mother treasured up all these things in her heart.*
2:52 *And Jesus increased in wisdom and in stature and in favor with God and man.*

2:42 (1) Joseph and Mary continued to obey the whole Law of Moses on Jesus' behalf as pious Jews (Ex 23:14-17). As a matter of fact, Mary was not obligated to go to the festival since only the men were required to go to three festivals in Jerusalem each year; however, by their own choice the women would often accompanied them. **2)** This trip was an essential part of Jesus' training so that he could take his place as an <u>adult</u> male Jew in the religious community the following year. It was a continuation of his normal physical and spiritual growth process referred to in verse 40 ([38]M. M. Lk 1:27).

2:43-50 As Jesus himself makes clear in verse 49, Joseph and Mary were still at times struggling to understand who Jesus was, what his mission was, and also just how they should be good parents to him along with their other children. If they had been more faithful they could no doubt have been more effective witnesses for him and his mission ([39]M. M. Mt 5:14). Unfortunately however, on this trip to Jerusalem they sinned by forgetting that he was the Son of God (v 49).

2:46-47 Verses 46-47 repeat the important idea, once again, that Jesus was both true God and true man (v 40; M. M. Lk 1:27 & [40]Lk 1:35). As a "normal" twelve year old boy, his general knowledge was perhaps not perfect, although it must have been far greater than other boys his age. But his knowledge of the Law of Moses must have been complete since he was able to *"amaze"* the teachers [of the Law] with his answers (v 47), and also obey it perfectly on behalf of his fellow men (4:21; 22:37; 24:44; [41]M. M. Mt 1:22).

2:48-49 Mary's words, *"your <u>father</u>"* in this verse stand in sharp contrast with Jesus' words, *"my Father"* in the next verse. The truth was that both were true because of his unique dual nature. It certainly is an interesting way for Luke to reemphasize this important truth. He wanted to make sure that his brothers and sisters, both Jews and Gentiles, would remember that Jesus had to be both true God and true man, so that God's salvation would apply to the entire human race ([42]M. M. Lk 1:27 & [43]Lk 1:35).

2:49 Jesus' two questions in verse 49: *"Why were you looking for me? Did you not know that I must be in my Father's house?"* indicate at least two things: **1)** His two questions demonstrate that by age 12, Jesus himself was obviously fully aware of the fact that he was both the Son of God and the adoptive son of Joseph, because he called God his heavenly Father. However, we can only speculate about how he knew that; and furthermore, we also can only speculate about why his parents had obviously forgotten who he was (1:47). Surely, his perfect obedience every single day must have stood out for them in sharp contrast to the sinful behavior of his brothers and sisters, so they would have been constantly reminded. Furthermore, this story is one more piece of clear evidence that, contrary to the opinion of some, Mary was indeed a sinful human being like everyone else (Ps 51:5; [44]M. M. Ro 3:26). **2)** And secondly, his words, *"my Father's house"* must also have been especially difficult for Joseph to hear. It would have been a great privilege and an extremely vital role to fill for the sake of all of humanity to be his adoptive father, and yet, on the other hand, it must also have been extremely difficult for both of his parents to deal with the many daily problems that they faced. How, indeed, could he, a simple carpenter, raise God's Son and his Savior? He had received direct guidance from an angel only three times that Matthew recorded (Mt 1:20; 2:13, 19; [45]M. M. Mt 5:14).

2:51-52 (1) While he recognized his own divinity, Jesus set aside his almighty nature, humbled himself and obeyed the fourth commandment (Phil 2:6). He *"was submissive to them"* perfectly (1:1) for the sake of all other children from every nation on earth, because no other child ever could have or can ever do so (4:21; 22:37; 24:44; [46]M. M. Mt 1:22). **2)** Verses 51-52 are almost identical to verse 40. Luke continues to emphasize Jesus' dual nature. Furthermore, verses 51-52 also fill a second long gap in Jesus' life between age 12 and about age 30 (3:23). There is no point in speculating why Joseph disappears from the account of Jesus' life during this period of time. Whether Joseph lived until he saw his death and resurrection and believed in him we will never know, but we do know for sure that Jesus continued to submit to the loving care of his pious mother and of his heavenly Father. And both were, of course, vital aspects of his mission because he was fulfilling the whole Law of God for the sake of all of his brothers and sisters (4:21; 19:10; M. M. Mt 1:22). **3)** Both verse 51 and verse 19 say essentially the same thing that *"his mother [Mary] treasured up all these things in her heart,"* although the Greek verbs for *"treasuring up"* are not the same verbs in the two verses. The Greek verb in verse 51 says more clearly that she continually pondered the wonder of what God was doing in their lives. As Mary *"treasured up"* or pondered so deeply about who Jesus truly was, the Holy Spirit prepared her for the future pain of her son's suffering and death (v 35). He would indeed be her Savior (1:47; [47]M. M. Lk 13:24). And what a beautiful example she still is for all who faithfully hear and ponder God's holy Word in a Bible translation that they can understand (Mt 13:19; [48]M. I. Ac 1:8 & [49]Ac 2:4).

---

[1] M. M. Lk 1:1: Jesus came to seek and save all lost people from every nation on earth.

[2] M. M. Ro 1:19: God clearly reveals four things in the universe: **a)** that he made it, **b)** that he exists, **c)** that he has almighty power and glory, **d)** and that he still controls it.

[3] M. M. Ac 4:28: The heavenly Father is always in full control of his mission to all nations of the world.

[4] M. M. Lk 1:26: The heavenly Father sent his Son, Jesus to be born and live in humble circumstances, so that everyone from every nation on earth would see his grace.

[5] M. M. Lk 1:27: Jesus had to be born as a true human being and as a true Jew in order to become the King of kings in his heavenly kingdom forever.

[6] M. M. Lk 1:27: Jesus had to be born as a true human being and as a true Jew in order to become the King of kings in his heavenly kingdom forever.

[7] M. M. Heb 9:12: As the great High Priest, Jesus offered his human and divine blood as the one perfect sacrifice for all of the sins of all of his brothers and sisters.

[8] M. M. Lk 1:26: The heavenly Father sent his Son, Jesus to be born and live in humble circumstances, so that everyone from every nation on earth would see his grace.

[9] M. M. Lk 1:27: Jesus had to be born as a true human being and as a true Jew in order to

become the King of kings in his heavenly kingdom forever.

[10] M. M. Lk 1:1: Jesus came to seek and save <u>all</u> lost people from <u>every</u> nation on earth.

[11] M. M. Ac 13:46: As he did with the old Israel, God <u>first of all</u> strengthens the faith of the new Israel, the Church with his Word and Sacraments, so that they can go and witness to the lost people of all nations.

[12] M. M. Lk 1:27: Jesus had to be born as a true human being and as a true Jew in order to become the King of kings in his heavenly kingdom forever.

[13] M. M. Lk 1:35: Jesus had to be born as true God, in order to rescue all of mankind from sin.

[14] M. M. Ro 3:24: Jesus lived a life of perfect obedience and shed his precious blood on the cross, in order to graciously set all nations free from sin, which a person only receives by faith in him.

[15] M. M. Ro 9:15: Before creation, God <u>foreknew</u> and graciously chose the people whom he would adopt as his children at their Baptisms; however, he did not predestine all of the other people to eternal condemnation, because he dearly loves <u>all</u> of the people he makes; and he therefore is <u>always</u> extremely patient with those who stubbornly persist in their sin, until in the end he reluctantly condemns them to eternal punishment.

[16] M. M. Ro 5:1: On the cross, Jesus earned <u>peace</u> with God for <u>all</u> of his brothers and sisters from every nation on earth.

[17] M. M. Lk 1:27: Jesus had to be born as a true human being and as a true Jew in order to become the King of kings in his heavenly kingdom forever.

[18] M. M. Ro 10:17a: The Holy Spirit <u>only</u> creates and preserves faith by using the message of God's grace in his holy Word.

[19] M. M. Lk 13:24: The <u>only</u> way to enter the Kingdom of God is to have <u>faith</u> in Jesus as one's Savior.

[20] M. M. Ac 13:46: As he did with the old Israel, God <u>first of all</u> strengthens the faith of the new Israel, the Church with his Word and Sacraments, so that they can go and witness to the lost people of all nations.

[21] M. M. Ac 17:11: When a person learns from the Bible how Jesus graciously fulfilled everything that God has promised him in the Bible, Jesus' grace fills him with eagerness to daily search for more proof in the Bible that Jesus did it for him.

[22] M. M. Mt 5:14: When the Holy Spirit creates faith in a person's heart, he also graciously gives him a new mission-heart that is eager to shine the light of the Gospel throughout the whole world.

[23] M. M. Lk 1:27: Jesus had to be born as a true human being and as a true Jew in order to become the King of kings in his heavenly kingdom forever.

[24] M. M. Ro 3:24: Jesus lived a life of perfect obedience and shed his precious blood on the cross, in order to graciously set all nations free from sin, which a person only receives by faith in him.

[25] M. M. Lk 1:1: Jesus came to seek and save all lost people from <u>every</u> nation on earth.

[26] M. M. Ac 13:46: As he did with the old Israel, God <u>first of all</u> strengthens the faith of the new Israel, the Church with his Word and Sacraments, so that they can go and witness to the lost people of all nations.

[27] M. M. Mt 5:14: When the Holy Spirit creates faith in a person's heart, he also graciously gives

him a new mission-heart that is eager to shine the light of the Gospel throughout the whole world.

[28] M. M. Ac 4:28: The heavenly Father is always in full control of his mission to all nations of the world.

[29] M. M. Ac 13:46: As he did with the old Israel, God <u>first of all</u> strengthens the faith of the new Israel, the Church with his Word and Sacraments, so that they can go and witness to the lost people of all nations.

[30] M. M. Ac 4:28: The heavenly Father is always in full control of his mission to all nations of the world.

[31] M. I. Ro 10:17c: Christians should grow in their Lord's grace by daily listening to his Word, and also by frequently eating his true body and drinking his true blood in Holy Communion.

[32] M. I. Lk 12:40: Christians should "eat" God's Word every day in order to keep their faith strong, so that they are always ready for their Lord's return.

[33] M. M. Ac 13:46: As he did with the old Israel, God <u>first of all</u> strengthens the faith of the new Israel, the Church with his Word and Sacraments, so that they can go and witness to the lost people of all nations.

[34] M. M. Mt 5:14: When the Holy Spirit creates faith in a person's heart, he also graciously gives him a new mission-heart that is eager to shine the light of the Gospel throughout the whole world.

[35] M. M. Mt 5:14: When the Holy Spirit creates faith in a person's heart, he also graciously gives him a new mission-heart that is eager to shine the light of the Gospel throughout the whole world.

[36] M. M. Lk 1:27: Jesus had to be born as a true human being and as a true Jew in order to become the King of kings in his heavenly kingdom forever.

[37] M. M. Lk 1:35: Jesus had to be born as true God, in order to rescue all of mankind from sin.

[38] M. M. Lk 1:27: Jesus had to be born as a true human being and as a true Jew in order to become the King of kings in his heavenly kingdom forever.

[39] M. M. Mt 5:14: When the Holy Spirit creates faith in a person's heart, he also graciously gives him a new mission-heart that is eager to shine the light of the Gospel throughout the whole world.

[40] M. M. Lk 1:35: Jesus had to be born as true God, in order to rescue all of mankind from sin.

[41] M. M. Mt 1:22: God sent his only Son, Jesus to be born as a true human being, so that he could save all of his brothers and sisters of all nations by fulfilling all of God's promises in the Old Testament.

[42] M. M. Lk 1:27: Jesus had to be born as a true human being and as a true Jew in order to become the King of kings in his heavenly kingdom forever.

[43] M. M. Lk 1:35: Jesus had to be born as true God, in order to rescue all of mankind from sin.

[44] M. M. Ro 3:26: God is just and fair to <u>everyone</u>, both when he condemns <u>all</u> people of all nations because all have sinned, and also when he <u>only</u> declares those people righteous who have faith in Jesus.

[45] M. M. Mt 5:14: When the Holy Spirit creates faith in a person's heart, he also graciously gives him a new mission-heart that is eager to shine the light of the Gospel throughout the whole world.

[46] M. M. Mt 1:22: God sent his only Son, Jesus to be born as a true human being, so that he could save all of his brothers and sisters of all nations by fulfilling all of God's promises in the Old Testament.

[47] M. M. Lk 13:24: The <u>only</u> way to enter the Kingdom of God is to have <u>faith</u> in Jesus as one's Savior.

[48] M. I. Ac 1:8: Christians should go and witness about Jesus to all who are lost from all languages and cultures by depending on the power of the Holy Spirit to help them bridge all of the language/cultural boundaries whether they are relatively easy, as in their own language, or extremely difficult.

[49] M. I. Ac 2:4: In cross-cultural situations, Christians should always focus on all of the needs of the target group by learning <u>their</u> heart-language and culture as deeply as possible, so that they can tell them the Gospel clearly in their own language and also help them with the true needs of their society.

Chapter 3

John the Baptist Prepares the Way 3:1-22

3:1 *In the fifteenth year of the reign of Tiberius Caesar, Pontius Pilate being governor of Judea, and Herod being tetrarch of Galilee, and his brother Philip tetrarch of the region of Ituraea and Trachonitis, and Lysanias tetrarch of Abilene,*

3:2 *during the high priesthood of Annas and Caiaphas, the word of God came to John the son of Zechariah in the wilderness.*

3:3 *And he went into all the region around the Jordan, proclaiming a baptism of repentance for the forgiveness of sins.*

3:4 *As it is written in the book of the words of Isaiah the prophet, "The voice of one crying in the wilderness: 'Prepare the way of the Lord, make his paths straight.*

3:5 *Every valley shall be filled, and every mountain and hill shall be made low, and the crooked shall become straight, and the rough places shall become level ways,*

3:6 *and all flesh shall see the salvation of God.'"*

3:7 *He said therefore to the crowds that came out to be baptized by him, "You brood of vipers! Who warned you to flee from the wrath to come?*

3:8 *Bear fruits in keeping with repentance. And do not begin to say to yourselves, 'We have Abraham as our father.' For I tell you, God is able from these stones to raise up children for Abraham.*

3:9 *Even now the axe is laid to the root of the trees. Every tree therefore that does not bear good fruit is cut down and thrown into the fire."*

3:10 *And the crowds asked him, "What then shall we do?"*

3:11 *And he answered them, "Whoever has two tunics is to share with him who has none, and whoever has food is to do likewise."*

3:12 *Tax collectors also came to be baptized and said to him, "Teacher, what shall we do?"*

3:13 *And he said to them, "Collect no more than you are authorized*

3:14 *Soldiers also asked him, "And we, what shall we do?" And he said to them, "Do not extort money from anyone by threats or by false accusation, and be content with your wages."*

3:15 *As the people were in expectation, and all were questioning in their hearts concerning John, whether he might be the Christ,*

3:16 *John answered them all, saying, "I baptize you with water, but he who is mightier than I is coming, the strap of whose sandals I am not worthy to untie. He will baptize you with the Holy Spirit and with fire.*

3:17 *His winnowing fork is in his hand, to clear his threshing floor and to gather the wheat into his barn, but the chaff he will burn with unquenchable fire."*

3:18 *So with many other exhortations he preached good news to the people.*

3:19 *But Herod the tetrarch, who had been reproved by him for Herodias, his brother's wife, and for all the evil things that Herod had done,*

3:20 *added this to them all, that he locked up John in prison.*

3:21 *Now when all the people were baptized, and when Jesus also had been baptized and was praying, the heavens were opened,*

3:22 *and the Holy Spirit descended on him in bodily form, like a dove; and a voice came from heaven, "You are my beloved Son; with you I am well pleased."*

3:1 Just like (2:1), verse 1 places Luke's account solidly within human history since all of these officials are well known by historians. Luke's account was not merely something that he made up or imagined; rather, the Holy Spirit moved him to record what God's mission-heart was doing in human history to rescue all of mankind from sin. This is vital information for all people of all nations, so that all may know that the Gospel is for them ([1]M. M. Lk 1:1).

3:2-4 (1) Verse 3 indicates that John's primary task was to *"proclaim a baptism of repentance"* to the nation of <u>Israel</u>. Generation after generation, God's mission-heart had sent many prophets to his people Israel, in order to call them to repentance and point them to a Messiah who would soon come to rescue them from sin. Now here was the last prophet of the Old Testament (v 4; 1:76; 7:26-27), John who *"prepared the way of the Lord"* (v 4), by calling God's people to repentance, in order to point them to Jesus. How gracious and patient God's heart is! How he longed for these stubborn people to repent and be the missionaries that he had called them to be (13:34; ²M. M. Ac 13:46)! And how eagerly he continues to call his people, the new Israel to go and plead with the lost people of every nation! It is a new mission imperative. M. I. Lk 3:3a: Christians should, in love, warn lost people who do not repent. **2)** Furthermore, note that John apparently emphasized the Law much more strongly than the Gospel. Perhaps God gave him this assignment, at least partly, because the Jews had had their own written Word for so many generations that clearly pointed to the Messiah. Especially their religious leaders should have been carefully studying their Scriptures and teaching their people; but sadly, they had obviously done neither. John needed to convict them of their sin of self-righteously depending on their blood relationship to their father Abraham, so that they would see their need for a Savior and be ready to hear the Gospel. Therefore, we can be sure that John depended on the Holy Spirit to guide him to emphasize the Law. Thus, it's vital that modern missionaries also depend on the Spirit's guidance for whether they should emphasize the Law or the Gospel, and which one to apply first. It is a new mission imperative. M. I. Lk 3:3b: Christians should always depend on the Holy Spirit's guidance for whether they should emphasize God's Law or the Gospel about Jesus, and which one to apply first.

3:5 All of the metaphors in this verse are from the prophet Isaiah, and they all have the same meaning of repentance, turning away from sin and turning toward the coming King. All people of all nations are equal before the Law and all stand condemned. Likewise, all are called to the same repentance and faith and to be baptized with the same Trinitarian Baptism. Note that verse 14 says that John also called Gentile soldiers to repentance and faith. It is very significant to note here that John mainly emphasized that all people urgently need to repent, so that they would look for someone to rescue them from their sin; therefore John apparently first proclaimed the Law. Whether or not John always <u>began</u> every message by proclaiming the Law certainly depended on the circumstances surrounding each opportunity that he had to witness, but it's always important for modern missionaries that at some point <u>every</u> hearer needs to hear the Law. (For example: Every hearer needs to be convicted of his sin, so that he feels the need for a rescue; however, the missionary may, in some cases, know that his hearer is already feeling very guilty before God and needs very little or even no reminder of his guilt.) The only issues are: how strongly should they emphasize both the Law and the Gospel, and in what sequence should they apply them in each situation ([3]M. I. Lk 3:3b)?

3:6 Luke, the <u>Gentile</u> Gospel writer, continues to emphasize that God sent his Son Jesus to save *"<u>all</u> flesh"* (v 6; 19:10). He uses every possible opportunity to make this point, so that no one from any culture in the world feels like he is left out ([4]M. M. Lk 1:1).

3:7 (1) *"The wrath to come,"* of course, refers to God's <u>final</u> judgment on Judgment Day on <u>all</u> people who have rejected his love (1 Thess 1:10). They will stand all <u>alone</u> to be condemned, because they rejected Jesus. And how terribly this will grieve God's mission-heart that day! How long and extremely patiently he had waited for each one of them to repent (Lk 15:20)! And how eagerly he had waited for his chosen nation Israel and for his Church to go and call them to repentance! But how slow and reluctant they were ([5]M. I. Ac 1:8)! **2)** However, on the other hand, all those who trusted in Jesus will be able to <u>stand</u> on that Judgment Day, because Jesus will stand <u>beside</u> them and say, "He is my brother," or "She is my sister." They trusted in me to cover them with the robe of my righteousness (Rev 6:11; [6]M. M. Lk 12:8).

3:8 (1) In spite of the fact that God chose the nation of Israel because of his rich grace alone, many Jews foolishly and stubbornly chose to <u>not</u> trust in his grace. Instead, they often became proud, doubted God's grace, chose the way of work righteousness, and foolishly depended on their <u>blood</u> relationship with Abraham. They loved to boast, as they did here, *"Abraham is <u>our</u> father."* However, God's gracious plan has always been that he would bless all nations <u>through</u> Abraham (Gen 12:1-3), and treat <u>all</u> of his children without discrimination. His mission-heart has always longed to graciously create a repentant heart and faith in himself in every lost sinner from every nation on earth; however, in his gracious will, only those who do, in fact, receive a repentant heart and faith in his Son Jesus are the true spiritual descendants of Abraham (Rom 4:16-25; Gal 3:7-9; [7]M. M. Ro 4:11). **2)** When John said, *"Do not begin to say to yourselves, 'We have Abraham as our father'"* he was publicly condemning the crowds for believing and teaching Satan's lies, so that people would turn away from the devil and learn to know the truth about Jesus. A very important part of proclaiming the Law is refuting false doctrine (2 Tim 3:16), so that Satan's lies and the truth of Jesus are thus set in juxtaposition for all to see. It's another new mission imperative. M. I. Lk 3:8: Christians should always be prepared to boldly and publicly refute false teaching, so that Satan cannot easily deceive people. **3)** John uses the powerful figure of speech of *"stones"* to give a very stern warning that everyone needs to repent. Stones are, of course, inanimate; and therefore, they cannot choose to either rebel against God or to return his love. Thus, humanly speaking, it would be easier for God to create repentance and faith in a stone than in a living human being (1:37)! But, of course, he doesn't do so, since his gracious mission-heart doesn't love stones in the same way that he loves all of the people whom he has made. Rather, God has made each one of his dear children with a pliable heart that he can change into a repentant heart that chooses to respond to his gracious call. Note that both repentance and faith are God's gracious gifts; his actions and not human actions, because a lost or spiritually dead person is just that—dead. (Note that God pleads with lost sinners to repent and believe; and then, contrary to our feeble human logic, he also graciously gives these two gifts to those who respond to his love. We all totally depend on his grace alone!) Therefore, because their Lord loves all of the people who are lost, Christians too should love them and hurry on their urgent mission to *"seek...the lost"* by calling them to repentance and faith in Jesus through their words and deeds (Mt 7:14; Jn 14:6; [8]M. I. Lk 3:3a).

3:9 Just as God's purpose in making all trees is that each type of tree would bear its own unique kind of fruit, likewise, God's purpose in graciously giving each person the gift of faith in Jesus is that he would produce his own <u>unique</u> kind of fruit—good deeds that he does within the context of his own <u>unique</u> language and culture. God's perfect plan is that these acts of faith would have wonderful <u>diversity</u> as each Christian glorifies his holy name as a witness to the lost (1 Cor 10:31; Rom 12:1-2). However, in sharp contrast, deeds done in unbelief dishonor his name and therefore deserve his condemnation ([9]M. I. Jn 14:15).

3:12-14 We see in verses 12 and 14 that, while John's primary call was to his fellow Jews (Rom 1:16), he was also faithful in calling <u>Gentiles</u> who came out to the desert to listen to his call to repentance and faith ([10]M. M. Ac 13:46). Both *"tax collectors"* who were Jews, and *"soldiers,"* who probably were Gentiles came to hear John. (However, some scholars such as W. F. Arndt in the Concordia Classic Commentary Series think that these soldiers may have been Jewish Temple guards. But that seems to be less likely.)

3:16-17 (1) John had received two gracious gifts from God: <u>faith</u> to trust in Jesus as the Messiah whom he was called to serve and also a special <u>call</u> to proclaim God's Law and Gospel message about Jesus. Therefore, he had been a faithful missionary, calling others to the same repentance and faith in Jesus that he had in him. Such a <u>servant</u> attitude is the kind of fruit that God hopes to see from every person who believes. These statements by John indicate that he had faithfully done all that he could in preparing the hearts of people to receive Jesus; and he could therefore now hand over his work to the <u>greatest</u> prophet of all, Jesus. Jesus was the God/man prophet who, not only proclaimed the same Law and Gospel message to *"the lost"* (Mk 1:14-15; 19:10), he himself <u>was</u> the Word of God incarnate (Jn 1:1-2, 10). Obviously the entire Jewish nation did not repent when they heard John's message, as the pagan Gentiles in Nineveh did (Jonah 3:6-9); therefore, it was necessary for Jesus to continue to preach the same message ([11]M. M. Ac 13:46). **2)** *"Fire"* in verse 16 most likely refers to God's judgment, since verse 17 says, *"the chaff he will burn with unquenchable fire,"* which is clearly a judgment theme (1 Cor 3:13). Furthermore, the message that the Lord Jesus has given to his missionaries to proclaim to *"the lost"* has two vital parts: the condemnation of the Law and his beautiful Gospel that comforts those who do repent and believe in Jesus as their Messiah; therefore, both John and Jesus always proclaimed both parts of the message (Mk 1:15); and the Church continues to do the same yet today (M. M. Ac 13:46).

3:19 John had <u>boldly</u> called King Herod to repentance by saying in (Mt 14:4) *"It is not lawful for you to have her [his brother's wife],"* even though he, no doubt, realized how extremely dangerous it was to do so. And we can be sure that John used the Scripture to clearly and boldly convict King Herod of his sin, because John was clearly sent by God to proclaim his message. He was only God's messenger, and he was willing to die for boldly delivering it, because it was <u>not</u> his own words ([12]M. I. Ac 4:20).

3:21 (1) In submitting to John's Baptism of repentance Jesus demonstrated his rich <u>grace</u> by willingly taking the first step of accepting the guilt of <u>our</u> sin, the sin of his brothers and sisters—even though he himself was holy (1 Jn 5:6; 2 Cor 5:21; Is 53:4-5). Then, in a few years, he willingly obeyed his Father's will (1:1; 4:21; 22;16; 24:44) and <u>fully</u> took all of our guilt on himself on the cross. Thus, already at his Baptism, he showed the true purpose of his coming to *"seek...and save the lost"* (19:10; [13]M. M. Heb 7:22). **2)** Luke is the only Gospel writer who notes in verse 21 that Jesus was <u>praying</u> at his Baptism. A common theme of his Gospel is that Jesus frequently prayed in order to know his Father's will in everything that he did. The author of the book of Hebrews talks in (10:5-10) about the relationship between Jesus and his Father before he gave Jesus a human body. The author speaks in human terms as if they had a discussion about what Jesus' role as the God/man would be in completing his Father's perfect plan of salvation. This "discussion," to some degree, helps us understand why Jesus felt the need to constantly be in prayer with his Father. Jesus obviously shared his Father's mission-heart and therefore loved him and his holy will unfailingly (22:42), so he sought to understand and follow his plan completely and perfectly. Thus, his constant prayers were essential to everything that Jesus did on his mission to the world ([14]M. I. Lk 11:10).

3:22 (1) Note how the <u>Holy Spirit</u> actively did <u>three</u> things: **a)** He *"descended on"* Jesus at his Baptism (v 22). **b)** He, then, compelled him to go into the wilderness (4:1). **c)** And then, he graciously compelled Jesus to return to Galilee (4:14). In addition, at his Baptism, Jesus' Father spoke and affirmed that he was his own *"beloved Son"* (v 22). Clearly all three persons of the holy Trinity shared the same mission-heart, and all were fully engaged in carrying out these most vital aspects of their plan of salvation, which culminated in Jesus' suffering, death and resurrection. Deep love and grace for rebellious mankind in their mission-heart, that is far beyond our feeble human comprehension, was obviously moving their every action to *"seek and to save the lost"* (19:10; Jn 3:16; Eph 3:18-19; [15]M. M. Lk 1:1). **2)** When the Holy Spirit "descended on" (v 22) Jesus at his Baptism, John was assured that his cousin, Jesus was indeed the Messiah; even though he did begin to doubt it later (7:18-23). John's work was, therefore, now finished since God had sent him to prepare the way for Jesus (Jn 1:33); and Jesus' Baptism marks a significant transition: the end of John's mission and the beginning of Jesus' mission (v 23, 19:10; [16]M. M. Mt 5:14). **3)** Since the Father himself addressed Jesus in verse 22, his words would also have been strong encouragement to Jesus as he began his mission, especially since Satan would very soon tempt him to doubt these very Words of his Father. God was *"pleased"* with Jesus (v 22) both because he trusted his Father (Gen 15:6; Heb 11:6; M. M. Lk 1:1) and also because he had willingly accepted a human body, in order to carry out his Father's plan to save sinful mankind (Heb 10:5-7; [17]M. M. Lk 1:26).

The Genealogy of Jesus Christ 3:23-38

3:23 *Jesus, when he began his ministry, was about thirty years of age, being the son (as was supposed) of Joseph, the son of Heli,*
3:24 *the son of Matthat, the son of Levi, the son of Melchi, the son of Jannai, the son of Joseph,*
3:25 *the son of Mattathias, the son of Amos, the son of Nahum, the son of Esli, the son of Naggai,*
3:26 *the son of Maath, the son of Mattathias, the son of Semein, the son of Josech, the son of Joda,*
3:27 *the son of Joanan, the son of Rhesa, the son of Zerubbabel, the*

- 3:28 *son of Shealtiel, the son of Neri,*
- 3:28 *the son of Melchi, the son of Addi, the son of Cosam, the son of Elmadam, the son of Er,*
- 3:29 *the son of Joshua, the son of Eliezer, the son of Jorim, the son of Matthat, the son of Levi,*
- 3:30 *the son of Simeon, the son of Judah, the son of Joseph, the son of Jonam, the son of Eliakim,*
- 3:31 *the son of Melea, the son of Menna, the son of Mattatha, the son of Nathan, the son of David,*
- 3:32 *the son of Jesse, the son of Obed, the son of Boaz, the son of Sala, the son of Nahshon,*
- 3:33 *the son of Amminadab, the son of Admin, the son of Arni, the son of Hezron, the son of Perez, the son of Judah,*
- 3:34 *the son of Jacob, the son of Isaac, the son of Abraham, the son of Terah, the son of Nahor,*
- 3:35 *the son of Serug, the son of Reu, the son of Peleg, the son of Eber, the son of Shelah,*
- 3:36 *the son of Cainan, the son of Arphaxad, the son of Shem, the son of Noah, the son of Lamech,*
- 3:37 *the son of Methuselah, the son of Enoch, the son of Jared, the son of Mahalaleel, the son of Cainan,*
- 3:38 *the son of Enos, the son of Seth, the son of Adam, the son of God.*

3:23 (1) Note that Luke says in verse 23 that Jesus *"began his ministry;"* however, the first place the Holy Spirit actually guides him is into the wilderness in (4:1). What a strange place that seems to be to *"seek...the lost!"* Yet, in the wilderness of sin is <u>exactly</u> where the lost human race is and where Christians continue to struggle yet today. After beginning to take on our sin at his Baptism, Jesus began to face the terrible temptations of Satan with a weakened body just like ours—just where weak sinners are. This was where he began to graciously share our suffering; thus, his passion actually began three years before the awful night in the garden of Gethsemane; and it, of course, culminated in his final terrible confrontation with the devil on the cross ([18]M. M. Lk 1:1). **2)** In the Jewish culture, a boy became a young man at age 12

(2:41-42), but he did not become a mature man until age 30. Note that (Num 4:47) says that the Levites began to serve in the temple at the age of 30. When he was a mature man, Jesus began to *"seek and save the lost"* full time. He was now mature because he had now fully *"increased in wisdom and in stature"* as a true human being (2:52). His heavenly Father had equipped him to do everything that he sent him to do (Heb 10:5-7; [19]M. M. 1 Cor 12:11).

3:24-38 (1) Some have argued that part of Luke's genealogy, from King David to Jesus, differs from that of Matthew since Luke traces the genealogy of Mary, while Matthew traces that of Joseph. (See W. F. Arndt in the Concordia Classic Commentary Series, as well as The Concordia Self Study Bible.) If this is correct, then Luke identifies Eli as the father of Mary; and thus Mary was also a descendant of King David; while Matthew identifies Jacob as the father of Joseph, making Joseph his descendant. And Luke's phrase here in verse 23, *"(as was supposed)"* certainly seems to support this idea. In any case, regardless of who Eli was, Luke's point is that *Jesus* was a full-blooded Jew, a vital fact that was necessary to carry out his dual mission to "seek and save the lost" ([20]M. M. Lk 1:27). **2)** Obviously, the main point of Luke's genealogy is to once again state the dual truth that Jesus was both true man, *"the son of Adam"* (v 38) and true God, *"the son of God"* (v 38). These two truths are so vital to Jesus being able to complete his mission to rescue all people from sin that Luke uses every possible opportunity to repeat both truths in many different ways, even though Luke himself was a Gentile (M. M. Lk 1:27 & [21]Lk 1:35). **3)** However, it's likewise very important to add that each time the two words, *"son of"* occur in verses 23-38, the Jews of that time understood them to mean two things: **a)** that one person was a physical descendant of another person. **b)** And in verses 23, these two words also meant that Jesus had all of the characteristics of being a human being (Heb 2:14-15; 4:15); and the same two words in verse 38 also meant that Jesus had all of the characteristics of being God (v 12). Note two examples. **a)** When Satan tempted Jesus in (4:1-13), Jesus had all of the characteristics of being a human being, which meant that all three temptations were very real temptations. As a true human being, he could have sinned and submitted to any one of them. But he graciously did not do so for the sake of all of his brothers and sisters (4:4, 8, 12). **b)** Likewise, when Satan tempted Jesus in (4:9-11) by setting him on the pinnacle of the temple, Jesus responded in (4:12) by calling himself <u>God</u>. He said, *"You shall not put the Lord your <u>God</u> to the test."* Even though he was true God, he graciously did not test his heavenly Father by recklessly throwing himself off and demanding that he save him. This too was a very real temptation; but he did not sin for the sake of all of his brothers and sisters (4:8; [22]M. I. Lk 11:4b).

---

[1] M. M. Lk 1:1: Jesus came to seek and save <u>all</u> lost people from <u>every</u> nation on earth.

[2] M. M. Ac 13:46: As he did with the old Israel, God <u>first of all</u> strengthens the faith of the new Israel, the Church with his Word and Sacraments, so that they can go and witness to the lost people of all nations.

[3] M. I. Lk 3:3b: Christians should always depend on the Holy Spirit's guidance for whether they should emphasize God's Law or the Gospel about Jesus, and which one to apply <u>first</u>.

[4] M. M. Lk 1:1: Jesus came to seek and save <u>all</u> lost people from <u>every</u> nation on earth.

[5] M. I. Ac 1:8: Christians should go and witness about Jesus to all who are lost from all languages and cultures by depending on the power of the Holy Spirit to help them bridge all of the language/cultural boundaries whether they are relatively easy, as in their own language, or extremely difficult.

[6] M. M. Lk 12:8: On Judgment Day, Jesus will acknowledge before his heavenly Father that all Christians are his brothers and sisters.

[7] M. M. Ro 4:11: All Christians from every nation on earth belong to the <u>spiritual family</u> of Abraham, the Church because they share the same faith in Jesus that their father had.

[8] M. I. Lk 3:3a: Christians should, in love, warn lost people who do not repent.

[9] M. I. Jn 14:15: Christians should obey all of Jesus' commands in grateful response to his love for them as they go on his mission to the world.

[10] M. M. Ac 13:46: As he did with the old Israel, God <u>first of all</u> strengthens the faith of the new Israel, the Church with his Word and Sacraments, so that they can go and witness to the lost people of all nations.

[11] M. M. Ac 13:46: As he did with the old Israel, God <u>first of all</u> strengthens the faith of the new Israel, the Church with his Word and Sacraments, so that they can go and witness to the lost people of all nations.

[12] M. I. Ac 4:20: Christians should boldly witness to the name of Jesus and allow nothing to stop their witness because it is the Holy Spirit's own message.

[13] M. M. Heb 7:22: As the great High Priest, Jesus guaranties by his holy life and holy sacrifice that his promise to forgive the sins of Christians is forever sure.

[14] M. I. Lk 11:10: Christians should <u>continuously</u> pray to their heavenly Father and <u>always</u>

depend on his grace, and not on their own feeble strength, because he <u>always</u> loves them.

[15] M. M. Lk 1:1: Jesus came to seek and save <u>all</u> lost people from <u>every</u> nation on earth.

[16] M. M. Mt 5:14: When the Holy Spirit creates faith in a person's heart, he also graciously gives him a new mission-heart that is eager to shine the light of the Gospel throughout the whole world.

[17] M. M. Lk 1:26: The heavenly Father sent his Son, Jesus to be born and live in <u>humble</u> circumstances, so that everyone from every nation on earth would see his <u>grace</u>.

[18] M. M. Lk 1:1: Jesus came to seek and save <u>all</u> lost people from <u>every</u> nation on earth.

[19] M. M. 1 Cor 12:11: When Christians baptize people the same Holy Spirit graciously gives each one faith in Jesus plus a unique set of spiritual gifts so that he can use them in order to expand the Lord's mission.

[20] M. M. Lk 1:27: Jesus had to be born as a true human being and as a true Jew in order to become the King of kings in his heavenly kingdom forever.

[21] M. M. Lk 1:35: Jesus had to be born as true God, in order to rescue all of mankind from sin.

[22] M. I. Lk 11:4b: Christians should ask their heavenly Father that he would not allow Satan to tempt them so severely that they lose their faith, and also that he would give them his strength to depend on his grace in all of their trials.

Chapter 4

The Temptation of Jesus 4:1-13

4:1   *And Jesus, full of the Holy Spirit, returned from the Jordan and was led by the Spirit in the wilderness*
4:2   *for forty days, being tempted by the devil. And he ate nothing during those days. And when they were ended, he was hungry.*
4:3   *The devil said to him, "If you are the Son of God, command this stone to become bread."*
4:4   *And Jesus answered him, "It is written, 'Man shall not live by bread alone.'"*
4:5   *And the devil took him up and showed him all the kingdoms of the world in a moment of time,*
4:6   *and said to him, "To you I will give all this authority and their glory, for it has been delivered to me, and I give it to whom I will.*
4:7   *If you, then, will worship me, it will all be yours."*
4:8   *And Jesus answered him, "It is written, "'You shall worship the Lord your God, and him only shall you serve.'"*
4:9   *And he took him to Jerusalem and set him on the pinnacle of the temple and said to him, "If you are the Son of God, throw yourself down from here,*
4:10 *for it is written, "'He will command his angels concerning you, to guard you,'*
4:11 *and "'On their hands they will bear you up, lest you strike your foot against a stone.'"*
4:12 *And Jesus answered him, "It is said, 'You shall not put the Lord your God to the test.'"*
4:13 *And when the devil had ended every temptation, he departed from him until an opportune time.*

4:1 Why did the Holy Spirit lead Jesus into the desert so that Satan could tempt him? He sent him there for at least <u>five</u> reasons: **a)** First of all, no mere human being can resist the temptations of the devil and obey God perfectly. All human beings (except for Jesus) are born with the same sinful human nature because our father, Adam sinned (Ps 51:5; Rom 5:12-14; [1]M. M. Ro 3:26). **b)** Therefore, someone had to do this for mankind; and thus, it was absolutely essential that Jesus also be born as a true human being, so that Satan's temptations would be real tests. And Jesus is a true human being because he has a human mother, Mary (2:7; [2]M. M. Mt 1:22). **c)** And furthermore, it was also absolutely essential that Jesus be born as true God, so that he would be able to obey his Father perfectly. And he is also true God and was born without sin because God is his Father (2:49; [3]M. M. Lk 1:35). **d)** Thus, in his rich grace, Jesus temporarily put aside the full power of his divine nature, and truly overcame the same temptations that all of his brothers and sisters face. He used the sword of his Spirit three times to defeat him in the desert and then continued to overcome him throughout the three years of his mission (vs 4, 8 & 12). What glorious Good News this is for all lost people in every culture of the world (22:37; 24:44; Heb 4:15; [4]M. I. Lk 11:4b)! **e)** And finally, he defeated Satan so that his Spirit would be able to graciously give all Christians the strength that they need to also defeat his evil plots. This evil world where Satan still lurks is also mankind's desert where Christians urgently need their Lord's grace to be able to say "No" to the devil. Anyone who tries to depend on his own feeble strength to stand against him will surely fail; but through faith in Jesus, our Brother we too are able to boldly defy him. Jesus' 40 days in the desert were another vital part of his mission ([5]M. I. Lk 4:4).

4:2 Jesus' 40 days of temptation in the desert was a reminder of the 40 years that God tested his chosen people, Israel in the desert of Sinai; nevertheless, Jesus' temptation was also far more than symbolic. Because the Israel of the Old Covenant failed to obey the covenant that God had established with them in that desert (Deu 8:2-3), Jesus suffered in this desert in the place of the old Israel and also the New Israel, the Church. How graciously he continued to display his mission-heart in this desert for all of his brothers and sisters to see! And Christians urgently need to depend on his rich grace every single day because that extremely dangerous *"lion"* is never far away (1 Pt 5:8; Rom 4:16; [6]M. M. Heb 7:17).

4:3, 9 (1) Satan stated a truth, but added *"if"* twice in verses 3 and 9 in order to plant the seed of doubt in Jesus' mind. This little word was so clever because it was an attack on the issue of Jesus' divinity; the devil tried to deceive him into questioning the same truth that Jesus' heavenly Father himself had stated just days earlier when he said, *"You are my beloved Son"* (3:22). Obviously, his Father had intended that his Words of assurance would still be very fresh in Jesus' memory when Satan questioned whether he was God's Son. From the devil's first temptation of Adam and Eve until today, he has always tried to deceive people by trying to plant doubt in his victim's minds. All of his temptations contain this same *"if."* In (Gen 3:1) he asked Eve, *"Did God actually say?"* And unfortunately, Eve wasn't so sure. He always says, *"If Jesus is not true God or true man, then listen to me."* But before these temptations of Jesus, his Father really did say, *"You are my beloved Son,"* and for our sakes, Jesus never doubted this truth ([7]M. M. Lk 1:27 & Lk 1:35). Therefore, all of his brothers and sisters who depend on his grace as true God and true man are also able to depend on the power of his Spirit to say "No" to Satan just as he did ([8]M. I. Lk 11:10). **2)** After a 40 day fast of no food and no water (v 2), Jesus would have been extremely weak, so Satan's temptation to use his divine power to make food for himself would have been very powerful. But this temptation was, of course, evil because, if he had done so, he would have: **a)** yielded to Satan's will to selfishly use his divine power, **b)** doubted his Father's love for him and his ability to care for his own Son, and **c)** he would not have obeyed his Father's mission-heart that he should overcome all temptations on behalf of all mankind. But Jesus did not yield to the temptation to be like God (Phil 2:6), as Adam did and as we also do, since every sin is a sin of pride, of worshipping ourselves instead of God. Therefore, the Good News for all of us is: because he did not yield to the devil, we too can, through faith in him, depend on his grace to resist all temptations (Heb 2:18, 19:10; [9]M. I. Lk 11:10). What a message he gives to all Christians to spread far and wide since we are all his missionaries!

4:4-12 (1) Jesus' answer to each temptation was to, three times, wield the mighty sword of God's Word, which is the power of his Spirit (Eph 6:17). Why did he do so? **a)** First of all, as a true human being, he knew that he was at that moment physically very weak; and the temptations were thus very real. He obviously willingly allowed himself to become weak for our sakes, so that he could overcome the devil on our behalf. He could not have done so if he had only been God. **b)** Secondly, he wanted to also teach us how we too would be able to defeat Satan because Jesus would soon be sending his Church on the same dangerous mission to *"seek...the lost"* (Mt 28:18-20; Ac 1:8). And how dangerous our Lord's mission is, since Satan hates it when Christians proclaim the Gospel! Therefore, Jesus did not depend on his own strength; he defeated Satan three times by depending on his Spirit's strength in his holy Word. It's a new mission imperative. M. I. Lk 4:4: When Satan attacks Christians on their mission they should wield the sword of God's Word by quoting from it, and not depend on their own strength. **2)** Furthermore, verse 4 strongly implies a very vital truth about his holy Word, since the spiritual "bread" that Jesus refers to here is, of course, his holy Word. This truth is that his Spirit only uses his holy Word as a mighty sword to condemn sin and to create, strengthen and preserve faith. St. Paul tells us in (Rom 10:17), *"So faith comes from hearing, and hearing through the word of Christ"* (2 Tim 3:16-17; [10]M. M. Ro 10:17a). And of course, his Spirit likewise used his Word to strengthen Jesus' faith in this bitter battle with the evil one. Therefore, it's obvious that we too should eagerly "eat" this precious food every day in our daily devotions and in regular worship in church, so that his Spirit can work in our hearts as well to strengthen our faith (11:3; Mt 6:11). And it is equally obvious that we Christians should hurry to the ends of the earth to share this sweet tasting food with the many, many people who are still lost all over the world (M. M. Ro 10:17a).

4:6 (1) Like all of Satan's temptations, the devil's statement in verse 6 was only half true. He was tempting Jesus who was the Word, and through whom God made the entire world. Nevertheless, the devil was then, and still is, *"the ruler of this world"* (Jn 12:31; 14:30; 16:11), even though God still controls the universe he made ([11]M. M. Ro 1:19). And when the devil deceived Adam and Eve, he tore them and all of their children away from serving God alone to serving the devil as his slaves. Likewise today, before a person has faith in Jesus, he is Satan's slave and has only one choice—to obey Satan (Rom 6:19, 22; Eph 2:1-2). But when Jesus overcame Satan in the desert and then died on the cross, he completely broke his power, so that through faith in Jesus the Holy Spirit enables Christians to choose to say "No" to Satan and to obey God ([12]M. I. Lk 4:4). **2)** This temptation for Jesus was to choose the easy way; to not obey his Father's will to walk the painful way of humility and suffering, the way of the cross. However, by obeying his Father he would receive his rightful crown from his Father, and not from Satan (v 6; Phil 2:6-9). Satan tempted Jesus to love the temporarily beautiful things of this world and to worship him. In his weak human condition this too would have been a powerful test. If he had followed Satan's way, he of course, would not have defeated Satan, and Satan would have continued to enslave all of mankind forever. Instead, Jesus wielded the sword of his Word and defeated him in order to *"save"* all of *"the lost"* (19:10; M. I. Lk 4:4).

4:7 (1) All sin is a violation of the first commandment, worshipping Satan and oneself instead of worshipping God (Ex 20:3). There is no such thing as a "small" sin or a "greater" sin. Sin is sin, and all sin rightfully angers God. Therefore, we thank and praise Jesus that he never once doubted his Father, never worshipped anyone but him alone. And he did so for us weak and foolish human beings, because no other human being could please our heavenly Father in this way. And what is so awesome is that Jesus not only did so in his weakened condition in the desert, he also did so some years later in his passion and on the cross. He did so for us because his mission-heart compelled him to love every person he has ever made equally, no matter how rebellious we all have been (19:10; [13]M. M. Ro 3:24 & [14]Ro 8:29b). **2)** Satan said, *"It will all be yours."* What a statement to the very person who had made all of it! All sin is also the proud desire to control God or others, which is, obviously once again, a violation of the first commandment. All pride is sin, while humility is an act of obedience to God. In his entire life, Jesus was never proud. By completely trusting his Father, he served him for our sake since we could not do so (Phil 2:5-8; [15]M. I. Lk 11:10).

4:9 The temptation in verse 9 was also very evil because Satan here tempted Jesus to test his Father's love for him. For a person to deliberately place oneself in harm's way is to <u>demand</u> a miracle from God, to proudly say that you <u>deserve</u> his help, that you do <u>not</u> <u>need</u> to depend on his grace and love. It's true that God did indeed promise to protect his people, but no one <u>deserves</u> his rescue. Note how Satan cleverly quotes one such promise from Scripture in verse 10, *"He [God] will command his angels concerning you, to guard you."* God rescues us as a free <u>gift</u> because his gracious mission-heart compels him to love us, in spite of our sins (M. I. Lk 11:10).

4:13 (1) When Luke says in verse 13 that the devil *"had ended every temptation,"* he seems to imply that Satan tempted him many times during the 40 days; and verse 13 likewise makes it clear that he also continued to tempt him <u>many more</u> times throughout Jesus' life. However, these three temptations were perhaps recorded for at least <u>three</u> reasons: **a)** to teach us how to defeat Satan with God's Word, **b)** to teach all human beings that Jesus experienced exactly the same clever temptations from Satan that we all experience; but for our sake he did not sin (Heb 4:15), **c)** and to demonstrate Satan's super-human cleverness as a warning to us. In this way, Jesus shows us in very practical ways how he rescues us when we depend on his grace when the devil tempts us ([16]M. I. Lk 4:4). **2)** All Christians should learn <u>two</u> things from Jesus' temptations in the desert: **a)** First, that all who live in this evil world are living in a <u>dangerous desert</u> where Satan is never very far away. He and his evil angels are a <u>constant</u> threat to all Christians, even though all of his demons are weaker than our Lord because he defeated them on the cross. **b)** Secondly, since Satan is eager to destroy all of our mission efforts, it is also extremely <u>dangerous</u> for us to go on our Lord's mission, especially if we try to depend on our own strength. But through prayerful dependence on him we go forth with courage and joy (1 Pet 5:8; Eph 6:10-18; [17]M. I. Lk 11:10 & Lk 4:4).

Jesus Begins His Ministry 4:14-15

4:14 *And Jesus returned in the power of the Spirit to Galilee, and a report about him went out through all the surrounding country.*
4:15 *And he taught in their synagogues, being glorified by all.*

4:14 Luke begins his narrative about how Jesus began to personally *"seek...the lost"* on his first missionary journey. Just as the Spirit first sent him into the wilderness, he now led him into Galilee. In his mission-heart, God was carefully carrying out his whole plan of salvation. However, verse 23 makes it clear that Jesus did not begin his mission in his hometown of Nazareth. In fact some scholars suggest that he carried out his mission elsewhere in Galilee for as long as a whole year before going "home." It's not clear why he began his mission in Galilee, but we do know that, in the nation of Israel, the largest concentrations of Gentiles lived in Galilee; therefore it's possible that Jesus deliberately went there to have opportunities to witness to Gentiles ([18]M. M. Lk 1:1).

Jesus Rejected at Nazareth 4:16-30

4:16 *And he came to Nazareth, where he had been brought up. And as was his custom, he went to the synagogue on the Sabbath day, and he stood up to read.*

4:17 *And the scroll of the prophet Isaiah was given to him. He unrolled the scroll and found the place where it was written,*

4:18 *"The Spirit of the Lord is upon me, because he has anointed me to proclaim good news to the poor. He has sent me to proclaim liberty to the captives and recovering of sight to the blind, to set at liberty those who are oppressed,*

4:19 to proclaim the year of the Lord's favor."

4:20 *And he rolled up the scroll and gave it back to the attendant and sat down. And the eyes of all in the synagogue were fixed on him.*

4:21 *And he began to say to them, "Today this Scripture has been fulfilled in your hearing."*

4:22 *And all spoke well of him and marveled at the gracious words that were coming from his mouth. And they said, "Is not this Joseph's son?"*

4:23 *And he said to them, "Doubtless you will quote to me this proverb, 'Physician, heal yourself.' What we have heard you*

	did at Capernaum, do here in your hometown as well."
4:24	*And he said, "Truly, I say to you, no prophet is acceptable in his hometown.*
4:25	*But in truth, I tell you, there were many widows in Israel in the days of Elijah, when the heavens were shut up three years and six months, and a great famine came over all the land,*
4:26	*and Elijah was sent to none of them but only to Zarephath, in the land of Sidon, to a woman who was a widow.*
4:27	*And there were many lepers in Israel in the time of the prophet Elisha, and none of them was cleansed, but only Naaman the Syrian."*
4:28	*When they heard these things, all in the synagogue were filled with wrath.*
4:29	*And they rose up and drove him out of the town and brought him to the brow of the hill on which their town was built, so that they could throw him down the cliff.*
4:30	*But passing through their midst, he went away.*

4:15-16 (1) Luke reports that Jesus *"taught in their synagogues"* in Galilee; and this may suggest that by his actions Jesus was teaching his disciples that God had called them to first tell the Law and the Gospel message to the Jews. Some years later, God continued to apply this mission message, when he began to first strengthen the new Israel, the Church with his holy Word, so that they would be able to go out into the world on his mission (Ac 13:46; [19]M. M. Ac 13:46). **2)** Even though Satan was always lurking about to try to deceive Jesus (v 13), the Holy Spirit was even nearer to Jesus, within his heart, to guide and strengthen him. As a true human being, he needed both his guidance and his strength in order to complete his mission with perfect obedience to his heavenly Father ([20]M. I. Lk 11:10). **3)** Verse 16 says that *"as was his custom, he [Jesus] went to the synagogue on the Sabbath day;"* which was the day of worship; and of course, he did so mainly because he always faithfully worshipped God there. But he also went there because it gave him opportunities to proclaim the Gospel message to people who were lost. All four Gospel writers record the fact that Jesus faithfully attended synagogues on the Sabbath. But why were the synagogues such excellent venues for him (and St. Paul) to proclaim the Gospel? There were at least four important reasons why: **a)** First of all, nearly every Jewish town (including Jerusalem) had a synagogue where devout Jews, as well as some pious Gentiles, went to worship. **b)** And secondly, the synagogues were the only places, except for the temple in Jerusalem, where copies of the Scriptures were kept; therefore, devout people went to their synagogues to study and hear the God's Word. Thus, Jesus went to the synagogues because he wanted to base his messages on his holy Word ([21]M. I. Lk 4:17). **c)** Thirdly, the synagogues were also a venue where all of the people considered the Scriptures to be God's Word, because it was inspired by his Spirit. They were therefore very open to hear how the speaker applied his Word to their lives ([22]M. M. Ro 10:17a & [23]Ac 13:46). **d)** And finally, on each Sabbath, the leader of the synagogue invited someone to read one reading from the Law and one from the Prophets and then expound on the meaning of both readings. And it was also common practice to invite a visiting teacher to do this. This created an opportunity for visitors to speak, which Jesus exploited on this Sabbath; and he no doubt did so much more often than the four Gospel writers have recorded. It's a new mission imperative. M. I. Lk 4:16: Christians should seize every opportunity to proclaim the Gospel message to lost people of all nations. **4)** Throughout Luke's account we see Jesus choose many different venues to proclaim the Good News. He taught by lake Galilee (5:1), in a private home (5:19) and on mountains (6:17). Jesus attracted large crowds who were eager to hear him for at least two reasons: **a)** because he spoke with such authority (v 32) **b)** and because he healed many sick people (v 36; [24]M. I. Lk 4:15).

4:17-18 (1) We can easily imagine Jesus' eagerness when he *"unrolled the scroll [of Isaiah]"* (v 17), so that he could begin to explain the true meaning of the passage. He must have been so eager for at least two reasons: **a)** Jesus knew that every passage of Scripture points to himself in some way, since he was the Messiah that they promised (24:27; [25]M. M. Mt 1:22). Even though this truth offended many of his hearers that day, they needed to hear it, repent and believe it in order to be saved by him. **b)** Secondly, he may also have based his message on a passage of

Scripture in order to teach his disciples that they should also base their own Law and Gospel messages on a passage of Scripture (Ac 13:15). And Jesus himself certainly continued to use this same method throughout his ministry. It's a new mission imperative. M. I. Lk 4:17: Christians should always base their messages on the Bible, so that the Holy Spirit can use his holy Word to convict their hearers of their sin and to create and strengthen faith in their hearts. **2)** One of the significant themes in Luke's account is that Jesus' mission-heart moved him to show special love to *"the poor…and those who are oppressed,"* as we see in this passage from Isaiah, and also throughout his ministry. He graciously loved those who received very little love from other people. These people were often both materially and also spiritually *"poor,"* since their spiritual leaders were probably not teaching them from the Scripture, as they should have been doing. Therefore, the poor were no doubt more eager than the wealthy people to depend on God's undeserved love (6:20; [26]M. I. Mt 19:14). Of course, Jesus also loved the rich; and he also preached to them, but they were very easily tempted to love their money more than anything else, therefore, the Gospels show that few of them repented and believed in him (18:24; [27]M. I. Lk 5:20). **4:19 (1)** While Isaiah was alluding to the Old Testament *"Year of Jubilee"* in verse 19, which was the year when the Israelites forgave all debts that people owed them once every 50 years, Jesus applied Isaiah's words to himself and to his own mission. He made the point that *"the year of the Lord's favor"* is now (v 21), the period of salvation when he himself would *"seek people who are lost"* by proclaiming liberation from sin to them, and *he* himself would *"save the lost"* on the cross by destroying sin's power and all its consequences (19:10; [28]M. M. Lk 1:1). **2)** Even though the people of Nazareth knew him from the time that he was a child, since he truly was their Messiah and Savior, he was, in fact, much, much more than he appeared to them to be. What wonderful Gospel that was for them! Nevertheless, the shock of these wonderful truths was only the first shock that they received that day. It was just too much for them, as we see in verse 22. (The second shock came in verses 26-27 when Jesus told them that his mission plan was to also go to the Gentiles, whom they hated.)

4:21 When Jesus began his message in verse 21 by saying, *"Today this Scripture has been fulfilled in your hearing"* he was very deliberately applying Isaiah's words to himself and thus teaching his hearers that, not only this passage, but also the entire Old Testament points to him as the Messiah for whom they had been waiting for many generations. It is very significant that Jesus begins his first recorded message in this way for at least two reasons: **a)** First of all, we can be certain that this was only the first time that he empathized this vital truth because he must have repeated it very frequently. And this is, no doubt, confirmed by the last chapter of Luke's Gospel. Luke says in (24:27), *"And beginning with Moses and all the Prophets, he [Jesus] interpreted to them in all the Scriptures the things concerning himself."* And in (24:44), Jesus himself says, *"everything written about me in the Law of Moses and the Prophets and the Psalms must be fulfilled."* (Verses 27 and 44 both refer to the entire Old Testament.) As the only true God and true man, Jesus is the only person who did indeed fulfill everything that God promised in the Old Testament. It's a new mission message. M. M. Lk 4:21: Every verse in the entire Bible points in some way to Jesus and his mission to seek and save the lost. **b)** Secondly, Jesus may have also deliberately chosen a synagogue as the first place where he said this, because the synagogues where obviously places of worship where the Jews heard and studied their written Scriptures (v 17). Their spiritual leaders should have been using the Scriptures to teach them about the coming Messiah. But obviously they had been doing so far too infrequently; and Jesus himself needed to do so ([29]M. I. Lk 12:40 & [30]Ro 1:17).

4:23 Jesus immediately explained the meaning of his proverb by saying in verse 23, *"What we have heard you did at Capernaum, do here in your hometown as well."* His hearers could only think of themselves, that he should heal them. But they did not trust in him as their Messiah nor depend on his grace. Instead, they felt that they deserved to be healed because of their blood relationship with him (3:8). However, all people are equal under God's grace; no one deserves his loving help, so he did not heal them. He did preach the Gospel to them, but they did not repent and believe in him ([31]M. I. Lk 3:3a).

4:26-28 (1) When he said in verses 26-28 that both the ancient prophets of Israel, Elijah and Elisha helped Gentiles by performing miracles instead of helping Israelites, Jesus deliberately gave the people of his hometown their second shock. He convicted them of their sin of thinking that they deserved God's grace ([32]M. M. Lk 1:26) and the Gentiles did not deserve it (M. M. Lk 1:26 & [33]M. I. Ac 1:8). **2)** Then, Jesus was probably not at all surprised when he saw in verse 28 that *"all in the synagogue were filled with wrath."* They, of course, knew that both *"Sidon"* and *"Syria"* were Gentile territories. Obviously, Jesus purposely emphasized the truth about God's mission-heart, that he never intended that he would bless only the nation of Israel. On the contrary, he has always healed whomever he graciously chooses to heal, because there is no human being who is sinless and deserves his help. No one who hears the Gospel deserves the gift of salvation it offers because God offers it by his grace alone. Since the people of Nazareth, in their pride as "God's chosen people" and blood relatives of Abraham, assumed that they deserved God's help more than pagan Gentiles, they were angry enough to want to kill Jesus. Such pride is the exact opposite of the humble faith of a small child (9:48; M. M. Lk 1:26).

4:30 It was obviously not the gracious will of the heavenly Father that Jesus' fellow Jews should, at this time, kill him in their proud anger (Jn 7:30). But when his right time did come (Rom 5:6; Gal 4:4), the unbelieving, proud spiritual leaders of the Jews would carry out the Father's will so that his Beloved Son would complete his gracious plan to save all nations on the cross (22:37; 24:44; M. M. Lk 1:26).

Jesus Heals a Man with an Unclean Demon 4:31-37

4:31 *And he went down to Capernaum, a city of Galilee. And he was teaching them on the Sabbath,*
4:32 *and they were astonished at his teaching, for his word possessed authority.*
4:33 *And in the synagogue there was a man who had the spirit of an unclean demon, and he cried out with a loud voice,*
4:34 *"Ha! What have you to do with us, Jesus of Nazareth? Have you come to destroy us? I know who you are--the Holy One of*

> *God."*
>
> 4:35 *But Jesus rebuked him, saying, "Be silent and come out of him!" And when the demon had thrown him down in their midst, he came out of him, having done him no harm.*
>
> 4:36 *And they were all amazed and said to one another, "What is this word? For with authority and power he commands the unclean spirits, and they come out!"*
>
> 4:37 *And reports about him went out into every place in the surrounding region.*

4:31-32 Luke continues to emphasize that Jesus was true God. Jesus spoke with *"authority"* (v 32) because the power of his Spirit was in the Words he spoke ([34]M. M. Lk 1:35). His Words created faith and drove out the enemy as he carried out his mission to *"seek...the lost"* (v 36; [35]M. M. Ro 10:17a).

4:33 While people in the so-called "Western world" may find this demon possession strange and unusual, people who live in cultures that practice Animism know exactly what Luke was talking about in verse 33. Christians in such cultures know that, yet today, evil spirits are constantly lurking about, especially at night; and while this knowledge is frightening, it nevertheless makes them better prepared for the struggle since they know exactly who their real enemy is. And equally important, they also know which weapon to use to defeat the demons, the mighty <u>sword</u> of God's Word, the Bible. Their Lord Jesus began to wield this sharp sword of his holy Word in the wilderness and drove Satan away (4:4-12), just as he wielded it again in verse 35. And therefore, they know that it can never grow dull ([36]M. I. Lk 4:4).

4:34 Note that the unbelieving Jews of Nazareth in verses 22-30 did not know who Jesus was. But in verse 34, the <u>demon</u> knew <u>exactly</u> who he was/is, that he was/is both true man and true God (Lk 1:27; 1:35). Therefore, the demon was, very rightly, terribly afraid of him (Jms 2:19; [37]M. M. Lk 1:27). More than any other group of people, the Jews <u>should have</u> known and believed both truths, because they had been hearing about him, their Messiah in their synagogues <u>all</u> of their lives. But sadly, their ears had been deaf all those years! Nevertheless, as God's Son, and in his Spirit's power, Jesus easily healed the man by driving out the demon (v 35; [38]M. I. Lk 11:10).

4:35 (1) In Luke's account, this is the first person that Jesus healed; and by doing so he taught his disciples an important new mission imperative. Jesus began to show them and us Christians in verse 35 that he viewed every person as a whole person, and therefore, he had deep compassion on them for all of their needs, both physical and spiritual (5:22-24). He never separated nor prioritized their needs, but simply had compassion on each whole person. It's a new mission imperative. M. I. Lk 4:35: Christians should view every person as a whole person, and show him compassion by caring for both his physical and spiritual needs as they go on their mission. **2)** Jesus' compassionate mission-heart for the sick man in verse 35 also shows clearly that it is never his will that one of his brothers or sisters would suffer any kind of sickness. All sickness is caused by mankind's sinful human nature and is not sent by God as punishment (Lam 3:33; [39]M. I. Mt 19:14). **3)** Why did Jesus order the demon to *"be silent?"* It may be because the demon asked in verse 34, *"Have you come to destroy us?"* He knew that Jesus came to earth in order to destroy the power of Satan and all of his demons; and perhaps Jesus did not yet want his plan to be widely known. Furthermore, why Jesus gave a similar command to some people (5:14) is even more uncertain, since all Christians are his missionaries ([40]M. M. Mt 5:14). (See the discussion at (Lk 5:14).) What is clear in this story, however, is that Jesus already knew that his death on the cross and his resurrection would destroy the power of these demons ([41]M. M. Ac 4:28).

Jesus Heals Many 4:38-41

4:38 *And he arose and left the synagogue and entered Simon's house. Now Simon's mother-in-law was ill with a high fever, and they appealed to him on her behalf.*
4:39 *And he stood over her and rebuked the fever, and it left her, and immediately she rose and began to serve them.*
4:40 *Now when the sun was setting, all those who had any who were*

> *sick with various diseases brought them to him, and he laid his hands on every one of them and healed them.*
> 4:41 *And demons also came out of many, crying, "You are the Son of God!" But he rebuked them and would not allow them to speak, because they knew that he was the Christ.*

4:39 Peter's mother-in-law was not like her fellow Jews in Nazareth. She trusted in Jesus' gracious will; and therefore, in his grace, he spoke his Word and immediately healed her. Faith in, or total dependence on, God's rich grace is always the key to a right relationship with God for all people. Jesus had found one more person who was *"lost"* and he will always eagerly receive all who have received the gracious gift of a repentant heart and humbly repent of their sins and seek his gracious will for their lives. He does not discriminate against anyone because of their cultural background ([42]M. I. Lk 4:35 & [43]Lk 4:40).

4:40 Note two significant ways in which Jesus showed his mission-heart in verse 40: **1)** First of all, it says that he *"laid his hands on every one of them,"* which means that he touched them one by one. He did not try to "save time" by saying a general blessing, as we impatient human beings might try to do. But of course, God has always shown his loving mission-heart to mankind. He has made every human being and loves each one of us (Ps 139:1-3, 13), even though we were born in sin (Ps 51:5). And therefore, he also knows just how sin has twisted each individual into his or her own unique distorted shape, so that each person is incredibly complex and unique. Both his or her personality and also the unique society that he or she lives in are so complex that no linguist or anthropologist can adequately describe them. What rich grace Jesus showed that day! And of course, he continues to show the same compassion, yet today, to each person that he has made. Therefore, what a powerful lesson his example is for all Christians on their mission to the lost world (15:6, 9, 24)! It's another new mission imperative: M. I. Lk 4:40: Christians should go and seek the lost one person at a time by focusing on each person's unique needs. **2)** Secondly, also note in verse 40 the time of day that Jesus healed these people. He patiently and lovingly did so *"when the sun was setting."* It was after the end of the Sabbath, which was the day of worship (about 6:00 p.m.) when people could start bringing their sick to him. Who knows how large the crowd must have been, and how tired he must have been! Yet there he stood touching <u>each one</u>, speaking his Words of grace, and healing them <u>one by one</u> ([44]M. I. Lk 4:35 & [45]Lk 4:40). What wonderful love and grace! He was truly teaching his disciples and us powerful mission imperatives.

Jesus Preaches in Synagogues 4:42-44

4:42 *And when it was day, he departed and went into a desolate place. And the people sought him and came to him, and would have kept him from leaving them,*
4:43 *but he said to them, "I must preach the good news of the kingdom of God to the other towns as well; for I was sent for this purpose."*
4:44 *And he was preaching in the synagogues of Judea.*

4:42 After a long hard day and night of work (vs 38-41), Jesus did not renew his strength by sleeping late; rather, he received more strength by going to his heavenly Father in <u>prayer</u>. He found true strength in "weakness," in increased <u>dependence</u> on him. He always sought to know his Father's mission-heart more fully ([46]M. M. Ro 8:29b). And he obviously prayed very frequently because his Father's will for his life was uppermost in his mind, so that he would be able to obey him completely in order to carry out every detail of his perfect plan of salvation for lost mankind ([47]M. I. Lk 11:10).

4:43 (1) Jesus was, of course, pointing to himself as God's chosen King who would soon reign fully over his people when he announced *"the good news of the kingdom of God"* (v 43; [48]M. M. Mt 2:6). **2)** And we likewise see Jesus himself pointing directly to the central theme of Luke's Gospel for the first time in verse 43 when he says, *"I was sent for this <u>purpose</u>," "to seek and to save the lost"* (19:10; [49]M. M. Lk 1:1). Obviously, Jesus displayed his mission-heart by showing deep compassion to each individual whom he met who was suffering from physical diseases; therefore, he healed many of them. We see examples of this in verse 40 and in many more verses throughout all of the Gospels. However, while these miracles showed that he was the Son of God ([50]M. M. Jn 1:49), the Holy Spirit does not use miracles to create faith; he has graciously chosen to only use his holy Word to do so ([51]M. M. Ro 10:17a). Therefore, the first part of Jesus' mission was not to heal people, but to *"seek the lost"* by proclaiming the Gospel message. (The second part of his mission, of course, was to *"save the lost"* (19:10) by dying for us and by the greatest miracle of rising from the dead for us.)

4:44 Exactly what the name *"Judea"* means in verse 44 is unclear. Therefore, just where did Jesus continue preaching? Some scholars suggest that Luke may have used *"Judea"* in verse 44 to mean *"the land of the Jews,"* since a Gentile, Luke was writing to a Gentile, Theophilus. However, some manuscripts do, in fact, read *"Galilee"* in verse 44 instead of *"Judea."* Furthermore, it's difficult to be certain whether the accounts in (Mt 4:23) and (Mk 1:39), which mention *"Galilee,"* are, in fact, parallel accounts. In any case, what is clear is that Jesus continued to use the opportunities to preach the Gospel to his fellow Jews, and perhaps also some devout Gentiles, in synagogues (M. M. Lk 1:1).

---

[1] M. M. Ro 3:26: God is just and fair to *everyone*, both when he condemns all people of all nations because all have sinned, and also when he only declares those people righteous who have faith in Jesus.

[2] M. M. Mt 1:22: God sent his only Son, Jesus to be born as a true human being, so that he could save all of his brothers and sisters of all nations by fulfilling all of God's promises in the Old Testament.

[3] M. M. Lk 1:35: Jesus had to be born as true God, in order to rescue all of mankind from sin.

[4] M. I. Lk 11:4b: Christians should ask their heavenly Father that he would not allow Satan to tempt them so severely that they lose their faith, and also that he would give them his strength to depend on his grace in all of their trials.

[5] M. I. Lk 4:4: When Satan attacks Christians on their mission they should wield the sword of God's Word by quoting from it, and not depend on their own strength.

[6] M. M. Heb 7:17: Jesus served his mission to Christians and to the world as an eternal High Priest by offering the holy sacrifice of his body in order to earn eternal forgiveness for all Christians.

[7] M. M. Lk 1:27: Jesus had to be born as a true human being and as a true Jew in order to become the King of kings in his heavenly kingdom forever.

[8] M. I. Lk 11:10: Christians should continuously pray to their heavenly Father and always

depend on his grace, and not on their own feeble strength, because he always loves them.

⁹ M. I. Lk 11:10: Christians should continuously pray to their heavenly Father and always depend on his grace, and not on their own feeble strength, because he always loves them.

¹⁰ M. M. Ro 10:17a: The Holy Spirit only creates and preserves faith by using the message of God's grace in his holy Word.

¹¹ M. M. Ro 1:19: God clearly reveals four things in the universe: **a)** that he made it, **b)** that he exists, **c)** that he has almighty power and glory, **d)** and that he still controls it.

¹² M. I. Lk 4:4: When Satan attacks Christians on their mission they should wield the sword of God's Word by quoting from it, and not depend on their own strength.

¹³ M. M. Ro 3:24: Jesus lived a life of perfect obedience and shed his precious blood on the cross, in order to graciously set all nations free from sin, which a person only receives by faith in him.

¹⁴ M. M. Ro 8:29b: Because God knew before he created the world that the people he would make in his perfect image would soon sin and tarnish his image, he therefore, already had a gracious predestination plan to send his Son Jesus to rescue them from sin, so that he could recreate the people he had chosen back into his perfect image.

¹⁵ M. I. Lk 11:10: Christians should continuously pray to their heavenly Father and always depend on his grace, and not on their own feeble strength, because he always loves them.

¹⁶ M. I. Lk 4:4: When Satan attacks Christians on their mission they should wield the sword of God's Word by quoting from it, and not depend on their own strength.

¹⁷ M. I. Lk 11:10: Christians should continuously pray to their heavenly Father and always depend on his grace, and not on their own feeble strength, because he always loves them.

¹⁸ M. M. Lk 1:1: Jesus came to seek and save all lost people from every nation on earth.

¹⁹ M. M. Ac 13:46: As he did with the old Israel, God first of all strengthens the faith of the new Israel, the Church with his Word and Sacraments, so that they can go and witness to the lost people of all nations.

²⁰ M. I. Lk 11:10: Christians should continuously pray to their heavenly Father and always depend on his grace, and not on their own feeble strength, because he always loves them.

²¹ M. I. Lk 4:17: Christians should always base their messages on the Bible, so that the Holy Spirit can use his holy Word to create and strengthen faith in their hearers.

²² M. M. Ro 10:17a: The Holy Spirit only creates and preserves faith by using the message of God's grace in his holy Word.

²³ M. M. Ac 13:46: As he did with the old Israel, God first of all strengthens the faith of the new Israel, the Church with his Word and Sacraments, so that they can go and witness to the lost people of all nations.

²⁴ M. I. Lk 4:15: Christians should seize every opportunity to proclaim the Gospel to lost people of all nations.

²⁵ M. M. Mt 1:22: God sent his only Son, Jesus to be born as a true human being, so that he could save all of his brothers and sisters of all nations by fulfilling all of God's promises in the Old Testament.

²⁶ M. I. Mt 19:14: Christians should show special love to people who are vulnerable in their society, so that they are able to come to Jesus and believe in him, because they belong in his Kingdom as his dear children.

^{27} M. I. Lk 5:20: Even when Christians proclaim the Gospel to large crowds, they should always remember that the crowds are made up of <u>individuals</u>; and that <u>each one</u> of them needs to repent and believe in Jesus.

^{28} M. M. Lk 1:1: Jesus came to seek and save <u>all</u> lost people from <u>every</u> nation on earth.

^{29} M. I. Lk 12:40: Christians should "eat" God's Word every day in order to keep their faith strong, so that they are always ready for their Lord's return.

^{30} M. M. Ro 1:17: God fully reveals both the Law and the Gospel <u>only</u> in his holy Word, the Bible.

^{31} M. I. Lk 3:3a: Christians should, in love, warn lost people who do not repent.

^{32} M. M. Lk 1:26: The heavenly Father sent his Son, Jesus to be born and live in <u>humble</u> circumstances, so that everyone from every nation on earth would see his <u>grace</u>.

^{33} M. I. Ac 1:8: Christians should go and witness about Jesus to all who are lost from all languages and cultures by depending on the power of the Holy Spirit to help them bridge all of the language/cultural boundaries whether they are relatively easy, as in their own language, or extremely difficult.

^{34} M. M. Lk 1:35: Jesus had to be born as true God, in order to rescue all of mankind from sin.

^{35} M. M. Ro 10:17a: The Holy Spirit <u>only</u> creates and preserves faith by using the message of God's grace in his holy Word.

^{36} M. I. Lk 4:4: When Satan attacks Christians on their mission they should wield the sword of God's Word by quoting from it, and not depend on their own strength.

^{37} M. M. Lk 1:27: Jesus had to be born as a true human being and as a true Jew in order to become the King of kings in his heavenly kingdom forever.

^{38} M. I. Lk 11:10: Christians should <u>continuously</u> pray to their heavenly Father and <u>always</u> depend on his grace, and not on their own feeble strength, because he <u>always</u> loves them.

^{39} M. I. Mt 19:14: Christians should show special love to people who are vulnerable in their society, so that they are able to come to Jesus and believe in him, because they belong in his Kingdom as his dear children.

^{40} M. M. Mt 5:14: When the Holy Spirit creates faith in a person's heart, he also graciously gives him a new mission-heart that is eager to shine the light of the Gospel throughout the whole world.

^{41} M. M. Ac 4:28: The heavenly Father is always in full control of his mission to all nations of the world.

^{42} M. I. Lk 4:35: Christians should view every person as a whole person, and show him compassion by caring for <u>both</u> his physical and spiritual needs as they go on their mission.

^{43} M. I. Lk 4:40: Christians should go and seek the lost <u>one</u> person at a time by focusing on each person's <u>unique</u> needs.

^{44} M. I. Lk 4:35: Christians should view every person as a whole person, and show him compassion by caring for *both* his physical and spiritual needs as they go on their mission.

^{45} M. I. Lk 4:40: Christians should go and seek the lost <u>one</u> person at a time by focusing on each person's <u>unique</u> needs.

^{46} M. M. Ro 8:29b: Because God knew before he created the world that the people he would make in his perfect image would soon sin and tarnish his image, he therefore, already had a gracious predestination <u>plan</u> to send his Son Jesus to rescue them from sin, so that he could recreate the people he had chosen back into his perfect image.

⁴⁷ M. I. Lk 11:10: Christians should continuously pray to their heavenly Father and always depend on his grace, and not on their own feeble strength, because he always loves them.

⁴⁸ M. M. Mt 2:6: Jesus was born in Bethlehem, so that he could be the King of the new Israel and rule over them as their dear Shepherd.

⁴⁹ M. M. Lk 1:1: Jesus came to seek and save all lost people from every nation on earth.

⁵⁰ M. M. Jn 1:49: Jesus' miracles prove that he is the Son of God.

⁵¹ M. M. Ro 10:17a: The Holy Spirit only creates and preserves faith by using the message of God's grace in his holy Word.

Chapter 5

Jesus Calls the First Disciples 5:1-11

5:1   *On one occasion, while the crowd was pressing in on him to hear the word of God, he was standing by the lake of Gennesaret,*

5:2   *and he saw two boats by the lake, but the fishermen had gone out of them and were washing their nets.*

5:3   *Getting into one of the boats, which was Simon's, he asked him to put out a little from the land. And he sat down and taught the people from the boat.*

5:4   *And when he had finished speaking, he said to Simon, "Put out into the deep and let down your nets for a catch."*

5:5   *And Simon answered, "Master, we toiled all night and took nothing! But at your word I will let down the nets."*

5:6   *And when they had done this, they enclosed a large number of fish, and their nets were breaking.*

5:7   *They signaled to their partners in the other boat to come and help them. And they came and filled both the boats, so that they began to sink.*

5:8   *But when Simon Peter saw it, he fell down at Jesus' knees, saying, "Depart from me, for I am a sinful man, O Lord."*

5:9   *For he and all who were with him were astonished at the catch of fish that they had taken,*

5:10 *and so also were James and John, sons of Zebedee, who were partners with Simon. And Jesus said to Simon, "Do not be afraid; from now on you will be catching men."*

5:11 *And when they had brought their boats to land, they left everything and followed him.*

5:3 Note that Jesus *"taught the people from the boat."* Until the time was right for Jesus to carry out the <u>second</u> part of his mission to *"<u>save</u> the lost"* by suffering and dying (19:10), the <u>first</u> part of his mission was to *"<u>seek</u>...the lost"* by *"proclaiming the good news to the poor...to*

announce the year of the Lord's favor" (4:18-19; 19:10; [1]M. M. Lk 1:1).
5:5-8 From the very first, Peter showed his impulsive nature, but he also very quickly showed that he believed that Jesus was God by saying in verse 5, *"But if you say so, I'll lower the nets."* And then *"he fell down at Jesus' knees, saying,"* in verse 8, *"Depart from me, for I am a sinful man, O Lord."* He recognized his sinfulness in his presence and confessed his sins, which is what Jesus, in his mission-heart, longs for all lost sinners everywhere to do, so that they see their need for his gracious forgiveness (Gen 18:27; Job 42:6; Is 6:5). He offers his salvation by his grace alone ([2]M. M. Lk 13:24 & [3]Ro 3:24).
5:10 When Jesus graciously called three men, Peter, James and John (Other Gospel writers also mention Andrew here, but Luke does not.) to *"catch men"* instead of fish he was giving them his gracious means or tool that they should begin to use to continue to *"seek...the lost,"* the same Law and Gospel message that he himself preached on his mission. His mission-heart compelled him to give his Church this one tool to use until the Last Day when he will return to judge all people. He gave all of his missionaries no other means to call people to faith except for God's holy Word, since it is his only, most gracious and powerful means of grace. There is no other Gospel apart from his cross and empty tomb (Gal 1:6-12; [4]M. I. Ro 1:16b & [5]M. M. Ro 10:17a).
5:11 It certainly was the Holy Spirit who used the Words of Jesus' gracious invitation to *"follow him"* to create faith in Jesus in the hearts of these fishermen. And, since their sinful human natures would have compelled them to refuse him, it could only have been the faith he gave them that compelled them to immediately take those first steps, abandon their livelihood and follow him (Heb 12:2; [6]M. M. Mt 5:14).

Jesus Cleanses a Leper 5:12-16

5:12 *While he was in one of the cities, there came a man full of leprosy. And when he saw Jesus, he fell on his face and begged him, "Lord, if you will, you can make me clean."*
5:13 *And Jesus stretched out his hand and touched him, saying, "I*

> 5:14 *will; be clean." And immediately the leprosy left him.*
> 5:14 *And he charged him to tell no one, but "go and show yourself to the priest, and make an offering for your cleansing, as Moses commanded, for a proof to them."*
> 5:15 *But now even more the report about him went abroad, and great crowds gathered to hear him and to be healed of their infirmities.*
> 5:16 *But he would withdraw to desolate places and pray.*

5:12-13 (1) When this man said, *"If you will,"* he was, in faith, placing himself under Jesus' gracious will; therefore, Jesus replied, *"I will"* and healed him. When Jesus sought the lost, it was this kind of humble submission to his gracious will, or faith, that he sought. It is always God's most gracious will to help and heal those who turn to him in humble faith (Rom 8:28, 32; Ps 103:8-14; [7]M. M. Ro 1:5). However, only God knows best when and how to help needy people. In this case, Jesus knew that immediate help would give the most glory to his Father and would be the most *holistic* healing for this man. Jesus had patiently found and rescued one more *"lost"* son of Abraham (19:9-10). **2)** On the other hand, however, when a person proudly demands God's help immediately and in his way, he is depending on his own proud will, not on God's grace. Such demands for a miracle are sinful because they are based upon unbelief (Mk 8:12; Ps 51:17; [8]M. I. Ac 8:12). Jesus at times met this same demanding attitude; nevertheless, he did heal many people because he loved each one. But the main purpose of his ministry was not to perform miracles of physical healing since, although such miracles point to him, they do not, by themselves, create faith. His Spirit only uses his Word to do so (Mk 8:11; [9]M. M. Ro 1:17). However, the greatest miracle of all time, Jesus' resurrection does have his almighty power to save, since he did it for us sinners (11:29; Rom 1:16; [10]M. M. Ro 1:16b).

5:14 (1) There has been much speculation about why Jesus gave this kind of a command to people *"to tell no one"* about himself. He gave a similar command to both demons (4:35, 41) and to people, as here; and all of them are puzzling, however, why he said it to people is especially puzzling since all who trust in him are his missionaries. There seem to be two possibilities: **a)** Jesus' main purpose in coming to earth was to deal with sin in two ways: *"seeking"* the lost by calling them to repentance and faith, and *"saving"* them by destroying the power of sin on the cross ([11]M. M. Lk 1:1). Therefore, if he had become known as a miracle worker, he no doubt could have spent all of his time healing physical sicknesses, especially since he had compassion on all people; and thus it would have hindered the purpose of his three-year ministry of preaching and teaching. Verse 15 seems to confirm this because, instead of obeying him, the people sinned by spreading the news about him *"now even more"* (v 15), but he avoided the large crowds. **b)** If Jesus would have become widely known as a miracle worker, it may have led to him dying prematurely, before his Father's entire plan was complete. This also seems to be confirmed by a similar command of Jesus in (9:21). There he commands his disciples to not tell anyone he is *"the Christ of God."* This makes it even clearer that the timing of Jesus' mission was very important to his Father's plan (19:10; [12]M. I. Ac 6:1). **2)** Jesus, no doubt, ordered this man to show himself to the priest for at least two reasons: **a)** Since Jesus came to fulfill the whole Law of God perfectly for sinful mankind (1:1; Lev 18:5); he could not fail to obey every detail of the Law for us by failing to urge this man to obey it. **b)** The man's sacrifices in the temple would verify his cleansing and restore him to society; and his healing would not be complete until he was restored to his family and society. Jesus loves every human being completely, and he came to save whole persons; and no one is whole unless he is living in a healthy family and society ([13]M. I. Lk 4:35).

5:16 This verse implies that Jesus' prayer life was both regular and frequent. As a true man who needed strengthening and encouragement, he faithfully turned to his heavenly Father for more strength. He also sought to know his Father's will fully and to submit to it. His mission *"to seek and to save the lost"* was of paramount importance to him; and only his Father could help him accomplish his will through the power of his Spirit in him ([14]M. M. Lk 1:1).

Jesus Heals a Paralytic 5:17 26

5:17 *On one of those days, as he was teaching, Pharisees and teachers of the law were sitting there, who had come from every village of Galilee and Judea and from Jerusalem. And the power of the Lord was with him to heal.*

5:18 *And behold, some men were bringing on a bed a man who was paralyzed, and they were seeking to bring him in and lay him before Jesus,*

5:19 *but finding no way to bring him in, because of the crowd, they went up on the roof and let him down with his bed through the tiles into the midst before Jesus.*

5:20 *And when he saw their faith, he said, "Man, your sins are forgiven you."*

5:21 *And the scribes and the Pharisees began to question, saying, "Who is this who speaks blasphemies? Who can forgive sins but God alone?"*

5:22 *When Jesus perceived their thoughts, he answered them, "Why do you question in your hearts?*

5:23 *Which is easier, to say, 'Your sins are forgiven you,' or to say, 'Rise and walk'?*

5:24 *But that you may know that the Son of Man has authority on earth to forgive sins"--he said to the man who was paralyzed-- "I say to you, rise, pick up your bed and go home."*

5:25 *And immediately he rose up before them and picked up what he had been lying on and went home, glorifying God.*

5:26 *And amazement seized them all, and they glorified God and were filled with awe, saying, "We have seen extraordinary things today."*

5:17 (1) While it may appear from this one verse 17 that these religious leaders of the Jews had the good intention of coming to hear Jesus preach the Gospel, verses 21 and 22 make it clear that they did <u>not</u> have the eyes of faith to see that Jesus was God's Son; and therefore they came with the evil purpose of exposing what they thought was Jesus' "lie" that he was the Messiah. The fact that they came from all parts of Israel also shows that it was a widespread evil plot to meet there. **2)** However, if these leaders of God's chosen people had been <u>faithful</u> to

God, they should have been doing all of the following things: **a)** helping their nation carry out God's original mission plan by teaching the Scriptures to them, so that they would have been waiting to see their heavenly Messiah, and the people would also have been busy telling all other nations about the coming Messiah (Gen 12:3), **b)** the leaders should have been the first ones to see Jesus' miracles, listen to his Gospel message and believe that he was the Messiah, **c)** the first ones to spread the Good News that their Messiah had come, **d)** and given Jesus every possible assistance on his mission. **3)** But instead, the leaders were doing none of these things. In fact, they were doing quite the opposite; they were unfaithful stewards of God's Kingdom who were seeking ways to kill the Son and heir of the Kingdom (20:8-19). Their pride in their powerful position in society and as "true" physical descendants of Abraham (3:8) blinded them to the truth, and prevented them from humbling themselves and submitting to the rule of their heavenly King ([15]M. M. Lk 1:27). **3)** And in sharp contrast to these unbelieving leaders, the paralyzed man and his friends in this story saw who Jesus was with the eyes of faith; they saw that *"the power of the Lord was with him to heal"* ([16]M. M. Lk 13:24).

5:19 Jesus was obviously much more popular than these spiritual leaders; and this would have been very painful to their pride. Crowds found Jesus even though he purposely did not advertise where he was. There must have been an enormous number of people who were sick since the only medicines they had at that time were some natural herbs and spices. It was, therefore, no doubt often very difficult for Jesus to carry out the main part of his mission of preaching and teaching (19:10; [17]M. I. Ac 6:1).

5:20 (1) We once again see in verse 20 the goal of Jesus' mission because he came, to *"seek and to save the lost"* by destroying and forgiving sin (19:10; [18]M. M. Lk 1:1). Furthermore, even though he was surrounded by many people at this time, Jesus focused on one lost, sick sinner. He saw the faith of the men who were bringing their sick friend to him, and he was eager to heal him. What a lesson this is for all who proclaim the Gospel! We should always remember that crowds are obviously made up of individuals; and we should focus on individuals.

It's a new mission imperative. M. I. Lk 5:20: Even when Christians proclaim the Gospel to large crowds, they should always remember that the crowds are made up of <u>individuals</u>; and that <u>each one</u> of them needs to repent and believe in Jesus. **2)** Note that Jesus *"saw <u>their</u> faith,"* then he said to the paralyzed man, *"<u>Your</u> sins are forgiven."* Jesus saw that they all had faith, but he especially saw that the sick man had faith because he had obviously urged his friends to help him. And therefore, Jesus healed him because he humbly depended on his grace. Jesus had patiently, one by one, found and rescued one more lost son of Abraham (19:9-10; [19]M. I. Lk 4:35 & [20]Lk 4:40). **3)** We also see how vital faith in Jesus is in this verse. Without this <u>personal</u> faith connection to Jesus he would not have been healed. Faith in Jesus is the only way into God's Kingdom (M. M. Lk 13:24). **4)** Furthermore, the faith of these men was very obvious because they expended extraordinary effort to get their friend into the presence of Jesus. Their faith was producing beautiful fruit that pleased their King who came to save them for this purpose (3:8). However, the spiritual leaders were producing rotten fruit. As John had said in (3:9), *"The ax is laid to the root of the trees. Every tree therefore that does not bear good fruit is cut down and thrown into the fire"* (Mt 23:13-36; [21]M. I. Jn 14:13).

5:21-23 (1) Jesus' rhetorical question in verse 23, *"Which is easier, to say, 'Your sins are forgiven you,' or to say, 'Rise and walk?'"* obviously implies the answer that both miracles are <u>equally</u> hard for human beings, but likewise <u>equally</u> easy for God (1:37). And Jesus was himself true God, therefore, he could <u>easily</u> do both miracles. He came to do both (v 17; [22]M. M. Lk 1:35 & [23]Jn 1:49). **2)** How could Jesus be so bold as to say, *"Your sins are forgiven you?"* **a)** The main reason, of course, was that he himself was God, as his Father had so recently assured him at his Baptism (3:22). **b)** The second reason was that saving mankind from sin was his main purpose in being born as a human being (19:10); and he already knew that he would have to endure terrible suffering and death to accomplish this on the cross (vs 34-35; 9:22; [24]M. M. Lk 1:27). **3)** By healing this man physically and, at the same time, forgiving his sins, Jesus taught a very important lesson. The original sin of mankind's parents, Adam and Eve, sickened all of their children, Jew and Gentile alike; and therefore, it causes all sicknesses, both spiritual and physical (Rom 5:13-14). Thus, when Jesus cured this man's spiritual sickness of sin, the physical sickness was gone as well (v 24). However, Jesus was not implying that any specific sin caused his sickness, but rather that his sinful human nature caused it (Jn 9:2). This is a Law message that all nations need to hear ([25]M. I. Ro 1:17). **4)** Furthermore, Jesus once again taught the truth in verses 21-23 that his mission to save the lost was a holistic mission. In his mission-heart, he created and loves each person in the world as a whole person: body, soul and spirit; but all parts of every person have been corrupted by sin; therefore, he came to save the whole person (19:10; 12:5; [26]M. I. Lk 4:35).

5:24 Jesus' statement here that *"the Son of Man has authority on earth to forgive sins"* is another very clear restatement of the second part of Luke's central theme (19:10): Jesus *"came to…save the lost"* by earning forgiveness for their sins on the cross. How, then, could he make this authoritative statement even though he had not yet died on the cross? **a)** The most obvious answer is that he was true God; and therefore, he had the right to call himself *"the Son of Man"* and make this claim of authority (M. M. Lk 1:35). **b)** Secondly, even though Jesus was also a true human being and he therefore could have yielded to the devil's temptations in the wilderness, he was also true God. And therefore, it was also true that the completion of his mission was inevitable or predestined. As a group of Christians' prayed in(Ac 4:28), *"The rulers [King Herod and Pontius Pilate] were gathered together, against the Lord and against his Anointed…to do whatever your [God's] hand and your plan had predestined to take place."* The whole purpose of Jesus' mission was *"to seek and to save the lost;"* and not even the devil and all his evil angels could stop him because his heavenly Father was in full control of his plan of salvation (19:10; [27]M. M. Ac 4:28).

5:25 When the man *"rose up before them"* in verse 25, the obvious conclusion, of course, was that Jesus was true God (M. M. Lk 1:35). But the spiritual leaders refused to see who he was and believe ([28]M. M. Jn 1:49).

5:26 The fact that the crowd *"glorified God"* showed that they believed that Jesus was God; and their amazement was a holy fear or awe (Heb

11:6; Ps 111:10). But obviously the word *"all"* here does not include the Pharisees and teachers of the law. No doubt it was some of these same men who finally succeeded in killing him, but only when Jesus' heavenly Father's time was right (20:15; [29]M. M. Ac 4:28).

Jesus Calls Levi 5:27-32

5:27 *After this he went out and saw a tax collector named Levi, sitting at the tax booth. And he said to him, "Follow me."*
5:28 *And leaving everything, he rose and followed him.*
5:29 *And Levi made him a great feast in his house, and there was a large company of tax collectors and others reclining at table with them.*
5:30 *And the Pharisees and their scribes grumbled at his disciples, saying, "Why do you eat and drink with tax collectors and sinners?"*
5:31 *And Jesus answered them, "Those who are well have no need of a physician, but those who are sick.*
5:32 *I have not come to call the righteous but sinners to repentance."*

5:27-28 (1) Jesus graciously called Levi (Matthew), one more *"lost person"* to follow him as his disciple ([30]M. I. Lk 4:40). Even though neither verses 27-28 nor Matthew's account in (Mt 9:9) mention any previous contact with Jesus, some scholars have argued that Matthew must have known Jesus before this day otherwise he could not have responded so quickly to Jesus' call. However, such arguments assume that God's Word is weak and that the Holy Spirit cannot create faith instantly. But St. Paul refutes this argument in (2 Cor 4:6) by illustrating the tremendous power of God's Word. He says that just as God's mighty Word instantly created light out of darkness (Gen 1:3), so likewise when he speaks Words such as, "Let there be the light of faith!" the Holy Spirit instantly creates faith in a person's dark heart. This is how Jesus has always and always will *"save the lost."* God's Word is the only means of grace, the only mighty sword of the Spirit ([31]M. M. Ro 10:17a). **2)** Human beings can't see faith except in the actions or fruit that faith produces; therefore, the miracle of <u>faith</u> does not appear to us to be very spectacular. But God views it very differently, as we have just seen above in (2 Cor 4: 6). When he creates faith in a person's heart it's a great miracle; and <u>only</u> Jesus' resurrection is an even greater miracle, because his resurrection proves that his heavenly Father accepted his holy sacrifice on the cross (2 Cor 1:20). The wonderful Gospel is that God wants <u>all</u> of the people from <u>all</u> nations to receive this gracious gift of his miracle of faith ([32]M. M. 1 Tim 2:3).

5:31 Jesus always sought *"those who are sick,"* who are *"the lost"* both physically and spiritually (19:10). He urged them to acknowledge that they were sick (to repent) and ask him for healing (forgiveness) through faith in him in verses 32 and 23. The Pharisees and their scribes, on the other hand, were in fact <u>not</u> the spiritually healthy people that they thought they were and should have been. They <u>thought</u> they were "the righteous" (v 32); therefore, this proud, self-righteous attitude prevented them from repenting. And so it is with all people. Even though, in his mission-heart, God graciously calls Christians to go and call the lost to repentance (vs 27-28), and even though the Holy Spirit is present with his mighty Word when they do so, self-righteous pride is the enemy that Satan often uses to prevent people from repenting and turning to God in faith ([33]M. I. Mt 7:14).

A Question About Fasting 5:33-39

5:33 *And they said to him, "The disciples of John fast often and offer prayers, and so do the disciples of the Pharisees, but yours eat and drink."*

5:34 *And Jesus said to them, "Can you make wedding guests fast while the bridegroom is with them?*

5:35 *The days will come when the bridegroom is taken away from them, and then they will fast in those days."*

5:36 *He also told them a parable: "No one tears a piece from a new garment and puts it on an old garment. If he does, he will tear the new, and the piece from the new will not match the old.*

5:37 *And no one puts new wine into old wineskins. If he does, the*

> *new wine will burst the skins and it will be spilled, and the skins will be destroyed.*
> 5:38 *But new wine must be put into fresh wineskins.*
> 5:39 *And no one after drinking old wine desires new, for he says, 'The old is good.'"*

5:34 The metaphor about a wedding that Jesus uses in verse 34 is very rich in meaning. When Jesus calls people to faith in him, he at the same time invites them to <u>return</u> his love for them, just as brides and grooms do. And his love is, indeed, very much like the love that a bride and groom have for each other (Eph 5:23-33). But the most important aspect of Jesus' love for his bride, the Church is that it springs from his mission-heart, his <u>grace</u> alone. No human being deserves to be invited into this wonderful personal relationship with Jesus because everyone is sinful. There is no nation or language or culture that deserves to be in this personal relationship with him more than any other. He calls no one because of any goodness in that person, since absolutely <u>no one</u> deserves it. His rich <u>grace alone</u> moves him to invite each and every human being into a personal relationship with him. And he completely and fully proved this to all mankind on the cross, because <u>he</u> did not deserve to die there; but, in deep love for us, he did so for the sake of <u>all</u> of his brothers and sisters (2 Cor 5:21). What a groom the Church, indeed, has (^{34}M. M. Ro 1:5)!

5:35 Jesus was born to die on the cross; and he already knew that he would soon have to endure suffering for all of mankind. Thus, when Jesus says in verse 35, *"When the bridegroom is taken away from them [his disciples],"* he is obviously referring to the day that he died on the cross a few years later. Therefore, there at the foot of his cross, <u>all</u> of his disciples, <u>all</u> Christians should, indeed, daily "fast" and repent of their sins because they know that he died for <u>their</u> sins (Is 53:4-6). To understand that our sins drove the nails into his body should make us hate both our sins and our sinful human nature that drives us to want to sin; we can never enjoy sinning again. That is the huge difference between a person who has received a <u>repentant</u> heart, a sinner who is kneeling at Jesus' cross and an <u>unrepentant</u> sinner who refuses to do so. An unrepentant person would never go through the painful struggle that

Paul describes in (Rom 7:14-25). How urgently the lost people of all nations need to hear this Law message ([35]M. I. Ro 1:17)!

5:36-38 (**1**) In Luke's account of Jesus' mission to *"seek the lost,"* this is the first of many illustrations and parables (a type of illustration) that Jesus used to teach new truths about himself and his Kingdom. And he used them so frequently because an illustration is such a powerful teaching tool. It begins with what the hearers <u>already know</u> about a concrete idea or a physical object in order to teach them a <u>new abstract</u>, spiritual truth. His illustration in verses 36-37 was culturally relevant; all of Jesus' hearers were very familiar with making and storing wine and would have understood the new spiritual truth about Jesus' Kingdom immediately. And yet today, illustrations that are culturally relevant can be very effective communication tools in all cultures around the world. It's a new mission imperative. M. I. Lk 5:36: Christians should use various kinds of illustrations that are culturally relevant in order to teach the Gospel, because illustrations begin with what their hearers <u>already know</u> about a concrete idea or a physical object in order to teach them a <u>new abstract</u>, spiritual truth. **2)** Jesus used the two illustrations in verses 36-38 to refer to the fact that Satan is a terrible taskmaster who holds his prisoners firmly in his evil kingdom. Furthermore, his prison has never truly changed since the day he tempted Adam and Eve, except that it has appeared all over the world with different <u>names</u>, such as: Animism, Islam, Hinduism and Buddhism. (And we can clearly see different forms of Animism throughout the Bible.) The lost people in many cultures around the world who yet today still practice these religions are, in fact, worshipping the devil and his demons, the "old" gods, *"old garments"* (v 36-37) and *"old wineskins"* (v 38). What a stern warning this is for all who still cling to the "old" gods by worshipping idols ([36]M. I. 2 Cor 11:14)!

5:39 In a religion like Animism, Satan holds his prisoners in his prison through terrible fear, and by constantly deceiving them as *"the father of lies"* (Jn 8:44), just as "an old garment" or an *"old wineskin"* deceives because it is unreliable. To try to escape by taking the leap of faith and begin trusting in the King of love is, indeed, a <u>terrifying</u> leap because it means that a new Christian will make the angry gods even angrier. They can, and often do, kill a person—especially if he tries to escape. Thus, the prisoner says, *"The old is good"* (v 39)! This is even truer if the leap of faith in Jesus means that his physical family will ostracize him for the rest of his life, or they may even hunt him down and kill him. This makes the support of that person's new spiritual family in the Body of Christ extremely important for keeping that person and his faith alive. How urgent, then, the message is that Jesus came to "save the lost" people who are bound in such an awful prison ([37]M. I. Lk 3:8)!

---

[1] M. M. Lk 1:1: Jesus came to seek and save all lost people from every nation on earth.

[2] M. M. Lk 13:24: The only way to enter the Kingdom of God is to have faith in Jesus as one's Savior.

[3] M. M. Ro 3:24: Jesus lived a life of perfect obedience and shed his precious blood on the cross, in order to graciously set all nations free from sin, which a person only receives by faith in him.

[4] M. M. Ro 1:16b: The Gospel is so powerful because it contains the central truth that Jesus rose from the dead with a glorified body in order to save all of his brothers and sisters from sin and death.

[5] M. M. Ro 10:17a: The Holy Spirit only creates and preserves faith by using the message of God's grace in his holy Word.

[6] M. M. Mt 5:14: When the Holy Spirit creates faith in a person's heart, he also graciously gives him a new mission-heart that is eager to shine the light of the Gospel throughout the whole world.

[7] M. M. Ro 1:5: The same Holy Spirit who creates faith and a new missionary nature in a person's heart also graciously empowers him to gratefully respond to his Lord's love by obeying him.

[8] M. I. Ac 8:12: Christians should only use miracles of healing in order to point to Jesus, and beware of people who use Satan's power to do miracles in order to point to themselves.

[9] M. M. Ro 1:17: God fully reveals both the Law and the Gospel only in his holy Word, the Bible.

[10] M. M. Ro 1:16b: The Gospel is so powerful because it contains the central truth that Jesus rose from the dead with a glorified body in order to save all of his brothers and sisters from sin and death.

[11] M. M. Lk 1:1: Jesus came to seek and save all lost people from every nation on earth.

[12] M. I. Ac 6:1: Christians should always remember that the main aspect of the mission is to proclaim the Law and Gospel message and should not allow any other aspect of the work to hinder this main work.

[13] M. I. Lk 4:35: Christians should view every person as a whole person, and show him compassion by caring for both his physical and spiritual needs as they go on their mission.

[14] M. M. Lk 1:1: Jesus came to seek and save all lost people from every nation on earth.

[15] M. M. Lk 1:27: Jesus had to be born as a true human being and as a true Jew in order to become the King of kings in his heavenly kingdom forever.

[16] M. M. Lk 13:24: The <u>only</u> way to enter the Kingdom of God is to have <u>faith</u> in Jesus as one's Savior.

[17] M. I. Ac 6:1: Christians should always remember that the main aspect of the mission is to proclaim the Law and Gospel message and should not allow any other aspect of the work to hinder this main work.

[18] M. M. Lk 1:1: Jesus came to seek and save <u>all</u> lost people from <u>every</u> nation on earth.

[19] M. I. Lk 4:35: Christians should view every person as a whole person, and show him compassion by caring for <u>both</u> his physical and spiritual needs as they go on their mission.

[20] M. I. Lk 4:40: Christians should go and seek the lost <u>one</u> person at a time by focusing on each person's <u>unique</u> needs.

[21] M. I. Jn 14:13: Christians should ask their heavenly Father for everything that they need in Jesus' name and he will do it; and then, everyone who sees God's grace will praise him in Jesus' name.

[22] M. M. Lk 1:35: Jesus had to be born as true God, in order to rescue all of mankind from sin.

[23] M. M. Jn 1:49: Jesus' miracles prove that he is the Son of God.

[24] M. M. Lk 1:27: Jesus had to be born as a true human being and as a true Jew in order to become the King of kings in his heavenly kingdom forever.

[25] M. M. Ro 1:17: God fully reveals both the Law and the Gospel <u>only</u> in his holy Word, the Bible.

[26] M. I. Lk 4:35: Christians should view every person as a whole person, and show him compassion by caring for <u>both</u> his physical and spiritual needs as they go on their mission.

[27] M. M. Ac 4:28: The heavenly Father is always in full control of his mission to all nations of the world.

[28] M. M. Jn 1:49: Jesus' miracles prove that he is the Son of God.

[29] M. M. Ac 4:28: The heavenly Father is always in full control of his mission to all nations of the world.

[30] M. I. Lk 4:40: Christians should go and seek the lost <u>one</u> person at a time by focusing on each person's <u>unique</u> needs.

[31] M. M. Ro 10:17a: The Holy Spirit *only* creates and preserves faith by using the message of God's grace in his holy Word.

[32] M. M. 1 Tim 2:3: It pleases God their Savior when Christians pray for all people because he desires all people to be saved and to come to the knowledge of the truth about Jesus.

[33] M. I. Mt 7:14: Christians should hurry on their mission to the world because people who are lost have many enemies who lure them away from Jesus; and therefore, few of them find faith in Jesus which is the only gate into his Kingdom of life.

[34] M. M. Ro 1:5: The same Holy Spirit who creates <u>faith</u> and a new missionary <u>nature</u> in a person's heart also graciously empowers him to gratefully respond to his Lord's love by <u>obeying</u> him.

[35] M. M. Ro 1:17: God fully reveals both the Law and the Gospel <u>only</u> in his holy Word, the Bible.

[36] M. I. 2 Cor 11:14: Christians should beware of Satan because he not only disguises himself as

an angel of light, but he also sends out false teachers who also disguise themselves as servants of the light, in order to deceive people by telling lies that appear to be the truth of the Gospel.

[37] M. I. Lk 3:8: Christians should always be prepared to boldly and publicly refute false teaching, so that Satan cannot easily deceive people.

Chapter 6

Jesus is Lord of the Sabbath 6:1-5

6:1   *On a Sabbath, while he was going through the grainfields, his disciples plucked and ate some heads of grain, rubbing them in their hands.*

6:2   *But some of the Pharisees said, "Why are you doing what is not lawful to do on the Sabbath?"*

6:3   *And Jesus answered them, "Have you not read what David did when he was hungry, he and those who were with him:*

6:4   *how he entered the house of God and took and ate the bread of the Presence, which is not lawful for any but the priests to eat, and also gave it to those with him?"*

6:5   *And he said to them, "The Son of Man is lord of the Sabbath."*

6:2 Is it possible that Jesus actually allowed his disciples to violate one of Moses' Laws, as verse 2 says? Of course, not! Since he came to fulfill all of God's Laws perfectly on behalf of sinful mankind, Jesus certainly never violated one of God's Laws himself; nor did he allow his disciples to do so (Lev 18:5). According to God's Laws, the Sabbath was a day of rest and worship (Ex 20:8-11). However, when "the disciples plucked and ate some the heads of grain" (v 1), it was <u>not</u> work according to <u>God's</u> Laws, but it was a violation of the <u>man-made</u> traditions of the Jews concerning the Sabbath. This is what the Pharisees were angry about. Furthermore, according to (Deu 23:25), the disciples were also not violating one of God's Laws, the seventh commandment by stealing the grain. They would only have been stealing if they had been cutting and harvesting it ([1]M. M. Mt 1:22).

6:3-5 (1) No, Jesus' disciples did not violate any of God's Laws; the Jews were angry because the disciples had violated their own <u>man-made</u> traditions concerning the Sabbath. Therefore, Jesus taught the Jews two things. **a)** First of all, in verses 3-4, he cited the case of an Old Testament priest who had compassion on David by obeying the Law of love and gave him consecrated bread to eat, which violated a Law of

God's tabernacle. Jesus' point was that the priest obeyed the more important Law of <u>love</u> because David was a desperately hungry man. Therefore, even if Jesus had allowed disciples to violate a Sabbath Law by eating the heads of grain, he would not have violated the greater Law of love because they also were very hungry (v 9). **b)** Secondly, Jesus taught the Jews in verse 5 that "the Son of Man is lord of the Sabbath." He was the King who was ruling in a <u>new</u> Kingdom that they knew nothing about. And as the King, he was teaching them a second time that the Law of love <u>fulfills</u> all other laws, because God gave all of his Laws to his people in order to show them how to <u>love</u> him and all other people by obeying his Laws, because they show them what pleases, or does not please him (Mt 22:37-40; Rom 13:8, 10: M. I. Lk 6:5). Thus, Jesus was also teaching his disciples a new mission imperative. M. I. Lk 6:5: Their faith in Jesus should move Christians to show Jesus' <u>love</u> in all circumstances even if their act of love breaks another less important human or even divine Law. **2)** The Law of love is even more important than any other Law of God; therefore, it is, of course, also more important than any other <u>human</u> law that people make for their own society/culture. However, it is sometimes very difficult for Christians to put Jesus' new mission imperative into practice, especially if the Bible does not speak to a specific issue (Rom 14:1; [2]M. I. Lk 6:5).

A Man with a Withered Hand 6:6-16

6:6   *On another Sabbath, he entered the synagogue and was teaching, and a man was there whose right hand was withered.*
6:7   *And the scribes and the Pharisees watched him, to see whether he would heal on the Sabbath, so that they might find a reason to accuse him.*
6:8   *But he knew their thoughts, and he said to the man with the withered hand, "Come and stand here." And he rose and stood there.*
6:9   *And Jesus said to them, "I ask you, is it lawful on the Sabbath to do good or to do harm, to save life or to destroy it?"*
6:10 *And after looking around at them all he said to him, "Stretch*

> *out your hand." And he did so, and his hand was restored.*
> 6:11 *But they were filled with fury and discussed with one another what they might do to Jesus.*

6:6-11 (1) Jesus' conflict with the scribes and Pharisees continued because he performed another miracle on a Sabbath, which was the day of worship. So they *"were filled with fury and discussed with one another what they might do to Jesus"* (v 7). However, Jesus' Law and Gospel message did not penetrate their hardened hearts because their hearts were harder than stones (3:8); and they violently resisted the truth. They persisted in their anger until they did eventually kill him. And of course, this was a necessary part of God's perfect plan to rescue all of mankind (19:10) since someone had to kill Jesus, but it did not <u>have</u> to be these particular men who chose to serve Satan by killing him. Nevertheless, Jesus loved them with his mission-heart as dearly as he loves all of his brothers and sisters from all nations; therefore, he was earnestly "seeking" them as well ([3]M. I. Lk 11:10). **2)** Likewise, in many countries yet today, the devil has such full control over some people that, not only do they resist the Gospel themselves, but they also kill those who do hear the Gospel and believe in Jesus (Rev 6:9). The devil hates it when Jesus' Kingdom continues to expand (M. I. Lk 11:10). **3)** In verse 9, Jesus repeats the truth from verses 1-5 that the Law of love is more important than any other Law of God or than any human law (Mt 22:37-40; [4]M. I. Lk 6:5).

The Twelve Apostles 6:12-16

> 6:12 *In these days he went out to the mountain to pray, and all night he continued in prayer to God.*
> 6:13 *And when day came, he called his disciples and chose from them twelve, whom he named apostles:*
> 6:14 *Simon, whom he named Peter, and Andrew his brother, and James and John, and Philip, and Bartholomew,*
> 6:15 *and Matthew, and Thomas, and James the son of Alphaeus, and Simon who was called the Zealot,*

> 6:16 *and Judas the son of James, and Judas Iscariot, who became a traitor.*

6:12 It is especially noteworthy that Jesus sought to know his Father's will <u>before</u> he chose twelve men to be his apostles, most especially his choice of Judas. As with the case of the religious leaders, it was a necessary part of God's perfect plan that <u>one</u> of the twelve should fulfill the Old Testament by betraying him, but Judas could have said no to the devil, as Peter did; but he did not do so. Furthermore, the fact that Jesus chose Judas at this time shows that he was indeed most earnestly also seeking him with his mission-heart, one-on-one, in a very personal way. Nevertheless, Satan began working in Judas's heart and eventually trapped him into loving money more than he loved his Lord ([5]M. I. Lk 4:40).

6:13 (1) By this action of choosing twelve men to train, Jesus began to teach his disciples another new mission imperative. M. I. Lk 6:13: Christians should choose new leaders and train them in order to multiply the work. **2)** When Jesus gave these twelve disciples this call to be his apostles, it was a special gift, an <u>extra</u> grace that he eventually personally gave to <u>only</u> fourteen men. (He called two other men later: Matthias to replace Judas (Ac 1:26) and Paul (Ac 9:3-19; Rom 1:1, 5).) Jesus, of course, graciously gives <u>all</u> Christians <u>two</u> gifts when he calls them to faith: the gift of faith and a <u>new</u> mission-heart that compels them to be holy priests/missionaries who daily proclaim the Gospel (1 Pet 2:9; [6]M. M. Mt 5:14). However, just as *"apostle"* (v 13) means "sent one," local congregations are guided by the Holy Spirit to give ministers of the Gospel an <u>additional</u> call from the Lord of the Church to <u>publicly</u> preach the Gospel <u>to</u> them and <u>for</u> them. In this way, the Lord of the Church maintains <u>good order</u> in everything that his Body, the Church does (1 Cor 14:33; [7]M. M. 1 Cor 12:12). **3)** This of course, still is Jesus' gracious means for continuing to *"seek...the lost"* <u>through</u> his missionary Church in every nation of the world, until he returns again on the Last Day. The Church also calls pastors in all of these lands who proclaim his Word <u>to</u> the Church and <u>for</u> the Church in <u>public</u> worship, as well as <u>privately</u>, of course ([8]M. M. Ac 13:46). And through the Word that all Christians proclaim, the Holy Spirit creates faith to strengthen and expand the Kingdom. God's Word is the only means of grace. There is no other way in which Jesus carries out his mission! Thus, the Church is the new Israel (Rom 11:26); and God continues to bless all nations through his new nation of chosen people (Gen 12:3: Rom 11:12; [9]M. M. Ro 10:17a).

Jesus Ministers to a Great Multitude 6:17-19

6:17 *And he came down with them and stood on a level place, with a great crowd of his disciples and a great multitude of people from all Judea and Jerusalem and the seacoast of Tyre and Sidon,*
6:18 *who came to hear him and to be healed of their diseases. And those who were troubled with unclean spirits were cured.*
6:19 *And all the crowd sought to touch him, for power came out from him and healed them all.*

6:14-19 Note three very significant things that Luke the Gentile Gospel writer, no doubt deliberately, added in this section to Matthew, the Jewish Gospel writer's account: **a)** First of all, probably because Tyre and Sidon were predominantly Gentile towns (4:26), Luke added in verse 17, *"and the seacoast of Tyre and Sidon."* In this way, Luke was careful to note that the news about Jesus' mission had already spread beyond the land of Israel (1:1; Mt 4:25). And it was no doubt Gentiles from these towns who had seen Jesus and returned home to spread the Good News to their fellow Gentiles about this great Jewish teacher. They must have told them that he was healing people and especially that he was telling people that all people from all nations are welcome in his Kingdom (19:10). **b)** Secondly, since Luke recorded portions of Jesus' "Sermon on the Mount" just a few verses later in (6:20-49), he may also be deliberately suggesting that both Jews and Gentiles were in the crowd who heard Jesus' sermon ([10]M. M. Ro 11:26). **c)** Thirdly, when Luke says in verse 19 that *"all the crowd sought to touch him,"* he was once again showing that Jesus' mission-heart never discriminated against anyone. Since both Jews and Gentiles were in the crowd listening to Jesus, he must have cured some from all of the nations who were there *"because power came out from him"* (v 19) as God's own beloved Son. His miracles proved that he was God. But we also see very clearly that Jesus never forgot the individuals in the crowds (M. M. Ro 11:26 & [11]M. I. Lk 5:20).

The Beatitudes 6:20-23

6:20 *And he lifted up his eyes on his disciples, and said: "Blessed are you who are poor, for yours is the kingdom of God.*
6:21 *"Blessed are you who are hungry now, for you shall be satisfied. "Blessed are you who weep now, for you shall laugh.*
6:22 *"Blessed are you when people hate you and when they exclude you and revile you and spurn your name as evil, on account of the Son of Man!*
6:23 *Rejoice in that day, and leap for joy, for behold, your reward is great in heaven; for so their fathers did to the prophets.*

6:20 Jesus began his sermon by teaching the only Way in which all people enter his Kingdom or come under his gracious rule. Luke records in verse 20, "Blessed are you who are poor," while Matthew says more clearly in (Mt 5:3), *"Blessed are the poor in spirit."* A person who is *"poor in spirit"* is spiritually dead and bankrupt, completely incapable of helping himself, completely dependent on God's grace. Martin Luther is reported to have written in his dying moments, "We are all beggars before God." King Jesus has a mission-heart and is full of grace; therefore, when a person hears the Gospel, his Holy Spirit uses this gracious message, in order to graciously give him three gifts: a repentant heart, a child-like faith in Jesus, and a new mission-heart. Therefore, a humble faith in Jesus is the only Way that a person can enter into a loving relationship with their true King. In his rich grace, our King of kings offers no other way (13:24; Mt 7:14; [12]M. M. Lk 13:24); therefore, all people from all nations have the same access into his Kingdom. He truly has a mission-heart that always compels him to love all the people

he has made <u>equally</u> ([13]M. M. Ro 1:5 & [14]1 Tim 2:3). (Note that God pleads with lost sinners to repent and believe; and then, contrary to our feeble human logic, he also graciously <u>gives</u> these three gifts to those who respond to his love. We all totally depend on his rich grace alone!)
6:21 The pagan religion of Animism is a religion of terrible and deadly <u>fear</u>; therefore, all people who practice it are, deep down, hungry for spiritual food that satisfies their *"weeping,"* (v 21) and terrified hearts. (Sadly, Animism is practiced in many different forms around the world.) And *"they shall [indeed] be satisfied"* and begin to *"laugh"* (v 21) <u>only</u> if they turn to Jesus in repentance and faith; and they will <u>only</u> hear about this nutritious *"bread of life"* (Jn 6:35) that Jesus offers them if a Christian goes to <u>tell</u> them this Good News in a language that they can hear and understand (Rom 10:14-17; Ac 1:8; [15]M. I. Ac 2:4).
6:22 (1) In verse 22, Jesus gives rich comfort to a Christian that he will surely *"bless"* him <u>in the midst</u> of his persecution *"on account of the Son of Man"* (v 22; Rom 5:3), and he will also "bless" him with eternal life in heaven if he remains faithful to him. What wonderful comfort this is, especially for a new Christian! To have the boldness and courage to confess Jesus in the face of persecution or death takes super-human strength; and this is precisely what Jesus is graciously offering to suffering Christians in this verse, his own almighty grace and blessing! It's a new mission message. M. M. Lk 6:22: The Lord Jesus will surely bless a Christian in the midst of suffering for his sake; and he will also bless him with eternal life if he remains faithful to him. **2)** In many cultures in the world today, people frequently hate and persecute Christians *"on account of the Son of Man"* (v 22). The devil is very angry when the Holy Spirit creates faith in the heart of someone whom he had bound in prison. It is he who stirs his slaves (both demons and humans) to mindless violence against those who have now become his enemy. And because family and cultural values are so powerful, Satan does, at times, use these powerful pressures to keep people in his clutches or pull them back into his prison. However, we praise Jesus because he himself faced terrible persecution in his passion and death, in order to destroy the power of *"the evil one"* (Col 2:5; Mt 6:13). He, therefore, now has far superior power to "bless" a Christian as he suffers

for him. Thus, it is a great privilege and even joy to be persecuted for his sake, and to also have the boldness to witness to others about his grace (Phil 3:10; Gal 6:14; [16]M. I. Ro 5:3b).

6:23 (1) God's mission-heart compelled him, even before he created the world and before mankind sinned, to create a mission plan of salvation, which, of course, included the need to sacrifice his own Son, Jesus in order to fulfill it (Heb 10:5-10). But God first graciously chose another man, Abraham, gave him faith and blessed him, in order to initiate his plan on earth to bless <u>all</u> nations through them (Gen 12:3). Yet, as verse 23 indicates, the nation of Israel frequently despised such a great privilege; and God had to send many prophets to them in order to try to keep them faithful to him. But, instead of embracing the prophets, they frequently <u>persecuted</u> and even killed them. And then, Jesus' generation was even more unfaithful—they even killed God's <u>greatest</u> prophet, his own Son Jesus; and in doing so, they ironically carried out the most important part of God's plan of salvation (20:9-19; 19:10). **2)** But why can Jesus urge Christians in verse 23 to *"rejoice in that day [of suffering], and leap for joy?"* St. Paul says in (Rom 5:1, 3), *"we have <u>peace</u> with God through our Lord Jesus Christ…and we rejoice in our sufferings."* His point is that Christians can *"rejoice,"* not <u>because</u> they suffer, but <u>in the</u> <u>midst</u> of suffering for Jesus' sake. Obviously, the holy Son of God did not deserve to endure such horrible suffering on the cross for us sinful human beings; but, as God's greatest prophet, the deep, deep love in his mission-heart moved him to willingly bear the suffering that we deserved, in order to make <u>peace</u> with God (Rom 5:10). Therefore, our hearts are now full of peace and *"joy"* (v 23) <u>in the midst</u> of suffering for him ([17]M. M. Lk 6:22)!

Jesus Pronounces Woes 6:24-26

6:24 *"But woe to you who are rich, for you have received your consolation.*
6:25 *"Woe to you who are full now, for you shall be hungry. "Woe to you who laugh now, for you shall mourn and weep.*
6:26 *"Woe to you, when all people speak well of you, for so their*

fathers did to the false prophets.

6:24-25 (1) This is the first of many times in Luke's account that Jesus warned people against the love of money. He continued to repeat the same warning many times in different forms: in <u>parables</u> (12:16-21; 16:1-31; 19:11-26; 21:1-4), in <u>discourse</u> (12:22-34), and in <u>dialogue</u> (18:18-30; 19:1-10). How eager his mission-heart was to warn everyone against this very common sin ([18]M. I. Lk 3:3a)! **2)** Because the rich people in many societies in the world often love their money more than anything else, far too often, the devil uses this sin to blind them from loving God and the poor people around them. They become so blind that it is almost impossible for them to find the narrow door of faith in Jesus and enter his Kingdom (13:24). However, their superior wealth, of course, gives them the strongest influence in their societies; therefore, Satan often deceives them into abusing their power, which causes them to do even worse sins: **a)** They too often oppress the poor and also make it difficult for them to hear the Gospel and find the narrow door of faith (16:19-31). **b)** And they also often make it very difficult for Christians to carry out their mission to *"seek the lost"* (19:10) by passing laws that hinder freedom of speech or laws that violate God's Laws ([19]M. M. Ro 5:1).

6:26 (1) In verse 22, Jesus said, *"Blessed are you when people hate you and when they exclude you and <u>revile</u> you;"* but here in verse 26 he says, *"Woe to you, when all people <u>speak well</u> of you."* People in every culture around the world often have the same problem: we often wonder what other people are saying about us. And sadly, far too often, this powerful fear of the opinion of others drives Christians to either hide their faith in Jesus, or to <u>deny</u> him completely. And how sad it will be on Judgment Day for those Christians who do yield to social pressure and <u>deny</u> Jesus, because he will also <u>deny</u> them on that Day ([20]M. I. Lk 9:54)! **2)** Especially in countries where a person's physical family means <u>everything</u> to him, if he becomes a Christian, the relative sizes of his physical and his new Christian family become crucial for whether his new faith in Jesus will survive the hatred of his physical family or not. If he has only a few Christians to support him, humanly speaking, it will take a tremendous amount of courage to cling to Jesus when his family ostracizes him or even tries to kill him. Yet, the Holy Spirit is far more powerful than any human fear; as the new Christian continues to hear and study God's holy Word, and as his new Christian family supports him, he will, by God's grace, be able to boldly cling to Jesus and even boldly spread the Gospel to his physical family. Therefore, how wonderful it will be for all Christians who faithfully <u>acknowledge</u> Jesus before others without fear, because he will also <u>acknowledge</u> them on that Last Day (Mt 10:32; M. I. Lk 9:54)! **3)** How it must have grieved Jesus' mission-heart to have to say in verse 26 that *"their fathers [his <u>own</u> ancestors]"* often spoke *"<u>well of the false prophets</u>,"* because the false prophets yielded to powerful social pressure and also spoke well of them (13:34)! The false prophets were afraid of their fellow Israelites, and therefore, they were also afraid to tell the truth and call them to repentance (Ezek 22:28-29). Furthermore, what was even sadder was the fact that the Jewish religious leaders of Jesus' day still loved false prophets so much that they thought that God's <u>greatest prophet</u>, Jesus (Heb 1:1-2) was a false prophet and eventually killed him (23:21). Even their High Priest, Caiaphas encouraged them to kill him (Jn 11:49-53). And ironically, in this way, God used these men to carry out his gracious plan of saving lost mankind, because it is he who is always in full control of every situation ([21]M. M. Ac 4:28).

Love Your Enemies 6:27-36

6:27 *"But I say to you who hear, Love your enemies, do good to those who hate you,*
6:28 *bless those who curse you, pray for those who abuse you.*
6:29 *To one who strikes you on the cheek, offer the other also, and from one who takes away your cloak do not withhold your tunic either.*
6:30 *Give to everyone who begs from you, and from one who takes away your goods do not demand them back.*
6:31 *And as you wish that others would do to you, do so to them.*
6:32 *"If you love those who love you, what benefit is that to you? For*

even sinners love those who love them.

6:33   *And if you do good to those who do good to you, what benefit is that to you? For even sinners do the same.*

6:34   *And if you lend to those from whom you expect to receive, what credit is that to you? Even sinners lend to sinners, to get back the same amount.*

6:35   *But love your enemies, and do good, and lend, expecting nothing in return, and your reward will be great, and you will be sons of the Most High, for he is kind to the ungrateful and the evil.*

6:36   *Be merciful, even as your Father is merciful.*

6:27-35 (1) Since verse 22 is part of the immediate context, the specific *"enemies"* that Jesus refers to in verses 27 and 35 are the <u>people</u> who persecute Christians. Thus, a new Christian may well ask, "Jesus, do you mean that I should <u>love</u> my unbelieving father even though he has told me that I am no longer his son because I trust in you? How can I *"love,"* *"bless"* and *"pray for"* him (vs 27-28, 35)? I will never again physically embrace my father, my mother, my brothers, my sisters—not one person in my family!" Obviously, this Christian's new Christian family is now incredibly important to him! Furthermore, he should also remember how much <u>Jesus</u> has always loved his human enemies. <u>All</u> human beings are born as God's enemies because we are all born in sin (Ps 51:5); yet it was <u>while</u> we all were his enemies that he died for us (Rom 5:10). And because we Christians have Jesus' love in our hearts we too are able to love our human enemies (even if they're our own physical family) by witnessing to them about our dear Lord, who's mission-heart longs to be their Lord as well ([22]M. I. Jn 14:15). **2)** Nevertheless, we Christians <u>do</u> have enemies that we should <u>not</u> love. We should <u>not</u> love our <u>spiritual</u> enemies, the devil and his demons. A person who loves Satan must hate Jesus because Satan is Jesus' archenemy. In his mission to *"seek and save the lost,"* Jesus never forgot that his worst enemy was *"the evil one,"* Satan. Therefore, we should always remember that Jesus did defeat him on the cross (Jn 19:30); yet we should also beware of the devil and his evil traps by depending on our Lord in constant prayer as

we go on our mission in this dark world ([23]M. I. Lk 11:10).
6:31 The love that Jesus places in the hearts of his disciples is the most radical love of all because he himself loved all mankind in the same way ([24]M. M. Ro 3:24). His indwelling Spirit makes his disciples both willing and able to witness to others by loving them as he loves us (Phil 2:13; [25]M. I. Jn 14:15).
6:35 (1) Jesus says in verse 35, *"Love your enemies…and your reward will be great, and you will be sons of the Most High."* To someone who chooses to love Jesus and thus make his father and mother and the rest of his family hate him, this promise of a reward or eternal inheritance, is incredibly important. Because he chose Jesus, it may mean that he will receive no inheritance here on earth, but his *"[eternal] reward will be great."* What a most gracious gift this is! And what an awesome inheritance it is! He will have a loving, eternal relationship with his heavenly Father as a son of *"the Most High [God]"* forever ([26]M. M. Lk 18:29)! **2)** Furthermore, this is a very unique *"reward"* since only one person could have earned it. The God/man Jesus earned it by obeying all of God's Laws perfectly for all of his brothers and sisters on earth (Lev 18:5). His mission-heart compelled him to give up his limitless riches as God and became poor like his brothers and sisters, so that he could *"reward"* those who trust in him with his riches (Tit 2:14). It is a most gracious gift that he gives to all who trust in him; therefore, no one should proudly think that he can do anything to try to earn this reward by his own strength or work righteousness; he must totally depend on the Lord Jesus' rich grace in order to receive it from him as a gift (2 Cor 8:9; M. M. Lk 18:29).

Judging Others 6:37-42

6:37 "Judge not, and you will not be judged; condemn not, and you will not be condemned; forgive, and you will be forgiven;
6:38 give, and it will be given to you. Good measure, pressed down, shaken together, running over, will be put into your lap. For with the measure you use it will be measured back to you."

6:39 *He also told them a parable: "Can a blind man lead a blind man? Will they not both fall into a pit?*

6:40 *A disciple is not above his teacher, but everyone when he is fully trained will be like his teacher.*

6:41 *Why do you see the speck that is in your brother's eye, but do not notice the log that is in your own eye?*

6:42 *How can you say to your brother, 'Brother, let me take out the speck that is in your eye,' when you yourself do not see the log that is in your own eye? You hypocrite, first take the log out of your own eye, and then you will see clearly to take out the speck that is in your brother's eye.*

6:37 When Jesus says in verse 37, *"Judge not, and you will not be judged,"* he is especially concerned about the honor of his holy <u>name</u>, since the Christian Church never lives in a vacuum. The objects of the Church's mission are watching them to see if they will actually live holy lives because they claim to be following holy Jesus. And when they judge others, their lives do <u>not</u> match their words, which brings shame on Jesus' name and drives people away from him instead of attracting them to him (Jn 12:32). No wonder Jesus warned his disciples against judging others, especially judging fellow Christians! If Christians proudly and hypocritically *"judge and condemn"* fellow Christians it causes not only serious problems within the Christian fellowship, it also has equally serious consequences in the unbelieving public in at least <u>three</u> ways: **a)** First of all, they will despise the Christians who are self-righteous judges because they see their pride and hypocrisy. **b)** Secondly, they will ridicule the unjustly condemned Christians for being part of the Christian Church. **c)** And finally, and worst of all, they will likewise despise the holy name of Jesus. It's a new mission imperative. M. I. Lk 6:37: Christians should beware of hypocritically judging their fellow Christians because it both destroys their unity in Jesus, and it may also bring shame on the holy name of Jesus before the unbelieving world that they are trying to reach.

6:37-38 (1) Jesus continues to make his <u>radical</u> claim on those who trust in him in verses 37-38. But why can he make such a radical claim on anyone? He can because, as the unique God/man, his mission-heart, deep love and grace for all of his fellow human beings is the greatest love the world will ever see. Who else would ever be able to match a God who loves people who are born as his enemies? Who else would ever be willing to die for people who hate him and proudly sin against him so that he could forgive them (Eph 3:18)? Therefore, the forgiveness that Jesus earned for us on the cross is a most gracious gift that he offers to all of mankind; and such a gift, therefore, also has the awesome power to empower anyone who takes up his own cross and follows Jesus to do the same thing, to likewise generously *"give"* (v 38) the gift of forgiveness to others, even forgive his enemies. The gift of forgiveness they then receive in return from the people who received their forgiveness would also be boundless, a *"good measure, pressed down, shaken together, running over, will be put into your lap"* (v 38; 17:3-4). This has always been in our Lord's mission-heart: that his love would flow like an endless river from his heart into the hearts of Christians and on and on into the hearts of countless others (2 Cor 1:3-7; Jn 4:14; [27]M. M. Lk 1:26). **2)** Unfortunately, some church leaders use verse 38 wrongly; they use it to try to motivate people to generously give money to their church. However, there is nothing in the context of verse 38 that refers to giving money! The whole context is all about giving the gift of forgiveness to others instead of proudly *"judging"* them (vs 32, 37).

6:41-42 (1) With his powerful metaphor about *"the speck"* or *"the log"* in a person's eye, Jesus repeats the same warning that he gave in verse 37 against judging others. It is sinful pride that compels a person to think that he is better than others and therefore he thinks that he has the right to judge them. In addition, the sin of judging others is often also a failure to forgive that person; and both sins obviously break the good personal relationship between them, as well as between them and God. And these broken relationships can cause very serious damage within the Church as well as hindering the Church's outreach to the lost world, as we saw at verse 37 ([28]M. I. Lk 6:37). **2)** Sin had broken the peaceful relationships between God and mankind and also between all human beings; therefore, Jesus' mission-heart had compelled him to be willing to be born as the God/man in order to restore all of these relationships.

And now as Jesus was beginning his ministry, his Spirit was already beginning to build the new Israel, the Church (Rom 11:26), which is a loving community of forgiven sinners who have learned how to forgive one another and even their enemies from their gracious Lord. The rich grace that Jesus poured out on all of mankind who were his enemies now compels Christians to forget any past prejudices against other races or cultures and to show the same grace and love to all people ([29]M. I. Ac 15:20).

A Tree and its Fruit 6:43-45

6:43 *"For no good tree bears bad fruit, nor again does a bad tree bear good fruit,*
6:44 *for each tree is known by its own fruit. For figs are not gathered from thornbushes, nor are grapes picked from a bramble bush.*
6:45 *The good person out of the good treasure of his heart produces good, and the evil person out of his evil treasure produces evil, for out of the abundance of the heart his mouth speaks.*

6:43-45 Jesus' mission-heart had moved him to make the radical commitment of setting aside his divine nature and becoming a humble human being (Phil 2:6-11) in order to make radical, total changes in the lives of his fellow human beings—not minor, superficial changes. He came to destroy the power of our inner sinful human nature through the waters of holy Baptism and his holy Word, so that our entire beings would be transformed from the inside-out ([30]M. M. Tit 3:5). Our new mission-hearts would then produce *"good fruit"* by his Spirit's power as a powerful witness to the world (3:8-9; Rom 6:1-10: Heb 11:6; [31]M. M. Lk 1:26 & [32]Lk 1:27).

Build Your House on the Rock 6:46-49

6:46 *"Why do you call me 'Lord, Lord,' and not do what I tell you?*

6:47 *Everyone who comes to me and hears my words and does them, I will show you what he is like:*

6:48 *he is like a man building a house, who dug deep and laid the foundation on the rock. And when a flood arose, the stream broke against that house and could not shake it, because it had been well built.*

6:49 *But the one who hears and does not do them is like a man who built a house on the ground without a foundation. When the stream broke against it, immediately it fell, and the ruin of that house was great."*

6:46-49 There is only one *"rock"* (v 48) that a person should build the *"house"* of his life on, since <u>Jesus</u> is that *"rock"* that can never be moved (Ps 18:31). All other gods are no gods at all (1 Cor 8:4-5). However, since the time of Adam and Eve, the devil has cleverly imprisoned countless numbers of people in the worship of gods that they themselves have made. People have worshipped and continue to worship stones, rivers, animals, stars, the sun, the moon, themselves, and other people in various forms of Animism (Is 44:6-20). However, if anyone builds his "house" on such a capricious, *"sandy"* god, his life can only end in total, eternal *"ruin,"* as Jesus concludes in verse 49, *"When the stream [of God's final judgment] broke against it, immediately it fell, and the ruin of that house [built on sand] was great."* Such a person is truly eternally *"lost."* Therefore, Jesus is the <u>only</u> *"rock"* to build one's house on because he came to save with the final solution to all of mankind's problems that are all caused by sin. He destroyed both sin and death on the cross and in his empty tomb (1 Cor 15). And faith in this *"rock"* is the gift that anyone can receive when the Holy Spirit works in a person's heart through his holy Word to turn him away from other *"sandy"* gods, and move him to repent and believe in Jesus ([33]M. M. Lk 13:24).

---

[1] M. M. Mt 1:22: God sent his only Son, Jesus to be born as a true human being, so that he could save all of his brothers and sisters of all nations by fulfilling all of God's promises in the Old

Testament.

[2] M. I. Lk 6:5: Their faith in Jesus should move Christians to show Jesus' <u>love</u> in all circumstances even if their act of love breaks another less important human or even divine Law.

[3] M. I. Lk 11:10: Christians should <u>continuously</u> pray to their heavenly Father and <u>always</u> depend on his grace, and not on their own feeble strength, because he <u>always</u> loves them.

[4] M. I. Lk 6:5: Their faith in Jesus should move Christians to show Jesus' <u>love</u> in all circumstances even if their act of love breaks another less important human or even divine Law.

[5] M. I. Lk 4:40: Christians should go and seek the lost <u>one</u> person at a time by focusing on each person's <u>unique</u> needs.

[6] M. M. Mt 5:14: When the Holy Spirit creates faith in a person's heart, he also graciously gives him a new mission-heart that is eager to shine the light of the Gospel throughout the whole world.

[7] M. M. 1 Cor 12:12: As Christians baptize each person the Holy Spirit graciously unites each one of them into one Body of Christ, which has many members.

[8] M. M. Ac 13:46: As he did with the old Israel, God <u>first of all</u> strengthens the faith of the new Israel, the Church with his Word and Sacraments, so that they can go and witness to the lost people of all nations.

[9] M. M. Ro 10:17a: The Holy Spirit <u>only</u> creates and preserves faith by using the message of God's grace in his holy Word.

[10] M. M. Ro 11:26: God graciously continues to graft Jews and Gentiles into the new Israel through the proclamation of the Gospel, until the remnant of Israel and the fullness of the Gentiles form one, holy Nation and are saved.

[11] M. I. Lk 5:20: Even when Christians proclaim the Gospel to large crowds, they should always remember that the crowds are made up of <u>individuals</u>; and that <u>each one</u> of them needs to repent and believe in Jesus.

[12] M. M. Lk 13:24: The <u>only</u> way to enter the Kingdom of God is to have <u>faith</u> in Jesus as one's Savior.

[13] M. M. Ro 1:5: The same Holy Spirit who creates <u>faith</u> and a new missionary <u>nature</u> in a person's heart also graciously empowers him to gratefully respond to his Lord's love by <u>obeying</u> him.

[14] M. M. 1 Tim 2:3: It pleases God their Savior when Christians pray for all people because he desires all people to be saved and to come to the knowledge of the truth about Jesus.

[15] M. I. Ac 2:4: In cross-cultural situations, they should always focus on all of the needs of the target group by learning <u>their</u> heart-language and culture as deeply as possible, so that they can tell them the Gospel clearly in their own language and also help them with the true needs of their society.

[16] M. I. Ro 5:3b: Christians should <u>rejoice</u> in the midst of <u>suffering</u> for Jesus' sake because unbelievers may see their joy, which may create opportunities to witness to Jesus.

[17] M. M. Lk 6:22: The Lord Jesus will surely bless a Christian in the midst of suffering for his sake; and he will also bless him with eternal life if he remains faithful to him.

[18] M. I. Lk 3:3a: Christians should, in love, warn lost people who do not repent.

[19] M. M. Ro 5:1: On the cross, Jesus earned <u>peace</u> with God for <u>all</u> of his brothers and sisters from every nation on earth.

[20] M. I. Lk 9:54: Christians should show patient love to people who unknowingly reject an opportunity to hear the Gospel.

[21] M. M. Ac 4:28: The heavenly Father is always in full control of his mission to all nations of the world.

[22] M. I. Jn 14:15: Christians should obey all of Jesus' commands in grateful response to his love for them as they go on his mission to the world.

[23] M. I. Lk 11:10: Christians should <u>continuously</u> pray to their heavenly Father and <u>always</u> depend on his grace, and not on their own feeble strength, because he <u>always</u> loves them.

[24] M. M. Ro 3:24: Jesus lived a life of perfect obedience and shed his precious blood on the cross, in order to graciously set all nations free from sin, which a person only receives by faith in him.

[25] M. I. Jn 14:15: Christians should obey all of Jesus' commands in grateful response to his love for them as they go on his mission to the world.

[26] M. M. Lk 18:29: All Christians will certainly receive rewards in heaven as gracious gifts, but not because they earned them by going into the lost world to proclaim the Gospel; rather, they went because they also received <u>grateful</u> mission-hearts from their Lord.

[27] M. M. Lk 1:26: The heavenly Father sent his Son, Jesus to be born and live in <u>humble</u> circumstances, so that everyone from every nation on earth would see his <u>grace</u>.

[28] M. I. Lk 6:37: Christians should beware of hypocritically judging their fellow Christians because it both destroys their unity in Jesus, and it may also bring shame on the holy name of Jesus before the unbelieving world that they are trying to reach.

[29] M. I. Ac 15:20: To preserve the unity of the Church and to make it possible to reach out to unbelievers from all cultural backgrounds, all they should show love to their fellow Christians and to all people of all cultures by refraining from actions that would easily offend them.

[30] M. M. Tit 3:5: When a person is baptized, God graciously saves him and gives him the gift of a new birth from his indwelling Holy Spirit; and he does this because his mercy is so great, and not because of any good deeds that that person has done.

[31] M. M. Lk 1:26: The heavenly Father sent his Son, Jesus to be born and live in <u>humble</u> circumstances, so that everyone from every nation on earth would see his <u>grace</u>.

[32] M. M. Lk 1:27: Jesus had to be born as a true human being and as a true Jew in order to become the King of kings in his heavenly kingdom forever.

[33] M. M. Lk 13:24: The <u>only</u> way to enter the Kingdom of God is to have <u>faith</u> in Jesus as one's Savior.

Chapter 7

Jesus Heals a Centurion's Servant 7:1-10

7:1 *After he had finished all his sayings in the hearing of the people, he entered Capernaum.*
7:2 *Now a centurion had a servant who was sick and at the point of death, who was highly valued by him.*
7:3 *When the centurion heard about Jesus, he sent to him elders of the Jews, asking him to come and heal his servant.*
7:4 *And when they came to Jesus, they pleaded with him earnestly, saying, "He is worthy to have you do this for him,*
7:5 *for he loves our nation, and he is the one who built us our synagogue."*
7:6 *And Jesus went with them. When he was not far from the house, the centurion sent friends, saying to him, "Lord, do not trouble yourself, for I am not worthy to have you come under my roof.*
7:7 *Therefore I did not presume to come to you. But say the word, and let my servant be healed.*
7:8 *For I too am a man set under authority, with soldiers under me: and I say to one, 'Go,' and he goes; and to another, 'Come,' and he comes; and to my servant, 'Do this,' and he does it."*
7:9 *When Jesus heard these things, he marveled at him, and turning to the crowd that followed him, said, "I tell you, not even in Israel have I found such faith."*
7:10 *And when those who had been sent returned to the house, they found the servant well.*

7:4-5 The way in which these Jewish leaders appealed to Jesus to help a Roman centurion (who was a Gentile, of course) is very telling. They said that *"he is worthy to have you do this for him"* because he had done good deeds to help them. What Luke does not say explicitly here is that these Jews, no doubt, also self-righteously assumed that they were *"worthy"* before God simply because they thought, "We have Abraham as our [physical] father" (3:8). Thus, Luke is saying that both assumptions that these Jews had made were completely sinful. <u>No one</u>, except the God/man Jesus, can <u>earn</u> God's grace by doing good deeds; and a self-righteous, doubting heart is only *"worthy"* of <u>condemnation</u> from God. Jesus here puts his Gospel into action by healing the centurion's servant; and he healed him, <u>not</u> because he <u>deserved</u> his help, but out of his pure <u>grace</u> alone. His mission-heart offers his gracious help to <u>all</u> people of <u>all</u> nations purely out of his grace alone and without any discrimination ([1]M. M. Ro 1:5).

7:6 This Gentile was in fact an important man (v 8), yet he demonstrates an entirely different attitude from the type of attitude that his Jewish friends displayed. He had a <u>humble</u>, child-like faith that moved him to say, *"I am <u>not worthy</u> to have you [Jesus] come under my roof."* What a sharp contrast in attitudes! Thus, we once again see that Jesus' mission-heart had moved him to set aside his divinity in order *"to seek and to save the lost"* on a truly <u>universal</u> mission to <u>all</u> nations on earth (19:10; [2]M. M. Lk 1:1). Moreover, he longs for his Church to continue to listen to their mission-hearts and hurry to every corner of the world to proclaim his Gospel message ([3]M. I. Ac 1:8 & [4]Ac 2:4).

7:9 The officer's faith was so *"great"* (NIV) because it was a <u>humble</u> and a child-like faith in Jesus (M. M. Lk 13:24). But the important question is: <u>Why</u> did Jesus find *"such faith <u>not even</u> in Israel?"* God had shown his grace to the nation of Israel <u>first</u>, gave them his holy Word in their own heart-language <u>first</u>, and gave them the responsibility of sharing his blessings with all other nations (Gen 12:1-3). The Israelites should have feasted on God's rich grace in his Word, especially since they could understand it so clearly (Is 25:6); then, they would have gone to the Gentile nations to share the glorious Gospel of a coming King of all kings. But obviously throughout their history very few of them did so (Rom 9:1-9; 11:1-32). But God's mission-heart could not be stopped by such stubborn sinfulness; from eternity, one key component of that plan was to create a <u>new</u> Israel, the Church in the new era of his Messiah. And he now <u>blesses</u> the new Israel with his holy Word as he had the old Israel, <u>so that</u> all Christians now have the same responsibility that he had entrusted to the old Israel to be a <u>blessing</u> to *"all the families of the earth"* (Gen 12:3; [5]M. M. Ac 13:46).

Jesus Raises a Widow's Son 7:11-17

7:11 *Soon afterward he went to a town called Nain, and his disciples and a great crowd went with him.*
7:12 *As he drew near to the gate of the town, behold, a man who had died was being carried out, the only son of his mother, and she was a widow, and a considerable crowd from the town was with her.*
7:13 *And when the Lord saw her, he had compassion on her and said to her, "Do not weep."*
7:14 *Then he came up and touched the bier, and the bearers stood still. And he said, "Young man, I say to you, arise."*
7:15 *And the dead man sat up and began to speak, and Jesus gave him to his mother.*
7:16 *Fear seized them all, and they glorified God, saying, "A great prophet has arisen among us!" and "God has visited his people!"*
7:17 *And this report about him spread through the whole of Judea and all the surrounding country.*

7:13 Jesus' mission-heart moved him to have compassion on *"the lost"* mother in verses 13-15; 2 Cor 1:3-5). And once again, Luke shows that Jesus did so very <u>personally</u>. First he comforted the mother with gentle Words in verse 13 by saying, *"Do not weep."* And then he put his Words into action by performing the wonderful miracle of raising her son from the dead (v 15). He always loves each and every person as an <u>individual</u>; and such personal love likewise compels his Church to have the same compassion on every individual that they meet on his mission ([6]M. I. Lk 4:40 & [7]Lk 5:20).

7:14-17 The resurrection miracle in verse 14 raises <u>three</u> issues regarding both Jesus' ministry and also the mission that he gave to his Church. **1)** Jesus performed many healing miracles; and <u>three</u> times (that are recorded in the Gospels) he even raised people from the dead (7:14; 8:54; Jn 11). However, there is only <u>one</u> resurrection miracle that can create and sustain saving faith: the resurrection of <u>Jesus</u> himself, because this miracle alone <u>proves</u> that his heavenly Father had accepted his perfect sacrifice which rescued all of mankind from its deepest <u>spiritual</u> enemies: sin, death and the devil (2 Cor 1:20; [8]M. M. Jn 20:8). **2)** By itself, however, <u>no</u> other miracle <u>can</u> create <u>saving</u> faith, because all other miracles rescue people from <u>physical</u> ailments. We see this truth clearly in at least two places: **a)** We see it in verse 16, where the people saw Jesus raise the young man from the dead, and they thought he was *"a great prophet"* (v 16), but not the <u>greatest</u> prophet; and they understood that *"God has visited his people"* (v 16), as a miracle worker, but <u>not</u> that he had come to rescue his people from sin. **b)** And we see it again in (Mk 8:11) where *"the Pharisees came…seeking from him [Jesus] a <u>sign</u> from heaven to <u>test</u> him;"* and they did this immediately <u>after</u> he had just miraculously fed 5,000 men! This miracle obviously had not created any kind of faith in their hard hearts—not even faith that he was God's Son ([9]M. I. Ac 6:1). **3)** Of course, all healing miracles did attract a lot of attention to Jesus (v 17); and they even attracted so much attention that he had to, at times, withdraw from the crowds (5:14, 16). Nevertheless, these miracles were important for his mission, since they created two kinds of opportunities for him and his disciples. First of all, the miracles showed that they had compassion on people in physical need, but they also provided venues for them to proclaim the Gospel message ([10]M. I. Lk 4:15). And miracles do, of course, still serve our Lord's mission by creating these <u>opportunities</u> yet today, but <u>only if</u> a Christian uses the name of Jesus to do them. Therefore, it is <u>only</u> God's gracious message of the <u>saving</u> Gospel that the Holy Spirit uses to touch the heart of each individual to create the new life of <u>saving</u> faith ([11]M. M. Ro 1:16b & [12]Ro 10:17a).

Messengers from John the Baptist 7:18-35

7:18 *The disciples of John reported all these things to him. And John,*
7:19 *calling two of his disciples to him, sent them to the Lord, saying, "Are you the one who is to come, or shall we look for*

another?"

7:20 *And when the men had come to him, they said, "John the Baptist has sent us to you, saying, 'Are you the one who is to come, or shall we look for another?'"*

7:21 *In that hour he healed many people of diseases and plagues and evil spirits, and on many who were blind he bestowed sight.*

7:22 *And he answered them, "Go and tell John what you have seen and heard: the blind receive their sight, the lame walk, lepers are cleansed, and the deaf hear, the dead are raised up, the poor have good news preached to them.*

7:23 *And blessed is the one who is not offended by me."*

7:24 *When John's messengers had gone, Jesus began to speak to the crowds concerning John: "What did you go out into the wilderness to see? A reed shaken by the wind?*

7:25 *What then did you go out to see? A man dressed in soft clothing? Behold, those who are dressed in splendid clothing and live in luxury are in kings' courts.*

7:26 *What then did you go out to see? A prophet? Yes, I tell you, and more than a prophet.*

7:27 *This is he of whom it is written, "'Behold, I send my messenger before your face, who will prepare your way before you.'*

7:28 *I tell you, among those born of women none is greater than John. Yet the one who is least in the kingdom of God is greater than he."*

7:29 *(When all the people heard this, and the tax collectors too, they declared God just, having been baptized with the baptism of John,*

7:30 *but the Pharisees and the lawyers rejected the purpose of God for themselves, not having been baptized by him.)*

7:31 *"To what then shall I compare the people of this generation, and what are they like?*

7:32 *They are like children sitting in the marketplace and calling to one another, "'We played the flute for you, and you did not dance; we sang a dirge, and you did not weep.'*

7:33 *For John the Baptist has come eating no bread and drinking no wine, and you say, 'He has a demon.'*

> 7:34 *The Son of Man has come eating and drinking, and you say, 'Look at him! A glutton and a drunkard, a friend of tax collectors and sinners!'*
> 7:35 *Yet wisdom is justified by all her children."*

7:18-19 John's question in verse 19 may indicate that he was starting to have doubts about who Jesus really was (v 23). His thoughts are strikingly similar to those of the people who saw the young man raised from the dead (v 16). But of course, even though John was very sure that he was the Messiah when he baptized Jesus, he was now languishing in prison and no doubt had good reason to fear for his life. He was suffering for the sake of witnessing to the truth, for the name of Jesus (v 23); and therefore, he urgently needed reassurance that Jesus was indeed the Messiah whom he had been longing for ([13]M. M. Lk 6:22).

7:22 Jesus answered John in verse 22, *"Go and tell John what you have seen and heard: the blind receive their sight, the lame walk, lepers are cleansed, and the deaf hear, the dead are raised up, the poor have good news preached to them."* We should note two things. **a)** First of all, Jesus was quoting parts of (Is 29:18-21; 35:5-6) in this verse, in order to teach John that by his ministry, he was fulfilling these wonderful promises that God made in Isaiah ([14]M. M. Mt 1:22). **b)** Secondly, note what the last item is in Jesus' list of what he had been doing on his mission: *"the poor have good news preached to them."* He thereby emphasized his most important work by listing it last. It was true that he was healing many people because they were suffering with many physical sicknesses and because he loved them as whole persons; but more importantly, he was preaching the Gospel to the *"poor"* (v 22; [15]M. M. Lk 1:1). These people were *"poor"* especially because they were *"lost"* spiritually (19:10; 4:18-19). And they were now hearing God's Word from the Word himself, so that the precious seed of the Gospel could now sprout and grow in their hearts (8:1-15) and rescue them from their deepest spiritual need ([16]M. M. Ro 10:17a).

7:23 It's clear here that John was indeed in danger of losing his faith because he feared for his life. Therefore, Jesus comforted him by saying in verse 22 *"the poor have Good News preached to them."* His Lord was continuing the mission work that he had begun; and he was, in fact, everything that John had been longing for. And Jesus' comforting Words did give John the strength that he would soon need to courageously witness to his Lord's name by becoming the first Christian martyr (Mt 14:10; [17]M. M. Lk 12:8).

7:26-27 (1) Near the end of John's mission, in Luke's account, Jesus announced the purpose of John's mission in verses 26, where he calls him *"a prophet…and more than a prophet."* It's possible that Jesus was referring here to the fact that John was the last of the Old Testament prophets, who *"prepared your [the Messiah, Jesus] way before you"* (v 27), which meant that Jesus himself was beginning a new era as the greatest prophet (Heb 1:1-2). John called the nation of Israel to repentance and initiated them into the new Kingdom through the water of holy Baptism (3:3-6). Repentant hearts would, then, be ready to receive Jesus their King, who would *"seek and save the lost"* (19:10; M. M. Lk 1:1). **2)** But why was it important in God's perfect plan of salvation that he had to send someone to *"prepare the way"* for the Messiah? There is at least one possibility. It was very important in the Hebrew judicial system that two or three witnesses must testify to the same truth or fact. Jesus himself said in (Mt 18:16), *"But if he [an unrepentant person] does not listen, take one or two others along with you, that every charge may be established by the evidence of two or three witnesses."* Therefore, John's testimony that Jesus was indeed God's Son and the Messiah confirmed Jesus' own testimony to the same truths. This should have provided more than sufficient evidence for every Jew that Jesus was indeed the long-promised Messiah. However, that was not always enough evidence for far too many Jews, as Jesus clearly indicates in verse 9, *"I tell you, not even in Israel have I found such faith."* By sending John to prepare the way for Jesus, God was truly in control of his mission ([18]M. M. Ac 4:28)!

7:28 For Jesus to say in verse 28, *"among those born of women none is greater than John"* is truly an extraordinary statement, especially since Jesus himself was also *"born of woman"* (Gal 4:4). Thus, scholars continue to debate just what Jesus may have meant by it. Nevertheless, Jesus may also be emphasizing in verse 28 the fact that John never pointed to himself in his ministry; he humbly did his mission work as a great prophet of God (v 26; 1:76; 9:48) by always pointing to Jesus as the Messiah/King ([19]M. I. Lk 11:10).

7:31-32 African drummers and dancers always respond to and interact with each other as they make music together. As the drummer changes his rhythm in subtle ways, the dancer expresses the new feeling or idea with his body. In a similar way, John led the way by first inviting *"the Pharisees and the lawyers"* to "dance to his tune" by repenting and being baptized, but they *"rejected the purpose of God for themselves"* (vs 30, 33). Next, Jesus came preaching the same message, *"Repent and believe in me;"* and thereby he confirmed John's witness (v 27); but they also refused to "dance to his tune," even though it's the most beautiful song in the universe about his glorious cross (Jn 12:32). Their self-righteous pride had made their ears deaf to the rhythm of both drummers (v 34; 3:8). Obviously, John and Jesus did not *"seek"* inanimate stones that could not respond to their tunes (3:8); instead, Jesus *"came to seek"* lost people (19:10). He played his music of love for them with his entire being—his life and his death—for thirty-three years; and he still waits for everyone who hears the same song from his missionaries, the Church to respond and dance to his tune in the same way with all of their love and with their whole being (1 Cor 10:31; Rom 12:1-2; [20]M. M. Lk 1:1).

A Sinful Woman Forgiven 7:36-50

7:36 *One of the Pharisees asked him to eat with him, and he went into the Pharisee's house and took his place at the table.*

7:37 *And behold, a woman of the city, who was a sinner, when she learned that he was reclining at table in the Pharisee's house, brought an alabaster flask of ointment,*

7:38 *and standing behind him at his feet, weeping, she began to wet his feet with her tears and wiped them with the hair of her head and kissed his feet and anointed them with the ointment.*

7:39 *Now when the Pharisee who had invited him saw this, he said to himself, "If this man were a prophet, he would have known who and what sort of woman this is who is touching him, for*

7:39 *...she is a sinner."*
7:40 *And Jesus answering said to him, "Simon, I have something to say to you." And he answered, "Say it, Teacher."*
7:41 *"A certain moneylender had two debtors. One owed five hundred denarii, and the other fifty.*
7:42 *When they could not pay, he cancelled the debt of both. Now which of them will love him more?"*
7:43 *Simon answered, "The one, I suppose, for whom he cancelled the larger debt." And he said to him, "You have judged rightly."*
7:44 *Then turning toward the woman he said to Simon, "Do you see this woman? I entered your house; you gave me no water for my feet, but she has wet my feet with her tears and wiped them with her hair.*
7:45 *You gave me no kiss, but from the time I came in she has not ceased to kiss my feet.*
7:46 *You did not anoint my head with oil, but she has anointed my feet with ointment.*
7:47 *Therefore I tell you, her sins, which are many, are forgiven--for she loved much. But he who is forgiven little, loves little."*
7:48 *And he said to her, "Your sins are forgiven."*
7:49 *Then those who were at table with him began to say among themselves, "Who is this, who even forgives sins?"*
7:50 *And he said to the woman, "Your faith has saved you; go in peace."*

7:40 It may be possible that Simon invited Jesus to a meal at his home because he wanted to hear his Gospel message, but unfortunately that's not very likely; it's much more likely that his intentions were evil because of the way we see this event unfold. He probably wanted to get him alone in order to deceive or trap him, since other Pharisees had already begun to try to do so. Nevertheless, Jesus accepted his invitation because he always seized <u>every</u> opportunity to "seek the lost" whether people seemed to be open to hearing him or not ([21]M. I. Lk 4:15).

7:47-50 What Luke said in narrative form about people dancing to Jesus' tune in verses 28-35 he now illustrates with a living example of how one lost sinner, this sinful woman in verses 36-50, responded to

Jesus' tune and received his forgiveness. The Pharisee who had invited Jesus to the meal was sadly deaf to his tune; but Jesus had found <u>one</u> more lost sinner; and in his rich grace, he forgave her huge debt by saying to her in verse 50, *"Your faith has saved you; go in peace."* And she responded with nothing less that her <u>whole</u> self (v 47; [22]M. I. Lk 4:40)! Obviously, faith in Jesus was the vital link to spiritual life and forgiveness that this woman needed; and what a powerful witness her faith was to all who were present that day—including the Pharisee ([23]M. M. Lk 13:24)!

---

[1] M. M. Ro 1:5: The same Holy Spirit who creates <u>faith</u> and a new missionary <u>nature</u> in a person's heart also graciously empowers him to gratefully respond to his Lord's love by <u>obeying</u> him.

[2] M. M. Lk 1:1: Jesus came to seek and save <u>all</u> lost people from <u>every</u> nation on earth.

[3] M. I. Ac 1:8: Christians should go and witness about Jesus to all who are lost from all languages and cultures by depending on the power of the Holy Spirit to help them bridge all of the language/cultural boundaries whether they are relatively easy, as in their own language, or extremely difficult.

[4] M. I. Ac 2:4: In cross-cultural situations, Christians should always focus on all of the needs of the target group by learning <u>their</u> heart-language and culture as deeply as possible, so that they can tell them the Gospel clearly in their own language and also help them with the true needs of their society.

[5] M. M. Ac 13:46: As he did with the old Israel, God <u>first of all</u> strengthens the faith of the new Israel, the Church with his Word and Sacraments, so that they can go and witness to the lost people of all nations.

[6] M. I. Lk 4:40: Christians should go and seek the lost <u>one</u> person at a time by focusing on each person's <u>unique</u> needs.

[7] M. I. Lk 5:20: Even when Christians proclaim the Gospel to large crowds, they should always remember that the crowds are made up of <u>individuals</u>; and that <u>each one</u> of them needs to repent and believe in Jesus.

[8] M. M. Jn 20:8: God gave faith in Jesus to people who personally saw that the tomb of Jesus was empty, because it proved that he was alive.

[9] M. I. Ac 6:1: Christians should always remember that the main aspect of the mission is to proclaim the Law and Gospel message and should not allow any other aspect of the work to hinder this main work.

[10] M. I. Lk 4:15: Christians should seize <u>every</u> opportunity to proclaim the Gospel to lost people of all nations.

[11] M. M. Ro 1:16b: The Gospel is so powerful because it contains the central truth that Jesus rose from the dead with a glorified body in order to save all of his brothers and sisters from sin and

death.

[12] M. M. Ro 10:17a: The Holy Spirit only creates and preserves faith by using the message of God's grace in his holy Word.

[13] M. M. Lk 6:22: The Lord Jesus will surely bless a Christian in the midst of suffering for his sake; and he will also bless him with eternal life if he remains faithful to him.

[14] M. M. Mt 1:22: God sent his only Son, Jesus to be born as a true human being, so that he could save all of his brothers and sisters of all nations by fulfilling all of God's promises in the Old Testament.

[15] M. M. Lk 1:1: Jesus came to seek and save all lost people from every nation on earth.

[16] M. M. Ro 10:17a: The Holy Spirit only creates and preserves faith by using the message of God's grace in his holy Word.

[17] M. M. Lk 12:8: On Judgment Day, Jesus will acknowledge before his heavenly Father that all Christians are his brothers and sisters.

[18] M. M. Ac 4:28: The heavenly Father is always in full control of his mission to all nations of the world.

[19] M. I. Lk 11:10: Christians should continuously pray to their heavenly Father and always depend on his grace, and not on their own feeble strength, because he always loves them.

[20] M. M. Lk 1:1: Jesus came to seek and save all lost people from every nation on earth.

[21] M. I. Lk 4:15: Christians should seize every opportunity to proclaim the Gospel to lost people of all nations.

[22] M. I. Lk 4:40: Christians should go and seek the lost one person at a time by focusing on each person's unique needs.

[23] M. M. Lk 13:24: The only way to enter the Kingdom of God is to have faith in Jesus as one's Savior.

Chapter 8

Women Accompanying Jesus 8:1-3

8:1 *Soon afterward he went on through cities and villages, proclaiming and bringing the good news of the kingdom of God. And the twelve were with him,*

8:2 *and also some women who had been healed of evil spirits and infirmities: Mary, called Magdalene, from whom seven demons had gone out,*

8:3 *and Joanna, the wife of Chuza, Herod's household manager, and Susanna, and many others, who provided for them out of their means.*

8:3 Luke says in verse 3 that the group of women who were following Jesus also *"provided for them out of their means."* Obviously, this <u>financial</u> support was very important for what must have been quite a large group of believers who were traveling with Jesus. An Old Testament law says that a laborer deserves to be paid (Lev 19:13); however, this situation was quite different. There were so many people following Jesus that he could not have depended on his hearers to support all of these people (9:4; 10:7; [1]M. I. Lk 10:7a & [2]Lk 10:7b).

The Parable of the Sower 8:4-8

8:4 *And when a great crowd was gathering and people from town after town came to him, he said in a parable:*

8:5 *"A sower went out to sow his seed. And as he sowed, some fell along the path and was trampled underfoot, and the birds of the air devoured it.*

8:6 *And some fell on the rock, and as it grew up, it withered away, because it had no moisture.*

8:7 *And some fell among thorns, and the thorns grew up with it and choked it.*

8:8 *And some fell into good soil and grew and yielded a hundredfold." As he said these things, he called out, "He who has ears to hear, let him hear."*

8:4-8 God has a most gracious mission-heart, therefore, when he made (and continues to make) mankind, he made Adam and Eve with a <u>free will</u>, because he wanted them to <u>respond</u> to his love by loving and serving him alone. But of course, they did not do so and sinned. (A robot cannot respond to its maker in love, just as a farmer does not expect the stones in his field to respond to the seed that he scatters there (v 6)!) However, God had already created a mission plan in order to rescue *"hard, rocky and weedy"* mankind; and he began to carry it out by choosing Abraham, gave him faith and blessed him and his descendants by revealing the Gospel to them, so that he could bless <u>all</u> nations as the Israelites proclaimed the Gospel to them (Gen 12:3). Then, the main part of his plan was to send their Messiah, his own Son, Jesus to *"seek and save"* them by revealing *"the secrets of the kingdom of God"* (v 10) to them, as a farmer scatters his seed—at times in parables (vs 4-8; [3]M. M. Lk 1:1).

The Purpose of the Parables 8:9-15

8:9 *And when his disciples asked him what this parable meant,*
8:10 *he said, "To you it has been given to know the secrets of the kingdom of God, but for others they are in parables, so that 'seeing they may not see, and hearing they may not understand.'*
8:11 *Now the parable is this: The seed is the word of God.*
8:12 *The ones along the path are those who have heard; then the devil comes and takes away the word from their hearts, so that they may not believe and be saved.*
8:13 *And the ones on the rock are those who, when they hear the word, receive it with joy. But these have no root; they believe for a while, and in time of testing fall away.*
8:14 *And as for what fell among the thorns, they are those who hear,*

> *but as they go on their way they are choked by the cares and riches and pleasures of life, and their fruit does not mature.*
>
> 8:15 *As for that in the good soil, they are those who, hearing the word, hold it fast in an honest and good heart, and bear fruit with patience.*

8:10 What does Jesus mean in verse 10, when he says that he revealed the secrets of his kingdom to his disciples in parables, so that *"seeing they [others, who were not his disciples] may not see, and hearing they may not understand?"* Scholars have long debated what he meant; however, the Scriptures give us clear truths about our gracious God and his mission to the world, which help to explain part of the meaning. (And verses 11-15 also help to explain some truths about those who hear the Gospel.) **a)** First of all, obviously, God's mission-heart has not changed, because he continues to make human beings with a free will (M. M. Ro 4:3). **b)** He also continues to send missionaries out to proclaim the same Gospel—at times in parables ([4]M. I. Ac 1:8). **c)** And he still longs for every person to respond to the Gospel in faith and obedience, therefore, he is like the anxious Father, who eagerly and patiently watches the road for his *"lost son"* to repent and return to him (15:20; [5]M. M. 1 Tim 2:3). Thus, Jesus was not implying in verse 10 that he desires that some people would hear a parable and not understand; rather he is sad that some do not respond in faith (1 Tim 2:4). And obviously, the stone-hearted Pharisees were living a lie because they thought they alone truly *"heard"* and *"understood"* the Scriptures correctly ([6]M. M. Ro 11:7).

8:11-15 Jesus himself teaches several truths in verses 11-15 with this extended metaphor. **1)** First of all, while Jesus taught a lesson in verse 10 about people who have no faith at all, note that three kinds of hearers in verses 12-14 had faith for a period of time. However, because original sin has corrupted everything that God made (Rom 5:17), three kinds of enemies hindered the Gospel from continuing to grow in their hearts: the devil (v 12), their sinful human nature (v 13), and the sinful world (v 14). And of course, the fourth category of hearers in verse 15 depended on their Lord's grace and did not lose their faith. **2)** Secondly, note that there was only one type of *"seed,"* one Law and Gospel message; therefore, it was not the seed that caused four different results. The results are the responsibility of the Holy Spirit who has the power to use his holy Word to graciously create faith as he wills (Mk 4:27-28; Jn 3:6; 1 Cor 6:11); and his Word is the only means of grace he uses to do so ([7]M. M. Ro 10:17a). Thus, in these verses, Jesus was teaching yet another new mission imperative. M. I. Lk 8:11: Christians should faithfully do their job of preaching and leave the results to the Holy Spirit. Also note that Jesus, no doubt, deliberately told this parable shortly before he sent his disciples out on their first missionary journey (9:1-6), so that they would learn to faithfully preach the Word and not be concerned about the results. **3)** Thirdly, note in the parable that the seed belongs to the farmer, which implies that the message belongs to the Lord of the mission, because, once again, his Spirit only uses his holy Word to graciously create faith (M. M. Ro 10:17a). And that is the reason why his faithful missionaries only base their messages on his Word in the Bible ([8]M. I. Lk 4:17). Also note once again that, a short time later, Jesus sent his twelve disciples out to "plant" or preach their Lord's Gospel message to "the lost" (9:1-9). **4)** And finally, note in the parable that the four types of hearers heard the message in four different ways, like four different kinds of soil. Some were ready to hear it and some were not; it was the hearers who failed to hear well; and it was not faulty seed. Therefore, verses 11-15 imply the same thing that Jesus says explicitly in verse 18, *"Take care then how you hear."* Every individual (every believer and unbeliever) is responsible for his own spiritual condition, whether he is ready to hear and obey the Gospel or not ([9]M. I. Lk 8:18).

A Lamp Under a Jar 8:16-18

8:16 *"No one after lighting a lamp covers it with a jar or puts it under a bed, but puts it on a stand, so that those who enter may see the light.*

8:17 *For nothing is hidden that will not be made manifest, nor is anything secret that will not be known and come to light.*

> 8:18 *Take care then how you hear, for to the one who has, more will be given, and from the one who has not, even what he thinks that he has will be taken away."*

8:16-17 The <u>first</u> thing that Jesus came to do was *"to <u>seek</u>...the lost"* (19:10; [10]M. M. Lk 1:1); therefore, he was not hiding *"the secrets of the kingdom of God"* (v 10). Rather, he was busy sowing the seed and putting his *"lamp on a stand, so that those who enter may see the light"* (v 16; Jn 8:12). And he would soon send his disciples out to do the same (9:1-6). His gracious will was that <u>all</u> people of <u>all</u> nations and cultures who were living in the darkness of sin would see his light and live ([11]M. M. Mt 5:14). If some people, such as the Pharisees, saw his light and did not understand its meaning, it was their own failure, their responsibility, and not his. Most of them had yielded to sin for so long that they had "rock" hard hearts (v 13), so that the darkness in their hearts was complete ([12]M. I. Lk 8:18).

8:18 (1) When Jesus says in verse 18, *"<u>Take care</u> then how you hear,"* he is saying very clearly that everyone who hears the Law and Gospel is <u>responsible</u> for how he hears it; therefore, <u>everyone</u> should listen very carefully. Furthermore, no one can trust in Jesus for another person—not his spouse or children or anyone else; <u>everyone</u> is responsible for the spiritual condition of his/her own faith. Therefore, on the Last Day, unbelievers will stand all <u>alone</u> before God and be condemned; but Jesus will stand there beside all Christians so that they are not condemned. It's a new mission imperative. M. I. Lk 8:18: Everyone is responsible for the spiritual condition of his own faith, because no one can believe for him. **2)** Therefore, every Christian has three <u>responsibilities</u> in his spiritual life: **a)** always be <u>alert</u> to the grave dangers that he faces from his three <u>spiritual enemies</u>: the devil (v 12), his own sinful human nature (v 13) and the sinful world around him (v 14; [13]M. I. Heb 1:14 & [14]Jms 4:7), **b)** and know how to <u>defeat</u> all three of them ([15]M. I. Lk 11:10), **c)** and keep his faith strong by <u>daily</u> listening to both the Law and the Gospel ([16]M. I. Lk 12:40 & [17]Ac 2:42). **3)** The issue of everyone being responsible for listening to the Gospel carefully obviously also raises other issues. During my missionary service in Nigeria, people asked me a few times:

"What will God do about my ancestors who never heard the Gospel?" "Or what about people who never heard it in their own heart language?" These questions are difficult to answer because the Bible obviously does not specifically address these issues; therefore, the best answer we can offer is that the true God is a <u>gracious</u> God who has a mission-heart that never changes because he is always faithful. We must, therefore, leave these difficult questions in his <u>gracious</u> hands ([18]M. M. Ro 3:26 & [19]Ro 9:15). **4)** But why would a gracious, mission-hearted God *"take away"* (v 18) the *"knowledge of the kingdom of God"* (v 10) from a person? He, of course, does not *"take [it] away"* immediately; but if a person <u>persistently</u> despises and rejects God's message of rich grace, he may ultimately and reluctantly <u>harden</u> his heart (Rom 9:13). This is the only sin that God <u>cannot</u> forgive because it is a sin against his Holy Spirit (12:10; Heb 6:4-6). Furthermore, no one who hears the Gospel <u>deserves</u> the gift of salvation that it offers because God offers it by his <u>grace</u> alone; and to despise his grace in Jesus is a terrible sin because that person is treating his death on the cross as <u>cheap</u> grace. God has a truly mission-heart; and he is, therefore, extremely patient; but his Spirit does not force his will on anyone. He patiently longs for each lost person to use the free will that he gave him to respond to his grace with love (15:20; [20]M. M. Ro 1:5).

Jesus' Mother and Brothers 8:19-21

8:19 *Then his mother and his brothers came to him, but they could not reach him because of the crowd.*
8:20 *And he was told, "Your mother and your brothers are standing outside, desiring to see you."*
8:21 *But he answered them, "My mother and my brothers are those who hear the word of God and do it."*

8:21 Obviously, Jesus was not despising his mother and sinning against the fourth commandment when he said, *"My mother and my brothers are those who hear the word of God and do it."* He always loved both his <u>physical</u> family and his <u>spiritual</u> family who trusted in him by hearing his Word and doing it (v 21). And he obviously always faithfully obeyed all of God's Laws on behalf of his fellow human beings. Rather, when he said this, he was emphasizing the truth that it is only a faith relationship with him that can save a person, and not a physical relationship—including his mother, who obviously had the closest physical relationship to him of any other person. Everyone receives his blessings through his grace alone. Therefore, if someone tries to depend on his blood relationship with Jesus or with his ancestor Abraham (3:8; 11:27-28), he is sinning in proud self-righteousness and is not depending on God's grace. However, a person who hears the gracious message of the Gospel, responds to Jesus' love in faith (v 15), and also *"does"* (v 21) what God's Word says, has already received two gracious gifts from the Holy Spirit: both a new mission-heart and also the Spirit's almighty power to obey his Lord (M. M. Ro 1:5).

Jesus Calms a Storm 8:22-25

8:22 *One day he got into a boat with his disciples, and he said to them, "Let us go across to the other side of the lake." So they set out,*

8:23 *and as they sailed he fell asleep. And a windstorm came down on the lake, and they were filling with water and were in danger.*

8:24 *And they went and woke him, saying, "Master, Master, we are perishing!" And he awoke and rebuked the wind and the raging waves, and they ceased, and there was a calm.*

8:25 *He said to them, "Where is your faith?" And they were afraid, and they marveled, saying to one another, "Who then is this, that he commands even winds and water, and they obey him?"*

8:23-25 Obviously, Jesus deliberately *"fell asleep"* (v 23) in order to test the faith of his disciples; but this was a most gracious test in order to strengthen their faith. He was also teaching them two new lessons about their faith. **1)** First of all, he wanted to teach them that Christians should expect their Lord to graciously test their faith, because a faith relationship with Jesus is a life and death matter. If a person has faith in Jesus he will live, but if not he will die eternally. Just as the muscles of an athlete will get flabby if he just sits on the bench, so likewise a person will get a flabby faith if he goes through life without God graciously testing his faith. He is in danger of losing his flabby faith. Jesus knew that the faith of his disciples would soon be tested much more severely because they would soon witness his horrible suffering and death. If they faced that with a flabby faith they would all easily completely despair and deny him as Judas did. Therefore, a person who *"hears the word of God and does it"* (v 21) should <u>expect</u> his loving Lord to graciously test his faith ([21]M. M. 1 Pe 1:7). **2)** Secondly, by the fact that he did not explicitly tell them that he was testing them, Jesus was also teaching them another lesson. He just did it; and this too was part of his tests. And this was only the <u>first</u> of several times that he tested their faith, but he never <u>explicitly</u> told them that he was testing them. He was teaching them that when they faced a test they should always listen very carefully to hear whether it was <u>his</u> voice or Satan's voice telling them to do it, because he would <u>never</u> tell them to do something that contradicts his holy Word (1 Jn 4:1). But Satan is extremely clever, and what he says almost always <u>sounds like</u> the truth, but is not. This is exactly how he tempted Jesus in the desert (4:1-13). He always <u>tempts</u> both believers and unbelievers to sin (v 12), but the Lord only <u>tests</u> Christians in order to strengthen their faith (M. M. 1 Pe 1:7). Furthermore, the devil loves to use a Christian's other two spiritual <u>enemies</u> in order to <u>tempt</u> him: his own sinful human nature (v 13) and the sinful world around him (v 14; [22]M. I. Jms 1:14).

Jesus Heals a Demon-Possessed Man 8:26-39

8:26   *Then they sailed to the country of the Gerasenes, which is opposite Galilee.*
8:27   *When Jesus had stepped out on land, there met him a man from the city who had demons. For a long time he had worn no clothes, and he had not lived in a house but among the tombs.*
8:28   *When he saw Jesus, he cried out and fell down before him and*

8:28 (cont.) *said with a loud voice, "What have you to do with me, Jesus, Son of the Most High God? I beg you, do not torment me."*

8:29 *For he had commanded the unclean spirit to come out of the man. (For many a time it had seized him. He was kept under guard and bound with chains and shackles, but he would break the bonds and be driven by the demon into the desert.)*

8:30 *Jesus then asked him, "What is your name?" And he said, "Legion," for many demons had entered him.*

8:31 *And they begged him not to command them to depart into the abyss.*

8:32 *Now a large herd of pigs was feeding there on the hillside, and they begged him to let them enter these. So he gave them permission.*

8:33 *Then the demons came out of the man and entered the pigs, and the herd rushed down the steep bank into the lake and were drowned.*

8:34 *When the herdsmen saw what had happened, they fled and told it in the city and in the country.*

8:35 *Then people went out to see what had happened, and they came to Jesus and found the man from whom the demons had gone, sitting at the feet of Jesus, clothed and in his right mind, and they were afraid.*

8:36 *And those who had seen it told them how the demon-possessed man had been healed.*

8:37 *Then all the people of the surrounding country of the Gerasenes asked him to depart from them, for they were seized with great fear. So he got into the boat and returned.*

8:38 *The man from whom the demons had gone begged that he might be with him, but Jesus sent him away, saying,*

8:39 *"Return to your home, and declare how much God has done for you." And he went away, proclaiming throughout the whole city how much Jesus had done for him.*

8:26 This was the first time that Luke recorded that Jesus left Israel and purposely went to a region of the Gentiles. However, Luke did not have to explicitly say that they were Gentiles because all of his hearers knew that Jews would never raise unclean animals such as pigs. And we can likewise be very sure that Luke recognized how significant it was that Jesus deliberately chose to go seek lost Gentiles. Jesus' action certainly spoke loud and clear to Luke, and hopefully to his disciples as well, that Jesus's mission-heart wants all people of all nations and cultures to hear the Gospel and be saved ([23]M. M. Lk 1:1).

8:33 Note in verse 33 that Jesus singled out one Gentile man and healed him ([24]M. I. Lk 4:35).

8:37 Such a powerful miracle of instantly driving thousands of demons away caused *"great fear"* (v 37) but the miracle did not create faith in their hearts. That would have to wait until the healed man went back home and began to proclaim the Gospel to his family and friends (v 39). Note that, because the preaching of God's Word produces invisible faith (2 Cor 4:6) (until faith produces visible actions) the proclamation of the Gospel often appears to be much weaker than visible, spectacular healing miracles. But how much more wonderful the miracle of faith is, because the final result of faith in Jesus is, not a temporary physical healing of a body, but eternal life with him ([25]M. I. 2 Cor 4:16)! Yet today, miracles that are done in the name of Jesus may attract people to Jesus, and therefore, create opportunities to witness to people about him, but they cannot create faith. God's Word is the only means that the Holy Spirit uses to create and preserve faith ([26]M. M. Ro 10:17a).

8:38-39 The fact that the healed man wanted to leave home and follow Jesus shows that *"what God has done for you"* (v 39) was that Jesus had not only healed his body, he had also given him two more gracious gifts: faith in himself, and a mission-heart. Therefore, Jesus would not allow him to follow him; rather he helped him to understand that he should follow his new mission-heart and return home to spread the Gospel about him (v 39; [27]M. M. Ac 13:46). And this new missionary would have been a powerful witness to his fellow Gentiles since his faith would have clearly demonstrated to them that the Lord of the mission always longs for his Church to proclaim the Gospel message to everyone from every nation on earth ([28]M. I. Ac 1:8).

Jesus Heals a Woman and Jairus's Daughter 8:40-56

8:40 *Now when Jesus returned, the crowd welcomed him, for they were all waiting for him.*

8:41 *And there came a man named Jairus, who was a ruler of the synagogue. And falling at Jesus' feet, he implored him to come to his house,*

8:42 *for he had an only daughter, about twelve years of age, and she was dying. As Jesus went, the people pressed around him.*

8:43 *And there was a woman who had had a discharge of blood for twelve years, and though she had spent all her living on physicians, she could not be healed by anyone.*

8:44 *She came up behind him and touched the fringe of his garment, and immediately her discharge of blood ceased.*

8:45 *And Jesus said, "Who was it that touched me?" When all denied it, Peter said, "Master, the crowds surround you and are pressing in on you!"*

8:46 *But Jesus said, "Someone touched me, for I perceive that power has gone out from me."*

8:47 *And when the woman saw that she was not hidden, she came trembling, and falling down before him declared in the presence of all the people why she had touched him, and how she had been immediately healed.*

8:48 *And he said to her, "Daughter, your faith has made you well; go in peace."*

8:49 *While he was still speaking, someone from the ruler's house came and said, "Your daughter is dead; do not trouble the Teacher any more."*

8:50 *But Jesus on hearing this answered him, "Do not fear; only believe, and she will be well."*

8:51 *And when he came to the house, he allowed no one to enter with him, except Peter and John and James, and the father and mother of the child.*

8:52 *And all were weeping and mourning for her, but he said, "Do not weep, for she is not dead but sleeping."*

8:53 *And they laughed at him, knowing that she was dead.*

8:54 *But taking her by the hand he called, saying, "Child, arise."*
8:55 *And her spirit returned, and she got up at once. And he directed that something should be given her to eat.*
8:56 *And her parents were amazed, but he charged them to tell no one what had happened.*

8:40 Jesus returned to his home territory of Galilee to resume his mission there; and verse 40 says that *"the crowd welcomed him."* This shows that they had faith in him, just as Jesus said in (9:48), *"whoever receives me receives him [his heavenly Father] who sent me."* In contrast to the Gentiles in verse 37 who had not yet heard the Gospel and asked Jesus to leave, these Jews had heard him preach the Gospel and believed in him ([29]M. M. Lk 13:24).

8:41 Not all of the Jewish religious leaders doubted that Jesus was their Messiah. Note that Jairus had a faith similar to the Roman centurion in (7:3). He too humbly asked Jesus to come to his home and heal his daughter because he depended on his grace alone. Sick and needy people continually surrounded Jesus as he continued on his mission; and his mission-heart was always full of compassion for whole persons, for both their physical and their spiritual needs, but he didn't allow healing their physical needs to hinder his main mission to *"seek the lost"* by proclaiming the Gospel message ([30]M. I. Lk 4:35 & [31]Ac 6:1).

8:48 (1) This sick woman did not touch Jesus accidentally, as the rest of the crowd was doing. She had heard the Gospel; and therefore, she merely touched *"the fringe of his garment"* (v 44) because she obviously believed that he was her Lord who had the power to heal her with just the slightest touch (M. M. Lk 13:24). And Jesus said, *"I perceive that power has gone out from me."* He was God and he healed her because she depended solely on his grace; and she went home at *"peace"* with God because Jesus had forgiven her sins as well (Rom 5:1; [32]M. I. Lk 4:35 & [33]Lk 4:40). **2)** When Jesus said in verse 46, *"I perceive that power has gone out from me,"* we see that he obviously knew that her touch was not at all accidental. In the midst of the crowd pressing in on him from every side, his compassionate mission-heart focused on just one lost person and her unique needs ([34]M. I. Lk 5:20).

8:50 Once again we see in verse 50 just how vital a faith connection to Jesus is, because Jesus urged him to *"only believe [in me], and she will be well."* Faith in Jesus has power only because a child-like faith depends on *his* gracious, almighty power, in this case, to even raise a person from the dead (v 55; [35]M. M. Lk 13:24).

8:55-56 (1) In Luke's account, this was the second person whom Jesus raised from the dead (7:15). Once again, because this miracle was so amazing, *"Jesus charged them to tell no one what had happened"* (v 56) probably because it would attract too much attention to him as a miracle-worker and hinder his main mission of seeking the lost (19:10; [36]M. I. Ac 6:1). **2)** Luke interwove the stories of Jesus healing these two people in a very interesting way; and thereby, Luke continued to emphasize the truth that Jesus healed them one by one because his mission-heart always loves each individual completely ([37]M. I. Lk 4:35 & [38]Lk 5:20).

---

[1] M. I. Lk 10:7a: When Christians go to a strange town on their mission, they should search for a family that welcomes them and their Gospel and stay with them, because that home may be an open door into the entire community.

[2] M. I. Lk 10:7b: Church leaders deserve to be paid for their work of preaching and teaching the Gospel.

[3] M. M. Lk 1:1: Jesus came to seek and save all lost people from every nation on earth.

[4] M. I. Ac 1:8: Christians should go and witness about Jesus to all who are lost from all languages and cultures by depending on the power of the Holy Spirit to help them bridge all of the language/cultural boundaries whether they are relatively easy, as in their own language, or extremely difficult.

[5] M. M. 1 Tim 2:3: It pleases God their Savior when Christians pray for all people because he desires all people to be saved and to come to the knowledge of the truth about Jesus.

[6] M. M. Ro 11:7: After patiently waiting for a person to repent, God may ultimately eternally condemn him by hardening his heart and closing his ears to hear and understand his holy Word.

[7] M. M. Ro 10:17a: The Holy Spirit only creates and preserves faith by using the message of God's grace in his holy Word.

[8] M. I. Lk 4:17: Christians should always base their messages on the Bible, so that the Holy Spirit can use his holy Word to create and strengthen faith in their hearers.

[9] M. I. Lk 8:18: Everyone is responsible for the spiritual condition of his own faith, because no one can do it for him.

[10] M. M. Lk 1:1: Jesus came to seek and save all lost people from every nation on earth.

[11] M. M. Mt 5:14: When the Holy Spirit creates faith in a person's heart, he also graciously gives

him a new mission-heart that is eager to shine the light of the Gospel throughout the whole world.

[12] M. I. Lk 8:18: Everyone is responsible for the spiritual condition of his own faith, because no one can do it for him.

[13] M. M. Heb 1:14: Christians will inherit salvation, and God sends out his holy angels to be with them and protect them; therefore, they should not be afraid of their spiritual enemies as they go on their mission.

[14] M. I. Jms 4:7: Christians should submit themselves to God completely; then resist the devil and he will run away from them.

[15] M. I. Lk 11:10: Christians should <u>continuously</u> pray to their heavenly Father and <u>always</u> depend on his grace, and not on their own feeble strength, because he <u>always</u> loves them.

[16] M. I. Lk 12:40: Christians should "eat" God's Word every day in order to keep their faith strong, so that they are always ready for their Lord's return.

[17] M. I. Ac 2:42: Christians should celebrate Holy Communion frequently in order to receive forgiveness and strength from their Lord's grace in order to continue on his mission.

[18] M. M. Ro 3:26: God is just and fair to <u>everyone</u>, both when he condemns <u>all</u> people of all nations because all have sinned, and also when he <u>only</u> declares those people righteous who have faith in Jesus.

[19] M. M. Ro 9:15: Before creation, God <u>foreknew</u> and graciously chose the people whom he would adopt as his children at their Baptisms; however, he did not predestine all of the other people to eternal condemnation, because he dearly loves <u>all</u> of the people he makes; and he therefore is <u>always</u> extremely patient with those who stubbornly persist in their sin, until in the end he reluctantly condemns them to eternal punishment.

[20] M. M. Ro 1:5: The same Holy Spirit who creates <u>faith</u> and a new missionary <u>nature</u> in a person's heart also graciously empowers him to gratefully respond to his Lord's love by <u>obeying</u> him.

[21] M. M. 1 Pe 1:7: God graciously allows Christians to suffer now for a little while so that their faith, which is as precious as gold that perishes even though it is tested by fire, may be proved genuine through the testing and also give glory and honor to Jesus Christ when God reveals him on the Last Day.

[22] M. I. Jms 1:14: Christians should beware that their own sinful human nature may tempt them with sinful desires; and these sinful desires may conceive and give birth to sin; and sin always gives birth to spiritual death.

[23] M. M. Lk 1:1: Jesus came to seek and save <u>all</u> lost people from <u>every</u> nation on earth.

[24] M. I. Lk 4:35: Christians should view every person as a whole person, and show him compassion by caring for <u>both</u> his physical and spiritual needs as they go on their mission.

[25] M. I. 2 Cor 4:16: Christians should not be discouraged, even though their temporary, physical nature is wasting away, because the Holy Spirit is daily renewing their eternal, spiritual nature.

[26] M. M. Ro 10:17a: The Holy Spirit <u>only</u> creates and preserves faith by using the message of God's grace in his holy Word.

[27] M. M. Ac 13:46: As he did with the old Israel, God <u>first of all</u> strengthens the faith of the new Israel, the Church with his Word and Sacraments, so that they can go and witness to the lost people of all nations.

[28] M. I. Ac 1:8: Christians should go and witness about Jesus to all who are lost from all languages and cultures by depending on the power of the Holy Spirit to help them bridge all of the language/cultural boundaries whether they are relatively easy, as in their own language, or extremely difficult.

[29] M. M. Lk 13:24: The only way to enter the Kingdom of God is to have faith in Jesus as one's Savior.

[30] M. I. Lk 4:35: Christians should view every person as a whole person, and show him compassion by caring for both his physical and spiritual needs as they go on their mission.

[31] M. I. Ac 6:1: Christians should always remember that the main aspect of the mission is to proclaim the Law and Gospel message and should not allow any other aspect of the work to hinder this main work.

[32] M. I. Lk 4:35: Christians should view every person as a whole person, and show him compassion by caring for both his physical and spiritual needs as they go on their mission.

[33] M. I. Lk 4:40: Christians should go and seek the lost one person at a time by focusing on each person's unique needs.

[34] M. I. Lk 5:20: Even when Christians proclaim the Gospel to large crowds, they should always remember that the crowds are made up of individuals; and that each one of them needs to repent and believe in Jesus.

[35] M. M. Lk 13:24: The only way to enter the Kingdom of God is to have faith in Jesus as one's Savior.

[36] M. I. Ac 6:1: Christians should always remember that the main aspect of the mission is to proclaim the Law and Gospel message and should not allow any other aspect of the work to hinder this main work.

[37] M. I. Lk 4:35: Christians should view every person as a whole person, and show him compassion by caring for both his physical and spiritual needs as they go on their mission.

[38] M. I. Lk 5:20: Even when Christians proclaim the Gospel to large crowds, they should always remember that the crowds are made up of individuals; and that each one of them needs to repent and believe in Jesus.

Chapter 9

Jesus Sends Out the Apostles 9:1-6

9:1 *And he called the twelve together and gave them power and authority over all demons and to cure diseases,*
9:2 *and he sent them out to proclaim the kingdom of God and to heal.*
9:3 *And he said to them, "Take nothing for your journey, no staff, nor bag, nor bread, nor money; and do not have two tunics.*
9:4 *And whatever house you enter, stay there, and from there depart.*
9:5 *And wherever they do not receive you, when you leave that town shake off the dust from your feet as a testimony against them."*
9:6 *And they departed and went through the villages, preaching the gospel and healing everywhere.*

9:1-2 Jesus now began to teach *"the twelve [disciples]"* (v 1) how to be his missionaries through practical experience. He gave them two assignments: *"to proclaim the kingdom of God and to heal"* (v 2). **1)** In this very practical way, Jesus taught them, first of all, that his Church would be able to expand his Kingdom more effectively, in the future, by training full time leaders who would guide others in their mission work ([1]M. I. Lk 6:13). **2)** Secondly, Jesus also taught his twelve disciples that he was giving them his almighty power so that they too could *"heal"* (v 2) physical ailments in his name. And he gave them this power for two reasons: **a)** so that they would show the sick people the same holistic compassion that he had been showing people everywhere he went [2](M. I. Lk 4:35), **b)** and so that, when they used his name to heal people, these miracles would point people to him and not to themselves ([3]M. I. Ac 3:6), and therefore, also create opportunities to witness to people about him ([4]M. I. Lk 4:15).

9:3-4 Jesus' disciples would obviously have physical needs on their missionary journey; however, he told them in verses 3-4, *"Take nothing for your journey...And whatever house you enter, stay there."* He thus, taught them to <u>depend on</u> their hearers to support them, as they would have, no doubt, remembered from their own Old Testament, which says that a laborer deserves to be paid (Lev 19:13; Deu 24:14-15; 10:4, 7). Part of his purpose was to establish a very important new personal <u>bond</u> between the missionary and his hearers; however, in (10:7) when he sent out the 72 disciples, he explained more reasons why he gave this command and established new mission imperatives ([5]M. I. Lk 10:7a & [6]Lk 10:7b).

9:5 Sadly, not all lost people who hear the Law and the Gospel repent and believe; therefore, when they do <u>not</u> do so, the missionary should give them a stern warning from God's Law that they are in the grave danger that, if they stubbornly persist in refusing to repent, God will condemn them to eternal punishment. Anyone who despises God's rich grace by rejecting his Gospel is committing a terrible sin that needs a very stern warning from the Law (8:18; [7]M. M. 2 Cor 2:15). In the Jewish culture, to *"shake off the dust from your feet as a testimony against them"* (v 5) would have been a very graphic warning to the Jews who refused to repent. Since Jesus had a mission-heart, he did all things in love for the lost; however, when someone stubbornly refuses to repent, true love demands using a stern <u>warning</u> in that person's own language/culture that he will not misunderstand, because Jesus does not want even one lost sinner to die eternally (2 Tim 4:4; Ezek 18:23; [8]M. M. 1 Tim 2:3).

Herod is Perplexed by Jesus 9:7-9

9:7   *Now Herod the tetrarch heard about all that was happening, and he was perplexed, because it was said by some that John had been raised from the dead,*

9:8   *by some that Elijah had appeared, and by others that one of the prophets of old had risen.*

9:9   *Herod said, "John I beheaded, but who is this about whom I hear such things?" And he sought to see him.*

9:9 King Herod *"sought to see him [Jesus];"* however, what King Herod probably didn't know was that Jesus <u>also</u> longed to see <u>him</u>! He was seeking him because the king was obviously lost ([9]M. M. Lk 1:1); as a matter of fact, the king may have been at the top of the list of those who needed to repent ([10]M. I. Lk 3:3a). However, when they did finally meet on Good Friday (23:8), the king was not eager to hear the Gospel; he only wanted to be <u>entertained</u> by a miracle. And since Jesus was in chains that sad day, it was too late for the king to be open to listening to his Law and Gospel message ([11]M. I. Ro 10:17b).

Jesus Feeds the Five Thousand 9:10-17

9:10   *On their return the apostles told him all that they had done. And he took them and withdrew apart to a town called Bethsaida.*

9:11   *When the crowds learned it, they followed him, and he welcomed them and spoke to them of the kingdom of God and cured those who had need of healing.*

9:12   *Now the day began to wear away, and the twelve came and said to him, "Send the crowd away to go into the surrounding villages and countryside to find lodging and get provisions, for we are here in a desolate place."*

9:13   *But he said to them, "You give them something to eat." They said, "We have no more than five loaves and two fish--unless we are to go and buy food for all these people."*

9:14   *For there were about five thousand men. And he said to his disciples, "Have them sit down in groups of about fifty each."*

9:15   *And they did so, and had them all sit down.*

9:16   *And taking the five loaves and the two fish, he looked up to heaven and said a blessing over them. Then he broke the loaves and gave them to the disciples to set before the crowd.*

9:17   *And they all ate and were satisfied. And what was left over was picked up, twelve baskets of broken pieces.*

9:10 After the twelve apostles returned from their first missionary journey, they simply reported in verse 10 *"all that they had done;"* however, when the seventy-two disciples returned from their mission journey in (10:17), their report was very different, because Luke says that *"the seventy-two returned with joy."* This contrast seems to imply that perhaps the twelve apostles did not see many visible results on their first mission attempt. In fact, their frustration became evident in John's complaint in verse 49, *"Master, we saw someone casting out demons in your name."* This man was doing what they evidently had not been able to do. Obviously, their faith was still weak; therefore, they needed both more training and, more importantly, to learn to depend more on their Lord's rich grace in order to carry out his mission ([12]M. I. Ac 6:1). Therefore, in order for Jesus to continue to *"seek the lost"* through his Church after his ascension, he continued to train his disciples until his death.

9:13 Jesus was obviously again testing the faith of his disciples with his command in verse 13, *"You give them something to eat."* In his grace, he wanted to see if they would turn to him as *"the Christ of God"* (v 20), and ask him to help the crowd by miraculously making food. But once again the disciples failed his test; they tried to solve the problem themselves by looking for food in their own supply (v 13b). Nevertheless, Jesus continued to test their faith so that they would be strong in the face of future suffering, especially at the time of his own suffering and death (8:23; [13]M. I. Ro 5:3a).

9:17 This miracle of multiplying food was the kind of entertainment that King Herod was seeking (v 9), but Jesus only sought to show his compassion for everyone by doing it (Mk 6:34); and he surely never forgot that every crowd was comprised of individuals who were lost ([14]M. I. Lk 4:35 & [15]Lk 5:20).

Peter Confesses Jesus As the Christ 9:18-20

> 9:18 *Now it happened that as he was praying alone, the disciples were with him. And he asked them, "Who do the crowds say that I am?"*

9:19 *And they answered, "John the Baptist. But others say, Elijah, and others, that one of the prophets of old has risen."*
9:20 *Then he said to them, "But who do you say that I am?" And Peter answered, "The Christ of God."*

9:18-20 (1) The five thousand hungry people whom Jesus fed no doubt saw Jesus as nothing but a miracle-worker; but Jesus was eager to teach his disciples that he was much, much more than that. He was, as Peter so correctly and boldly confessed in verse 20, *"The Christ of God,"* their Savior (1:47). Jesus had not come to merely rescue a few people from physical problems. In his mission-heart, he obviously had compassion on whole persons, and therefore, he could not ignore the physical suffering that he saw every day, but his even greater compassion to rescue his fellow human beings from their much deeper spiritual needs compelled him to focus on his main dual mission of proclaiming the Gospel and going to the cross in order to destroy the power of sin and Satan (19:10; [16]M. I. Ac 6:1 & [17]M. M. Ro 3:24). **2)** Therefore, when the Holy Spirit inspired Peter, the leader of the disciples to make this confession (1 Cor 12:3), the Holy Spirit was beginning to train him to be a bold leader of the very young Church to witness this vital truth to the whole world (13:24; Ac 4:19-20; [18]M. M. Ac 4:12).

Jesus Foretells His Death 9:21-22

9:21 *And he strictly charged and commanded them to tell this to no one,*
9:22 *saying, "The Son of Man must suffer many things and be rejected by the elders and chief priests and scribes, and be killed, and on the third day be raised."*

9:21-22 (1) Jesus knew that he would soon be the suffering Messiah, therefore, he told his disciples privately in verse 22 that *"the Son of Man must suffer many things."* Even though he knew that they would not yet comprehend what he was telling them, he was beginning to gradually teach them more explicitly what would happen to him for at least three reasons: **a)** so that they themselves would be better <u>prepared</u> to suffer in order to follow him ([19]M. M. Lk 6:22), **b)** so that they would be able to remain faithful to him when they saw his terrible suffering and death ([20]M. I. Lk 9:54), **c)** and so that they, in turn, would, teach others to be prepared to follow a <u>suffering</u> Savior ([21]M. I. Lk 9:23). **2)** However, he also *"strictly charged and commanded them [his disciples] to tell this [Peter's confession] to <u>no one</u>"* (v 21). Obviously, Jesus knew that the time was not yet right for the crowds to know this, since they themselves were, no doubt, not yet ready to endure suffering in order to follow him (vs 23-26; [22]M. I. Ro 5:3a).

Take Up Your Cross and Follow Jesus 9:23-27

9:23   *And he said to all, "If anyone would come after me, let him deny himself and take up his cross daily and follow me.*
9:24   *For whoever would save his life will lose it, but whoever loses his life for my sake will save it.*
9:25   *For what does it profit a man if he gains the whole world and loses or forfeits himself?*
9:26   *For whoever is ashamed of me and of my words, of him will the Son of Man be ashamed when he comes in his glory and the glory of the Father and of the holy angels.*
9:27   *But I tell you truly, there are some standing here who will not taste death until they see the kingdom of God."*

9:23-26 (1) What would compel a person to *"deny himself and take up his cross daily"* (v 23) in order to follow Jesus? The truth is that no one has power <u>in himself</u> to repent. However, <u>innocent</u> Jesus was compelled by his mission-heart to love his lost brothers, who <u>deserve</u> eternal death, and to carry his cross <u>for them</u>, and to die on his cross <u>for their sins</u>. Therefore, it is only the message of his undeserved love that his Spirit uses to graciously do <u>four</u> things: **a)** create a repentant heart in a person who hears the Gospel ([23]M. I. Lk 15:7), **b)** create faith in Jesus in his heart ([24]M. M. Ro 1:16b), **c)** compel him to gladly *"deny himself and* *take up his cross daily"* (v 23; [25]M. M. Jn 6:44), **d)** and give him a new mission-heart, which, of course, compels him and all Christians to *go* to all nations and tell this same Gospel to all people of all nations ([26]M. M. Mt 5:14). And his Gospel will thus continue to spread, since their hearers too will repent, follow Jesus, and then tell others as well (Lk 18:29). **2)** It is very important to note that Jesus gives two warnings in verses 23-26. **a)** When he says in verse 23 that a person must *"take up his cross daily and follow me,"* he is saying that if they follow him, they may have to suffer for his sake. **b)** And he says in verse 26 that, on Judgment Day, he will be ashamed of a person who was ashamed of him and of his holy Word. Both are certainly hard truths to tell to people who may already be reluctant to follow Jesus; and these truths may offend some of them. In some cases, their own family may hate them if they follow Jesus. But, since these warnings are both true, no Christian should hesitate to tell them to their hearers. The message that Christians tell to the world should always be the whole truth about Jesus; and to hide the parts that may be discouraging is both lying, since it's not the whole truth, and also foolish since telling them the whole truth later would be even more discouraging. It is a new mission imperative. M. I. Lk 9:23: Christians should deceive no one by only telling them the Gospel about Jesus, but rather they should also give them two warnings: a) that they may have to suffer for the sake of Jesus if they follow him, b) and that, on Judgment Day, Jesus will be ashamed of people who were ashamed of him.

9:27 Jesus said in verse 27, *"But I tell you truly, there are some standing here who will not taste death until they see the kingdom of God."* And then, Luke placed the Transfiguration story in his narrative (9:28-36) immediately after this statement of Jesus. This shows that Luke understood that Jesus was predicting that in just eight days (v 28) Peter, John and James would stand on a different mountain and *"see his [Jesus'] glory"* as the King of kings in his kingdom (v 32). By showing these three leaders of his disciples his glory in his kingdom, Jesus was not only giving them the encouragement that they would soon need when they saw him suffer and die, but he was also training them to be the future leaders of his Church ([27]M. I. Lk 6:13).

The Transfiguration 9:28-36

9:28 *Now about eight days after these sayings he took with him Peter and John and James and went up on the mountain to pray.*
9:29 *And as he was praying, the appearance of his face was altered, and his clothing became dazzling white.*
9:30 *And behold, two men were talking with him, Moses and Elijah,*
9:31 *who appeared in glory and spoke of his departure, which he was about to accomplish at Jerusalem.*
9:32 *Now Peter and those who were with him were heavy with sleep, but when they became fully awake they saw his glory and the two men who stood with him.*
9:33 *And as the men were parting from him, Peter said to Jesus, "Master, it is good that we are here. Let us make three tents, one for you and one for Moses and one for Elijah"--not knowing what he said.*
9:34 *As he was saying these things, a cloud came and overshadowed them, and they were afraid as they entered the cloud.*
9:35 *And a voice came out of the cloud, saying, "This is my Son, my Chosen One; listen to him!"*
9:36 *And when the voice had spoken, Jesus was found alone. And they kept silent and told no one in those days anything of what they had seen.*

9:28 Jesus continued to pray <u>daily</u> for at least <u>two</u> reasons: in order to fully understand his heavenly Father's will for carrying out every aspect of his mission on earth, and also in order to receive the strength that he would need in order to faithfully obey him. Therefore, his frequent prayers and the vision that is recorded in the following verses gave him much-needed strength for the severe suffering that he, no doubt, knew was coming soon ([28]M. I. Lk 11:10).

9:31-32 (1) The vision in verses 31-32 was an extraordinary set of miracles that God graciously granted to Jesus and three of his disciples as strong encouragement for all of them. At this point, the three disciples had no idea how much they would soon need this strength; and Peter's reaction shows that they had no idea at all what the future held for them. They had a great deal to learn; and Jesus was patiently and wisely teaching them bit-by-bit ([29]M. I. Lk 6:13). **2)** But Jesus certainly knew all too well what lay in the future. As a true human being, Jesus obviously <u>needed</u> strength to even think about his approaching *"departure"* or death (v 31). Death is mankind's last enemy; and that is frightening enough, but the death that Jesus faced would have been frightening far beyond anything that our feeble human minds can comprehend. How could he face being abandoned by his heavenly Father? How could God himself die? Yet this was precisely the death that he was born to die; his main purpose for living and dying was *"to… save the lost"* from sin (19:10). How he needed this encouraging vision (M. I. Lk 11:10)!

9:33 Peter's idea to stay in order to see more of Jesus' glory was not sinful, but it was premature, since Jesus had much more work to accomplish on his mission to *"seek and to save the lost"* (19:10; [30]M. M. Lk 1:1). Peter would have to wait for his own physical death, in order to see Jesus' glory fully and eternally in a manner that, yet today, far outshines this brief vision ([31]M. M. Lk 6:22).

9:35 (1) The heavenly Father's statement in verse 35 is almost precisely the same words of encouragement that the Father spoke at Jesus' Baptism (3:22), *"This is my Son, my Chosen One; listen to him!"* However, here it's quite clear that the disciples also heard him; and all four of them must have been greatly encouraged at this affirmation that Jesus was indeed God's Chosen Son. Nevertheless, it was also necessary for his Father to abandon Jesus on the cross, in order for his *"Chosen One"* to carry out his Father's will and for him to accomplish his mission (Ac 2:31; Mt 27:46; [32]M. M. Ro 3:24). **2)** The Father's mission call, *"Listen to him!"* continues to ring down through the centuries throughout his holy Church and throughout the whole world! What a cry this is! Through his Church, <u>all</u> people everywhere should indeed listen to *"the Word of life"* (Jn 4:14; 1 Jn 1:1). He alone feeds the world with his "daily bread" (11:3). <u>All</u> people everywhere should listen to him because it is <u>only</u> his holy Word that the Holy Spirit uses to create and sustain faith. Through his Word alone he continues to "seek the lost"

[33](M. M. Ro 10:17a).

9:36 (1) The heavenly Father was in full control of every aspect of the <u>timing</u> of his plan of salvation ([34]M. M. Ac 4:28); and it was not yet time for Jesus to complete his mission. Therefore, in verse 36, Luke records that the three disciples obediently told no one what they saw on the mountain until after his resurrection, although Luke does not record Jesus' instruction to not tell others. (Matthew does record it in his Gospel in (Mt 17:9).) **2)** Furthermore, Jesus' command here is consistent with verse 21 where he ordered them to tell <u>no one</u> that he was *"the Christ of God"* (v 20). We feeble human beings will never fully understand why he gave this command at this time; nevertheless, Jesus' mission could only have been fully completed with <u>precise</u> timing. And we will never know all of these details, even though this knowledge would give us even more reasons to give our Father more glory (M. M. Ac 4:28).

Healing of a Boy with an Unclean Spirit 9:37-43a

9:37 *On the next day, when they had come down from the mountain, a great crowd met him.*

9:38 *And behold, a man from the crowd cried out, "Teacher, I beg you to look at my son, for he is my only child.*

9:39 *And behold, a spirit seizes him, and he suddenly cries out. It convulses him so that he foams at the mouth, and shatters him, and will hardly leave him.*

9:40 *And I begged your disciples to cast it out, but they could not."*

9:41 *Jesus answered, "O faithless and twisted generation, how long am I to be with you and bear with you? Bring your son here."*

9:42 *While he was coming, the demon threw him to the ground and convulsed him. But Jesus rebuked the unclean spirit and healed the boy, and gave him back to his father.*

9:43a *And all were astonished at the majesty of God.*

9:41 What a stern warning Jesus gives in verse 41! *"O faithless and twisted generation, how long am I to be with you and bear with you?"*

Jesus, once again, publicly and powerfully refuted the lie that (especially the religious leaders of the Jews) believed, that they deserved God's salvation because they were blood relatives of Abraham. How stubborn and blind they were ([35]M. I. Lk 3:3a)!

Jesus Again Foretells His Death 9:43b-45

9:43b *But while they were all marveling at everything he was doing, Jesus said to his disciples,*
9:44 *"Let these words sink into your ears: The Son of Man is about to be delivered into the hands of men."*
9:45 *But they did not understand this saying, and it was concealed from them, so that they might not perceive it. And they were afraid to ask him about this saying.*

9:44-45 Note that, in verses 44-45, Jesus predicts his betrayal by Judas and his arrest, but he did not repeat what he had said in verse 22, that he would die and rise again. Also note that *"it [the details of his passion, including Judas' name] was concealed from them"* by God (v 45). Apparently it was important that the disciples not yet understand that one of them would betray him or know who he was. The heavenly Father was in full control of the timing of his plan of salvation and was carrying out his will perfectly and very precisely (19:10; [36]M. M. Ac 4:28).

Who is the Greatest? 9:46-48

9:46 *An argument arose among them as to which of them was the greatest.*
9:47 *But Jesus, knowing the reasoning of their hearts, took a child and put him by his side*
9:48 *and said to them, "Whoever receives this child in my name receives me, and whoever receives me receives him who sent me. For he who is least among you all is the one who is great."*

9:46-48 Jesus' disciples made it very obvious that they didn't understand many things. To argue about whom among them *"was the greatest"* (v 46) was exactly the opposite of their Lord's thinking. Instead, *"he who is least among you all"* (v 48) or who is *"poor in spirit"* (Mt 5:3) is *"greatest"* because he has received the gift of a repentant heart; therefore, he has repented of his pride and humbly submitted himself to his Lord with the faith of a child. To have a child-like faith means to *"deny himself and take up his cross daily"* (v 23). It's truly amazing how patiently Jesus taught his disciples and prepared them for their future mission to the world ([37]M. I. Lk 6:13).

Anyone Not Against Us Is For Us 9:49-50

9:49 *John answered, "Master, we saw someone casting out demons in your name, and we tried to stop him, because he does not follow with us."*

9:50 *But Jesus said to him, "Do not stop him, for the one who is not against you is for you."*

9:49-50 Since the person who was casting out demons used the power of *"your [Jesus'] name,"* he must have had faith in Jesus. But John was apparently jealous because he and the others had not been able to heal in Jesus' name (vs 10, 40). In other words, John was afraid that this other person would be *"greater"* than he was (v 46). Nevertheless, Jesus used this situation as a teaching tool and answered him very patiently, in order to try to teach him, once again, to be humble ([38]M. I. Lk 6:13).

A Samaritan Village Rejects Jesus 9:51-56

9:51 *When the days drew near for him to be taken up, he set his face to go to Jerusalem.*

9:52 *And he sent messengers ahead of him, who went and entered a village of the Samaritans, to make preparations for him.*

9:53 *But the people did not receive him, because his face was set*

> *toward Jerusalem.*
> 9:54 *And when his disciples James and John saw it, they said, "Lord, do you want us to tell fire to come down from heaven and consume them?"*
> 9:55 *But he turned and rebuked them.*
> 9:56 *And they went on to another village.*

9:51 (1) The first part of verse 51 is strikingly similar to (Heb 12:2) where the author says of Jesus, *"who for the joy that was set before him endured the cross, despising the shame, and is seated at the right hand of the throne of God."* Jesus had firm faith that his Father would raise him from the dead again and take him back to himself in heaven. This all-surpassing joy would give Jesus the strength that he would soon need, in order to endure horrible suffering and death for all mankind. In his heart he was already suffering, but his mission-heart *"is love"* (1 Jn 4:16) and he was not focused on his own needs but the needs of his lost brothers and sisters. All of this he would joyfully do because he loved us so much ([39]M. M. Ro 8:35 & [40]Mt 1:22). **2)** Even after Biblical scholars attempt to carefully combine all four Gospel accounts, the exact timing and the directions of the routes that Jesus took through the land of Israel and through Gentile territories on his mission to *"seek the lost"* are not completely clear. However, it is apparent that Jesus' journey to Jerusalem in verse 51 was probably not his final journey there. Nevertheless, he clearly continued to have the final purpose of his life and mission foremost in his thoughts. He knew his Fathers' gracious plan of salvation, that he was born to die for all of his brothers and sisters everywhere; and he also knew that he must die in Jerusalem, in order to fulfill all of the Scriptures (1:1; 13:33; 19:10; [41]M. M. Lk 1:1).
9:52-53 (1) Many Jews, if not all Jews (except for Jesus, of course), despised the Samaritans because they had mixed Gentile and Jewish blood. And therefore, the Jews would not hesitate to travel great distances in order to avoid taking even one step into Samaritan territory. But here we see that, when Jesus and his disciples started their journey to Jerusalem, Jesus went straight into Samaritan territory. He obviously deliberately planned to make this into a mission trip into Gentile

territory. It was a bold plan for Jesus to purposely want to sleep in a "disgusting" Samaritan village. The Pharisees would consider him and his disciples unclean for doing this, but <u>not</u> according to God's Laws, of course. Jesus loves <u>all</u> lost sheep regardless of what language or culture they come from. He harbors absolutely no prejudice whatsoever! What deep <u>love</u> he has shown for <u>everyone</u> (^{42}M. M. 1 Tim 2:3)! **2)** It's unclear why the Samaritans did not welcome them in their homes (v 53). But, in doing so, they both unknowingly rejected their Savior and King and also missed an opportunity to hear the Gospel from their gracious Lord himself (^{43}M. M. Lk 1:1).

9:54-56 James and John became angry at the Samaritans' rejection and wanted God to punish them with his final condemnation immediately. However, Jesus showed his love for these lost people because he saw that it was their cultural background that had blinded them from seeing a wonderful opportunity to hear the Gospel from the Word of life himself. They simply didn't know what they were doing, so Jesus did not condemn them. But, in patient love, he simply continued his mission journey to another Samaritan village. And furthermore, Jesus saw his disciples' angry question as another opportunity to teach a new mission imperative to them. M. I. Lk 9:54: Christians should show patient love to people who unknowingly reject an opportunity to hear the Gospel.

The Cost of Following Jesus 9:57-62

9:57 *As they were going along the road, someone said to him, "I will follow you wherever you go."*

9:58 *And Jesus said to him, "Foxes have holes, and birds of the air have nests, but the Son of Man has nowhere to lay his head."*

9:59 *To another he said, "Follow me." But he said, "Lord, let me first go and bury my father."*

9:60 *And Jesus said to him, "Leave the dead to bury their own dead. But as for you, go and proclaim the kingdom of God."*

9:61 *Yet another said, "I will follow you, Lord, but let me first say farewell to those at my home."*

9:62 *Jesus said to him, "No one who puts his hand to the plow and looks back is fit for the kingdom of God."*

9:57-62 In verses 57-62, Jesus taught <u>three</u> lessons about three men who wanted to follow him; and each one of them had his own unique, wrong sense of priorities ([44]M. I. Lk 4:40).

9:57-58 The first man was focused on the sinful idea of having a <u>physical</u> home that would give him earthly security. Therefore, Jesus warned him that he himself had <u>no</u> earthly home because his real home was in <u>heaven</u>; however, by calling himself "the Son of Man" (v 58), Jesus promised him that, if he trusted in him as his Savior, he would live with him there forever ([45]M. M. 2 Pe 3:13).

9:59-60 (1) The second man was focused on burying his father; however, Jesus knew that this man believed in him, but his whole family was <u>spiritually</u> dead; therefore, he told him that his <u>first</u> priority should be to go back home and *"proclaim the kingdom of God"* to his lost family (v 60). Lost people, who are still <u>physically</u> alive, still have a chance to hear the Gospel and repent, while those who are physically dead can no longer repent. This is the reason why Satan rejoices when a lost person dies, because he now has him as his own forever. Therefore, since every Christian has received a mission-heart, and since the situation is urgent, their <u>top</u> priority should be spreading the kingdom of God to lost people everywhere ([46]M. M. Mt 5:14 & [47]M. I. Mt 7:14). **2)** Jesus was, of course, not telling this man to dishonor his father, and thereby violating the fourth commandment; rather, he was using a hyperbole to teach this very important lesson.

9:61-62 (1) Once again, in verse 61, Jesus was obviously not teaching this man to dishonor his family by not even saying farewell to them; rather he used a hyperbole to compare <u>physical</u> family relationships with a <u>faith</u> relationship with himself. Even though physical family relationships are the most important and strongest <u>human</u> relationships, faith in him is even more important because human relationships are <u>temporary</u>, but his love is <u>eternal</u> ([48]M. M. Lk 13:24). **2)** For people who live in cultures that strongly emphasize the importance of a person's physical <u>family</u>, the two warnings in verses 57-62 that emphasize that a <u>faith</u> relationship with Jesus is far more important than family relationships can be very hard lessons to follow. In such cultures, people are very easily offended if someone even suggests to you that something may be more important than your physical family. Yet, even though God himself placed us all in physical families (Ps 68:6), our families are only temporary relationships. However, it is far too often these same powerful physical family relationships that may prevent a person from obeying Jesus' call to faith in him. If an unbelieving father is firmly controlling his family, and one of his family members becomes a Christian, he may threaten to disown or even kill him. It can be a terrible choice that the new Christian may have to make; yet it is a serious sin with eternal consequences to deny Jesus. Jesus warned this man because he obviously loves all human beings and does not want anyone to be eternally lost because that person considers physical family relationships more important than faith in him ([49]M. I. 2 Tim 2:12). **3)** Jesus' warning that Christians may have to reject their own physical family to follow him may, of course, be especially offensive to many people. However, he is telling his disciples, once again, that they should tell people the whole truth about following him and not hide the parts of their message that may discourage them. Jesus always wants people to follow him for all of the right reasons. Unlike Satan, Jesus never deceives anyone—not even for a moment; nor should his disciples do so ([50]M. I. Lk 9:23). **4)** Then, Jesus used a powerful metaphor about a farmer, in verse 62, in order to teach the same lesson that he taught in verse 60. Since all Christians have a mission-heart, by their very nature, they should be faithfully plowing in the kingdom of God by proclaiming the Gospel message at every opportunity they have ([51]M. M. Mt 5:14).

---

[1] M. I. Lk 6:13: Christians should choose new leaders and train them in order to multiply the work.

[2] M. I. Lk 4:35: Christians should view every person as a whole person, and show him compassion by caring for both his physical and spiritual needs as they go on their mission.

[3] M. I. Ac 3:6: Christians should heal a person's physical problem by speaking the name of Jesus, so that everyone knows that it was the divine power of Jesus that healed him.

[4] M. I. Lk 4:15: Christians should seize every opportunity to proclaim the Gospel to lost people of all nations.

[5] M. I. Lk 10:7a: When Christians go to a strange town on their mission, they should search for a family that welcomes them and their Gospel and stay with them, because that home may be an <u>open</u> door into the <u>entire</u> community.

[6] M. I. Lk 10:7b: Church leaders deserve to be paid for their work of preaching and teaching the Gospel.

[7] M. M. 2 Cor 2:15: When Christians proclaim the sweet fragrance of the Gospel, it will become the fragrance of eternal death for some people who stubbornly reject it, but for those who hear it, repent and believe in Jesus it is the fragrance of eternal life.

[8] M. M. 1 Tim 2:3: It pleases God their Savior when Christians pray for all people because he desires all people to be saved and to come to the knowledge of the truth about Jesus.

[9] M. M. Lk 1:1: Jesus came to seek and save <u>all</u> lost people from <u>every</u> nation on earth.

[10] M. I. Lk 3:3a: Christians should, in love, warn lost people who do not repent.

[11] M. I. Ro 10:17b: Christians should continuously and earnestly pray that the Holy Spirit would open the <u>hearts</u> of everyone around the world who is <u>hearing</u> the Gospel, so that they will repent and believe in Jesus.

[12] M. I. Ac 6:1: Christians should always remember that the main aspect of the mission is to proclaim the Law and Gospel message and should not allow any other aspect of the work to hinder this main work.

[13] M. I. Ro 5:3a: Christians should <u>rejoice</u> in the midst of <u>suffering</u> for Jesus' sake because suffering teaches them to depend on their Lord's rich grace, and thus continue to grow in more spiritual gifts.

[14] M. I. Lk 4:35: Christians should view every person as a whole person, and show him compassion by caring for <u>both</u> his physical and spiritual needs as they go on their mission.

[15] M. I. Lk 5:20: Even when Christians proclaim the Gospel to large crowds, they should always remember that the crowds are made up of <u>individuals</u>; and that <u>each one</u> of them needs to repent and believe in Jesus.

[16] M. I. Ac 6:1: Christians should always remember that the main aspect of the mission is to proclaim the Law and Gospel message and should not allow any other aspect of the work to hinder this main work.

[17] M. M. Ro 3:24: Jesus lived a life of perfect obedience and shed his precious blood on the cross, in order to graciously set all nations free from sin, which a person only receives by faith in him.

[18] M. M. Ac 4:12: <u>Only</u> the power of Jesus' name can save a person from sin.

[19] M. M. Lk 6:22: The Lord Jesus will surely bless a Christian in the midst of suffering for his sake; and he will also bless him with eternal life if he remains faithful to him.

[20] M. I. Lk 9:54: Christians should show patient love to people who unknowingly reject an opportunity to hear the Gospel.

[21] M. I. Lk 9:23: Christians should deceive no one by <u>only</u> telling them the Gospel about Jesus, but rather they should <u>also</u> give them two warnings: a) that they may have to suffer for the sake of Jesus if they follow him, b) and that, on Judgment Day, Jesus will be ashamed of people who were ashamed of him.

[22] M. I. Ro 5:3a: Christians should <u>rejoice</u> in the midst of <u>suffering</u> for Jesus' sake because suffering teaches them to depend on their Lord's rich grace, and thus continue to grow in more

spiritual gifts.

[23] M. I. Lk 15:7: Christians should rejoice together with the heavenly Father and his angels when just <u>one</u> lost person hears the Law and Gospel, and then receives the gracious gifts of a repentant heart and faith in Jesus.

[24] M. M. Ro 1:16b: The Gospel is so powerful because it contains the central truth that Jesus rose from the dead with a glorified body in order to save all of his brothers and sisters from sin and death.

[25] M. M. Jn 6:44: People who are lost cannot come to faith in Jesus by their own power; <u>only</u> the heavenly Father, who sent Jesus to die for them can draw them to Jesus by sending Christians to proclaim the Gospel to them.

[26] M. M. Mt 5:14: When the Holy Spirit creates faith in a person's heart, he also graciously gives him a new mission-heart that is eager to shine the light of the Gospel throughout the whole world.

[27] M. I. Lk 6:13: Christians should choose new leaders and train them in order to multiply the work.

[28] M. I. Lk 11:10: Christians should <u>continuously</u> pray to their heavenly Father and <u>always</u> depend on his grace, and not on their own feeble strength, because he <u>always</u> loves them.

[29] M. I. Lk 6:13: Christians should choose new leaders and train them in order to multiply the work.

[30] M. M. Lk 1:1: Jesus came to seek and save <u>all</u> lost people from <u>every</u> nation on earth.

[31] M. M. Lk 6:22: The Lord Jesus will surely bless a Christian in the midst of suffering for his sake; and he will also bless him with eternal life if he remains faithful to him.

[32] M. M. Ro 3:24: Jesus lived a life of perfect obedience and shed his precious blood on the cross, in order to graciously set all nations free from sin, which a person only receives by faith in him.

[33] M. M. Ro 10:17a: The Holy Spirit <u>only</u> creates and preserves faith by using the message of God's grace in his holy Word.

[34] M. M. Ac 4:28: The heavenly Father is always in full control of his mission to all nations of the world.

[35] M. I. Lk 3:3a: Christians should, in love, warn lost people who do not repent.

[36] M. M. Ac 4:28: The heavenly Father is always in full control of his mission to all nations of the world.

[37] M. I. Lk 6:13: Christians should choose new leaders and train them in order to multiply the work.

[38] M. I. Lk 6:13: Christians should choose new leaders and train them in order to multiply the work.

[39] M. M. Ro 8:35: God has proven the depth of his love for <u>all</u> whom he has chosen, who trust in Jesus, by sending his Son, Jesus to die for them; therefore, <u>nothing</u> in all creation can separate them from his love.

[40] M. M. Mt 1:22: God sent his only Son, Jesus to be born as a true human being, so that he could save all of his brothers and sisters of all nations by fulfilling all of God's promises in the Old Testament.

[41] M. M. Lk 1:1: Jesus came to seek and save <u>all</u> lost people from <u>every</u> nation on earth.

⁴² M. M. 1 Tim 2:3: It pleases God their Savior when Christians pray for all people because he desires all people to be saved and to come to the knowledge of the truth about Jesus.

⁴³ M. M. Lk 1:1: Jesus came to seek and save <u>all</u> lost people from <u>every</u> nation on earth.

⁴⁴ M. I. Lk 4:40: Christians should go and seek the lost <u>one</u> person at a time by focusing on each person's <u>unique</u> needs.

⁴⁵ M. M. 2 Pe 3:13: God has promised all Christians that he will create new heavens and a new earth, the eternal home of righteousness.

⁴⁶ M. M. Mt 5:14: When the Holy Spirit creates faith in a person's heart, he also graciously gives him a new mission-heart that is eager to shine the light of the Gospel throughout the whole world.

⁴⁷ M. I. Mt 7:14: Christians should hurry on their mission to the world because people who are lost have many enemies who lure them away from Jesus; and therefore, few of them find faith in Jesus which is the only gate into his Kingdom of life.

⁴⁸ M. M. Lk 13:24: The <u>only</u> way to enter the Kingdom of God is to have <u>faith</u> in Jesus as one's Savior.

⁴⁹ M. I. 2 Tim 2:12: If Christians endure their suffering patiently they will surely reign with their Lord Jesus forever in heaven; but if they deny him before people, Jesus will also deny them before his heavenly Father on Judgment Day.

⁵⁰ M. I. Lk 9:23: Christians should deceive no one by <u>only</u> telling them the Gospel about Jesus, but rather they should <u>also</u> give them two warnings: a) that they may have to suffer for the sake of Jesus if they follow him, b) and that, on Judgment Day, Jesus will be ashamed of people who were ashamed of him.

⁵¹ M. M. Mt 5:14: When the Holy Spirit creates faith in a person's heart, he also graciously gives him a new mission-heart that is eager to shine the light of the Gospel throughout the whole world.

Chapter 10

Jesus Sends Out the Seventy-Two 10:1-12

10:1 *After this the Lord appointed seventy-two others and sent them on ahead of him, two by two, into every town and place where he himself was about to go.*

10:2 *And he said to them, "The harvest is plentiful, but the laborers are few. Therefore pray earnestly to the Lord of the harvest to send out laborers into his harvest.*

10:3 *Go your way; behold, I am sending you out as lambs in the midst of wolves.*

10:4 *Carry no moneybag, no knapsack, no sandals, and greet no one on the road.*

10:5 *Whatever house you enter, first say, 'Peace be to this house!'*

10:6 *And if a son of peace is there, your peace will rest upon him. But if not, it will return to you.*

10:7 *And remain in the same house, eating and drinking what they provide, for the laborer deserves his wages. Do not go from house to house.*

10:8 *Whenever you enter a town and they receive you, eat what is set before you.*

10:9 *Heal the sick in it and say to them, 'The kingdom of God has come near to you.'*

10:10 *But whenever you enter a town and they do not receive you, go into its streets and say,*

10:11 *'Even the dust of your town that clings to our feet we wipe off against you. Nevertheless know this, that the kingdom of God has come near.'*

10:12 *I tell you, it will be more bearable on that day for Sodom than for that town.*

10:1 (1) Once more, Jesus expanded the work of his mission by sending out some of his disciples to *"seek the lost."* Instead of sending the twelve apostles this time, he *"appointed 72 others."* (Some manuscripts say 70.) This practical experience would, of course, be very important for the future expansion of his Church ([1]M. I. Lk 6:13). **2)** He told them in verse 1 to travel *"two by two."* (Note that Luke did not add this same command when Jesus sent out the twelve disciples in (9:1-6); and Mark is the only other Gospel writer who did add it when he sent out the twelve disciples.) With this command Jesus taught them a new mission imperative. M. I. Lk 10:1: Christians should go on their mission to all nations two by two in order to affirm each other's witness. **3)** Jesus does not give a reason for this command, but he may have said this because of what Moses' wrote in (Deu 19:15) which says, *"Only on the evidence of two witnesses or of three witnesses shall a charge be established"* (Jn 8:17). Jesus knew that, especially if a missionary is <u>all alone</u> in a totally different language/culture, and especially if it is a "face-to-face" society where everyone knows everyone else, his hearers may seriously question his testimony about Jesus. However, if the missionary goes there with one or two other missionaries, their hearers will probably take their <u>combined</u> testimony much more seriously. Furthermore, in many languages/cultures around the world yet today, the people still have never heard the Gospel about Jesus and it may be a strange new idea that needs verification. Thus, Jesus' wisdom in training his disciples is again evident (M. I. Lk 6:13).

10:2 Jesus taught <u>three</u> very significant mission lessons in verse 2. **1)** First of all, he said that *"the harvest is <u>plentiful</u>."* He saw that, in his own day, there still were many, many people who were lost in sin. How could this be? It had been about 2,000 years since God had called Abraham and given him and the whole nation of Israel mission-hearts, so that they would spread the Gospel in their own land and then also do the same in other nations (Gen 12:1-3). But obviously they had failed miserably on both counts! Yet, the Church today has no reason whatsoever to point an accusing finger at them, since our own record in the past 2,000 years has been equally miserable on both counts. How it must grieve our dear Lord's mission-heart! *"The harvest [truly] is <u>plentiful</u>!"* **2)** Secondly, Jesus said that *"the laborers are few."* Obviously, the first issue is, at least to a large degree, caused by the second issue. Every Christian receives the gracious gift of a mission-heart at his Baptism ([2]M. M. Mt 5:14); therefore, the next urgent question is: "Why do so few Christians listen to their mission-heart and seek opportunities to tell others the Gospel? Sadly, we all try to invent all kinds of excuses for not doing so, but the bottom line is that all of our excuses are sinful; and we need to repent. How it must grieve our dear Lord's mission-heart! *"The laborers [truly] are few!"* It's a new mission message. M. M. Lk 10:2a: There are many people who are lost; and there are too few Christians who are eager to tell them the Gospel. **3)** Thirdly, Jesus therefore urged his disciples to *"pray earnestly to the Lord of the harvest to send out [more and more] laborers into his harvest."* But why did he urge us to ask him for more *"laborers?"* Just as with many other types of prayers, this prayer is all about him changing *us*, and has nothing to do with our Lord changing, since **a)** it is he himself who graciously gives all Christians both faith in himself and also a mission-heart at our Baptisms (M. M. Mt 5:14); **b)** and secondly, he himself is already eager to send his *"laborers"* out, since he did so twice in (9:1-6) and here in verses 1-12, and he continues to do so. This prayer is all about our Lord increasing our faith and increasing the zeal of our mission-hearts. **4)** In (17:5), Jesus' disciples realized that they needed more faith in order to be able to forgive repeated offenses; therefore, they wisely asked Jesus, *"Lord, Increase our faith"* (Mk 9:24)! Likewise here in verse 2, when Jesus urged his Church to ask him for more *"laborers,"* he was reminding his whole Church that it needs both more faith in order to be able to depend more and more on his gracious power to expand his mission (v 3), and also more and more zeal in our mission-hearts. With more faith and more zeal, his *"laborers"* will then multiply because more and more Christians will be more and more eager to daily seek more opportunities to be his missionaries. It's a second new mission imperative in verse 2. M. I. Lk 10:2b: Christians should ask their Lord for more faith and more zeal, so that more of them will be eager to be his missionaries.

10:3 (1) Jesus called his missionary laborers "lambs" because lambs are, of course, completely helpless against wolves; they are totally dependent on him as their Shepherd, just as a lamb cannot survive without its shepherd. Yet, by depending on his grace, they could go on his mission full of courage because they went in his strength and not their own strength (³M. I. Lk 11:10). **2)** The *"wolves,"* of course, were at that time, and still are: the devil himself, his evil angels, and also all lost people whom Satan has deceived into becoming enemies of the Lord's mission. All of them are extremely dangerous spiritual enemies, who are eager to destroy both the missionaries and their mission; and they have many, many clever and devious ways of trying to do so. Satan especially hates two things: all proclamation of the Gospel and all Bible translation work. However, the *"lambs"* do not go alone since they go together with the Lord of the mission who sent them out, since they depend on his almighty power to defeat their enemies and not on their own feeble strength (Mt 28:20). **3)** Furthermore, while lost people are *"wolves"* because they too are dangerous spiritual enemies, they are also *"lost;"* and they are, therefore, the objects of the Lord's mission. Thus, the Church obviously does not try to destroy its human spiritual enemies (It is Satan who is eager to kill them as quickly as he can, so that they will belong to him forever.); rather we try to reach them with the Law and Gospel because they are *"lost"* and urgently need to hear it and trust in Jesus (⁴M. M. Ac 13:46).

10:4 (1) Note that Jesus' command to his 70 missionaries in verse 4 is similar to his command to his 12 missionaries in (9:3), where he said, *"Take nothing for your journey, no staff, nor bag, nor bread, nor money; and do not have two tunics"* in that both commands are filled with a sense of urgency. Jesus did not want them to allow anything to delay their mission. Nothing was more urgent than going to complete their assignment to reach the lost! It's a new mission imperative. M. I. Lk 10:4: Their mission is urgent; therefore, Christians should go on their mission quickly and not allow anything to distract them. **2)** Furthermore, when Jesus said, *"greet no one on the road,"* he was, no doubt, implying that they should not engage in idle conversation. In other words, they should give people friendly greetings as they went on their way because they have a genuine interest in their welfare, but they should not stop and waste time by talking about things that aren't important. Their mission task was much too urgent to be wasting precious time on other trivial matters (M. I. Lk 10:4). He would certainly never tell his disciples to be so <u>rude</u> as to not give people friendly greetings. In fact, in verse 5 he told them to greet people at their doors by saying, *"Peace be to this house!"* If they had failed to greet people they would have offended people and risked <u>closing</u> doors of <u>opportunity</u> to tell them the Gospel rather than opening them ([5]M. I. Lk 4:15). (Too often we Americans take simple, every-day greetings for granted, but not so people in the hundreds of cultures in the "developing world." I know that this is certainly true in Africa; and I strongly suspect that the Jewish culture of Jesus' day was also quite similar.)

10:6 (1) Who was Jesus calling *"a son of peace"* (v 6)? **a)** First of all, the missionaries would have recognized a person as *"a son of peace"* by the way in which he answered their normal, every-day greeting, *"Peace be to this house"* (v 5), because *"a son of peace"* would have been someone who was waiting for the Messiah to bring <u>peace</u> to Israel (1:79; 2:14; 19:42). Clearly, Simeon and Anna were such persons (2:25, 38). Such a person would have been very happy to welcome two disciples of Jesus who came to tell his family that *"the kingdom of God has come near you"* (v 9)! **b)** Secondly, *"a son of peace"* would definitely <u>not</u> have been a hostile wolf, who Jesus warned them about in verse 3, *"behold, I am sending you out as lambs in the midst of <u>wolves</u>."* Nevertheless, these spiritual enemies were also the targets of their mission, whom they hoped to reach by staying in their friends' house (v 7; [6]M. I. Lk 10:7a). **2)** In addition, these verses seem to imply that there may have been "a son of peace" in *"<u>every</u> town and place where he himself [Jesus] was about to go"* (v 1). Evidently there still was *"a remnant"* in Israel who was still faithfully waiting for their King (1 Kng 19:18; [7]M. I. Lk 4:15 & [8]Lk 8:11). **3)** Furthermore, this method of finding an open door to preach the Gospel by finding *"a son of peace"* is likewise similar to the mission method of going <u>first</u> to the local synagogue that both Jesus (4:16) and St. Paul frequently used, since they probably went there partly because they knew that they would find *"devout men"* there (Ac 2:5). Such Jews and Gentiles who were worshipping in a synagogue would also have been longing for their King to finally appear (Ac 13:15; M. I. Lk 4:15).

10:7 (1) Therefore, Jesus continued in verse 7, *"Remain in the same* *house, eating and drinking what they provide... Do not go from house to house."* Some people in the towns were *"wolves"* (v 6); however, if these disciples who were <u>strangers</u> were staying in their relative's or friend's home, they would probably have been more likely to listen to them. Therefore, <u>one</u> *"son of peace,"* <u>one</u> open door would have been a way for the missionaries to find an <u>open</u> door into the <u>entire</u> community. They would have expended less effort by quickly leaving a home where they were not welcomed and continuing their search for an open door into the community. (Jesus gave this same command to his disciples in (9:4), but he explains the reasons why they should do this much more clearly here in verse 7.) Thus, Jesus established a new mission imperative. M. I. Lk 10:7a: When Christians go to a strange town on their mission, they should search for a family that welcomes them and their Gospel message and stay with them, because that home may be an <u>open</u> door into the <u>entire</u> community. **2)** And Jesus likewise added in verse 7 that *"the laborer deserves his wages."* His disciples and their Jewish hosts would probably have recognized this truth since Jesus is, in fact, referring to an Old Testament law in (Lev 19:13; Deu 24:14-15), which he once again applies to the missionaries that he has sent out. It is, therefore, another new mission imperative. M. I. Lk 10:7b: Church leaders deserve to be paid for their work of preaching and teaching the Gospel.

10:8 Jesus also commanded his disciples to *"eat what is set before you"* in verse 7 and then he repeated the same command in verse 8; and it may, in fact, be very noteworthy that he repeated it. **1)** Jesus was sending them on their very first missionary journey; therefore, it's very doubtful that he sent them into <u>Gentile</u> territories, where they would have been offered unclean food. (They obviously had not yet learned that God considers all food clean (Ac 10:28).) Rather, he sent them to their fellow Jews; and depending on how far they traveled, some of their fellow Jews may indeed have offered them strange, but *"clean"* food, which would have been a much easier challenge for them. Furthermore, it's very likely that Jesus repeated this command because eating and drinking food was, no doubt, a strong sign of good <u>fellowship</u> in their Jewish culture. And if they had refused what their hosts offered them, they would have been highly offended. And obviously, Jesus wanted them to maintain good fellowship with their hosts, so that they would remain open to hearing the Gospel. Thus, he was giving them more gentle experiences in their own Jewish culture, in order to teach them a new cross-cultural mission imperative. M. I. Lk 10:8: When Christians go on their mission into a cross-cultural situation they should eat what is offered to them, in order to maintain good fellowship with their hosts, so that they will remain open to hearing the Gospel. **2)** Jesus' command may at first appear to be rather insignificant to us Americans, since, in our culture, the cook may or may not be offended if a guest doesn't eat what he cooked. However, in many "developing world" cultures, both food and drink are also signs of fellowship; therefore, if a guest refuses either food or drink, it means that that person is rejecting the fellowship that their host has offered. It can be a very serious matter indeed! Therefore, a cross-cultural missionary today would be wise to at least try to eat or drink whatever his host offers him, no matter how strange or even repulsive the food may appear to him. If he eats it, it can be a very significant breakthrough in identifying with the target culture and may open opportunities to share the Gospel (M. I. Lk 10:8), since his hosts will feel like he is interested in learning about them and their culture. Furthermore, as he lives there longer, he will, no doubt, learn more and more polite ways to refuse food; and he may eventually even learn to enjoy the food!

10:9 (1) Jesus was always concerned about the whole person who was lost, physically, spiritually and mentally, but he knew that their physical and mental needs were only temporary while their spiritual needs were eternal. Therefore, he wanted his disciples to do both: *"heal the sick"* and also tell them that *"the kingdom of God has come near to you"* (v 9). However, as we have seen above, telling the Gospel message was the heart and core of their mission; and it will continue to be so until the Lord of the Harvest returns ([9]M. M. Mt 5:14 & [10]M. I. Lk 4:35). **2)** *"The kingdom of God has come near to you"* (v 9) is, of course, the central message of the Gospel because it means that King Jesus is present (1:32-33) *"to seek and to save the lost"* (19:10; [11]M. M. Lk 1:1).

10:10-11 It is a terrible sin to hear the most gracious Good News in the history of mankind, that the King of kings himself has come to seek and to save you, and yet to stubbornly refuse to repent and believe. This sin is so terrible that Jesus gave several serious warnings against it in verses 10-16, as well as elsewhere (3:8; 9:5; [12]M. M. 2 Cor 2:15).

Woe to Unrepentant Cities 10:13-16

10:13 *"Woe to you, Chorazin! Woe to you, Bethsaida! For if the mighty works done in you had been done in Tyre and Sidon, they would have repented long ago, sitting in sackcloth and ashes.*
10:14 *But it will be more bearable in the judgment for Tyre and Sidon than for you.*
10:15 *And you, Capernaum, will you be exalted to heaven? You shall be brought down to Hades.*
10:16 *"The one who hears you hears me, and the one who rejects you rejects me, and the one who rejects me rejects him who sent me."*

10:12-15 (1) Jesus mentioned two groups of cities in verses 12-15; and everyone who heard him that day would have immediately understood why he grouped them as he did, while we today must carefully study his Words in order to understand his subtle meaning. They knew that *"Chorazin, Bethsaida and Capernaum"* were cities in Israel, while *"Sodom, Tyre and Sidon"* were Gentile cities. **2)** Therefore, his point was that the cities in *Israel* had the *first* chance to hear Good News that *"the kingdom of God has come near"* (v 9); and yet they did not repent and believe in him. The King of kings himself or his missionaries came to their towns, preached the Gospel and healed many people to prove that he was God; yet they did not *"dance"* to the song that he sang (7:32). In his rich grace, God had chosen little Israel first; and this was an awesome privilege, but together with the privilege they also received the awesome responsibilities to both hear it themselves and to share it with all of the Gentiles nations. *"Woe to them"* indeed ([13]M. M. Lk 13:24)! **3)** But the Gentile cities, on the other hand, most likely did not see the King himself, nor did they see him perform any miracles; and they too did not repent and believe in him. Therefore, Jesus taught us here that God is always completely just in all of his judgments (12:47-48). He will punish everyone in hell, who does not believe in Jesus as their Savior, but there will be degrees of punishment. He will have a more terrible judgment for those who hear his gracious Gospel message (especially in their heart-language) and reject his amazing grace. But *"It will be more bearable in the judgment for [these Gentile cities]"* (v 14) because they did not receive the same gracious message and did not believe ([14]M. M. Lk 12:48 & [15]Ro 1:16b).

10:16 Jesus implied here that there is a Lord of the Harvest who is even greater than himself—his heavenly Father. It is his gracious heavenly Father who sent Jesus as the greatest prophet (Heb 1:1-2) to announce, *"The kingdom of God has come near to you"* (v 9; 4:18)! As such, the Father is the source of all grace. It is he who made the choice of using the Law and Gospel as the only means to call people of all nations to repentance and faith. If a person rejects this means of grace he is rejecting the source of that grace; and what an awful choice that is ([16]M. M. Ro 10:17a)!

The Return of the Seventy-Two 10:17-20

10:17 *The seventy-two returned with joy, saying, "Lord, even the demons are subject to us in your name!"*
10:18 *And he said to them, "I saw Satan fall like lightning from heaven.*
10:19 *Behold, I have given you authority to tread on serpents and scorpions, and over all the power of the enemy, and nothing shall hurt you.*
10:20 *Nevertheless, do not rejoice in this, that the spirits are subject to you, but rejoice that your names are written in heaven."*

10:17 The report of the seventy-two disciples was much more encouraging than that of the twelve apostles, where Luke simply said, *"On their return the apostles told him all that they had done"* (9:10). Perhaps these disciples had learned through observing Jesus' own mission work how to carry out their own mission ([17]M. M. Mt 5:14). In faith, they used the power of *"your [Jesus'] name"* (v 17). Having faith in him meant depending on his power, not theirs; and using his powerful name meant that they were invoking his presence (2 Chr 6:20). They were invoking the presence of the creator of the universe and of the Lord of the Harvest (v 2; [18]M. I. Lk 10:2b & [19]M. M. Ro 1:16b).

10:18 Once again, Jesus spoke here about his defeat of Satan on the cross as if it had already happened, since he knew that, in his gracious mission-heart, his heavenly Father had already planned his Son's total mission on earth even before Adam and Eve sinned (Rev 13:8). Thus, Jesus was born to destroy the devil (1:32, 47; Mt 1:21); and since the Father is far more powerful than Satan, nothing could stop Jesus from carrying it out (Ac 4:28). On the cross, Jesus cut off Satan's head; and, like the snake that he is, his body continues to thrash around for a long, long time—up until now, about 2,000 years. And it is especially we missionaries who feel his throes and suffer much bitter pain as a result. But our Brother, Jesus destroyed the *power* of sin, death and the devil, the sources of all of our problems ([20]M. M. Ro 3:24 & [21]Ro 5:1).

10:19 Satan continues to thrash about like a snake; and he attacks us because he hates everything that we do in order to expand our Lord's mission. However, our Brother Jesus has given us the power to use his holy name in order to daily win these minor skirmishes with the devil. Therefore, when the devil or his demons hear his name, they run away in abject terror. We may suffer painful wounds and deformities (physical, emotional and/or spiritual) in these struggles, but these are ultimately insignificant because our Brother won the final battle long ago on the cross ([22]M. M. Lk 6:22).

10:20 But the real joy is that, although these minor and temporary struggles with sin and Satan are very painful for us, ultimately they don't really matter. What really matters is the sure fact that our *"names are written in heaven"* (v 20), in the Lamb's book of life (Rev 21:27). How could Jesus be so bold as to make such a statement that our names are already written there? And how can we be so sure that our names are written there? Both statements are 1,000 % sure because the tomb of Jesus is empty! His empty tomb shouts that our Brother has fulfilled everything that he came to earth to do. That is the most important miracle in the history of the world because he did it <u>for us</u> (18:31; 2 Cor 1:20; Lev 18:5; [23]M. M. Jn 20:8).

Jesus Rejoices in the Holy Spirit 10:21-24

10:21 *In that same hour he rejoiced in the Holy Spirit and said, "I thank you, Father, Lord of heaven and earth, that you have hidden these things from the wise and understanding and revealed them to little children; yes, Father, for such was your gracious will.*
10:22 *All things have been handed over to me by my Father, and no one knows who the Son is except the Father, or who the Father is except the Son and anyone to whom the Son chooses to reveal him."*
10:23 *Then turning to the disciples he said privately, "Blessed are the eyes that see what you see!*
10:24 *For I tell you that many prophets and kings desired to see what you see, and did not see it, and to hear what you hear, and did not hear it."*

10:21-24 (1) Jesus' prayer in verses 21-24 has three similarities to his prayer in (Jn 17). **a)** First of all, he obviously allowed his disciples to listen to both prayers, because he was praying for them and their mission to the world (vs 22-24; Jn 17:18, 20). **b)** And secondly, in both prayers, he showed his total dependence on his Father's rich <u>grace</u> so that he could carry out his mission on earth (vs 21, 22; [24]M. I. Lk 11:10). **c)** Thirdly, both prayers are all about who *"knows," "sees"* and *"hears,"* or doesn't *"know"* and *"see"* (v 21, 23, 24; Jn 17:3, 7, 8, 23-26) the truth about the heavenly Father's plan of salvation, because he *"revealed"* it to them or *"hid"* it from them (v 21; Jn 17:5, 6). **2)** Therefore, since it was the mission-heart of God that compelled him to create a mission plan to rescue mankind from sin, why would a just and loving God "hide" his Law and Gospel message from some people and "reveal" it to others? It appears to defeat the very purpose of his mission.

Note that verse 21 says that "you [the Holy Spirit] have hidden these things from the <u>wise</u> and <u>understanding</u> and revealed them to little children." No amount of <u>human</u> *"wisdom"* or *"understanding"* (v 21) can ever discover the true wisdom of the *"Lord of heaven and earth"* (v 21; 1 Cor 1:18-31); rather by his Spirit, he *"reveals"* (v 21) his gracious will through his holy Word alone ([25]M. M. Ro 10:17a), and he gives faith in Jesus as a gracious <u>gift</u> to those who become his *"little children"* ([26]M. M. Ro 1:5). This is the reason why Jesus immediately began training twelve men to be his missionaries. Through them, he established his holy Church, the new Israel (1 Pe 2:9), who would carry on his mission of strengthening the faith of the Church, so that they all would be able to proclaim the Gospel to the whole world (Gen 12:1-3; [27]M. M. Ac 13:46).

10:23-24 (1) In verse 23, Jesus addressed his disciples privately and called them *"blessed;"* then he continued in verse 24, *"many prophets and kings desired to see what you see, and did not see it."* What they longed to see was Jesus, the Messiah. In other words, this special gift and privilege of physically *"seeing and touching"* Jesus (1 Jn 1-3) was not, in fact, *"hidden"* (v 21) from these prophets and kings; rather they simply lived at a different time, just as we today do; nevertheless, many of them were blessed (as we are), because they believed in him without seeing him with their physical eyes (Jn 20:29). They (and other Israelites) heard God's Word in their own heart-language (Hebrew, not a translation) and believed. What a blessing that was, and still is for the Jews today! Therefore, <u>both</u> ways of seeing are special <u>gifts</u> of the Holy Spirit's rich grace. No one deserves to receive either one (M. M. Ro 1:5). Furthermore, we today are especially blessed in another way, because we have the <u>whole</u> Bible to read in order to understand God's entire plan of salvation ([28]M. M. 2 Tim 3:16). **2)** Yet, sadly, there were many people who were also blessed in the same way as these disciples were, because they too saw Jesus with their <u>physical</u> eyes. But unfortunately for them, pride in their own human *"wisdom"* (v 21) or pride in their <u>physical</u> relationship with Abraham hindered them from truly "seeing" him with the eyes of faith (11:42-47; 20:19). This also highlights the truth that faith is a gracious <u>gift</u> of the Holy Spirit;

however, he never forces his grace on anyone if they resist him. Faith is a mystery that no human being can understand ([29]M. M. Ac 10:45). **3)** Obviously, the Holy Spirit does not use physical seeing to create faith; rather, he <u>only</u> uses physical <u>hearing</u> of his holy Word to perform this wonderful miracle of faith (2 Cor 4:6). And he can be most "effective" when his Word has been translated into the heart-language of the hearers, because everyone understands everything that we hear in our own heart-language. Bible translation work is obviously extremely important (Mt 13:19; [30]M. I. Ac 2:4).

The Parable of the Good Samaritan 10:25-37

10:25 *And behold, a lawyer stood up to put him to the test, saying, "Teacher, what shall I do to inherit eternal life?"*
10:26 *He said to him, "What is written in the Law? How do you read it?"*
10:27 *And he answered, "You shall love the Lord your God with all your heart and with all your soul and with all your strength and with all your mind, and your neighbor as yourself."*
10:28 *And he said to him, "You have answered correctly; do this, and you will live."*
10:29 *But he, desiring to justify himself, said to Jesus, "And who is my neighbor?"*
10:30 *Jesus replied, "A man was going down from Jerusalem to Jericho, and he fell among robbers, who stripped him and beat him and departed, leaving him half dead.*
10:31 *Now by chance a priest was going down that road, and when he saw him he passed by on the other side.*
10:32 *So likewise a Levite, when he came to the place and saw him, passed by on the other side.*
10:33 *But a Samaritan, as he journeyed, came to where he was, and when he saw him, he had compassion.*
10:34 *He went to him and bound up his wounds, pouring on oil and wine. Then he set him on his own animal and brought him to an inn and took care of him.*

10:35 *And the next day he took out two denarii and gave them to the innkeeper, saying, 'Take care of him, and whatever more you spend, I will repay you when I come back.'*
10:36 *Which of these three, do you think, proved to be a neighbor to the man who fell among the robbers?"*
10:37 *He said, "The one who showed him mercy." And Jesus said to him, "You go, and do likewise."*

10:25-29 (1) In verses 25-29, Jesus taught his disciples to understand the proper relationship between the Law and the Gospel. This *"lawyer"* thought that he was *"wise"* (v 21) and expected Jesus to confirm his sinful belief that he could do something to earn eternal life. And, on the surface, it at first may appear that Jesus agreed with him, because he told him to obey God's Law that says that he should love God and his fellow man. But then Jesus concluded in verse 28, *"You have answered correctly; do this, and you will live."* Jesus, thus, told him that, where he was wrong was in proudly thinking that he could, in fact, obey the Law perfectly; and therefore would deserve eternal life. However, he apparently did not catch Jesus' point that no sinful human being is able to keep the whole Law perfectly. Jesus himself, as true man and true God, was the only person who could and ever did do so, in order to earn eternal life as a free gift for all of his brothers and sisters (22:37; 24:44; [31]M. M. Mt 1:22). (Theologians call this truth: "objective justification." He graciously offers this free gift; but a person only receives this gift by faith in him alone. Theologians call this truth: "subjective justification.")
2) Jesus was, of course, *"seeking"* this lost lawyer as he spoke (19:10); and he was at that moment also continuing to obey the whole Law for his sake. Jesus longed for him to hear both the Law that he should repent of his sin of trying to earn forgiveness, and also the Gospel that he would soon earn forgiveness for him. How Jesus longed for him to repent and believe in him! This is the reason why he went on to tell him the story about the Good Samaritan in verses 30-37 (22:37; 24:44; M. M. Mt 1:22).
10:33 Obviously, it's important to note here that the Samaritans were enemies of the Jews, since the Samaritans were Jews with mixed Gentile blood; therefore, many Jews hated them even more than Gentiles. How

Jesus longed for this man to understand in his illustration that <u>he</u> himself was the Good Samaritan! It was when mankind was sinful, rebellious and <u>enemies</u> of God that the mission-heart of God moved Jesus to come to earth, in order to love and rescue his enemies (Rom 5:6-11). There is no other love greater than this (Jn 15:13). In his gracious mission-heart, Jesus did what his brothers and sisters could never do; he obeyed the whole Law perfectly, including shedding his divine/human blood to earn complete salvation. This was the eternal life that this man longed for, but refused to accept as a free gift, because pride blinded him to Jesus' rich grace (v 21; 22:37; 24:44; [32]M. M. Mt 1:22 & [33]Ro 3:24).

10:37 (1) Obviously, when Jesus told the lawyer in verse 37, *"You go, and do likewise,"* he was <u>not</u> contradicting himself by now telling the man to go and try to *earn* salvation for himself. Rather, he was urging him to love his enemies out of <u>gratitude</u> for the free gift of salvation that he would receive through faith in Jesus, just as he, the Good Samaritan loved his enemy, the wounded Jew. **2)** It's also possible that Jesus gave this command to this man in verse 37 because the man had heard this story and had received the gracious gifts of a repentant heart and faith in Jesus; however, sadly, there is no indication in the text that he did, in fact, repent and believe ([34]M. M. Ro 3:26). **3)** Furthermore, Jesus also urges us Christians, *"You go, and do likewise."* And we do strive to obey his Law of love perfectly, but <u>not</u> in order to <u>earn</u> anything; <u>only</u> Jesus has already obeyed it perfectly for us (M. M. Ro 3:24).

Martha and Mary 10:38-42

10:38 *Now as they went on their way, Jesus entered a village. And a woman named Martha welcomed him into her house.*

10:39 *And she had a sister called Mary, who sat at the Lord's feet and listened to his teaching.*

10:40 *But Martha was distracted with much serving. And she went up to him and said, "Lord, do you not care that my sister has left me to serve alone? Tell her then to help me."*

10:41 *But the Lord answered her, "Martha, Martha, you are anxious and troubled about many things,*

> 10:42 *but one thing is necessary. Mary has chosen the good portion, which will not be taken away from her."*

10:39 What a wonderful opportunity for Mary! She was Jesus himself present in her home and teaching her <u>one-on-one</u>. Mary truly was *"wise"* (v 21) because she showed that she knew that she was "lost;" and she showed her child-like faith in seeing whom Jesus was, ignoring all other concerns and seizing this precious opportunity to hear from Jesus himself (8:18). Very few people in all of history have had such a wonderful chance to hear from the Word of Life himself (24:13-35; Jn 6:63; 1 Jn 1:1). Furthermore, Jesus was, of course, very eager to personally *"seek"* this one person who clearly knew that she was *"lost."* And he likewise did not miss the opportunity to teach her and the other disciples that they too should carry out their mission one person at a time ([35]M. I. Lk 4:40).

10:40 Martha, on the other hand, was thinking just like the three men in (9:57-62), who wanted to follow Jesus for wrong reasons, since her priorities were also misdirected and sinful. She was focused too much on what she was doing to please him and not on humbly listening to his Gospel message, as Mary was doing. Jesus was there to *"seek"* her as well, and to call her to repentance. Furthermore, Jesus no doubt knew that her brother Lazarus would soon die, which would severely test Martha's faith in him. Therefore, she needed to repent, and trust him more surely ([36]M. I. Lk 3:3a).

10:42 Since God has provided no other means for creating and strengthening faith except through his holy Word (Heb 12:2), there truly was only <u>one</u> thing, *"the good portion"* that Mary needed (v 42). The Holy Spirit graciously uses <u>only</u> the Gospel as his mighty tool for creating faith (Rom 1:16; [37]M. M. Ro 10:17a); and this is the <u>only</u> tool because there is only <u>one</u> cross that saves. This is also the reason why Jesus, the Lord of the mission will never *"take away"* (v 42) this precious tool of his holy Word; rather, he always has and always will carefully <u>preserve</u> it as his Church's vital mission tool for *"seeking the lost"* ([38]M. M. Ac 13:46).

[1] M. I. Lk 6:13: Christians should choose new leaders and train them in order to multiply the work.

[2] M. M. Mt 5:14: When the Holy Spirit creates faith in a person's heart, he also graciously gives him a new mission-heart that is eager to shine the light of the Gospel throughout the whole world.

[3] M. I. Lk 11:10: Christians should <u>continuously</u> pray to their heavenly Father and <u>always</u> depend on his grace, and not on their own feeble strength, because he <u>always</u> loves them.

[4] M. M. Ac 13:46: As he did with the old Israel, God <u>first of all</u> strengthens the faith of the new Israel, the Church with his Word and Sacraments, so that they can go and witness to the lost people of all nations.

[5] M. I. Lk 4:15: Christians should seize <u>every</u> opportunity to proclaim the Gospel to lost people of all nations.

[6] M. I. Lk 10:7a: When Christians go to a strange town on their mission, they should search for a family that welcomes them and their Gospel and stay with them, because that home may be an <u>open</u> door into the <u>entire</u> community.

[7] M. I. Lk 4:15: Christians should seize <u>every</u> opportunity to proclaim the Gospel to lost people of all nations.

[8] M. I. Lk 8:11: Christians should faithfully do their job of preaching and leave the <u>results</u> to the Holy Spirit.

[9] M. M. Mt 5:14: When the Holy Spirit creates faith in a person's heart, he also graciously gives him a new mission-heart that is eager to shine the light of the Gospel throughout the whole world.

[10] M. I. Lk 4:35: Christians should view every person as a whole person, and show him compassion by caring for <u>both</u> his physical and spiritual needs as they go on their mission.

[11] M. M. Lk 1:1: Jesus came to seek and save <u>all</u> lost people from <u>every</u> nation on earth.

[12] M. M. 2 Cor 2:15: When Christians proclaim the sweet fragrance of the Gospel, it will become the fragrance of eternal death for some people who stubbornly reject it, but for those who hear it, repent and believe in Jesus it is the fragrance of eternal life.

[13] M. M. Lk 13:24: The <u>only</u> way to enter the Kingdom of God is to have <u>faith</u> in Jesus as one's Savior.

[14] M. M. Lk 12:48: God will justly condemn to eternal punishment all people who do not trust in Jesus as their Savior, but he will punish them by different <u>degrees</u>, according to how well they knew his will.

[15] M. M. Ro 1:16b: The Gospel is so powerful because it contains the central truth that Jesus rose from the dead with a glorified body in order to save all of his brothers and sisters from sin and death.

[16] M. M. Ro 10:17a: The Holy Spirit <u>only</u> creates and preserves faith by using the message of God's grace in his holy Word.

[17] M. M. Mt 5:14: When the Holy Spirit creates faith in a person's heart, he also graciously gives him a new mission-heart that is eager to shine the light of the Gospel throughout the whole world.

[18] M. I. Lk 10:2b: Christians should ask their Lord for more <u>faith</u> and more <u>zeal</u>, so that more of them will be eager to be his missionaries.

[19] M. M. Ro 1:16b: The Gospel is so powerful because it contains the central truth that Jesus rose from the dead with a glorified body in order to save all of his brothers and sisters from sin and death.

[20] M. M. Ro 3:24: Jesus lived a life of perfect obedience and shed his precious blood on the cross, in order to graciously set all nations free from sin, which a person only receives by faith in him.

[21] M. M. Ro 5:1: On the cross, Jesus earned <u>peace</u> with God for <u>all</u> of his brothers and sisters from every nation on earth.

[22] M. M. Lk 6:22: The Lord Jesus will surely bless a Christian in the midst of suffering for his sake; and he will also bless him with eternal life if he remains faithful to him.

[23] M. M. Jn 20:8: God gave faith in Jesus to people who personally saw that the tomb of Jesus was empty, because it proved that he was alive.

[24] M. I. Lk 11:10: Christians should <u>continuously</u> pray to their heavenly Father and <u>always</u> depend on his grace, and not on their own feeble strength, because he <u>always</u> loves them.

[25] M. M. Ro 10:17a: The Holy Spirit <u>only</u> creates and preserves faith by using the message of God's grace in his holy Word.

[26] M. M. Ro 1:5: The same Holy Spirit who creates <u>faith</u> and a new missionary <u>nature</u> in a person's heart also graciously empowers him to gratefully respond to his Lord's love by <u>obeying</u> him.

[27] M. M. Ac 13:46: As he did with the old Israel, God <u>first of all</u> strengthens the faith of the new Israel, the Church with his Word and Sacraments, so that they can go and witness to the lost people of all nations.

[28] M. M. 2 Tim 3:16: The Holy Spirit inspired the entire Bible; and therefore, the whole Bible is useful for teaching people the truth, for teaching them how to live a life that pleases God, for rebuking their errors, and for correcting their faults.

[29] M. M. Ac 10:45: When God graciously gives the gift of faith in his Son, Jesus to a person from any nation on earth, he also graciously gives him his Holy Spirit who now lives in his new mission-heart.

[30] M. I. Ac 2:4: In cross-cultural situations, Christians should always focus on all of the needs of the target group by learning <u>their</u> heart-language and culture as deeply as possible, so that they can tell them the Gospel clearly in their own language and also help them with the true needs of their society.

[31] M. M. Mt 1:22: God sent his only Son, Jesus to be born as a true human being, so that he could save all of his brothers and sisters of all nations by fulfilling all of God's promises in the Old Testament.

[32] M. M. Mt 1:22: God sent his only Son, Jesus to be born as a true human being, so that he could save all of his brothers and sisters of all nations by fulfilling all of God's promises in the Old Testament.

[33] M. M. Ro 3:24: Jesus lived a life of perfect obedience and shed his precious blood on the cross, in order to graciously set all nations free from sin, which a person only receives by faith in him.

[34] M. M. Ro 3:26: God is just and fair to <u>everyone</u>, both when he condemns <u>all</u> people of all nations because all have sinned, and also when he <u>only</u> declares those people righteous who have faith in Jesus.

[35] M. I. Lk 4:40: Christians should go and seek the lost <u>one</u> person at a time by focusing on each person's <u>unique</u> needs.

[36] M. I. Lk 3:3a: Christians should, in love, warn lost people who do not repent.

[37] M. M. Ro 10:17a: The Holy Spirit <u>only</u> creates and preserves faith by using the message of God's grace in his holy Word.

[38] M. M. Ac 13:46: As he did with the old Israel, God <u>first of all</u> strengthens the faith of the new Israel, the Church with his Word and Sacraments, so that they can go and witness to the lost people of all nations.

Chapter 11

The Lord's Prayer 11:1-13

11:1   *Now Jesus was praying in a certain place, and when he finished, one of his disciples said to him, "Lord, teach us to pray, as John taught his disciples."*
11:2   *And he said to them, "When you pray, say: "Father, hallowed be your name. Your kingdom come.*
11:3   *Give us each day our daily bread,*
11:4   *and forgive us our sins, for we ourselves forgive everyone who is indebted to us. And lead us not into temptation."*
11:5   *And he said to them, "Which of you who has a friend will go to him at midnight and say to him, 'Friend, lend me three loaves,*
11:6   *for a friend of mine has arrived on a journey, and I have nothing to set before him';*
11:7   *and he will answer from within, 'Do not bother me; the door is now shut, and my children are with me in bed. I cannot get up and give you anything'?*
11:8   *I tell you, though he will not get up and give him anything because he is his friend, yet because of his impudence he will rise and give him whatever he needs.*
11:9   *And I tell you, ask, and it will be given to you; seek, and you will find; knock, and it will be opened to you.*
11:10 *For everyone who asks receives, and the one who seeks finds, and to the one who knocks it will be opened.*
11:11 *What father among you, if his son asks for a fish, will instead of a fish give him a serpent;*
11:12 *or if he asks for an egg, will give him a scorpion?*
11:13 *If you then, who are evil, know how to give good gifts to your children, how much more will the heavenly Father give the Holy Spirit to those who ask him!"*

11:1 (1) Jesus continued to pray in order to faithfully seek his Father's will for his mission to the world, so that he could faithfully obey him perfectly. He was, at the same time, teaching his disciples by his example that it was also vital for them to continue to pray as they carried out their mission to *"seek the lost."* And the disciples' request to learn how to pray in verse 1 shows that they had begun to learn this lesson ([1]M. I. Lk 11:10). **2)** Likewise, in (Ac 2:42) we see that the disciples did not forget to continue to make prayer a vital part of the life of the community of Christians after Jesus' ascension. There we read that the Christians *"devoted themselves to the apostles' teaching and fellowship, to the breaking of bread and the prayers"* (M. I. Lk 11:10).

11:2 (1) The fact that Jesus taught his disciples to address his Father as their *"Father"* at this time in his mission is further indication that Jesus knew that his mission to *"save the lost"* would not fail. Without his death on the cross and his empty tomb, no one has any right to call the righteous judge of the world their *"Father"* because all human beings are spiritually dead and are his rebellious enemies. But he was even at that moment carrying out his Father's will to remove that barrier and replace it with a "peaceful" relationship (Rom 5:1, 10; 10:33). Because of this mighty saving action, all who trust in him can come to his Father as their own Father because they too are now his own beloved sons and daughters (Rom 8:14-17; [2]M. M. Ro 8:15). **2)** The heavenly Father is love, which means that he has a mission-heart that forever longs to have all mankind living under his gracious rule forever (v 2; 10:9; 1 Tim 2:4). Therefore, Jesus taught his disciples to pray in verse 2 that their heavenly Father would enable them to keep their Father's name holy by obeying his gracious will and follow their own mission-hearts to continuously seek opportunities to proclaim the Gospel. In this way, his kingdom will *"come"* (v 2) quickly among all of the *"lost"* people he has made in all nations on earth (Ezek 18:23; [3]M. I. Lk 4:15).

11:3 (1) The fact that this petition of the Lord's Prayer occurs immediately after the story of Mary sitting at the feet of Jesus to hear his Word is very striking, since this petition is a humble request to be able to sit at Jesus' feet and "eat" his living Word *"every day"* (Jn 6:68; [4]M. I. Lk 12:40). But even more than that, it is a request to be able to receive his holy sacraments as well—*"daily"* forgiveness in the waters of Holy Baptism, and frequent forgiveness in our Lord's very body and blood and. All of this food is so rich in <u>grace</u> because it is connected with God's holy Word (^{5}M. M. Tit 3:5). Our heavenly Father longs to feed his dear children with the richest food he has made, with his holy Word (Is 25:6), so that they can carry out their mission to the world (^{6}M. I. Ro 10:17c). **2)** In addition, this is, of course, also a prayer to daily receive the <u>physical</u> food that we need in order to have the physical strength to carry out our mission. It's a new mission imperative. M. I. Lk 11:3: Christians should daily ask their heavenly Father for the physical and spiritual food that they need every day, in order to be able to carry out their mission to the world.

11:4 (1) Verse 4 begins: *"and forgive us our sins [Father], for we ourselves forgive everyone who is indebted to us."* While the greatest desire of our heavenly Father's mission-heart is to be at peace with <u>all</u> human beings because he has <u>forgiven</u> all of their sins (v 4), his second greatest desire is that <u>all</u> the people he has made would live in peace with one another because they have <u>forgiven</u> each other (2:14; 24:36; Jn 14:27). However, since all human beings are sinful, his second desire is only possible if we Christians <u>first</u> forgive others. There should be three steps. **a)** We should <u>first of all</u> depend on the gracious power of his Holy Spirit to forgive people who have sinned against us (v 4), since that broken relationship also breaks our loving relationship with our heavenly Father. **b)** Then, our heavenly Father is eager to forgive us and restore our broken relationship with him by giving us repentant hearts and faith in our Lord Jesus (v 4). **c)** And we can then, once again, be in mission to the people we have forgiven by helping them with all of their needs. It's a new mission imperative. M. I. Lk 11:4a: Christians should depend on the power of the Holy Spirit to forgive people who have sinned against them so that their heavenly Father will also forgive them. **2)** And especially if we Christians forgive an <u>unbeliever</u> who has sinned against us, it can be a very powerful Gospel for that person because he will wonder how we are able to forgive so freely. It therefore creates a wonderful <u>opportunity</u> to tell him that we were able to forgive him because our heavenly Father first forgave us (^{7}M. I. Lk 4:15). **3)** Verse 4 then continues, *"And lead us not into temptation."* As Martin Luther said, *"God indeed tempts no one [to sin];"* however, he does graciously test our faith in order to strengthen it, as we go out into this dark world on his mission where Satan lurks ([8]M. M. 1 Pe 1:7). And, of course, Satan certainly does frequently try to tempt us to sin by obeying him instead of our heavenly Father. Therefore, Jesus our Shepherd taught us to pray here that our heavenly Father would not allow Satan to tempt us so severely that we lose our faith (Job 1:8-12), as we, his *"lambs"* go on his mission to preach his Gospel message among many fierce *"wolves"* (10:3). When we continually pray this prayer, it shows our dependence on our Father's strength to help us avoid and overcome all of the clever traps of the devil and his evil *"wolves."* It's a new mission imperative. M. I. Lk 11:4b: Christians should ask their heavenly Father that he would not allow Satan to tempt them so severely that they lose their faith, and also that he would give them his strength to depend on his grace in all of their trials.

11:8 Jesus used a negative example in this parable about a friend who was in need, in order to teach a powerful lesson about praying to our heavenly Father. The wealthy *"friend"* in the parable obviously did not love his needy friend and only helped him after prolonged pleading. However, in sharp contrast to his lack of love, the heavenly Father is the *"God of all comfort"* (2 Cor 1:3). His mission-heart is full of grace and mercy and is eager to answer all who call on him in humble faith ([9]M. I. Lk 11:3).

11:9-10 The fact that Jesus repeated three different ways of asking in verse 9 teaches us that every child of the heavenly Father should pray to him continuously, because, in his mission-heart, he always loves them (1 Jn 4:16). Once again, his love stands in sharp contrast to the lack of love of the wealthy friend in the parable in verses 5-8 who did not care about his friend's needs. Therefore, instead of forgetting about their heavenly Father's love and depending on their own feeble strength, his continuous love and grace should move them to continuously turn to him for all of their needs. It's a new mission imperative. M. I. Lk 11:10: Christians should continuously pray to their heavenly Father and always depend on his grace, and not on their own feeble strength, because he always loves them.

11:11-12 Jesus again used negative examples in these two verses to powerfully teach the <u>positive</u> truth that the heavenly Father has a mission-heart that is full of <u>grace</u> and mercy for his dear children, and therefore, he always eagerly answers their prayers. Therefore, his children should always depend on him alone in prayer as they carry out his mission to this dangerous world ([10]M. I. Lk 11:10).

11:13 (1) The mission-heart of God is full of <u>gracious</u> and <u>generous</u> spiritual gifts that he eagerly gives to *"those who ask him."* However, since all unbelievers are spiritually <u>dead</u>, they cannot by their own strength ask him for anything ([11]M. M. Eph 2:2). Therefore, his rich grace is abundantly clear, since he alone does <u>all</u> of the action in the process of giving his Spiritual gifts. **a)** The <u>first</u> gift that the Holy Spirit gives a spiritually <u>dead</u> person is the gracious gift of <u>faith</u>, or the spiritual life of a new mission-heart (2 Cor 4:6). And he has graciously chosen to use only <u>one</u> means to give this gift: his holy <u>Word</u> ([12]M. M. Ro 10:17a). Therefore, he may give this first gift at two different times: **b)** He will create faith in a person's heart when a <u>child</u> is baptized (M. M. Ro 10:17a). **c)** Or he will create faith in a person's heart when the person hears the Gospel and believes, and then he is baptized (8:15). **d)** This person's faith, then, is like a hand that receives all other spiritual blessings that the Spirit gives him ([13]M. M. Ro 3:26). As the mission-heart of each Christian moves him to seek opportunities to share the Gospel message, he also naturally <u>asks</u> his heavenly Father for both more spiritual gifts and also the strength that he needs to share the Gospel. And, of course, his Father is eager to *"give[s] the Holy Spirit to those who ask him"* (v 13). **2)** Obviously, every step of this process is a gracious <u>miracle</u>; and especially the miraculous gift of faith is, perhaps, second in importance only to the greatest miracle in history—the resurrection of Jesus. Nevertheless, as great as these miracles are, it's a process that no human being can <u>see</u>; therefore, sadly, many people doubt that any part of it has even happened. And most often, even some Christians refuse to believe that a person receives any spiritual gifts when he is <u>baptized</u>. It's incredibly sad, especially since this unbelief <u>divides</u> the Church. And, of course, the unbelieving world is often offended by these sinful divisions ([14]M. M. Eph 1:13 & [15]Eph 1:14).

Jesus and Beelzebul 11:14-23

11:14 *Now he was casting out a demon that was mute. When the demon had gone out, the mute man spoke, and the people marveled.*
11:15 *But some of them said, "He casts out demons by Beelzebul, the prince of demons,"*
11:16 *while others, to test him, kept seeking from him a sign from heaven.*
11:17 *But he, knowing their thoughts, said to them, "Every kingdom divided against itself is laid waste, and a divided household falls.*
11:18 *And if Satan also is divided against himself, how will his kingdom stand? For you say that I cast out demons by Beelzebul.*
11:19 *And if I cast out demons by Beelzebul, by whom do your sons cast them out? Therefore they will be your judges.*
11:20 *But if it is by the finger of God that I cast out demons, then the kingdom of God has come upon you.*
11:21 *When a strong man, fully armed, guards his own palace, his goods are safe;*
11:22 *but when one stronger than he attacks him and overcomes him, he takes away his armor in which he trusted and divides his spoil.*
11:23 *Whoever is not with me is against me, and whoever does not gather with me scatters.*

11:14 Jesus was continuing his mission of *"seeking the lost"* by using his own divine presence in his holy name to drive out a demon, as he had just recently empowered his disciples to do ([16]M. I. Lk 4:35).
11:15-16 *"The Lamb of God"* himself (Jn 1:29) now encountered some of the same *"wolves"* whom he had just warned his disciples about (10:3). In spite of the miracle that Jesus had just performed, which should have clearly proven to everyone present that he was true God, the devil inspired some of his human *"wolves"* to, not only doubt Jesus'

divinity, but also to even accuse him of using <u>Satan's</u> power to drive out the demon. How absurd is that ([17]M. I. Lk 3:8)! Their evil accusations lacked any subtlety at all, but, in that respect, these accusations were just as blatant as the devil's three temptations of Jesus in the desert (4:3-11). Perhaps Satan's attempt at deception in all of these temptations actually lay in the element of <u>surprise</u> at such blatant lies. However, throughout his life, Jesus obviously saw through every attempt by the devil and by every one of his *"wolves"* to lure him away from his mission in serving his heavenly Father. He himself, of course, is *"the truth"* (Jn 14:6; [18]M. I. Lk 11:10 & [19]Lk 4:4).

11:20 Jesus' miracle of driving out a demon proclaimed the message that *"the kingdom of God has come near to you"* (10:9). And it was, of course, the same message that he had told his disciples to proclaim on their second mission trip (10:1-12). The King of kings himself was, indeed, present as *"Immanuel, God with us"* (Mt 1:23). And anyone who saw what he did and persisted in his unbelief was despising the heavenly Father's rich <u>grace</u>, since he is the one who had sent his royal Son on this mission. Obviously, the heavenly Father and his Son shared the same mission-heart, which had moved Jesus to briefly set his divinity aside and humble himself for the sake of his human brothers and sisters. Therefore, his healing of this <u>one</u> man was only one example of what he had come to do *"to seek the lost"* by focusing on this man's urgent spiritual and physical needs ([20]M. I. Lk 4:35).

11:23 In Jesus' kingdom of grace, the invisible Church, there are no unbelievers; if a person trusts in Jesus alone, he is under his loving rule ([21]M. M. Mt 2:6). However, another person who doubts that Jesus is his Lord has chosen to follow the arch-enemy, Satan, who is the evil ruler of this dark world (Jn 12:31). There is <u>no</u> neutral ground ([22]M. M. Eph 2:2). When Jesus told a man in (Mk 12:34), *"You're not far from the kingdom of God,"* he was sternly warning him that he was still <u>outside</u> of his holy kingdom because he did not believe in him. Therefore, <u>all</u> unbelievers are Satan's *"wolves"* and his slaves. And anything that they do in unbelief they are doing in <u>opposition</u> to King Jesus; what they do <u>hinders</u> and can never advance the mission of Jesus (4:16; 24:47-48; [23]M. M. Lk 13:24).

Return of an Unclean Spirit 11:24-26

> 11:24 *"When the unclean spirit has gone out of a person, it passes through waterless places seeking rest, and finding none it says, 'I will return to my house from which I came.'*
> 11:25 *And when it comes, it finds the house swept and put in order.*
> 11:26 *Then it goes and brings seven other spirits more evil than itself, and they enter and dwell there. And the last state of that person is worse than the first."*

11:24-26 Satan is so evil that he continues to fill the heart of an unrepentant person with even more of his demons, so that he enslaves him even more completely (v 26). However, Jesus does not empty a person's heart of demons in order to allow even more demons access into his heart; rather, his Spirit graciously enters his heart, so that he no longer serves the devil; he now serves Jesus and begins advancing his kingdom (M. M. Lk 13:24 & [24]Eph 1:21).

True Blessedness 11:27-28

> 11:27 *As he said these things, a woman in the crowd raised her voice and said to him, "Blessed is the womb that bore you, and the breasts at which you nursed!"*
> 11:28 *But he said, "Blessed rather are those who hear the word of God and keep it!"*

11:27-28 (1) God did indeed *"bless"* Jesus' mother, Mary (v 27), because it was a great honor to conceive, give birth to and raise God's own beloved Son (1:42); however, Jesus answered this woman in the same way that he answered a similar question in (8:21), when he said, *"My mother and my brothers are those who hear the word of God and do it."* Mary's blood relationship to Jesus and the many things that she did for him in raising him could do nothing to save her from her sins. Only if she trusted in him as her Savior would she receive a much greater blessing, his free gift of forgiveness. And of course, it is quite apparent in all of the Gospels that she did in fact receive the Holy Spirit's gracious gift of faith in her Son as her dear Lord (1:47; [25]M. M. Lk 13:24). **2)** Note that Luke, the Gentile was careful to repeat this very important lesson that all people of all nations have but one equal way to receive God's rich blessing of complete forgiveness for all of their sins, through faith in Jesus (19:10). No Jew, not even Mary, has any advantage because he is related to Jesus by blood (19:9). What a gracious gift this is for all people because faith only comes by hearing the Law and Gospel about Jesus (v 28; [26]M. M. Ro 10:17a & [27]Ro 4:11).

The Sign of Jonah 11:29-32

11:29 *When the crowds were increasing, he began to say, "This generation is an evil generation. It seeks for a sign, but no sign will be given to it except the sign of Jonah.*
11:30 *For as Jonah became a sign to the people of Nineveh, so will the Son of Man be to this generation.*
11:31 *The queen of the South will rise up at the judgment with the men of this generation and condemn them, for she came from the ends of the earth to hear the wisdom of Solomon, and behold, something greater than Solomon is here.*
11:32 *The men of Nineveh will rise up at the judgment with this generation and condemn it, for they repented at the preaching of Jonah, and behold, something greater than Jonah is here.*

11:29-30 (1) It is sinful to demand that God should perform a miracle (v 16), because it too is a gracious gift from his merciful mission-heart; therefore, Jesus publicly refuted this lie of Satan that anyone can demand anything from God ([28]M. I. Lk 3:8). **2)** However, Jesus did, of course, heal many people physically as gracious gifts to them. But the very special *"sign of Jonah"* that Jesus gave as a gracious gift to, not only *"his generation"* (v 30), but to all people of all time was his resurrection from the dead. Just as the prophet Jonah was *"in the belly of the fish for three days and three nights"* (Jonah 1:17), so Jesus was in the belly of the earth three days. This was the greatest of all miracles for at least two reasons: **a)** First of all, it is the greatest of all because it says to the person who hears and believes his holy Word, "I died and rose again for you." His resurrection is a miracle that no human being demanded of God nor deserved from him, because he raised his own beloved Son from the dead as a most gracious gift to the entire sinful human race (^{29}M. M. Jn 20:8). **b)** Secondly, his empty tomb shouts, "Yes" to all of God's promises to his people, Israel (1 Cor 2:2; 2 Cor 1:20). The historical fact of his resurrection is absolutely vital prove for everyone's faith that God does truly have a mission-heart and does indeed love them and will richly *"bless"* (v 28) all who come to him in the name of Jesus (^{30}M. M. Ro 1:16b).

11:31-32 (1) First of all, God's gracious mission-heart moved him to choose Abraham and his descendants as his own people (Gen 12:1-3). Then, he inspired men from their midst such as King Solomon (v 31) to write down *"the wisdom"* (v 31; 1 Kng 4:29) of his holy Word in their own heart-language. Therefore, they had the high privilege of hearing the Gospel first and very clearly; so that they would repent and believe; and so that their mission-hearts would move them to share the Gospel message with the Gentile nations (^{31}M. M. Ac 13:46). **2)** Secondly, *"the [Gentile] queen of the South"* (Queen Sheba, 1 Kng 10:1) "came from the ends of the earth to hear the wisdom of Solomon," and she heard about his wisdom, repented and believed; even though (apparently) no Israelite missionary had gone to her country in order to proclaim the Gospel to them. Then later, God chose another Israelite, Jonah as his prophet; yet, he only very reluctantly went to the Gentile city of Nineveh to proclaim the coming Messiah to them (Jonah 1:1-3:3). And he was even angry with God when they repented (v 32; Jonah 4:1-11). In short, over a period of about 2,000 years, the people of Israel were sadly very, very poor missionaries to Gentile nations. **3)** Thirdly, nevertheless, God's gracious mission-heart never gives up on his people. In order to fully reveal the physical embodiment of his *"wisdom,"* he sent *"something greater"* (vs 31-32), his Son, Jesus to be born as a Jew; therefore, he graciously gave his people yet another awesome responsibility, the honor of being the first people to see and hear Jesus, the Wisdom of God (1 Cor 1:24; ^{32}M. M. Lk 1:1). Yet, many of them repeatedly refused to repent and believe (vs 42-52). **4)** Therefore, on Judgment Day, these <u>Gentiles</u>: *"the queen from the south"* (v 31) and *"the men of Nineveh"* (v 32) will rightfully bear witness before God that these Jews deserve God's terrible, eternal punishment. These Jews despised God's bountiful grace, even though they were eye witnesses of Jesus' life, death and resurrection. But these <u>Gentiles</u>, on the other hand, repented when they heard a Gospel message that was far less clear than the glorious Gospel of Jesus' resurrection, which is greatest of all miracles (vs 29, 31-32; [33]M. M. Lk 12:48).

The Lamp of the Body 11:33-36

11:33 *"No one after lighting a lamp puts it in a cellar or under a basket, but on a stand, so that those who enter may see the light.*
11:34 *Your eye is the lamp of your body. When your eye is healthy, your whole body is full of light, but when it is bad, your body is full of darkness.*
11:35 *Therefore be careful lest the light in you be darkness.*
11:36 *If then your whole body is full of light, having no part dark, it will be wholly bright, as when a lamp with its rays gives you light."*

11:33-36 (1) The gift of <u>faith</u> that the Holy Spirit graciously gives to a person is not simply a spiritual treasure that he now has to keep for himself, it is a precious treasure to <u>share</u>. His *"whole body is [now] full of light"* (v 34); his new light is a <u>mission-heart</u>. Therefore, Jesus' said in verse 33, *"No one after lighting a lamp puts it in a cellar or under a basket, but on a stand, so that those who enter may see the light"* (8:1-15; Mt 5:14). Jesus had been going from city to city *"seeking the lost"* by preaching both the Law and *"the light"* of the Gospel. And he had very purposely sent his disciples out on two mission trips to proclaim the same message of *"light"* (9:1; 10:1; [34]M. M. Lk 1:1). **2)** But sadly, *"the bodies"* of many of the Jews who saw his light were *"full of darkness"* (v 34; 37-54). They were blind to the <u>brightest</u> light the world has ever seen—Jesus, *"the light of the world"* (Jn 8:12). Thus, Jesus' statement in verse 35 that they should *"be careful lest the light in you be darkness"* was a stern <u>warning</u> to these people that they were <u>personally</u> responsible for <u>how</u> they listen to the Law and Gospel message. This is true because <u>no other</u> person can believe for someone else—no matter how close his personal relationship may be, such as spouse, brother or sister (8:21; v 52). The Spirit of Jesus is eager to use the Gospel to create and strengthen faith, but if the heart of the hearer is like rocky or weedy soil (8:12-14), it is the hearer, not God or the preacher, who is responsible for how he feeds his faith with the light of the Gospel (^{35}M. I. Lk 8:18).

Woes to the Pharisees and Lawyers 11:37-54

11:37 *While Jesus was speaking, a Pharisee asked him to dine with him, so he went in and reclined at table.*
11:38 *The Pharisee was astonished to see that he did not first wash before dinner.*
11:39 *And the Lord said to him, "Now you Pharisees cleanse the outside of the cup and of the dish, but inside you are full of greed and wickedness.*
11:40 *You fools! Did not he who made the outside make the inside also?*
11:41 *But give as alms those things that are within, and behold, everything is clean for you.*
11:42 *"But woe to you Pharisees! For you tithe mint and rue and every herb, and neglect justice and the love of God. These you ought to have done, without neglecting the others.*
11:43 *Woe to you Pharisees! For you love the best seat in the synagogues and greetings in the marketplaces.*
11:44 *Woe to you! For you are like unmarked graves, and people walk over them without knowing it."*
11:45 *One of the lawyers answered him, "Teacher, in saying these things you insult us also."*
11:46 *And he said, "Woe to you lawyers also! For you load people*

> with burdens hard to bear, and you yourselves do not touch the burdens with one of your fingers.
>
> 11:47 *Woe to you! For you build the tombs of the prophets whom your fathers killed.*
> 11:48 *So you are witnesses and you consent to the deeds of your fathers, for they killed them, and you build their tombs.*
> 11:49 *Therefore also the Wisdom of God said, 'I will send them prophets and apostles, some of whom they will kill and persecute,'*
> 11:50 *so that the blood of all the prophets, shed from the foundation of the world, may be charged against this generation,*
> 11:51 *from the blood of Abel to the blood of Zechariah, who perished between the altar and the sanctuary. Yes, I tell you, it will be required of this generation.*
> 11:52 *Woe to you lawyers! For you have taken away the key of knowledge. You did not enter yourselves, and you hindered those who were entering."*
> 11:53 *As he went away from there, the scribes and the Pharisees began to press him hard and to provoke him to speak about many things,*
> 11:54 *lying in wait for him, to catch him in something he might say.*

11:37 Instead of avoiding this Pharisee, whom he knew was one of his spiritual enemies, Jesus accepted his invitation to his home because his mission-heart made him eager to take this wonderful opportunity to "seek," not only this one "lost" person, but also his evil cronies (vs 42-54), whom he had also invited to this meal ([36]M. M. Lk 1:1 & [37]M. I. Lk 4:15).

11:38 Once again, Jesus was, of course, not breaking a Law of *God* by "not first wash[ing] before dinner," since this was a man-made rule which was made by the Pharisees themselves. Therefore, it's obvious that Jesus now deliberately broke this rule in order to start an opportunity for a conversation that he could direct toward a clear witness to his own love or *"light"* (v 33) for the man. He always focused on the unique needs of individuals and sought them personally ([38]M. I. Lk 4:40

& Lk 4:15).

11: 40-52 (1) In these six *"Woes"* or calls to repentance, Jesus openly condemned the religious leaders of the Jews with the harsh Law because of the very things that he had been warning all of his hearers about in verses 14-36. Such severe condemnation may not seem to be loving words from Jesus (Mt 23:37), but he was in fact *"seeking"* these *"lost"* people because they obviously needed to hear the Law *first* before the brilliant light of the Gospel could penetrate their *"dark"* hearts (v 35) or their rocky or weedy soil (8:12-14). Like their ancestors, they were *"a stubborn people"* (Deu 9:13; Lk 20:9-19; [39]M. I. Lk 3:3a). **2)** Jesus' condemnation in verse 52, *"You did not enter yourselves, and you hindered those who were entering"* is, perhaps, his most severe warning. These men were *"the tenants,"* the spiritual leaders of the Jews (20:10), who had the responsibility to teach God's Word to their people (Gen 12:1-3: [40]M. M. Ac 13:46). Yet, they not only failed to heed his Word themselves and be responsible for caring for their own faith, but even worse, they likewise hindered other people from hearing God's holy Word. They were actively taking *"away the key of knowledge"* (v 52), the true *"light"* (v 33). That is incredibly evil! They were full slaves of Satan himself, true *"wolves"* who were trying to destroy the precious lambs that they should have been guarding (10:3). *"Woe"* to them indeed (17:2; 20:16; [41]M. I. Lk 3:3a)!

11:53-54 Nevertheless, Jesus' Words of warning and condemnation fell on deaf ears. As a matter of fact, his heavenly Father soon used these same men to kill his own beloved Son in order to carry out his plan of salvation (23:18-21). His gracious plan had to be fulfilled, but how terrible for them that they were the very ones who were responsible for being the terrible instruments that the Father used to murder their own Messiah and Lord (5:17; [42]M. I. Lk 8:18)!

---

[1] M. I. Lk 11:10: Christians should continuously pray to their heavenly Father and always depend on his grace, and not on their own feeble strength, because he always loves them.

[2] M. M. Ro 8:15: God the Father has adopted all people from all nations, who trust in Jesus, as his own dear children.

³ M. I. Lk 4:15: Christians should seize every opportunity to proclaim the Gospel to lost people of all nations.

⁴ M. I. Lk 12:40: Christians should "eat" God's Word every day in order to keep their faith strong, so that they are always ready for their Lord's return.

⁵ M. M. Tit 3:5: When a person is baptized, God graciously saves him and gives him the gift of a new birth from his indwelling Holy Spirit; and he does this because his mercy is so great, and not because of any good deeds that that person has done.

⁶ M. I. Ro 10:17c: Christians should grow in their Lord's grace by daily listening to his Word, and also by frequently eating his true body and drinking his true blood in Holy Communion.

⁷ M. I. Lk 4:15: Christians should seize every opportunity to proclaim the Gospel to lost people of all nations.

⁸ M. M. 1 Pe 1:7: God graciously allows Christians to suffer now for a little while so that their faith, which is as precious as gold that perishes even though it is tested by fire, may be proved genuine through the testing and also give glory and honor to Jesus Christ when God reveals him on the Last Day.

⁹ M. I. Lk 11:3: Christians should daily ask their heavenly Father for the physical and spiritual food that they need every day, in order to be able to carry out their mission to the world.

¹⁰ M. I. Lk 11:10: Christians should continuously pray to their heavenly Father and always depend on his grace, and not on their own feeble strength, because he always loves them.

¹¹ M. M. Eph 2:2: All unbelievers follow the world's evil way; and instead of obeying God, they obey Satan, who controls them as his slaves because he is the evil ruler of the spiritual powers in space.

¹² M. M. Ro 10:17a: The Holy Spirit only creates and preserves faith by using the message of God's grace in his holy Word.

¹³ M. M. Ro 3:26: God is just and fair to everyone, both when he condemns all people of all nations because all have sinned, and also when he only declares those people righteous who have faith in Jesus.

¹⁴ M. M. Eph 1:13: When a person believes in Jesus because he has heard the true Gospel that Jesus has saved him, and he is baptized, God graciously gives him his promised in-dwelling Holy Spirit, so that everyone can see that he now belongs to God alone.

¹⁵ M. M. Eph 1:14: When the Holy Spirit dwells in a Christian's mission-heart, he is sure proof that that person will receive his eternal inheritance in heaven, which will bring all praise to God alone.

¹⁶ M. I. Lk 4:35: Christians should view every person as a whole person, and show him compassion by caring for both his physical and spiritual needs as they go on their mission.

¹⁷ M. I. Lk 3:8: Christians should always be prepared to boldly and publicly refute false teaching, so that Satan cannot easily deceive people.

¹⁸ M. I. Lk 11:10: Christians should continuously pray to their heavenly Father and always depend on his grace, and not on their own feeble strength, because he always loves them.

¹⁹ M. I. Lk 4:4: When Satan attacks Christians on their mission they should wield the sword of God's Word by quoting from it, and not depend on their own strength.

²⁰ M. I. Lk 4:35: Christians should view every person as a whole person, and show him compassion by caring for both his physical and spiritual needs as they go on their mission.

[21] M. M. Mt 2:6: Jesus was born in Bethlehem, so that he could be the King of the new Israel and rule over them as their dear Shepherd.

[22] M. M. Eph 2:2: All unbelievers follow the world's evil way; and instead of obeying God, they obey Satan, who controls them as his slaves because he is the evil ruler of the spiritual powers in space.

[23] M. M. Lk 13:24: The only way to enter the Kingdom of God is to have faith in Jesus as one's Savior.

[24] M. M. Eph 1:21: God has given Jesus his almighty power to rule as King of all kings over Satan and all of his evil angels and demons until the Last Day and forever.

[25] M. M. Lk 13:24: The only way to enter the Kingdom of God is to have faith in Jesus as one's Savior.

[26] M. M. Ro 10:17a: The Holy Spirit only creates and preserves faith by using the message of God's grace in his holy Word.

[27] M. M. Ro 4:11: All Christians from every nation on earth belong to the spiritual family of Abraham, the Church because they share the same faith in Jesus that their father had.

[28] M. I. Lk 3:8: Christians should always be prepared to boldly and publicly refute false teaching, so that Satan cannot easily deceive people.

[29] M. M. Jn 20:8: God gave faith in Jesus to people who personally saw that the tomb of Jesus was empty, because it proved that he was alive.

[30] M. M. Ro 1:16b: The Gospel is so powerful because it contains the central truth that Jesus rose from the dead with a glorified body in order to save all of his brothers and sisters from sin and death.

[31] M. M. Ac 13:46: As he did with the old Israel, God first of all strengthens the faith of the new Israel, the Church with his Word and Sacraments, so that they can go and witness to the lost people of all nations.

[32] M. M. Lk 1:1: Jesus came to seek and save all lost people from every nation on earth.

[33] M. M. Lk 12:48: God will justly condemn to eternal punishment all people who do not trust in Jesus as their Savior, but he will punish them by different degrees, according to how well they knew his will.

[34] M. M. Lk 1:1: Jesus came to seek and save all lost people from every nation on earth.

[35] M. I. Lk 8:18: Everyone is responsible for the spiritual condition of his own faith, because no one can do it for him.

[36] M. M. Lk 1:1: Jesus came to seek and save all lost people from every nation on earth.

[37] M. I. Lk 4:15: Christians should seize every opportunity to proclaim the Gospel to lost people of all nations.

[38] M. I. Lk 4:40: Christians should go and seek the lost one person at a time by focusing on each person's unique needs.

[39] M. I. Lk 3:3a: Christians should, in love, warn lost people who do not repent.

[40] M. M. Ac 13:46: As he did with the old Israel, God first of all strengthens the faith of the new Israel, the Church with his Word and Sacraments, so that they can go and witness to the lost people of all nations.

[41] M. I. Lk 3:3a: Christians should, in love, warn lost people who do not repent.

[42] M. I. Lk 8:18: Everyone is responsible for the spiritual condition of his own faith, because no

one can do it for him.

Chapter 12

Beware of the Leaven of the Pharisees 12:1-3

12:1 *In the meantime, when so many thousands of the people had gathered together that they were trampling one another, he began to say to his disciples first, "Beware of the leaven of the Pharisees, which is hypocrisy.*

12:2 *Nothing is covered up that will not be revealed, or hidden that will not be known.*

12:3 *Therefore whatever you have said in the dark shall be heard in the light, and what you have whispered in private rooms shall be proclaimed on the housetops.*

12:1-2 (1) *"The leaven of the Pharisees"* was, and still is, so dangerous and evil since it is, in essence, a theology of work-righteousness. It is Satan's own evil idea that a person can earn God's favor by obeying man-made rules or even God's Laws. The Pharisees were so hypocritical because they so proudly thought that they were perfect (18:11), that they had actually obeyed all of God's Laws. And this idea is so dangerous because mankind's proud, sinful human nature loves to think that he can do something that is worthy of God's praise. But it's all Satan's lie, because all so-called "good" deeds that a person does that are not based on faith (Heb 11:6) are *"like a polluted garment"* before God (Is 64:6). Since there is only one Way to enter God's Kingdom—through faith in Jesus ([1]M. M. Lk 13:24), there obviously is also only *one wrong* way—Satan's way of work-righteousness. And therefore, all other religions, whatever many, many names sinful people may give them, follow this wrong way (M. M. Gal 3:10). (However, when a Christian obeys God out of gratitude for receiving his grace in Christ, he is doing a truly "good" deed that pleases God ([2]M. M. Ro 1:5).) **2)** But when will this lie of Satan finally be exposed as evil *"leaven"* (v 1)? At the final judgment, it will be God, the righteous judge who will eternally condemn all who tried to earn their own salvation by work-righteousness. He will, once and for all, reveal his final judgment that his own beloved Son, Jesus is the only person who was able to, and did obey all of his Laws perfectly on behalf of all of his brothers and sisters (Jn 19:30). And only those who trusted in him will enter his eternal, glorious Kingdom (M. M. Lk 13:24 & [3]Ro 3:24).

The One to Fear 12:4-7

12:4 *"I tell you, my friends, do not fear those who kill the body, and after that have nothing more that they can do.*
12:5 *But I will warn you whom to fear: fear him who, after he has killed, has authority to cast into hell. Yes, I tell you, fear him!*
12:6 *Are not five sparrows sold for two pennies? And not one of them is forgotten before God.*
12:7 *Why, even the hairs of your head are all numbered. Fear not; you are of more value than many sparrows.*

12:4 (1) In verse 12:1, Jesus warned his disciples about *"the leaven of the Pharisees;"* then, here, in verse 4, he warned them about the Pharisees a second time, "do not fear those who kill the [physical] body, and after that have nothing more that they can do." Jesus was, of course, a bitter enemy of the Pharisees, because he was becoming far more popular than they were which probably reduced their illegal "earnings" at the temple and elsewhere. And they therefore also hated anyone who followed Jesus. Thus, Jesus knew that these Pharisees would soon try to do his disciples physical harm by bringing them *"before the synagogues and the rulers and the authorities"* (v 11). Since they had full control of everything in their society, they could punish them physically and even murder them, but they could do nothing to take away the eternal life that their dear *"friend"* (v 4) had promised them. Therefore, his disciples should not be afraid of them because of the physical harm that they may do to them. It's a new mission imperative. M. I. Lk 12:4: Christians should not be afraid of the physical harm that their human or spiritual enemies may do to them, because they can only harm them physically, but they cannot take away their eternal life with Jesus, their dear friend. **2)** If a Christian is afraid that his government may physically harm him because of his faith, that is serious enough, but if it is his own <u>father or mother</u> that he is afraid of, it is far more agonizing. It may be possible for him to leave his country to escape persecution, but his family is <u>always</u> his family whether he leaves them or stays at home; yet if his parents disown and disinherit him because he is a Christian, his whole life is finished, <u>done</u>. He may as well be dead. However, sadly, this very thing is still happening all over the world. The vast majority of the world today is the so-called "developing world" where the extended family means <u>everything</u> in a person's life; and it is in these same parts of the world where Christianity is still a minority religion. Therefore, unfortunately, Christian persecution is still rampant; and these suffering Christians urgently need the prayers of the Church ([4]M. I. Lk 11:10 & [5]M. M. Lk 6:22).

12:5 (1) But who is Jesus warning his disciples about in verse 5? He says, *"Yes, I tell you, fear <u>him</u>!"* It is God, of course, whom they should fear, because he will, on the final Judgment Day, *"cast into hell"* those who do not trust in Jesus. Therefore, everyone who does not trust in God or fear or obey him should be filled with terrible fear of his final, eternal condemnation ([6]M. M. Ro 3:26). Sadly, however, some people never do have faith in Jesus, but others may have had faith in him at one time but lost it: some have lost their faith because they feared their human and spiritual enemies more than they feared God (v 4), while others lost their faith because they did not faithfully feed their faith with God's holy Word (8:12-14; [7]M. I. Lk 12:40). **2)** However, it's also very important to add *two* more truths. **a)** First of all, when Jesus says in verse 5, *"Yes, I tell you, fear him [God]!"* he is emphasizing that, on one hand, his heavenly Father is a <u>just</u> God who hates *sin*, but, on the other hand, he dearly loves the <u>sinner</u> (Rom 5:8). In fact, he hates sin so much that he was willing to sacrifice the life of his own <u>innocent</u> Son, Jesus in order to pay the awful price of mankind's sin (2 Cor 5:21)! However, the heavenly Father has also <u>always</u> had a mission-heart that <u>always</u> compels him to love <u>all</u> people. He never wants to have to *"cast"* even one person *"into hell"* (v 5; 1 Tim 2:4). No, he is <u>not</u> an angry God who is eagerly waiting for the day when he can finally destroy sinners forever. **b)** Secondly, the *"fear"* that Jesus is talking about in verse 5 is one kind of fear, that God will punish a person who has disobeyed him; however, there are other Bible passages, such as (Ps 111:10), that talk about different kind of fear of God. It says that *"the fear of the LORD is the beginning of wisdom."* This kind of fear is the only kind of fear that a Christian should have for his heavenly Father; it is an awe of his almighty power and authority because it is far beyond the ability of any mere human being to know and understand him (Is 40:28; Rom 11:33-34). But a Christian's fear of him is combined with a humble trust in him, a faith that his gracious God has placed in his heart. Therefore, this kind of fear also emphasizes God's amazing grace for us sinners, because no one deserves his amazing love—no one. "We are all beggars before him," as Martin Luther is reported to have once said ([8]M. M. Ro 3:26 & [9]Ro 4:3).

Acknowledge Christ Before Men 12:8-12

12:8   *"And I tell you, everyone who acknowledges me before men, the Son of Man also will acknowledge before the angels of God,*
12:9   *but the one who denies me before men will be denied before the angels of God.*
12:10 *And everyone who speaks a word against the Son of Man will be forgiven, but the one who blasphemes against the Holy Spirit will not be forgiven.*
12:11 *And when they bring you before the synagogues and the rulers and the authorities, do not be anxious about how you should defend yourself or what you should say,*
12:12 *for the Holy Spirit will teach you in that very hour what you ought to say."*

12:8-9 (1) Fear of one's spiritual enemies is extremely powerful; it can make even the strongest Christian become a feeble coward, so that he even *"denies"* his Lord Jesus (v 9). And a Christian who goes on his Lord's mission and tries to tough it out against his enemies on his own strength will surely fail. But the heavenly Father's love is far more powerful than any other force in the universe; therefore, when a

Christian depends on his Father's proven love and grace, his dear Lord Jesus will *"acknowledge him"* (v 8) as his own brother or sister on the Last Day. Therefore, a Christian's personal relationship with his Lord Jesus is the most precious personal relationship that he can ever have ([10]M. M. Lk 13:24), especially since his Lord's love is <u>eternal</u>; while all other human relationships—as precious as they are—are only temporary. It's a new mission message. M. M. Lk 12:8: On Judgment Day, Jesus will acknowledge before his heavenly Father that all Christians are his brothers and sisters. **2)** However, it's obvious that not all people *"acknowledge"* Jesus as their Lord. Some of them have heard about him, yet, for various reasons, have *"denied"* him (v 9); however, others have, also for various reasons, never even heard his name. How incredibly sad that is! And who is to blame? Obviously it is the Christian Church that has utterly failed! Just like ancient Israel utterly failed, even though they received the same call from God through Abraham (Gen 12: 1-3) to spread the Gospel message about the coming Messiah, the new Israel, the Church has likewise sinned in the same way ([11]M. M. Ac 13:46). And yet one of the main reasons why the Lord Jesus came to this earth was *"to seek and to save the lost"* (19:10; [12]M. M. Lk 1:1). When will the Church finally wake up, begin to listen to the mission-heart that the Holy Spirit has given them, and obediently depend on their Lord's grace to go and seek the lost by using their own heart languages ([13]M. M. Ro 1:5)?

12:10 (1) It's important to understand verse 10 in the context of verses (4-12) where Jesus warns Christians to not lose their faith because they are afraid of their spiritual enemies. When Christians boldly tell the Gospel about Jesus, the Holy Spirit uses their message to create faith in the hearts of their hearers. Therefore, a person who is afraid of his spiritual enemies and *"denies"* that he knows Jesus (v 9) *"blasphemes against the Holy Spirit,"* since it was the Spirit who gave him the gracious <u>gift</u> of faith in Jesus. Thus, it's a terrible sin to spurn such an undeserved gift by denying him (vs 52-53; 8:18; 22:55-62; Heb 6:4-6). However, our gracious God always has a loving mission-heart, and therefore, he is extremely patient with those who persistently deny their Lord. He only very reluctantly may eventually harden a person's stony heart and confirm his eternal condemnation (Eph 4:30; [14]M. M. Ro 11:7). **2)** At times Christians become worried that they have committed this unforgivable sin against the Holy Spirit (v 10), however, their concern should, in fact, be a sure sign that they have <u>not</u> done so, since no one commits this sin unknowingly. It's always a <u>deliberate</u> sin or a sin of <u>conscious</u> indifference (11:42-52; 8:12-14; Mt 18:17; [15]M. I. Lk 3:3a).

12:11-12 No doubt Luke was thinking about his fellow missionaries, Peter and John (Ac 4) as well as his fellow missionary traveler, Paul (Ac 21 and 24) as he wrote verses 11-12. It was not until after Jesus' resurrection and ascension that his disciples finally and fully realized that everything that Jesus had said and done were, in fact, true; they now knew that he was exactly who he said he was, their gracious Lord and Savior (18:31; 2 Cor 1:20). Therefore, this knowledge filled them with the bold faith to stand before their religious and secular leaders *"to acknowledge"* Jesus as their Lord (v 8; Ac 4:13). They did so, just as Jesus said in verse 12, *"The Holy Spirit will teach you...what you ought to say."* He was, of course, the one who sent them on this mission and gave them this message to proclaim (Ac 1:5, 8; 9:1; [16]M. M. Mt 5:14). It's another new mission imperative. M. I. Lk 12:12: Christians should go and tell the Gospel depending on the Holy Spirit to teach them what they should say.

The Parable of the Rich Fool 12:13-21

12:13 *Someone in the crowd said to him, "Teacher, tell my brother to divide the inheritance with me."*
12:14 *But he said to him, "Man, who made me a judge or arbitrator over you?"*
12:15 *And he said to them, "Take care, and be on your guard against all covetousness, for one's life does not consist in the abundance of his possessions."*
12:16 *And he told them a parable, saying, "The land of a rich man produced plentifully,*
12:17 *and he thought to himself, 'What shall I do, for I have nowhere*

12:18 *And he said, 'I will do this: I will tear down my barns and build larger ones, and there I will store all my grain and my goods.*
12:19 *And I will say to my soul, Soul, you have ample goods laid up for many years; relax, eat, drink, be merry.'*
12:20 *But God said to him, 'Fool! This night your soul is required of you, and the things you have prepared, whose will they be?'*
12:21 *So is the one who lays up treasure for himself and is not rich toward God."*

Do Not Be Anxious 12:22-34

12:22 *And he said to his disciples, "Therefore I tell you, do not be anxious about your life, what you will eat, nor about your body, what you will put on.*
12:23 *For life is more than food, and the body more than clothing.*
12:24 *Consider the ravens: they neither sow nor reap, they have neither storehouse nor barn, and yet God feeds them. Of how much more value are you than the birds!*
12:25 *And which of you by being anxious can add a single hour to his span of life?*
12:26 *If then you are not able to do as small a thing as that, why are you anxious about the rest?*
12:27 *Consider the lilies, how they grow: they neither toil nor spin, yet I tell you, even Solomon in all his glory was not arrayed like one of these.*
12:28 *But if God so clothes the grass, which is alive in the field today, and tomorrow is thrown into the oven, how much more will he clothe you, O you of little faith!*
12:29 *And do not seek what you are to eat and what you are to drink, nor be worried.*
12:30 *For all the nations of the world seek after these things, and your Father knows that you need them.*
12:31 *Instead, seek his kingdom, and these things will be added to you.*

12:32 *"Fear not, little flock, for it is your Father's good pleasure to give you the kingdom.*
12:33 *Sell your possessions, and give to the needy. Provide yourselves with moneybags that do not grow old, with a treasure in the heavens that does not fail, where no thief approaches and no moth destroys.*
12:34 *For where your treasure is, there will your heart be also.*

12:13-34 Jesus warned his disciples against worrying about having enough food and shelter in these two long sections, verses 13-21 & 22-34, since material *"possessions"* are another enemy that Satan often uses to try to hinder Christians from carrying out their Lord's mission. The love of money can *"choke them"* so that *"their fruit does not mature"* (8:14); and the fruit that his mission-heart longs most earnestly for them to bear is more and more seeds of his holy Word that have sprouted in the hearts of many lost people. Even though money itself is not sinful, human pride teams up with the love of money and power (1 Tim 6:10) in order to completely change a Christian's priorities. Then, when he has many material *"possessions,"* he may be in grave danger of losing his true *"treasure in the heavens"* (v 33). And this is incredibly sad, since his Lord Jesus gave up his riches in heaven, in order to make that person truly, eternally rich through faith in him alone (2 Cor 8:9; [17]M. M. Ro 10:17a).

12:31-32 When Jesus urges us Christians to *"seek his kingdom"* (v 31), he is saying the same thing as telling us to *"pray earnestly to the Lord of the harvest to send out laborers into his harvest"* (10:2). When the King of kings rules in the heart of a person, his Lord does not want him to be just sitting around and enjoying his blessings; rather, his King has graciously given him a mission-heart, so that his new heart would continuously move him to gratefully seek every opportunity to expand his kingdom (v 43). This includes both telling the Gospel through his words and his deeds and also by praying that his kingdom would expand in many other ways ([18]M. M. Mt 5:14 & [19]Lk 10:2a).

You Must Be Ready 12:35-48

12:35 *"Stay dressed for action and keep your lamps burning,*
12:36 *and be like men who are waiting for their master to come home from the wedding feast, so that they may open the door to him at once when he comes and knocks.*
12:37 *Blessed are those servants whom the master finds awake when he comes. Truly, I say to you, he will dress himself for service and have them recline at table, and he will come and serve them.*
12:38 *If he comes in the second watch, or in the third, and finds them awake, blessed are those servants!*
12:39 *But know this, that if the master of the house had known at what hour the thief was coming, he would not have left his house to be broken into.*
12:40 *You also must be ready, for the Son of Man is coming at an hour you do not expect."*
12:41 *Peter said, "Lord, are you telling this parable for us or for all?"*
12:42 *And the Lord said, "Who then is the faithful and wise manager, whom his master will set over his household, to give them their portion of food at the proper time?*
12:43 *Blessed is that servant whom his master will find so doing when he comes.*
12:44 *Truly, I say to you, he will set him over all his possessions.*
12:45 *But if that servant says to himself, 'My master is delayed in coming,' and begins to beat the male and female servants, and to eat and drink and get drunk,*
12:46 *the master of that servant will come on a day when he does not expect him and at an hour he does not know, and will cut him in pieces and put him with the unfaithful.*
12:47 *And that servant who knew his master's will but did not get ready or act according to his will, will receive a severe beating.*
12:48 *But the one who did not know, and did what deserved a beating, will receive a light beating. Everyone to whom much was given, of him much will be required, and from him to whom they entrusted much, they will demand the more.*

12:35-46 (1) The work that the *"Master,"* Jesus (v 43) had given his disciples in (9:1-6) and in (10:1-12) was to go and proclaim the Gospel. Then, before his ascension, he repeated his gracious assignment in (Ac 1:8) when he told his disciples, *"you will be my witnesses."* But the Master of the Church will one day soon return on the Last Day, after we too have finished our assignments in every corner of the lost world. In verses 35-46, then, Jesus repeatedly urged his servants to always *"be ready"* (v 40) because he *"will come on a [the Last] day when he does not expect him"* ([20]M. I. Lk 12:40). **2)** Some have suggested, quite wrongly, that a loving Master would not make his servants wonder when he will return (Mt 24:36; Mk 13:32; Ac 1:7). However, if we, his servants knew exactly when he will return, our sinful human natures would most likely make us lazy and quick to doubt his promise to come again; therefore, it's doubtful that very many of us would be ready with a strong faith on the day that he returns. That is why Jesus most graciously urged us in verse 40, *"You also must be ready, for the Son of Man is coming at an hour you do not expect."* And the only way for us to *"be ready"* every moment of every day is to always have a strong faith in our Lord—always depending on his rich grace. And there is only one food that supplies the strength that our faith needs—his holy Word ([21]M. M. Ro 10:17a). By daily "eating" God's Word in order to keep our faith strong, we will also *"stay dressed for action"* (v 35) and on the job of spreading the Gospel because *"the harvest is plentiful, but the laborers are few"* (10:2). It's a new mission imperative. M. I. Lk 12:40: Christians should "eat" God's Word every day in order to keep their faith strong, so that they are always ready for their Lord's return.

12:47-48 Jesus talks in verses 47-48 about people who know or do not know God's will; and therefore, this raises at least three issues about how human beings know God's will. **a)** First of all, when God makes every human being in his image, he gives them natural knowledge of his will, his Law—knowing what is right and wrong (Col 3:10; [22]M. M. Ro 2:15a). However, original sin and actual sin corrupts this natural knowledge (Rom 1:21); therefore, only God's holy Word can correct this natural knowledge because it is the only source of truth ([23]M. M. Jn 14:6). **b)** Secondly, Jesus talks about those who *"know their Master's will"* in verse 47 and then talks about those who don't know it in verse

48. Obviously, he is not talking about the natural knowledge that everyone has. Rather, he's talking about knowledge that God revealed in the Bible—hearing and understanding his Word. Therefore, this raises some issues about how people actually hear and understand God's holy Word, because, in the history of the world, **aa)** some people have heard it in their own heart language so that they truly heard it and understood both the Law and the Gospel, **bb)** some have heard it less clearly in a second language, **cc)** and some people have not received it in any form at all.

12:47 In verse 47, Jesus refers to two groups of people: *"that servant who knew his master's will;"* and in verse 48 he refers to the same groups: *"everyone to whom much was given."* The two groups of people are: **a)** The first group that he most obviously was referring to was the nation of Israel, because God certainly most graciously blessed them more than any other nation in the world by directly revealing his holy Word to them through his prophets in their own heart-language. What a huge blessing that was! They received the full knowledge of God's will—not in a foreign language, and not only in spoken words that they would have to try to remember—but written down in their own mother tongue and inspired directly by his Holy Spirit! How earnestly the mission-heart of God has sought them! And furthermore, what a high privilege and responsibility it was for them as well! God richly blessed them, so that they would be a blessing to each other and to all other Gentile nations (Gen 12:1-3). Yet, for most of their history they seldom did so (7:9; 10:12; 11:31). **b)** The second group that Jesus was referring to was all people who have had the privilege of receiving a translation of the Bible (or at least portions of it) in their own heart-language or in a second language that they can understand (Mt 13:19). This too is a privilege that only a limited number of people have enjoyed in the history of the world. (And no other language has received more translations than the English language.) **aa)** Sadly, we only hear about one Bible translation in the Old Testament era; the Old Testament was translated in the 3rd century BC into Koine Greek, which is called "The Septuagint." "Koine" means common, therefore, it was a common language that people used as a second language; and it was not a first, heart-language for anyone in that era. **bb)** Then, in the New Testament era, the Holy Spirit inspired men to write the New Testament in another form of Koine Greek, because it was a language that many, many people understood. But, once again, it was not a first, heart-language for anyone in that era. **cc)** And then, for sixteen centuries, the Church translated the Bible into only <u>one</u> language: Latin. St. Jerome was commissioned to translate the Bible into Latin in 382, which is called "the Vulgate." And it became the official Bible of the Church; but Latin was no longer anyone's heart-language. It was not until after the Reformation in the 16th century that the Church finally began to put serious effort into translating the Bible into a significant number of languages. It's a sad, sad history! So very many people in this long, sad history never had a chance to hear and understand the Bible clearly! How incredibly sad God's mission-heart must be ([24]M. M. Ac 13:46)!

12:48 (1) *"The servant who did not know his Master's will"* that Jesus refers to in verse 48 is a person who has <u>never</u> heard the Law and the Gospel about Jesus; therefore, he has no way of knowing God's holy will. Once again, Jesus is obviously not referring to the partial knowledge of God's will that everyone has at his birth, as was discussed above. Rather he is referring to the countless numbers of people from every generation in the history of the world who never heard the Gospel because the nation of Israel in the Old Testament era was <u>not</u> faithful in telling it to them, nor has the new Israel, the Church been faithful in spreading the Gospel message. (What a terrible sin both the old and the new Israel have committed and continue to commit!) How sad it is for all of these people who <u>never</u> had a chance to hear the Gospel! And how will God, who has a mission-heart that is both gracious and righteous, judge these people on the Last Day? Jesus answers this question in verse 48 when he says that he <u>will</u> punish them (because he did give them partial knowledge of his will at birth), but they *"will receive a <u>light</u> beating"* ([25]M. M. Ro 3:26). **2)** From time to time, Africans asked me whether God will condemn their ancestors because they never heard the Gospel and did not believe in Jesus. Verse 48 makes it clear that God will give some punishment to <u>all</u> people who do not believe in Jesus as their Savior, no matter what the reason for their unbelief may have been.

However, the following true story makes one wonder whether it's possible that many more people have heard the Gospel than we are aware of. An expatriate missionary to the Yala people in Nigeria in the late 1950's, who did not know their language, tried to preach the Gospel to them by using a Yala interpreter for some months. But then he began to notice that the interpreter never said the name of Jesus. However, when the missionary sternly confronted him with his apparent failure to interpret accurately, the interpreter said that his people already knew who Jesus was! But his Yala name was "Orede." He then told the missionary everything that the Yala people knew about Orede; and it was obvious that Orede was Jesus; but the pronunciation of Jesus' name had become distorted. So when and how did the Yala people hear about Jesus? We can only wonder. But this story should also make us very cautious about saying that a certain group of people never had a chance to hear the Gospel about Jesus (M. M. Ro 3:26).

12:47-48 Therefore, we learn from verses 47-48 that God, the <u>righteous</u> judge, will, on the Last Judgment Day, condemn to eternal punishment <u>all</u> people who did not obey him and trust in Jesus as their Savior. However, he will separate them into two groups and the <u>degrees</u> of their punishment will not be the same. **a)** The first group is in verse 47, *"that servant who <u>knew</u> his master's will but did not get ready or act according to his will, will receive a severe beating."* Of course, these people did <u>not</u> deserve to receive the gracious gift of hearing and understanding God's will clearly and fully in his holy Word; but because they failed to obey him and believe in his son, Jesus, they <u>do</u> deserve <u>severe</u> punishment (v 47). **b)** And the second group is in verse 48, *"the one who did <u>not</u> know, and did what deserved a beating, will receive a <u>light</u> beating."* God is a righteous judge and will also have to give some punishment to those who didn't know his will completely, but disobeyed him. Perhaps they didn't hear the Law and Gospel in their own mother tongue, or perhaps they heard it in a language that they understood poorly (Mt 13:19), or perhaps they didn't hear it at all. At first, it may seem that God is not just and fair when he condemns them; however, these people will, in fact, have no excuse, because God has graciously made every human being in his image with some knowledge of what is right and wrong (Rom 14:23; [26]M. M. Ro 2:15a). However, even though original sin has corrupted this natural knowledge (Ps 51:5), every human being has some sense of what is right and wrong. It's a new mission message. M. M. Lk 12:48: On Judgment Day, God will justly condemn all people who disobeyed him to eternal punishment in hell; but those who knew his will the best will receive the most punishment.

Not Peace, but Division 12:49-53

12:49 *"I came to cast fire on the earth, and would that it were already kindled!*
12:50 *I have a Baptism to be baptized with, and how great is my distress until it is accomplished!*
12:51 *Do you think that I have come to give peace on earth? No, I tell you, but rather division.*
12:52 *For from now on in one house there will be five divided, three against two and two against three.*
12:53 *They will be divided, father against son and son against father, mother against daughter and daughter against mother, mother-in-law against her daughter-in-law and daughter-in-law against mother-in-law."*

12:49-50 When Jesus says, *"I have a Baptism to be baptized with"* in verse 50, he indicates that he was already beginning to suffer by just thinking about the *"fire"* (v 49) of the horrible suffering that he would soon have to endure on the cross. His deep love for all lost people was, therefore, already apparent, since he willingly suffered, to some degree, for us, his brothers and sisters for about 33 <u>years</u>—not just for a few days. Therefore, when Jesus refers to his future suffering by calling it his *"Baptism"* in verse 50, he is using a very fitting figure of speech, since a person does literally <u>die</u> spiritually when he is baptized in the name of the Triune God. In fact, Jesus endured two Baptisms of suffering. **a)** First, he began to die to sin for sinful mankind in his own water Baptism (3:21; Rom 6:3). **b)** His cross, then, was his second Baptism, where, as the true God/man, he did literally die both physically and spiritually in

order to *"save the lost"* (23:46; [27]M. M. Lk 1:27 & [28]Heb 13:20).
12:51-53 (1) Since Jesus obviously has a mission-heart and purposely came to earth *"to seek and to save the lost"* (19:10), why would he now say that he came to *"cast fire on the earth"* (v 49) and bring *"division"* in families (v 51)? How can a God who *"is love"* (1 Jn 4:17) show love by causing the *"fire"* of division? Jesus is, of course, not dishonoring the fourth commandment here; rather, he is using a hyperbole to emphasize a vital truth. Even though family relationships are the most important human relationships in all cultures, if a Christian's family tries to force him to deny his spiritual relationship with Jesus, he must suffer the severe pain of breaking his family relationships in order to cling to his much more important, eternal relationship with Jesus. There can be no room for compromise; he must face either the *"fire"* of division in his family (v 49) or the literal fire in hell (3:17; Heb 10:27) and eternal separation from Jesus—there is no middle ground (vs 8-9; 14:26; [29]M. M. Lk 13:24 & [30]M. I. Lk 12:51). **2)** It's painful to have other human enemies, but it's far more painful to make your own family your bitter enemies because of your faith in Jesus. Everyone in every culture rightfully expects their family to love them; therefore, for a Christian to be afraid of their family because they want to kill you is terrible for anyone, but it's even more terrible in "developing world" cultures where the extended family is often the most important unit in the society. Nevertheless, the value of an eternal, loving relationship with Jesus is beyond comparison. Who can measure the value of what Jesus did *"to save the lost"* and say that the love of their human father is more important than that (1 Pet 1:18-19; Heb 12:14)? It's a new mission imperative. M. I. Lk 12:51: Christians should cling to their faith relationship with Jesus at all costs, even if it means suffering the pain of breaking their loving, but temporary family relationships, so that they can live with him in heaven forever. **3)** Furthermore, Jesus once again proclaimed the whole truth and hid nothing from his hearers, so that people would not follow him because they thought that, if they followed him, they would always live a peaceful life, and then be surprised later when they faced suffering because of their faith in him. Rather, Jesus always wants people to follow him because they respond to his deep

love for them and love him more than anyone else, even though it may make their family angry, and even though it may mean suffering here on earth ([31]M. M. Lk 6:22).

Interpreting the Time 12:54-56

12:54 *He also said to the crowds, "When you see a cloud rising in the west, you say at once, 'A shower is coming.' And so it happens.*
12:55 *And when you see the south wind blowing, you say, 'There will be scorching heat,' and it happens.*
12:56 *You hypocrites! You know how to interpret the appearance of earth and sky, but why do you not know how to interpret the present time?*

12:56 *"The present time"* that Jesus refers to in verse 56 was the years that he lived on earth; and it was obviously the most vital and important time in the whole history of mankind. *"The Christ of God"* (9:20) was standing there in the presence of a crowd as their *"Immanuel"* (Mat 1:23); and they were the very *"lost"* people whom he was at that very moment *"seeking"* (19:10); yet many of his hearers lacked the faith of Peter to see who he was and confess his name (9:20). Now was their time to repent and believe in him, because tomorrow may be too late (v 20; 3:9; 7:31; 11:50; 19:42). As the saying goes, "They were so close, and yet oh so far!" The moment that any lost person hears the Gospel of Jesus is his or her "now" that may never return, even though, with his mission-heart, Jesus never ceases *"to seek the lost"* through his Church. Thus, the question for us is: Does the present day Church have the mission-heart to see the urgent need of lost people all over the world and then respond to his love by going out quickly on his mission ([32]M. I. Mt 7:14 & [33]M. M. Ac 13:46)?

Settle with your Accuser 12:57-59

12:57 *"And why do you not judge for yourselves what is right?*

12:58 *As you go with your accuser before the magistrate, make an effort to settle with him on the way, lest he drag you to the judge, and the judge hand you over to the officer, and the officer put you in prison.*

12:59 *I tell you, you will never get out until you have paid the very last penny."*

12:57-59 Beginning with verse 54, Jesus was speaking to the unbelieving crowd before him; and he condemns many of them in verses 57-59 for their failure to forgive others before it becomes a legal matter and they have to pay a fine. By implication, he was also warning his disciples to not follow their bad example. Rather, they should shine the bright light in their own mission-hearts into the evil society around them by quickly forgiving others, as their gracious Lord has forgiven them (Mt 5:21-26). Thus, their actions would be a powerful witness to them, which hopefully would lead to opportunities to tell them who Jesus really is ([34]M. I. 1 Thess 5:5).

---

[1] M. M. Lk 13:24: The only way to enter the Kingdom of God is to have faith in Jesus as one's Savior.

[2] M. M. Ro 1:5: The same Holy Spirit who creates faith and a new missionary nature in a person's heart also graciously empowers him to gratefully respond to his Lord's love by obeying him.

[3] M. M. Ro 3:24: Jesus lived a life of perfect obedience and shed his precious blood on the cross, in order to graciously set all nations free from sin, which a person only receives by faith in him.

[4] M. I. Lk 11:10: Christians should continuously pray to their heavenly Father and always depend on his grace, and not on their own feeble strength, because he always loves them.

[5] M. M. Lk 6:22: The Lord Jesus will surely bless a Christian in the midst of suffering for his sake; and he will also bless him with eternal life if he remains faithful to him.

[6] M. M. Ro 3:26: God is just and fair to everyone, both when he condemns all people of all nations because all have sinned, and also when he only declares those people righteous who have faith in Jesus.

[7] M. I. Lk 12:40: Christians should "eat" God's Word every day in order to keep their faith strong, so that they are always ready for their Lord's return.

[8] M. M. Ro 3:26: God is just and fair to everyone, both when he condemns all people of all nations because all have sinned, and also when he only declares those people righteous who have faith in Jesus.

[9] M. M. Ro 4:3: Faith in Jesus is a free <u>gift</u> that a person graciously receives from God and he does not earn.

[10] M. M. Lk 13:24: The <u>only</u> way to enter the Kingdom of God is to have <u>faith</u> in Jesus as one's Savior.

[11] M. M. Ac 13:46: As he did with the old Israel, God <u>first of all</u> strengthens the faith of the new Israel, the Church with his Word and Sacraments, so that they can go and witness to the lost people of all nations.

[12] M. M. Lk 1:1: Jesus came to seek and save <u>all</u> lost people from <u>every</u> nation on earth.

[13] M. M. Ro 1:5: The same Holy Spirit who creates <u>faith</u> and a new missionary <u>nature</u> in a person's heart also graciously empowers him to gratefully respond to his Lord's love by <u>obeying</u> him.

[14] M. M. Ro 11:7: After patiently waiting for a person to repent, God may ultimately eternally condemn him by hardening his heart and closing his ears to hear and understand his holy Word.

[15] M. I. Lk 3:3a: Christians should, in love, warn lost people who do not repent.

[16] M. M. Mt 5:14: When the Holy Spirit creates faith in a person's heart, he also graciously gives him a new mission-heart that is eager to shine the light of the Gospel throughout the whole world.

[17] M. M. Ro 10:17a: The Holy Spirit <u>only</u> creates and preserves faith by using the message of God's grace in his holy Word.

[18] M. M. Mt 5:14: When the Holy Spirit creates faith in a person's heart, he also graciously gives him a new mission-heart that is eager to shine the light of the Gospel throughout the whole world.

[19] M. M. Lk 10:2a: There are many people who are lost; and there are too few Christians who are eager to tell them the Gospel.

[20] M. I. Lk 12:40: Christians should "eat" God's Word every day in order to keep their faith strong, so that they are always ready for their Lord's return.

[21] M. M. Ro 10:17a: The Holy Spirit <u>only</u> creates and preserves faith by using the message of God's grace in his holy Word.

[22] M. M. Ro 2:15a: At his birth, and as part of his own image, God graciously gives knowledge of his moral Law to each human being: however, sin corrupts this knowledge.

[23] M. M. Jn 14:6: As the only Son of the heavenly Father, Jesus is the <u>only</u> Way to go to his Father, the <u>only</u> source of all Truth, and the <u>only</u> source of all Life.

[24] M. M. Ac 13:46: As he did with the old Israel, God <u>first of all</u> strengthens the faith of the new Israel, the Church with his Word and Sacraments, so that they can go and witness to the lost people of all nations.

[25] M. M. Ro 3:26: God is just and fair to <u>everyone</u>, both when he condemns <u>all</u> people of all nations because all have sinned, and also when he <u>only</u> declares those people righteous who have faith in Jesus.

[26] M. M. Ro 2:15a: At his birth, and as part of his own image, God graciously gives knowledge of his moral Law to each human being: however, sin corrupts this knowledge.

[27] M. M. Lk 1:27: Jesus had to be born as a true human being and as a true Jew in order to become the King of kings in his heavenly kingdom forever.

[28] M. M. Heb 13:20: As the great Shepherd, Jesus has proven his love for all nations by <u>dying</u> as

a holy sacrifice on the cross and <u>rising</u> from the dead for all.

[29] M. M. Lk 13:24: The <u>only</u> way to enter the Kingdom of God is to have <u>faith</u> in Jesus as one's Savior.

[30] M. I. Lk 12:51: Christians should cling to their faith relationship with Jesus at all costs, even if it means suffering the pain of breaking their loving, but temporary family relationships, so that they can live with him in heaven forever.

[31] M. M. Lk 6:22: The Lord Jesus will surely bless a Christian in the midst of suffering for his sake; and he will also bless him with eternal life if he remains faithful to him.

[32] M. I. Mt 7:14: Christians should hurry on their mission to the world because people who are lost have many enemies who lure them away from Jesus; and therefore, few of them find faith in Jesus which is the only gate into his Kingdom of life.

[33] M. M. Ac 13:46: As he did with the old Israel, God <u>first of all</u> strengthens the faith of the new Israel, the Church with his Word and Sacraments, so that they can go and witness to the lost people of all nations.

[34] M. I. 1 Thess 5:5: Christians should always witness to people who are living in spiritual darkness by living as children of light because their mission-hearts move them to share the love of Jesus.

Chapter 13

Repent or Perish 13:1-5

13:1 *There were some present at that very time who told him about the Galileans whose blood Pilate had mingled with their sacrifices.*
13:2 *And he answered them, "Do you think that these Galileans were worse sinners than all the other Galileans, because they suffered in this way?*
13:3 *No, I tell you; but unless you repent, you will all likewise perish.*
13:4 *Or those eighteen on whom the tower in Siloam fell and killed them: do you think that they were worse offenders than all the others who lived in Jerusalem?*
13:5 *No, I tell you; but unless you repent, you will all likewise perish."*

13:1-5 In the two tragic cases cited in verses 1-5, many people wrongly assumed that it was only the people who were killed who deserved their tragic death; but Jesus warned them in verses 3 and 5 that *"unless you repent, you will all likewise perish."* He said this because all people deserve to die because all people are sinful ([1]M. M. Ro 3:26). Therefore, instead of pointing their accusing fingers at others, they should repent of their own sins and turn to him since he is the only way to be saved. Jesus' mission-heart and his deep love for all lost people from all nations moved him to once again urge everyone to repent and believe in him to receive forgiveness for their sins ([2]M. I. Lk 3:3a).

The Parable of the Barren Fig Tree 13:6-9

13:6 *And he told this parable: "A man had a fig tree planted in his vineyard, and he came seeking fruit on it and found none.*
13:7 *And he said to the vinedresser, 'Look, for three years now I*

> *have come seeking fruit on this fig tree, and I find none. Cut it down. Why should it use up the ground?'*
>
> 13:8 *And he answered him, 'Sir, let it alone this year also, until I dig around it and put on manure.*
>
> 13:9 *Then if it should bear fruit next year, well and good; but if not, you can cut it down.'"*

13:6-9 In this parable in verses 6-9, Jesus himself is the owner of the vineyard who lovingly and patiently *"seeks the lost"* by waiting for them to bear the fruit of faith ([3]M. M. Lk 1:1 & [4]M. I. Lk 4:40). And the meaning of this parable is essentially the same whether *"the fig tree"* is a Christian or an unbeliever, since all people are lost and need to receive a repentant heart. All Christians are both saints and sinners; therefore, their life is a daily cycle of repentance and faith that is "fertilized" by the Law and the Gospel as they daily "eat" God's rich Word (Rom 6:4; [5]M. I. Lk 12:40). Likewise, an unbeliever too needs to respond to the same "fertilizer" of God's Word by repenting and believing in order to start the same cycle that other Christians live in ([6]M. M. Ro 10:17a).

A Woman with a Disabling Spirit 13:10-17

> 13:10 *Now he was teaching in one of the synagogues on the Sabbath.*
>
> 13:11 *And there was a woman who had had a disabling spirit for eighteen years. She was bent over and could not fully straighten herself.*
>
> 13:12 *When Jesus saw her, he called her over and said to her, "Woman, you are freed from your disability."*
>
> 13:13 *And he laid his hands on her, and immediately she was made straight, and she glorified God.*
>
> 13:14 *But the ruler of the synagogue, indignant because Jesus had healed on the Sabbath, said to the people, "There are six days in which work ought to be done. Come on those days and be healed, and not on the Sabbath day."*
>
> 13:15 *Then the Lord answered him, "You hypocrites! Does not each of you on the Sabbath untie his ox or his donkey from the manger*

> *and lead it away to water it?*
> 13:16 *And ought not this woman, a daughter of Abraham whom Satan bound for eighteen years, be loosed from this bond on the Sabbath day?"*
> 13:17 *As he said these things, all his adversaries were put to shame, and all the people rejoiced at all the glorious things that were done by him.*

13:10-17 (1) Obviously, Jesus both sought and healed people every day of the week, but when he did so on the Sabbath day, which was the day of worship it violated the man-made rules of the Pharisees since he was doing work. But of course, he never violated any of God's Laws; he continued to obey all of his Laws perfectly for our sakes, his brothers and sisters ([7]M. I. Lk 6:5). **2)** Jesus called this woman, *"a daughter of Abraham"* in verse 16. He meant it first of all in the literal sense to emphasize that she was a fellow Jew, whom the synagogue leader should naturally pity as a sister. But Jesus also meant that she was Abraham's spiritual daughter, just as he later called Lazarus a son of Abraham (16:22), and he also called Zacchaeus *"a son of Abraham"* (19:9) because all three of them had faith in God, and therefore, they were Abraham's true spiritual descendants (Gal 3:7). They all bore fruit (6:44) not because of their blood relationship to Abraham, but rather because of their faith relationship to Jesus, Abraham's God and Lord. And this woman was now physically free to return to blessing others on her mission as she had been blessed (Gen 12:1-3; [8]M. M. Ro 4:11). **3)** Jesus once again showed his power over the devil by setting the woman free from Satan's bonds (v 16). Therefore, once again he taught her and his disciples that they would not need to fear the devil when they went on his mission to the world ([9]M. M. Ro 3:24 & [10]Ro 5:1).

The Mustard Seed and the Leaven 13:18-21

> 13:18 *He said therefore, "What is the kingdom of God like? And to what shall I compare it?*
> 13:19 *It is like a grain of mustard seed that a man took and sowed in*

his garden, and it grew and became a tree, and the birds of the air made nests in its branches."

13:20 *And again he said, "To what shall I compare the kingdom of God?*

13:21 *It is like leaven that a woman took and hid in three measures of flour, until it was all leavened."*

13:18-21 (1) The person who plants *"a mustard seed"* (v 19) and the woman who puts the *"leaven"* in the dough (v 21) do not make them grow; although they do do the very significant mission work of planting God's Word. But, while both *"a mustard seed"* and "leaven" are small and appear to have little potential, the unbelievable growth of both of them shows that part of their very nature is the power to grow. How apt these stories are, then, to teach a powerful lesson to all who proclaim the Gospel of Jesus about the reign of the King of kings. Those who go and tell the Gospel are not the ones who make Jesus' Kingdom grow; rather it is the work of the Holy Spirit in using the Law and Gospel that they proclaim as his mighty and gracious sword to move a person to repentance and faith (8:11; 21:33; [11]M. I. Lk 8:11 & [12]M. M. Ro 10:17a). **2)** Nevertheless, the fact that the growth of Jesus' Kingdom does not depend on how a Christian uses his abilities to proclaim the Gospel does not give him the excuse to make a sloppy or careless presentation of the Gospel. The Holy Spirit has given each Christian his unique set of physical and spiritual abilities so that he would be able to do two things: **a)** He has the responsibility to depend on his Lord's grace to use all of his abilities to the fullest extent in order to seize every opportunity that he has to tell others about his dear Lord. **b)** And he has the responsibility to always focus his hearers' attention on Jesus and not on himself. The Holy Spirit can, then, most quickly and easily use his beautiful presentation of the message to touch the hearts of his hearers (M. I. Lk 8:11). And obviously, the Holy Spirit often does his amazing work even when we feel like we have made a poor presentation or when we are afraid that we may have said the wrong thing (2 Cor 4:6; M. I. Lk 8:11).

The Narrow Door 13:22-30

13:22 *He went on his way through towns and villages, teaching and journeying toward Jerusalem.*

13:23 *And someone said to him, "Lord, will those who are saved be few?" And he said to them,*

13:24 *"Strive to enter through the narrow door. For many, I tell you, will seek to enter and will not be able.*

13:25 *When once the master of the house has risen and shut the door, and you begin to stand outside and to knock at the door, saying, 'Lord, open to us,' then he will answer you, 'I do not know where you come from.'*

13:26 *Then you will begin to say, 'We ate and drank in your presence, and you taught in our streets.'*

13:27 *But he will say, 'I tell you, I do not know where you come from. Depart from me, all you workers of evil!'*

13:28 *In that place there will be weeping and gnashing of teeth, when you see Abraham and Isaac and Jacob and all the prophets in the kingdom of God but you yourselves cast out.*

13:29 *And people will come from east and west, and from north and south, and recline at table in the kingdom of God.*

13:30 *And behold, some are last who will be first, and some are first who will be last."*

13:22 (1) In verse 22, Luke says that Jesus deliberately continued his mission travels in order to *"to seek the lost"* (19:10); and, by his actions, he was, of course, also continuing to train his disciples to be his missionaries ([13]M. M. Lk 1:1 & [14]M. I. Lk 6:13). **2)** Furthermore, Luke also says in verse 22 that Jesus was likewise deliberately *"journeying toward Jerusalem"* to complete the second part of his mission *"to save the lost"* (v 33; 9:31; 5:1; 19:10). His disciples obviously could not do this part of Jesus' mission; and therefore, this was not part of his training process. However, his faithful determination to go to his death in Jerusalem should have given them a very powerful <u>example</u> of his mission-heart and his deep love for all of lost mankind, so that they could also see it and learn from it (M. I. Lk 6:13).

13:23-24 (1) First of all, it surely must have been very painful for Jesus to even hear this question in verse 23 verbalized, *"Lord, will those who are saved be few?"* Jesus willingly *"made himself nothing, taking the form of a servant, being born in the likeness of men"* (Phil 2:7), in order *"to seek and to save [all of] the lost"* (19:10). He therefore was at that very moment continuing to seek them one by one, so that not even one would be lost (2 Pet 3:9; 1 Tim 2:4; [15]M. I. Lk 4:40). Yet he at the same time knew that most people who are lost would not respond to his love with repentance, faith and love. This certainly dramatically increased his sorrow (v 34). **2)** *"The narrow door"* in verse 24 is the truth that a person can only receive the gracious gift of forgiveness by faith in Jesus as one's Savior. And the implied *"wide gate"* (Mt 7:13) to salvation is the sin of depending on one's own *work-righteousness*; and unfortunately, it's *"wide"* because it appears to be a very *easy* way to please God, therefore, most people choose that gate. Therefore, there are, in fact, only *two* kinds of religion in the world. **a)** The only true religion is for a person to trust in what Jesus has done for him to please God. **b)** In all other religions, people depend on their own work-righteousness to please God. And the sad truth is that all people who *"seek to enter"* the door to the Kingdom by work-righteousness *"will not be able"* to do so (v 24) because people who try to earn God's favor by doing good deeds only earn his eternal condemnation. It is the evil way of the *"leaven of the Pharisees"* (12:1). Furthermore, Jesus can say with certainty that they *"will not be able"* to enter, since he, the God/man is the only person who was able to earn salvation by obeying all of God's Laws perfectly since he was both true God and true man (10:25-37; 12:1; [16]M. M. Lk 1:27 & [17]Mt 1:22). His heavenly Father accepted only *his* sacrifice on the cross (Heb 10:9). Thus, *"the door"* of faith in Jesus truly is a very *"narrow door,"* but it must be so since there truly is no other way and there never will be another way. It is the only possible Way for a person to depend on God's grace alone (Jn 14:6). It's a new mission message. M. M. Lk 13:24: The only way to enter the Kingdom of God is to have faith in Jesus as one's Savior. **3)** Truly, there is only one *"narrow door"* (v 24) through which a person can enter the

Father's Kingdom. And this is the one vital reason why Jesus so urgently sought *"the lost,"* and why he continues this search for them through his holy Church yet today (19:10). Furthermore, this is the vital link between the two parts of Luke's Central Theme: Jesus *"came to seek and to save the lost."* It would have been pointless for him to seek them without saving them, in order to make those who trust in him his own dear brothers and sisters and live with him forever ([18]M. M. Lk 1:1).
13:25-30 Verses 25-30, Jesus teaches us that, on Judgment Day, God will judge two groups of people very differently. **a)** By his grace alone, the first group will enter through *"the narrow door"* of faith in Jesus and *"recline at table in the kingdom of God"* (v 29). These people will be from every nation on earth: both Jews, such as *"Abraham, Isaac, Jacob, and all the prophets"* (v 28), and also Gentiles who are *"from east and west, and from north and south"* (v 29; Rom 11:25-26). They heard the Law and the Gospel; and the Holy Spirit used this message to move them to repent of their sins and believe in Jesus, the only Way. They are the true sons and daughters of Abraham, not by blood, but by faith in God alone (Rom 4:11-13; [19]M. M. Ro 3:26). **b)** And on Judgment Day, God will condemn all of the people in the second group because they tried to enter his Kingdom through *"the wide gate"* (Mt 7:13) of earning salvation by their own self-righteous good deeds. They will be living in hell outside of God's Kingdom, which is a place of eternal suffering, of terrible *"weeping and gnashing of teeth"* (v 28). Some of them will be Jews who had the high privilege of actually seeing Jesus and hearing the Gospel from the King himself, but they did not repent and believe in him. They will proudly say on Judgment Day, *"We ate and drank in your presence, and you taught in our streets"* (v 26). But *"woe to"* them (10:13)! They proudly clung to the belief that their blood relationship with Abraham made them worthy of the Kingdom (3:8), or they tried other proud ways to try to earn the Kingdom by their own feeble human power ([20]M. M. Lk 12:48).

Lament over Jerusalem 13:31-35

13:31 *At that very hour some Pharisees came and said to him, "Get away from here, for Herod wants to kill you."*

13:32 *And he said to them, "Go and tell that fox, 'Behold, I cast out demons and perform cures today and tomorrow, and the third day I finish my course.*

13:33 *Nevertheless, I must go on my way today and tomorrow and the day following, for it cannot be that a prophet should perish away from Jerusalem.'*

13:34 *O Jerusalem, Jerusalem, the city that kills the prophets and stones those who are sent to it! How often would I have gathered your children together as a hen gathers her brood under her wings, and you would not!*

13:35 *Behold, your house is forsaken. And I tell you, you will not see me until you say, 'Blessed is he who comes in the name of the Lord!'"*

13:31-33 (1) Verses 32-33 are full of Jesus' resolute and faithful determination that he was going to complete both parts of his mission: "*seek* the lost" in King Herod's territory in spite of any danger from the king (vs 31-32), and "*save* the lost" in Jerusalem (v 22; 9:22, 31, 51; 17:11, 25; 18:31; 19:10, 28). These verses also imply that not even Satan could stop him from completing his mission ([21]M. M. Lk 1:1). **2)** It could only have been Jesus' mission-heart that is full of amazing grace and love for all of his brothers and sisters from all nations on earth that drove him with such faithful determination on his last journey to Jerusalem to die. If it had been any one of us who knew that we were facing such a horrendous death, we feeble human beings would only have been focused on ourselves, thinking constantly about how horrible the pain was going to be; but not so our dear Lord. One could almost say that the closer that that day came, and then the more intensely his pain increased, he thought less and less about his own needs. He only felt more and more compassion for others, for "*the lost*" around him. It's likewise incredible to observe, during his last journey, how often he focused on the needs of others—one person at a time (12:10; [22]M. I. Lk 4:35 & [23]Lk 4:40)! His love is far beyond our human comprehension (Eph 3:18). And furthermore, how deeply his amazing grace moves us to likewise eagerly seek the lost, one by one!

13:34 We may well wonder whether St. Paul may have been thinking of these words of Jesus when he wrote in (Rom 9:3), *"I could wish that I myself were accursed and cut off from Christ for the sake of my brothers, my kinsmen according to the flesh."* But of course, Jesus not only expressed deep love for his fellow Jews in this verse, but he actually carried it out by accepting his heavenly Father's curse on the cross for the sake of his Jewish brothers and sisters—as well as all of his Gentile brothers and sisters, of course (1:1). Paul also says in (Gal 3:13), *"Christ redeemed us from the curse of the Law by becoming a curse for us—for it is written, 'Cursed is everyone who is hanged on a tree'"* ([24]M. M. Lk 12:48). **2)** Nevertheless, it does not diminish Jesus' grace for all nations to add that Jesus did have a special love for his fellow Jews, as he clearly says in verse 34. In his mission-heart, God did graciously choose the nation of Israel to experience his grace first, although this high privilege came with great responsibility (1:54). It was also Jesus' responsibility to *"seek"* the people of Israel first (19:10; 1:2; Rom 1:16; [25]M. M. Ac 13:46).

13:35 Jesus knew that the capital city of his nation, Jerusalem would one day soon welcome him into the city as their King with these words, *"Blessed is the King who comes in the name of the Lord"* (19:38)! However, since apparently some of these same Jews also cursed him and condemned him to die on the cross a few days later (23:18-25), it seems very likely that many of them did not trust in him as their spiritual King at all (v 27). Therefore, Jesus had to very sadly say in verse 35, *"Your house is forsaken."* On the final Judgment Day, God will have to abandon them forever because they refused to trust in his Son, whom he did abandon for their sake on the cross (v 25, 12:9, Mt 27:46). How terrible, to spurn such amazing grace and love (M. M. Lk 12:48)!

---

[1] M. M. Ro 3:26: God is just and fair to everyone, both when he condemns all people of all nations because all have sinned, and also when he only declares those people righteous who have faith in Jesus.

[2] M. I. Lk 3:3a: Christians should, in love, warn lost people who do not repent.

³ M. M. Lk 1:1: Jesus came to seek and save all lost people from every nation on earth.

⁴ M. I. Lk 4:40: Christians should go and seek the lost *one* person at a time by focusing on each person's unique needs.

⁵ M. I. Lk 12:40: Christians should "eat" God's Word every day in order to keep their faith strong, so that they are always ready for their Lord's return.

⁶ M. M. Ro 10:17a: The Holy Spirit only creates and preserves faith by using the message of God's grace in his holy Word.

⁷ M. I. Lk 6:5: Their faith in Jesus should move Christians to show Jesus' love in all circumstances even if their act of love breaks another less important human or even divine Law.

⁸ M. M. Ro 4:11: All Christians from every nation on earth belong to the spiritual family of Abraham, the Church because they share the same faith in Jesus that their father had.

⁹ M. M. Ro 3:24: Jesus lived a life of perfect obedience and shed his precious blood on the cross, in order to graciously set all nations free from sin, which a person only receives by faith in him.

¹⁰ M. M. Ro 5:1: On the cross, Jesus earned peace with God for all of his brothers and sisters from every nation on earth.

¹¹ M. I. Lk 8:11: Christians should faithfully do their job of preaching and leave the results to the Holy Spirit.

¹² M. M. Ro 10:17a: The Holy Spirit only creates and preserves faith by using the message of God's grace in his holy Word.

¹³ M. M. Lk 1:1: Jesus came to seek and save all lost people from every nation on earth.

¹⁴ M. I. Lk 6:13: Christians should choose new leaders and train them in order to multiply the work.

¹⁵ M. I. Lk 4:40: Christians should go and seek the lost one person at a time by focusing on each person's unique needs.

¹⁶ M. M. Lk 1:27: Jesus had to be born as a true human being and as a true Jew in order to become the King of kings in his heavenly kingdom forever.

¹⁷ M. M. Mt 1:22: God sent his only Son, Jesus to be born as a true human being, so that he could save all of his brothers and sisters of all nations by fulfilling all of God's promises in the Old Testament.

¹⁸ M. M. Lk 1:1: Jesus came to seek and save all lost people from every nation on earth.

¹⁹ M. M. Ro 3:26: God is just and fair to everyone, both when he condemns all people of all nations because all have sinned, and also when he only declares those people righteous who have faith in Jesus.

²⁰ M. M. Lk 12:48: God will justly condemn to eternal punishment all people who do not trust in Jesus as their Savior, but he will punish them by different degrees, according to how well they knew his will.

²¹ M. M. Lk 1:1: Jesus came to seek and save all lost people from every nation on earth.

²² M. I. Lk 4:35: Christians should view every person as a whole person, and show him compassion by caring for both his physical and spiritual needs as they go on their mission.

²³ M. I. Lk 4:40: Christians should go and seek the lost one person at a time by focusing on each person's unique needs.

²⁴ M. M. Lk 12:48: God will justly condemn to eternal punishment all people who do not trust in Jesus as their Savior, but he will punish them by different degrees, according to how well they

knew his will.

[25] M. M. Ac 13:46: As he did with the old Israel, God <u>first of all</u> strengthens the faith of the new Israel, the Church with his Word and Sacraments, so that they can go and witness to the lost people of all nations.

Chapter 14

Healing of a Man on the Sabbath 14:1-6

14:1   One Sabbath, when he went to dine at the house of a ruler of the Pharisees, they were watching him carefully.
14:2   And behold, there was a man before him who had dropsy.
14:3   And Jesus responded to the lawyers and Pharisees, saying, "Is it lawful to heal on the Sabbath, or not?"
14:4   But they remained silent. Then he took him and healed him and sent him away.
14:5   And he said to them, "Which of you, having a son or an ox that has fallen into a well on a Sabbath day, will not immediately pull him out?"
14:6   And they could not reply to these things.

14:1-6 (1) Jesus faithfully continued to *"seek the lost"* by accepting a Pharisee's invitation to a meal (7:36; 11:37). Even though Jesus knew that this Pharisee and his guests were his enemies, he accepted his invitation in order to seize the opportunity to personally tell them the Law and Gospel message ([1]M. I. Lk 4:40). **2)** He then also took this opportunity to once again teach all who were present there that love for one's fellow human beings is far more important than any other law, especially if it is merely a man-made law for the Sabbath, which was the day of worship (v 3; [2]M. I. Lk 6:5).

The Parable of the Wedding Feast 14:7-11

14:7   Now he told a parable to those who were invited, when he noticed how they chose the places of honor, saying to them,
14:8   "When you are invited by someone to a wedding feast, do not sit down in a place of honor, lest someone more distinguished than you be invited by him,
14:9   and he who invited you both will come and say to you, 'Give

> *your place to this person,' and then you will begin with shame to take the lowest place.*
> 14:10 *But when you are invited, go and sit in the lowest place, so that when your host comes he may say to you, 'Friend, move up higher.' Then you will be honored in the presence of all who sit at table with you.*
> 14:11 *For everyone who exalts himself will be humbled, and he who humbles himself will be exalted."*

14:7-11 Jesus' next lesson was about humility. While humility is an important lesson to learn for attending banquets of physical food, Jesus' mention in verse 16 of *"a great banquet"* makes it clear that he was teaching a spiritual lesson. The heavenly Father has indeed invited all of his children to a feast, as the prophet Isaiah says in (Is 25:6), *"On this mountain the LORD of hosts will make for all peoples a feast of rich food, a feast of well-aged wine, of rich food full of marrow, of aged wine well refined."* His feast has two parts. **a)** The great feast begins with eating and drinking the very body and blood of his own beloved Son in holy Communion, since he came to earth to offer this feast in order *"to save the lost"* (19:10). This rich, rich food builds up and strengthens the humble faith of the Christian who eats it frequently in order to humbly serve his Lord on his mission ([3]M. I. Ac 2:42). **b)** And the feasting will continue forever at his royal banquet in his heavenly home (Rev 19:9). What a feast! But, while the Father's mission-heart longs for all of his children to come in, there is only one *"narrow door"* whereby a person can enter—through *"humble"* faith in Jesus (v 11). True faith is humble faith because that person knows that he does not deserve to enter either banquet hall. It is the only door, but the Pharisees present at the meal were trying to enter the banquet by the opposite *"wide"* door of proud work-righteousness ([4]M. M. Lk 12:48 & [5]M. I. Mt 7:14).

The Parable of the Great Banquet 14:12-24

> 14:12 *He said also to the man who had invited him, "When you give a dinner or a banquet, do not invite your friends or your brothers*

or your relatives or rich neighbors, lest they also invite you in return and you be repaid.

14:13 *But when you give a feast, invite the poor, the crippled, the lame, the blind,*

14:14 *and you will be blessed, because they cannot repay you. You will be repaid at the resurrection of the just."*

14:15 *When one of those who reclined at table with him heard these things, he said to him, "Blessed is everyone who will eat bread in the kingdom of God!"*

14:16 *But he said to him, "A man once gave a great banquet and invited many.*

14:17 *And at the time for the banquet he sent his servant to say to those who had been invited, 'Come, for everything is now ready.'*

14:18 *But they all alike began to make excuses. The first said to him, 'I have bought a field, and I must go out and see it. Please have me excused.'*

14:19 *And another said, 'I have bought five yoke of oxen, and I go to examine them. Please have me excused.'*

14:20 *And another said, 'I have married a wife, and therefore I cannot come.'*

14:21 *So the servant came and reported these things to his master. Then the master of the house became angry and said to his servant, 'Go out quickly to the streets and lanes of the city, and bring in the poor and crippled and blind and lame.'*

14:22 *And the servant said, 'Sir, what you commanded has been done, and still there is room.'*

14:23 *And the master said to the servant, 'Go out to the highways and hedges and compel people to come in, that my house may be filled.*

14:24 *For I tell you, none of those men who were invited shall taste my banquet.'"*

14:12-14 In these verses, Jesus used the imagery of a banquet to reinforce the truth that true faith in him is also humble faith because <u>no one</u> deserves to go in to the Father's feast in heaven, because every human being (except for Jesus, of course) is born in sin (Ps 51:5). Therefore, everyone must depend on God's grace alone (Gen 15:6; [6]M. M. Lk 1:26 & [7]Lk 1:27). In verse 14, Jesus' words, *"You will be repaid at the resurrection of the just"* may sound like he is saying that the Father's eternal feast is a reward for those who do good deeds. Rather, the true meaning is that a Christian does loving deeds for others out of deep gratitude for what his Lord has done for him; and he knows that no one can earn their way into the banquet by doing them. God's rich, rich grace that we can see most clearly in the cross of Jesus is the powerful force that the Holy Spirit uses to move a Christian to show love to others. And the greatest love anyone can show another person is to tell him the Gospel about Jesus ([8]M. M. Ro 1:5).

14:16-23 (1) When Jesus said in verse 16 that the heavenly Father first invited *"many,"* he was referring to the nation of Israel (Gen 12:1-3). However, these invitees gave all kinds of excuses why they couldn't come because they thought that they deserved the invitation as sons and daughters of Abraham (9:59-61). They sinfully assumed that, because they deserved it, God would repeat the invitation at a more convenient time for them (3:8; 13:34). Jesus certainly especially directed this severe warning toward his host at this meal and toward all of the guests who were Pharisees. Many times throughout his ministry, Jesus showed his deep love for the lost Jewish religious leaders by trying to warn them against the grave danger of committing the unforgivable sin against the Holy Spirit, even though his warnings exposed him to grave danger (v 24; 12:10; 13:31-35; [9]M. M. Lk 12:48). **2)** On the other hand, when Jesus said in verse 21 that *"the poor and crippled and blind and lame"* and the people in *"the highways and hedges"* in verse 23 were invited, he was talking about the Gentiles. In sharp contrast to the Jews, many of them gladly came to the banquet in humble faith because they knew that it was a gracious invitation that they did not deserve at all (7:9). It should, in fact, have been the Pharisees who invited the Gentiles to their Father's banquet, since it was part of their responsibilities as the spiritual leaders of the Jews; however, they themselves refused their heavenly Father's invitations. It was a sad and tragic failure of Israel's spiritual leaders throughout nearly their entire history that they did not spread the

Gospel to other nations. But then, it's equally unfortunate and sad that, throughout its history, the Christian Church has likewise done a very poor job of proclaiming the Gospel message around the world ([10]M. M. Ac 13:46 & [11]Ro 4:11).

The Cost of Discipleship 14:25-33

14:25 *Now great crowds accompanied him, and he turned and said to them,*
14:26 *"If anyone comes to me and does not hate his own father and mother and wife and children and brothers and sisters, yes, and even his own life, he cannot be my disciple.*
14:27 *Whoever does not bear his own cross and come after me cannot be my disciple.*
14:28 *For which of you, desiring to build a tower, does not first sit down and count the cost, whether he has enough to complete it?*
14:29 *Otherwise, when he has laid a foundation and is not able to finish, all who see it begin to mock him,*
14:30 *saying, 'This man began to build and was not able to finish.'*
14:31 *Or what king, going out to encounter another king in war, will not sit down first and deliberate whether he is able with ten thousand to meet him who comes against him with twenty thousand?*
14:32 *And if not, while the other is yet a great way off, he sends a delegation and asks for terms of peace.*
14:33 *So therefore, any one of you who does not renounce all that he has cannot be my disciple.*

14:25-27 (1) All people are born sinful (Ps 51:5), and every human being lives in his sinful human body as long as he is alive. Therefore, not only did Jesus *"seek the lost"* throughout his ministry with a two-part message: repent, and then also believe the Gospel (Mk 1:15), he continues to seek them through his Church yet today (19:10; [12]M. M. Lk 1:1). However, he adds a warning in verse 27, *"Whoever does not bear his own cross and come after me cannot be my disciple."* Why did he do so, since a warning might drive some people away, instead of attracting them ([13]M. I. Lk 9:23)? He warns them so that each one of them would be very realistic and first count the cost of *"bear[ing] his own cross [of suffering for Jesus' sake]"* (v 27) before following him. They should follow him because they love him more than *"[their] own [lives]"* (v 26) or more than any other person in their lives, and not because they expect him to fill their lives with blessings, while they continue to cling to sin and to their unbelieving family (v 26). If their family hates Jesus, they will have to *"hate"* their families (v 26) and cling to him, even if their family tries to kill them (12:49-53; M. I. Lk 9:23). (Obviously, Jesus used a hyperbole when he used the strong word *"hate"* in verse 26, because a Christian also continues to love his unbelieving family, and therefore, continues to seek them.) **2)** Everyone who chooses to follow Jesus must be prepared to *"bear his own cross"* (v 27) by daily repeating the cycle of repenting of his sins in order to receive daily forgiveness (9:23), since all Christians are both forgiven saints and sinners. However, we are not alone in our constant struggle with sin, because Jesus also helps us to carry our burdens. As our dear Brother, he literally carried his cross for our sakes (23:26; Jn 19:17). Such undeserved love for us enables us to carry our own crosses much more easily, as we daily "eat" his holy Word, where we hear his beautiful Gospel (Mt 11:29-30; [14]M. I. Lk 12:40).

14:28-33 With these two parables in verses 28-32, Jesus further emphasized the need for everyone to carefully *"count the cost"* (v 28) before following him, because the decision to follow him is the most important decision anyone will ever make. It means *"renounc[ing] all that he has"* (v 33) because Jesus himself renounced everything for the sake of his brothers and sisters of the entire human race, in order *"to seek and to save"* us (19:10; 2 Cor 8:9). However, this is not a blind commitment to him, from two opposite points of view. **a)** First, it's a joyous commitment, because it is the choice of returning love in response to the deepest love that the person will ever know (Eph 3:17-19; [15]M. M. Jn 6:44). How beautiful the cross of Jesus is! The depth of his grace for rebellious mankind is beyond understanding (Rom 5:6-10). **b)** Secondly, when a person chooses to follow Jesus, there will always be a *"cost"* (v 28), which, at the very least, will be daily repentance, which means saying "No" to one's sinful desires. And the cost may be even higher—suffering rejection from one's family, or public shame, or even death for the name of Jesus ([16]M. I. Lk 9:23 & [17]M. M. Lk 6:22).

Salt without Taste is Worthless 14:34-35

14:34 *"Salt is good, but if salt has lost its taste, how shall its saltiness be restored?*
14:35 *It is of no use either for the soil or for the manure pile. It is thrown away. He who has ears to hear, let him hear."*

14:34-35 (1) A person's faith relationship with Jesus is like salt, because salt has a completely unique flavor, just as a person's faith relationship with Jesus is completely unique among all human relationships and can be found nowhere else in the world. It *"tastes"* uniquely sweet, because no one deserves it and the taste will last forever! Therefore, before taking the first step in following Jesus, everyone should carefully consider what a treasure his faith relationship with him is; and then firmly decide to cling to him alone forever. It's a new mission message. M. M. Lk 14:34: A Christian's faith relationship with Jesus is a precious treasure and a completely unique personal relationship, because no one deserves it and it will last forever. **2)** However, if a person loses this wonderful relationship, his whole life has become even worse than useless (14:35) because he has become like "salt that has lost its taste" (v 34), a follower of Jesus in name only, or even a bitter enemy of the cross. Sadly, Jesus will be ashamed of him on the Last Day, because he is ashamed of Jesus before others. How can anyone see the cross of Jesus, understand its grace for him, and still reject him? How can it possibly happen? Yet, sadly, it does happen. Satan is extremely clever and is able to deceive many unwary people (9:26; [18]M. I. Lk 9:54 & [19]2 Cor 11:14).

---

[1] M. I. Lk 4:40: Christians should go and seek the lost <u>one</u> person at a time by focusing on each person's <u>unique</u> needs.

[2] M. I. Lk 6:5: Their faith in Jesus should move Christians to show Jesus' <u>love</u> in all circumstances even if their act of love breaks another less important human or even divine Law.

[3] M. I. Ac 2:42: Christians should celebrate Holy Communion frequently in order to receive forgiveness and strength from their Lord's grace in order to continue on his mission.

[4] M. M. Lk 12:48: God will justly condemn to eternal punishment all people who do not trust in Jesus as their Savior, but he will punish them by different <u>degrees</u>, according to how well they knew his will.

[5] M. I. Mt 7:14: Christians should hurry on their mission to the world because people who are lost have many enemies who lure them away from Jesus; and therefore, few of them find faith in Jesus which is the only gate into his Kingdom of life.

[6] M. M. Lk 1:26: The heavenly Father sent his Son, Jesus to be born and live in <u>humble</u> circumstances, so that everyone from every nation on earth would see his <u>grace</u>.

[7] M. M. Lk 1:27: Jesus had to be born as a true human being and as a true Jew in order to become the King of kings in his heavenly kingdom forever.

[8] M. M. Ro 1:5: The same Holy Spirit who creates <u>faith</u> and a new missionary <u>nature</u> in a person's heart also graciously empowers him to gratefully respond to his Lord's love by <u>obeying</u> him.

[9] M. M. Lk 12:48: God will justly condemn to eternal punishment all people who do not trust in Jesus as their Savior, but he will punish them by different <u>degrees</u>, according to how well they knew his will.

[10] M. M. Ac 13:46: As he did with the old Israel, God <u>first of all</u> strengthens the faith of the new Israel, the Church with his Word and Sacraments, so that they can go and witness to the lost people of all nations.

[11] M. M. Ro 4:11: All Christians from every nation on earth belong to the <u>spiritual family</u> of Abraham, the Church because they share the same faith in Jesus that their father had.

[12] M. M. Lk 1:1: Jesus came to seek and save <u>all</u> lost people from <u>every</u> nation on earth.

[13] M. I. Lk 9:23: Christians should deceive no one by <u>only</u> telling them the Gospel about Jesus, but rather they should <u>also</u> give them two warnings: a) that they may have to suffer for the sake of Jesus if they follow him, b) and that, on Judgment Day, Jesus will be ashamed of people who were ashamed of him.

[14] M. I. Lk 12:40: Christians should "eat" God's Word every day in order to keep their faith strong, so that they are always ready for their Lord's return.

[15] M. M. Jn 6:44: People who are lost cannot come to faith in Jesus by their own power; <u>only</u> the heavenly Father, who sent Jesus to die for them can draw them to Jesus by sending Christians to proclaim the Gospel to them.

[16] M. I. Lk 9:23: Christians should deceive no one by <u>only</u> telling them the Gospel about Jesus, but rather they should <u>also</u> give them two warnings: a) that they may have to suffer for the sake of Jesus if they follow him, b) and that, on Judgment Day, Jesus will be ashamed of people who were ashamed of him.

[17] M. M. Lk 6:22: The Lord Jesus will surely bless a Christian in the midst of suffering for his sake; and he will also bless him with eternal life if he remains faithful to him.

[18] M. I. Lk 9:54: Christians should show patient love to people who unknowingly reject an opportunity to hear the Gospel.

[19] M. I. 2 Cor 11:14: Christians should beware of Satan because he not only disguises himself as an angel of light, but he also sends out false teachers who also disguise themselves as servants of the light, in order to deceive people by telling lies that appear to be the truth of the Gospel.

Chapter 15

The Parable of the Lost Sheep 15:1-7

15:1 *Now the tax collectors and sinners were all drawing near to hear him.*
15:2 *And the Pharisees and the scribes grumbled, saying, "This man receives sinners and eats with them."*
15:3 *So he told them this parable:*
15:4 *"What man of you, having a hundred sheep, if he has lost one of them, does not leave the ninety-nine in the open country, and go after the one that is lost, until he finds it?*
15:5 *And when he has found it, he lays it on his shoulders, rejoicing.*
15:6 *And when he comes home, he calls together his friends and his neighbors, saying to them, 'Rejoice with me, for I have found my sheep that was lost.'*
15:7 *Just so, I tell you, there will be more joy in heaven over one sinner who repents than over ninety-nine righteous persons who need no repentance.*

The Parable of the Lost Coin 15:8-10

15:8 *"Or what woman, having ten silver coins, if she loses one coin, does not light a lamp and sweep the house and seek diligently until she finds it?*
15:9 *And when she has found it, she calls together her friends and neighbors, saying, 'Rejoice with me, for I have found the coin that I had lost.'*
15:10 *Just so, I tell you, there is joy before the angels of God over one sinner who repents."*

15:1-31 Luke places the three parables in chapter 15 in a setting where the Pharisees and the scribes complained that *"this man [Jesus] receives sinners and eats with them"* (v 2). And this setting helps us to learn the same three lessons in all three parables: **a)** First of all, all people are lost sinners who need to repent. On the one hand, the tax collectors and sinners *"were all drawing near to hear"* Jesus (v 1), because they knew that they were sinful and needed to repent. However, the Pharisees and the scribes, on the other hand, were self-righteous and *"grumbled"* (v 2) because they thought that they did not need to repent. **b)** Secondly, all Christians should go seek *"the lost"* one by one. In each parable, it is, of course, Jesus himself (or his heavenly Father in the third parable) who *"seeks"* and finds one *"lost"* sheep (v 5), one *"lost"* coin (v 8), and one *"lost"* son (v 12). Because God made each one of the countless number of people who have ever lived and ever will live as unique individuals, he loves each one of them, even though they all have sinned and rebelled against him. However, because of his deep love for them he does not want even one of them to remain *"lost"* forever (1 Tim 2:4); therefore, he lovingly and patiently *"seeks"* each *"lost"* sinner one by one. Obviously this includes all Jews and all Gentiles of all nations (Jn 3:16-17; [1]M. I. Lk 4:40 & [2]Lk 5:20). **c)** In verses 7, 10 and 24, we see the same rejoicing when just one lost sheep, one lost coin, and one lost person is found. Obviously, we have no idea how many people God has made; however, we do know for sure that every one of them is born in original sin (Ps 51:5). And we also know that this sad fact grieves the mission-heart of our gracious God so much that he was willing to sacrifice his own Beloved Son, Jesus, in order to save us undeserving sinners. It's no wonder, then, that our heavenly Father and his holy angels rejoice so much when just one lost person hears the Law and the Gospel and then repents and believes. It's a new mission imperative. M. I. Lk 15:7: Christians should rejoice together with the heavenly Father and his angels when just one lost person hears the Law and the Gospel and then receives the gracious gifts of a repentant heart and faith in Jesus.

15:7 Who were the *"ninety-nine righteous people who need no repentance"* that Jesus was referring to in verse 7? The Pharisees' words in verse 2, *"This man receives sinners and eats with them"* were spoken with great disdain for "other" people who were so obviously *"sinners."* This suggests that the ninety-nine people were unrepentant Israelites or

Jews of his day, such as the Pharisees who <u>thought</u> that they <u>didn't</u> need to repent. Therefore, Jesus was using very powerful <u>irony</u> here, in order to say that <u>everyone</u> needs to repent; and therefore, no one can rightly look down on others with a self-righteous attitude (3:8-9). The Pharisees and the scribes were lost and unrepentant; and what was worse, they were unhappy when even <u>one</u> person did repent, because it meant that that person was no longer under their evil control. They were obviously serving Satan. Jesus had been repeatedly seeking them and warning them very sternly because they were in grave danger of God confirming them in eternal condemnation (14:24; Eph 4:30). This understanding of verse 7 likewise supports the idea that the older son in the third parable represents the Pharisees, because the older son too thought that he did not need to repent, he never went to search for his lost brother, and he was angry when his brother did repent (vs 28-29; [3]M. I. Lk 3:3a).

The Parable of the Lost Son 15:11-32

15:11 *And he said, "There was a man who had two sons.*
15:12 *And the younger of them said to his father, 'Father, give me the share of property that is coming to me.' And he divided his property between them.*
15:13 *Not many days later, the younger son gathered all he had and took a journey into a far country, and there he squandered his property in reckless living.*
15:14 *And when he had spent everything, a severe famine arose in that country, and he began to be in need.*
15:15 *So he went and hired himself out to one of the citizens of that country, who sent him into his fields to feed pigs.*
15:16 *And he was longing to be fed with the pods that the pigs ate, and no one gave him anything.*
15:17 "But when he came to himself, he said, 'How many of my father's hired servants have more than enough bread, but I perish here with hunger!*
15:18 *I will arise and go to my father, and I will say to him, "Father, I have sinned against heaven and before you.*

15:19 *I am no longer worthy to be called your son. Treat me as one of your hired servants."'*

15:20 *And he arose and came to his father. But while he was still a long way off, his father saw him and felt compassion, and ran and embraced him and kissed him.*

15:21 *And the son said to him, 'Father, I have sinned against heaven and before you. I am no longer worthy to be called your son.'*

15:22 *But the father said to his servants, 'Bring quickly the best robe, and put it on him, and put a ring on his hand, and shoes on his feet.*

15:23 *And bring the fattened calf and kill it, and let us eat and celebrate.*

15:24 *For this my son was dead, and is alive again; he was lost, and is found.' And they began to celebrate.*

15:25 *"Now his older son was in the field, and as he came and drew near to the house, he heard music and dancing.*

15:26 *And he called one of the servants and asked what these things meant.*

15:27 *And he said to him, 'Your brother has come, and your father has killed the fattened calf, because he has received him back safe and sound.'*

15:28 *But he was angry and refused to go in. His father came out and entreated him,*

15:29 *but he answered his father, 'Look, these many years I have served you, and I never disobeyed your command, yet you never gave me a young goat, that I might celebrate with my friends.*

15:30 *But when this son of yours came, who has devoured your property with prostitutes, you killed the fattened calf for him!'*

15:31 *And he said to him, 'Son, you are always with me, and all that is mine is yours.*

15:32 *It was fitting to celebrate and be glad, for this your brother was dead, and is alive; he was lost, and is found.'"*

15:12-21 Verses 12-21 paint a picture of the <u>younger son</u>. **1)** There apparently were at least <u>three</u> reasons why he rebelled and ran away from home: **a)** First of all, he obviously loved money and the pleasures of this sinful world above everything else, because, as soon as he got the money that he wanted, he ran away to satisfy these desires (vs 13-14). **b)** Secondly, it's also obvious that the two brothers were disputing over their inheritance rights, as verse 12 indicates. Of course, it's also possible that the younger son forgot that he too would inherit part of his father's property, and simply rebelled. **c)** And thirdly, of course, the underlying problem was a lack of love between the brothers, which prompted them to fight over their inheritance; and also prompted the older son to refuse to go seek his brother. Those who are lost have no reason to search for others who are lost ([4]M. M. Mt 5:14). And this is most evident when the older brother became angry and refused to join in the celebration (v 28). **2)** If Christians also sin by acting like the older brother and do not love a person or a certain group of people who are lost, they too will not go to look for them. However, it is their mission-heart and <u>love</u> for their Lord and for others that should motivate them to be in mission to seek the lost, whether those who are lost are unbelievers or fellow Christians who have fallen into sin ([5]M. M. Lk 18:29). **3)** When the younger son left and his brother refused to go look for him, the father could only depend on one thing, that his lost son would <u>remember</u> who he was and then <u>remember</u> how much his father loved him. Would he remember? That was the only hope that he had. At least his firstborn son was still at home and had a chance to <u>remember</u> his love, but he too was lost. So the father's heart ached as he waited and watched the empty road! How do people today, who once were Christians, <u>remember</u> their Father's love, in order to repent and believe in Jesus again? They only have fellow Christians who use God's Word to <u>remind</u> them since, obviously, unbelievers will only lead them further away from him ([6]M. M. Ro 10:17a). **4)** Verse 17 says that *"he [the younger son] came to himself."* It was mere <u>physical</u> hunger that finally stimulated him to <u>remember</u> who he was, because back at home even his father's servants had plenty to eat. His father loved both of his sons as well as his whole household; and, of course, he continued to care for them; therefore, the lost son <u>remembered</u> his father's <u>love</u>. He also now knew that he didn't <u>deserve</u> his love. Sadly, no one reminded him with a message of Law from God's Word, since his own brother did not come to look for him to call him to repentance ([7]M. I. Lk 3:3a).

15:25-30 (1) Jesus described the <u>older son</u> in verses 25-30. The fact that the older son did not love his brother was certainly one of the reasons why his brother left home in the first place; and it also obviously explains why he did not go look for him, and why he refused to celebrate with the rest of the family ([8]M. M. Lk 13:24 & [9]Mt 5:14). He said in verse 29, *"I never disobeyed your command;"* but this was obviously <u>not</u> true, since it's clear that he had no love for his father either since he did nothing to search for his brother, even though he knew perfectly well that his father was waiting for <u>him</u> to go looking for him. Then, when his brother did return, he wasn't even willing to call him his brother; instead, in verse 30, he called him, *"this son of yours."* In short, the older son sadly never did repent. **2)** It's quite evident that Jesus intended that the older son should represent the <u>unrepentant</u> Jews of his day, such as the Pharisees, since he acted like he <u>deserved</u>, not just the <u>first</u> right to his father's inheritance, but perhaps <u>all</u> of it; and if he would be able to drive his brother away, he would get it all. Obviously, some Jews thought that, since the Gentiles were not sons of Abraham like they were, they didn't deserve any blessings from the heavenly Father in any case. Therefore, if they didn't share the Gospel with the Gentiles, <u>they</u> would get <u>all</u> of God's blessings; but they didn't realize that they didn't deserve it either ([10]M. M. Ac 13:46). **3)** Some Christians today may protest that they are not prejudiced against a certain group of people who are from a different language and culture; yet, just like the older son in the parable, their actions of refusing to go look for the lost in that group, or their actions of hindering others who want to do so, clearly arise from their <u>lack of love</u> for them. The same Christians, again like the older son, often resent it when these people do repent and receive the Father's gracious forgiveness. They obviously need to hear the warning that they too are lost in sin ([11]M. I. Lk 3:3a). **4)** Thus, if the older son represents the <u>unrepentant</u> Israelites or Jews of Jesus' day, then, the younger son represents the Gentile nations. These are the nations whom the heavenly Father always longs to bless <u>through</u> his older son, the Church, the new Israel. In the Old Testament era, how the heavenly Father longed for his chosen people, Israel to love the Gentile nations around them enough to go and seek them! And yet today, how his mission-heart still eagerly waits for his Church to go as well ([12]M. M. Ac 13:46)!

15:12, 20-24, 28, 31-32 Jesus paints a beautiful picture of his heavenly Father in all of these verses. **1)** Throughout this parable we see <u>three</u> things very clearly about the father: **a)** He loved <u>both</u> of his sons very dearly, especially because both of them were lost. **b)** He therefore went beyond what God's Laws require when he gave both of them their inheritance (v 12). **c)** He also longed for his sons to love each other completely and to be in mission to each other. Likewise, throughout the Bible we see that there is no question that our heavenly Father has a mission-heart that moves him to love <u>every one</u> of his children, from Adam and Eve down to the last child who will ever be born on earth. Furthermore, he made all of his children with the hope that they would all love each other completely. And finally, he also has a fabulous inheritance in heaven that he will give to all of his children who trust in Jesus. **2)** The father was sad enough when his youngest son left, but he was even more brokenhearted when, every morning, he asked his oldest son, "Son, are you leaving today to go look for your brother?" (It's true that the father never explicitly says this in the parable, but it is very strongly implied.) But every day he was greeted by the same stony silence. The oldest son too was disobedient and lost. Verse 30 indicates that the older son probably even knew where his brother was, because he knew what he had been doing, but he refused to go look for him. Thus, as the father stood at his door day after long day, it wasn't just one son he was watching for—<u>both</u> of his sons were lost, spiritually <u>dead</u> in sin (v 32)! How his heart grieved (1 Jn 4:16-17)! Our heavenly Father loves all of his children equally; and he wants all of them to find ways to show love for each other by seeking the lost ([13]M. M. Mt 5:14). **3)** In verse 20, we see the most beautiful picture in this parable. Every day, the father had been standing at his door eagerly watching the road, longing to see his son return. Then he finally saw him! And he *"felt compassion, and ran and embraced him and kissed him"* (v 20); his son still reeked of the pungent odor of "unclean" pigs but he didn't even notice the smell because this was his own <u>dear</u>, repentant son. Ever since Adam and Eve sinned, our heavenly Father has been standing at his door eagerly watching the road, longing for <u>all</u> of his children to repent and return home. In societies where it's against the law to convert to any other religion, it can be fatal to confess your love for Jesus and your heavenly Father (Ezek 18:23). Yet, such amazing love from our heavenly Father can give a person the courage to confess his love for Jesus and for his <u>heavenly</u> Father even though it may make his <u>physical</u> father angry. And when that happens, what a powerful testimony that is to the power of our Father's grace and love ([14]M. M. Ro 4:11)! **4)** In verse 23, the father joyfully announced a celebration (vs 7, 10). To <u>finally</u> see his youngest son turn the last corner in the road just overwhelmed him! His heart was so full of forgiveness and joy that he just <u>had</u> to share his joy with his entire household. He shouted, *"Let us eat and celebrate"* (v 23; [15]M. M. Lk 13:24)! We all reek of the pungent odor of unclean pigs (our sin) and totally depend on him in his rich <u>grace</u> to raise us from both physical and spiritual death. <u>Of course</u>, our heavenly Father stands waiting at his door with a heart full of pain! What a <u>gracious</u> message we have that we are eager to go and share with all of our brothers and sisters everywhere ([16]M. M. Ro 1:5)!

---

[1] M. I. Lk 4:40: Christians should go and seek the lost <u>one</u> person at a time by focusing on each person's <u>unique</u> needs.

[2] M. I. Lk 5:20: Even when Christians proclaim the Gospel to large crowds, they should always remember that the crowds are made up of <u>individuals</u>; and that <u>each one</u> of them needs to repent and believe in Jesus.

[3] M. I. Lk 3:3a: Christians should, in love, warn lost people who do not repent.

[4] M. M. Mt 5:14: When the Holy Spirit creates faith in a person's heart, he also graciously gives him a new mission-heart that is eager to shine the light of the Gospel throughout the whole world.

[5] M. M. Lk 18:29: All Christians will certainly receive rewards in heaven as gracious gifts, but not because they earned them by going into the lost world to proclaim the Gospel; rather, they went because they also received <u>grateful</u> mission-hearts from their Lord.

[6] M. M. Ro 10:17a: The Holy Spirit <u>only</u> creates and preserves faith by using the message of God's grace in his holy Word.

[7] M. I. Lk 3:3a: Christians should, in love, warn lost people who do not repent.

[8] M. M. Lk 13:24: The <u>only</u> way to enter the Kingdom of God is to have <u>faith</u> in Jesus as one's Savior.

[9] M. M. Mt 5:14: When the Holy Spirit creates faith in a person's heart, he also graciously gives him a new mission-heart that is eager to shine the light of the Gospel throughout the whole world.

[10] M. M. Ac 13:46: As he did with the old Israel, God <u>first of all</u> strengthens the faith of the new Israel, the Church with his Word and Sacraments, so that they can go and witness to the lost people of all nations.

[11] M. I. Lk 3:3a: Christians should, in love, warn lost people who do not repent.

[12] M. M. Ac 13:46: As he did with the old Israel, God <u>first of all</u> strengthens the faith of the new Israel, the Church with his Word and Sacraments, so that they can go and witness to the lost people of all nations.

[13] M. M. Mt 5:14: When the Holy Spirit creates faith in a person's heart, he also graciously gives him a new mission-heart that is eager to shine the light of the Gospel throughout the whole world.

[14] M. M. Ro 4:11: All Christians from every nation on earth belong to the <u>spiritual family</u> of Abraham, the Church because they share the same faith in Jesus that their father had.

[15] M. M. Lk 13:24: The <u>only</u> way to enter the Kingdom of God is to have <u>faith</u> in Jesus as one's Savior.

[16] M. M. Ro 1:5: The same Holy Spirit who creates <u>faith</u> and a new missionary <u>nature</u> in a person's heart also graciously empowers him to gratefully respond to his Lord's love by <u>obeying</u> him.

Chapter 16

The Parable of the Dishonest Manager 16:1-13

16:1 *He also said to the disciples, "There was a rich man who had a manager, and charges were brought to him that this man was wasting his possessions.*

16:2 *And he called him and said to him, 'What is this that I hear about you? Turn in the account of your management, for you can no longer be manager.'*

16:3 *And the manager said to himself, 'What shall I do, since my master is taking the management away from me? I am not strong enough to dig, and I am ashamed to beg.*

16:4 *I have decided what to do, so that when I am removed from management, people may receive me into their houses.'*

16:5 *So, summoning his master's debtors one by one, he said to the first, 'How much do you owe my master?'*

16:6 *He said, 'A hundred measures of oil.' He said to him, 'Take your bill, and sit down quickly and write fifty.'*

16:7 *Then he said to another, 'And how much do you owe?' He said, 'A hundred measures of wheat.' He said to him, 'Take your bill, and write eighty.'*

16:8 *The master commended the dishonest manager for his shrewdness. For the sons of this world are more shrewd in dealing with their own generation than the sons of light.*

16:9 *And I tell you, make friends for yourselves by means of unrighteous wealth, so that when it fails they may receive you into the eternal dwellings.*

16:10 *"One who is faithful in a very little is also faithful in much, and one who is dishonest in a very little is also dishonest in much.*

16:11 *If then you have not been faithful in the unrighteous wealth, who will entrust to you the true riches?*

16:12 *And if you have not been faithful in that which is another's, who will give you that which is your own?*

16:13 *No servant can serve two masters, for either he will hate the one and love the other, or he will be devoted to the one and despise the other. You cannot serve God and money."*

16:1-13 To begin with, note that, because there are a number of ideas in this parable that seem to conflict with some truths that Jesus taught clearly elsewhere, it's difficult to interpret this parable with complete satisfaction. Nevertheless, the following thoughts seem to clarify most of the difficulties: **a)** First of all, God most graciously gives Christians both spiritual and material wealth so that they can carry out their mission outreach to others ([1]M. M. 1 Cor 12:11). **b)** Secondly, because Christians receive their spiritual wealth through faith in Jesus, he wants them to show their complete devotion to him by <u>managing</u> all of their wealth wisely (v 8), in order to share both the priceless treasure of their <u>spiritual</u> wealth with others, as well as sharing their <u>material</u> wealth with others who are in need. It's a new mission imperative. M. I. Lk 16:13: Christians should manage both their spiritual and material wealth wisely, in order to be able to most effectively proclaim the Gospel and also be able to share their material wealth with others who are in need. **c)** Thirdly, because Christians show through a life of repentance and faith in Jesus that they depend on the righteousness of Jesus (the spiritual wealth that Jesus has earned for them) in order to receive the <u>gift</u> of God's favor, God will reward them with eternal, spiritual wealth in heaven on the Last Day (v 9; [2]M. M. Ro 1:5). However, unbelievers will, instead, receive the curse of eternal condemnation from God on that Day, because, in their life, they depended on their material wealth or on their own spiritual wealth (their own work-righteousness) in order to earn God's favor ([3]M. M. Gal 3:10 & [4]Ro 3:26).

The Law and the Kingdom of God 16:14-17

> 16:14 *The Pharisees, who were lovers of money, heard all these things, and they ridiculed him.*
> 16:15 *And he said to them, "You are those who justify yourselves before men, but God knows your hearts. For what is exalted among men is an abomination in the sight of God.*

> 16:16 *"The law and the Prophets were until John; since then the Good News of the kingdom of God is preached, and everyone forces his way into it.*
>
> 16:17 *But it is easier for heaven and earth to pass away than for one dot of the law to become void.*

16:14-16 Because the Pharisees *"were lovers of money"* (v 14) more than anything else, they did not miss the point that Jesus made in his parable in verses 1-13, that they should love spiritual wealth more than material wealth. Satan had full control of them in several ways. **a)** First, they obviously had not received God's gracious gift of Jesus' righteousness through faith in him. They should have been able to find this treasure in *"the law and the Prophets"* (v 16) and especially through hearing it from Jesus, *"the Word of life"* himself (Phil 2:16), because he had been seeking them again and again throughout his ministry ([5]M. M. Lk 1:1). **b)** Secondly, it was, therefore, spiritually impossible for them to faithfully share this priceless treasure with others. As the spiritual leaders of Israel, they were primarily responsible for spreading the Gospel message among their own nation and also share it with all Gentile nations ([6]M. M. Ac 13:46); but, instead, they were spreading the devil's evil lies and even hindering others from obeying God (11:46). **c)** Thirdly, they did much worse than make only *"one dot of the Law... void"* (v 17); they showed that they even despised it by disobeying God's Laws (v 18) and by adding their own evil, elaborate set of rules to it. **d)** And finally, they were trying to *"force their way into the kingdom of God"* (v 16) by self-righteously obeying their own man-made rules; they trusted in their own prideful "wealth" of work-righteousness (13:24). Nevertheless, because Jesus loved them so dearly, he continued to seek these lost Pharisees in verses 14-16 by trying to break their hard hearts with God's Law ([7]M. I. Lk 3:3a).

16:16 Before God made the universe and before mankind fell into sin, his mission-heart compelled him to plan how he would rescue all of mankind, so that they would once again be his own forever (1 Tim 2:4). Therefore, he began carrying out his plan by first choosing Abraham (Gen 12:1-3; [8]M. M. Ac 13:46). Then, in the Old Testament era, the prophets preached a Law and Gospel message that warned sinners to repent and also promised a future rescue by the Messiah. And then, the prophet, John made the transition into a new era by *"telling the Good News of the kingdom of God"* (v 16). And now, the greatest Prophet, Jesus began to fully launch a vigorous mission campaign to proclaim the Law and the Gospel that the King of kings had finally come to *"seek and save the lost."* And he also called 12 disciples and continues to call his disciples, the Church to eagerly carry out his mission to the world (Heb 1:1-2; [9]M. M. Lk 1:1 & [10]Ro 1:5).

16:17 (1) Even as Jesus continued to seek these lost Pharisees in verse 17, he himself was, of course, likewise obeying every *"dot of the Law"* perfectly by doing so, since the very purpose of God's Word is to *"seek the lost"* (19:10; Ps 119:89; Is 40:8; Is 55:11; Mt 5:18; Mk 13:31; M. M. Lk 1:1). Furthermore, by his perfect obedience of the Law, he was earning the spiritual treasure of his righteousness (vs 1-15) for the sake of all of his brothers and sisters from all nations ([11]M. M. Ro 5:1). **2)** What Jesus said in verse 17 about *"the Law"* he was, of course, likewise applying to all of Scripture since all of Scripture is a sharp sword that can never fail (21:33; Ps 119:89; Is 40:8; Is 55:11). Therefore, as Christians proclaim his Law and Gospel message throughout the world yet today, they do so with full confidence in it, because the Holy Spirit will use his sword of the Word to do his work of creating and sustaining faith. He does not depend on feeble human abilities to do so (Heb 4:12; Rom 1:16; [12]M. I. Lk 8:11). It's another new mission imperative. M. I. Lk 16:17: Christians should wield the sword of the Spirit with confidence as they go and tell the Gospel because his Word can never fail.

Divorce and Remarriage 16:18

16:18 *"Everyone who divorces his wife and marries another commits adultery, and he who marries a woman divorced from her husband commits adultery.*

16:18 In verse 18, Jesus warned against a false teaching taught by the

Pharisees that a man is allowed to divorce his wife, since Moses commanded the Israelites to not divorce their spouse (Mt 19:1-11; [13]M. I. Mt 19:9 & [14]Lk 3:8). And in this verse, he also added another command that *"everyone who divorces his wife and marries another commits adultery, and he who marries a woman divorced from her husband commits adultery."* Our Lord always has at least <u>three</u> concerns in this matter: **a)** First of all, he is always concerned that Christians should follow his perfect example by showing patient <u>love</u> in all circumstances. Because married couples live together so closely, personal conflicts can arise very quickly and very often; therefore, marriage always demands a great deal of love and patience. However, by depending on their Lord's rich grace, couples can learn to love and forgive each other more and more often ([15]M. I. Lk 11:10). **b)** Secondly, our Lord is also concerned that if a Christian gets a divorce and <u>quickly</u> marries someone else, he or she is not giving their spouse a chance to repent and return to them. Their divorce could shock their spouse into realizing his or her errors and realizing how much they actually do love each other ([16]M. I. Lk 15:7). **c)** Thirdly, if a Christian man or a woman is continually divorcing someone and marrying someone else, they are essentially practicing polygamy. And Jesus himself condemned polygamy in (Jn 4:16-18). **d)** And finally, our Lord is always concerned that unbelievers are watching Christians to see if their lives are truly different from theirs. Everything that a Christian says and does is a good or a bad witness to unbelievers; and bad behavior always destroys a Christian's witness to Jesus' holy name. Therefore, especially our married lives should always match our verbal witness to unbelievers. It's not at all easy to do, but it's obviously very important to try to do so ([17]M. I. Tit 2:7).

The Rich Man and Lazarus 16:19-31

> 16:19 *"There was a rich man who was clothed in purple and fine linen and who feasted sumptuously every day.*
> 16:20 *And at his gate was laid a poor man named Lazarus, covered*

with sores,

16:21 *who desired to be fed with what fell from the rich man's table. Moreover, even the dogs came and licked his sores.*

16:22 *The poor man died and was carried by the angels to Abraham's side. The rich man also died and was buried,*

16:23 *and in Hades, being in torment, he lifted up his eyes and saw Abraham far off and Lazarus at his side.*

16:24 *And he called out, 'Father Abraham, have mercy on me, and send Lazarus to dip the end of his finger in water and cool my tongue, for I am in anguish in this flame.'*

16:25 *But Abraham said, 'Child, remember that you in your lifetime received your good things, and Lazarus in like manner bad things; but now he is comforted here, and you are in anguish.*

16:26 *And besides all this, between us and you a great chasm has been fixed, in order that those who would pass from here to you may not be able, and none may cross from there to us.'*

16:27 *And he said, 'Then I beg you, father, to send him to my father's house--*

16:28 *for I have five brothers--so that he may warn them, lest they also come into this place of torment.'*

16:29 *But Abraham said, 'They have Moses and the Prophets; let them hear them.'*

16:30 *And he said, 'No, father Abraham, but if someone goes to them from the dead, they will repent.'*

16:31 *He said to him, 'If they do not hear Moses and the Prophets, neither will they be convinced if someone should rise from the dead.'"*

16:19-31 (1) Jesus taught three main lessons in this parable: **a)** First, only faith in God's promises saves. Both of the men in the story were Jews or physical sons of Abraham; however, only Lazarus was a true son of Abraham since he trusted in God, as his spiritual father, Abraham did (Gen 15:6; v 22; 13:16; 19:9; [18]M. M. Lk 13:24). **b)** Secondly, the Holy Spirit only uses his holy Word as his means of grace to create and strengthen faith (v 31; [19]M. M. Ro 10:17a). **c)** Thirdly, he uses

Christians to proclaim his Word because he gives them a mission-heart when he gives them faith in Jesus (1:13-20, 28-37; 2:1-14). Therefore, the rich man's brothers could only receive his gift of faith by either listening to his Word from other people in their synagogue or in the temple (vs 29, 31; 8:11-15; 9:2, 35). **2)** Jesus taught these three lessons by contrasting the temporary earthly lives and eternal lives of the two men. In his miserable life on earth, Lazarus heard the Law and Gospel message of the Scriptures, then, he repented and believed in God's promises; therefore he enjoyed eternal life with his spiritual father, Abraham and God (v 22). On the other hand, the rich man apparently barely heard the same Word of God in the midst of his partying; and instead of repenting, he **a)** chose to trust in his blood relationship with Abraham (v 24; 3:8), and he **b)** chose to trust in his earthly wealth (v 13). He proudly assumed that God had given him his money because he deserved it since God was pleased with him (v 19; 12:20-21), and he **c)** despised God's Word because he thought that miracles create faith (vs 29-30). Therefore, he suffered eternal misery in hell (v 24; M. M. Ro 10:17a).

16:30-31 In verse 30, the rich man asked that Lazarus be raised from the dead in order to convince his brothers to repent. However, even though such a miracle would have been impressive, that alone could not have created repentance and faith in a person's heart. Therefore, Jesus said in verse 31 *"neither will they be convinced if someone should rise from the dead."* He meant that, even his own resurrection is only an historical fact and will not convince anyone until a Christians tells a person that Jesus rose from the dead for you. He died and was raised again for us sinners even though we do not deserve his forgiveness. Then, the historical fact of his resurrection becomes pure Gospel because it is sure proof that his sacrifice paid for all of the sins of all mankind. And it therefore has God's awesome power to create faith in a person's heart ([20]M. M. Ro 3:24).

---

[1] M. M. 1 Cor 12:11: When Christians baptize people the same Holy Spirit graciously gives each one faith in Jesus plus a unique set of spiritual gifts so that he can use them in order to expand

the Lord's mission.

[2] M. M. Ro 1:5: The same Holy Spirit who creates <u>faith</u> and a new missionary <u>nature</u> in a person's heart also graciously empowers him to gratefully respond to his Lord's love by <u>obeying</u> him.

[3] M. M. Gal 3:10: All people who try to please God by their own good deeds are under God's curse because only Jesus, God's Son was able to obey God perfectly for the sake of all of his fellow human beings.

[4] M. M. Ro 3:26: God is just and fair to <u>everyone</u>, both when he condemns <u>all</u> people of all nations because all have sinned, and also when he <u>only</u> declares those people righteous who have faith in Jesus.

[5] M. M. Lk 1:1: Jesus came to seek and save <u>all</u> lost people from <u>every</u> nation on earth.

[6] M. M. Ac 13:46: As he did with the old Israel, God <u>first of all</u> strengthens the faith of the new Israel, the Church with his Word and Sacraments, so that they can go and witness to the lost people of all nations.

[7] M. I. Lk 3:3a: Christians should, in love, warn lost people who do not repent.

[8] M. M. Ac 13:46: As he did with the old Israel, God <u>first of all</u> strengthens the faith of the new Israel, the Church with his Word and Sacraments, so that they can go and witness to the lost people of all nations.

[9] M. M. Lk 1:1: Jesus came to seek and save <u>all</u> lost people from <u>every</u> nation on earth.

[10] M. M. Ro 1:5: The same Holy Spirit who creates <u>faith</u> and a new missionary <u>nature</u> in a person's heart also graciously empowers him to gratefully respond to his Lord's love by <u>obeying</u> him.

[11] M. M. Ro 5:1: On the cross, Jesus earned <u>peace</u> with God for <u>all</u> of his brothers and sisters from every nation on earth.

[12] M. I. Lk 8:11: Christians should faithfully do their job of preaching and leave the <u>results</u> to the Holy Spirit.

[13] M. I. Mt 19:9: Christians should not divorce their spouse unless their spouse is unfaithful and stubbornly refuses to repent.

[14] M. I. Lk 3:8: Christians should always be prepared to boldly and publicly refute false teaching, so that Satan cannot easily deceive people.

[15] M. I. Lk 11:10: Christians should <u>continuously</u> pray to their heavenly Father and <u>always</u> depend on his grace, and not on their own feeble strength, because he <u>always</u> loves them.

[16] M. I. Lk 15:7: Christians should rejoice together with the heavenly Father and his angels when just *one* lost person hears the Law and Gospel, and then receives the gracious gifts of a repentant heart and faith in Jesus.

[17] M. I. Tit 2:7: Christians should always be sure that their <u>actions</u> match their <u>verbal</u> witness to the name of Jesus, because if they do <u>not</u> match they will destroy their <u>verbal</u> witness, especially for <u>unbelievers</u>.

[18] M. M. Lk 13:24: The <u>only</u> way to enter the Kingdom of God is to have <u>faith</u> in Jesus as one's Savior.

[19] M. M. Ro 10:17a: The Holy Spirit <u>only</u> creates and preserves faith by using the message of God's grace in his holy Word.

[20] M. M. Ro 3:24: Jesus lived a life of perfect obedience and shed his precious blood on the

cross, in order to graciously set all nations free from sin, which a person only receives by faith in him.

Chapter 17

Temptations to Sin 17:1-4

17:1 *And he said to his disciples, "Temptations to sin are sure to come, but woe to the one through whom they come!*
17:2 *It would be better for him if a millstone were hung around his neck and he were cast into the sea than that he should cause one of these little ones to sin.*
17:3 *Pay attention to yourselves! If your brother sins, rebuke him, and if he repents, forgive him,*
17:4 *and if he sins against you seven times in the day, and turns to you seven times, saying, 'I repent,' you must forgive him."*

17:1-2 Jesus warns all Christians about two dangers when he says in verse 3, *"Pay attention to yourselves."* **1)** The first danger is that *"temptations to sin are sure to come"* (v 1). Obviously, Satan and the evil world around us are constantly working mightily to destroy the faith of all Christians, but especially the young faith of *"these little ones"* (v 2). They are Christians who are vulnerable because they are either young in age or young in their faith. Likewise, Satan knows how vital faith in Jesus is; and he also knows how unprepared *"these little ones"* are to face his incredibly evil and clever temptations. The danger is very real and unrelenting ([1]M. I. 2 Cor 11:14). **2)** Jesus adds the second danger in verse 1, *"but woe to the one through whom they come!"* He knew that this happens in several different ways—both intentionally and unintentionally. **a)** First of all, our spiritual enemies are obviously always busy attacking *"these little ones"* intentionally. St. Paul frequently warned against at least two ways that they do so: First, he very frequently warned against false teachers who were apparently quite common in some churches at that time (2 Cor 11:13; Gal 2:4), and of course are still common today as well. Secondly, in (Rom 1:18), he also warned against people who deliberately suppress the truth about who God is. Unfortunately, this sin is very prevalent today, especially in American public schools in many different ways. Satan is still very busy.

b) Secondly, Christians may, perhaps <u>unintentionally</u>, sin by tempting "these little ones" as well. Most frequently they may do so by their <u>bad examples</u>, since "actions speak louder than words." Not only are unbelievers watching how Christians behave, but so are *"these little ones."* Therefore, instead of being bad examples, it's vitally important that their parents and older Christians should help *"these little ones"* (18:16) by always showing them <u>good examples</u> of loving others ([2]M. I. Tit 2:7).

17:3-4 Christians are at times confused about why Jesus said in verse 4 that we *"must forgive him"* <u>seven</u> times in one day. And it's even more confusing when Jesus told Peter in (Mt 18:22), *"I do not say to you [forgive him] seven times, but <u>seventy times</u> seven."* It's confusing to us today because our cultures are all very different from the Jewish culture of Jesus' day. For them, two numbers: seven and ten, or multiples of both numbers, as in (Mt 18:22), symbolized perfection or completion; but for us they have no secondary meaning. Therefore, our gracious Lord was saying in both verses that his disciples should forgive him an <u>unlimited</u> number of times, *"seven times,"* just as he himself has been eager to most <u>graciously</u> forgive them. How can we do otherwise, since he is so overwhelmingly gracious and generous to us? Do we <u>deserve</u> his forgiveness? Does our brother or sister, who is one of *"these little ones,"* deserve our forgiveness? Therefore, genuine forgiveness is always a generous <u>gift</u> that we give to others out of gratitude to our dear Lord (6:38; 2 Cor 1:3-5; [3]M. M. Eph 1:7). And what a powerful example this is to our children and especially also to the sinful world, because it is completely impossible for unbelievers to truly forgive others. Unbelievers do not have the power of the Holy Spirit in their hearts ([4]M. I. Ro 12:20).

Increase Our Faith 17:5-6

17:5 *The apostles said to the Lord, "Increase our faith!"*
17:6 *And the Lord said, "If you had faith like a grain of mustard seed, you could say to this mulberry tree, 'Be uprooted and planted in the sea,' and it would obey you.*

17:5-6 (1) This was probably the most significant request that Jesus' disciples ever asked him since it shows that they realized how much they <u>needed</u> his mighty grace if they were going to carry out his mission to the world successfully ([5]M. M. Ro 1:5). However, in another sense, they didn't really know what they were asking him, since our Lord often uses gracious <u>testing</u> in order to strengthen the faith of his disciples. They were actually asking him to <u>test</u> their faith ([6]M. M. 1 Pe 1:7)! **2)** How could the faith of a mere human being be so powerful as to command a tree to move (v 6)? It's only possible because faith in Jesus <u>connects</u> him to the rich grace of his almighty Lord. The size of the person's faith does not matter, because it is his Lord Jesus who does it according to his gracious will. Furthermore, the tree that Jesus was, no doubt, talking about here was a stubborn <u>heart</u> that <u>only</u> his Spirit can move to repentance and faith in Jesus through his holy Word ([7]M. M. Ro 10:17a).

Unworthy Servants 17:7-10

17:7 *"Will any one of you who has a servant plowing or keeping sheep say to him when he has come in from the field, 'Come at once and recline at table'?*

17:8 *Will he not rather say to him, 'Prepare supper for me, and dress properly, and serve me while I eat and drink, and afterward you will eat and drink'?*

17:9 *Does he thank the servant because he did what was commanded?*

17:10 *So you also, when you have done all that you were commanded, say, 'We are unworthy servants; we have only done what was our duty.'"*

17:7-10 Some people make two wrong assumptions about Christians whom they call, "<u>foreign</u> missionaries." **a)** First of all, some people wrongly assume that "<u>foreign</u> missionaries" deserve more praise because they have left their families and gone so far to proclaim the Gospel.

However, this is not true for at least two reasons: Christians who go one mile and Christians who go thousands of miles to do their duty of proclaiming the Gospel are the same *"unworthy servants"* (v 10) who have *"only done what was our [their] duty"* (v 10). Neither servant has done more than the other one, and therefore, has earned more of God's favor than the other one. As a matter of fact, no Christian earns God's favor by obeying him, since we do so in grateful response to his gracious love for us (Eph 2:8-10; [8]M. M. Ro 1:5). **b)** Secondly, others may argue that "foreign missionaries" must have more faith than those who go one mile, but Jesus taught his disciples in verses 5 and 6 that the size of one's faith does not matter. What does matter is the *size* of their Lord's almighty power. The Holy Spirit not only gives us the gift of faith, he also graciously empowers us to use our faith and our mission-hearts to go where he sends us on our Lord's mission—whether our target person or target group is nearby or far away (Eph 2:10; [9]M. M. Mt 5:14 & Ro 1:5).

Jesus Cleanses Ten Lepers 17:11-19

17:11 *On the way to Jerusalem he was passing along between Samaria and Galilee.*
17:12 *And as he entered a village, he was met by ten lepers, who stood at a distance*
17:13 *and lifted up their voices, saying, "Jesus, Master, have mercy on us."*
17:14 *When he saw them he said to them, "Go and show yourselves to the priests." And as they went they were cleansed.*
17:15 *Then one of them, when he saw that he was healed, turned back, praising God with a loud voice;*
17:16 *and he fell on his face at Jesus' feet, giving him thanks. Now he was a Samaritan.*
17:17 *Then Jesus answered, "Were not ten cleansed? Where are the nine?*
17:18 *Was no one found to return and give praise to God except this foreigner?"*

17:19 *And he said to him, "Rise and go your way; your faith has made you well."*

17:11 Jesus never forgot, as he continued to *"seek the lost,"* that he also came to *"save"* them; therefore, he was *"on the way to Jerusalem"* (v 1), in order to die for all Samaritans, all Jews and all Gentiles (19:10; 13:33; [10]M. M. Lk 1:1).

17:12-19 (1) In his account, Luke did not miss the fact that nine of the sick men were Jews and <u>one</u> was a Samaritan or a <u>Gentile</u> like himself. But why did the Gentile man return to thank Jesus and the others did not? He no doubt thanked Jesus since he knew for sure that, as a Gentile, he did not <u>deserve</u> such help from a Jew, while the others sinfully assumed that they deserved it because they were Jews (7:4-6). It's obvious from Luke's account here and elsewhere that many Jews of Jesus' day proudly depended on their <u>blood</u> relationship with Abraham for God's favor; it was not only the Pharisees and scribes who did so (3:8). Therefore, it's clear, once again, that a person's race and culture do not matter before God, rather <u>all</u> human beings are equally sinful and deserve his wrath; and likewise <u>all</u> receive the gracious gift of his forgiveness by the same *"narrow door"* of faith in Jesus ([11]M. M. Lk 13:24 & [12]Ro 3:26). **2)** Why did Jesus tell them in verse 14, *"Go and show yourselves to the priests?"* He had at least two reasons: **a)** First, he ordered them to obey the Law, so that he himself could continue to obey the whole Law of God perfectly for us (Lev 13:2-3), since <u>no</u> other human being could do so, in order to save us (19:10; [13]M. M. Mt 1:22). **b)** Secondly, he told the nine Jews to do this, so that they could be <u>fully</u> healed by being restored to their families and their society. Only a priest could verify that they were healed and allow them to return home (Lev 14:1-9). Obviously, the Samaritan, on the other hand, would not have gone to the priests, since the Samaritans did not worship in the temple in Jerusalem (Jn 4:20; [14]M. I. Lk 4:35 & [15]M. M. Ro 3:31).

The Coming of the Kingdom 17:20-37

17:20 *Being asked by the Pharisees when the kingdom of God would come, he answered them, "The kingdom of God is not coming with signs to be observed,*

17:21 *nor will they say, 'Look, here it is!' or 'There!' for behold, the kingdom of God is in the midst of you."*

17:22 *And he said to the disciples, "The days are coming when you will desire to see one of the days of the Son of Man, and you will not see it.*

17:23 *And they will say to you, 'Look, there!' or 'Look, here!' Do not go out or follow them.*

17:24 *For as the lightning flashes and lights up the sky from one side to the other, so will the Son of Man be in his day.*

17:25 *But first he must suffer many things and be rejected by this generation.*

17:26 *Just as it was in the days of Noah, so will it be in the days of the Son of Man.*

17:27 *They were eating and drinking and marrying and being given in marriage, until the day when Noah entered the ark, and the flood came and destroyed them all.*

17:28 *Likewise, just as it was in the days of Lot--they were eating and drinking, buying and selling, planting and building,*

17:29 *but on the day when Lot went out from Sodom, fire and sulfur rained from heaven and destroyed them all--*

17:30 *so will it be on the day when the Son of Man is revealed.*

17:31 *On that day, let the one who is on the housetop, with his goods in the house, not come down to take them away, and likewise let the one who is in the field not turn back.*

17:32 *Remember Lot's wife.*

17:33 *Whoever seeks to preserve his life will lose it, but whoever loses his life will keep it.*

17:34 *I tell you, in that night there will be two in one bed. One will be taken and the other left.*

17:35 *There will be two women grinding together. One will be taken and the other left."*

17:36 *[Two men will be in the field; one will be taken and the other left.]*

> 17:37 *And they said to him, "Where, Lord?" He said to them, "Where the corpse is, there the vultures will gather."*

17:20-21 No doubt, when the Pharisees asked about *"when the kingdom of God would come"* in verse 20, they were thinking in terms of a Messiah who would restore political power to the Jews, which would have given them even more power over the people. However, they could not see the *"kingdom of God"* (v 20) in this mere man, Jesus, since they lacked the faith to see him as their King of kings. Once again, faith in Jesus is the only door into the kingdom of God (13:23). However, what they also did not know was that Jesus was *"seeking"* them and longed to graciously rule over them (19:10); but they were too proud to humble themselves and receive the gift of child-like faith (v 2) from him. Quite to the contrary, they were the ones who deserved to have a millstone hung around their necks and be cast into the sea (v 2) because they were the worst human enemies of Jesus and his *"little ones"* (17:2; [16]M. I. Lk 3:3a)

17:22-35 (1) While the disciples were also blind to much of what was happening, the Spirit of Jesus was in their hearts to give them the strength to carry their own crosses and to endure, in order to become the leaders of the Church that would continue to carry out their mission to people all over the world who did not yet know Jesus as their King ([17]M. M. Ro 1:5). **2)** We have no way of knowing how long Jesus, as a human being, knew so many details of his heavenly Father's mission plan to send him to rescue mankind from sin (19:10; v 11). Nevertheless, in verse 25, he once again graciously warned his disciples that he would *"suffer many things [by dying]"* and that he would leave them by ascending. But then he also gave them the wonderful promise that he would, one day soon, suddenly and publicly returned to them in all of his brilliant glory on the Last Day (v 24). He both warned them and also gave them hope, so that they would not be totally surprised when each phase of his Father's plan happened (12:35-48; [18]M. M. 1 Cor 15:20 & [19]1 Cor 15:51). And they did, in fact, repeatedly forget his many warnings and promises (24:11, 19-24); but after his resurrection and ascension, they did have his words of warning and hope to recall and comfort them (24:8; [20]M. I. Lk 11:10). **3)** The majority of the Pharisees were trying to *"preserve"* (v 33) their lives by work-righteousness (3:8); and they would therefore sadly *"lose"* (v 33) their lives eternally. Their King and Savior was at that very moment patiently seeking them, but they proudly persisted in their blindness. Nicodemus (Jn 19:39) and Joseph (23:50) were apparently the only two members of the Jewish Council who received the gracious gift of faith in Jesus. They *"lost their lives"* in child-like repentance, and would therefore also receive the gracious gift of eternal salvation (v 33; [21]M. I. Lk 15:7).

17:37 Jesus' warnings were filled with so many bewildering details that the disciples could only ask in verse 37, *"Where, Lord?"* Therefore, Jesus comforted them with the assurance that his sudden return with full power and glory (v 24) as their King would be as obvious as seeing vultures circling over a dead body (v 37). The complete fulfillment of his Father's gracious mission plan (1:1; Lev 18:5) was so certain that it was as if it had already happened. Jesus would most certainly do everything that he had just told them he would do to *"seek and save the lost"* (19:10; [22]M. M. Lk 1:1).

---

[1] M. I. 2 Cor 11:14: Christians should beware of Satan because he not only disguises himself as an angel of light, but he also sends out false teachers who also disguise themselves as servants of the light, in order to deceive people by telling lies that appear to be the truth of the Gospel.

[2] M. I. Tit 2:7: Christians should always be sure that their <u>actions</u> match their <u>verbal</u> witness to the name of Jesus, because if they do <u>not</u> match they will destroy their <u>verbal</u> witness, especially for <u>unbelievers</u>.

[3] M. M. Eph 1:7: Instead of punishing mankind for our sins, in his great wisdom and knowledge, God himself most graciously and generously paid our debt by sacrificing his own Son Jesus, in order to forgive us all of our sins.

[4] M. I. Ro 12:20: Christians should respond to God's grace by always showing love (and not cursing or taking revenge against) their enemies, so that their enemies may be ashamed of harming them; and they, then, may have opportunities to witness the Gospel to them.

[5] M. M. Ro 1:5: The same Holy Spirit who creates <u>faith</u> and a new missionary <u>nature</u> in a person's heart also graciously empowers him to gratefully respond to his Lord's love by <u>obeying</u> him.

[6] M. M. 1 Pe 1:7: God graciously allows Christians to suffer now for a little while so that their faith, which is as precious as gold that perishes even though it is tested by fire, may be proved genuine through the testing and also give glory and honor to Jesus Christ when God reveals him

on the Last Day.

⁷ M. M. Ro 10:17a: The Holy Spirit <u>only</u> creates and preserves faith by using the message of God's grace in his holy Word.

⁸ M. M. Ro 1:5: The same Holy Spirit who creates <u>faith</u> and a new missionary <u>nature</u> in a person's heart also graciously empowers him to gratefully respond to his Lord's love by <u>obeying</u> him.

⁹ M. M. Mt 5:14: When the Holy Spirit creates faith in a person's heart, he also graciously gives him a new mission-heart that is eager to shine the light of the Gospel throughout the whole world.

¹⁰ M. M. Lk 1:1: Jesus came to seek and save <u>all</u> lost people from <u>every</u> nation on earth.

¹¹ M. M. Lk 13:24: The <u>only</u> way to enter the Kingdom of God is to have *faith* in Jesus as one's Savior.

¹² M. M. Ro 3:26: God is just and fair to <u>everyone</u>, both when he condemns <u>all</u> people of all nations because all have sinned, and also when he <u>only</u> declares those people righteous who have faith in Jesus.

¹³ M. M. Mt 1:22: God sent his only Son, Jesus to be born as a true human being, so that he could save all of his brothers and sisters of all nations by fulfilling all of God's promises in the Old Testament.

¹⁴ M. I. Lk 4:35: Christians should view every person as a whole person, and show him compassion by caring for <u>both</u> his physical and spiritual needs as they go on their mission.

¹⁵ M. M. Ro 3:31: Christianity <u>fulfills</u> the Jewish religion because the Holy Spirit empowers Christians to <u>obey</u> God's Law and thus also obey Jesus who fulfilled all of God's Laws for them.

¹⁶ M. I. Lk 3:3a: Christians should, in love, warn lost people who do not repent.

¹⁷ M. M. Ro 1:5: The same Holy Spirit who creates <u>faith</u> and a new missionary <u>nature</u> in a person's heart also graciously empowers him to gratefully respond to his Lord's love by <u>obeying</u> him.

¹⁸ M. M. 1 Cor 15:20: As the only God/man, Jesus is the first human being whom God raised from the dead; and therefore, on the Last Day, he will also raise all of his brothers and sisters who died believing in him.

¹⁹ M. M. 1 Cor 15:51: The wonderful mystery is that not all Christians will die; however, when the trumpet sounds on the Last Day, God will quickly change the perishable bodies of all Christians into imperishable bodies.

²⁰ M. I. Lk 11:10: Christians should <u>continuously</u> pray to their heavenly Father and <u>always</u> depend on his grace, and not on their own feeble strength, because he <u>always</u> loves them.

²¹ M. I. Lk 15:7: Christians should rejoice together with the heavenly Father and his angels when just <u>one</u> lost person hears the Law and Gospel, and then receives the gracious gifts of a repentant heart and faith in Jesus.

²² M. M. Lk 1:1: Jesus came to seek and save <u>all</u> lost people from <u>every</u> nation on earth.

Chapter 18

The Parable of the Persistent Widow 18:1-8

18:1 *And he told them a parable to the effect that they ought always to pray and not lose heart.*
18:2 *He said, "In a certain city there was a judge who neither feared God nor respected man.*
18:3 *And there was a widow in that city who kept coming to him and saying, 'Give me justice against my adversary.'*
18:4 *For a while he refused, but afterward he said to himself, 'Though I neither fear God nor respect man,*
18:5 *yet because this widow keeps bothering me, I will give her justice, so that she will not beat me down by her continual coming.'"*
18:6 *And the Lord said, "Hear what the unrighteous judge says.*
18:7 *And will not God give justice to his elect, who cry to him day and night? Will he delay long over them?*
18:8 *I tell you, he will give justice to them speedily. Nevertheless, when the Son of Man comes, will he find faith on earth?"*

18:1-8 (1) While Jesus used this powerful illustration to teach his disciples to *"always to pray and not lose heart"* (v 1; 11:5-10), we can be very sure that he was also teaching them the same lesson by the perfect example of his own *"continual"* (v 5) prayer life. Through constant prayer, he kept his own mission-heart completely focused on his Father's gracious will, so that he could completely fulfill his mission to *"seek and to save the lost"* (19:10; [1]M. M. Lk 1:1).

18:6 This illustration is so powerful because, in his mission-heart, the heavenly Father is always completely the <u>opposite</u> of this stubborn *"unrighteous"* judge (v 6). He is constantly full of compassion for *"his elect"* (v 7), who are the true <u>spiritual</u> sons and daughters of Abraham because they have faith in his Son, Jesus (2 Cor 1:3; [2]M. M. Ro 4:11).

18:7 What is the *"justice"* (v 7) that the heavenly Father's *"elect"* (v 7) need so urgently? As Christians today continue to go about their task of proclaiming Jesus' Law and Gospel message, their hearers may be <u>offended</u> both by God's Law that condemns them and also by the Gospel that insists that there is only <u>one</u> *"narrow door"* to enter God's Kingdom. Many people do not like to hear either truth, because neither one of these two truths are *"just"* or right (vs 7-8) in their sinful human eyes. Therefore, some of these unbelieving hearers who are serving Satan (vs 2, 4) often persecute and kill those who preach this "offensive" Law and Gospel message. Thus, every Christian's urgent and persistent prayer should always be that the Last Day when God will reveal the Son of Man (v 8) will come very soon (17:30). On that Day, he will give the final *"judgment"* (v 7) that his Word stands <u>true</u> forever. All of Jesus' enemies will then know that they believed a lie and that his missionaries were indeed proclaiming his truth ([3]M. M. Ro 3:26 & [4]Lk 12:48).

18:8 (1) The widow who was begging before the judge was just like the disciples of Jesus who were *"lambs among wolves"* (10:3) as they went out to proclaim the Gospel. As the weak *"lambs"* continue to proclaim the Gospel yet today in a world full of *"wolves,"* we may appear to be helpless before our enemies, but, as we *"cry to him day and night"* (v 7), our Lord gives us the strength and courage we need to face our enemies. Through constant prayer, we remain totally within our Lord's gracious will; and by his almighty grace, *"he will give justice to them [us] speedily"* (v 8; [5]M. I. Lk 11:10 & [6]Lk 10:2b). **2)** Jesus then warns in verse 8, *"Will he [the Son of Man] find faith on earth?"*
Even though the heavenly Father's mission-heart has been patiently waiting for and seeking lost mankind ever since Adam and Eve sinned (15:20), it surely painfully grieves his heart that only a *"few"* (v 8) people who hear the Law and Gospel will repent and believe in his Son (v 8; 13:23; [7]M. I. Mt 7:14). However, by giving this dire prediction, Jesus was obviously not trying to discourage his disciples (either then or now) whom he was sending out; instead, he gave them and us this sober assessment of the final result of his mission, in order to give us a sense of <u>urgency</u> on our mission. By implication, he was urging us: **a)** First of all, we should pray for more Christians because all Christians are missionaries ([8]M. M. Mt 5:14 & [9]Ro 1:5). **b)** And then, we should also carefully choose and train more leaders for his mission ([10]M. I. Lk 6:13).

The Pharisee and the Tax Collector 18:9-14

18:9 *He also told this parable to some who trusted in themselves that they were righteous, and treated others with contempt:*
18:10 *"Two men went up into the temple to pray, one a Pharisee and the other a tax collector.*
18:11 *The Pharisee, standing by himself, prayed thus: 'God, I thank you that I am not like other men, extortioners, unjust, adulterers, or even like this tax collector.*
18:12 *I fast twice a week; I give tithes of all that I get.'*
18:13 *But the tax collector, standing far off, would not even lift up his eyes to heaven, but beat his breast, saying, 'God, be merciful to me, a sinner!'*
18:14 *I tell you, this man went down to his house justified, rather than the other. For everyone who exalts himself will be humbled, but the one who humbles himself will be exalted."*

18:9-14 Certainly, a number of Pharisees (v 10) were listening to Jesus at this time; therefore, Jesus, yet again, used a powerful illustration to continue to seek these lost people (19:10; [11]M. M. Lk 1:1). His message of Law to them was always the same: *"Humble yourselves; repent and believe that I am your King"* (Mk 1:15). However, very few of them had the ears to hear him, since they thought that they <u>deserved</u> God's blessings (7:30; 11:43; [12]M. I. Lk 3:3a). The tax collectors (v 13) and other well-known sinners, on the other hand, heard the same message and repented, because they <u>knew</u> that they were sinners and did <u>not</u> deserve God's forgiveness (15:2; 17:20; [13]M. M. Ro 4:3).

Let the Children Come to Me 18:15-17

18:15 *Now they were bringing even infants to him that he might touch them. And when the disciples saw it, they rebuked them.*
18:16 *But Jesus called them to him, saying, "Let the children come to me, and do not hinder them, for to such belongs the kingdom of*

God.
18:17 *Truly, I say to you, whoever does not receive the kingdom of God like a child shall not enter it."*

18:15-17 (1) First of all, in verses 15-17, Jesus was obviously talking to his disciples about the children whom he was holding, and he was telling them that the children also needed his forgiveness because they too were born in sin. However, these verses do not say whether Jesus added that the children also needed to be baptized; but, yet today, we baptize children because they are born in sin (Ps 51:5; [14]M. M. Tit 3:5). **2)** A person who has the faith of *"a child"* (vs 16-17) has entered *"the narrow door"* (13:24) into the Kingdom of God because he knows that he is *"poor"* before his heavenly Father (6:20) and he must depend completely on his rich grace for him. The tax collector in verse14 had this kind of faith and was a true spiritual son of Abraham, just as Mary did in (1:28), the woman did in (13:16), Lazarus did in (16:23) and Zacchaeus did in (19:9). In short, Luke did not merely talk about true faith as an abstract idea that came into being as a result of hearing God's Word; rather, throughout his account, he repeatedly illustrated true faith with personal examples to drive this truth home. Childlike faith is the only *"narrow door"* that God's Word opens into the Kingdom. As our Lord's mission expands, his Kingdom will never grow by any other means (Jn 14:6; Ac 4:12; [15]M. M. Lk 13:24). **3)** Jesus' mission-heart longs for all lost people who hear his Gospel to listen to it carefully and then believe in him (1 Tim 2:4). Nevertheless, his heart must have been filled with grief when he told us that *"many…will seek to enter [my Kingdom] and will not be able"* (13:24); therefore, when he returns on the Last Day, he will find only a few people on earth who have a childlike faith (v 8). Thus, we are compelled to ask two questions: Why then, is there only one, narrow door into the Kingdom? The truth is that there can be no other way because there can be no other sacrifice for the sins of mankind (Heb 10:9-10). In his rich grace, he alone has done everything for us, in order to make peace between us and our heavenly Father (Rom 5:1). And secondly, why do so few people find this one, narrow door? **a)** First of all, it is the responsibility of the hearer to listen carefully to both the Law and the Gospel, because our gracious Lord never forces his grace on anyone. Faith is always a free gift; yet many people don't have a chance to hear it or many do not listen carefully to such a vital message (8:4-15; Rom 10:14-15; [16]M. I. Lk 3:3a & [17]M. M. Ro 4:3). **b)** Secondly, this exclusive truth offends many people; and they then refuse to believe in him and are lost forever. Today, for example, some people take offense at the fact that the Gospel is so "narrow minded;" and Satan uses this as a clever trap to confuse them (8:12, 14). **c)** And thirdly, Satan deceives many into believing that there are many gods, therefore, there must be many ways to get to heaven. How evil and confusing that is ([18]M. M. Lk 13:24)!

The Rich Ruler 18:18-30

18:18 *And a ruler asked him, "Good Teacher, what must I do to inherit eternal life?"*
18:19 *And Jesus said to him, "Why do you call me good? No one is good except God alone.*
18:20 *You know the commandments: 'Do not commit adultery, Do not murder, Do not steal, Do not bear false witness, Honor your father and mother.'"*
18:21 *And he said, "All these I have kept from my youth."*
18:22 *When Jesus heard this, he said to him, "One thing you still lack. Sell all that you have and distribute to the poor, and you will have treasure in heaven; and come, follow me."*
18:23 *But when he heard these things, he became very sad, for he was extremely rich.*
18:24 *Jesus, looking at him with sadness, said, "How difficult it is for those who have wealth to enter the kingdom of God!*
18:25 *For it is easier for a camel to go through the eye of a needle than for a rich person to enter the kingdom of God."*
18:26 *Those who heard it said, "Then who can be saved?"*
18:27 *But he said, "What is impossible with men is possible with God."*
18:28 *And Peter said, "See, we have left our homes and followed*

> *you."*
> 18:29 *And he said to them, "Truly, I say to you, there is no one who has left house or wife or brothers or parents or children, for the sake of the kingdom of God,*
> 18:30 *who will not receive many times more in this time, and in the age to come eternal life."*

18:18-27 (1) Jesus was earnestly seeking this young man who was lost because he loved money more than anything else. His life was focused on earning both material and spiritual wealth; therefore, in his self-righteousness, he claimed that he had always obeyed all of God's Laws. Jesus countered by trying to make him realize that he had in fact not been able to obey all of God's Laws perfectly. But he did not understand, and turned away from his Savior, Jesus, still lost in prideful self-righteousness ([19]M. I. Lk 3:3a). **2)** However, those who were present that day had not learned Jesus' lesson either; and thus they asked in verse 26, *"Then who can be saved?"* Therefore, Jesus told them a further truth by answering in verse 27, *"What is impossible with men is possible with God."* In other words, Jesus told them that salvation is entirely God's work. Jesus himself, as true God and true man, was at that very moment doing what the young man was totally incapable of doing because he was a sinful human being ([20]M. M. Lk 1:27 & [21]Lk 1:35). Holy Jesus was continuing to earn his Father's favor by obeying all of his Laws for the sake of all of his fellow human beings, including this young man. However, his obedience was, by no means, a "cheap" grace, because it also cost him a horrible death on the cross. Furthermore, in his rich grace, our heavenly Father, then, gives the righteousness that Jesus earned to all who trust in his Son, as a free gift. How it must have grieved Jesus' mission-heart that day that his hearers were so blind to his rich grace for them (22:37; 24:44; Rom 5:19; [22]M. M. Mt 1:22)!

18:28-30 (1) Likewise, Jesus' disciples had not learned the lesson that Jesus just tried to teach them that salvation from sin is a gracious gift from God. They still thought that they were earning God's favor by following Jesus, because Peter said in verse 28, *"See, we have left our* *homes and followed you."* However, when Jesus then promised his disciples rewards in verse 29-30, he was <u>not</u> saying that they were <u>earning</u> anything by their obedience. Rather he was saying that, by his love and grace, the Holy Spirit had not only created faith in their hearts, he had also graciously given them <u>grateful</u> mission-hearts that moved them to love Jesus, obey him and follow him (Eph 2:8-10; [23]M. M. Ro 1:5). It's a new mission message. M. M. Lk 18:29: All Christians will certainly receive rewards in heaven as gracious gifts, but not because they earned them by going into the lost world to proclaim the Gospel message; rather, they went because they also received <u>grateful</u> mission-hearts from their Lord. **2)** It's true that especially foreign missionaries must leave their *"house or wife or brothers or parents or children, for the sake of the kingdom of God"* (v 29); however, they may not have to wait to receive all of their rewards (v 30) in heaven. Many times missionaries receive the gracious reward of seeing the fruits of their labors on the mission field. As our Lord graciously promises in verse 30, they may *"receive many times more [family] in this time [on earth]"* (v 30) because they receive <u>spiritual</u> brothers and sisters, who heard the Law and Gospel they preached, repented and now believe in Jesus. And what a great joy <u>that</u> is that they don't have to wait for all of their rewards! It's a heavenly joy that they share with their heavenly Father, with their dear Lord and with all of his angels (15:6, 10, 23-24). It's a new mission message. M. M. Lk 18:30: God may graciously reward missionaries with the joy of seeing the fruit of their labors on earth by giving them a new family of <u>spiritual</u> brothers and sisters who heard the Gospel they preached and now believe in Jesus.

Jesus Foretells His Death a Third Time 18:31-34

18:31 *And taking the twelve, he said to them, "See, we are going up to Jerusalem, and everything that is written about the Son of Man by the prophets will be accomplished.*
18:32 *For he will be delivered over to the Gentiles and will be mocked and shamefully treated and spit upon.*
18:33 *And after flogging him, they will kill him, and on the third day*

> *he will rise."*
> 18:34 *But they understood none of these things. This saying was hidden from them, and they did not grasp what was said.*

18:31-34 (1) Jesus continued to <u>not</u> focus on his *own* horrible pain and death that was looming ever nearer; rather he continued to focus on his <u>disciples'</u> needs and *"seek"* them by, once again, warning them in verse 31 that this was his <u>last</u> journey to Jerusalem. But they were focused on themselves and their own needs so much that, once again, *"this saying was hidden from them, and they did not grasp what was said"* (v 34). But of course, this was neither the first nor the last time that they misunderstood him (9:22, 43-45; 12:50; 17:25). Therefore, they had no idea how soon and how great their own needs would be; they would have to carry their own crosses of suffering far more often and far sooner than they then realized. And no doubt, they likewise still did not realize that suffering for their dear Lord was an inevitable part of serving him on his mission, because they were feeble *"sheep"* among *"wolves"* who were serving Satan (10:3; [24]M. M. Lk 6:22). However, as true God, their dear Lord obviously knew about all that they would have to endure, and he therefore, continued to focus on them and their needs and not his own. His grace is so amazing ([25]M. M. Lk 1:35 & [26]Ro 3:24)! **2)** Why did Jesus continue to warn them even though they wouldn't understand? Perhaps he was trying to jar their memories. As pious Jews, they should have recalled many passages in the Old Testament like Isaiah 53 that says very plainly that the Messiah would be the Lord's *"<u>suffering Servant</u>."* Therefore, even though it made no sense to them at the time, after he rose from the dead, he himself taught two of his disciples how his words and actions perfectly fulfilled the words of all of Scripture (24:25-27). Then finally, the Holy Spirit used his holy Word to produce the fruit of much stronger faith, as his disciples carefully studied the Scripture in order to confirm that everything that Jesus had told them was indeed true ([27]M. M. Ro 10:17a). And this filled them with a boldness that no one could silence (Ac 4:29).

Jesus Heals a Blind Beggar 18:35-43

18:35 *As he drew near to Jericho, a blind man was sitting by the roadside begging.*
18:36 *And hearing a crowd going by, he inquired what this meant.*
18:37 *They told him, "Jesus of Nazareth is passing by."*
18:38 *And he cried out, "Jesus, Son of David, have mercy on me!"*
18:39 *And those who were in front rebuked him, telling him to be silent. But he cried out all the more, "Son of David, have mercy on me!"*
18:40 *And Jesus stopped and commanded him to be brought to him. And when he came near, he asked him,*
18:41 *"What do you want me to do for you?" He said, "Lord, let me recover my sight."*
18:42 *And Jesus said to him, "Recover your sight; your faith has made you well."*
18:43 *And immediately he recovered his sight and followed him, glorifying God. And all the people, when they saw it, gave praise to God.*

18:35-43 (1) The fact that the blind man called Jesus, *"Son of David"* is significant for two reasons: **a)** First of all, the name, *"Son of David"* is a Messianic title of royalty; his mission-heart had moved him to come to earth in order to expand his Kingdom by *"seeking and saving the lost."* Thus, the blind man trusted in Jesus as his God and King; and therefore, he received the gracious gift of healing from him ([28]M. I. Lk 4:35). **b)** Secondly, by using this Messianic title he showed his faith in his King. Then, in (19:9), Jesus called Zacchaeus *"a son of Abraham."* Therefore, both this man and Zacchaeus were true spiritual sons of Abraham, because they had received the same gift of faith in God's promises that their father Abraham had ([29]M. M. Ro 4:11 & [30]Lk 14:34). **2)** Also note that the first fruit of faith that came out of this man's heart was gratitude and praise; verse 43 says, *"Immediately he recovered his sight and followed him, glorifying God."* And the people who were present heard him praise God and also *"gave praise to God"* (v 43). He had a new mission-heart that immediately turned him into a powerful witness about his Lord's rich grace ([31]M. M. Mt 5:14).

[1] M. M. Lk 1:1: Jesus came to seek and save all lost people from every nation on earth.

[2] M. M. Ro 4:11: All Christians from every nation on earth belong to the spiritual family of Abraham, the Church because they share the same faith in Jesus that their father had.

[3] M. M. Ro 3:26: God is just and fair to everyone, both when he condemns all people of all nations because all have sinned, and also when he only declares those people righteous who have faith in Jesus.

[4] M. M. Lk 12:48: God will justly condemn to eternal punishment all people who do not trust in Jesus as their Savior, but he will punish them by different degrees, according to how well they knew his will.

[5] M. I. Lk 11:10: Christians should continuously pray to their heavenly Father and always depend on his grace, and not on their own feeble strength, because he always loves them.

[6] M. I. Lk 10:2b: Christians should ask their Lord for more faith and more zeal, so that more of them will be eager to be his missionaries.

[7] M. I. Mt 7:14: Christians should hurry on their mission to the world because people who are lost have many enemies who lure them away from Jesus; and therefore, few of them find faith in Jesus which is the only gate into his Kingdom of life.

[8] M. M. Mt 5:14: When the Holy Spirit creates faith in a person's heart, he also graciously gives him a new mission-heart that is eager to shine the light of the Gospel throughout the whole world.

[9] M. M. Ro 1:5: The same Holy Spirit who creates faith and a new missionary nature in a person's heart also graciously empowers him to gratefully respond to his Lord's love by obeying him.

[10] M. I. Lk 6:13: Christians should choose new leaders and train them in order to multiply the work.

[11] M. M. Lk 1:1: Jesus came to seek and save all lost people from every nation on earth.

[12] M. I. Lk 3:3a: Christians should, in love, warn lost people who do not repent.

[13] M. M. Ro 4:3: Faith in Jesus is a free gift that a person graciously receives from God and he does not earn.

[14] M. M. Tit 3:5: When a person is baptized, God graciously saves him and gives him the gift of a new birth from his indwelling Holy Spirit; and he does this because his mercy is so great, and not because of any good deeds that that person has done.

[15] M. M. Lk 13:24: The only way to enter the Kingdom of God is to have faith in Jesus as one's Savior.

[16] M. I. Lk 3:3a: Christians should, in love, warn lost people who do not repent.

[17] M. M. Ro 4:3: Faith in Jesus is a free gift that a person graciously receives from God and he does not earn.

[18] M. M. Lk 13:24: The only way to enter the Kingdom of God is to have faith in Jesus as one's Savior.

[19] M. I. Lk 3:3a: Christians should, in love, warn lost people who do not repent.

[20] M. M. Lk 1:27: Jesus had to be born as a true human being and as a true Jew in order to become the King of kings in his heavenly kingdom forever.

[21] M. M. Lk 1:35: Jesus had to be born as true God, in order to rescue all of mankind from sin.

[22] M. M. Mt 1:22: God sent his only Son, Jesus to be born as a true human being, so that he

could save all of his brothers and sisters of all nations by fulfilling all of God's promises in the Old Testament.

[23] M. M. Ro 1:5: The same Holy Spirit who creates <u>faith</u> and a new missionary <u>nature</u> in a person's heart also graciously empowers him to gratefully respond to his Lord's love by <u>obeying</u> him.

[24] M. M. Lk 6:22: The Lord Jesus will surely bless a Christian in the midst of suffering for his sake; and he will also bless him with eternal life if he remains faithful to him.

[25] M. M. Lk 1:35: Jesus had to be born as true God, in order to rescue all of mankind from sin.

[26] M. M. Ro 3:24: Jesus lived a life of perfect obedience and shed his precious blood on the cross, in order to graciously set all nations free from sin, which a person only receives by faith in him.

[27] M. M. Ro 10:17a: The Holy Spirit <u>only</u> creates and preserves faith by using the message of God's grace in his holy Word.

[28] M. I. Lk 4:35: Christians should view every person as a whole person, and show him compassion by caring for <u>both</u> his physical and spiritual needs as they go on their mission.

[29] M. M. Ro 4:11: All Christians from every nation on earth belong to the <u>spiritual family</u> of Abraham, the Church because they share the same faith in Jesus that their father had.

[30] M. M. Lk 14:34: A Christian's faith relationship with Jesus is a precious <u>treasure</u> and a completely <u>unique</u> personal relationship, because no one deserves it and it will last forever.

[31] M. M. Mt 5:14: When the Holy Spirit creates faith in a person's heart, he also graciously gives him a new mission-heart that is eager to shine the light of the Gospel throughout the whole world.

Chapter 19

Jesus and Zacchaeus 19:1-10

19:1 *He entered Jericho and was passing through.*
19:2 *And there was a man named Zacchaeus. He was a chief tax collector and was rich.*
19:3 *And he was seeking to see who Jesus was, but on account of the crowd he could not, because he was small of stature.*
19:4 *So he ran on ahead and climbed up into a sycamore tree to see him, for he was about to pass that way.*
19:5 *And when Jesus came to the place, he looked up and said to him, "Zacchaeus, hurry and come down, for I must stay at your house today."*
19:6 *So he hurried and came down and received him joyfully.*
19:7 *And when they saw it, they all grumbled, "He has gone in to be the guest of a man who is a sinner."*
19:8 *And Zacchaeus stood and said to the Lord, "Behold, Lord, the half of my goods I give to the poor. And if I have defrauded anyone of anything, I restore it fourfold."*
19:9 *And Jesus said to him, "Today salvation has come to this house, since he also is a son of Abraham.*
19:10 *For the Son of Man came to seek and to save the lost."*

19:1-8 (1) Out of the many people living in Jericho, and out of the huge crowd that was following him, Jesus' loving mission-heart focused on one person who was *"lost"* ([1]M. I. Lk 4:40 & [2]Lk 5:20). **2)** Presumably Zacchaeus embarrassed himself by climbing a tree—a childish thing for an adult to do, and he was a very rich man at that! Therefore, his bold action shows that he had already received the gracious gift of faith. And his faith is what Jesus saw, because he was looking for it. His mission-heart was constantly seeking individuals who were eager to receive his invitation into his Kingdom, seeking opportunities to share his Gospel message (M. I. Lk 5:20 & [3]Lk 4:15). **3)** Therefore, another extraordinary thing happened—Jesus invited himself into Zacchaeus' home; but of course, he had seen that he was already a welcome guest in Zacchaeus' heart. Then, Zacchaeus did something else that the other people present that day must have thought was quite extraordinary—he gave away and returned much of his ill-gotten money (v 8). However, for Jesus, it was, of course, not extraordinary at all, since his Spirit had given Zacchaeus a mission-heart along with his faith, therefore, it was a very normal fruit of his repentance and faith (v 13; [4]M. M. Mt 5:14). Zacchaeus' new life became another powerful personal witness for who Jesus was ([5]M. I. Ro 12:1).

19:9 (1) Jesus added in verse 9, *"He [Zacchaeus] also is a son of Abraham."* Obviously he meant that Zacchaeus was a true spiritual son of Abraham, since everyone there knew that he was his descendant by blood (14:16; 13:16; 16:22; [6]M. M. Ro 4:11). **2)** Luke was very careful to record this statement of Jesus in verse 9 that Zacchaeus was a true spiritual son of Abraham, because Luke recognized how vital this truth was for *all* people, but especially vital for Gentiles like himself and Theophilus, who was the recipient of his Gospel message. But where did Luke learn this vital truth that the Jews do not have a more privileged way to enter God's Kingdom than any other nation? He had almost certainly learned it during his journeys with St. Paul, because Paul himself had to be completely turned around by his gracious Lord in a powerful vision, in order to understand that no one deserves to enter God's Kingdom except by God's grace alone (Ac 9:4-6). He then proclaimed to the Gentiles the rich Gospel that all people from all nations are equal before God since all people, Jew and Gentiles alike, are able to enter God's Kingdom by only one *"narrow door,"* which is faith in Jesus alone (Rom 4:11-12; 11:26; Gal 3:7; [7]M. M. Mt 7:14 & [8]Lk 13:24).

19:10 (1) It's important to note that the two parts of Luke's central theme are intimately linked; he did both: *"seek the lost"* and also *"save the lost."* **2)** It was vital that Jesus had to be born as a true human being for at least two reasons: **a)** so that he could *"seek...the lost"* by proclaiming his Law and Gospel message, as his heavenly Father's last and greatest prophet, and as a fellow human being. (4:21; 24:26-27, 44; Heb 1:2; [9]M. M. Ro 16:25). And the way in which Jesus sought out and found Zacchaeus is a perfect example of this (vs 1-10; [10]M. M. Lk 1:1). **b)** And he also had to be born as a true human being so that he could *"save the lost"* by offering a truly human sacrifice for sin for all of his fellow human beings ([11]M. M. Lk 1:27 & [12]Heb 2:17). **3)** And it was equally vital for both parts of his mission that Jesus was also true God for at least three reasons: **a)** He had to be true God in order to be able to *"seek...the lost"* by pointing to himself as the Messiah, *"the Son of Man,"* whom his heavenly Father had sent ([13]M. M. Lk 1:27 & [14]Ac 2:24). **b)** He also had to be true God in order to *"save the lost"* by offering a holy sacrifice for sin that his Father would accept on behalf of all of his sinful brothers and sisters from all nations (24:26, 46; [15]M. M. Heb 9:12). **c)** And he also had to be true God so that his heavenly Father would raise him from the dead as his own Beloved Son in order to prove that he had accepted his holy sacrifice and truly *"saved the lost"* (2 Cor 1:20; [16]M. M. Lk 1:35 & [17]Heb 7:17).

The Parable of the Ten Minas 19:11-27

> 19:11 *As they heard these things, he proceeded to tell a parable, because he was near to Jerusalem, and because they supposed that the kingdom of God was to appear immediately.*
> 19:12 *He said therefore, "A nobleman went into a far country to receive for himself a kingdom and then return.*
> 19:13 *Calling ten of his servants, he gave them ten minas, and said to them, 'Engage in business until I come.'*
> 19:14 *But his citizens hated him and sent a delegation after him, saying, 'We do not want this man to reign over us.'*
> 19:15 *When he returned, having received the kingdom, he ordered these servants to whom he had given the money to be called to him, that he might know what they had gained by doing business.*
> 19:16 *The first came before him, saying, 'Lord, your mina has made ten minas more.'*
> 19:17 *And he said to him, 'Well done, good servant! Because you*

have been faithful in a very little, you shall have authority over ten cities.'
19:18 *And the second came, saying, 'Lord, your mina has made five minas.'*
19:19 *And he said to him, 'And you are to be over five cities.'*
19:20 *Then another came, saying, 'Lord, here is your mina, which I kept laid away in a handkerchief;*
19:21 *for I was afraid of you, because you are a severe man. You take what you did not deposit, and reap what you did not sow.'*
19:22 *He said to him, 'I will condemn you with your own words, you wicked servant! You knew that I was a severe man, taking what I did not deposit and reaping what I did not sow?*
19:23 *Why then did you not put my money in the bank, and at my coming I might have collected it with interest?'*
19:24 *And he said to those who stood by, 'Take the mina from him, and give it to the one who has the ten minas.'*
19:25 *And they said to him, 'Lord, he has ten minas!'*
19:26 *'I tell you that to everyone who has, more will be given, but from the one who has not, even what he has will be taken away.*
19:27 *But as for these enemies of mine, who did not want me to reign over them, bring them here and slaughter them before me.'"*

19:11-27 (1) In this parable, Jesus himself is the gracious King who entrusts all of his subjects with both spiritual and material wealth, so that they would use their gifts to glorify his holy name, and thus he would receive *"interest"* (v 23) on his investments (Jms 2:14, 17). St. Paul also says in (1 Cor 10:31), *"So, whether you eat or drink, or whatever you do, do all to the glory of God."* And the King, of course, also gave his servants mission-hearts, so that they can use all of their wealth in order to proclaim their King's Law and Gospel message to others (16:1-13; [18]M. I. Lk 16:13). **2)** However, on Judgment Day, Jesus will also rightfully condemn the subjects (v 22) who hid their gifts and did not use them to glorify their Lord's holy name. Instead, they despised his gracious gifts because they thought that they deserved them (v 20; [19]M. M. Ro 3:26).

The Triumphal Entry 19:28-40

19:28 *And when he had said these things, he went on ahead, going up to Jerusalem.*

19:29 *When he drew near to Bethphage and Bethany, at the mount that is called Olivet, he sent two of the disciples,*

19:30 *saying, "Go into the village in front of you, where on entering you will find a colt tied, on which no one has ever yet sat. Untie it and bring it here.*

19:31 *If anyone asks you, 'Why are you untying it?' you shall say this: 'The Lord has need of it.'"*

19:32 *So those who were sent went away and found it just as he had told them.*

19:33 *And as they were untying the colt, its owners said to them, "Why are you untying the colt?"*

19:34 *And they said, "The Lord has need of it."*

19:35 *And they brought it to Jesus, and throwing their cloaks on the colt, they set Jesus on it.*

19:36 *And as he rode along, they spread their cloaks on the road.*

19:37 *As he was drawing near--already on the way down the Mount of Olives--the whole multitude of his disciples began to rejoice and praise God with a loud voice for all the mighty works that they had seen,*

19:38 *saying, "Blessed is the King who comes in the name of the Lord! Peace in heaven and glory in the highest!"*

19:39 *And some of the Pharisees in the crowd said to him, "Teacher, rebuke your disciples."*

19:40 *He answered, "I tell you, if these were silent, the very stones would cry out."*

19:28-40 (1) This whole event shows very clearly how <u>purposeful</u> Jesus was in his entire mission, as he *"sought the lost"* one person at a time (v 10), and as he traveled to Jerusalem to die (18:32), because, as he says in (18:31), "everything that is written about the Son of Man by the prophets <u>will be</u> accomplished" (24:44). His loving mission-heart moved him to come to earth in order to fulfill his Father's gracious will (1:1; Lev 18:5); and nothing—neither Satan nor the Pharisees nor the scribes—could stop him ([20]M. M. Lk 1:1). **2)** Jesus commended those who praised him that joyful day as "the King who comes in the name of the Lord" (v 38) because they had heard his Gospel message, seen his miracles, and believed in him. However, even though Jesus had lovingly sought the Pharisees in the crowd many times, and in many different ways, not even his holy Word had been able to penetrate their hearts of stone (3:8; [21]M. I. Lk 3:3a). **3)** Of course, it's also true that *"nothing will be impossible with God"* (1:37), therefore, God certainly could make *"the stones...cry out"* (v 40) in praise of Jesus, the King of kings. However, just as he does not want to create faith in inanimate stones (3:8), he also does not want to make the stones *"cry out"* joyfully singing his praise, as if they were human beings. Rather, unlike inanimate stones, he made all human beings with a free will, so that they would praise him willingly out of gratitude for all of his gracious gifts to them. All of the rest of nature (which obviously includes stones) does indeed sing God's praise because its beauty clearly shows that he made it (Ps 98:7-9; [22]M. M. Ro 1:19); however, he is most pleased when praise springs from a mission-heart that his Spirit has filled with faith and from a new flexible will that his Spirit controls ([23]M. I. Jn 14:15).

Jesus Weeps over Jerusalem 19:41-44

19:41 *And when he drew near and saw the city, he wept over it,*
19:42 *saying, "Would that you, even you, had known on this day the things that make for peace! But now they are hidden from your eyes.*
19:43 *For the days will come upon you, when your enemies will set up a barricade around you and surround you and hem you in on every side*
19:44 *and tear you down to the ground, you and your children within you. And they will not leave one stone upon another in you, because you did not know the time of your visitation."*

19:41-44 How deep Jesus' love was for the city of Jerusalem! How his mission-heart grieved over it! It was, and still is, his capital city where he will reign forever (Rev 21:2). How could he <u>not</u> be sad to see his dear fellow Jews reject their King? They had received three gracious <u>gifts</u> from him: **a)** God's Word in their own (untranslated) heart-language that promised them that their *"Prince of Peace"* would soon come (Is 9:6). **b)** They actually saw their Savior and King with their physical eyes many times. **c)** And they also would soon see his death and empty tomb with their physical eyes. However, their hard hearts prevented them from seeing with the eyes of <u>faith</u> that he was in fact their Messiah. They *"did not know the time of your [their] visitation"* (v 44). Therefore, God would one day soon *"tear you [them] down to the ground"* (v 44). Yet, it still was not too late for them. How many of them would heed his last warnings to repent ([24]M. I. Lk 3:3a)?

Jesus Cleanses the Temple 19:45-48

> 19:45 *And he entered the temple and began to drive out those who sold,*
> 19:46 *saying to them, "It is written, 'My house shall be a house of prayer,' but you have made it a den of robbers."*
> 19:47 *And he was teaching daily in the temple. The chief priests and the scribes and the principal men of the people were seeking to destroy him,*
> 19:48 *but they did not find anything they could do, for all the people were hanging on his words.*

19:45-48 As a 12-year-old boy, Jesus went to the temple for the first time, because it was his "home," his heavenly *"Father's house"* (2:49). That day, he found activity in the temple that <u>pleased</u> his Father, because the teachers of the Law were doing their duty by <u>teaching</u> the people; and he joined them as a learner and as a teacher (2:46). However, now, many years later, when he went to the temple to *"teach"* the people (v 47) he found people <u>selling</u> things—an activity that was making his Father very <u>angry</u>. Therefore, in righteous anger, he physically removed their evil behavior. But why did this make *"the chief priests and the scribes and the principal men of the people"* so angry that they *"were seeking to destroy him"* (v 47) even more than before? No doubt it was because Jesus had ruined a very nice source of extra income for them, even though they surely knew that it violated God's Laws. Obviously they loved money far more than they loved God! However, Jesus never disobeyed his heavenly Father—not one time. Right up to the day that he was arrested and died, he continued to faithfully obey all of his Father's Laws perfectly for the sake of all of his brothers and sisters, and also to faithfully *"seek the lost,"* including his evil enemies who killed him ([25]M. M. Lk 1:1 & [26]Mt 1:22).

---

[1] M. I. Lk 4:40: Christians should go and seek the lost one person at a time by focusing on each person's unique needs.

[2] M. I. Lk 5:20: Even when Christians proclaim the Gospel to large crowds, they should always remember that the crowds are made up of individuals; and that each one of them needs to repent and believe in Jesus.

[3] M. I. Lk 4:15: Christians should seize every opportunity to proclaim the Gospel to lost people of all nations.

[4] M. M. Mt 5:14: When the Holy Spirit creates faith in a person's heart, he also graciously gives him a new mission-heart that is eager to shine the light of the Gospel throughout the whole world.

[5] M. I. Ro 12:20: Christians should respond to God's grace by always showing love (and not cursing or taking revenge against) their enemies, so that their enemies may be ashamed of harming them; and they, then, may have opportunities to witness the Gospel to them.

[6] M. M. Ro 4:11: All Christians from every nation on earth belong to the spiritual family of Abraham, the Church because they share the same faith in Jesus that their father had.

[7] M. I. Mt 7:14: Christians should hurry on their mission to the world because people who are lost have many enemies who lure them away from Jesus; and therefore, few of them find faith in Jesus which is the only gate into his Kingdom of life.

[8] M. M. Lk 13:24: The only way to enter the Kingdom of God is to have faith in Jesus as one's Savior.

[9] M. M. Ro 16:25: The wonderful mystery is that even though both Jews and Gentiles were disobedient to God in the past, God has now shown all nations his unlimited grace by revealing the Gospel about his Son Jesus to his apostles and prophets so that they would write it down for all nations to read and hear.

[10] M. M. Lk 1:1: Jesus came to seek and save all lost people from every nation on earth.

[11] M. M. Lk 1:27: Jesus had to be born as a true human being and as a true Jew in order to

become the King of kings in his heavenly kingdom forever.

[12] M. M. Heb 2:17: Jesus had to become like his fellow human beings in every way, so that he could serve God as their merciful and faithful High Priest in order to earn forgiveness for all of their sins.

[13] M. M. Lk 1:27: Jesus had to be born as a true human being and as a true Jew in order to become the King of kings in his heavenly kingdom forever.

[14] M. M. Ac 2:24: Our Lord Jesus loosed the pangs of death for us mortal human beings when God raised him from the dead, because it was not possible for him to be held by death.

[15] M. M. Heb 9:12: As the great High Priest, Jesus offered his human and divine blood as the one perfect sacrifice for all of the sins of all of his brothers and sisters.

[16] M. M. Lk 1:35: Jesus had to be born as true God, in order to rescue all of mankind from sin.

[17] M. M. Heb 7:17: Jesus served his mission to Christians and to the world as an eternal High Priest by offering the holy sacrifice of his body in order to earn eternal forgiveness for all Christians.

[18] M. I. Lk 16:13: Christians should manage both their spiritual and material wealth wisely, in order to be able to most effectively proclaim the Gospel and also be able to share their material wealth with others who are in need.

[19] M. M. Ro 3:26: God is just and fair to everyone, both when he condemns all people of all nations because all have sinned, and also when he only declares those people righteous who have faith in Jesus.

[20] M. M. Lk 1:1: Jesus came to seek and save all lost people from every nation on earth.

[21] M. I. Lk 3:3a: Christians should, in love, warn lost people who do not repent.

[22] M. M. Ro 1:19: God clearly reveals four things in the universe: **a)** that he made it, **b)** that he exists, **c)** that he has almighty power and glory, **d)** and that he still controls it.

[23] M. I. Jn 14:15: Christians should obey all of Jesus' commands in grateful response to his love for them as they go on his mission to the world.

[24] M. I. Lk 3:3a: Christians should, in love, warn lost people who do not repent.

[25] M. M. Lk 1:1: Jesus came to seek and save all lost people from every nation on earth.

[26] M. M. Mt 1:22: God sent his only Son, Jesus to be born as a true human being, so that he could save all of his brothers and sisters of all nations by fulfilling all of God's promises in the Old Testament.

Chapter 20

The Authority of Jesus Challenged 20:1-8

20:1 *One day, as Jesus was teaching the people in the temple and preaching the Gospel, the chief priests and the scribes with the elders came up*
20:2 *and said to him, "Tell us by what authority you do these things, or who it is that gave you this authority."*
20:3 *He answered them, "I also will ask you a question. Now tell me,*
20:4 *Was the Baptism of John from heaven or from man?"*
20:5 *And they discussed it with one another, saying, "If we say, 'From heaven,' he will say, 'Why did you not believe him?'*
20:6 *But if we say, 'From man,' all the people will stone us to death, for they are convinced that John was a prophet."*
20:7 *So they answered that they did not know where it came from.*
20:8 *And Jesus said to them, "Neither will I tell you by what authority I do these things."*

20:1-8 Even during the last week of his brief life on earth, Jesus never stopped "seeking the lost" by *"teaching the people in the temple and preaching the Gospel"* (v 1; [1]M. M. Lk 1:1); nevertheless, *"the chief priests and the scribes with the elders"* demanded to know who gave Jesus the authority to teach and preach and to destroy their tidy source of illegal income in the temple (v 2). In other words, instead of using their powerful leadership position to assist the mission of their Messiah, they were using their power to stop it; and they were also even using it to satisfy their own greed for more power and money. This is the reason why Jesus asked them in verse 4 why they had not listened to John, who was God's last *"prophet"* in the Old Testament era (v 6). John had taught them that Jesus was God's Son, his greatest prophet and their Messiah (Heb 1:2). But they refused to repent and believe in him. Therefore, they also rejected Jesus, even though he was the greatest teacher in all human history; and then, unfortunately for them, the heavenly Father used these same evil men to send his Son to the cross just a few days later (22:66; 23:13; ²M. I. Lk 3:3a).

The Parable of the Wicked Tenants 20:9-18

<u>20:9</u> *And he began to tell the people this parable: "A man planted a vineyard and let it out to tenants and went into another country for a long while.*
<u>20:10</u> *When the time came, he sent a servant to the tenants, so that they would give him some of the fruit of the vineyard. But the tenants beat him and sent him away empty-handed.*
<u>20:11</u> *And he sent another servant. But they also beat and treated him shamefully, and sent him away empty-handed.*
<u>20:12</u> *And he sent yet a third. This one also they wounded and cast out.*
20:13 *Then the owner of the vineyard said, 'What shall I do? I will send my beloved son; perhaps they will respect him.'*
20:14 *But when the tenants saw him, they said to themselves, 'This is the heir. Let us kill him, so that the inheritance may be ours.'*
20:15 *And they threw him out of the vineyard and killed him. What then will the owner of the vineyard do to them?*
20:16 *He will come and destroy those tenants and give the vineyard to others." When they heard this, they said, "Surely not!"*
20:17 *But he looked directly at them and said, "What then is this that is written: "'The stone that the builders rejected has become the cornerstone'?*
20:18 *Everyone who falls on that stone will be broken to pieces, and when it falls on anyone, it will crush him."*

20:9-18 (1) Jesus' parable in verses 9-18 shows, first of all, that this present generation of religious leaders was not the first generation of Jewish leaders who killed the prophets. Sadly, they were following a long, evil pattern. When God called Abraham, he launched his gracious mission plan to rescue mankind from sin by first blessing him and his descendants, so that they would be a blessing to all other nations (Gen 12:1-3; ³M. M. Ac 13:46). And he sent them many prophets who proclaimed his holy Word to them (16:29); and of course, their religious leaders were responsible to teach his Word to the people and, <u>first of all</u>, spread it to their entire nation. However, over the many years, instead of carrying out this <u>first</u> part of God's plan, they repeatedly even killed God's messengers, the prophets (Neh 9:26; Jer 7:25-26; 25:4-7). Therefore, very seldom did any of the Jewish leaders even remember the <u>second</u> part of their mission, to tell this Gospel to the Gentiles; instead of that, most of the time in their history, they <u>hated</u> all other nations. Thus, it's not surprising that both the nation of Israel as well as all other nations suffered from a <u>famine</u> of hearing God's Word (6:23; Amos 8:11; M. M. Ac 13:46). How sad is that! **2)** In verse 13 in this parable, Jesus is, of course, *"the son"* whom the tenants killed. And, as verse 19 implies, the Jewish leaders who heard this parable knew very well that Jesus was talking about himself. However, their hearts were much too hard to believe that he was God's own beloved Son (v 13), and thus be the first ones to spread this wonderful Good News. Instead, they were leading their people away from Jesus. And, for some time already, they had been plotting to kill him, as Jesus said they would in verses 14-15. In fact, the four Gospels record that only two members of the Jewish Council believed in Jesus: Nicodemus and Joseph from Arimathea (23:50; Jn 19:39; [4]M. M. Ac 2:24).

Paying Taxes to Caesar 20:19-26

20:19 *The scribes and the chief priests sought to lay hands on him at that very hour, for they perceived that he had told this parable against them, but they feared the people.*
20:20 *So they watched him and sent spies, who pretended to be sincere, that they might catch him in something he said, so as to deliver him up to the authority and jurisdiction of the governor.*
20:21 *So they asked him, "Teacher, we know that you speak and teach rightly, and show no partiality, but truly teach the way of God.*
20:22 *Is it lawful for us to give tribute to Caesar, or not?"*
20:23 *But he perceived their craftiness, and said to them,*
20:24 *"Show me a denarius. Whose likeness and inscription does it*

> have?" They said, "Caesar's."
> 20:25 *He said to them, "Then render to Caesar the things that are Caesar's, and to God the things that are God's."*
> 20:26 *And they were not able in the presence of the people to catch him in what he said, but marveling at his answer they became silent.*

20:19 Luke adds a final sad note following this parable in verse 19, *"They perceived that he had told this parable against them."* This makes it very clear that these leaders knew that they were responsible for managing God's Kingdom as the religious leaders of the nation of Israel, and they also knew very well that Jesus was right in condemning them for failing in this responsibility. Jesus had done his job of confronting them with their sin in this powerful way; but their pride and greed was so enormous that not even God's Law could break their stone, cold hearts (19:40; [5]M. I. Lk 3:3a & [6]Lk 3:8).

20:20-26 (1) Jesus certainly knew that these men were spies, as verse 23 indicates, but he also saw it as yet another opportunity to seek these men who were obviously lost. His loving mission-heart would not allow him to ever stop trying to reach out to them ([7]M. I. Lk 4:15). **2)** This exchange between Jesus and the spies would perhaps not be very significant except for the fact that, at his trial a few days later, Jesus' enemies deliberately misquoted his statement in verse 25. They had to misquote him because he, of course, had not said or done anything illegal that they could use against him. Their previous efforts to trap him concerned religious matters, but here they were trying to get him in political trouble, so that they could get rid of him and retain their power and wealth. Obviously, the devil was busy using these men; nevertheless, as a matter of fact, it was the heavenly Father who was in full control and using these evil men; he was carrying out his gracious plan of salvation right down to its last beautiful details ([8]M. M. Ac 4:28). **3)** Furthermore, Jesus taught a very important set of truths in verse 25 when he said, *"Then render to Caesar the things that are Caesar's, and to God the things that are God's."* Jesus was teaching two truths: **a)** First of all, God himself establishes all secular governments

(*"Caesar"* or the Roman Empire; Rom 13:1). Everyone lives under a secular government whether it obeys God's Laws or not. **b)** Secondly, when God graciously gives a person faith in his Son Jesus, he also places him under their Lord's own gracious authority in his eternal Kingdom. However, Jesus' disciples could not have even imagined that day what these truths would soon mean for them as they began to carry out their Lord's mission in this evil Roman Empire. History tells us that nearly all of the 12 apostles were eventually martyred by it. It's a new mission message. M. M. Lk 20:25: God establishes all secular governments, so that everyone lives under a secular authority; and God also places all Christians under his own gracious authority in his eternal kingdom; therefore, all Christians should gladly give everything that they owe to both kingdoms.

Sadducees Ask About the Resurrection 20:27-40

20:27 *There came to him some Sadducees, those who deny that there is a resurrection,*
20:28 *and they asked him a question, saying, "Teacher, Moses wrote for us that if a man's brother dies, having a wife but no children, the man must take the widow and raise up offspring for his brother.*
20:29 *Now there were seven brothers. The first took a wife, and died without children.*
20:30 *And the second*
20:31 *and the third took her, and likewise all seven left no children and died.*
20:32 *Afterward the woman also died.*
20:33 *In the resurrection, therefore, whose wife will the woman be? For the seven had her as wife."*
20:34 *And Jesus said to them, "The sons of this age marry and are given in marriage,*
20:35 *but those who are considered worthy to attain to that age and to the resurrection from the dead neither marry nor are given in marriage,*

20:36 *for they cannot die anymore, because they are equal to angels and are sons of God, being sons of the resurrection.*
20:37 *But that the dead are raised, even Moses showed, in the passage about the bush, where he calls the Lord the God of Abraham and the God of Isaac and the God of Jacob.*
20:38 *Now he is not God of the dead, but of the living, for all live to him."*
20:39 *Then some of the scribes answered, "Teacher, you have spoken well."*
20:40 *For they no longer dared to ask him any question.*

20:27-38 The Sadducees' unrealistic question about the resurrection veiled the fact that they did not believe in God's mercy and grace for them. Even though they claimed to be *"experts in the Law,"* they did not understand a central teaching of Scripture that there is a resurrection. God gives physical life to all people of all nations; and because his mission-heart is full of grace and mercy, he longs to raise every one of them from the dead in order to live with him in eternity. Therefore, Jesus reached out to these men by quoting from the five books of Moses in verse 37, their favorite portion of Scripture, so that the mighty sword of God's Word could penetrate their hard hearts. His point was that Moses taught them the same truth that he himself was teaching them that there is a resurrection. God will, in fact raise those who trust in him as their Messiah from the dead; they too could have the free gift of a resurrected body and eternal life with him by trusting in him. However, Satan had trapped them so completely that they could not see either the heavenly Father's grace or Jesus' deep love for them ([9]M. M. Lk 4:21).

20:39-40 In spite of the fact that verse 39 shows that there was much animosity between the scribes and Sadducees, the words in verse 40, *"they no longer dared to ask him any question"* seem to apply to all of Jesus' enemies. The fact that the religious leaders of the Jews took so long to give up on trying to trap Jesus gives just one indication of just how thoroughly Satan had ensnared them in his evil web, the love of money and power. The devil had created a situation that he thought he could use to defeat God's plan to rescue mankind from sin by the cross of Jesus, but his cleverness was no match for the heavenly Father's almighty wisdom and power. The Father would soon carry it out no matter how clever *"the father of lies"* may be (Jn 8:44; [10]M. M. Ac 4:28)!

Whose Son is the Christ? 20:41-44

20:41 *But he said to them, "How can they say that the Christ is David's son?*
20:42 *For David himself says in the Book of Psalms, "'The Lord said to my Lord, Sit at my right hand,*
20:43 *until I make your enemies your footstool.'*
20:44 *David thus calls him Lord, so how is he his son?"*

20:41-44 Verses 41-44 seem to be an additional answer that Jesus addressed to the Sadducees. Nevertheless, even though he had silenced both groups, Jesus made one more attempt to *"seek"* the Sadducees by telling them the Gospel. In verses 41-44, he taught them from the Scripture that he was in fact both a true man, *"David's son"* (v 41), and he was at the same time true God, David's *"Lord"* (v 42; [11]M. M. Lk 1:27 & [12]Lk 1:35). What wonderful Gospel this is! However, this amazing paradox was far beyond the understanding of anyone who did not have the gracious gift of faith in Jesus. Unfortunately, Jesus apparently sought them in vain ([13]M. I. Lk 3:3a & [14]M. M. Lk 4:21). (Then, in verses 45-47, he used the Law to warn the scribes to repent.)

Beware of the Scribes 20:45-47

20:45 *And in the hearing of all the people he said to his disciples,*
20:46 *"Beware of the scribes, who like to walk around in long robes, and love greetings in the marketplaces and the best seats in the synagogues and the places of honor at feasts,*
20:47 *who devour widows' houses and for a pretense make long prayers. They will receive the greater condemnation."*

20:45-47 Jesus tried one last time to seek the scribes by giving them a very stern warning from the Law. They understood his previous effort to warn them perfectly well in his parable in verses 9-19, but they did not want to understand. So he again warned them in verse 47 that *"they will receive the greater condemnation"* on Judgment Day because their pride and terrible abuse of power were so evil. Satan had full control of their hearts. At the same time, he also warned his disciples to avoid these grave sins ([15]M. I. Lk 3:3a & [16]Lk 3:8).

---

[1] M. M. Lk 1:1: Jesus came to seek and save all lost people from every nation on earth.

[2] M. I. Lk 3:3a: Christians should, in love, warn lost people who do not repent.

[3] M. M. Ac 13:46: As he did with the old Israel, God first of all strengthens the faith of the new Israel, the Church with his Word and Sacraments, so that they can go and witness to the lost people of all nations.

[4] M. M. Ac 2:24: Our Lord Jesus loosed the pangs of death for us mortal human beings when God raised him from the dead, because it was not possible for him to be held by death.

[5] M. I. Lk 3:3a: Christians should, in love, warn lost people who do not repent.

[6] M. I. Lk 3:8: Christians should always be prepared to boldly and publicly refute false teaching, so that Satan cannot easily deceive people.

[7] M. I. Lk 4:15: Christians should seize every opportunity to proclaim the Gospel to lost people of all nations.

[8] M. M. Ac 4:28: The heavenly Father is always in full control of his mission to all nations of the world.

[9] M. M. Lk 4:21: Every verse in the entire Bible points in some way to Jesus and his mission to seek and save the lost.

[10] M. M. Ac 4:28: The heavenly Father is always in full control of his mission to all nations of the world.

[11] M. M. Lk 1:27: Jesus had to be born as a true human being and as a true Jew in order to become the King of kings in his heavenly kingdom forever.

[12] M. M. Lk 1:35: Jesus had to be born as true God, in order to rescue all of mankind from sin.

[13] M. I. Lk 3:3a: Christians should, in love, warn lost people who do not repent.

[14] M. M. Lk 4:21: Every verse in the entire Bible points in some way to Jesus and his mission to seek and save the lost.

[15] M. I. Lk 3:3a: Christians should, in love, warn lost people who do not repent.

[16] M. I. Lk 3:8: Christians should always be prepared to boldly and publicly refute false teaching, so that Satan cannot easily deceive people.

Chapter 21

The Widow's Offering 21:1-4

21:1 *Jesus looked up and saw the rich putting their gifts into the offering box,*
21:2 *and he saw a poor widow put in two small copper coins.*
21:3 *And he said, "Truly, I tell you, this poor widow has put in more than all of them.*
21:4 *For they all contributed out of their abundance, but she out of her poverty put in all she had to live on."*

21:1-4 (1) This is the last chapter in Luke's account before Jesus' arrest. It contains teachings of Jesus that he addressed to his disciples in the temple courtyard (vs 37-38); however, he apparently no longer tried to seek his enemies, the religious leaders of the Jews by warning them to repent. He was, however, still training his disciples by giving them last-minute instructions on how to carry out his mission after he left them ([1]M. I. Lk 6:13). **2)** Jesus used the obvious sharp contrast between the material wealth, but spiritual poverty of the Jewish religious leaders and the abject material poverty, but spiritual wealth of the widow to teach some very powerful lessons to his disciples. She was living in abject poverty, yet *"she out of her poverty put in all she had to live on"* (v 4). His lessons must have been especially meaningful to his disciples since they, no doubt, knew that these were some of the same men who often *"robbed widows"* (20:47) of the very few possessions that they did have. However, the Holy Spirit had given her a *"child-like faith"* (18:17) and a mission-heart that produced abundant fruit (8:8, 15) in a tiny, but extremely generous gift to her dear Lord. In deep gratitude to him for his rich grace for her, she cast her whole life at her Lord's feet in total dependence on his abundant grace. She was truly spiritually *"rich"* like Lazarus in Jesus' parable; but the Jewish religious leaders were truly spiritually *"poor"* like that rich man (16:19-31; [2]M. M. Ro 1:5). What a lesson this was that his disciples would urgently need—and very soon! In just a few days, they saw their dear Lord die; and they also soon faced the anger of these same religious leaders as they went on their Lord's mission (^{3}M. I. Lk 6:13).

Jesus Foretells Destruction of the Temple 21:5-9

21:5 *And while some were speaking of the temple, how it was adorned with noble stones and offerings, he said,*
21:6 *"As for these things that you see, the days will come when there will not be left here one stone upon another that will not be thrown down."*
21:7 *And they asked him, "Teacher, when will these things be, and what will be the sign when these things are about to take place?"*
21:8 *And he said, "See that you are not led astray. For many will come in my name, saying, 'I am he!' and, 'The time is at hand!' Do not go after them.*
21:9 *And when you hear of wars and tumults, do not be terrified, for these things must first take place, but the end will not be at once."*

21:5-28 Jesus was obviously very much concerned about the future of his Church, the new Israel, because he had already begun to entrust his few disciples with carrying out his mission to the Church itself and also to the lost world (^{4}M. M. Ac 13:46). And he certainly knew how weak their faith was; therefore, he continued to warn them in the next long section in verses 5-28 about the future troubles and persecutions in order to prepare them for the future. He was no doubt especially concerned because, very soon, he would no longer be with them <u>physically</u> after his ascension (Ac 1:9; Mt 28:20).
21:6-8 He first warned them about the future destruction of the temple in verse 6 and then about false teachers in verse 8. (He again warned them about the destruction of Jerusalem in verses 20-24.) Their admiration of the beautiful temple that King Herod had built demonstrated that they were still focused too much on <u>material</u> beauty and not thinking at all about spiritual issues. But Jesus knew very well that Satan and his

demons were very near; and that his death and resurrection would very soon fill them with despair and terrible wrath. To him, the spiritual danger must have been palpable; and they were like helpless sheep who were totally unaware of the spiritual danger. They would need a *"child-like faith"* like the widow had in order to face Satan's extremely clever attacks. Therefore, in deep compassion for them and for the future mission of his Church, he warned them of the grave danger that they would lose their faith in him by following one of the many deceivers, who *"will come in my name"* (v 8). Such people would use Satan's favorite trick of imitating the truth with a lie (Jn 8:44; 2 Cor 11:14). And this trick would be so clever because Jesus would no longer be with them physically; therefore, like the widow they would have to depend on his almighty grace through his Holy Spirit (^{5}M. I. Ro 5:3a).

Nation Will Rise Against Nation 21:10-19

21:10 *Then he said to them, "Nation will rise against nation, and kingdom against kingdom.*
21:11 *There will be great earthquakes, and in various places famines and pestilences. And there will be terrors and great signs from heaven.*
21:12 *But before all this they will lay their hands on you and persecute you, delivering you up to the synagogues and prisons, and you will be brought before kings and governors for my name's sake.*
21:13 *This will be your opportunity to bear witness.*
21:14 *Settle it therefore in your minds not to meditate beforehand how to answer,*
21:15 *for I will give you a mouth and wisdom, which none of your adversaries will be able to withstand or contradict.*
21:16 *You will be delivered up even by parents and brothers and relatives and friends, and some of you they will put to death.*
21:17 *You will be hated by all for my name's sake.*
21:18 *But not a hair of your head will perish.*
21:19 *By your endurance you will gain your lives.*

21:9-11 In verses 9-11, Jesus also prepared his disciples and his Church for the future by warning them that Satan will cause chaos, many terrifying things such as wars, earthquakes and famines all over the world. However, he urged them to *"do not be terrified"* in verse 9. Obviously, they would be able to continue to find opportunities to witness to him in the midst of the chaos, because he is always in full control of his mission ([6]M. M. Ac 4:28).

21:12-19 Next, Jesus warned his disciples in verses 12-19 that they would have to face two different kinds of persecution: **a)** from people in authority over them, in verses 12-15, and from their families and friends, in verses16-19.

21:12-15 In verse 12, he warned them that they would soon face persecution from people in authority over them. However, instead of hindering his mission, he quickly added that, *"this will be your opportunity to bear witness"* (v 13; [7]M. I. Ro 5:3b). All Christians receive a new mission-heart when the Holy Spirit graciously gives them faith ([8]M. M. Mt 5:14). Therefore, Jesus now promised his disciples that his Spirit would not only guide them to see opportunities to witness in the midst of suffering, he would also *"give you [them] a mouth and wisdom, which none of your adversaries will be able to withstand or contradict"* (v 15). And, true to his Word, within a few months, Peter and John found themselves standing before the Jewish council accused of preaching and healing in the name of Jesus (Ac 4:10). And the Spirit of Jesus did indeed give them powerful words to witness before them (Ac 4:12, 20). Likewise, within a few years, it's likely that Luke himself may have witnessed how Paul stood before the Jewish council and before kings and boldly witnessed to the name of Jesus. Therefore, Jesus commended and encouraged Paul in (Ac 23:11), *"Take courage, for as you have testified to the facts about me in Jerusalem, so you must testify also in Rome"* ([9]M. I. Lk 11:10 & [10]Lk 12:12).

21:16-19 (1) Then, Jesus warned his disciples in verses 16-17 that they would have to face persecution from their families and friends. This was the second time that Jesus warned his disciples that a faith relationship with him may cause even their own families to hate and kill them (12:51-53). The bitterest test of the endurance of a Christian's faith may, indeed, come from the day that he must choose between the strong love that he has for his physical family and the love that he now has for his <u>dearest</u> Brother Jesus. It's hard enough to be able to boldly witness before *"kings and governors"* (v 12), but if it's your own father or mother who will hate you for confessing him (vs 16-17), it's terrible indeed. **2)** Therefore, in verses 18-19, Jesus quickly assured them that *"not a hair of your head will perish. By your endurance you will gain your lives."* Their gracious Lord is fully able to protect his missionaries from both their physical and spiritual enemies, so that the devil will not be able to harm even one (spiritual) hair. And the clearest proof of his almighty power is in his own resurrection from the dead ([11]M. I. Lk 12:4). **3)** Obviously, when Jesus says in verse 19 that *"by your endurance you will gain your lives,"* he is not saying that his disciples can save themselves. Rather, the meaning is clearer in (Mk 13:13), *"the one who endures to the end will be saved."* The passive form of the verb in Mark, *"will <u>be</u> saved"* means that their <u>Lord</u> will do the action of graciously saving them. Jesus never could deny, nor did he ever deny who he is, a most <u>gracious</u> and loving God (2 Cor 5:21). He himself would strengthen his disciples in the coming dark days as they depended on him in constant prayer ([12]M. I. Lk 11:10). **4)** Persecution from one's own family is a serious problem in all cultures of the world, but in some cultures they place even more emphasis on their family relationships since their entire lives are centered on their extended family. In such situations, only their gracious Lord will be able to give them the endurance that they need to be able to hold on to their faith in Jesus and to their eternal life (v 18; [13]M. M. Lk 6:22).

Jesus Foretells Destruction of Jerusalem 21:20-24

21:20 *"But when you see Jerusalem surrounded by armies, then know that its desolation has come near.*
21:21 *Then let those who are in Judea flee to the mountains, and let those who are inside the city depart, and let not those who are out in the country enter it,*
21:22 *for these are days of vengeance, to fulfill all that is written.*

21:23 *Alas for women who are pregnant and for those who are nursing infants in those days! For there will be great distress upon the earth and wrath against this people.*

21:24 *They will fall by the edge of the sword and be led captive among all nations, and Jerusalem will be trampled underfoot by the Gentiles, until the times of the Gentiles are fulfilled.*

21:20-24 Just as the temple in Jerusalem was Jesus' "home" because it was his *"Father's house"* (2:49), so likewise, the city of Jerusalem was his Capital City, as the King of kings and Lord of his mission to the world ([14]M. M. Eph 1:21 & [15]Ac 4:28). Therefore, it must have grieved him deeply to have to predict the physical destruction of both; even though both were merely *"copies"* of the *"more perfect"* spiritual temple and capital city in heaven (Heb 9:11, 23-24; 12:22; Rev 21:2). Furthermore, when both were destroyed by the Roman Empire in A.D. 70, it must have been a terrible shock for all Jews; nevertheless, the Christians living in Israel at that time were also carried away to Gentile nations, where they would have many opportunities to witness to their Lord. Sadly, the history of the Church records very few times when the new Israel has obeyed their Lord and gone to Gentile nations with the Gospel, as God graciously planned even before he created the world ([16]M. M. Ac 13:46).

The Coming of the Son of Man 21:25-28

21:25 *"And there will be signs in sun and moon and stars, and on the earth distress of nations in perplexity because of the roaring of the sea and the waves,*

21:26 *people fainting with fear and with foreboding of what is coming on the world. For the powers of the heavens will be shaken.*

21:27 *And then they will see the Son of Man coming in a cloud with power and great glory.*

21:28 *Now when these things begin to take place, straighten up and raise your heads, because your redemption is drawing near."*

21:25-28 In verse 27, Jesus said, *"they [all people who are alive on the Last Day] will see the Son of Man coming in a cloud with power and great glory."* It was the second time (17:30) that he comforted his disciples with his assurance that he will certainly return very soon on the Last Day. On that great Day, all persecution and suffering of Christians will end because his mission to the lost will end; there will be no more need for hope for an eternal life with him. That is the Day that our full, eternal life with him will begin in a new heaven and a new earth. Thus, Jesus wanted us to never be discouraged as we carried out our mission to the whole world ([17]M. M. Lk 12:8).

The Lesson of the Fig Tree 21:29-33

21:29 *And he told them a parable: "Look at the fig tree, and all the trees.*
21:30 *As soon as they come out in leaf, you see for yourselves and know that the summer is already near.*
21:31 *So also, when you see these things taking place, you know that the kingdom of God is near.*
21:32 *Truly, I say to you, this generation will not pass away until all has taken place.*
21:33 *Heaven and earth will pass away, but my words will not pass away.*

21:29-33 The comforting Words of Jesus in verse 33 that *"heaven and earth will pass away, but my words will not pass away"* mean that every precious Word that he ever spoke is on the same holy level as every precious written Word of the Bible, both the Old and New Testaments. (The New Testament obviously does not record every Word that he spoke as a human being (Jn 21:25).) Every one of his Words is true forever and can never fail (16:17; Ps 119:89; Is 40:8; 55:11). This is the reason why the Holy Spirit is able to use the mighty, sharp sword of his holy Word to carry out his mission of creating and sustaining faith in the hearts of people (Heb 4:12; Rom 1:16; [18]M. M. Ro 10:17a). Therefore, as we Christians continue to proclaim his Word all over the world yet today, we do not depend on our own power, but rather we wield the sword of the Spirit, which is the Word of God (Eph 6:17). Furthermore, this truth is also very comforting because it obviously means that the <u>results</u> of our mission efforts do not depend on anything that we say or do. The Holy Spirit graciously uses his holy Word to produce the results that he desires (8:8; Rom 10:17; [19]M. I. Lk 8:11 & [20]Lk 16:17).

Watch Yourselves 21:34-38

21:34 *"But watch yourselves lest your hearts be weighed down with dissipation and drunkenness and cares of this life, and that day come upon you suddenly like a trap.*
21:35 *For it will come upon all who dwell on the face of the whole earth.*
21:36 *But stay awake at all times, praying that you may have strength to escape all these things that are going to take place, and to stand before the Son of Man."*
21:37 *And every day he was teaching in the temple, but at night he went out and lodged on the mount called Olivet.*
21:38 *And early in the morning all the people came to him in the temple to hear him.*

21:34-36 Jesus here repeated his warning to his disciples that they would be proclaiming his Law and Gospel message in a <u>hostile</u> world in which the devil uses sinful human beings to constantly create chaos (vs 9-26). However, he urged them that, by *"stay [ing] awake at all times,"* *"praying"* to him (v 36) and depending on the power of his grace, they would be able to do two things: **a)** *"escape all these things that are going to take place;"* **b)** and also *"stand before the Son of Man [on the Last Day]"* (v 36). Jesus, of course, knew how difficult it would be for all of his disciples, the Church in the new era, as he sent us out to seek the lost in a <u>dark</u> world. Not all Christians would be able to endure the terrible suffering; and not all Christians would be able to endure his Father's judgment on the Last Day either. However, if we *"stay awake"* and pray to our gracious Lord *"at all times"* we are depending on his grace (v 36), and he is always eager to give us his almighty grace during our struggles; and, in his rich grace, he will surely cover us with his robe of righteousness, so that we will stand fully justified before our heavenly Father on that glorious Judgment Day (Rev 6:11; [21]M. I. Lk 11:10 & [22]M. M. 2 Tim 4:8).

21:37-38 Every single day of his earthly life, Jesus' mission-heart filled him with compassion for the lost. Verses 37-38 emphasize that, even though he knew that his horrible passion was just days away, *"every day he was teaching in the temple…And early in the morning all the people came to him in the temple to hear him."* He taught the people right down to the day that he was arrested. He always used every possible opportunity to proclaim his Law and Gospel message ([23]M. M. Lk 1:1). Also note that he was, of course, even focused on the lost and not on himself during his entire passion (chapters 22-23) and even on the cross (23:32-43)—down to the very last breath he took. His grace is beyond our feeble comprehension ([24]M. M. Ro 11:26).

---

[1] M. I. Lk 6:13: Christians should choose new leaders and train them in order to multiply the work.

[2] M. M. Ro 1:5: The same Holy Spirit who creates faith and a new missionary nature in a person's heart also graciously empowers him to gratefully respond to his Lord's love by obeying him.

[3] M. I. Lk 6:13: Christians should choose new leaders and train them in order to multiply the work.

[4] M. M. Ac 13:46: As he did with the old Israel, God first of all strengthens the faith of the new Israel, the Church with his Word and Sacraments, so that they can go and witness to the lost people of all nations.

[5] M. I. Ro 5:3a: Christians should rejoice in the midst of suffering for Jesus' sake because suffering teaches them to depend on their Lord's rich grace, and thus continue to grow in more spiritual gifts.

[6] M. M. Ac 4:28: The heavenly Father is always in full control of his mission to all nations of the world.

[7] M. I. Ro 5:3b: Christians should rejoice in the midst of suffering for Jesus' sake because unbelievers may see their joy, which may create opportunities to witness to Jesus.

[8] M. M. Mt 5:14: When the Holy Spirit creates faith in a person's heart, he also graciously gives him a new mission-heart that is eager to shine the light of the Gospel throughout the whole world.

[9] M. I. Lk 11:10: Christians should continuously pray to their heavenly Father and always depend on his grace, and not on their own feeble strength, because he always loves them.

[10] M. I. Lk 12:12: Christians should go and tell the Gospel depending on the Holy Spirit to teach them what they should say.

[11] M. I. Lk 12:4: Christians should not be afraid of the physical harm that their human or spiritual enemies may do to them, because they can only harm them physically, but they cannot take away their eternal life with Jesus, their dear friend.

[12] M. I. Lk 11:10: Christians should continuously pray to their heavenly Father and always depend on his grace, and not on their own feeble strength, because he always loves them.

[13] M. M. Lk 6:22: The Lord Jesus will surely bless a Christian in the midst of suffering for his sake; and he will also bless him with eternal life if he remains faithful to him.

[14] M. M. Eph 1:21: God has given Jesus his almighty power to rule as King of all kings over Satan and all of his evil angels and demons until the Last Day and forever.

[15] M. M. Ac 4:28: The heavenly Father is always in full control of his mission to all nations of the world.

[16] M. M. Ac 13:46: As he did with the old Israel, God first of all strengthens the faith of the new Israel, the Church with his Word and Sacraments, so that they can go and witness to the lost people of all nations.

[17] M. M. Lk 12:8: On Judgment Day, Jesus will acknowledge before his heavenly Father that all Christians are his brothers and sisters.

[18] M. M. Ro 10:17a: The Holy Spirit only creates and preserves faith by using the message of God's grace in his holy Word.

[19] M. I. Lk 8:11: Christians should faithfully do their job of preaching and leave the results to the Holy Spirit.

[20] M. I. Lk 16:17: Christians should wield the sword of the Spirit with confidence as they go and tell the Gospel because his Word can never fail.

[21] M. I. Lk 11:10: Christians should continuously pray to their heavenly Father and always depend on his grace, and not on their own feeble strength, because he always loves them.

[22] M. M. 2 Tim 4:8: On the Last Day, the Lord Jesus, the righteous Judge, will graciously award a crown of righteousness to Christians who have fought the good fight, finished the race, kept the faith, have loved him and longed for that Day when he will appear again.

[23] M. M. Lk 1:1: Jesus came to seek and save all lost people from every nation on earth.

[24] M. M. Ro 11:26: God graciously continues to graft Jews and Gentiles into the new Israel through the proclamation of the Gospel, until the remnant of Israel and the fullness of the Gentiles form one, holy Nation and are saved.

Chapter 22

The Plot to Kill Jesus 22:1-2

22:1 *Now the Feast of Unleavened Bread drew near, which is called the Passover.*
22:2 *And the chief priests and the scribes were seeking how to put him to death, for they feared the people.*

Judas to Betray Jesus 22:3-6

22:3 *Then Satan entered into Judas called Iscariot, who was of the number of the twelve.*
22:4 *He went away and conferred with the chief priests and officers how he might betray him to them.*
22:5 *And they were glad, and agreed to give him money.*
22:6 *So he consented and sought an opportunity to betray him to them in the absence of a crowd.*

22:1-6 Satan was obviously plotting to destroy Jesus by using the evil Jewish religious leaders and one of his disciples, Judas; and they thought that they would be powerful enough to have their own way in order to completely destroy him. But it was, of course, the heavenly <u>Father</u> who was in full control (Jn 13:3). It was <u>he</u> who was using them to carry out his perfect, gracious plan (v 22) in order to destroy the power of Satan, sin and death through the sacrificial death of his Holy One, Jesus (Ac 2:27). "The Son of Man" had, indeed, come *"to <u>seek</u> and to <u>save</u> the lost"* (19:10; [1]M. M. Lk 1:1 & [2]Ac 4: 28)!

The Passover with the Disciples 22:7-13

22:7 *Then came the day of Unleavened Bread, on which the Passover lamb had to be sacrificed.*

22:8   *So Jesus sent Peter and John, saying, "Go and prepare the Passover for us, that we may eat it."*
22:9   *They said to him, "Where will you have us prepare it?"*
22:10 *He said to them, "Behold, when you have entered the city, a man carrying a jar of water will meet you. Follow him into the house that he enters*
22:11 *and tell the master of the house, 'The Teacher says to you, Where is the guest room, where I may eat the Passover with my disciples?'*
22:12 *And he will show you a large upper room furnished; prepare it there."*
22:13 *And they went and found it just as he had told them, and they prepared the Passover.*

22:7-13 Jesus makes it very clear to his disciples in verses 7-13 that he was in full control of everything down to the last detail, but he was mainly focused on preparing his disciples for the spiritual and physical dangers and for the shock of his arrest that night. His disciples, on the other hand, were probably only thinking about all of the preparations that they had to make for the Passover and were totally unaware of any spiritual and physical danger ([3]M. M. Ac 4: 28).

22:7 Note exactly what Luke says in (v 7): *"Then came the day of Unleavened Bread on which the Passover lamb had to be sacrificed."* Even though Luke (the <u>Gentile</u> author) did not grow up experiencing the Jewish sacrificial system, he understood how very significant this day was for all of mankind. All of the thousands of lambs that had been sacrificed on this day in the long history of the nation of Israel pointed to this fulfilment, this one sacrifice of the very Lamb of God (Jn 1:29). The great Day had, indeed, finally come for the Son of Man to save the lost from every nation on earth (19:10; [4]M. M. Lk 1:1 & [5]Mt 1:22)!

(H30Institution of the Lord's Supper 22:14-23

22:14 *And when the hour came, he reclined at table, and the apostles with him.*

22:15 *And he said to them, "I have earnestly desired to eat this Passover with you before I suffer.*
22:16 *For I tell you I will not eat it until it is fulfilled in the kingdom of God."*
22:17 *And he took a cup, and when he had given thanks he said, "Take this, and divide it among yourselves.*
22:18 *For I tell you that from now on I will not drink of the fruit of the vine until the kingdom of God comes."*
22:19 *And he took bread, and when he had given thanks, he broke it and gave it to them, saying, "This is my body, which is given for you. Do this in remembrance of me."*
22:20 *And likewise the cup after they had eaten, saying, "This cup that is poured out for you is the new covenant in my blood.*
22:21 *But behold, the hand of him who betrays me is with me on the table.*
22:22 *For the Son of Man goes as it has been determined, but woe to that man by whom he is betrayed!"*
22:23 *And they began to question one another, which of them it could be who was going to do this.*

22:19-20 (1) Jesus clearly knew how horribly his enemies were going to torture him in the next few hours, and he likewise knew how frightening his passion and death would be for his disciples. However, the deep compassion of his mission-heart would not allow him to focus on his own far greater needs; quite to the contrary, he continued to focus on strengthening not only the shaky faith of these twelve disciples, but also the faith of *all* of his future disciples during the long new era of the Church. Therefore, he now gave all Christians the most gracious gift of his own body and blood in, with and under the bread and wine that he gave them to eat and drink that last evening. He graciously promised all Christians, in verse 19, *"This is my body;"* and then he added in verse 20, *"This cup is…the new covenant in my blood."* Note that Luke clearly quoted our Lord's gracious Words in a literal historical account; and therefore, they should be understood very literally: *"This is my body,"* and *"This cup [wine] is…my blood."* Furthermore, he adds a gracious promise to his meal when he says in verse 19, *"which is given* *for you."* In these three Words, he promises us, *"I died for you, in order to give you the forgiveness of all of your sins."* He offers complete forgiveness in Holy Communion to those who trust in this most gracious promise. Therefore, a person who repents of his sin and knows that he does not deserve to partake of his true body and blood in this holy meal (1 Cor 11:28-29) will surely receive full forgiveness for all of his sin. It's a new mission message. M. M. Lk 22:19a: The Lord Jesus graciously offers full forgiveness for all of his sins to a person who repents of his sin and knows that he does not deserve to partake of his Lord's true body and true blood in Holy Communion. **2)** Sadly, however, our Lord's mission has been greatly harmed by the fact that some Christian groups interpret Jesus' Words to be merely symbolic. They say that the unleavened bread and wine merely symbolize his body and blood; and in this way, they seriously diminish the meaning of his holy meal. They do not believe that they receive forgiveness of their sins in this meal; and therefore, they do not take it seriously and only celebrate it infrequently. Therefore, these false teachings destroy the unity in the Church, and they also display a divided witness to the lost world. And, of course, this sin surely makes Satan very happy because it destroys faith and prevents opportunities to witness to Jesus love for all people ([6]M. I. Ac 15:20). **3)** Jesus continues in verse 19 by urging us: *"Do this in remembrance of me."* What does he want us to remember when we partake of his true body and true blood in Holy Communion? Clearly, he longs for us to always remember his cross, where he graciously died for us (2 Cor 5:21). His cross is the heart and core of the Gospel, the main focus of all of human history because he died there for all humanity; therefore, he longs for every human being to remember that he died for them, so that they would be drawn to his cross alone ([7]M. M. Jn 6:44). We have no other Gospel to proclaim to the lost world ([8]M. I. Ro 1:16a). Our Lord helps and blesses us in many, many other ways; and these are also Gospel messages, but he only offers complete forgiveness through his cross. It's another new mission imperative. M. I. Lk 22:19b: As they partake of Holy Communion, they should always remember that Jesus graciously died on the cross for the forgiveness of all of their sins. (Note: Jesus died for *all* of his brothers and sisters from all nations (objective justification); however, he will only forgive those who trust in him and in his gracious promise of forgiveness (subjective justification).) **4)** Jesus gave his truly human and truly divine body and blood as a most gracious gift of forgiveness to all people from all nations and cultures on earth. Therefore, as we Christians, yet today, celebrate Holy Communion together with our brothers and sisters from all nations on the earth, and also witness to the presence of his true body and his true blood, we continue to affirm our unity as one Body under Jesus, our Lord and Brother. Thus, in spite of the disunity noted above, this meal continues to erase all sinful barriers that human beings erect between nations and cultures *"until the kingdom of God comes"* (v 18). On that Last Day, our Lord Jesus will return in great glory, riding on a cloud as our victorious King (21:27; [9]M. M. Lk 22:19a).

22:21-22 (1) As Jesus says in verse 22, it was his own beloved Father who planned how his Son would die, *"as it has been determined"* (Heb 10:5-10). And his plan was driven by his mission-heart, his deep compassion for all of lost mankind; yet, when we see one of his own disciples betray him (vs 21-22), it may appear to us feeble human beings to be the worst possible plan that he could have made. However, since his plan shows his rich, rich grace so clearly, it surely could not have been a more perfect plan. Thus, Luke carefully records Jesus' holy life from his holy conception to his glorious ascension some thirty years later, in order to teach us how glorious God's plan was and how beautifully it showed forth his amazing grace (1:1; 19:10; [10]M. M. Ro 1:16b). **2)** When Jesus said in verse 22, *"The Son of Man goes [to die] as it has been determined,"* his disciples no doubt did not, at that time, understand a Gospel message at all. However, his Words are indeed a very beautiful Gospel message that they would soon joyfully spread to all nations (19:10). And Christians in all ages and in all cultures have the most beautiful and glorious Gospel in the entire history of mankind to proclaim. Therefore, the mission-heart of every Christian should compel him to eagerly proclaim it far and wide in all languages and cultures on the earth. But how often we neglect to do so ([11]M. I. Ac 1:8 & [12]Ro 1:16a). **3)** And *"woe to that man [Judas] by whom he is betrayed"* (v 22), indeed! Judas was one of "the Twelve" who heard his Lord seeking him personally, one-on-one with his Truth, with his gracious, holy Words day after day for about three years. And no doubt he trusted in Jesus when he first called him, but instead of continuing to trust in him, he believed the lies of Satan and learned to love money more than his Lord and Savior! Not only did he hear Jesus' beautiful Gospel, but he also heard Jesus' very stern warnings against loving money that he repeatedly addressed to the Pharisees and scribes. *"Woe to"* Judas, indeed (v 22)! Obviously, his heart was even harder than the hearts of the religious leaders of the Jews; he was the worst kind of enemy, a traitor within the inner group; he was *"against"* Jesus instead of for him (9:50). Yet, Jesus continued to warn Judas so clearly in verse 22 because he loved him as dearly as he loved all of the other disciples; and he never gave up seeking him. Even though he did not use Judas' name in this warning, he surely made eye contact with him, so that Judas could not miss his meaning; just as he warned Peter a few hours later with direct eye contact (v 61). (Although none of the four Gospel accounts are completely clear about just when Judas left the room that evening, this warning of Jesus makes the most sense if Judas was still present.) As a matter of fact, Jesus gave him one last warning in verse 48, *"Judas, would you betray the Son of Man with a kiss?"* The Lord of the mission never gives up on anyone who is lost as long as that person is still alive and has a chance to repent; and that is precisely why Satan is always so eager to destroy those whom he holds in his prison as quickly as he can ([13]M. I. Lk 3:3a & [14]Ac 1:8).

Who is the Greatest? 22:24-30

22:24 *A dispute also arose among them, as to which of them was to be regarded as the greatest.*

22:25 *And he said to them, "The kings of the Gentiles exercise lordship over them, and those in authority over them are called benefactors.*

22:26 *But not so with you. Rather, let the greatest among you become as the youngest, and the leader as one who serves.*

22:27 *For who is the greater, one who reclines at table or one who*

> *serves? Is it not the one who reclines at table? But I am among you as the one who serves.*
> 22:28 *"You are those who have stayed with me in my trials,*
> 22:29 *and I assign to you, as my Father assigned to me, a kingdom,*
> 22:30 *that you may eat and drink at my table in my kingdom and sit on thrones judging the twelve tribes of Israel.*

22:24-27 (1) Obviously, all twelve disciples had failed to learn this lesson about humility because this was not Jesus' first warning about this (9:45-48). Just like Judas, the other eleven disciples too had heard Jesus' most gracious Words daily for three years as he personally sought each one of them one-on-one; yet, here they were experiencing the last few hours of physical contact with their Lord Jesus, and they still failed to understand all of his warnings against sinful pride (vs 26-27). In short, their weak faith was not all that stronger than Judas' lack of faith, since they all had the same basic problem of sinful human pride (M. I. Lk 3:3a). **2)** But of course, in verse 27, Jesus added very beautiful Gospel to his Words of warning, *"I am among you as the one who serves"* others (v 27), and not a proud lord (v 25). He not only served his disciples by *"seeking"* them for three years, John tells us in his Gospel that he also served them by washing their feet (Jn 13:4-11). And most importantly, he would also in a few hours be their humble servant and *"save"* them by dying for them and all people (19:10; vs 29-30; Phil 2:5-11; [15]M. M. Lk 1:1). And his deep compassion for them as a servant soon compelled them to go out into the dark world as quickly as they could in order to serve others by seeking them (M. I. Ac 1:8).

22:28-30 After warning his disciples to be humble servants and not proud lords here on earth in verses 25-27, Jesus promised them in verse 30 that, after they had suffered here with him, they would receive the gracious gift of a role-reversal. They would one day soon reign with him in his kingdom in heaven forever, sitting *"on thrones judging the twelve tribes of Israel."* How this wonderful promise must have encouraged them in the next three terrible days! However, although his promise may sound like they were earning this reward by their obedience, he obviously was not saying this because he alone could earn any eternal rewards by his perfect obedience ([16]M. M. Lk 18:29). Furthermore, he was doing just that even as he spoke; and in just a few hours, he would complete that work on the cross. In the near future, they would continue to *"seek the lost,"* as he also had done throughout his life, but he <u>alone</u> could *"<u>save</u> the lost"* by his perfect obedience (19:10; [17]M. M. Ro 3:24 & [18]Lk 1:1).

Jesus Foretells Peter's Denial 22:31-34

> 22:31 *"Simon, Simon, behold, Satan demanded to have you, that he might sift you like wheat,*
> 22:32 *but I have prayed for you that your faith may not fail. And when you have turned again, strengthen your brothers."*
> 22:33 *Peter said to him, "Lord, I am ready to go with you both to prison and to death."*
> 22:34 *Jesus said, "I tell you, Peter, the rooster will not crow this day, until you deny three times that you know me."*

22:31-34 (1) Satan may or may not have already known that he would <u>only</u> be able to *"<u>strike</u> (NIV) his [Jesus'] heel,"* but Jesus would *"<u>crush</u> [his] head"* (Gen 3:15) on the cross, but there is little doubt that Jesus knew <u>three</u> things: how fierce his final, awful battle with him would be, that the final result of his passion would be the total defeat of his arch-enemy, and he also knew how extremely vulnerable his disciples would be for at least three days, especially since they would personally see and touch his dead body. They would not be able to deny the apparent total end to all that he had promised them. Therefore, Jesus was, of course, still focusing on <u>them</u>, on <u>their</u> vulnerability and not on his own much graver danger. And right now, the devil was about to attack their leader, Peter, who had already proven to be quite fickle (v 31). Satan had already overcome Judas, and now his much larger target was Peter. Thus, Jesus' warning to Peter in verse 34 is very blunt and clear. Yet, somehow Peter totally missed it! He seemed to be totally unaware of the grave spiritual danger that they all faced and how vulnerable they were. How urgently Peter would very soon need to totally depend on the power of his Lord's rich grace by remembering his promises ([19]M. I. Lk 4:4 & [20]Lk 11:4b)! **2)** Thus, Jesus especially prayed for Peter (v 32) for at least two reasons: **a)** He had given Peter the special mission of being the main leader of his disciples. **b)** However, Peter was also perhaps the most proud among the disciples. Therefore, Jesus "sought" Peter not only by warning him about pride in verses 25-27, but he also gave him a very direct and clear warning that he would soon deny him (v 34; [21]M. I. Lk 3:3a). However, the very good news for our Lord's mission is that both Jesus' warnings and his Gospel messages to Peter did bear fruit in his heart. When Jesus *"turned and looked at Peter"* (v 61) a few hours later, Peter did remember what his Lord had said and "wept bitterly" (v 62) in repentance. And, after further urging by Jesus in (Jn 21:15-17), he did later also *"feed my [his Lord's] sheep"* by leading the other disciples and by spreading the Gospel as his Lord's missionary to the Jews (Gal 2:7; [22]M. I. Ac 20:19).

Scripture Must Be Fulfilled in Jesus 22:35-38

> 22:35 *And he said to them, "When I sent you out with no moneybag or knapsack or sandals, did you lack anything?" They said, "Nothing."*
> 22:36 *He said to them, "But now let the one who has a moneybag take it, and likewise a knapsack. And let the one who has no sword sell his cloak and buy one.*
> 22:37 *For I tell you that this Scripture must be fulfilled in me: 'And he was numbered with the transgressors.' For what is written about me has its fulfillment."*
> 22:38 *And they said, "Look, Lord, here are two swords." And he said to them, "It is enough."*

22:35-38 (1) First of all, since Jesus' death loomed ever closer, we can readily understand why he comforted his disciples by reminding them in verse 35 that they didn't *"lack anything"* on their first mission journey (9:1-6) because their Lord supplied <u>all</u> of their needs—with spiritual strength, with courage, with a mighty message, and with their physical needs, which he gave them through their hosts ([23]M. I. Lk 11:10 & [24]M. M. Ac 4:28). **2)** Secondly, however, Jesus' disciples misunderstood his Words in verse 36, *"But now let the one who has a moneybag take it, and likewise a knapsack. And let the one who has no <u>sword</u> sell his cloak and buy one."* It's obvious from their reply in verse 38, *"Look, Lord, here are two swords"* that they thought that he meant that they would need physical swords as they went on his mission to proclaim the Gospel. But they did, of course, understand some time later that he meant *"the <u>sword</u> of the Spirit,"* which is his holy Word (Eph 6:17). This is the only weapon that his disciples would in fact use on their mission, so that the Holy Spirit could create and strengthen faith in the hearts of their hearers; and it's also the only weapon that they could use to defeat both their human enemies (21:15) and their worst, spiritual enemy, Satan (Eph 6:11; Jms 4:7; [25]M. M. Ro 10:17a). **3)** Thirdly, Jesus' Words in verse 37, *"For what is written about me has its fulfillment"* is almost precisely what Jesus said to the two Emmaus disciples after he rose from the dead in (24:44), where he said, *"These are my words that I spoke to you while I was still with you, that everything written about me in the Law of Moses and the Prophets and the Psalms must be fulfilled"* (1:1; 9:44; 18:31-33; Lev 18:5). Thus, Jesus again teaches us here in verse 37 that <u>every</u> verse in the Old Testament points to Jesus and his mission on earth *"to seek and to save the lost."* From before his creation of the world, the heavenly Father has been carrying out this gracious plan of salvation; and the Old Testament revealed this plan bit by bit in ever greater clarity. Therefore, the Old Testament (along with the New Testament) is likewise a vital part of *"the sword of the Spirit"* for us disciples of Jesus to wield as we go to all nations to proclaim its message ([26]M. I. Lk 4:17 & [27]Ac 2:4).

Jesus Prays on the Mount of Olives 22:39-46

22:39 *And he came out and went, as was his custom, to the Mount of Olives, and the disciples followed him.*
22:40 *And when he came to the place, he said to them, "Pray that you may not enter into temptation."*

22:41 *And he withdrew from them about a stone's throw, and knelt down and prayed,*
22:42 *saying, "Father, if you are willing, remove this cup from me. Nevertheless, not my will, but yours, be done."*
22:43 *And there appeared to him an angel from heaven, strengthening him.*
22:44 *And being in an agony he prayed more earnestly; and his sweat became like great drops of blood falling down to the ground.*
22:45 *And when he rose from prayer, he came to the disciples and found them sleeping for sorrow,*
22:46 *and he said to them, "Why are you sleeping? Rise and pray that you may not enter into temptation."*

22:39-46 (1) It's completely impossible for us mere human beings to even begin to imagine the *"agony"* (v 44) that Jesus felt at this terrible moment in the garden. Although he was indeed a true human being; yet, as true God, he also knew exactly what his human and spiritual enemies were going to do to him. Most importantly, he knew the full extent of his Father's righteous anger against sin (Nah 1:2); and thus he also knew just how unbelievably enormous the load of mankind's sin would be that he was about to carry all alone (2 Cor 5:21). Furthermore, he had known all of this for a long time and had already been carrying this cross daily. Thus, he offered *"earnest"* prayers (v 44) to his Father, in order to know if there could possibly be any other way that this saving work could be accomplished. But, even as he prayed and submitted his will to his gracious Father's will, he already knew that there was no other way except for the way of the cross. He had come for this very purpose, *"to…save the lost."* In addition, he also did this, so that his disciples, the new Israel would have a glorious Gospel to share with the lost world ([28]M. M. Ro 5:1). **2)** However, in the midst of all of this, we still see his own rich, rich grace as well. He was not just thinking of himself, or just thinking of the success of his mission; he likewise continued to repeatedly focus on the weaknesses and fears of his disciples. He continued on his mission of *"seeking"* them and urged them to do as he was doing, to turn to their heavenly Father in prayer and depend on his strength, and not on their own strength. They were the only ones who could carry on his mission to the world in the future; therefore, it was vital that they too should not lose their faith, and therefore not be able to carry out his mission to the world ([29]M. I. Lk 11:10).

Betrayal and Arrest of Jesus 22:47-53

22:47 *While he was still speaking, there came a crowd, and the man called Judas, one of the twelve, was leading them. He drew near to Jesus to kiss him,*
22:48 *but Jesus said to him, "Judas, would you betray the Son of Man with a kiss?"*
22:49 *And when those who were around him saw what would follow, they said, "Lord, shall we strike with the sword?"*
22:50 *And one of them struck the servant of the high priest and cut off his right ear.*
22:51 *But Jesus said, "No more of this!" And he touched his ear and healed him.*
22:52 *Then Jesus said to the chief priests and officers of the temple and elders, who had come out against him, "Have you come out as against a robber, with swords and clubs?*
22:53 *When I was with you day after day in the temple, you did not lay hands on me. But this is your hour, and the power of darkness."*

22:47-53 (1) The 11 disciples were, no doubt, thinking about nothing but their <u>physical</u> danger when their enemies came, because they were weak human beings just like we are; but not so Jesus, because he now focused on <u>one</u> lost sinner, Judas when he came up to greet him. He <u>still</u> tried to *"seek"* Judas, one-on-one, by jarring his conscience one last time. His own awful hour had arrived, yet his compassionate mission-heart did not allow him to think about himself. It was his last opportunity, and he didn't fail in his mission to try to personally "seek" this one lost sinner by warning him, *"Judas, would you betray the Son of Man with a kiss"* (v 48)? And no doubt Jesus likewise tried to *"seek"* him with up-close-and-personal *eye contact*, just as he did a short time later with Peter (v

61). But Satan had already totally imprisoned Judas with his lies; therefore, Judas lied by kissing Jesus. And he was, no doubt, also careful to avoid his compassionate eyes ([30]M. I. Lk 4:35 & [31]Lk 4:40). **2)** Then, Jesus likewise sought one more of his human enemies, one-on-one, by graciously healing one of the soldiers (v 51). He knew that it still wasn't too late to try to reach this one man and his fellow soldiers who saw this miracle. It's truly amazing that he was still so compassionately focused on the needs of others and not his own needs ([32]M. I. Lk 4:35 & [33]Lk 4:40). **3)** And now Jesus' compassionate mission-heart turned to his main human enemies in verse 52, *"the chief priests and officers of the temple and elders."* The very spiritual leaders of his people who should have been embracing and supporting his mission on earth were, instead, his main enemies. They had been plotting to destroy him for at least three years; and today was *"their hour"* (v 53; 20:15). Yet in the compassionate eyes of Jesus, it was also *"his hour,"* his opportunity to try once again, to *"seek"* them. No matter the circumstances, he always faithfully seized every opportunity for that! Jesus was also very blunt with these men in verse 53 when he reminded them that they were in league with the devil, *"the power of darkness."* They were putting all of their energy and power into advancing the wrong kingdom, the kingdom of darkness. Do we need to point out that they despised his warning instead of heeding it ([34]M. I. Lk 4:15)? (Note that it was likewise the heavenly Father's *"hour"* (v 53) when he could, at long last, carry out the final details of his master plan of salvation. He was in complete control of every perfect detail ([35]M. M. Ac 4:28).) **4)** When Jesus said in verse 53, *"But this is your hour, and the power of darkness,"* he saw far more than a few hired soldiers surrounding him; he also saw legions of evil angels led by his arch-enemy, the devil. For these few hours *"darkness"* did indeed rule, even though his Father was still ultimately in control. Yet, even if these had been his only enemies, Jesus obviously could have destroyed them himself, if he had chosen to do so, and even without the help of his holy angels (Mt 26:53). But no, they were not even his worst enemies, since he had made his dear Father his archenemy by taking the burden of mankind's sins on himself (Is 53:3-12). His Father was the enemy to whom he graciously yielded himself as a holy sacrifice. What amazing grace we see in our Lord! And what a gracious Gospel this is that we carry to the desperately lost world (Mt 27:46; Rom 5:10; Col 1:21; [36]M. M. Ro 3:24)!

Peter Denies Jesus 22:54-62

22:54 *Then they seized him and led him away, bringing him into the high priest's house, and Peter was following at a distance.*
22:55 *And when they had kindled a fire in the middle of the courtyard and sat down together, Peter sat down among them.*
22:56 *Then a servant girl, seeing him as he sat in the light and looking closely at him, said, "This man also was with him."*
22:57 *But he denied it, saying, "Woman, I do not know him."*
22:58 *And a little later someone else saw him and said, "You also are one of them." But Peter said, "Man, I am not."*
22:59 *And after an interval of about an hour still another insisted, saying, "Certainly this man also was with him, for he too is a Galilean."*
22:60 *But Peter said, "Man, I do not know what you are talking about." And immediately, while he was still speaking, the rooster crowed.*
22:61 *And the Lord turned and looked at Peter. And Peter remembered the saying of the Lord, how he had said to him, "Before the rooster crows today, you will deny me three times."*
22:62 *And he went out and wept bitterly.*

22:54-62 (1) By boldly entering the courtyard near Jesus' trial, Peter was not only placing himself in much more grave danger than all of the disciples already faced, he was also very foolishly depending on his own feeble strength. And even more importantly, he was also jeopardizing the entire future of Jesus' mission to the whole world, because, if their enemies had also killed the leader of the disciples, the remaining ten disciples would have been even more fearful and discouraged ([37]M. I. Lk 11:10). **2)** However, Jesus continued to *"seek"* Peter (19:10) with an extremely powerful message by using very deliberate eye contact (v 61).

His look brought all of Jesus' warnings (v 34) and all of Jesus' love roaring back into Peter's memory. It touched his heart as no mere words could have. With just a look, Jesus "sought" Peter and found him ([38]M. I. Lk 3:3a).

Jesus is Mocked 22:63-65

> 22:63 *Now the men who were holding Jesus in custody were mocking him as they beat him.*
> 22:64 *They also blindfolded him and kept asking him, "Prophesy! Who is it that struck you?"*
> 22:65 *And they said many other things against him, blaspheming him.*

22:63-65 By placing Peter's denial immediately before the guards mocking Jesus (v 63), Luke teaches his readers that Peter's actions and their actions meant exactly the same thing to Jesus. (Note that Matthew and Mark made the same linkage, but in their Gospels they placed the guards beating Jesus <u>before</u> Peter's denial.) What a sad choice that was for Peter, to act like the guards and Judas and make himself an enemy of Jesus by denying him! It's no wonder, then, that Peter *"wept bitterly"* (v 62; 9:50; Phil 3:18; M. I. Lk 11:10).

Jesus Before the Council 22:66-71

> 22:66 *When day came, the assembly of the elders of the people gathered together, both chief priests and scribes. And they led him away to their council, and they said,*
> 22:67 *"If you are the Christ, tell us." But he said to them, "If I tell you, you will not believe,*
> 22:68 *and if I ask you, you will not answer.*
> 22:69 *But from now on the Son of Man shall be seated at the right hand of the power of God."*
> 22:70 *So they all said, "Are you the Son of God, then?" And he said to them, "You say that I am."*

22:71 Then they said, "What further testimony do we need? We have heard it ourselves from his own lips."

22:66-71 And now here in the Jewish council were some of the same men who were there when they arrested Jesus. And, as Jesus stood before them, his compassionate mission-heart saw yet another opportunity to *"seek"* them, even as they were seeking to complete their evil plot to destroy him. He, of course, was not afraid of them nor was he even thinking about what they were about to do to him; rather he was still concerned about their lost hearts. Therefore, he "sought" them by making a very bold confession before them that he was both *"the Christ"* (v 67) and *"the Son of God"* (v 70; 1:32-33). They all had heard about his many miracles, especially when they heard, just a few days earlier, that he had raised Lazarus from the dead. That should have been solid proof to them that he was true God (Jn 11:45-47). But did that convince them? Obviously not! Now standing before them was an added witness to the same truth from "the Truth" himself (Jn 14:6). Did this convince them? Obviously not! Sadly, all of their hearts, except for the hearts of Nicodemus and Joseph of Arimathea, were already as hard as stone (3:8; [39]M. I. Lk 4:15).

---

[1] M. M. Lk 1:1: Jesus came to seek and save all lost people from every nation on earth.

[2] M. M. Ac 4:28: The heavenly Father is always in full control of his mission to all nations of the world.

[3] M. M. Ac 4:28: The heavenly Father is always in full control of his mission to all nations of the world.

[4] M. M. Lk 1:1: Jesus came to seek and save all lost people from every nation on earth.

[5] M. M. Mt 1:22: God sent his only Son, Jesus to be born as a true human being, so that he could save all of his brothers and sisters of all nations by fulfilling all of God's promises in the Old Testament.

[6] M. I. Ac 15:20: To preserve the unity of the Church and to make it possible to reach out to unbelievers from all cultural backgrounds, all they should show love to their fellow Christians and to all people of all cultures by refraining from actions that would easily offend them.

[7] M. M. Jn 6:44: People who are lost cannot come to faith in Jesus by their own power; only the heavenly Father, who sent Jesus to die for them can draw them to Jesus by sending Christians to proclaim the Gospel to them.

⁸ M. I. Ro 1:16a: Christians should not be ashamed to proclaim the Gospel, even though it may appear to be weak and foolish; rather, they should be proud to proclaim it because it is the almighty power that the Holy Spirit uses to create faith in Jesus.

⁹ M. M. Lk 22:19a: The Lord Jesus graciously offers full forgiveness for all of his sins to a person who repents of his sin and knows that he does not deserve to partake of his Lord's true body and true blood in Holy Communion.

¹⁰ M. M. Ro 1:16b: The Gospel is so powerful because it contains the central truth that Jesus rose from the dead with a glorified body in order to save all of his brothers and sisters from sin and death.

¹¹ M. I. Ac 1:8: Christians should go and witness about Jesus to all who are lost from all languages and cultures by depending on the power of the Holy Spirit to help them bridge all of the language/cultural boundaries whether they are relatively easy, as in their own language, or extremely difficult.

¹² M. I. Ro 1:16a: Christians should not be ashamed to proclaim the Gospel, even though it may appear to be weak and foolish; rather, they should be proud to proclaim it because it is the almighty power that the Holy Spirit uses to create faith in Jesus.

¹³ M. I. Lk 3:3a: Christians should, in love, warn lost people who do not repent.

¹⁴ M. I. Ac 1:8: Christians should go and witness about Jesus to all who are lost from all languages and cultures by depending on the power of the Holy Spirit to help them bridge all of the language/cultural boundaries whether they are relatively easy, as in their own language, or extremely difficult.

¹⁵ M. M. Lk 1:1: Jesus came to seek and save <u>all</u> lost people from <u>every</u> nation on earth.

¹⁶ M. M. Lk 18:29: All Christians will certainly receive rewards in heaven as gracious gifts, but not because they earned them by going into the lost world to proclaim the Gospel; rather, they went because they also received <u>grateful</u> mission-hearts from their Lord.

¹⁷ M. M. Ro 3:24: Jesus lived a life of perfect obedience and shed his precious blood on the cross, in order to graciously set all nations free from sin, which a person only receives by faith in him.

¹⁸ M. M. Lk 1:1: Jesus came to seek and save <u>all</u> lost people from <u>every</u> nation on earth.

¹⁹ M. I. Lk 4:4: When Satan attacks Christians on their mission they should wield the sword of God's Word by quoting from it, and not depend on their own strength.

²⁰ M. I. Lk 11:4b: Christians should ask their heavenly Father that he would not allow Satan to tempt them so severely that they lose their faith, and also that he would give them his strength to depend on his grace in all of their trials.

²¹ M. I. Lk 3:3a: Christians should, in love, warn lost people who do not repent.

²² M. I. Ac 20:19: Christians should humbly serve their hearers and their Lord Jesus because he first humbly served all of them.

²³ M. I. Lk 11:10: Christians should <u>continuously</u> pray to their heavenly Father and <u>always</u> depend on his grace, and not on their own feeble strength, because he <u>always</u> loves them.

²⁴ M. M. Ac 4:28: The heavenly Father is always in full control of his mission to all nations of the world.

²⁵ M. M. Ro 10:17a: The Holy Spirit <u>only</u> creates and preserves faith by using the message of God's grace in his holy Word.

[26] M. I. Lk 4:17: Christians should always base their messages on the Bible, so that the Holy Spirit can use his holy Word to create and strengthen faith in their hearers.

[27] M. I. Ac 2:4: In cross-cultural situations, Christians should always focus on all of the needs of the target group by learning their heart-language and culture as deeply as possible, so that they can tell them the Gospel clearly in their own language and also help them with the true needs of their society.

[28] M. M. Ro 5:1: On the cross, Jesus earned peace with God for all of his brothers and sisters from every nation on earth.

[29] M. I. Lk 11:10: Christians should continuously pray to their heavenly Father and always depend on his grace, and not on their own feeble strength, because he always loves them.

[30] M. I. Lk 4:35: Christians should view every person as a whole person, and show him compassion by caring for both his physical and spiritual needs as they go on their mission.

[31] M. I. Lk 4:40: Christians should go and seek the lost one person at a time by focusing on each person's unique needs.

[32] M. I. Lk 4:35: Christians should view every person as a whole person, and show him compassion by caring for *both* his physical and spiritual needs as they go on their mission.

[33] M. I. Lk 4:40: Christians should go and seek the lost one person at a time by focusing on each person's unique needs.

[34] M. I. Lk 4:15: Christians should seize every opportunity to proclaim the Gospel to lost people of all nations.

[35] M. M. Ac 4:28: The heavenly Father is always in full control of his mission to all nations of the world.

[36] M. M. Ro 3:24: Jesus lived a life of perfect obedience and shed his precious blood on the cross, in order to graciously set all nations free from sin, which a person only receives by faith in him.

[37] M. I. Lk 11:10: Christians should continuously pray to their heavenly Father and always depend on his grace, and not on their own feeble strength, because he always loves them.

[38] M. I. Lk 3:3a: Christians should, in love, warn lost people who do not repent.

[39] M. I. Lk 4:15: Christians should seize every opportunity to proclaim the Gospel to lost people of all nations.

Chapter 23

Jesus Before Pilate 23:1-5

23:1 *Then the whole company of them arose and brought him before Pilate.*
23:2 *And they began to accuse him, saying, "We found this man misleading our nation and forbidding us to give tribute to Caesar, and saying that he himself is Christ, a king."*
23:3 *And Pilate asked him, "Are you the King of the Jews?" And he answered him, "You have said so."*
23:4 *Then Pilate said to the chief priests and the crowds, "I find no guilt in this man."*
23:5 *But they were urgent, saying, "He stirs up the people, teaching throughout all Judea, from Galilee even to this place."*

23:3-4 (1) The first two charges that the members of the Jewish Council brought against Jesus before Pilate were mere fabrications, but not the third one in verse 2 that he was *"saying that he himself is Christ, a king,"* since Jesus was indeed a spiritual king—the King of all kings. And all of them were serious accusations for political reasons that Pilate would naturally pay attention to; but for some reason he focused on the only one that was actually true. Therefore, this choice gave Jesus a perfect opportunity to *"seek"* this Gentile who was lost. Instead of thinking about the grave danger that he was in, Jesus was focused on one more lost sinner, Pilate. He therefore said, *"You have said so"* (v 3), so that Pilate would hear the Gospel about him. (John records a much longer dialogue in his account in (Jn 18:28-38); therefore, Jesus did apparently have a much longer opportunity to "seek" Pilate than it would appear here in Luke.) Since the religious leaders of the Jews were not even doing their job of first teaching God's Word to their fellow Jews (11:52; 20:19; [1]M. M. Ac 13:46), let alone proclaim it to the Romans, their Gentile oppressors, Pilate was perhaps hearing the Gospel for the first time. Of course, these Council members didn't even notice that Jesus was doing their job; and that he was doing it in spite of the fact that he stood before Pilate as a prisoner accused of being a traitor to the Empire (²M. M. Lk 1:1 & ³M. I. Lk 4:15). **2)** It's amazing to realize that even in these very stressful circumstances, Jesus was thinking about Pilate's needs, not his own. He faithfully and patiently continued to seek one more person who was lost (⁴M. I. Lk 4:40).

Jesus Before Herod 23:6-16

23:6 *When Pilate heard this, he asked whether the man was a Galilean.*
23:7 *And when he learned that he belonged to Herod's jurisdiction, he sent him over to Herod, who was himself in Jerusalem at that time.*
23:8 *When Herod saw Jesus, he was very glad, for he had long desired to see him, because he had heard about him, and he was hoping to see some sign done by him.*
23:9 *So he questioned him at some length, but he made no answer.*
23:10 *The chief priests and the scribes stood by, vehemently accusing him.*
23:11 *And Herod with his soldiers treated him with contempt and mocked him. Then, arraying him in splendid clothing, he sent him back to Pilate.*
23:12 *And Herod and Pilate became friends with each other that very day, for before this they had been at enmity with each other.*
23:13 *Pilate then called together the chief priests and the rulers and the people,*
23:14 *and said to them, "You brought me this man as one who was misleading the people. And after examining him before you, behold, I did not find this man guilty of any of your charges against him.*
23:15 *Neither did Herod, for he sent him back to us. Look, nothing deserving death has been done by him.*
23:16 *I will therefore punish and release him."*

23:7-11 Here was Jesus' first opportunity to personally *"seek"* King

Herod by proclaiming the Law and Gospel message to him; therefore, why didn't Jesus answer him? There are at least <u>two</u> possibilities: **a)** First of all, at one time, King Herod wanted to kill Jesus (13:31), perhaps because he had killed John the Baptist; and the king was afraid that John had reincarnated as Jesus. However, at this time, King Herod was apparently only hoping that Jesus would <u>entertain</u> him with a miracle (v 8). But the only sign that Jesus would soon provide to his skeptics such as the king was the very heart of the Gospel, his <u>resurrection</u> from the dead (11:29). As the Lord of his mission, Jesus obviously knew that not even the incredibly sharp sword of his Law would now penetrate this king's heart. Furthermore, his resurrection is the only miracle that can create and sustain faith, because he would soon rise from the dead <u>for</u> the king's salvation ([5]M. M. Ro 1:16b). **b)** Secondly, Jesus was silent before the king, so that the king would not set him free but returned him to Pilate who alone could crucify him. Therefore, in this way, he would be able to *"save the lost"* (19:10; [6]M. M. Lk 1:1). And this, of course, was the result that both he himself and his heavenly Father desired, because his Father's mission-heart had long planned this very carefully, and he was controlling every essential detail in order to carry it out ([7]M. M. Heb 6:19).

Pilate Delivers Jesus to Be Crucified 23:17-25

23:17 *[Now he was obliged to release <u>one</u> man to them at the festival.]*
23:18 *But they all cried out together, "Away with this man, and release to us Barabbas"--*
23:19 *a man who had been thrown into prison for an insurrection started in the city and for murder.*
23:20 *Pilate addressed them once more, desiring to release Jesus,*
23:21 *but they kept shouting, "Crucify, crucify him!"*
23:22 *A third time he said to them, "Why, what evil has he done? I have found in him no guilt deserving death. I will therefore punish and release him."*
23:23 *But they were urgent, demanding with loud cries that he should*

> *be crucified. And their voices prevailed.*
> 23:24 *So Pilate decided that their demand should be granted.*
> 23:25 *He released the man who had been thrown into prison for insurrection and murder, for whom they asked, but he delivered Jesus over to their will.*

23:18-25 It was, of course, actually the religious leaders of the Jews who pressured Pilate to kill him by inciting the crowd. And once again, they thought that <u>they</u> were the ones who were in control of the situation; however, it was the heavenly Father who was the author of the plan of salvation; and he himself was very carefully orchestrating every moment, so that his holy sacrifice would be perfect and complete. Furthermore, every Word of Scripture had to be fulfilled for this to take place (1:1; 18:31; 22:37; 24:46-47). When *"Pilate decided that their demand should be granted"* (v 24), he, in fact, did the Father's gracious will, in order to make it possible for Jesus to defeat Satan's evil will forever. The devil was extremely powerful, but he was helpless to prevent his own total defeat, since *"the Son of Man came to seek and to <u>save</u> the lost"* (19:10; [8]M. M. Lk 1:1).

The Crucifixion 23:26-43

> 23:26 *And as they led him away, they seized one Simon of Cyrene, who was coming in from the country, and laid on him the cross, to carry it behind Jesus.*
> 23:27 *And there followed him a great multitude of the people and of women who were mourning and lamenting for him.*
> 23:28 *But turning to them Jesus said, "Daughters of Jerusalem, do not weep for me, but weep for yourselves and for your children.*
> 23:29 *For behold, the days are coming when they will say, 'Blessed are the barren and the wombs that never bore and the breasts that never nursed!'*
> 23:30 *Then they will begin to say to the mountains, 'Fall on us,' and to the hills, 'Cover us.'*
> 23:31 *For if they do these things when the wood is green, what will*

happen when it is dry?"

23:32 Two others, who were criminals, were led away to be put to death with him.

23:33 And when they came to the place that is called The Skull, there they crucified him, and the criminals, one on his right and one on his left.

23:34 And Jesus said, "Father, forgive them, for they know not what they do." And they cast lots to divide his garments.

23:35 And the people stood by, watching, but the rulers scoffed at him, saying, "He saved others; let him save himself, if he is the Christ of God, his Chosen One!"

23:36 The soldiers also mocked him, coming up and offering him sour wine

23:37 and saying, "If you are the King of the Jews, save yourself!"

23:38 There was also an inscription over him, "This is the King of the Jews."

23:39 One of the criminals who were hanged railed at him, saying, "Are you not the Christ? Save yourself and us!"

23:40 But the other rebuked him, saying, "Do you not fear God, since you are under the same sentence of condemnation?

23:41 And we indeed justly, for we are receiving the due reward of our deeds; but this man has done nothing wrong."

23:42 And he said, "Jesus, remember me when you come into your kingdom."

23:43 And he said to him, "Truly, I say to you, today you will be with me in Paradise."

23:26 Simon of Cyrene was apparently a Jew living in Africa; and the soldiers evidently conscripted him quite randomly. Nevertheless, it appears that their choice led to a once-in-a-lifetime opportunity for Simon to hear the Gospel by seeing it actually carried out with his very own eyes. Therefore, it's not surprising that Jesus' gracious action for him apparently moved him to trust in such a Savior. And ultimately it appears that Simon also shared this tremendous Gospel with his family since we have some sketchy, but quite compelling, evidence in (Rom 16:13; Mk 15:21) that indicates that Simon's sons, Rufus and Alexander and their mother were part of the church in Rome some years later ([9]M. M. Mt 5:14).

23:27-30 Even though Jesus' agony was so great and he was so weak that he could no longer carry the crossbeam of his cross (Jn 19:17), his mission-heart still moved him to not focus on himself, but to have compassion on some <u>women</u> who were crying over his terrible suffering. Therefore, he "sought" them in verses 28-31 by giving them another warning about the imminent destruction of Jerusalem by Roman soldiers. Jesus did not explicitly say that these women were his disciples, but it appears that they were. Therefore, he longed for them to remember during their own time of suffering in the future that he was now suffering and dying <u>for them</u>, so that they would remain faithful to him at that time. It's absolutely incredible that he was focused on the future needs of these women in the midst of his own unbelievable agony. How deeply his mission-heart compelled him to completely obey his heavenly Father's will in order to carry out even this detail of his mission to the lost ([10]M. M. Lk 1:1 & [11]M. I. Lk 3:3a).

23:31 (1) In (3:9), John the Baptist had warned the religious leaders of the Jews, *"Every tree therefore that does not bear good fruit is cut down and thrown into the fire."* He warned them that the anger of the heavenly Father against sinful mankind is like a fire that consumes a <u>dry</u> or unfruitful tree (17:29). But here in verse 31, Jesus said that his Father's righteous anger was consuming a *"green"* tree—that is Jesus himself. He was *"green"* or not yet ready for the fire in the sense that God was destroying an <u>innocent</u> man (Rom 8:32). How much more so, then, will his Father's righteous anger more rapidly consume trees that are <u>truly dry</u> and ready for the fire, people who are <u>guilty</u> of rejecting his rich grace for them! Therefore, this warning to repent that Jesus gave to the women in verses 28-31 was even sterner than John's warning (M. I. Lk 3:3a). **2)** Thus, the Father was, of course, at that very moment, making Jesus *"dry"* or guilty by placing all of mankind's sin on him and consuming him, the *"green"* tree instead of the dry trees. Paul said the same thing in a completely different and beautiful way in (2 Cor 5:21), *"For our sake he [God] made him to be sin who knew no sin, so that in him we might become the righteousness of God"* ([12]M. M. Heb 7:22).

What amazing grace that we once again see in the cross of Jesus ([13]M. M. Ro 5:1)!

23:33-38 (1) Jesus said in verse 34, *"Father, forgive them, for they know not what they do."* Any weak human being like us would be thinking so much about our own agony that we couldn't even begin to think about anyone else; but not so the mission-heart of our gracious, compassionate Lord. Here was yet another opportunity to carry out his mission to the same lost members of the Council who were killing him (22:68-70). His amazing Words of forgiveness for them, no doubt, refer to the *"dry"* tree in verse 31. Even as his Father was consuming the *"green"* tree, Jesus "sought" these evil men with Words of forgiveness, which he was at that very moment earning for them (11:4; 2 Cor 5:21). As true God, who is love (1 Jn 4:16), Jesus could not deny his mission-heart, even in the midst of innocently dying for them (Jn 15:13; [14]M. M. Mt 1:22). **2)** Nevertheless, instead of repenting, his enemies continued to taunt him (v 35). However, they abused him with the truth about who he was, *"the King of the Jews"* (v 37), even though they, of course, believed that it was a lie, blasphemy before God. And sadly, the soldiers learned very quickly from their evil example and chimed right in with more taunts (vs 36-37). Yet, it was, in fact, the responsibility of these religious leaders to teach the Gospel to these soldiers instead of leading them into more sin (2:31-32). Their failure to be faithful stewards of God's kingdom was, of course, also some of the sins that Jesus was at that moment bearing for them (20:19; [15]M. M. Heb 7:17).

23:39-43 (1) Even though Matthew says that initially both criminals insulted Jesus (Mt 27:44), verses 41-42 tell us that one of them, then, heard the gracious Words of Jesus and was moved by the Holy Spirit to repent and believe in Jesus in the very last moments of his life. Any of Jesus' Words could have touched his heart, of course, but his gracious Words in verse 34, *"Father, forgive them, for they know not what they do"* must have been extremely powerful to such a man, since they make it clear that Jesus was also innocently dying for him, a guilty criminal. Then of course, Jesus' wonderfully comforting Gospel for him in verse 43 would have touched his heart very personally, *"Truly, I say to you, today you will be with me in Paradise"* ([16]M. I. Lk 4:40). **2)** We all would have to admit that none of us would be thinking of anyone but ourselves while hanging on a cross; but look at the amazing grace of Jesus' mission-heart! In the very last moments of his life, as he endured infinitely more suffering than the two criminals, he was still seeking one more person who was lost. Furthermore, he was still doing this very personally and compassionately (M. I. Lk 4:40). His faithful mission-heart had compelled him to complete the first part of his mission while he still lived on the earth *"to seek the lost"* ([17]M. M. Lk 1:1). And obviously, he continues on this part of his mission yet today through his Church ([18]M. M. Ac 13:46).

The Death of Jesus 23:44-49

23:44 *It was now about the sixth hour, and there was darkness over the whole land until the ninth hour,*
23:45 *while the sun's light failed. And the curtain of the temple was torn in two.*
23:46 *Then Jesus, calling out with a loud voice, said, "Father, into your hands I commit my spirit!" And having said this he breathed his last.*
23:47 *Now when the centurion saw what had taken place, he praised God, saying, "Certainly this man was innocent!"*
23:48 *And all the crowds that had assembled for this spectacle, when they saw what had taken place, returned home beating their breasts.*
23:49 *And all his acquaintances and the women who had followed him from Galilee stood at a distance watching these things.*

23:44-46 It was obviously the heavenly Father who caused the darkness, the earthquake and the people to rise from the dead (Mt 27:51-54). And each one of these events would have been a message from him that the death of Jesus was a very unique and special event that everyone should pay attention to. However, he also caused yet another event, *"the curtain of the temple was torn in two"* (v 45). This miraculous event would have sent a much more specific message to all pious Jews who were continually worshipping in the temple, but most especially to the religious leaders of the Jews. This message was truly extraordinary, since it was the Father himself who was *"seeking"* Jesus' enemies, who were obviously *"lost."* This was an unmistakable warning, but it was also very wonderful Gospel. The torn curtain should have told them that the Father himself was both offering and receiving the holy sacrifice of his own beloved Son for mankind's sin in the most holy place of the temple; and therefore, he would accept no more animal or food sacrifices for sin (Heb 9:8; 10:10, 19-22; [19]M. M. Heb 9:12). The holy curtain was now gone together with all of the worship and sacrifices that the Father had commanded in the Old Testament. The death of Jesus now opened the way for all Christians to pray to the heavenly Father in the name of Jesus, the great High Priest ([20]M. M. Heb 4:14). We can be sure, then, that, as the religious leaders gave orders to have the curtain repaired, they were thinking about the meaning of this message from God; however, it sadly, no doubt, fell on hearts that were still completely hardened ([21]M. I. Lk 3:3a).

23:46 Since none of the Gospel writers recorded all of Jesus' Words on the cross, it's difficult to know what their exact sequence was; nevertheless, his Words, *"Father, into your hands I commit my spirit"* in verse 46 are his last Words in Luke's account. These Words, then, make it abundantly clear that he, of course, never wavered in his trust in his heavenly Father. His faithful mission-heart moved him to perfectly obey every part of his gracious will, even though that will brought him to this terrible moment (22:42). By entrusting his entire being into his Father most gracious care, he finally also completed the second part of his mission *"to save the lost"* (19:10; [22]M. M. Heb 6:19). His sacrifice for all sinners was complete; and his Gospel to the world is true forever, the only Gospel that can truly save a person, because his Gospel tells the entire world that he died for all of sinful mankind ([23]M. M. Lk 13:24).

23:47 The fact that this Gentile soldier *"praised God"* in verse 47, tells us that this was a confession of faith in Jesus and not just a casual comment (1 Cor 12:3; Heb 11:6). Furthermore, obviously some of Jesus' disciples must have overheard his confession and made sure that it was recorded in some of the Gospels. Like the one criminal, he *"saw what* *had taken place"* (v 47) and certainly heard the gracious Words of Jesus as well. The cases of the two men are parallel except that the soldier was a Gentile, while the criminal was probably a Jew, since Roman citizens could not be crucified. Jesus' gracious Words of *"seeking the lost"* (19:10; [24]M. M. Lk 1:1 & [25]M. I. Lk 4:40) continued to have impact even after he was apparently completely defeated and dead. Satan had destroyed him physically, but, by his almighty power, Jesus had destroyed the devil spiritually forever (Gen 3:15; M. M. Heb 6:19 & [26]Heb 7:22).

23:48-49 (1) Not all of the people who heard Jesus' gracious Words on the cross were *"good soil"* (8:5-7). The religious leaders of the Jews and most of the soldiers jeered at Jesus. And now part of the crowd reacts by *"beating their breasts [crying]"* (v 48). Hopefully some of them had seen his terrible suffering for them, repented and were now grieving over their own sins. They had witnessed the most significant event in the history of mankind, and yet they totally missed its true meaning. There is little doubt that we must, once again, lay the blame for their unbelief at the feet of the religious leaders of the Jews. If they had been faithfully keeping the people of Israel focused on *"waiting for the kingdom of God"* (v 51), these same people would surely have recalled Old Testament passages like Isaiah 53 on this horrible day, and they too may have repented ([27]M. M. Ac 13:46 & [28]M. I. Lk 3:3a). **2)** Verse 49 says that *"all of his [Jesus'] acquaintances and the women who had followed him from Galilee"* (8:2-3) were also there near the cross, but they *"stood at a distance watching these things."* It's difficult for us to imagine just what Jesus' disciples were thinking and feeling as they stood there, but this was the moment that Jesus had warned them about several times, so that they would not give in to Satan's evil taunting, lose their faith and fail to carry out his mission to the world. As they stood there in shock, the entire future of his mission seemed to be completely ended. In (22:31-32), Jesus had warned Peter, *"Simon, Simon, behold, Satan demanded to have you, that he might sift you like wheat, but I have prayed for you that your faith may not fail. And when you have turned again, strengthen your brothers."* This was indeed a terrible moment for all of them to be able to recover from. Would the devil defeat them and their mission? What a risk for Jesus to entrust the entire future of his mission into the hands of this shaky crew! Yet, Jesus himself had fed them his holy, almighty Words and had trained them for three years. Obviously, he knew that, when he would soon fully give them his Spirit, they would be ready to be his witnesses to the lost people of all nations (24:47-48; Ac 1:5; 2:4; M. M. Ac 13:46 & [29]Lk 6:22).

Jesus is Buried 23:50-56

> 23:50 *Now there was a man named Joseph, from the Jewish town of Arimathea. He was a member of the council, a good and righteous man,*
> 23:51 *who had not consented to their decision and action; and he was looking for the kingdom of God.*
> 23:52 *This man went to Pilate and asked for the body of Jesus.*
> 23:53 *Then he took it down and wrapped it in a linen shroud and laid him in a tomb cut in stone, where no one had ever yet been laid.*
> 23:54 *It was the day of Preparation, and the Sabbath was beginning.*
> 23:55 *The women who had come with him from Galilee followed and saw the tomb and how his body was laid.*
> 23:56 *Then they returned and prepared spices and ointments. On the Sabbath they rested according to the commandment.*

23:50 Just two men who were members of the Jewish council, Joseph and Nicodemus, were secretly disciples of Jesus. Perhaps we should not judge their secrecy too harshly, since it would have been extremely dangerous for them to raise any objections to condemning Jesus. Nicodemus had been bold enough to defend Jesus with just one question (Jn 7:50-51); but after they silenced him, apparently they both were silenced. Now however, Joseph was bold enough to ask Pilate for the body of Jesus; and John mentions in his account that Nicodemus also helped with the burial (Jn 19:39). As pious Jews, they showed their love for Jesus in the best way that they could by taking care of his body, even though his body would seem to be clear physical evidence that Jesus had utterly failed in his mission. Therefore, obviously without their realizing it, and just like Jesus' parents in (2:21-35), they obeyed God's Laws <u>on his behalf</u> since he obviously, once again, could not do so ([30]M. M. Mt 1:22 & [31]M. I. Jn 14:15).

23:51 Furthermore, Luke says that Joseph was "looking for the kingdom of God" (v 51). Thus, in this way, Luke points out the parallel between Joseph near the <u>end</u> of his Gospel and Simeon near the <u>beginning</u> of his Gospel since Simeon too was *"waiting for the consolation of Israel"* (2:25). These two men, then, represented the faithful remnant in Israel in Jesus' day, who continued to patiently wait for God to "console" Israel with his Messiah, in spite of the fact that their religious leaders were not teaching them this Gospel message ([32]M. M. Ac 13:46).

23:52 Luke's explicit reference in verse 52 to the <u>body</u> of Jesus is very significant for at least four reasons: **a)** First of all, this is clear evidence from God's holy Word that Jesus was indeed <u>dead</u> and buried. Jesus' disciples clearly did <u>not</u> run away with and hide a <u>nearly</u> dead Jesus, as some later claimed ([33]M. M. Heb 2:17). **b)** Secondly, this is the holy, <u>truly human</u> body that his heavenly Father had prepared for him as the one perfect sacrifice for the sins of all of his fellow human beings (Heb 10:5-10; [34]M. M. Heb 7:27). **c)** Thirdly, this is the body that Jesus himself still <u>literally</u>, not just figuratively, graciously gives to us Christians in his Holy Communion yet today. His true body and true blood in this holy meal assure us that he offered this very body and the blood that it contained for the forgiveness of all of our sins ([35]M. I. Ac 2:42). **d)** And finally, this body also <u>symbolizes</u> his holy Church (1 Cor 12:12-31), which he has established, enables and sends out on his mission into the entire world, in order to spread this same Gospel that unifies us in his one body (M. M. Ac 13:46).

23:55-56 Like Joseph and Nicodemus, the women in verses 55-56, who had faithfully followed Jesus for two years or more still showed great faith and courage by helping to prepare to care for Jesus' body. And again, they too did so, in spite of having to touch a corpse, which was stark, and apparently devastating physical evidence of the total defeat of Jesus' mission. And they too, like the two men, carefully obeyed all of God's Laws by resting on the Sabbath, which was the day of worship (v 56; M. I. Jn 14:15).

¹ M. M. Ac 13:46: As he did with the old Israel, God <u>first of all</u> strengthens the faith of the new Israel, the Church with his Word and Sacraments, so that they can go and witness to the lost people of all nations.

² M. M. Lk 1:1: Jesus came to seek and save <u>all</u> lost people from <u>every</u> nation on earth.

³ M. I. Lk 4:15: Christians should seize <u>every</u> opportunity to proclaim the Gospel to lost people of all nations.

⁴ M. I. Lk 4:40: Christians should go and seek the lost <u>one</u> person at a time by focusing on each person's <u>unique</u> needs.

⁵ M. M. Ro 1:16b: The Gospel is so powerful because it contains the central truth that Jesus rose from the dead with a glorified body in order to save all of his brothers and sisters from sin and death.

⁶ M. M. Lk 1:1: Jesus came to seek and save <u>all</u> lost people from <u>every</u> nation on earth.

⁷ M. M. Heb 6:19: Through his sacrifice as the great High Priest, Jesus gives Christians <u>sure hope</u> for an eternal inheritance with him.

⁸ M. M. Lk 1:1: Jesus came to seek and save <u>all</u> lost people from <u>every</u> nation on earth.

⁹ M. M. Mt 5:14: When the Holy Spirit creates faith in a person's heart, he also graciously gives him a new mission-heart that is eager to shine the light of the Gospel throughout the whole world.

¹⁰ M. M. Lk 1:1: Jesus came to seek and save <u>all</u> lost people from <u>every</u> nation on earth.

¹¹ M. I. Lk 3:3a: Christians should, in love, warn lost people who do not repent.

¹² M. M. Heb 7:22: As the great High Priest, Jesus guaranties by his holy life and holy sacrifice that his promise to forgive the sins of Christians is forever sure.

¹³ M. M. Ro 5:1: On the cross, Jesus earned <u>peace</u> with God for <u>all</u> of his brothers and sisters from every nation on earth.

¹⁴ M. M. Mt 1:22: God sent his only Son, Jesus to be born as a true human being, so that he could save all of his brothers and sisters of all nations by fulfilling all of God's promises in the Old Testament.

¹⁵ M. M. Heb 7:17: Jesus served his mission to Christians and to the world as an <u>eternal</u> High Priest by offering the holy sacrifice of his body in order to earn <u>eternal</u> forgiveness for all Christians.

¹⁶ M. I. Lk 4:40: Christians should go and seek the lost <u>one</u> person at a time by focusing on each person's <u>unique</u> needs.

¹⁷ M. M. Lk 1:1: Jesus came to seek and save <u>all</u> lost people from <u>every</u> nation on earth.

¹⁸ M. M. Ac 13:46: As he did with the old Israel, God <u>first of all</u> strengthens the faith of the new Israel, the Church with his Word and Sacraments, so that they can go and witness to the lost people of all nations.

¹⁹ M. M. Heb 9:12: As the great High Priest, Jesus offered his <u>human</u> and <u>divine</u> blood as the one perfect sacrifice for <u>all</u> of the sins of <u>all</u> of his brothers and sisters.

²⁰ M. M. Heb 4:14: As the great High Priest, Jesus has ascended into heaven with his sacrifice to open the way for all Christians to approach God's throne with confidence.

²¹ M. I. Lk 3:3a: Christians should, in love, warn lost people who do not repent.

²² M. M. Heb 6:19: Through his sacrifice as the great High Priest, Jesus gives Christians <u>sure hope</u> for an eternal inheritance with him.

[23] M. M. Lk 13:24: The <u>only</u> way to enter the Kingdom of God is to have <u>faith</u> in Jesus as one's Savior.

[24] M. M. Lk 1:1: Jesus came to seek and save <u>all</u> lost people from <u>every</u> nation on earth.

[25] M. I. Lk 4:40: Christians should go and seek the lost <u>one</u> person at a time by focusing on each person's <u>unique</u> needs.

[26] M. M. Heb 7:22: As the great High Priest, Jesus guaranties by his holy life and holy sacrifice that his promise to forgive the sins of Christians is forever sure.

[27] M. M. Ac 13:46: As he did with the old Israel, God <u>first of all</u> strengthens the faith of the new Israel, the Church with his Word and Sacraments, so that they can go and witness to the lost people of all nations.

[28] M. I. Lk 3:3a: Christians should, in love, warn lost people who do not repent.

[29] M. M. Lk 6:22: The Lord Jesus will surely bless a Christian in the midst of suffering for his sake; and he will also bless him with eternal life if he remains faithful to him.

[30] M. M. Mt 1:22: God sent his only Son, Jesus to be born as a true human being, so that he could save all of his brothers and sisters of all nations by fulfilling all of God's promises in the Old Testament.

[31] M. I. Jn 14:15: Christians should obey all of Jesus' commands in grateful response to his love for them as they go on his mission to the world.

[32] M. M. Ac 13:46: As he did with the old Israel, God <u>first of all</u> strengthens the faith of the new Israel, the Church with his Word and Sacraments, so that they can go and witness to the lost people of all nations.

[33] M. M. Heb 2:17: Jesus had to become like his fellow human beings in every way, so that he could serve God as their merciful and faithful High Priest in order to earn forgiveness for all of their sins.

[34] M. M. Heb 7:27: Because Jesus is a holy High Priest he was able to offer <u>one</u> sacrifice for <u>all</u> people.

[35] M. I. Ac 2:42: Christians should celebrate Holy Communion frequently in order to receive forgiveness and strength from their Lord's grace in order to continue on his mission.

Chapter 24

The Resurrection 24:1-12

24:1 *But on the first day of the week, at early dawn, they went to the tomb, taking the spices they had prepared.*
24:2 *And they found the stone rolled away from the tomb,*
24:3 *but when they went in they did not find the body of the Lord Jesus.*
24:4 *While they were perplexed about this, behold, two men stood by them in dazzling apparel.*
24:5 *And as they were frightened and bowed their faces to the ground, the men said to them, "Why do you seek the living among the dead?*
24:6 *He is not here, but has risen. Remember how he told you, while he was still in Galilee,*
24:7 *that the Son of Man must be delivered into the hands of sinful men and be crucified and on the third day rise."*
24:8 *And they remembered his words,*
24:9 *and returning from the tomb they told all these things to the eleven and to all the rest.*
24:10 *Now it was Mary Magdalene and Joanna and Mary the mother of James and the other women with them who told these things to the apostles,*
24:11 *but these words seemed to them an idle tale, and they did not believe them.*
24:12 *But Peter rose and ran to the tomb; stooping and looking in, he saw the linen cloths by themselves; and he went home marveling at what had happened.*

24:1-10 (1) The most significant words in Luke's account in verses 1-10 are in verse 3, *"they did not find the body of the Lord Jesus"* and in verse 6, *"he is not here."* The body that these same women came to prepare for burial was <u>gone</u>. This historical <u>fact</u> is the most important fact in human history ever since God made the <u>first</u> bodies for Adam and

Eve; and then they sinned. This fact means that every promise that the Father gave to his people in the Old Testament (18:31) is true and is surely fulfilled (2 Cor 1:20). This historical fact is also *"the sign of Jonah"* that Jesus spoke about in (11:29-30), since it is the final proof that the heavenly Father did indeed raise his beloved Son from the dead to show that he accepted the holy sacrifice of this human and divine body. If anyone were to find the actual bones of Jesus buried anywhere, then, Jesus would be a worse liar than his archenemy, the devil. But there are no bones of Jesus in any grave; and therefore, Jesus is *"the truth"* (Jn 14:6); and Satan is *"the father of lies"* (Jn 8:44). What a glorious message this is for all lost human beings everywhere (^{1}M. M. Jn 20:8)! **2)** However, another historical fact is vital here. This was the same human and divine body that the heavenly Father had prepared for Jesus in the womb of Mary. This means that everything that Jesus did on his mission in this Body was thoroughly grounded in human history. His sacrifice was not a myth that someone invented, but rather, it was as real as all of the animal sacrifices of the Old Testament. But, unlike these sacrifices that were effective only temporarily, his was fully effective for paying the price of all of the sins of all of his brothers and sisters since his Body was both truly human and truly divine (19:10; ^{2}M. M. Heb 2:17). **3)** The actions of these women in preparing the spices and perfumes and in going to the tomb very early show that they loved their Lord, even though they believed that he was still dead and that everything he told them must have been false. But the moment that the angels reminded them of Jesus' promise that he would rise again they *"remembered his [Jesus'] words"* (v 8; Jn 2:22). This reminder, then, was Jesus himself still *"seeking"* them through a repetition of his gracious Words of warning that he would have to suffer and die and Words of promise that he would rise again (9:22; 18:32-33; ^{3}M. M. Lk 1:1). And through the memory of his mighty Words, his Spirit, as *"the perfecter"* of their faith, restored and strengthened their faith (Heb 12:2; Rom 10:17; ^{4}M. M. Ro 10:17a). **4)** Likewise today, when Christians proclaim their Lord's Law and Gospel message as his witnesses throughout the world (v 48), his Spirit uses his mighty Word to do two things. **a)** As *"the founder"* of faith (Heb 12:2), he creates faith in the hearts of <u>unbelievers</u> (2 Cor 4:6). **b)** And as the *"perfecter of our faith"* (Heb 12:2), his Spirit also uses the processes of reading and remembering God's promises in his holy Word to <u>recreate</u> or strengthen the faith in the hearts of <u>Christians</u> (M. M. Ro 10:17a). **5)** By telling *"all these things to the eleven and to all the rest"* (v 9), the women, of course, were faithful in immediately carrying out their risen Lord's mission to the world. They had just received such tremendous Gospel that their dear Lord was <u>alive</u> instead of dead, and they could not keep it to themselves. They apparently were the <u>first</u> missionaries in the new era of the Church who did their duty (Ac 4:20; [5]M. M. Mt 5:14).

24:11-12 Unlike the women, the eleven apostles did <u>not remember</u> what Jesus had promised them just hours earlier; therefore, *"they didn't believe them"* (v 11). Even Peter did not remember! In spite of the fact that he had just met his Lord's accusing eyes and repented of denying him; and in spite of seeing the physical evidence that his Lord's Body was gone, Peter was <u>still</u> left *"marveling at what had happened"* (v 12)! What was left to wonder about, Peter? Yet, no one should chide him or any of the others too severely. They had just been through a series of extremely stressful events that would traumatize anyone. It took them several more <u>reminders</u> of Jesus' promises before his Spirit would be able to penetrate their hearts with Jesus' gracious Words of promise ([6]M. M. Ro 6:18).

On the Road to Emmaus 24:13-35

> 24:13 *That very day two of them were going to a village named Emmaus, about seven miles from Jerusalem,*
> 24:14 *and they were talking with each other about all these things that had happened.*
> 24:15 *While they were talking and discussing together, Jesus himself drew near and went with them.*
> 24:16 *But their eyes were kept from recognizing him.*
> 24:17 *And he said to them, "What is this conversation that you are holding with each other as you walk?" And they stood still, looking sad.*

24:18 Then one of them, named Cleopas, answered him, "Are you the only visitor to Jerusalem who does not know the things that have happened there in these days?"

24:19 And he said to them, "What things?" And they said to him, "Concerning Jesus of Nazareth, a man who was a prophet mighty in deed and word before God and all the people,

24:20 and how our chief priests and rulers delivered him up to be condemned to death, and crucified him.

24:21 But we had hoped that he was the one to redeem Israel. Yes, and besides all this, it is now the third day since these things happened.

24:22 Moreover, some women of our company amazed us. They were at the tomb early in the morning,

24:23 and when they did not find his body, they came back saying that they had even seen a vision of angels, who said that he was alive.

24:24 Some of those who were with us went to the tomb and found it just as the women had said, but him they did not see."

24:25 And he said to them, "O foolish ones, and slow of heart to believe all that the prophets have spoken!

24:26 Was it not necessary that the Christ should suffer these things and enter into his glory?"

24:27 And beginning with Moses and all the Prophets, he interpreted to them in all the Scriptures the things concerning himself.

24:28 So they drew near to the village to which they were going. He acted as if he were going farther,

24:29 but they urged him strongly, saying, "Stay with us, for it is toward evening and the day is now far spent." So he went in to stay with them.

24:30 When he was at table with them, he took the bread and blessed and broke it and gave it to them.

24:31 And their eyes were opened, and they recognized him. And he vanished from their sight.

24:32 They said to each other, "Did not our hearts burn within us while he talked to us on the road, while he opened to us the Scriptures?"

> 24:33 *And they rose that same hour and returned to Jerusalem. And they found the eleven and those who were with them gathered together,*
> 24:34 *saying, "The Lord has risen indeed, and has appeared to Simon!"*
> 24:35 *Then they told what had happened on the road, and how he was known to them in the breaking of the bread.*

24:13-24 Here were two more disciples of Jesus who did <u>not</u> yet <u>remember</u> his gracious Words of promise that he would rise again; and therefore their faith had not yet been restored. However, they did remember an ancient hope that the prophets of the Old Testament had given their nation. They said, *"We had hoped that he was the one to redeem Israel"* (v 21; 68-69; 1:54-55). In short, during the time that they had followed Jesus on his mission, they obviously must have believed that Jesus was *"the one"* who fulfilled this *"hope"* of eternal salvation. But his horrible crucifixion and death had dashed this *"hope."* In fact, witnessing his terrible death had totally obliterated their whole wonderful experience with him. Therefore, Jesus began to once again graciously and gently *"seek"* them by asking a question, *"What is this conversation that you are holding with each other as you walk"* (v 17)? He met them where they were in their thinking with this question, and in this way he tried to restore their <u>memory</u> and their *"hope"* that he was indeed *"the one"* (16:31; [7]M. I. Lk 4:40).

24:26 Jesus then continued to *"seek"* these two disciples by reminding them once again of what the Scriptures said about him. He said, *"Was it not necessary that the Christ should suffer these things and enter into his glory"* (v 26)? The most important things they had forgotten were the many Old Testament prophecies that *"the Christ"* would have to suffer and die before the heavenly Father returned all glory and honor to him (v 44). If they had remembered that they would not have begun to doubt that he was *"the one."* But since they failed to remember both the Scriptures and Jesus' own Words, the Holy Spirit was not able to recreate their faith because he uses no other means ([8]M. M. Ro 10:17a).

24:27 (1) But Jesus did not stop with just a few words; he continued to *"seek"* them with the most wonderful Bible lesson that anyone could imagine. Just as he had patiently taught Mary one-on-one (10:39), he gently used the private time that they had on the road to Emmaus and *"interpreted to them in all the Scriptures the things concerning himself"* (v 27; [9]M. M. Lk 4:21 & Ro 10:17a). **2)** Note how clearly verse 27 teaches us once again that Jesus and his mission are the <u>central focus</u> of <u>all</u> of Scripture. <u>Every</u> verse of Scripture, both Old and New Testaments, points to Jesus' mission to *"seek and to save the lost."* A person who is studying the Bible has not fully expounded the meaning of each verse until he has shown at least one connection between that verse and the mission of Jesus (4:21; [10]M. M. Lk 1:1). This is the reason why <u>every</u> verse of Scripture is the mighty sword that the Holy Spirit can use to create and recreate faith (Heb 12:2; Rom 1:16). And this is also the reason why Jesus gave all Christians, the Church only <u>one</u> mission, to proclaim his holy Word, the Holy Spirit's <u>one</u> mighty tool, to the lost people of all nations (v 47; M. M. Ro 10:17a).

24:28-35 (1) In Luke's account, this is the first post resurrection appearance of the Immanuel, God with us, as their Lord Jesus "went in to stay with them" (v 29). Yet they <u>still</u> did not yet recognize him and remember his Words of promise until *"he broke it [the bread] and gave it to them"* (v 30). Perhaps this act of breaking the bread jarred their memories because they had seen their dear Lord do it so many times. It was a Jewish tradition to bless their food in this way before every meal (Mt 14:19; 15:36). Jesus was *"seeking"* them very lovingly and personally, <u>one-on-one</u>, through this common, every-day action (M. I. Lk 4:40). **2)** The true source of these two disciples' hearts burning in them (v 32) when Jesus taught them on the road was the fact that, as he also <u>reminded</u> them of the innumerable promises of God in the Old Testament Scriptures, his Spirit was <u>renewing</u> their faith and hope. <u>Now</u> they remembered that <u>all</u> that they had learned in God's Word to hope for was sure and true because their dear Lord was indeed alive again ([11]M. M. Ro 5:2b)! **3)** Before these two disciples could rush back to Jerusalem to share this tremendous Gospel, Jesus had also appeared to some women who had followed him (Mt 28:9-10), as well as to *"Simon [Peter]"* (v 34; 1 Cor 15:5). And even before the Emmaus disciples could tell their story, the eleven disciples burst out with their own story. Now that all of them remembered Jesus' promises, and they were now sure that he was truly alive again, they had such an exciting message to tell that they could not contain it. The Holy Spirit had planted this fire of faith and hope in their hearts. However, at this point, they seemed to be thinking about sharing this Gospel message only within their small group since the day of Pentecost had not yet come ([12]M. M. Mt 5:14).

Jesus Appears to His Disciples 24:36-49

24:36 *As they were talking about these things, Jesus himself stood among them, and said to them, "Peace to you!"*
24:37 *But they were startled and frightened and thought they saw a spirit.*
24:38 *And he said to them, "Why are you troubled, and why do doubts arise in your hearts?*
24:39 *See my hands and my feet, that it is I myself. Touch me, and see. For a spirit does not have flesh and bones as you see that I have."*
24:40 *And when he had said this, he showed them his hands and his feet.*
24:41 *And while they still disbelieved for joy and were marveling, he said to them, "Have you anything here to eat?"*
24:42 *They gave him a piece of broiled fish,*
24:43 *and he took it and ate before them.*
24:44 *Then he said to them, "These are my words that I spoke to you while I was still with you, that everything written about me in the law of Moses and the Prophets and the Psalms must be fulfilled."*
24:45 *Then he opened their minds to understand the Scriptures,*
24:46 *and said to them, "Thus it is written, that the Christ should suffer and on the third day rise from the dead,*
24:47 *and that repentance and forgiveness of sins should be proclaimed in his name to all nations, beginning from Jerusalem.*

24:48 *You are witnesses of these things.*

24:49 *And behold, I am sending the promise of my Father upon you. But stay in the city until you are clothed with power from on high."*

24:36-43 By suddenly *"standing among"* his disciples (v 36), telling them to *"touch"* his body (v 39), and *"eating"* a fish (v 43), Jesus taught them at least three very important things about his newly transformed body: **a)** He convinced them that *"it is I myself"* (v 39). He was the very same Jesus, their dear Lord and God (Jn 20:28). This was the same truly human body that his Father had given to him to use to carry out his dual mission of *"seeking and saving the lost"* (19:10; Heb 10:5-10; [13]M. M. Lk 1:27). **b)** Yet his body was now different. His Father had transformed it into an eternally glorified body, as he had promised to do on the mountain (9:29). Primarily, this was sure proof that the heavenly Father had accepted his holy sacrifice; and therefore, Jesus had fulfilled the second part of his mission of *"saving the lost"* (19:10; Lev 18:5; 2 Cor 1:20). **c)** Thirdly, by showing them his glorified body, Jesus likewise began to teach them that his personal relationship with them was now different. They would never again physically follow him from town to town as they had done, although, until after his ascension, they did at times see and touch him (v 39); but, even more significantly, he promised them in verse 49 that his Spirit would soon be with them every step of the way on their mission to the world (Ac 2:1-4; Mt 28:20). He therefore continued to patiently teach them how to carry out their mission, so that their loving personal relationship could always continue ([14]M. I. Lk 6:13).

24:44 In verse 44, Jesus repeated the very important lesson that he had just taught the two men from Emmaus (vs 26-27), that *"everything written about me [Jesus]"* in the entire Scriptures *"must be fulfilled."* His heavenly Father's very purpose in giving him a human body was to fulfill *"everything"* that he had promised his chosen people in his holy Word (1:1; Lev 18:5; 1 Cor 2:20; M. M. Lk 1:27).

24:45 Once again, Jesus *"opened their minds to understand the Scriptures"* (v 45) by teaching them a wonderful Bible lesson, as he had done for the Emmaus disciples on the road (v 27). Through this lesson, his Spirit was <u>reminding</u> them of the many, many promises that they all had studied and memorized their whole lives as God's chosen people, so that they could share his promises with all nations (1:2, 4; [15]M. M. Ac 13:46). Before creation, the heavenly Father's mission-heart had formed a perfect plan for rescuing sinful mankind; and in the <u>Scriptures</u>, his prophets had predicted many of the details of how his Beloved Son, Jesus would carry it out. And now, he had just perfectly carried out the most vital parts of his plan in Jesus' death and resurrection. Therefore, the disciples should have remembered the Scriptures, but they needed a <u>reminder</u>. Thus, Jesus used this lesson in his holy Word to restore their faith and hope ([16]M. M. Ro 10:17a).

24:46-47 Most importantly, Jesus reminded them in this lesson, one last time, of both parts of the central theme of Luke's Gospel: **a)** Verse 46 says, *"Thus it is written [in Scripture], that the Christ should suffer and on the third day rise from the dead."* This clearly points to, *"the Son of Man has come…to <u>save</u> the lost"* (19:10; [17]M. M. Lk 1:1). **b)** Verse 47 then says, *"Thus it is written…repentance and forgiveness of sins should be proclaimed in his name to all nations."* This clearly points to the same verse (19:10), *"the Son of Man has come to <u>seek</u>…the lost"* (M. M. Lk 1:1).

24:47-48 (1) Jesus says in verses 47 and 48 that the Gospel *"should be proclaimed in his name to all nations, beginning from Jerusalem. You are witnesses of these things."* And then in (Ac 1:8), he says, *"But you will receive power when the Holy Spirit has come upon you, and you will be my witnesses in Jerusalem and in all Judea and Samaria, and to the end of the earth"* (Mt 28:18-20). Twice in these verses, Jesus repeats his command that <u>all</u> of his disciples should be his *"witnesses."* The Greek term, *"witness"* has a two meanings: **a)** A witness first <u>sees</u> (or hears) what has happened (v 48), **b)** and he then faithfully <u>tells</u> others what he has seen (v 8; 1:1-4). This is the same seeing or hearing and then telling process that Paul describes so well in (Rom 10:14-15, 17). And this was likewise the task that Luke himself set out to faithfully do in his two books (1:3-4; Ac 1:1). Furthermore, while Luke strongly implies throughout both of his books that <u>all</u> Christians have a mission-heart, and therefore, are his witnesses, verse 48 is the first time that he explicitly states it in Jesus' own Words ([18]M. M. Mt 5:14). Therefore, yet today, all Christians are still his witnesses, because we hear in the Bible what the Old Testament prophets and *"the twelve"* disciples (1 Jn 1:1-4) saw and heard; and then we tell others what we too have heard ([19]M. I. Ac 1:8). **2)** And what had *"the twelve"* disciples seen as Jesus' witnesses? They saw everything that Jesus did from the first day to the last day of his mission (Ac 1:22). And most importantly, they saw and touched his resurrected and glorified body (v 39; 1 Jn 1:1-4). This was tremendous Gospel in their eyes and ears; and therefore, it was the spark that the Holy Spirit used to ignite, not only their own mission-hearts to renewed faith, but also the hearts of all who would hear this Gospel in the future. This Gospel is what started Jesus' disciples on his mission to *"seek the lost"* in all nations, because it is eternally true, and because our gracious Lord sent them and us out with this same Gospel message to proclaim to all people everywhere (vs 47-48; M. I. Ac 1:8).

24:49 However, in his rich grace, Jesus does not send out his disciples, the Church as his witnesses to the lost people of all nations with only our feeble human strength to depend on. He graciously promises us in verse 49, *"And behold, I am sending the promise of my Father upon you. But stay in the city until you are clothed with power from on high."* His promise is a wonderful reminder of another promise that our heavenly Father gave us in (Joel 2:28-29) that he would send us the gracious gift of his Holy Spirit. Therefore, it is his Spirit's almighty power that does three things: **a)** First, he protects us from all of our spiritual enemies because we are weak lambs among wolves (10:3; [20]M. I. Lk 11:10). **b)** Secondly, he gives us the very words that we should speak in every situation as we witness to the lost (21:15; [21]M. I. Lk 12:12). **c)** And thirdly, he uses the words that we speak as we witness to others, because they are from him, in order to create and strengthen faith in the hearts of our hearers (Rom 1:16; [22]M. M. Ro 10:17a).

The Ascension 24:50-53

> 24:50 *Then he led them out as far as Bethany, and lifting up his hands he blessed them.*
> 24:51 *While he blessed them, he parted from them and was carried up into heaven.*

24:50-51 It was crucial for the full completion of the heavenly Father's plan of salvation that Jesus' disciples should witness the physical ascension of their resurrected Lord. When they actually saw him ascend, there would be no doubt in their minds that a totally new phase had begun in their personal relationship with him; although that relationship would not be complete until they had received the gracious gift of his indwelling Spirit ten days later (Ac 2:1-4). If they had not witnessed his physical ascension, they would have been left wondering how soon he would appear to them again; but now this possibility was erased from their minds. His glorified body was gone, and his mission on earth had ended; therefore, he passed his mission on to his *"witnesses,"* his Church ([23]M. I. Ac 1:8).

> 24:52 *And they worshiped him and returned to Jerusalem with great joy,*
> 24:53 *and were continually in the temple blessing God.*

24:52-53 (1) The last two verses in Luke's Gospel account do not end in a dramatic fashion, because they are not actually the end of his account; instead, these verses form a transition to the beginning of his second book, the Acts of the Apostles (Ac 1:1). As a matter of fact, there is some historical evidence that his two books were at times circulated together. **2)** The fact that the disciples did not go back into hiding in Jerusalem shows that they were no longer afraid of either their religious leaders or of Pilate. And the fact that they *"were continually in the temple blessing God"* (v 53) shows that they were still pious Old Testament Jews continuing to worship God in their heavenly Father's house (2:49). Jesus' gracious Words had clearly restored their faith in him; but without his physical presence, and without his indwelling Spirit during these ten days, they were still living in a training period in-between the old covenant and the new ([24]M. I. Lk 6: 13).

[1] M. M. Jn 20:8: God gave faith in Jesus to people who personally saw that the tomb of Jesus was empty, because it proved that he was alive.

[2] M. M. Heb 2:17: Jesus had to become like his fellow human beings in every way, so that he could serve God as their merciful and faithful High Priest in order to earn forgiveness for all of their sins.

[3] M. M. Lk 1:1: Jesus came to seek and save all lost people from every nation on earth.

[4] M. M. Ro 10:17a: The Holy Spirit only creates and preserves faith by using the message of God's grace in his holy Word.

[5] M. M. Mt 5:14: When the Holy Spirit creates faith in a person's heart, he also graciously gives him a new mission-heart that is eager to shine the light of the Gospel throughout the whole world.

[6] M. M. Ro 6:18: In his Baptism, Jesus graciously sets a new Christian free from his slavery to sin and gives him the power of his Spirit to gratefully obey his new Lord by doing good deeds.

[7] M. I. Lk 4:40: Christians should go and seek the lost one person at a time by focusing on each person's unique needs.

[8] M. M. Ro 10:17a: The Holy Spirit only creates and preserves faith by using the message of God's grace in his holy Word.

[9] M. M. Lk 4:21: Every verse in the entire Bible points in some way to Jesus and his mission to seek and save the lost.

[10] M. M. Lk 1:1: Jesus came to seek and save all lost people from every nation on earth.

[11] M. M. Ro 5:2b: On the cross, Jesus earned the joy of hoping for a glorious eternal life with him for all of his brothers and sisters from every nation on earth.

[12] M. M. Mt 5:14: When the Holy Spirit creates faith in a person's heart, he also graciously gives him a new mission-heart that is eager to shine the light of the Gospel throughout the whole world.

[13] M. M. Lk 1:27: Jesus had to be born as a true human being and as a true Jew in order to become the King of kings in his heavenly kingdom forever.

[14] M. I. Lk 6:13: Christians should choose new leaders and train them in order to multiply the work.

[15] M. M. Ac 13:46: As he did with the old Israel, God first of all strengthens the faith of the new Israel, the Church with his Word and Sacraments, so that they can go and witness to the lost people of all nations.

[16] M. M. Ro 10:17a: The Holy Spirit only creates and preserves faith by using the message of God's grace in his holy Word.

[17] M. M. Lk 1:1: Jesus came to seek and save all lost people from every nation on earth.

[18] M. M. Mt 5:14: When the Holy Spirit creates faith in a person's heart, he also graciously gives him a new mission-heart that is eager to shine the light of the Gospel throughout the whole world.

[19] M. I. Ac 1:8: Christians should go and witness about Jesus to all who are lost from all languages and cultures by depending on the power of the Holy Spirit to help them bridge all of the language/cultural boundaries whether they are relatively easy, as in their own language, or extremely difficult.

[20] M. I. Lk 11:10: Christians should continuously pray to their heavenly Father and always

depend on his grace, and not on their own feeble strength, because he <u>always</u> loves them.

[21] M. I. Lk 12:12: Christians should go and tell the Gospel depending on the Holy Spirit to teach them what they should say.

[22] M. M. Ro 10:17a: The Holy Spirit <u>only</u> creates and preserves faith by using the message of God's grace in his holy Word.

[23] M. I. Ac 1:8: Christians should go and witness about Jesus to all who are lost from all languages and cultures by depending on the power of the Holy Spirit to help them bridge all of the language/cultural boundaries whether they are relatively easy, as in their own language, or extremely difficult.

[24] M. I. Lk 6:13: Christians should choose new leaders and train them in order to multiply the work.

The Acts of the Apostles

Chapter 1

The Promise of the Holy Spirit 1:1-5

1:1 *In the first book, O Theophilus, I have dealt with all that Jesus began to do and teach,*
1:2 *until the day when he was taken up, after he had given commands through the Holy Spirit to the apostles whom he had chosen.*
1:3 *To them he presented himself alive after his suffering by many proofs, appearing to them during forty days and speaking about the kingdom of God.*
1:4 *And while staying with them he ordered them not to depart from Jerusalem, but to wait for the promise of the Father, which, he said, "you heard from me;*
1:5 *for John baptized with water, but you will be baptized with the Holy Spirit not many days from now."*

1:1-2 As the "Introduction to the Book of Acts" (The Lutheran Study Bible, p. 1651) indicates, both Luke, the author of his Gospel and the book of Acts and also the very early Christian Church felt that the two books belong together (1:1-2; Luke (1:1-3). Thus, Luke faithfully recorded in his Gospel that the most vital phase of the heavenly Father's plan of salvation had already been fully *"accomplished"* by the Lord Jesus (Lk 1:1); and in this way, the mission of Israel in the Old Testament era <u>ended</u>. Now Luke begins to record the beginnings of a totally <u>new</u> era of the mission of the <u>new</u> Israel in his second book (Rom 11: 25-26; [25]M. M. Ac 13:46). And it was, of course, Jesus himself who made the transition. As he was *"accomplishing"* the final phases of his mission on earth, he gave *"<u>commands</u> through the Holy Spirit to the apostles whom he had chosen"* to continue his mission of seeking the lost in every nation on earth (v 2; 1:8; Lk 24:47; [26]Mt 28:18-20). He then returned to his Father, so that he could send them his Spirit (2:4) who would empower their mission-hearts to go quickly and boldly on their way ([27]M. I. Ac 1:8).

1:3-4 If Jesus was, in fact, still rotting in a tomb somewhere, it would have meant that he did <u>not</u> truly *"seek the lost"* because he did <u>not</u> truly *"save the lost"* (Lk 19:10). However, Luke boldly refutes this lie and testifies to the truth in verse 3, *"To them [the 11 apostles] he [Jesus] presented himself alive after his suffering by many proofs, appearing to them during forty days and speaking about the kingdom of God."* Their Lord's resurrection was the main proof that the heavenly Father had kept all of his promises through him, in order to carry out his gracious plan of salvation. Therefore, the 11 apostles could, indeed, be faithful *"<u>witnesses</u>"* about the truth of his resurrection on their mission to people of all nations ([28]M. I. Ac 1:8).

1:5 When Jesus says in verse 5, *"you will be baptized with the Holy Spirit not many days from now,"* he was obviously using the word *"baptized"* <u>figuratively</u> and was not referring to water Baptism, such as the work that John the Baptist had done (Lk 3:16). He was referring to the one-time gift that the Holy Spirit graciously gave to the 12 apostles ten days later on Pentecost Day to <u>speak human</u> languages that they had not studied (2:1-4). On that one very special day, they were able to proclaim the <u>Gospel</u> in at least 12 different languages. And as a result, thousands of people returned to their homes in many different countries eager to spread this glorious new and wonderful Gospel about Jesus. (See the long discussion of this gift at (2:1).)

The Ascension 1:6-11

1:6   *So when they had come together, they asked him, "Lord, will you at this time restore the kingdom to Israel?"*
1:7   *He said to them, "It is not for you to know times or seasons that the Father has fixed by his own authority.*
1:8   *But you will receive power when the Holy Spirit has come upon you, and you will be my witnesses in Jerusalem and in all Judea and Samaria, and to the end of the earth."*

1:9 *And when he had said these things, as they were looking on, he was lifted up, and a cloud took him out of their sight.*
1:10 *And while they were gazing into heaven as he went, behold, two men stood by them in white robes,*
1:11 *and said, "Men of Galilee, why do you stand looking into heaven? This Jesus, who was taken up from you into heaven, will come in the same way as you saw him go into heaven."*

1:6-7 (1) Even after Jesus had taught his apostles for three years that his mission to the world was only about serving *"the lost"* by going out to *"seek"* them, the apostles' question in verse 6, *"Lord, will you at this time restore the kingdom to Israel?"* was glaring evidence that they still did not understand that his kingdom was not about having worldly power over others. Perhaps when he told them to stay in Jerusalem in verse 4 they assumed that he was about to restore it as his capital city; instead, it would be there that he would very soon empower them to go out into the world on his mission (v 8; M. I. Ac 1:8). **2)** However, Jesus did once again promise them in verse 7 that his Father did have all power and authority over his entire creation, but only he knew when and how he would, in his gracious mission-heart, carry out the final stage of his plan to fully restore his rightful reign over his entire creation (Ps 102:13; Mk 13:32). Until then, their only concern should be to go and carry out his mission (M. I. Ac 1:8).

1:8 (1) The sequence in verse 8 is, of course, vital: first Jesus promised to empower his apostles by saying in verse 8, *"You will receive power when the Holy Spirit has come upon you;"* and then, he commanded them to go out into the world by adding, *"and you will be my witnesses."* They could do nothing on their own without his Spirit's power, because the Spirit would help them in at least three ways: **a)** He would empower them on their mission (2:6). **b)** At times, he would have to use persecution in order to force them out of their comfort zones to actually leave their homes (8:1). **c)** And he would also lead them in the directions that he wanted them to go (16:10). **2)** Hence, Jesus' words in verse 8, *"And you will be my witnesses"* are not a mere wish but a direct command of Jesus, since the apostles needed to be repeatedly pushed into cross-cultural situations where they were not yet comfortable. It has long been assumed that, because Jesus used geographical terms in his command, he was sending his witnesses out to progressively greater geographical distances; however, we will soon see in Luke's account that Jesus was, in fact, pushing them out of their own cultural comfort zone in order to cross progressively more difficult cross-cultural boundaries. His mission-heart was, of course, fully in tune with his heavenly Father's heart, because when his Father chose Abraham in order to begin to carry out his plan of salvation, he first sent him away from his home culture and called him to use his blessings in order to bless all other Gentile nations with the Gospel (Gen 12:1-3; [29]M. M. Ac 13:46). Thus, Jesus also sent his apostles out across three levels of cultural difficulty. **a)** Level 1 was *"Jerusalem and in all Judea"* or their own language and culture, the nation of Israel. (In this period of history, the Jews mainly spoke Hebrew or Aramaic; however, chapter 6 informs us that, at least in the capital city of Jerusalem, the Jews were not a homogeneous group, since some Jews spoke mainly Greek.) **b)** Level 2 was *"Samaria,"* their close neighbors whom the Jews hated so much. **c)** And Level 3 was *"to the end of the earth"* or to all Gentile nations (v 8). Therefore, in verse 8, Jesus taught his apostles a new mission imperative. M. I. Ac 1:8: The Christian Church should go and witness about Jesus to all who are lost from all languages and cultures by depending on the power of the Holy Spirit to help them bridge all of the language/cultural boundaries whether they are relatively easy, as in their own language, or extremely difficult. **3)** Furthermore, a closer, chapter-by-chapter, examination of Luke's account in Acts indicates that the Holy Spirit did not actually send them out in progressively greater geographical distances; rather his plan was much more random over time, which indicates that he continuously tried to push them out of their cultural comfort zone into ever more different cultures. Two examples illustrate this: **a)** We immediately see the Holy Spirit carrying out all three levels of the mission on one day, on Pentecost Day (2:4-11). **b)** And again in chapters 8 and 9 we see him sending the believers out on all three levels instead of just on Level 2 to Samaria. Furthermore, these are only two very obvious examples; we will document several more in Acts. **4)** What did it mean for the very early Jewish believers to be Jesus' witnesses in different languages/cultures? **a)** On his mission in Level 1, *"Jerusalem and in all Judea,"* the Jewish believers would have had relatively few problems communicating with their fellow Jews. **b)** And on his mission in Level 2, *"Samaria,"* the Samaritan culture had changed quite extensively from the Jewish culture because the Samaritans had intermarried with Gentiles for many generations; and this made many Jews hate them bitterly. However, they still shared many of their religious and cultural practices through their common Old Testament. Therefore, the believers actually had many cultural and theological bridges or connecting points where they could begin a conversation with the Samaritans. Jesus' conversation with the woman at the well in (Jn 4) demonstrates this clearly. Note that his references to *"living water,"* to marriage laws, to *"the place where people ought to worship,"* and of course, her reference to *"the Messiah"* all come from their common Old Testament. **c)** However, when the Jewish believers were on his mission in Level 3, *"to the end of the earth,"* they obviously faced many major linguistic and cultural barriers between themselves and the Gentiles. The main barrier was that they considered the Gentiles unclean because they were uncircumcised; and they would not touch anything unclean, since they would then become unclean themselves and not be able to perform any sacrifices (Ch. 10). Nevertheless, there also were at least three bridges or connecting points that they could use to witness to the Gentiles. **aa)** First of all, the common or "Koine" Greek language was a useful but somewhat limited tool of cross-cultural communication, since most people, Jews and Gentiles alike, in the Roman Empire spoke it. The term *"Gentile"* was a very generic term because it referred to anyone who was not a Jew. They were people living both outside the Roman Empire (e.g., Ethiopia (8:27) and inside it, who were from many different languages and cultures (2:8), which, of course, included Latin, the language of the Roman rulers. Therefore, "Koine" Greek was a second, trade language for most people that they had a limited knowledge of, which made it a limited tool to use in witnessing. **bb)** Secondly, all of the early Jewish believers were, no doubt, somewhat familiar with the Greco-Roman culture, as we note in Paul's message in Athens in (17:22-31). **cc)** And thirdly, the first thing we see Saul do after his conversion in (9:20) was to preach in the synagogues partly because he knew that Gentile converts to Judaism would be worshipping there. And after they heard the Gospel and were converted they would become effective cross-cultural bridges who could witness to other lost Gentiles, since they lived within two cultures (8:27; ch.10; [30]M. I. Ac 1:8).

1:9-11 (1) A faithful *"witness"* (v 8) both sees a person or an event and then also tells others about what he has seen. Therefore, the key fact in verse 9 is that the apostles *"were looking on"* as Jesus left them; they were eye *"witnesses"* of the historical fact that his Father was taking his physical/glorified body back to heaven. Because they saw this with their own eyes, just as they had seen his entire mission on earth, they could then also *"witness"* with complete sincerity and truth to other people who were lost. And they could likewise confidently tell them about the promise that the angels gave them in verse 11 that, one day soon, Jesus will certainly return *"in the same way,"* with his same physical yet glorified body. What glorious Gospel that is for all who are lost (M. I. Ac 1:8)! **2)** Again note that, since the apostles "*saw*" Jesus leave with his physical/glorified *body*, the life and mission of Jesus was thoroughly grounded in human history from the very beginning at his birth to the very end at his ascension. They had not been seeing a vision either now or when they first met him, nor was he some kind of a spirit that might suddenly disappear again. Their witness was the full truth; and they were not lying. His mission was and still is a true mission because he was and still is true God and true man ([31]M. M. Lk 1:26 & [32]Ac 2:24).

Matthias Chosen to Replace Judas 1:12-26

1:12   *Then they returned to Jerusalem from the mount called Olivet, which is near Jerusalem, a Sabbath day's journey away.*

1:13   *And when they had entered, they went up to the upper room, where they were staying, Peter and John and James and Andrew, Philip and Thomas, Bartholomew and Matthew, James the son of Alphaeus and Simon the Zealot and Judas the son of James.*

1:14   *All these with one accord were devoting themselves to prayer, together with the women and Mary the mother of Jesus, and his brothers.*

1:15 *In those days Peter stood up among the brothers (the company of persons was in all about 120) and said,*

1:16 *"Brothers, the Scripture had to be fulfilled, which the Holy Spirit spoke beforehand by the mouth of David concerning Judas, who became a guide to those who arrested Jesus.*

1:17 *For he was numbered among us and was allotted his share in this ministry."*

1:18 *(Now this man bought a field with the reward of his wickedness, and falling headlong he burst open in the middle and all his bowels gushed out.*

1:19 *And it became known to all the inhabitants of Jerusalem, so that the field was called in their own language Akeldama, that is, Field of Blood.)*

1:20 *"For it is written in the Book of Psalms, "'May his camp become desolate, and let there be no one to dwell in it'; and "'Let another take his office.'*

1:21 *So one of the men who have accompanied us during all the time that the Lord Jesus went in and out among us,*

1:22 *beginning from the baptism of John until the day when he was taken up from us--one of these men must become with us a witness to his resurrection."*

1:23 *And they put forward two, Joseph called Barsabbas, who was also called Justus, and Matthias.*

1:24 *And they prayed and said, "You, Lord, who know the hearts of all, show which one of these two you have chosen*

1:25 *to take the place in this ministry and apostleship from which Judas turned aside to go to his own place."*

1:26 *And they cast lots for them, and the lot fell on Matthias, and he was numbered with the eleven apostles.*

1:12-14 The apostles obeyed their Lord by returning to Jerusalem to wait for his gift of the Holy Spirit. They likewise displayed unity and the faith to depend on his grace through devoted prayer. Jesus was continuing to prepare them to begin to go and carry out his mission to the world ([33]M. I. Lk 11:10 & [34]Lk 6:13).

1:15-26 Obviously, the eleven apostles felt incomplete because Judas was dead. They understood why Jesus had deliberately chosen <u>twelve</u> men to be his apostles (and not any other number), since the new Israel, his Church must have the same number of leaders as the <u>twelve</u> patriarchs of the old Israel. Therefore, in verse 20, Peter quoted from the Book of Psalms in order to make it clear to everyone present that it was the Holy Spirit who was guiding them in choosing a replacement. Furthermore, the criterion for choosing a new apostle was very significant for Jesus' mission, because he had to be a *"<u>witness</u>."* And, in order to be a faithful witness, he had to have seen the historical facts in this case: **a)** first of all, by being *"one of the men who have accompanied us during all the time that the Lord Jesus went in and out among us"* (v 21). He had to have seen *"the things that have been accomplished among us [by Jesus]"* (Lk 1:1), the fact that Jesus did fulfill everything that his heavenly Father had sent him to do. **b)** And secondly, he also had to be *"a <u>witness</u> to his [Jesus'] resurrection"* (v 22); he had to have seen his resurrected body, which proved that his Father had accepted the holy sacrifice of his body. And then he could faithfully *"witness"* to others what he had seen ([35]M. I. Ac 1:8).

---

[25] M. M. Ac 13:46: As he did with the old Israel, God <u>first of all</u> strengthens the faith of the new Israel, the Church with his Word and Sacraments, so that they can go and witness to the lost people of all nations.

[26] M. I. Mt 28:19: Christians should go and proclaim God's Law and Gospel to all nations; then, baptize all who repent and believe after teaching them the meaning of holy Baptism.

[27] M. I. Ac 1:8: Christians should go and witness about Jesus to all who are lost from all languages and cultures by depending on the power of the Holy Spirit to help them bridge all of the language/cultural boundaries whether they are relatively easy, as in their own language, or extremely difficult.

[28] M. I. Ac 1:8: Christians should go and witness about Jesus to all who are lost from all languages and cultures by depending on the power of the Holy Spirit to help them bridge all of the language/cultural boundaries whether they are relatively easy, as in their own language, or extremely difficult.

[29] M. M. Ac 13:46: As he did with the old Israel, God <u>first of all</u> strengthens the faith of the new Israel, the Church with his Word and Sacraments, so that they can go and witness to the lost people of all nations.

[30] M. I. Ac 1:8: Christians should go and witness about Jesus to all who are lost from all languages and cultures by depending on the power of the Holy Spirit to help them bridge all of the language/cultural boundaries whether they are relatively easy, as in their own language, or extremely difficult.

[31] M. M. Lk 1:26: The heavenly Father sent his Son, Jesus to be born and live in humble circumstances, so that everyone from every nation on earth would see his grace.

[32] M. M. Ac 2:24: Our Lord Jesus loosed the pangs of death for us mortal human beings when God raised him from the dead, because it was not possible for him to be held by death.

[33] M. I. Lk 11:10: Christians should continuously pray to their heavenly Father and *always* depend on his grace, and not on their own feeble strength, because he always loves them.

[34] M. I. Lk 6:13: Christians should choose new leaders and train them in order to multiply the work.

[35] M. I. Ac 1:8: Christians should go and witness about Jesus to all who are lost from all languages and cultures by depending on the power of the Holy Spirit to help them bridge all of the language/cultural boundaries whether they are relatively easy, as in their own language, or extremely difficult.

Chapter 2

The Coming of the Holy Spirit 2:1-13

2:1 *When the day of Pentecost arrived, they were all together in one place.*
2:2 *And suddenly there came from heaven a sound like a mighty rushing wind, and it filled the entire house where they were sitting.*
2:3 *And divided tongues as of fire appeared to them and rested on each one of them.*
2:4 *And they were all filled with the Holy Spirit and began to speak in other tongues as the Spirit gave them utterance.*
2:5 *Now there were dwelling in Jerusalem Jews, devout men from every nation under heaven.*
2:6 *And at this sound the multitude came together, and they were bewildered, because each one was hearing them speak in his own language.*
2:7 *And they were amazed and astonished, saying, "Are not all these who are speaking Galileans?*
2:8 *And how is it that we hear, each of us in his own native language?*
2:9 *Parthians and Medes and Elamites and residents of Mesopotamia, Judea and Cappadocia, Pontus and Asia,*
2:10 *Phrygia and Pamphylia, Egypt and the parts of Libya belonging to Cyrene, and visitors from Rome,*
2:11 *both Jews and proselytes, Cretans and Arabians--we hear them telling in our own tongues the mighty works of God."*
2:12 *And all were amazed and perplexed, saying to one another, "What does this mean?"*
2:13 *But others mocking said, "They are filled with new wine."*

2:1-13 It was very significant that the first gift that the Holy Spirit gave to the believers gathered on Pentecost Day was the ability to <u>speak human</u> languages (for a very short period of time) that they had not studied (v 4) and with just one important purpose—to proclaim the Gospel. (The Holy Spirit may have given all of the believers other special gifts that day; however, neither verse 4 nor any other verse in this context explicitly says anything about any other gifts.) Obviously, he was in this way also teaching his Church some very important lessons, which are discussed below at (2:4). And it's likewise helpful for us today to attempt to understand which languages the 12 apostles spoke that day. However, verses 1-13 leave us with several significant questions about exactly what happened, but for our purposes, we will only discuss the linguistic and cultural issues. (Some of the following points clarify some issues but others are by no means certain.) **1)** When Luke says in verse 4 that *"they were all filled with the Holy Spirit and began to speak in other tongues,"* verse 14 makes it explicit that it was only the 12 apostles who received this one-time gift. Verse 14 says, *"But Peter, standing with the eleven, lifted up his voice and addressed them."* **2)** Who were these *"devout men"* in verses 5 and 11 and what languages did they understand? **a)** First of all, most of them were, no doubt, Jews (v 5), but verse 11 adds that they were *"both Jews and proselytes;"* and proselytes were Gentile converts to Judaism. **b)** Secondly, because they were *"devout"* believers, they had, no doubt, been waiting for the Messiah and were ready to hear the Gospel about Jesus. The Holy Spirit had already prepared their hearts for the Gospel. They were ready and waiting for him just as devout Simeon and Anna had been eagerly waiting (Lk 2:25-38). **c)** Thirdly, they showed that they were *"devout"* by their willingness to travel to Jerusalem—some of them great distances (vs 9-11), *"from every nation under heaven"* (v 5). **d)** Fourthly, most of these pilgrims would soon be leaving Jerusalem because the Festival ended that day and they were only temporarily *"dwelling in Jerusalem"* (v 5), in order to attend the fifty days of the Passover Festival. (However, as verse 14 indicates, some of them were also permanent residents in Jerusalem and in other parts of Israel.) **e)** Fifthly, even though the Greek text in verse 5 explicitly says, *"devout men,"* some of them must also have been women and children. **aa)** First of all, it was normal in all cultures in that time period for the authors of all types of material to use the term "men" in order to refer to both men and women. **bb)** Secondly, surely everyone—men, women and children

—must have heard the wind, and they <u>all</u> would have rushed to see what was happening; and then <u>all</u> of them also heard 12 men speaking in at least 12 different languages (vs 2, 6). **cc)** And thirdly, we know from (Lk 2:41) that <u>whole families</u> went to this Festival every year, although, no doubt, women and children did not travel there from distant countries. **g)** And finally, it's likewise very significant that most, if not all, of the pilgrims in the crowd were <u>bi-lingual</u> and spoke one of these foreign languages in addition to Aramaic. Gentile nations had carried the ancestors of the Jewish pilgrims off as slaves to their own countries; and there they lived for many years and learned their <u>foreign languages</u>. Therefore, on this day, they heard the Gospel in two languages: both in their own language, Aramaic (from Peter, vs 14-40) and also in the <u>foreign languages</u> that they had learned (v 4). **3)** In verses 15-21, Peter, no doubt, used <u>Aramaic</u> to answer the criticism of some of the people in the crowd, because he saw that it was not pilgrims from foreign lands but *"men of Judea and all who dwell in Jerusalem"* (v 14) who were mocking the miracle of them speaking foreign languages (v 4). **4)** Finally, two verses indicate that Peter continued to use <u>Aramaic</u> in verses 22-40 to address the whole crowd. In verse 22, he explicitly addressed them as *"men of Israel;"* and then, in verse 23, he specifically accused his fellow Jews of crucifying their Messiah, because he knew that the Gentile proselytes in his audience were not included in the awful curse that the Jewish religious leaders had placed on their whole nation at Jesus' crucifixion when they said, *"His blood be on us and on our children"* (Mt 27:25)! Furthermore, Peter, no doubt, also knew that the Gentile proselytes had also learned Aramaic as a second language.

2:1 Why did the Holy Spirit choose Pentecost Day (v 1) in order to begin to empower his Church to quickly go on its mission to all nations? There are at least <u>six</u> significant answers: **1)** First of all, Pentecost Day marked the <u>end</u> of the Passover Festival cycle. *"Pentecost"* is the name that the Greek speaking Jews gave to the Jewish Feast of Weeks; and as verse 1 indicates, it was fifty days after the Passover. This meant that *"about three thousand"* pilgrims (v 41) would be <u>soon</u> be <u>returning home</u>. **2)** Secondly, this meant that many of these pilgrims heard the Gospel and received the gracious gift of <u>faith</u>. Everyone must have listen with rapt attention when they heard them speak their own local languages (v 12); and, for the first time for the majority of them, they heard about the cross and empty tomb of Jesus in their own language. Both parts of this experience must have been utterly amazing! And what a mighty tool this was! The Holy Spirit used the Gospel about the cross and empty tomb of Jesus in order to penetrate into their very hearts and give them his gracious gift of faith in Jesus (Heb 4:12). **3)** Thirdly, these pilgrims were now new <u>missionaries</u>. They all now had a glorious, unforgettable message that they would eagerly and boldly share wherever they went ([1]M. M. Mt 5:14 & [2]M. I. Ac 1:8). They would now give the Church's mission a huge jump-start on all three levels of the mission all over the Empire, and perhaps beyond ([3]M. M. Ac 13:46). **4)** In addition, the regions and cities in the list in verses 9-11 were scattered all over the Roman Empire; therefore, we clearly see how quickly and easily the Holy Spirit accomplished his purpose of spreading the Gospel on Level 3 to many Gentile nations very rapidly. How it must have pleased his mission-heart (M. M. Ac 13:46)! **e)** Furthermore, they already knew the foreign languages in all of these lands, so that they could communicate effectively with many lost people in their <u>own heart-languages</u>. **5)** And finally, in this way, the Holy Spirit made sure that the mission of the Church would <u>no longer</u> completely depend on a few <u>Jewish</u> apostles. Sadly, Luke's accounts in Luke and Acts clearly indicate that the apostles had often been slow to leave their comfort zone on Level 1 (8:1), in order to go to Samaria on Level 2, let alone also go to the Gentile nations on Level 3 ([4]M. I. Lk 10:4).

2:4 (1) The Holy Spirit's mission-heart had been longing for the people of Israel to go to Gentile lands in order to proclaim the Gospel to them in their own languages for hundreds of years, but they very seldom obeyed him ([5]M. M. Ac 13:46); therefore, this dramatic public act in verse 4 finally ended this drought. It is likewise clear from the list of regions and cities in verses 9-11 that the apostles briefly spoke <u>local</u> languages; and only Peter, no doubt, used Aramaic in his longer message (vs 14-40). The Holy Spirit was teaching the very new Church two mission lessons: First of all, he was reminding them that his own mission-heart has always been focused on all of the needs of all of the people whom he has made by loving them unconditionally (M. M. Ac 13:46). And his second lesson was that especially believers who are trying to communicate the Gospel in cross-cultural situations should always focus on all of the needs of their target group by learning the heart-language and culture of the target group as deeply as possible for two reasons: Of primary importance, so that they will be able to tell them the Gospel clearly in their own language. But, in addition, they will also be able to help them in other ways because they understand the true needs of their society. It's a new mission imperative. M. I. Ac 2:4: In cross-cultural situations, Christians should always focus on all of the needs of the target group by learning their heart-language and culture as deeply as possible, so that they can tell them the Gospel clearly in their own language and also help them with the true needs of their society. **2)** It's also very important to point out a very important distinction between three very different gifts that the Holy Spirit began to give to his very young Church. **a)** He began to give some believers the ability to study and learn how to speak the language and culture of a target group, in order to be able to proclaim the Gospel in their heart-language (obviously a human language). He gave this unique gift to the apostles only on that one day, even though they obviously had not studied them; however he still continues to graciously give this gift to some cross-cultural missionaries. The Holy Spirit's second and third gifts are a set of gifts: **b)** the gift of speaking in tongues (10:46) **c)** and third, the gift of interpreting this unintelligible language to other worshippers (1 Cor 14:6). The gift of speaking in tongues is different from the ability to learn another human language in four significant ways: **aa)** Speaking in tongues is the ability to speak a "heavenly" or non-human language in order to praise God, which only benefits that one person (1 Cor 14:4). **bb)** Therefore, it requires a second person to interpret it, so that the whole worshiping group can also praise God. **cc)** It is typically a brief experience. **dd)** And it is only used to praise God in a worship setting and not to proclaim the Gospel. Therefore, Paul warned believers in the early Church about misusing the gift of speaking in tongues because: first of all, some believers who claimed to have it became proud and thought that they were "better" believers than others; and secondly if no one interpreted it, it only benefited one person; and thirdly, when more than one person used it at the same time, it caused confusion in the service (1 Cor 14:1-25).

Furthermore, it is very sad that some believers continue to cause these same problems in the Church yet today (1 Cor 14:2, 23; [6]M. I. 1 Cor 14:2).

2:11 The messages that the apostles preached that day were about *"the mighty works of God"* (v 11). Which miracles did they preach about? We can be very certain that they emphasized the two most significant *"works of God"* in the entire history of mankind: the cross and the empty tomb of Jesus (Lk 11:29). These *"works of God"* are obviously the very heart and core of Jesus' Gospel message, because his empty tomb shouts, "Yes, here is the final proof that I have kept all of the many promises that I made to my people, Israel in the Scriptures" (2 Cor 1:20). Therefore, in the book of Acts, we continue to see all of the disciples, and especially St. Paul, continue to emphasize these two *"works of God,"* as Paul says in (1 Cor 2:2), *"I decided to know nothing among you except Jesus Christ and him crucified"* (1 Cor 2:2; [7]M. I. Ro 1:16a & [8]1 Cor 1:17).

Peter's Sermon at Pentecost 2:14-41

2:14 *But Peter, standing with the eleven, lifted up his voice and addressed them, "Men of Judea and all who dwell in Jerusalem, let this be known to you, and give ear to my words.*
2:15 *For these men are not drunk, as you suppose, since it is only the third hour of the day.*
2:16 *But this is what was uttered through the prophet Joel:*
2:17 *"'And in the last days it shall be, God declares, that I will pour out my Spirit on all flesh, and your sons and your daughters shall prophesy, and your young men shall see visions, and your old men shall dream dreams;*
2:18 *even on my male servants and female servants in those days I will pour out my Spirit, and they shall prophesy.*
2:19 *And I will show wonders in the heavens above and signs on the earth below, blood, and fire, and vapor of smoke;*
2:20 *the sun shall be turned to darkness and the moon to blood, before the day of the Lord comes, the great and magnificent*

day.

2:21 *And it shall come to pass that everyone who calls upon the name of the Lord shall be saved.'*

2:22 *"Men of Israel, hear these words: Jesus of Nazareth, a man attested to you by God with mighty works and wonders and signs that God did through him in your midst, as you yourselves know--*

2:23 *this Jesus, delivered up according to the definite plan and foreknowledge of God, you crucified and killed by the hands of lawless men.*

2:24 *God raised him up, loosing the pangs of death, because it was not possible for him to be held by it.*

2:25 *For David says concerning him, "'I saw the Lord always before me, for he is at my right hand that I may not be shaken;*

2:26 *therefore my heart was glad, and my tongue rejoiced; my flesh also will dwell in hope.*

2:27 *For you will not abandon my soul to Hades, or let your Holy One see corruption.*

2:28 *You have made known to me the paths of life; you will make me full of gladness with your presence.'*

2:29 *"Brothers, I may say to you with confidence about the patriarch David that he both died and was buried, and his tomb is with us to this day.*

2:30 *Being therefore a prophet, and knowing that God had sworn with an oath to him that he would set one of his descendants on his throne,*

2:31 *he foresaw and spoke about the resurrection of the Christ, that he was not abandoned to Hades, nor did his flesh see corruption.*

2:32 *This Jesus God raised up, and of that we all are witnesses.*

2:33 *Being therefore exalted at the right hand of God, and having received from the Father the promise of the Holy Spirit, he has poured out this that you yourselves are seeing and hearing.*

2:34 *For David did not ascend into the heavens, but he himself says, "'The Lord said to my Lord, Sit at my right hand,*

2:35 *until I make your enemies your footstool.'*

2:36 *Let all the house of Israel therefore know for certain that God has made him both Lord and Christ, this Jesus whom you crucified."*

2:37 *Now when they heard this they were cut to the heart, and said to Peter and the rest of the apostles, "Brothers, what shall we do?"*

2:38 *And Peter said to them, "Repent and be baptized every one of you in the name of Jesus Christ for the forgiveness of your sins, and you will receive the gift of the Holy Spirit.*

2:39 *For the promise is for you and for your children and for all who are far off, everyone whom the Lord our God calls to himself."*

2:40 *And with many other words he bore witness and continued to exhort them, saying, "Save yourselves from this crooked generation."*

2:41 *So those who received his word were baptized, and there were added that day about three thousand souls.*

2:14-16 We can probably assume that Peter also first spoke in one local language during the time that the other 11 apostles did so; then Peter stepped up to a prominent position, with the other 11 apostles around him, and he spoke to the entire crowd in a language that they <u>all</u> understood. The text does not say which language he used, but it was most likely Aramaic and not Greek, since the majority of them were Jews; and, as was common practice, he would have used the Septuagint, which is a Greek translation of the Old Testament, when he quoted from the prophet Joel (vs 16-21). Therefore, in these ways, the Holy Spirit also moved Peter to maximize the effectiveness of his message in order to change the hearts of about 3,000 people (v 41; Heb 4:12; [9]M. M. Ro 1:16b).

2:15 When Peter said in verse 15 that it was too early for the disciples to be drunk, his purpose was to very quickly defuse any criticism of the apostles that would have distracted the crowd from focusing on <u>Jesus</u> as their Messiah and Savior ([10]M. M. Lk 4:21).

2:17-21 (1) Since both the Jews and the devout Gentile converts to Judaism who were in Peter's audience studied the <u>same</u> Scriptures in their synagogues, he began the main body of his message with the quotation in verses 17-21 from their common Greek Septuagint Scriptures. In this way, he tried to overcome some of the cultural barriers between his audience and himself ([11]M. I. Ac 2:4). **2)** Peter's quotation from the prophet Joel indicates that a key element of God's gracious mission-heart has always been eager to empower his people with his indwelling Holy Spirit (v 17), since, without his power, they cannot carry out any part of his mission to spread the Gospel either to their own nation or to all Gentiles nations ([12]M. M. Ac 13:46). Furthermore, by quoting from their own Scriptures throughout his message, Peter proved to them that Jesus was indeed the Messiah whom they had been longing to see for so many years (M. M. Lk 4:21 & [13]M. I. Ac 1:8). **3)** When the Holy Spirit inspired the prophet Joel to say that *"they shall prophesy"* (v 17) he was, of course, revealing nothing new about what God's mission-heart has always longed to do in order to restore the people of all nations to his family. The proclamation of the Gospel is the only gracious means that the Holy Spirit has chosen to use in order to create faith in a person's heart. Therefore, the prophet Joel went and proclaimed the Gospel; Jesus himself did so (Lk 4:15); his disciples did so (Lk 5:10), and, of course, Peter was likewise doing so as he quoted Joel in his message (vs 14-40). And obviously the response that the Holy Spirit's mission-heart has always longed to see in those who hear his message is: *"everyone who calls upon the name of the Lord shall be saved"* (v 21). This wonderful promise, of course, refers to the final, eternal salvation that all believers from all nations will receive as a most gracious gift from their heavenly Father ([14]M. M. Lk 1:1 & [15]Ro 10:17a, b). **4)** The *"wonders"* and *"signs"* (v 19) that God will display *"before the day of the Lord comes"* (v 20), on the other hand, are warnings of the final Judgment Day that cause fear of God's almighty power, and therefore, only point to the need for some kind of rescue ([16]M. I. Lk 3:3a & [17]Lk 3:8); and they, therefore, cannot by themselves create faith. Thus, these miracles are quite different from the greatest miracle of all time: Jesus' resurrection from the dead (vs 24-32; Lk 11:29). This is the only miracle that the Holy Spirit graciously uses to create a repentant heart and faith in Jesus, because his resurrection is the only answer to mankind's need for rescue from their sin. It is the final proof that the heavenly Father accepted Jesus' holy sacrifice on the cross for mankind's sin, which no other miracle proves (2 Cor 1:20; [18]M. M. Ro 10:17a). (Of course, the Holy Spirit also graciously uses other Gospel messages, such as the cross of Jesus, in order to create faith (4:33).)

2:22-36 (1) In the heart of Peter's message in verses 22-36, he makes a sharp contrast between what sinful men did to Jesus by killing him and what our gracious heavenly Father did through Jesus to carry out his most gracious plan of salvation for all mankind. Peter said in several different ways, *"you sinful people crucified Jesus, but God did this…and this…and this…"* Thus, Peter very correctly followed his Lord's example (Lk 4:25-28; Phil 2:6-11) and taught them both the Law and the Gospel. No doubt some of these same people were the ones who had so glibly said to Pilate in (Mt 27:25), *"His blood be on us and on our children!"* His dual message was so powerful for Peter's hearers, since it both convicted them of their need for a Savior from sin and also pointed them to Jesus as their true Messiah, whom they had learned about in their Scriptures and had longed to see their whole lives. Most importantly, the key miracle of the final proof that this was so was the fact that their heavenly Father raised him from the dead (vs 24; Lk 11:29; 24:1-12). Every human being naturally knows that one day he will die, therefore, everyone is afraid of dying, whether he admits it or not. And this is the reason why the fact that our Lord Jesus conquered death is such a vital and comforting truth. It's a new mission message. M. M. Ac 2:24: Our Lord Jesus loosed the pangs of death for us mortal human beings when God raised him from the dead, because it was not possible for him to be held by death. **2)** Furthermore, in verses 22-36, Peter affirmed two vital truths about Jesus: that he is both true man and true God. He was a true human being because he was born in Nazareth (v 22), he died like every other human being (v 23), and he had human *"flesh"* (v 31). Likewise, in nearly every verse in this section, Peter cites more evidence that Jesus was also true God. He had to be both in order to fulfill his Father's plan of salvation completely for us ([19]M. M. Lk 1:26).

2:25-31 Why did Peter use such a long quotation from King David in verses 25-31; and why did he emphasize so strongly that King David believed that God would raise the Messiah from the dead? King David was the greatest king of Israel whom God himself had chosen to be king; and, more importantly, God chose him to be the forefather of Jesus, his Messiah. King David was also *"a prophet"* (v 30), whom God inspired to write many Psalms that Peter's audience loved so dearly. All of this knowledge about King David was planted very deeply in the hearts of the people listening to Peter; and therefore, the Holy Spirit moved Peter to use this common knowledge to move them to faith. The Holy Spirit can, of course, use any Law and Gospel to create faith, but humanly speaking, he can most effectively use a message that touches the hearts of the hearers fully in their own language and culture ([20]M. I. Ac 2:4).
2:37-38 (1) The fact that these men asked, *"Brothers, what shall we do?"* in verse 37 indicates that they had already received the gracious gift of faith from the Holy Spirit, since a spiritually dead person cannot spring to life by their own power ([21]M. M. Ro 10:17a). However, verses 37-38 refer to a new element in the new Christian era, holy Baptism, which is a new means of grace and the new public mark of faith. God's Word offers two promises in Holy Baptism: God forgives the person's sins ([22]M. M. Ro 6:18), and he *"will receive the gift of the Holy Spirit [from God]"* ([23]M. M. Tit 3:5). The new public mark of faith in the water of holy Baptism thus replaces the Old Testament mark of faith in physical circumcision. John the Baptist first began baptizing; and then Jesus himself commanded his disciples, *"Go therefore and make disciples of all nations, baptizing them in the name of the Father and of the Son and of the Holy Spirit, teaching them to observe all that I have commanded you"* (Mt 28:19-20). **2)** However, note that Peter said in verse 38, *"be baptized every one of you in the name of Jesus Christ,"* and he did not say, *"in the name of the Trinity."* Obviously he was not blatantly disobeying Jesus' express command in ([24]M. I. Mt 28:19; Acts 8:16). Rather, he was emphasizing the unique nature of this new Baptism (8:16; 10:48; 19:5). **3)** Furthermore, why did God wait until this specific Pentecost Day in order to begin to give the gift of his Spirit in holy Baptism? John explains in his Gospel in (Jn 7:39), *"Now this he*

[Jesus] said about the Spirit, whom those who believed in him were to receive, for as yet the Spirit had not been given, because Jesus was not yet glorified." And Luke reported in (1:9), *"And when he [Jesus] had said these things, as they [his disciples] were looking on, he was lifted up, and a cloud took him out of their sight."* Thus, on this very special day, God now began to graciously give the gracious gift of his Holy Spirit in the new sacrament of holy Baptism (M. M. Tit 3:5).

2:39 In verse 39, Peter refers to (Gen 12:1-3) where God, for the first time, revealed his mission-heart to mankind by choosing Abraham as the father of the nation of Israel, so that God could first bless them, as verse 39 says, *"For the promise [of God] is for you [the nation of Israel] and for your children."* And then, verse 39 continues by referring to the second part of God's original plan when it says, *"and for all [Gentiles] who are far off."* God's plan was that the nation of Israel should share his blessings by proclaiming the Gospel to all Gentile nations (1:8; [25]M. M. Ac 13:46). Therefore, in verse 39, Peter was announcing a very significant shift in the history of mankind on this important day. God was shifting the responsibility to proclaim the Gospel to the Gentile nations from the old Israel to the new Israel, the Church. And beginning with the mighty miracle in verse 4 of the apostles doing this very thing in many different languages, the Holy Spirit began to continuously empower his Church in many wonderful ways ([26]M. I. Ac 1:8 & [27]Mt 28:19).

2:41 (1) As verse 41 says, on this Pentecost day, the apostles baptized *"those who received his word"* in the name of the holy Trinity. And, of course, they continued to do so on many subsequent occasions (8:38; 9:18; 16:15, 33). However, the fact that Luke records so many details of Peter's message implies that, in the portions of his message that he did not record, Peter also taught them the meaning of holy Baptism before they baptized them, as their Lord Jesus had taught them (M. I. Mt 28:19). **2)** Verse 41 then continues, *"and there were added that day about three thousand souls."* It's a record of the amazing results of how the Holy Spirit used the messages that the 11 apostles and also Peter himself spoke to them in their own languages in order to create faith in 3,000 hearts. And it was, of course, the main purpose of everything that happened that day. These 3,000 people would now be eager to begin to carry out the mission of Jesus to all of the nations where they lived (M. I. Ac 1:8). And therefore, Pentecost Day must have filled the mission-heart of God with pure joy, as Jesus himself said in (Lk 15:10), *"Just so, I tell you, there is joy before the angels of God over one sinner who repents"* ([28]M. I. Lk 15:7). **3)** Furthermore, this "progress report" in verse 41 is the first of nine progress reports that Luke lists in his account (2:41; 4:4; 5:14; 6:7; 9:31; 12:24; 16:5; 19:20; 28:31). Thus, the Holy Spirit obviously continued to use his holy Word in order to work faith in the hearts of many hearers as the Church was faithfully proclaiming the Gospel ([29]M. M. Ro 10:17a).

The Fellowship of the Believers 2:42-47

> 2:42 *And they devoted themselves to the apostles' teaching and fellowship, to the breaking of bread and the prayers.*
> 2:43 *And awe came upon every soul, and many wonders and signs were being done through the apostles.*
> 2:44 *And all who believed were together and had all things in common.*
> 2:45 *And they were selling their possessions and belongings and distributing the proceeds to all, as any had need.*
> 2:46 *And day by day, attending the temple together and breaking bread in their homes, they received their food with glad and generous hearts,*
> 2:47 *praising God and having favor with all the people. And the Lord added to their number day by day those who were being saved.*

2:42 (1) When verse 42 says that the believers *"devoted themselves to the apostles' teaching"* it represents a significant shift from the believers studying only the Old Testament to now also studying what the apostles taught them—truths that the apostles soon wrote down as parts of the New Testament. The Holy Spirit had been busy for many centuries inspiring his prophets to write down both Law and Gospel messages in order to teach his will to his people; and in the coming years he continued to guide the apostles and their disciples to write down *"the apostles' teaching"* ([30]M. M. 2 Tim 3:16). And eventually, one of the main criteria for including these written truths in the New Testament canon was that an apostle or his disciple had written them. And just two examples of this are: the Gospel and the book of Acts by Luke, who was a disciple of Paul and the Gospel by Mark, who was a disciple of Peter. Furthermore, yet today, of course, both the Old and New Testaments continue to be the <u>only</u> source of spiritual food for the Church that the Holy Spirit uses to create and strengthen faith (Phil 1:6; [31]M. M. Ro 10:17a). **2)** Not many years later, the "*<u>fellowship</u>*" (v 42) of the believers became increasingly important when the Church began to suffer from many different kinds of persecution. They would soon need each other's support very urgently ([32]M. I. 1 Cor 12:26 & [33]2 Cor 1:5). **3)** The phrase, *"the breaking of bread"* in verse 42 almost certainly refers to Holy Communion since it would not make sense to refer to every day meals here (20:7; Lk 22:19; 1 Cor 10:16; 11:20). Furthermore, this is most likely the meaning that Luke intended in this verse in spite of the fact that a similar phrase in verse 46 refers to everyday meals. The apostles obviously would not have forgotten to eat the precious, powerful spiritual food that their Lord had so graciously provided for all believers, since they knew that they needed this continual strength of complete forgiveness from the Holy Spirit. This is the first reference to Holy Communion in the book of Acts, and there are only a few more references; however, the scarcity of these references certainly does not indicate anything about how important it was to them, nor how frequently they celebrated this holy meal. In fact, this verse is a new mission imperative because this holy meal was another powerful means of God's grace and source of strength that the Church needed very frequently. M. I. Ac 2:42: Christians should celebrate Holy Communion frequently in order to receive forgiveness and strength from their Lord's grace in order to continue on his mission. **4)** The apostles likewise did not forget to make prayer (v 42) an important part of their everyday life since they had seen the powerful example of their Lord doing so. In prayer, they continued to depend on their Lord's rich grace ([34]M. I. Lk

11:10).
2:47 When Luke says in verse 47 that *"the Lord added to their number day by day those who were being saved,"* he was talking about the results of the mission work of *two* groups of believers. Both groups were busy following their mission-hearts and eagerly spreading the Gospel ([35]M. M. Mt 5:14). **a)** The first group was the believers who were living in Jerusalem. The first assignment that their Lord had given them was to spread the Gospel on Level 1 in Jerusalem and in all of Judea (1:8). The amazing work that the Holy Spirit had done on Pentecost Day had created an atmosphere of good will in Jerusalem; therefore, verse 47 says that the believers who were living there were *"having favor with all the people."* And since this favorable atmosphere had created many opportunities to spread the Gospel, they were now busy carrying out their Lord's mission ([36]M. I. Lk 4:15). And of course, the Holy Spirit was also busy *"adding to their number"* ([37]M. M. Ro 10:17a). **b)** The second group of missionaries was the 3,000 new believers (v 41), who were returning to their homes in other countries during this period of time and also eagerly spreading the Gospel (M. M. Mt 5:14). New Christians, who have just received the gracious gifts of mission-hearts are often the most eager missionaries wherever they go; and how this pleases the mission-heart of their Lord ([38]M. I. Ro 12:1)!

---

[1] M. M. Mt 5:14: When the Holy Spirit creates faith in a person's heart, he also graciously gives him a new mission-heart that is eager to shine the light of the Gospel throughout the whole world.

[2] M. I. Ac 1:8: Christians should go and witness about Jesus to all who are lost from all languages and cultures by depending on the power of the Holy Spirit to help them bridge all of the language/cultural boundaries whether they are relatively easy, as in their own language, or extremely difficult.

[3] M. M. Ac 13:46: As he did with the old Israel, God first of all strengthens the faith of the new Israel, the Church with his Word and Sacraments, so that they can go and witness to the lost people of all nations.

[4] M. I. Lk 10:4: Their mission is urgent; therefore, Christians should go on their mission quickly and not allow anything to distract them.

[5] M. M. Ac 13:46: As he did with the old Israel, God first of all strengthens the faith of the new Israel, the Church with his Word and Sacraments, so that they can go and witness to the lost

people of all nations.

⁶ M. I. 1 Cor 14:2: Christians should not use the Holy Spirit's gift of speaking in a strange language in a worship service when no one is present to interpret his message for other members, because obviously he is only speaking to God, and he is not using this gift to build up the members who cannot understand him.

⁷ M. I. Ro 1:16a: Christians should not be ashamed to proclaim the Gospel, even though it may appear to be weak and foolish; rather, they should be proud to proclaim it because it is the almighty power that the Holy Spirit uses to create faith in Jesus.

⁸ M. I. 1 Cor 1:17: Christians should always proclaim the Gospel by focusing very clearly on the gracious power of the cross of Jesus, so that the faith of their hearers is based on its power; and they should not try to persuade people by using clever arguments, which would rob his cross of its power because the faith of their hearers would then be based on human wisdom.

⁹ M. M. Ro 1:16b: The Gospel is so powerful because it contains the central truth that Jesus rose from the dead with a glorified body in order to save all of his brothers and sisters from sin and death.

¹⁰ M. M. Lk 4:21: Every verse in the entire Bible points in some way to Jesus and his mission to seek and save the lost.

¹¹ M. I. Ac 2:4: In cross-cultural situations, Christians should always focus on all of the needs of the target group by learning *their* heart-language and culture as deeply as possible, so that they can tell them the Gospel clearly in their own language and also help them with the true needs of their society.

¹² M. M. Ac 13:46: As he did with the old Israel, God first of all strengthens the faith of the new Israel, the Church with his Word and Sacraments, so that they can go and witness to the lost people of all nations.

¹³ M. I. Ac 1:8: Christians should go and witness about Jesus to all who are lost from all languages and cultures by depending on the power of the Holy Spirit to help them bridge all of the language/cultural boundaries whether they are relatively easy, as in their own language, or extremely difficult.

¹⁴ M. M. Lk 1:1: Jesus earned salvation for all lost people from every nation on earth.

¹⁵ M. M. Ro 10:17a: The Holy Spirit only creates and preserves faith by using the message of God's grace in his holy Word.

¹⁶ M. I. Lk 3:3a: Christians should, in love, warn lost people who do not repent.

¹⁷ M. I. Lk 3:8: Christians should always be prepared to boldly and publicly refute false teaching, so that Satan cannot easily deceive people.

¹⁸ M. M. Ro 10:17a: The Holy Spirit only creates and preserves faith by using the message of God's grace in his holy Word.

¹⁹ M. M. Lk 1:26: The heavenly Father sent his Son, Jesus to be born and live in humble circumstances, so that everyone from every nation on earth would see his grace.

²⁰ M. I. Ac 2:4: In cross-cultural situations, Christians should always focus on all of the needs of the target group by learning their heart-language and culture as deeply as possible, so that they can tell them the Gospel clearly in their own language and also help them with the true needs of their society.

²¹ M. M. Ro 10:17a: The Holy Spirit only creates and preserves faith by using the message of God's grace in his holy Word.

[22] M. M. Ro 6:18: In his Baptism, Jesus graciously sets a new Christian free from his slavery to sin and gives him the power of his Spirit to gratefully obey his new Lord by doing good deeds.

[23] M. M. Tit 3:5: When a person is baptized, God graciously saves him and gives him the gift of a new birth from his indwelling Holy Spirit; and he does this because his mercy is so great, and not because of any good deeds that that person has done.

[24] M. I. Mt 28:19: Christians should go and proclaim God's Law and Gospel to all nations; then, baptize all who repent and believe after teaching them the meaning of holy Baptism.

[25] M. M. Ac 13:46: As he did with the old Israel, God <u>first of all</u> strengthens the faith of the new Israel, the Church with his Word and Sacraments, so that they can go and witness to the lost people of all nations.

[26] M. I. Ac 1:8: Christians should go and witness about Jesus to all who are lost from all languages and cultures by depending on the power of the Holy Spirit to help them bridge all of the language/cultural boundaries whether they are relatively easy, as in their own language, or extremely difficult.

[27] M. I. Mt 28:19: Christians should go and proclaim God's Law and Gospel to all nations; then, baptize all who repent and believe after teaching them the meaning of holy Baptism.

[28] M. I. Lk 15:7: Christians should rejoice together with the heavenly Father and his angels when just <u>one</u> lost person hears the Law and Gospel and then receives the gracious gifts of a repentant heart and faith in Jesus.

[29] M. M. Ro 10:17a: The Holy Spirit <u>only</u> creates and preserves faith by using the message of God's grace in his holy Word.

[30] M. M. 2 Tim 3:16: The Holy Spirit inspired the entire Bible; and therefore, the whole Bible is useful for teaching people the truth, for teaching them how to live a life that pleases God, for rebuking their errors, and for correcting their faults.

[31] M. M. Ro 10:17a: The Holy Spirit <u>only</u> creates and preserves faith by using the message of God's grace in his holy Word.

[32] M. I. 1 Cor 12:26: In the one Body of Christ there should be no divisions, but instead each member should care for the other members, so that if one member suffers, all should suffer together; and if one member is honored, all should rejoice together.

[33] M. I. 2 Cor 1:5: Since their Lord Jesus graciously suffered and died in order to give them eternal comfort in the midst of their suffering, Christians should also generously share his comfort with other people in the midst of their suffering.

[34] M. I. Lk 11:10: Christians should <u>continuously</u> pray to their heavenly Father and <u>always</u> depend on his grace, and not on their own feeble strength, because he <u>always</u> loves them.

[35] M. M. Mt 5:14: When the Holy Spirit creates faith in a person's heart, he also graciously gives him a new mission-heart that is eager to shine the light of the Gospel throughout the whole world.

[36] M. I. Lk 4:15: Christians should seize <u>every</u> opportunity to proclaim the Gospel to lost people of all nations.

[37] M. M. Ro 10:17a: The Holy Spirit <u>only</u> creates and preserves faith by using the message of God's grace in his holy Word.

[38] M. I. Ro 12:1: Christians should respond to God's mercy by offering their total bodies as living sacrifices to their Lord, which will please him only because they offer them with grateful

hearts.

Chapter 3

The Lame Beggar Healed 3:1-10

3:1 *Now Peter and John were going up to the temple at the hour of prayer, the ninth hour.*
3:2 *And a man lame from birth was being carried, whom they laid daily at the gate of the temple that is called the Beautiful Gate to ask alms of those entering the temple.*
3:3 *Seeing Peter and John about to go into the temple, he asked to receive alms.*
3:4 *And Peter directed his gaze at him, as did John, and said, "Look at us."*
3:5 *And he fixed his attention on them, expecting to receive something from them.*
3:6 *But Peter said, "I have no silver and gold, but what I do have I give to you. In the name of Jesus Christ of Nazareth, rise up and walk!"*
3:7 *And he took him by the right hand and raised him up, and immediately his feet and ankles were made strong.*
3:8 *And leaping up he stood and began to walk, and entered the temple with them, walking and leaping and praising God.*
3:9 *And all the people saw him walking and praising God,*
3:10 *and recognized him as the one who sat at the Beautiful Gate of the temple, asking for alms. And they were filled with wonder and amazement at what had happened to him.*

3:1-10 (1) After the general description of the communal life of the believers in Jerusalem in Luke's account in (2:42-47), the next significant event in the mission of the Church after Pentecost Day was the miracle of physical healing that Peter and John did (v 6). Obviously this miracle created so much excitement because Peter spoke the <u>name</u> of Jesus in order to heal him, so that everyone knew that he did not heal him, but that it was the divine power of <u>Jesus</u> that healed him. Peter said, *"In the <u>name</u> of Jesus Christ of Nazareth, rise up and walk!"* It's a new mission imperative. M. I. Ac 3:6: Christians should heal a person's physical problem by speaking the name of Jesus, so that everyone knows that it was the divine power of Jesus that healed him. **2)** Of course, the Holy Spirit also used this miracle to advance the mission of the Church in two other ways: **a)** It showed the people that the Lord Jesus always has compassion for all of the needs of all people ([1]M. I. Lk 4:35a). **b)** And it created two opportunities for Peter and John to witness to Jesus ([2]M. I. Lk 4:15), by attracting an audience of worshipers in the temple (v 11) and later an audience before the Jewish Council (4:7). Furthermore, the Holy Spirit *only* uses the message of two miracles, the cross and empty tomb of Jesus in order to create faith in the hearts of people (4:4; [3]M. M. Ro 10:17a).

Peter Speaks in Solomon's Portico 3:11-26

3:11 *While he clung to Peter and John, all the people ran together to them in the portico called Solomon's, astounded.*
3:12 *And when Peter saw it he addressed the people: "Men of Israel, why do you wonder at this, or why do you stare at us, as though by our own power or piety we have made him walk?*
3:13 *The God of Abraham, the God of Isaac, and the God of Jacob, the God of our fathers, glorified his servant Jesus, whom you delivered over and denied in the presence of Pilate, when he had decided to release him.*
3:14 *But you denied the Holy and Righteous One, and asked for a murderer to be granted to you,*
3:15 *and you killed the Author of life, whom God raised from the dead. To this we are witnesses.*
3:16 *And his name--by faith in his name--has made this man strong whom you see and know, and the faith that is through Jesus has given the man this perfect health in the presence of you all.*
3:17 *"And now, brothers, I know that you acted in ignorance, as did also your rulers.*
3:18 *But what God foretold by the mouth of all the prophets, that his Christ would suffer, he thus fulfilled.*

3:19 *Repent therefore, and turn again, that your sins may be blotted out,*
3:20 *that times of refreshing may come from the presence of the Lord, and that he may send the Christ appointed for you, Jesus,*
3:21 *whom heaven must receive until the time for restoring all the things about which God spoke by the mouth of his holy prophets long ago.*
3:22 *Moses said, 'The Lord God will raise up for you a prophet like me from your brothers. You shall listen to him in whatever he tells you.*
3:23 *And it shall be that every soul who does not listen to that prophet shall be destroyed from the people.'*
3:24 *And all the prophets who have spoken, from Samuel and those who came after him, also proclaimed these days.*
3:25 *You are the sons of the prophets and of the covenant that God made with your fathers, saying to Abraham, 'And in your offspring shall all the families of the earth be blessed.'*
3:26 *God, having raised up his servant, sent him to you first, to bless you by turning every one of you from your wickedness."*

3:13-26 (1) Once again, no doubt, Peter now used Aramaic to speak to his fellow Jews since it was their common, every-day language; he likewise quoted their own Scriptures to them (vs 22-25). Therefore, humanly speaking, they <u>all</u> should have responded very positively to his Law and Gospel message. However, Luke gives both a good and a bad report in (4:1-4) that about 5,000 people had received a repentant heart and faith in Jesus as their Lord; however, their spiritual leaders responded with anger and arrested Peter and John (4:3). This wonderful response must have pleased the Holy Spirit's mission-heart, since it was he who had planned that the new Church should begin their new mission on Level 1 in Jerusalem and in all of Judea (1:8; Lk 15; [4]M. I. Lk 15:7 & [5]M. M. Mt 5:14). **2)** Peter especially noticed that some in his audience were his religious leaders; and therefore, as guided by the Holy Spirit, **a)** he first used the <u>Law</u> to convict them of their sin in verses 13-15 by saying, *"whom [Jesus] you delivered over and denied in the presence of*

Pilate…you killed the Author of life" ([6]M. I. Lk 3:3b). **b)** However, Peter *then* strongly emphasized the Gospel in most of his message. His message was all about *Jesus* and his dual nature as both true man and true God. He emphasized his divinity in verse 14 when he called him, *"the Holy and Righteous One,"* and in verse 15 when he called him, *"the Author of life,"* and in verse 16 when he said, *"the faith that is through Jesus has given the man this perfect health."* But he likewise referred to Jesus' humanity in verse 18 when he said, *"his Christ would suffer,"* and in verse 22 when he said, "a prophet like me [Moses] from your brothers" ([7]M. M. Ac 2:24). In addition, note that Peter continued to quote Scripture to teach his hearers that Jesus was the Messiah ([8]M. I. Lk 4:17). **2)** In verse 25, Peter says, *"You are the sons…of the covenant that God made with your fathers."* He was reminding his hearers that, in (Gen 12:1-3), God had first shown his mission-heart by calling Abraham to repentance and faith, so that God could bless him and his descendants, and so that he could also bless all Gentile nations through them. Then, in verse 26 Peter also made it very clear to them that since *"[God] sent him [Jesus] to you [Jews] first."* God had clearly *not* changed his original mission plan of reaching the Gentile nations through the nation of Israel. And now perhaps, Peter had already begun to realize that God had passed this responsibility on to the new Israel, the Church to be his missionaries. But how miserably the Jews had failed to do so in the past! Therefore, how he longed for his Church to now begin to first be a blessing to each other so that they could then also be a blessing to the Gentile nations ([9]M. M. Ac 13:46)!

---

[1] M. I. Lk 4:35a: Christians should view every person as a whole person, and show him compassion by caring for *both* his physical and spiritual needs as they go on their mission.

[2] M. I. Lk 4:15: Christians should seize every opportunity to proclaim the Gospel to lost people of all nations.

[3] M. M. Ro 10:17a: The Holy Spirit only creates and preserves faith by using the message of God's grace in his holy Word.

[4] M. I. Lk 15:7: Christians should rejoice together with the heavenly Father and his angels when just one lost person hears the Law and Gospel and then receives the gracious gifts of a repentant heart and faith in Jesus.

[5] M. M. Mt 5:14: When the Holy Spirit creates faith in a person's heart, he also graciously gives him a new mission-heart that is eager to shine the light of the Gospel throughout the whole world.

[6] M. I. Lk 3:3b: Christians should always depend on the Holy Spirit's guidance for whether they should emphasize God's Law or the Gospel about Jesus, and which one to apply <u>first</u>.

[7] M. M. Ac 2:24: Our Lord Jesus loosed the pangs of death for us mortal human beings when God raised him from the dead, because it was not possible for him to be held by death.

[8] M. I. Lk 4:17: Christians should always base their messages on the Bible, so that the Holy Spirit can use his holy Word to create and strengthen faith in their hearers.

[9] M. M. Ac 13:46: As he did with the old Israel, God <u>first of all</u> strengthens the faith of the new Israel, the Church with his Word and Sacraments, so that they can go and witness to the lost people of all nations.

Chapter 4

Peter and John Before the Council 4:1-22

4:1 *And as they were speaking to the people, the priests and the captain of the temple and the Sadducees came upon them,*
4:2 *greatly annoyed because they were teaching the people and proclaiming in Jesus the resurrection from the dead.*
4:3 *And they arrested them and put them in custody until the next day, for it was already evening.*
4:4 *But many of those who had heard the word believed, and the number of the men came to about five thousand.*
4:5 *On the next day their rulers and elders and scribes gathered together in Jerusalem,*
4:6 *with Annas the high priest and Caiaphas and John and Alexander, and all who were of the high-priestly family.*
4:7 *And when they had set them in the midst, they inquired, "By what power or by what name did you do this?"*
4:8 *Then Peter, filled with the Holy Spirit, said to them, "Rulers of the people and elders,*
4:9 *if we are being examined today concerning a good deed done to a crippled man, by what means this man has been healed,*
4:10 *let it be known to all of you and to all the people of Israel that by the name of Jesus Christ of Nazareth, whom you crucified, whom God raised from the dead--by him this man is standing before you well.*
4:11 *This Jesus is the stone that was rejected by you, the builders, which has become the cornerstone.*
4:12 *And there is salvation in no one else, for there is no other name under heaven given among men by which we must be saved."*
4:13 *Now when they saw the boldness of Peter and John, and perceived that they were uneducated, common men, they were astonished. And they recognized that they had been with Jesus.*
4:14 *But seeing the man who was healed standing beside them, they had nothing to say in opposition.*

4:15 *But when they had commanded them to leave the council, they conferred with one another,*

4:16 *saying, "What shall we do with these men? For that a notable sign has been performed through them is evident to all the inhabitants of Jerusalem, and we cannot deny it.*

4:17 *But in order that it may spread no further among the people, let us warn them to speak no more to anyone in this name."*

4:18 *So they called them and charged them not to speak or teach at all in the name of Jesus.*

4:19 *But Peter and John answered them, "Whether it is right in the sight of God to listen to you rather than to God, you must judge,*

4:20 *for we cannot but speak of what we have seen and heard."*

4:21 *And when they had further threatened them, they let them go, finding no way to punish them, because of the people, for all were praising God for what had happened.*

4:22 *For the man on whom this sign of healing was performed was more than forty years old.*

4:1-3 (1) Since Peter and John were *"teaching the people and proclaiming in Jesus the resurrection from the dead"* (v 2; 3:26; [1]M. I. Lk 3:8); some of the same religious leaders who had crucified Jesus were now moved by the devil to *"arrested them and put them in custody until the next day"* (v 3). It's very evident that it was Satan who was attacking the very young mission of the Church. He cannot stop the work of the Holy Spirit once someone has proclaimed the Gospel; therefore, he must slow down the Lord's mission, either by attacking those who hear the Gospel, or by trying to stop those who proclaim the Gospel ([2]M. M. 2 Cor 4:4 & [3]M. I. Lk 4:4). And of course, Satan was easily able to use these men to attack the apostles since some of them were Sadducees, who believed that there is no resurrection from the dead. In spite of the overwhelming evidence that God had indeed raised Jesus from the dead, they still did not believe that he was God's Son and their Messiah. **2)** And Jesus had, of course, lovingly warned his disciples that some people would persecute them because they are carrying out his mission to the world; he said in (Lk 21:12). *"But before all this they will* *lay their hands on you and persecute you, delivering you up to the synagogues and prisons, and you will be brought before kings and governors for my name's sake."* Thus here at the very beginning of their mission, they should not have been surprised that they already had begun to face suffering for his sake, and they surely remembered that they must depend on their gracious Lord to protect them ([4]M. I. Lk 11:10).

4:5-8 How quickly Peter and John found themselves before the Jewish Council! How quickly they had a wonderful opportunity to bear witness to Jesus and his resurrection before the highest religious court of their land, before the very men who had just murdered their Lord! And how quickly the Holy Spirit showed his presence in them by giving them the very words that they should say that would have the greatest impact on these men! In faith, they were thrust into the mission at the very linguistic/cultural point where Jesus had commanded them to begin, on Level 1 in Jerusalem and in all of Judea. The Holy Spirit did not allow them to get comfortable in their group and content to say that they had already done enough on Jesus' mission ([5]M. M. Ac 13:46 & [6]M. I. Mt 28:19).

4:8-12 (1) Peter boldly witnessed before the Council to the name of Jesus as the only gate into the kingdom of God (Mt 7:13). He said in verse 12, *"There is salvation in no one else, for there is no other name under heaven given among men by which we must be saved,"* which clearly echoes Jesus' own Words in (Jn 14:6), *"I am the way, and the truth, and the life. No one comes to the Father except through me."* Just as the power of Jesus' name healed the crippled man, so also only the power of his name can save from sin. It's a new mission message. M. M. Ac 4:12: Only the power of Jesus' name can save a person from sin. In his Gospel, Luke also strongly emphasized this truth, as we see in (Lk 3:22; 9:20, 35; 13:24; 18:17) and elsewhere. **2)** Yet it is this truth more than any other that stirs up opposition because it totally rejects all other ways since they are all prideful man-made ways that Satan has always used and continues to use in order to deceive people every single day ([7]M. M. Gal 1:6). In fact, it was precisely because Peter said these words and then his bold refusal to stop witnessing to the name of Jesus in verse

20 that the Council began to *persecute* him and all of the believers in Jerusalem ([8]M. I. Ac 4:20).

4:13-17 How could Peter and John be so bold before the highest religious court in their land? They stood before the men who had the power of life and death over them, as evidenced by how they had so recently murdered their Lord. There were at least four reasons: **a)** First of all, verse 8 says that Peter was *"filled with the Holy Spirit;"* therefore, he did not stand in front of them all alone at all (M. I. Ac 4:20 & [9]Lk 16:17). **b)** Secondly, and of course, they also *"had been with Jesus"* for about three years (v 13) and carefully listening to his gracious Words that had filled their hearts with faith and a mission-heart like his (Lk 10:39; [10]M. I. Ro 1:16a); and they had also heard their Lord boldly condemn and warn these same men to repent of their evil ways many, many times (Lk 11:42-52; 20:9-20; Mt 23:13-29; [11]M. M. Ro 3:26). **c)** Thirdly, Peter knew that he had not healed the man in the temple by his own power, since he boldly said in (3:16) that he had healed him in the name of Jesus ([12]M. I. Ac 3:6). **d)** And finally, what had especially filled them with boldness was that they had seen and touched his glorified body after his resurrection (Lk 24:39; 1 Jn 1:1-4; [13]M. I. Ac 1:8 & [14]M. M. Jn 20:8).

4:18-22 (1) Obviously these merely human judges were not speaking God's Words, as they should have been, since they were the spiritual leaders of the Jews (Lk 20:9-19). Rather, the fact was that they were inspired by Satan to speak these words, because Satan is always angry when Christians witness to Jesus' almighty name. Ever since Jesus' resurrection destroyed his power, he knows that he cannot stand up against the almighty power of the Holy Spirit; therefore, he tries to fight back by using the people whom he has under his evil control in order to try to stop those who proclaim the Gospel. Thus, the true Law and Gospel witness of the Church will always encounter his bitter opposition ([15]M. I. Lk 11:10 & [16]M. M. Mt 5:14). **2)** Nevertheless, in the face of such an extremely dangerous enemy, the two apostles were filled with anther gift of boldness from the Holy Spirit, as noted in (vs 8, 13). With his almighty power filling their mission-hearts, no mere human being could silence them, nor could terrible Satan stop them, since his power had just been *"bruise [d]"* (Gen 3 15) forever by the cross and empty tomb of Jesus (Lk 24:6). Therefore, Peter and John answered them <u>very boldly</u> in (vs 19-20), *"Whether it is right in the sight of God to listen to you rather than to God, you must judge, for we cannot but speak of what we have seen and heard."* <u>Nothing</u> could ever stop them again from boldly witnessing to his holy name! This is another new mission imperative. M. I. Ac 4:20: Christians should boldly witness to the name of Jesus and allow nothing to stop their witness because it is the Holy Spirit's own message.

The Believers Pray for Boldness 4:23-31

4:23 *When they were released, they went to their friends and reported what the chief priests and the elders had said to them.*
4:24 *And when they heard it, they lifted their voices together to God and said, "Sovereign Lord, who made the heaven and the earth and the sea and everything in them,*
4:25 *who through the mouth of our father David, your servant, said by the Holy Spirit, "'Why did the Gentiles rage, and the peoples plot in vain?*
4:26 *The kings of the earth set themselves, and the rulers were gathered together, against the Lord and against his Anointed'--*
4:27 *for truly in this city there were gathered together against your holy servant Jesus, whom you anointed, both Herod and Pontius Pilate, along with the Gentiles and the peoples of Israel,*
4:28 *to do whatever your hand and your plan had predestined to take place.*
4:29 *And now, Lord, look upon their threats and grant to your servants to continue to speak your word with all boldness,*
4:30 *while you stretch out your hand to heal, and signs and wonders are performed through the name of your holy servant Jesus."*
4:31 *And when they had prayed, the place in which they were gathered together was shaken, and they were all filled with the*

Holy Spirit and continued to speak the word of God with boldness.

4:23 Peter and John quickly went to their fellow believers and *"reported what the chief priests and the elders had said to them"* (v 23), which showed that the apostles, of course, understood how very important it was for all of them to depend on each other in the face of physical and spiritual danger ([17]M. I. Lk 11:10 & [18]M. M. Ro 12:2b).

4:24-30 Then, the response of the group was also very significant because they immediately turned to their heavenly Father in joint prayer (vs 24-28), because they knew that they only had his almighty grace to depend on in the face of persecution as they went on their mission to the world. Their mission-hearts were in tune with the fact that the heavenly Father had *"plan[ned]"* and *"predestined"* (v 28) before he created the world how he would rescue sinful mankind from sin and how he would continue to control and guide his mission to all lost mankind (Ps 2:1-2). And his full control of human history was most evident as he sacrificed his own beloved Son, because, when the religious leaders of the Jews murdered him, they did *"whatever…your [God's] plan had predestined to take place"* (v 28). Therefore, yet today, when God's faithful people prayerfully go forth proclaiming the name of Jesus to the lost, it is always the heavenly Father who is in full control of his mission. It's a new mission message. M. M. Ac 4:28: The heavenly Father is always in full control of his mission to all nations of the world.

4:29-31 Then, based on their conviction that their heavenly Father was in full control of his mission, they continued their prayer by asking for two things: **a)** the same kind of boldness that Peter and John had displayed before the Jewish Council (v 20). They prayed in verse 29, *"grant to your servants to continue to speak your word with all boldness."* **b)** And they also asked God to likewise use them to continue to point to the name of Jesus through miracles of healing (v 30). These *"signs and wonders"* (v 30) would assist the mission in at least two ways. They would attract attention to the name of Jesus, and they would also demonstrate that the believers were proclaiming the Gospel in the name of Jesus and by the power of his Spirit ([19]M. I. Ac 3:6). Therefore, verse 31 says that *"they were all filled with the Holy Spirit and continued to speak the word of God with <u>boldness</u>."* Not only Peter and John, but <u>all</u> of them could now boldly witness to the name of Jesus ([20]M. I. Ac 4:20).

They Had Everything in Common 4:32-37

4:32 *Now the full number of those who believed were of one heart and soul, and no one said that any of the things that belonged to him was his own, but they had everything in common.*
4:33 *And with great power the apostles were giving their testimony to the resurrection of the Lord Jesus, and great grace was upon them all.*
4:34 *There was not a needy person among them, for as many as were owners of lands or houses sold them and brought the proceeds of what was sold*
4:35 *and laid it at the apostles' feet, and it was distributed to each as any had need.*
4:36 *Thus Joseph, who was also called by the apostles Barnabas (which means son of encouragement), a Levite, a native of Cyprus,*
4:37 *sold a field that belonged to him and brought the money and laid it at the apostles' feet.*

4:33 Why does Luke emphasize in verse 33 that the heart of the message that the apostles continued to proclaim was the <u>empty</u> tomb of Jesus? They obviously knew that it is the most significant miracle in the history of mankind. Other kinds of miracles like miracles of healing can point to Jesus' name and to this greatest miracle, but the Holy Spirit does not use healing miracles to create faith. He <u>only</u> graciously uses the Gospel about the miracle of his resurrection to create faith in him (2:24; Rom 10:17). His resurrection proves that his heavenly Father accepted his sacrifice on the cross as full payment for all of the sins of mankind; and no other miracle proves that (2 Cor 1:20; [21]M. M. Ac 2:24 & [22]Ro 1:16b & [23]Jn 20:8). (Of course, the Holy Spirit also graciously uses other

Gospel messages, such as the cross of Jesus, in order to create faith (2:24).)

4:32-37 The large group of believers in Jerusalem was inspired by the Holy Spirit to live in a very closely-knit group, having *"everything in common"* (vs 32-37; 2:44). And they already numbered much more than five thousand people, since verse 4 specifies that *"the number of the men came to about five thousand,"* which would not include women and children. Perhaps, the Holy Spirit's purpose was at least threefold: In this way, **a)** he, of course, helped to foster unity among them in the face of persecution ([24]M. M. Ac 5:1). **b)** He also helped to focus all of the physical and spiritual resources of the group on carrying out Level 1 of their mission to their fellow Jews in Jerusalem and in all of Judea (Lk 8:1-3; 2 Cor 11:9). **c)** And by pooling their resources they were able to publicly show their love for their fellow believers by caring for those who were poor in their group (vs 34-37). This would have been a powerful witness in a society where there were many poor people who were forced to beg; and their religious leaders were oppressing them instead of caring for them (Lk 20:47). Therefore, this loving action by the believers not only helped the poor, but, no doubt, also created opportunities for them to tell the Gospel to others. It's another new mission imperative. M. I. Ac 4:34: Christians should care for needy people, so that they can not only help them, but the public would also see their love for them, which could also create opportunities for them to tell them the Gospel. **3)** Luke does not indicate how long this group of believers continued to live in this way; therefore, it's impossible for us to know today whether this arrangement was useful to carry out their Level 1 mission beyond Jerusalem and in all of Judea to include all of Israel, or even beyond that to Levels 2 and 3. Thus, we cannot say with any degree of confidence that the Holy Spirit intended this to be a new mission imperative.

4:36-37 In verses 36-37, Luke introduced Barnabas as a man who demonstrated his love and faith in actions; therefore, his actions contrast sharply with Ananias and Sapphira in (5:1-11), since they sinned because they obviously loved money more than they loved the Lord Jesus (9:27; 11:22, 30; 13:2).

[1] M. I. Lk 3:8: Christians should always be prepared to boldly and publicly refute false teaching, so that Satan cannot easily deceive people.

[2] M. M. 2 Cor 4:4: Jesus is the Light of the world and the perfect image of God; and Christians have proclaimed this Gospel message to the lost world; however, Satan, the evil god of this world, has blinded the minds of their hearers so that they do not believe in Jesus.

[3] M. I. Lk 4:4: When Satan attacks Christians on their mission they should wield the sword of God's Word by quoting from it, and not depend on their own strength.

[4] M. I. Lk 11:10: Christians should <u>continuously</u> pray to their heavenly Father and *always* depend on his grace, and not on their own feeble strength, because he <u>always</u> loves them.

[5] M. M. Ac 13:46: As he did with the old Israel, God <u>first of all</u> strengthens the faith of the new Israel, the Church with his Word and Sacraments, so that they can go and witness to the lost people of all nations.

[6] M. I. Mt 28:19: Christians should go and proclaim God's Law and Gospel to all nations; then, baptize all who repent and believe after teaching them the meaning of holy Baptism.

[7] M. M. Gal 1:6: Jesus was the only person who was able to graciously earn God's favor by his perfect obedience; therefore, it is very foolish for anyone to reject God's gracious call to trust in Jesus, and believe the lie taught by false teachers that a person can earn God's favor by their own imperfect obedience.

[8] M. I. Ac 4:20: Christians should boldly witness to the name of Jesus and allow nothing to stop their witness because it is the Holy Spirit's own message.

[9] M. I. Lk 16:17: Christians should wield the sword of the Spirit with confidence as they go and tell the Gospel because his Word can never fail.

[10] M. I. Ro 1:16a: Christians should not be ashamed to proclaim the Gospel, even though it may appear to be weak and foolish; rather, they should be proud to proclaim it because it is the almighty power that the Holy Spirit uses to create faith in Jesus.

[11] M. M. Ro 3:26: God is just and fair to <u>everyone</u>, both when he condemns <u>all</u> people of all nations because all have sinned, and also when he <u>only</u> declares those people righteous who have faith in Jesus.

[12] M. I. Ac 3:6: Christians should heal a person's physical problem by speaking the <u>name</u> of Jesus, so that everyone knows that it was the divine power of Jesus that healed him.

[13] M. I. Ac 1:8: Christians should go and witness about Jesus to all who are lost from all languages and cultures by depending on the power of the Holy Spirit to help them bridge all of the language/cultural boundaries whether they are relatively easy, as in their own language, or extremely difficult.

[14] M. M. Jn 20:8: God gave faith in Jesus to people who personally saw that the tomb of Jesus was empty, because it proved that he was alive.

[15] M. I. Lk 11:10: Christians should <u>continuously</u> pray to their heavenly Father and <u>always</u> depend on his grace, and not on their own feeble strength, because he <u>always</u> loves them.

[16] M. M. Mt 5:14: When the Holy Spirit creates faith in a person's heart, he also graciously gives him a new mission-heart that is eager to shine the light of the Gospel throughout the whole world.

[17] M. I. Lk 11:10: Christians should <u>continuously</u> pray to their heavenly Father and <u>always</u> depend on his grace, and not on their own feeble strength, because he <u>always</u> loves them.

[18] M. M. Ro 12:2b: The Lord Jesus has <u>united</u> the Church into one Body in himself; and he has also given it many members who have <u>different</u> functions, so that they can be in mission to each other and to the unbelieving world.

[19] M. I. Ac 3:6: Christians should heal a person's physical problem by speaking the <u>name</u> of Jesus, so that everyone knows that it was the divine power of Jesus that healed him.

[20] M. I. Ac 4:20: Christians should boldly witness to the name of Jesus and allow nothing to stop their witness because it is the Holy Spirit's own message.

[21] M. M. Ac 2:24: Our Lord Jesus loosed the pangs of death for us mortal human beings when God raised him from the dead, because it was not possible for him to be held by death.

[22] M. M. Ro 1:16b: The Gospel is so powerful because it contains the central truth that Jesus rose from the dead with a glorified body in order to save all of his brothers and sisters from sin and death.

[23] M. M. Jn 20:8: God gave faith in Jesus to people who personally saw that the tomb of Jesus was empty, because it proved that he was alive.

[24] M. M. Ac 5:1: The Holy Spirit often uses personal relationships in order to strengthen the unity of the family of the Church.

Chapter 5

Ananias and Sapphira 5:1-11

5:1 *But a man named Ananias, with his wife Sapphira, sold a piece of property,*
5:2 *and with his wife's knowledge he kept back for himself some of the proceeds and brought only a part of it and laid it at the apostles' feet.*
5:3 *But Peter said, "Ananias, why has Satan filled your heart to lie to the Holy Spirit and to keep back for yourself part of the proceeds of the land?*
5:4 *While it remained unsold, did it not remain your own? And after it was sold, was it not at your disposal? Why is it that you have contrived this deed in your heart? You have not lied to men but to God."*
5:5 *When Ananias heard these words, he fell down and breathed his last. And great fear came upon all who heard of it.*
5:6 *The young men rose and wrapped him up and carried him out and buried him.*
5:7 *After an interval of about three hours his wife came in, not knowing what had happened.*
5:8 *And Peter said to her, "Tell me whether you sold the land for so much." And she said, "Yes, for so much."*
5:9 *But Peter said to her, "How is it that you have agreed together to test the Spirit of the Lord? Behold, the feet of those who have buried your husband are at the door, and they will carry you out."*
5:10 *Immediately she fell down at his feet and breathed her last. When the young men came in they found her dead, and they carried her out and buried her beside her husband.*
5:11 *And great fear came upon the whole church and upon all who heard of these things.*

5:1-11 (1) In this sad story in verses 1-11, Luke records Satan's second major attack on the very new mission of the Church. He was able to tempt this couple into committing two sins in this attack: the love of money and telling lies. If the Holy Spirit had not exposed their sins, other believers would have also been tempted to commit the same sins, which would have continued to divide the group. And Satan, of course, continues to use the same two weapons very effectively yet today in order to try to destroy the mission of the Church (^{1}M. M. Ac 4:28 & ^{2}M. I. Lk 4:4). **2)** It's very significant to compare this story in verses 1-11 with the Old Testament story of Achan in (Josh 7:1-26), because, in the case of Achan, the Holy Spirit likewise exposed these same two sins within a relatively small family. He used personal relationships by family groupings, in a culturally relevant way, in order to expose the sins of Achan *within* the physical and spiritual family of Israel, because Achan's sins had begun to destroy the unity of the family of Israel. And the sins of this couple in Acts had likewise begun to destroy the unity of the new spiritual family of the Church. Furthermore, these divisions were potentially so devastating for both families (Israel and the Church), since both families were small groups that were surrounded by much larger cultural groups that were threatening them. Therefore, both families urgently needed the support of each other in their families. And thus, we learn from both cases that, yet today, the Holy Spirit still uses Christians to build up the faith of their fellow Christians through their loving personal relationships. And of course, our personal relationships are complex physical and spiritual relationships, which he uses in many wonderful ways (Gal 6:10; Eph 2:19; 1 Pet 4:17). It's another new mission message. M. M. Ac 5:1: The Holy Spirit uses Christians to build up the faith of their fellow Christians in the family of the Church through their loving personal relationships that are both physical and spiritual. **2)** Yet today in many parts of the world, the unity of the family of the Church is still absolutely vital to the mission of the Church, because it is so vastly outnumbered in so many countries. Many societies in the world are "lineage kinship systems," which means that their entire lives, including their religions, are centered on their physical families. Therefore, for example, when the Holy Spirit uses the message of the Gospel in order to create repentance and faith in the heart of just one person in a family, the new Christian must either keep his new faith a secret from his entire physical family or boldly confess his faith in Jesus and become a lonely target of persecution from them. It's extremely frightening and dangerous; and he urgently needs the fellowship of the person or persons who told him about Jesus, who are his new family, the Church—if he has the courage to fellowship with or even worship with them ([3]M. M. Ac 4:20 & [4]Ac 5:1).

Many Signs and Wonders Done 5:12-16

5:12 *Now many signs and wonders were regularly done among the people by the hands of the apostles. And they were all together in Solomon's Portico.*
5:13 *None of the rest dared join them, but the people held them in high esteem.*
5:14 *And more than ever believers were added to the Lord, multitudes of both men and women,*
5:15 *so that they even carried out the sick into the streets and laid them on cots and mats, that as Peter came by at least his shadow might fall on some of them.*
5:16 *The people also gathered from the towns around Jerusalem, bringing the sick and those afflicted with unclean spirits, and they were all healed.*

5:12, 15-16 (1) The miracles that the Holy Spirit did through the apostles contributed to the mission in at least four ways: **a)** People saw that they were disciples of Jesus because they did the miracles in his name ([5]M. I. Ac 3:6). **b)** Many people were attracted to the family of the Church so that they also had the opportunity to hear the Gospel about Jesus ([6]M. I. Lk 4:15). **c)** The miracles also strengthened the apostles' faith in Jesus because he had promised them that he would give them this power (Lk 9:1; 10:19; Mk 16:17-18). **d)** And the miracles also obviously helped many needy people and showed the compassion of the apostles ([7]M. I. Lk 4:35).
5:13-14 Luke says in verse 13 that *"none of the rest [of the Jews living*

in Jerusalem] dared join them, but the people held them in high esteem;" however, he then adds in verse 14, *"And more than ever believers were added to the Lord, multitudes of both men and women."* Obviously, some people, who were merely curious or pretending to be interested, were afraid to join the new family of believers because of the dramatic deaths of Ananias and Sapphira. The issue, of course, was that the members of their highest religious court, the Council, were the most powerful people in their society, and they had already murdered the Lord Jesus, and then they next arrested Peter and John. And later, another group of Jews, who *"belonged to the synagogue of the Freedmen"* (6:9), also became so violently angry with Stephen, one of the leaders of the Church that they also murdered him (7:54-60). Since the small family of believers faced such powerful enemies, any break in the unity of this new family was a grave threat to the whole group. This, at least in part, explains why the Holy Spirit's judgment on this couple was so severe; a gentle rebuke would not have preserved the unity in the Church. Nevertheless, many people were so attracted by the healing miracles that the apostles were doing that their hearts were ready to hear the powerful Gospel that Jesus was indeed their Messiah and Savior ([8]M. I. Ac 4:34).

The Apostles Arrested and Freed 5:17-42

5:17 *But the high priest rose up, and all who were with him (that is, the party of the Sadducees), and filled with jealousy*
5:18 *they arrested the apostles and put them in the public prison.*
5:19 *But during the night an angel of the Lord opened the prison doors and brought them out, and said,*
5:20 *"Go and stand in the temple and speak to the people all the words of this Life."*
5:21 *And when they heard this, they entered the temple at daybreak and began to teach. Now when the high priest came, and those who were with him, they called together the council and all the senate of Israel and sent to the prison to have them brought.*
5:22 *But when the officers came, they did not find them in the prison,*

so they returned and reported,

5:23 *"We found the prison securely locked and the guards standing at the doors, but when we opened them we found no one inside."*

5:24 *Now when the captain of the temple and the chief priests heard these words, they were greatly perplexed about them, wondering what this would come to.*

5:25 *And someone came and told them, "Look! The men whom you put in prison are standing in the temple and teaching the people."*

5:26 *Then the captain with the officers went and brought them, but not by force, for they were afraid of being stoned by the people.*

5:27 *And when they had brought them, they set them before the council. And the high priest questioned them,*

5:28 *saying, "We strictly charged you not to teach in this name, yet here you have filled Jerusalem with your teaching, and you intend to bring this man's blood upon us."*

5:29 *But Peter and the apostles answered, "We must obey God rather than men.*

5:30 *The God of our fathers raised Jesus, whom you killed by hanging him on a tree.*

5:31 *God exalted him at his right hand as Leader and Savior, to give repentance to Israel and forgiveness of sins.*

5:32 *And we are witnesses to these things, and so is the Holy Spirit, whom God has given to those who obey him."*

5:33 *When they heard this, they were enraged and wanted to kill them.*

5:34 *But a Pharisee in the council named Gamaliel, a teacher of the Law held in honor by all the people, stood up and gave orders to put the men outside for a little while.*

5:35 *And he said to them, "Men of Israel, take care what you are about to do with these men.*

5:36 *For before these days Theudas rose up, claiming to be somebody, and a number of men, about four hundred, joined him. He was killed, and all who followed him were dispersed and came to nothing.*

5:37 *After him Judas the Galilean rose up in the days of the census*

> *and drew away some of the people after him. He too perished, and all who followed him were scattered.*
> 5:38 *So in the present case I tell you, keep away from these men and let them alone, for if this plan or this undertaking is of man, it will fail;*
> 5:39 *but if it is of God, you will not be able to overthrow them. You might even be found opposing God!" So they took his advice,*
> 5:40 *and when they had called in the apostles, they beat them and charged them not to speak in the name of Jesus, and let them go.*
> 5:41 *Then they left the presence of the council, rejoicing that they were counted worthy to suffer dishonor for the name.*
> 5:42 *And every day, in the temple and from house to house, they did not cease teaching and preaching Jesus as the Christ.*

5:17-18 Satan attacked the mission of the Church, once again, by continuing to use the evil members of the powerful Council of the Jews, who hated Jesus and his family, the Church, in order to try to stop the believers from proclaiming the Gospel. Part of the reason why they hated all believers was because they thought that they were starting a new religion and denying the Jewish faith of their ancestors. Their religion was, of course, everything that all Jews had always believed. However, the true message of the new family of believers was that they were, in reality, not leaving their old family of believers at all. Rather, the believers tried to demonstrate from their common Scriptures that their faith in Jesus was not a new religion at all, but rather the wonderful fulfillment of everything they all had long believed ([9]M. M. Lk 4:21 & [10]Jn 16:13). But the evil members of the Council would have none of it and refused to listen to them; and the devil was, of course, enjoying himself!

5:20-21 The angel did indeed free the apostles; however, he did not tell them to go into fearful hiding. On the contrary, he sent them out once again on their Level 1 mission to the Jews, specifically to those who were worshipping in the temple. He sent them there because the temple courtyard was an excellent venue for proclaiming the Gospel to pious

Jews. And he perhaps also sent them there because, by their worship in the temple, they were showing that they still faithfully believed everything that the Scriptures said about the Messiah—except that they believed that he had already come in the person of Jesus, of course (Lk 2:25-38; [11]M. I. Lk 4:15 & [12]Ac 2:4).

5:28 The apostles continued to be very bold and *"filled Jerusalem with their teaching"* (v 28), which certainly contained both the Law and the Gospel, since they were not afraid to condemn their religious leaders and to refute their lies. Likewise, the first time Peter had stood before this Council he also boldly proclaimed the Law as well as the Gospel (4:7-20); therefore, when the chief priest now said, *"You intend to bring this man's blood upon us"* (v 28), he was showing that the Law had struck home in his heart so that he now had a guilty conscience. Unfortunately however, Satan had possessed him and the other evil members of the Council so completely that the Gospel had no impact on any of them ([13]M. I. Lk 3:3a & [14]Lk 11:10).

5:29 Level 1 of the apostles' mission was, of course, very frightening because they faced bitter opposition from the Council. However, it was the Holy Spirit who convinced them of two things: **a)** that they were *"obey[ing] God"* (v 29) in their mission, and they were not merely following their own human plans and wishes; **b)** and that the Council was opposing, not just them, but *God* himself. Therefore, the Spirit inspired Peter and the apostles to boldly defy their religious leaders by saying in verse 29, *"We must obey God rather than men."* Their Lord Jesus had taught them in (Lk 20:25) to always obey those who are in authority over them ([15]M. M. Lk 20:25); however, this situation was different, because their religious leaders had ordered them to disobey their Lord's clear commands to go to all nations, in order to proclaim the Gospel ([16]M. I. Ac 1:8 & [17]Mt 28:19). Therefore, the apostles had to obey God and boldly defy their merely human religious leaders. It's a new mission imperative. M. I. Ac 5:29: Christians should always obey those who have authority over them, unless they order them to disobey God; then, they must obey God and not mere human beings.

5:38-40 Just as God had earlier used the chief priest Caiaphas to assure that the Council did not arrest Jesus prematurely (Jn 11:51), God, once again, demonstrated that he was in full control of his mission by using another member of the Council, Gamaliel to assure that the Council would *"keep away from these men and let them alone"* (v 38). The Council, once again, *"charged them not to speak in the name of Jesus,"* (v 40) even though they knew that this was their own human wish, and *not* God's will. The truth was, of course, that it was God who was once again using them to carry out his perfect plan, so that the apostles could continue Level 1 of their mission without their powerful opposition ([18]M. I. Ac 4:20 & [19]M. M. Ac 4:28).

5:41 Verse 41 raises two questions concerning the mission of the Church. **a)** Why did the majority of the Council hate the apostles? Jesus himself told the parable in (Lk 20:9-19) as a severe warning to these men. God had given these men the responsibility of leading God's mission to the world; therefore, they should have been the ones who were leading their people to follow their Messiah or the Name (v 41). Instead, Satan was controlling their hearts, so that they first of all hated the Name of Jesus and thereby they also hated the heavenly Father who had sent him and anyone who witnessed to his Name or healed someone in his Name (3:6; Lk 6:22-23; Jn 15:18-27). Nevertheless, the Council feared the people whom they should have been serving; and therefore, they reluctantly released the apostles; however, out of frustration that they couldn't have them killed, they had them flogged as severely as their Law allowed (v 40). **b)** And why did the apostles leave the Council *"rejoicing that they were counted worthy to suffer dishonor for the name"* (v 41)? These 12 men had, very recently, been eyewitnesses when their dear Lord suffered terrible pain and death on the cross; and they knew that he had graciously done it for them? His profound grace and love for them in that act had moved them deeply to gladly witness to his Name, and to cling to his Name alone in the midst of suffering (Rom 5:3). Furthermore, as they shared in his suffering and death, they knew that they would also surely share in his glorious resurrection (Rom 6:5; [20]M. M. Lk 6:22). Therefore, all believers are full of joy as we go on his mission and thereby gladly suffer for his glorious Name. It's a new mission imperative. M. I. Ac 5:41: Christians should consider it a great honor to be persecuted for proclaiming the name of Jesus.

5:42 Luke mentions two venues for proclaiming the Gospel in verse 42: *"in the temple and from house to house."* Clearly, the early Church often used the temple as a venue to proclaim the Gospel; however, this is the first of only two references in the book of Acts to this mission method of proclaiming the Gospel *"from house to house."* The other reference is in (20:20), where Paul reminded the elders of the church in Ephesus that he had been *"teaching you [them] in public and from house to house."* In both towns, the disciples took the mission <u>initiative</u> and went *"from house to house"* in order to witness to people where they lived ([21]M. I. Ac 1:8).

---

[1] M. M. Ac 4:28: The heavenly Father is always in full control of his mission to all nations of the world.

[2] M. I. Lk 4:4: When Satan attacks Christians on their mission they should wield the sword of God's Word by quoting from it, and not depend on their own strength.

[3] M. I. Ac 4:20: Christians should boldly witness to the name of Jesus and allow nothing to stop their witness because it is the Holy Spirit's own message.

[4] M. M. Ac 5:1: The Holy Spirit often uses personal relationships in order to strengthen the unity of the family of the Church.

[5] M. I. Ac 3:6: Christians should heal a person's physical problem by speaking the <u>name</u> of Jesus, so that everyone knows that it was the divine power of Jesus that healed him.

[6] M. I. Lk 4:15: Christians should seize <u>every</u> opportunity to proclaim the Gospel to lost people of all nations.

[7] M. I. Lk 4:35a: Christians should view every person as a whole person, and show him compassion by caring for <u>both</u> his physical and spiritual needs as they go on their mission.

[8] M. I. Ac 4:34: Christians should care for needy people, so that they can not only help them, but the public would also see their love for them, which could also create opportunities for them to tell them the Gospel.

[9] M. M. Lk 4:21: <u>Every</u> verse in the entire Bible points in some way to Jesus and his mission to seek and save the lost.

[10] M. M. Jn 16:13: The Holy Spirit came on Pentecost Day in order to teach all Christians <u>all</u> of the truth about God by reading and studying his holy Word, the Bible.

[11] M. I. Lk 4:15: Christians should seize <u>every</u> opportunity to proclaim the Gospel to lost people of all nations.

[12] M. I. Ac 2:4: In cross-cultural situations, Christians should always focus on all of the needs of the target group by learning *their* heart-language and culture as deeply as possible, so that they can tell them the Gospel clearly in their own language and also help them with the true needs of their society.

[13] M. I. Lk 3:3a: Christians should, in love, warn lost people who do not repent.

[14] M. I. Lk 11:10: Christians should <u>continuously</u> pray to their heavenly Father and <u>always</u> depend on his grace, and not on their own feeble strength, because he <u>always</u> loves them.

[15] M. M. Lk 20:25: God establishes all secular governments, so that everyone lives under a secular authority; and God also places all Christians under his own gracious authority in his eternal kingdom; therefore, all Christians should gladly give everything that they owe to both rulers.

[16] M. I. Ac 1:8: Christians should go and witness about Jesus to all who are lost from all languages and cultures by depending on the power of the Holy Spirit to help them bridge all of the language/cultural boundaries whether they are relatively easy, as in their own language, or extremely difficult.

[17] M. I. Mt 28:19: Christians should go and proclaim God's Law and Gospel to all nations; then, baptize all who repent and believe after teaching them the meaning of holy Baptism.

[18] M. I. Ac 4:20: Christians should boldly witness to the name of Jesus and allow nothing to stop their witness because it is the Holy Spirit's own message.

[19] M. M. Ac 4:28: The heavenly Father is always in full control of his mission to all nations of the world.

[20] M. M. Lk 6:22: The Lord Jesus will surely bless a Christian in the midst of suffering for his sake; and he will also bless him with eternal life if he remains faithful to him.

[21] M. I. Ac 1:8: Christians should go and witness about Jesus to all who are lost from all languages and cultures by depending on the power of the Holy Spirit to help them bridge all of the language/cultural boundaries whether they are relatively easy, as in their own language, or extremely difficult.

Chapter 6

Seven Chosen to Serve 6:1-7

6:1 *Now in these days when the disciples were increasing in number, a complaint by the Hellenists arose against the Hebrews because their widows were being neglected in the daily distribution.*

6:2 *And the twelve summoned the full number of the disciples and said, "It is not right that we should give up preaching the word of God to serve tables.*

6:3 *Therefore, brothers, pick out from among you seven men of good repute, full of the Spirit and of wisdom, whom we will appoint to this duty.*

6:4 *But we will devote ourselves to prayer and to the ministry of the word."*

6:5 *And what they said pleased the whole gathering, and they chose Stephen, a man full of faith and of the Holy Spirit, and Philip, and Prochorus, and Nicanor, and Timon, and Parmenas, and Nicolaus, a proselyte of Antioch.*

6:6 *These they set before the apostles, and they prayed and laid their hands on them.*

6:7 *And the word of God continued to increase, and the number of the disciples multiplied greatly in Jerusalem, and a great many of the priests became obedient to the faith.*

6:1 In Satan's third attack on the young mission of the Church, he used the sin of racial prejudice to try to slow down the main work of the mission and to divide the Church. He attacked two aspects of the mission: **1)** Most importantly, he attacked the main work of proclaiming the Gospel. He knew that, once the believers had proclaimed it, the Holy Spirit would begin to wield the mighty sword of his holy Word; and he could do nothing against his vastly superior power (Eph 6:17). The sin of racial prejudice had begun to hinder the work of *"preaching the word of God"* (v 2) because the apostles were spending part of their time dealing with the problem of food distribution and not nurturing the spiritual needs of the widows and others full time ([1]M. M. Ac 13:46). The work of *"preaching the word of God"* was the most important work, because the Holy Spirit has graciously chosen to only care for spiritual needs through his means of grace, through his holy Word and Sacraments. Thus, the Holy Spirit moved the apostles to begin to apply a new mission imperative. M. I. Ac 6:1: Christians should always remember that the main aspect of the mission is to proclaim the Law and Gospel message and should not allow any other aspect of the work to hinder this main work. **2)** Secondly, Satan also used this sin of racial prejudice to attack the unity of the group of believers in Jerusalem. Verse 1 says that there were two main groups among the believers who were labeling each other, *"the Hebrews,"* that is Hebrew/Aramaic-speaking Jews and *"Hellenists,"* that is Greek-speaking Jews. It is not at all surprising to learn that there were a significant number of "foreigners" living in a big, capital city like Jerusalem. And some of these foreigners were Hellenistic Jews, who had been born in foreign countries and had moved back to Israel; hence, they may have understood very little Hebrew or Aramaic, and they had likewise adopted many "strange, foreign" customs. And Satan always very easily uses misunderstanding and miscommunication for his evil purposes. Who was "right" or "wrong" in this dispute didn't really matter; what mattered was that the sin of racial prejudice had destroyed the unity of the group. The language/culture issues had led them to focus on what divided them and to forget about the much more important things that they still shared: **a)** especially their common love for their Lord Jesus, **b)** the Old Testament that they all shared, **c)** and God's promises in Scripture that Jesus had fulfilled for all of them. Once again, they had to depend on the guidance of the Holy Spirit in order to find a solution to the problem of disunity, as they had in the tragic case of Ananias and Sapphira (5:1-11; [2]M. I. Ac 6:1 & [3]Ac 15:2).

6:2-6 (1) The Holy Spirit led the apostles to solve the two problems of neglecting the main work of proclaiming the Gospel and of the lack of unity by advising the group to do three things: **a)** First of all, note that it was not the apostles who chose the seven men; rather they advised them that *"the whole gathering"* should choose them (v 5); and then the apostles *"prayed and laid their hands on them"* (v 6), in order to commission them to serve ([4]M. I. Lk 6:13). If the apostles had "hand-picked" them, the group could have easily accused the seven men of serving the apostles instead of serving the whole group. It's another important mission imperative. M. I. Ac 6:3: The local group of Christians should choose men who will lead them; and then those in authority should publicly commission them before they begin their work. **b)** Secondly, the apostles advised the group to *"pick out from among you seven men of good repute, full of the Spirit and of wisdom"* (v 3). They recognized that this problem of racial prejudice required more than mere human wisdom to overcome it; it required the wisdom of the Holy Spirit. Cross-cultural problems can be especially complicated because, as noted above, the devil loves to use miscommunication, since it often does two things: It creates mistrust and disunity; and it causes emotions to run high, which causes even more confusion ([5]M. I. Ac 2:4). **c)** Thirdly, it's very significant that seven men that the group chose were all Gentiles. Note in the list in verse 5 that all seven men had Greek names. And one of them, Nicolaus was *"a proselyte"* (v 5), which means that he had converted to Judaism before he became a believer. They chose Gentiles to deal with the complaints of the Greek-speaking widows since they knew their language and culture; and equally important, they also knew the language and culture of the Jews who spoke Hebrew and Aramaic. They were perfectly suited to bridge the gaps of misunderstanding and bias. It's a new mission imperative. M. I. Ac 6:5: Christians should choose spiritually wise leaders who know the language and culture of both the target language group and the source language group to deal with cross-cultural problems. **2)** Secondly, we see in Luke's account after verse 6 that he says nothing more about this type of work. Even though this food distribution must have been quite a large operation and helped many people, Luke continues to place the most emphasis on the main work of proclaiming the Gospel. Instead, Luke does record that two of the seven men, Stephen and Philip also served as missionaries of the Gospel. Stephen became a powerful public speaker and the first martyr of the

Church (v 8-7:60); and Philip was the first person whom the Holy Spirit later sent on a mission trip to witness to a Gentile proselyte (8:5-7; 21:8). **3)** Obviously, this first cross-cultural problem in the young Church was relatively easy to overcome, since they were still mainly witnessing on Level 1 in Jerusalem and Judea. However, as they went on the remaining two levels of the mission, the language and cultural distances obviously increased more and more, and would have, of course, created more and more difficult cross-cultural problems. Therefore, the Holy Spirit had wisely begun to guide the Church in how to, first of all, resolve this relatively easier problem in Jerusalem by beginning to choose more leaders who were spiritually wise ([6]M. I. Ac 6:5 & Lk 6:13).

6:7 (1) The fact that Luke makes the specific point in verse 7 that *"a great many of the priests became obedient to the faith"* raises a significant issue about what life-changing decision this would have been for them, since he is silent about whether they continued to serve in the temple or not. It, of course, had been their families' entire livelihood. And now, the apostles and Stephen must have been proclaiming the truth that when the curtain in the temple tore at the crucifixion (v 11; Mt 27:51), it proved that their sacrifices were no longer needed. They now believed that Jesus was, indeed, their Messiah, and that his one holy sacrifice on the cross had fulfilled all of these sacrifices. Their unbelieving colleagues certainly continued to perform their daily sacrifices, but if they boldly put their new faith into action, they would have to find a new livelihood. What a life-changing decision! And whatever they decided to do about that, they also had to learn to depend on the new spiritual food of their Lord's holy Word and Sacraments ([7]M. I. Lk 12:40 & [8]M. M. Ro 1:16b). **2)** Nevertheless, since these priests had actually performed sacrifices many times, and not just observed them, they brought a unique perspective to the witness of the new mission of the Church. They understood very deeply what it means that Jesus' one, perfect sacrifice had fulfilled and replaced all of the Old Testament sacrifices. Therefore, when they witnessed to their fellow Jews, and especially to their fellow priests about Jesus' holy sacrifice it must have made a unique and powerful impression on them ([9]M. M. Ac

13:46).

Stephen is Seized 6:8-15

6:8   *And Stephen, full of grace and power, was doing great wonders and signs among the people.*
6:9   *Then some of those who belonged to the synagogue of the Freedmen (as it was called), and of the Cyrenians, and of the Alexandrians, and of those from Cilicia and Asia, rose up and disputed with Stephen.*
6:10 *But they could not withstand the wisdom and the Spirit with which he was speaking.*
6:11 *Then they secretly instigated men who said, "We have heard him speak blasphemous words against Moses and God."*
6:12 *And they stirred up the people and the elders and the scribes, and they came upon him and seized him and brought him before the council,*
6:13 *and they set up false witnesses who said, "This man never ceases to speak words against this holy place and the Law,*
6:14 *for we have heard him say that this Jesus of Nazareth will destroy this place and will change the customs that Moses delivered to us."*
6:15 *And gazing at him, all who sat in the council saw that his face was like the face of an angel.*

6:8-15 (1) Satan once again showed his extremely crafty and evil nature in order to attack two important aspects of the Church's mission, by *"secretly instigate[ing] men"* (v 11) to tell lies about what Stephen was proclaiming. **a)** His main attack was against the proclamation of God's Word, since he knows that the Holy Spirit only uses his mighty Word to create faith ([10]M. M. Ro 10:17a). In addition to helping with the food distribution, Stephen was so filled with the Holy Spirit that he was also *"doing great wonders and signs"* (v 8), which attracted crowds, so that he could proclaim the Gospel ([11]M. I. Lk 4:15 & [12]Ro 1:16a). **b)** Secondly, he attacked the truth itself about Jesus that Stephen was proclaiming, which shows the importance of publicly refuting Satan's lies ([13]M. I. Lk 3:8). In this way, Stephen was brought before the Jewish Council (v 12). This was, of course, the same tactic that Satan had used successfully against Jesus before the same evil men in the Council. And now, just like at Jesus' trial, the Council murdered Stephen's <u>physical</u> body (7:58, Lk 23:24), but they could not touch his soul, nor could they silence the proclamation of the Gospel. Verse 10 says that *"they could not withstand the wisdom and the Spirit with which he was speaking"* ([14]M. I. Lk 11:10 & [15]Ac 5:41). **2)** The fact that *"all who sat in the council saw that his face was like the face of an angel"* (v 15) should have been a warning to them that Stephen was full of the Holy Spirit and that they were obviously serving Satan. But their hearts were still so evil and hard that it apparently meant nothing to them. Furthermore, this was another fulfillment of Jesus' promise in (Lk 21:15), *"I will give you a mouth and wisdom, which none of your adversaries will be able to withstand or contradict"* ([16]M. I. Lk 12:12).

---

[1] M. M. Ac 13:46: As he did with the old Israel, God <u>first of all</u> strengthens the faith of the new Israel, the Church with his Word and Sacraments, so that they can go and witness to the lost people of all nations.

[2] M. I. Ac 6:1: Christians should always remember that the main aspect of the mission is to proclaim the Law and Gospel message and should not allow any other aspect of the work to hinder this main work.

[3] M. I. Ac 15:2: For the sake of unity in the Church, Christians should act as one unit in order to settle internal disputes, and not allow small groups to act on their own.

[4] M. I. Lk 6:13: Christians should choose new leaders and train them in order to multiply the work.

[5] M. I. Ac 2:4: In cross-cultural situations, Christians should always focus on all of the needs of the target group by learning <u>their</u> heart-language and culture as deeply as possible, so that they can tell them the Gospel clearly in their own language and also help them with the true needs of their society.

[6] M. I. Ac 6:5: Christians should choose spiritually wise leaders who know the language and culture of both the target language group and the source language group to deal with cross-cultural problems.

[7] M. I. Lk 12:40: Christians should "eat" God's Word every day in order to keep their faith strong, so that they are always ready for their Lord's return.

[8] M. M. Ro 1:16b: The Gospel is so powerful because it contains the central truth that Jesus rose

from the dead with a glorified body in order to save all of his brothers and sisters from sin and death.

⁹ M. M. Ac 13:46: As he did with the old Israel, God first of all strengthens the faith of the new Israel, the Church with his Word and Sacraments, so that they can go and witness to the lost people of all nations.

¹⁰ M. M. Ro 10:17a: The Holy Spirit only creates and preserves faith by using the message of God's grace in his holy Word.

¹¹ M. I. Lk 4:15: Christians should seize every opportunity to proclaim the Gospel to lost people of all nations.

¹² M. I. Ro 1:16a: Christians should not be ashamed to proclaim the Gospel, even though it may appear to be weak and foolish; rather, they should be proud to proclaim it because it is the almighty power that the Holy Spirit uses to create faith in Jesus.

¹³ M. I. Lk 3:8: Christians should always be prepared to boldly and publicly refute false teaching, so that Satan cannot easily deceive people.

¹⁴ M. I. Lk 11:10: Christians should continuously pray to their heavenly Father and always depend on his grace, and not on their own feeble strength, because he always loves them.

¹⁵ M. I. Ac 5:41: Christians should consider it a great honor to be persecuted for proclaiming the name of Jesus.

¹⁶ M. I. Lk 12:12: Christians should go and tell the Gospel depending on the Holy Spirit to teach them what they should say.

Chapter 7

Stephen's Speech 7:1-53

7:1   And the high priest said, "Are these things so?"
7:2   And Stephen said: "Brothers and fathers, hear me. The God of glory appeared to our father Abraham when he was in Mesopotamia, before he lived in Haran,
7:3   and said to him, 'Go out from your land and from your kindred and go into the land that I will show you.'
7:4   Then he went out from the land of the Chaldeans and lived in Haran. And after his father died, God removed him from there into this land in which you are now living.
7:5   Yet he gave him no inheritance in it, not even a foot's length, but promised to give it to him as a possession and to his offspring after him, though he had no child.
7:6   And God spoke to this effect--that his offspring would be sojourners in a land belonging to others, who would enslave them and afflict them four hundred years.
7:7   'But I will judge the nation that they serve,' said God, 'and after that they shall come out and worship me in this place.'
7:8   And he gave him the covenant of circumcision. And so Abraham became the father of Isaac, and circumcised him on the eighth day, and Isaac became the father of Jacob, and Jacob of the twelve patriarchs.
7:9   "And the patriarchs, jealous of Joseph, sold him into Egypt; but God was with him
7:10 and rescued him out of all his afflictions and gave him favor and wisdom before Pharaoh, king of Egypt, who made him ruler over Egypt and over all his household.
7:11 Now there came a famine throughout all Egypt and Canaan, and great affliction, and our fathers could find no food.
7:12 But when Jacob heard that there was grain in Egypt, he sent out our fathers on their first visit.
7:13 And on the second visit Joseph made himself known to his

brothers, and Joseph's family became known to Pharaoh.
7:14 *And Joseph sent and summoned Jacob his father and all his kindred, seventy-five persons in all.*
7:15 *And Jacob went down into Egypt, and he died, he and our fathers,*
7:16 *and they were carried back to Shechem and laid in the tomb that Abraham had bought for a sum of silver from the sons of Hamor in Shechem.*
7:17 *"But as the time of the promise drew near, which God had granted to Abraham, the people increased and multiplied in Egypt*
7:18 *until there arose over Egypt another king who did not know Joseph.*
7:19 *He dealt shrewdly with our race and forced our fathers to expose their infants, so that they would not be kept alive.*
7:20 *At this time Moses was born; and he was beautiful in God's sight. And he was brought up for three months in his father's house,*
7:21 *and when he was exposed, Pharaoh's daughter adopted him and brought him up as her own son.*
7:22 *And Moses was instructed in all the wisdom of the Egyptians, and he was mighty in his words and deeds.*
7:23 *"When he was forty years old, it came into his heart to visit his brothers, the children of Israel.*
7:24 *And seeing one of them being wronged, he defended the oppressed man and avenged him by striking down the Egyptian.*
7:25 *He supposed that his brothers would understand that God was giving them salvation by his hand, but they did not understand.*
7:26 *And on the following day he appeared to them as they were quarreling and tried to reconcile them, saying, 'Men, you are brothers. Why do you wrong each other?'*
7:27 *But the man who was wronging his neighbor thrust him aside, saying, 'Who made you a ruler and a judge over us?*
7:28 *Do you want to kill me as you killed the Egyptian yesterday?'*
7:29 *At this retort Moses fled and became an exile in the land of Midian, where he became the father of two sons.*

7:30 "Now when forty years had passed, an angel appeared to him in the wilderness of Mount Sinai, in a flame of fire in a bush.

7:31 When Moses saw it, he was amazed at the sight, and as he drew near to look, there came the voice of the Lord:

7:32 'I am the God of your fathers, the God of Abraham and of Isaac and of Jacob.' And Moses trembled and did not dare to look.

7:33 Then the Lord said to him, 'Take off the sandals from your feet, for the place where you are standing is holy ground.

7:34 I have surely seen the affliction of my people who are in Egypt, and have heard their groaning, and I have come down to deliver them. And now come, I will send you to Egypt.'

7:35 "This Moses, whom they rejected, saying, 'Who made you a ruler and a judge?'--this man God sent as both ruler and redeemer by the hand of the angel who appeared to him in the bush.

7:36 This man led them out, performing wonders and signs in Egypt and at the Red Sea and in the wilderness for forty years.

7:37 This is the Moses who said to the Israelites, 'God will raise up for you a prophet like me from your brothers.'

7:38 This is the one who was in the congregation in the wilderness with the angel who spoke to him at Mount Sinai, and with our fathers. He received living oracles to give to us.

7:39 Our fathers refused to obey him, but thrust him aside, and in their hearts they turned to Egypt,

7:40 saying to Aaron, 'Make for us gods who will go before us. As for this Moses who led us out from the land of Egypt, we do not know what has become of him.'

7:41 And they made a calf in those days, and offered a sacrifice to the idol and were rejoicing in the works of their hands.

7:42 But God turned away and gave them over to worship the host of heaven, as it is written in the book of the prophets: "'Did you bring to me slain beasts and sacrifices, during the forty years in the wilderness, O house of Israel?

7:43 You took up the tent of Moloch and the star of your god Rephan, the images that you made to worship; and I will send you into exile beyond Babylon.'

7:44 *"Our fathers had the tent of witness in the wilderness, just as he who spoke to Moses directed him to make it, according to the pattern that he had seen.*

7:45 *Our fathers in turn brought it in with Joshua when they dispossessed the nations that God drove out before our fathers. So it was until the days of David,*

7:46 *who found favor in the sight of God and asked to find a dwelling place for the God of Jacob.*

7:47 *But it was Solomon who built a house for him.*

7:48 *Yet the Most High does not dwell in houses made by hands, as the prophet says,*

7:49 *"'Heaven is my throne, and the earth is my footstool. What kind of house will you build for me, says the Lord, or what is the place of my rest?*

7:50 *Did not my hand make all these things?'*

7:51 *"You stiff-necked people, uncircumcised in heart and ears, you always resist the Holy Spirit. As your fathers did, so do you.*

7:52 *Which of the prophets did not your fathers persecute? And they killed those who announced beforehand the coming of the Righteous One, whom you have now betrayed and murdered,*

7:53 *you who received the Law as delivered by angels and did not keep it."*

7:1-43 From one point of view it may be surprising that Stephen spent so much time describing the history of the nation of Israel to men who themselves knew every single detail. **1)** However, two main points soon become clear in his message: **a)** He was, in fact, making a strong point that it was God, and not Abraham or any of the other patriarchs, who had planned all of these details. His gracious mission-heart had compelled him, from before the creation of the world, to very carefully plan how he was going to rescue sinful mankind, even before Adam and Eve sinned ([1]M. M. Ac 13:46). **b)** And secondly, it was *God* who was in full control of history and carrying out his most gracious plan of salvation through the nation of Israel ([2]M. M. Ac 4:28). Everything that he planned and carried out had to be as it was, so that his beloved Son could be born as true man and true God—a son of Abraham and a son of King David in order to offer his holy sacrifice for all of mankind (^{3}M. I. Lk 1:27). **2)** Furthermore, it was God who had given these same men the responsibility to help carry out the most important details of his plan, because they were the current religious leaders of the Jews (Lk 20:9). Unfortunately however, because Satan possessed their hearts, God was forced to use them to carry it out in a negative way. Therefore, Stephen very boldly warned them to repent two times: **a)** First of all, he told them in verse 37, *"This is the Moses who said to the Israelites, 'God will raise up for you a prophet like me from your brothers.'"* It must have been especially galling to these men to hear Stephen boldly tell them that Moses himself also pointed to Jesus as the Messiah. They very proudly thought that they had studied Moses more thoroughly than any other Jews. But Stephen used their own Scriptures to lovingly but boldly condemn them (^{4}M. I. Lk 3:3a). **b)** Secondly, Stephen also warned them that it was not a mere man whom they had just *"betrayed and murdered"* (v 52); he was none other than Jesus, *"the Righteous One"* (v 52). God's mission-heart had graciously chosen this very God/man to offer as a sacrifice for them and for all mankind (^{5}M. M. Ro 8:29b). But their wicked hearts were harder than stone and totally incapable of receiving God's gift of repentance (Lk 20:15; M. I. Lk 3:3a).

7:44, 48-49 In verses 44, 48-49, Stephen continued to use their own Scripture to warn the Jewish Council that their responsibility as spiritual leaders of Israel was to lead their people away from worship in the temporary temple in Jerusalem to the eternal temple in heaven. Jesus' one, holy sacrifice had made the sacrifices that were offered there obsolete, because it had fulfilled the purpose of that temporary building. Stephen used three verses of Scripture: **a)** First of all, Stephen deliberately did not use the word temple in verse 44; rather he used the word *"the tent of witness in the wilderness"* to refer to the mobile tent where the priests served God in the desert because obviously a tent is temporary. **b)** Secondly, he quoted King Solomon in verse 48 by saying that *"the Most High does not dwell in houses made by hands."* **c)** And he then quoted the prophet Isaiah in verse 49, *"Heaven is my throne, and the earth is my footstool. What kind of house will you build for me?"*

Stephen was emphasizing that both the tent of witness and the temple in Jerusalem temporarily focused the worship of Israel on a physical building. However, Jesus, our great High Priest, ended the need for all other sacrifices by offering his own holy sacrifice in the eternal temple in heaven (Heb 9:1-10; [6]M. M. Heb 8:1 & [7]Heb 9:12).

7:52 However, Stephen's boldest warning is in verse 52: *"Which of the prophets did your fathers not persecute? And they killed those who announced beforehand the coming of the Righteous One, whom you have now betrayed and murdered..."* He very boldly accused them of betraying and <u>murdering</u> God's holy prophet, Jesus. He was echoing God's own warning to them, because at the moment that Jesus died, God tore open the curtain in the temple from the top down (Lk 23:45; Mt 27:51). They should have pondered deeply what that meant; however, their evil minds were not able to comprehend why God did that any more than they could understand Stephen's warning. However, it was, no doubt, this bold warning and then Stephen's vision of heaven (v 56) that made them so angry that they also *murdered* him (58-59; [8]M. I. Lk 11:10 & [9]Lk 4:4).

The Stoning of Stephen 7:54-60

7:54 *Now when they heard these things they were enraged, and they ground their teeth at him.*
7:55 *But he, full of the Holy Spirit, gazed into heaven and saw the glory of God, and Jesus standing at the right hand of God.*
7:56 *And he said, "Behold, I see the heavens opened, and the Son of Man standing at the right hand of God."*
7:57 *But they cried out with a loud voice and stopped their ears and rushed together at him.*
7:58 *Then they cast him out of the city and stoned him. And the witnesses laid down their garments at the feet of a young man named Saul.*
7:59 *And as they were stoning Stephen, he called out, "Lord Jesus, receive my spirit."*
7:60 *And falling to his knees he cried out with a loud voice, "Lord,*

do not hold this sin against them." And when he had said this, he fell asleep.

7:56, 60 Stephen was equally bold in proclaiming the Gospel about Jesus as he was bold in proclaiming the Law. He especially witnessed to Jesus' death and resurrection and his eternal glory in verse 56, *"Behold, I see the heavens opened, and the Son of Man standing at the right hand of God."* Then, in verse 60 Luke says, *"And falling to his knees he cried out with a loud voice, 'Lord, do not hold this sin against them.'"* With his last breath, Stephen tried one last time to penetrate the hard hearts of his murderers, but it too fell on deaf ears ([10]M. I. Ac 4:20 & [11]M. M. Ac 2:24).

7:58, 8:1 Luke first mentions Saul in verse 58, because he was participating in the murder of Stephen. He says that *"the witnesses laid down their garments at the feet of a young man named Saul."* This was, of course, the missionary to the Gentiles who was later named Paul. Even though Saul was probably not a member of the Council, (although some scholars do suggest that he was a member), he obviously was not only present as an observer but he also zealously supported their actions. And then, when Saul saw that the murder of Stephen did not cause any open opposition from the public, he must have volunteered to take further action by persecuting and attempting to completely wipe out this new group, the Church because he thought that it was heretical. And it was these evil actions against the Church that, of course, later made Saul feel that he was the worst of sinners and completely unworthy of his Lord's call to serve him as a missionary to the Gentiles (1 Tim 1:15; [12]M. M. 1 Cor 15:10).

---

[1] M. M. Ac 13:46: As he did with the old Israel, God first of all strengthens the faith of the new Israel, the Church with his Word and Sacraments, so that they can go and witness to the lost people of all nations.

[2] M. M. Ac 4:28: The heavenly Father is always in full control of his mission to all nations of the world.

[3] M. M. Lk 1:27: Jesus had to be born as a true human being and as a true Jew in order to become the King of kings in his heavenly kingdom forever.

⁴ M. I. Lk 3:3a: Christians should, in love, warn lost people who do not repent.

⁵ M. M. Ro 8:29b: Because God knew before he created the world that the people he would make in his perfect image would soon sin and tarnish his image, he therefore, already had a gracious predestination <u>plan</u> to send his Son Jesus to rescue them from sin, so that he could <u>recreate</u> the people he had chosen back into his perfect <u>image</u>.

⁶ M. M. Heb 8:1: As our Royal High Priest, Jesus sits at the right hand of the throne in the <u>heavenly</u> temple ruling over and praying for his mission on earth.

⁷ M. M. Heb 9:12: As the great High Priest, Jesus offered his <u>human</u> and <u>divine</u> blood as the one perfect sacrifice for <u>all</u> of the sins of <u>all</u> of his brothers and sisters.

⁸ M. I. Lk 11:10: Christians should <u>continuously</u> pray to their heavenly Father and <u>always</u> depend on his grace, and not on their own feeble strength, because he <u>always</u> loves them.

⁹ M. I. Lk 4:4: When Satan attacks Christians on their mission they should wield the sword of God's Word by quoting from it, and not depend on their own strength.

¹⁰ M. I. Ac 4:20: Christians should boldly witness to the name of Jesus and allow nothing to stop their witness because it is the Holy Spirit's own message.

¹¹ M. M. Ac 2:24: Our Lord Jesus loosed the pangs of death for us mortal human beings when God raised him from the dead, because it was not possible for him to be held by death.

¹² M. M. 1 Cor 15:10: God has graciously made every Christian to be who he is, and he is therefore unworthy of God's call to proclaim the Gospel; therefore all Christians should depend completely on God's rich grace to work hard as his missionary to all nations.

Chapter 8

Saul Ravages the Church 8:1-3

8:1   *And Saul approved of his execution. And there arose on that day a great persecution against the church in Jerusalem, and they were all scattered throughout the regions of Judea and Samaria, except the apostles.*

8:2   *Devout men buried Stephen and made great lamentation over him.*

8:3   *But Saul was ravaging the church, and entering house after house, he dragged off men and women and committed them to prison.*

8:1, 4 The fact that *"there arose on that day a great persecution against the church in Jerusalem"* (v 1) would, no doubt, have made some people afraid to join the group of believers. Nevertheless, it was still *God* who was in control, since this persecution actually had the opposite effect from what Satan and these mere men had intended ([1]M. M. Ac 4:28). Luke continues in verse 1, *"and they were all scattered throughout the regions of Judea and Samaria."* It was like trying to stomp out a fire; instead of putting it out, you scatter it, because they went out proclaiming the Gospel with mission-hearts on fire. Luke adds in verse 4, *"now those who were scattered went about preaching the word."* The Holy Spirit forced them to leave their homes and *go* out of their "comfort zone" on Level 1 in Jerusalem to begin to expand the mission on Level 2 in *"Samaria"* (vs 1, 5). And then, (11:19) says that *"those who were scattered because of the persecution...traveled as far as Phoenicia and Cyprus and Antioch"* on Level 3 ([2]M. I. Ro 5:3a, b & [3]M. M. Lk 6:22).

8:1 Note that Luke continues in verse 1 by saying, *"except the apostles."* However, there is no indication in Luke's account why it was only the apostles who stayed in Jerusalem. But we do know that the Holy Spirit was, of course, in full control of his mission, and he certainly had very good reasons for keeping them in Jerusalem (vs 1, 14; [4]M. M. Ac 4:28).

Philip Proclaims Christ in Samaria 8:4-8

8:4 *Now those who were scattered went about preaching the word.*
8:5 *Philip went down to the city of Samaria and proclaimed to them the Christ.*
8:6 *And the crowds with one accord paid attention to what was being said by Philip when they heard him and saw the signs that he did.*
8:7 *For unclean spirits came out of many who were possessed, crying with a loud voice, and many who were paralyzed or lame were healed.*
8:8 *So there was much joy in that city.*

8:4-8 (1) One of the believers who fled from Jerusalem because of the persecution was Philip (v 4). This Philip was one of the seven men whom the believers in Jerusalem had chosen to oversee the food distribution (6:5; 21:8); he was not one of the apostles (v 1). Furthermore, much like Stephen, the Holy Spirit also chose him to be his missionary on two different occasions: to Samaria on Level 2 of the mission; and there Philip *"proclaimed to them the Christ"* (v 5). Later, he also sent him on Level 3 of the mission to witness to a Gentile, an Ethiopian eunuch (vs 26-40). Philip, therefore, was the first missionary to the Samaritans that Luke recorded. **2)** Also note that Philip performed healing miracles in Jesus' name (v 6), which attracted people's attention so that they heard the Gospel about Jesus their Messiah ([5]M. I. Ac 3:6).

Simon the Magician Believes 8:9-25

8:9 *But there was a man named Simon, who had previously practiced magic in the city and amazed the people of Samaria, saying that he himself was somebody great.*

8:10 *They all paid attention to him, from the least to the greatest, saying, "This man is the power of God that is called Great."*
8:11 *And they paid attention to him because for a long time he had amazed them with his magic.*
8:12 *But when they believed Philip as he preached good news about the kingdom of God and the name of Jesus Christ, they were baptized, both men and women.*
8:13 *Even Simon himself believed, and after being baptized he continued with Philip. And seeing signs and great miracles performed, he was amazed.*
8:14 *Now when the apostles at Jerusalem heard that Samaria had received the word of God, they sent to them Peter and John,*
8:15 *who came down and prayed for them that they might receive the Holy Spirit,*
8:16 *for he had not yet fallen on any of them, but they had only been baptized in the name of the Lord Jesus.*
8:17 *Then they laid their hands on them and they received the Holy Spirit.*
8:18 *Now when Simon saw that the Spirit was given through the laying on of the apostles' hands, he offered them money,*
8:19 *saying, "Give me this power also, so that anyone on whom I lay my hands may receive the Holy Spirit."*
8:20 *But Peter said to him, "May your silver perish with you, because you thought you could obtain the gift of God with money!*
8:21 *You have neither part nor lot in this matter, for your heart is not right before God.*
8:22 *Repent, therefore, of this wickedness of yours, and pray to the Lord that, if possible, the intent of your heart may be forgiven you.*
8:23 *For I see that you are in the gall of bitterness and in the bond of iniquity."*
8:24 *And Simon answered, "Pray for me to the Lord, that nothing of what you have said may come upon me."*
8:25 *Now when they had testified and spoken the word of the Lord, they returned to Jerusalem, preaching the Gospel to many*

villages of the Samaritans.

8:9-13 (1) The difference between the miracles that Philip performed and Simon's magic would have been obvious since Philip used them to point people to <u>Jesus</u> (v 12), but Simon, in sinful pride, used Satan's power to do them in order to point to <u>himself</u> (v 9). This illustrates a new mission imperative. M. I. Ac 8:12: Christians should <u>only</u> use miracles of healing in order to point to Jesus, and beware of people who use Satan's power to do miracles in order to point to themselves. **2)** However, it, of course, was not these miracles, but the Gospel about the greatest miracle of all time, the resurrection of Jesus that the Spirit of Jesus used to create faith ([6]M. M. Ac 2:24 & [7]Ro 10:17a).

8:14 (1) There is some uncertainty in Luke's account about whether there was some formal structure in the Church in Jerusalem during this early period, and what that structure was: **a)** In (6:2-6), the apostles advised the Church to choose seven men to oversee the distribution of food. **b)** Then, in (8:5) Luke implies that the Holy Spirit was using the persecution in Jerusalem in order to fulfill Jesus' command in (1:8) that his disciples should go on all <u>three</u> levels of his mission to the lost world. Therefore, he sent Philip to Samaria on Level 2. **c)** However, verse 14 implies that, sometime later, the apostles met together and apparently they themselves decided to send Peter and John as missionaries to Samaria. **d)** And then, (9:32) says, *"Now as Peter went here and there among them all, he came down also to the saints who lived at Lydda,"* which suggests that Peter was still working as a missionary or leader among the believers. Nevertheless, we do know two important things about the early Church: Peter was their dynamic leader in Luke's account up until chapter 13, when he begins to focus on the great missionary, Paul. And we also, of course, know with full certainly that it was the heavenly Father who was still in full control; his mission-heart never fails to lead and guide all human affairs, so that his gracious will is always done ([8]M. M. Ac 4:28). **2)** Verse 14 says that *"Samaria had received the word of God,"* which indicates that the Gospel had produced fruit there (Lk 8:5-8). Philip was a Gentile (6:5); and therefore, there, no doubt, were cultural gaps such as racial prejudice that Philip had to overcome while witnessing to Samaritans; however, he did share a devotion to the Old Testament as God's holy Word with them. It may have been that Philip had become a proselyte in Judaism; and then he would have begun to learn from the Old Testament in a synagogue. Or it may have been that he was not a proselyte but became a believer; and then he would have begun to learn from his fellow believers how his Lord Jesus fulfilled the entire Old Testament (5:42; [9]M. M. Mt 1:22).

8:16 Verse 16 is unclear in two ways: **a)** First of all, Luke says in verse 12 that *"when they [the Samaritans] believed Philip as he preached good news about the kingdom of God and the name of Jesus Christ, they were baptized, both men and women."* And all who have faith in Jesus have received the gracious gift the indwelling Holy Spirit (Titus 3:5; [10]M. M. Tit 3:5). However, Luke then says in verse 16 that *"he [the Holy Spirit] had not yet fallen on any of them [the Samaritans]."* Therefore, we can only conclude that Luke must be referring to the spectacular gifts of the Holy Spirit in verse 16 ([11]M. I. 1 Cor 14:2). Furthermore, they received these spectacular gifts when Peter and John *"laid their hands on them"* (v 17). **b)** Secondly, Luke says in verse 16 that *"they [the Samaritans] had only been baptized in the name of the Lord Jesus."* He is obviously referring to the Trinitarian Baptism that Jesus commanded in (Mt 28:19); and Peter and John emphasized the new nature of this Baptism that now focused on Jesus (2:38; 10:48; 19:5).

8:20 When Peter called Simon to repentance in verse 20, because Simon thought that he could buy the gifts of the Holy Spirit, he was teaching him the very important truth that no one can buy his gifts. All of the gifts that the Holy Spirit gives to Christians are just that, most gracious gifts that no one deserves. Whether it's the gift of faith, or the gifts of abilities to serve others, or spectacular gifts, he gives them all to whomever he graciously chooses to give them ([12]M. M. 1 Cor 12:11 & [13]Ro 6:18).

Philip and the Ethiopian Eunuch 8:26-40

8:26 *Now an angel of the Lord said to Philip, "Rise and go toward the south to the road that goes down from Jerusalem to Gaza." This is a desert place.*

8:27 *And he rose and went. And there was an Ethiopian, a eunuch, a court official of Candace, queen of the Ethiopians, who was in charge of all her treasure. He had come to Jerusalem to worship*

8:28 *and was returning, seated in his chariot, and he was reading the prophet Isaiah.*

8:29 *And the Spirit said to Philip, "Go over and join this chariot."*

8:30 *So Philip ran to him and heard him reading Isaiah the prophet and asked, "Do you understand what you are reading?"*

8:31 *And he said, "How can I, unless someone guides me?" And he invited Philip to come up and sit with him.*

8:32 *Now the passage of the Scripture that he was reading was this: "Like a sheep he was led to the slaughter and like a lamb before its shearer is silent, so he opens not his mouth.*

8:33 *In his humiliation justice was denied him. Who can describe his generation? For his life is taken away from the earth."*

8:34 *And the eunuch said to Philip, "About whom, I ask you, does the prophet say this, about himself or about someone else?"*

8:35 *Then Philip opened his mouth, and beginning with this Scripture he told him the good news about Jesus.*

8:36 *And as they were going along the road they came to some water, and the eunuch said, "See, here is water! What prevents me from being baptized?"*

8:37 *[And Philip said, "If you believe with all your heart, you may." And he replied, "I believe that Jesus Christ is the Son of God."]*

8:38 *And he commanded the chariot to stop, and they both went down into the water, Philip and the eunuch, and he baptized him.*

8:39 *And when they came up out of the water, the Spirit of the Lord carried Philip away, and the eunuch saw him no more, and went on his way rejoicing.*

8:40 *But Philip found himself at Azotus, and as he passed through he preached the Gospel to all the towns until he came to Caesarea.*

8:26-31 (1) When *"an angel of the Lord"* commanded Philip to go to *"a desert place"* (v 26), he apparently did not yet know that he would be the first missionary whom the Holy Spirit was sending to proclaim the Gospel to one specific Gentile on Level 3 of the mission. But when Philip saw that the man was a Gentile (v 27), he did not disobey the Lord, as the prophet Jonah had done many years before (Jonah 1:3). The Holy Spirit had sent many new missionaries to return home to many Gentile nations on Pentecost Day, but not to specific people. Now he was expanding the Church's mission to a whole new continent of Gentiles, Africa ([14]M. M. Ac 4:28). **2)** Secondly, there were at least eight reasons why the Holy Spirit chose this specific Gentile man to be the first one to hear the Gospel. **a)** First, he knew that he was a proselyte who had converted to the Jewish religion and who took his new religion seriously enough that he had traveled all of the way to Jerusalem to practice it (v 27). **b)** Second, he knew that the official also had become a student of the Old Testament, the Greek Septuagint; and the Holy Spirit had used his holy Word to create faith in his heart. In fact, he was so diligent about it that he was even reading it while he traveled (v 28). **c)** Third, the Spirit, therefore, also knew that the official would be very open to hearing the Gospel, especially since the man did not yet fully understand what he was reading (vs 30-31). **d)** Fourth, the Spirit also knew that both men spoke the Greek language, so that Philip could clearly apply the Gospel to him ([15]M. M. Lk 4:21). **e)** Fifth, the Spirit knew that the cultural gap that Philip would now experience in witnessing to this Gentile proselyte was essentially the same as he had recently experienced in witnessing to the Samaritans (v 5) because they too shared the same Scriptures. **f)** Six, the Holy Spirit had guided the official to read verse 32, *"Like a sheep he was led to the slaughter"* because both Jews and Gentiles were very familiar with animal sacrifices. Therefore, Philip was easily able to help this Gentile understand that Jesus was the Lamb of God whom God had graciously sacrificed specifically for him (the official) and also for all nations. **g)** Seventh, Philip had obviously not only effectively told the official that Jesus died for him, he also taught him about the meaning of holy

Baptism; and therefore, he very promptly baptized him. Therefore, the official left Philip full of the joy of the Holy Spirit (v 8; 9:18; 16:33; [16]M. M. Tit 3:5). **h)** And finally, the Spirit knew that this man would likewise become an effective cultural bridge from the Jewish faith on Level 1 to his fellow Gentiles on Level 3, since he was both a *proselyte* and also a Gentile from Africa. Like the *"devout men"* (2:5), who first heard the Gospel about Jesus on Pentecost Day and then went home and shared it with their Gentile neighbors, he too would now be eager to share this tremendous Gospel with his Gentile family and friends. And we can, of course, say with some confidence that he did, indeed, do so, because a Christian church that has very ancient roots is still thriving in Ethiopia yet today. Thus the Holy Spirit was, of course, still very much in control of his mission and guiding it exactly where his Word would have the most effect on people who heard it ([17]M. M. Ac 4:28 & [18]M. I. Ac 1:8 & [19]Ac 2:4).

8:40 Azotus (or Ashdod) was not far from Caesarea in Judea, and of course, many Jews lived in both cities (Level 1 of the mission to the Jews). However, the Roman government had made Caesarea the headquarters of that Province; therefore, no doubt, there also were many Gentiles living in both cities (Level 2 of the mission to Gentiles). Thus, we see that the Holy Spirit was guiding the Church on two levels of the mission simultaneously. He did not intend that the believers should go out on their mission in a strictly geographical progression ([20]M. M. Mt 5:14 & [21]Ac 13:46).

---

[1] M. M. Ac 4:28: The heavenly Father is always in full control of his mission to all nations of the world.

[2] M. I. Ro 5:3a: Christians should rejoice in the midst of suffering for Jesus' sake because suffering teaches them to depend on their Lord's rich grace, and thus continue to grow in more spiritual gifts.

[3] M. M. Lk 6:22: The Lord Jesus will surely bless a Christian in the midst of suffering for his sake; and he will also bless him with eternal life if he remains faithful to him.

[4] M. M. Ac 4:28: The heavenly Father is always in full control of his mission to all nations of the world.

[5] M. I. Ac 3:6: Christians should heal a person's physical problem by speaking the name of

Jesus, so that everyone knows that it was the divine power of Jesus that healed him.

⁶ M. M. Ac 2:24: Our Lord Jesus loosed the pangs of death for us mortal human beings when God raised him from the dead, because it was not possible for him to be held by death.

⁷ M. M. Ro 10:17a: The Holy Spirit only creates and preserves faith by using the message of God's grace in his holy Word.

⁸ M. M. Ac 4:28: The heavenly Father is always in full control of his mission to all nations of the world.

⁹ M. M. Mt 1:22: God sent his only Son, Jesus to be born as a true human being, so that he could save all of his brothers and sisters of all nations by fulfilling all of God's promises in the Old Testament.

¹⁰ M. M. Tit 3:5: When a person is baptized, God graciously saves him and gives him the gift of a new birth from his indwelling Holy Spirit; and he does this because his mercy is so great, and not because of any good deeds that that person has done.

¹¹ M. I. 1 Cor 14:2: Christians should not use the Holy Spirit's gift of speaking in a strange language in a worship service when no one is present to interpret his message for other members, because obviously he is only speaking to God, and he is not using this gift to build up the members who cannot understand him.

¹² M. M. 1 Cor 12:11: When Christians baptize people the same Holy Spirit graciously gives each one faith in Jesus plus a unique set of spiritual gifts so that he can use them in order to expand the Lord's mission.

¹³ M. M. Ro 6:18: In his Baptism, Jesus graciously sets a new Christian free from his slavery to sin and gives him the power of his Spirit to gratefully obey his new Lord by doing good deeds.

¹⁴ M. M. Ac 4:28: The heavenly Father is always in full control of his mission to all nations of the world.

¹⁵ M. M. Lk 4:21: Every verse in the entire Bible points in some way to Jesus and his mission to seek and save the lost.

¹⁶ M. M. Tit 3:5: When a person is baptized, God graciously saves him and gives him the gift of a new birth from his indwelling Holy Spirit; and he does this because his mercy is so great, and not because of any good deeds that that person has done.

¹⁷ M. M. Ac 4:28: The heavenly Father is always in full control of his mission to all nations of the world.

¹⁸ M. I. Ac 1:8: Christians should go and witness about Jesus to all who are lost from all languages and cultures by depending on the power of the Holy Spirit to help them bridge all of the language/cultural boundaries whether they are relatively easy, as in their own language, or extremely difficult.

¹⁹ M. I. Ac 2:4: In cross-cultural situations, Christians should always focus on all of the needs of the target group by learning their heart-language and culture as deeply as possible, so that they can tell them the Gospel clearly in their own language and also help them with the true needs of their society.

²⁰ M. M. Mt 5:14: When the Holy Spirit creates faith in a person's heart, he also graciously gives him a new mission-heart that is eager to shine the light of the Gospel throughout the whole world.

²¹ M. M. Ac 13:46: As he did with the old Israel, God first of all strengthens the faith of the new Israel, the Church with his Word and Sacraments, so that they can go and witness to the lost

people of all nations.

Chapter 9

The Conversion of Saul 9:1-19a

9:1 *But Saul, still breathing threats and murder against the disciples of the Lord, went to the high priest*

9:2 *and asked him for letters to the synagogues at Damascus, so that if he found any belonging to the Way, men or women, he might bring them bound to Jerusalem.*

9:3 *Now as he went on his way, he approached Damascus, and suddenly a light from heaven flashed around him.*

9:4 *And falling to the ground he heard a voice saying to him, "Saul, Saul, why are you persecuting me?"*

9:5 *And he said, "Who are you, Lord?" And he said, "I am Jesus, whom you are persecuting.*

9:6 *But rise and enter the city, and you will be told what you are to do."*

9:7 *The men who were traveling with him stood speechless, hearing the voice but seeing no one.*

9:8 *Saul rose from the ground, and although his eyes were opened, he saw nothing. So they led him by the hand and brought him into Damascus.*

9:9 *And for three days he was without sight, and neither ate nor drank.*

9:10 *Now there was a disciple at Damascus named Ananias. The Lord said to him in a vision, "Ananias." And he said, "Here I am, Lord."*

9:11 *And the Lord said to him, "Rise and go to the street called Straight, and at the house of Judas look for a man of Tarsus named Saul, for behold, he is praying,*

9:12 *and he has seen in a vision a man named Ananias come in and lay his hands on him so that he might regain his sight."*

9:13 *But Ananias answered, "Lord, I have heard from many about this man, how much evil he has done to your saints at Jerusalem.*

9:14 *And here he has authority from the chief priests to bind all who call on your name."*
9:15 *But the Lord said to him, "Go, for he is a chosen instrument of mine to carry my name before the Gentiles and kings and the children of Israel.*
9:16 *For I will show him how much he must suffer for the sake of my name."*
9:17 *So Ananias departed and entered the house. And laying his hands on him he said, "Brother Saul, the Lord Jesus who appeared to you on the road by which you came has sent me so that you may regain your sight and be filled with the Holy Spirit."*
9:18 *And immediately something like scales fell from his eyes, and he regained his sight. Then he rose and was baptized;*
9:19a *and taking food, he was strengthened.*

9:1 Verse 1 describes the intense zeal that God had given to Saul; however, at this time, Satan was using it for his evil purposes. But it was, in fact, God who was in control. Therefore, sometime later, he grabbed ahold of this fierce enemy of his mission (vs 3-4), and, by his grace alone, he gave him two gracious gifts: the gift of faith in him (vs 17, 20) and the gift of apostleship (Rom 1:5) to serve him with even greater zeal and faithfulness ([1]M. M. Ac 4:28). All of mankind is sinful, as Saul's early life illustrates; therefore, no one deserves to be called by God to serve him. And some years after God had called him, Saul himself confessed in (1 Cor 15:9-10): *"I am the least of the apostles, unworthy to be called an apostle, because I persecuted the church of God. But by the grace of God I am what I am"* ([2]M. M. Lk 14:34).

9:2 (1) It is very significant that, after just a few years, verse 2 indicates that the Church had already become known as *"the Way."* This name obviously reflects Jesus' own words in (Jn 14:6) *"I am the way, and the truth, and the life."* Why, then, did people start giving the Church this name? Obviously, when the believers witnessed to them, they must have quoted these Words of Jesus as they proclaimed his name. Therefore, in doing so, they were confessing two truths: **a)** that Jesus was their Lord,

b) and that they would joyfully follow his Way even if it meant persecution and death, since <u>only he</u> could lead them to their heavenly Father (Lk 13:24; ³M. M. Ac 4:12). **2)** Furthermore, this new name, *"the Way"* illustrates two other facts: **a)** It often identified the new Church as *distinct* from the Jewish religion. As a matter of fact, the religious leaders of the Jews had recognized very quickly, that the Church was a *new* religion that threatened their power over the people. Already in (5:17), we see that they were *"<u>jealous</u>"* of the popularity of the Church (5:13); therefore they arrested the apostles. **b)** Secondly however, everyone could, no doubt, also see that this new *"Way"* was also <u>connected</u> to the Jewish religion. When the believers witnessed to their new faith, they always quoted from their common Jewish Scriptures (⁴M. I. Lk 4:15). **3)** Therefore, as time passed, people began to wonder more and more, what was the <u>true</u> status of *"the Way?"* Was this yet another new Jewish <u>sect</u> or a completely new <u>religion</u>? Of course, most people did not see the true connection; and therefore, this issue eventually raised two more serious issues: **a)** A few years later it became a very serious issue <u>within</u> the Church. Some Jewish believers wanted to circumcise new Gentile believers because they believed that they should still obey the whole Law as Gentile converts or proselytes to the <u>Jewish</u> religion (15:5). **b)** And a few years after that, an <u>external</u> issue arose. Many people considered *"the Way"* a new religion, which was <u>illegal</u> according to Roman law (16:19-24; 18:12-17). This led to severe persecution by the Roman government (Rom 8:35; ⁵M. I. Lk 9:23).
9:3-6 Jesus himself <u>graciously</u> appeared to Saul in all of his glory as the Lord of the mission, in order to give him the two gifts of faith and apostleship (Rom 1:1, 5). On Pentecost day, his Spirit had sent out 3,000 *"devout men"* (2:5) with the Gospel to expand the mission as quickly as possible on all three levels; and then, he sent Philip to expand his mission on Level 2 to Samaria (8:5-8) and on Level 3 to the Gentiles on the continent of Africa (8:26-39). Meanwhile, the twelve apostles were content with staying in their comfort zone on Level 1 in Jerusalem and Judea; and it took three visions to move their leader, Peter on to Level 3 (10:10-16). Therefore, the Lord Jesus <u>graciously</u> chose (v 15) and completely changed the heart of a violent enemy of the Church into a

mission-heart, so that he would go on Level 3 of his mission to the Gentiles. How amazing is his grace! He wanted to use the many abilities that he had given to this new, dynamic leader as his 13th apostle; he chose Saul ([6]M. M. Ro 6:18).

9:15 (1) The Lord Jesus graciously called Saul to *"carry my name before the Gentiles and kings"* (v 15), that is mainly before Gentiles; and he also graciously called Peter to witness mainly to the Jews (Gal 2:7). However, as we examine the record of their separate missions, we often see overlap; Saul also witnessed to Jews, and Peter also witnessed to Gentiles. There were at least three reasons for this: **a)** First of all, all Christians have the same call to go to all nations ([7]M. M. Mt 5:14). **b)** Secondly, it's also significant in verse 15 that the Lord included *"the children of Israel,"* the Jews in Saul's call; and in the next chapter, he sent Peter to Cornelius, a Gentile. **c)** And thirdly, throughout his mission journeys, Saul often first went to the synagogue in a new town (See the discussion at (13:5)) and witnessed to the Jews and to the Gentile proselytes who were worshipping there (13:14-16; [8]M. M. Ac 13:46). **2)** Why did Jesus specifically command Saul to *"carry my name"* in verse 15? Throughout the Scriptures, the name of a person evoked the presence of that person. This was especially true for the personal name of God, which is, *"I AM WHO I AM"* (Ex 3:14). Thus, he called Saul to *"carry my name"* before Gentiles by telling them that Jesus was *present* with them in his holy Word as the great *"I AM,"* both true God and true man. And this is precisely what Saul, almost immediately, did (vs 20-22)! And because it was this holy presence that Jesus willingly offered on the cross, his heavenly Father accepted his sacrifice (1 Cor 2:20); and Saul, therefore, only witnessed to his name and his cross (1 Cor 2:2; [9]M. M. Heb 9:12). **3)** When did Saul witness to the name of Jesus before kings (v 15)? While Saul had a only few opportunities to do so on his first three mission journeys (13:7), it's very significant that he did do so on a much more consistent basis as a prisoner of the Roman Empire on his fourth missionary journey (23:11; Chs 21-28; Lk 10:24; Lk 21:12; [10]M. I. Ac 1:8)

9:16 In verse 16, the Lord Jesus told Ananias that *"I will show him [Saul] how much he must suffer for the sake of my name."* And very soon (v 23), Saul did indeed begin to experience persecution wherever he went because he proclaimed Jesus' holy name; and since Jesus was actually present with him in his holy Word, Satan inspires people who hate Jesus to also hate those who witness to his holy name. However, Saul soon learned to rejoice in the midst of persecution no matter how violent it became (Rom 5:3; Phil 4:4). But his joy and fearlessness in suffering did not spring from his own human strength; it was, rather, clear evidence that he was indeed *"filled with the Holy Spirit"* (v 17) and depending on his Lord's rich grace ([11]M. I. Lk 11:10).

9:18 Verse 18 says that Saul *"was baptized"* immediately, which would seem to indicate that this had already become regular practice in the Church ([12]M. I. Mt 28:19).

Saul Proclaims Jesus in Synagogues 9:19b-22

9:19b *For some days he was with the disciples at Damascus.*
9:20 *And immediately he proclaimed Jesus in the synagogues, saying, "He is the Son of God."*
9:21 *And all who heard him were amazed and said, "Is not this the man who made havoc in Jerusalem of those who called upon this name? And has he not come here for this purpose, to bring them bound before the chief priests?"*
9:22 *But Saul increased all the more in strength, and confounded the Jews who lived in Damascus by proving that Jesus was the Christ.*

9:20-22 Saul also quickly demonstrated that the Holy Spirit (v 17) had, indeed, given him a mission-heart by doing *three* things: **a)** First of all, his mission-heart moved him, so that *"immediately he proclaimed Jesus"* (v 20; [13]M. M. Mt 5:14). **b)** Secondly, he boldly witnessed to Jesus' holy name by saying that Jesus *"is the Son of God"* (v 20); and he likewise *"confounded the Jews who lived in Damascus by proving that Jesus was the Christ"* (v 22). He was, without a doubt, quoting from their own Scriptures in order to prove this because God's entire holy Word points to Jesus (Lk 24:27, 44; [14]M. I. Lk 4:17). **c)** And thirdly, verse 20 says that Saul quickly seized every <u>opportunity</u> to proclaim the name of Jesus to both devout Jews and Gentiles by going to the synagogues in Damascus ([15]M. I. Lk 4:15).

Saul Escapes from Damascus 9:23-25

9:23 *When many days had passed, the Jews plotted to kill him,*
9:24 *but their plot became known to Saul. They were watching the gates day and night in order to kill him,*
9:25 *but his disciples took him by night and let him down through an opening in the wall, lowering him in a basket.*

9:24 It was, of course, Satan who was inspiring these people in their plot to kill Paul (v 24), because he hates all forms of proclaiming the Gospel. If people hear it, he is angry because he knows two things: **a)** that the Holy Spirit can use his Word to graciously create faith in their hearts and rescue them from his terrifying power ([16]M. M. Ro 1:16b). **b)** And he, of course, also knows that the Holy Spirit has awesome power far greater than his own. Therefore the devil is constantly doing everything that he can to stop all aspects of the Lord's mission. And any Christian who is unaware of this danger or ignores it is especially vulnerable to his evil attacks ([17]M. I. Eph 6:10).

9:25-26 It may appear from Luke's account that Saul left Damascus in verse 25 and went straight to Jerusalem in verse 26. However, Saul himself tells us in (Gal 1:17-18) that he first went to Arabia for about <u>three</u> years, and then he returned to Damascus, before he went to Jerusalem for the first time. But why did he go to Arabia for such a long time? His new mission-heart would certainly have compelled him to witness to others at every opportunity while he was there. However, his main purpose may have been to find a significant period of time when he could meditate on the <u>Scriptures,</u> in order to find more evidence that his new Lord Jesus was, indeed, the Messiah whom he had so earnestly longed for ([18]M. M. Lk 4:21 & [19]M. I. Lk 12:40). There are at least two pieces of strong evidence that this was his main purpose: **a)** First of all, we know that he was already extremely zealous for the Law of Moses, because, in (23:6) and (Phil 3:5), he describes himself as the <u>strictest</u> of Pharisees before his conversion. **b)** And secondly, throughout his four missionary journeys, we see him using the mighty sword of God's holy Word, again and again, in order to try to persuade others who were equally devoted to the Scriptures that Jesus was also their Messiah (18:28; [20]M. I. Lk 16:17).

Saul in Jerusalem 9:26-31

9:26 *And when he had come to Jerusalem, he attempted to join the disciples. And they were all afraid of him, for they did not believe that he was a disciple.*

9:27 *But Barnabas took him and brought him to the apostles and declared to them how on the road he had seen the Lord, who spoke to him, and how at Damascus he had preached boldly in the name of Jesus.*

9:28 *So he went in and out among them at Jerusalem, preaching boldly in the name of the Lord.*

9:29 *And he spoke and disputed against the Hellenists. But they were seeking to kill him.*

9:30 *And when the brothers learned this, they brought him down to Caesarea and sent him off to Tarsus.*

9:31 *So the church throughout all Judea and Galilee and Samaria had peace and was being built up. And walking in the fear of the Lord and in the comfort of the Holy Spirit, it multiplied.*

9:26 It is not at all surprising that the disciples in Jerusalem were afraid of Saul when he tried to join their group since he had persecuted and killed some of them (v 1). Furthermore, it is likewise not at all surprising that *"<u>Barnabas</u> took him [Saul] and brought him to the apostles"* (v 27a), since the name Barnabas means *"son of encouragement"* (4:36; 11:22, 30). And then a short time later, the Holy Spirit chose these same two men, Barnabas and Saul as his first mission team to send out from Antioch, because he had given them many wonderful gifts and abilities for this task (13:2; [21]M. M. 1 Cor 12:11).

9:29 Obviously, Saul's mission-heart was greatly enriched by his study of Scripture in Arabia because he was so filled with the Holy Spirit that he zealously spread Jesus' holy name everywhere he went. He also *"spoke and disputed against the Hellenists [Greek-speaking Jews]"* (v 29), which meant that he was also publicly refuting false teaching ([22]M. I. Lk 3:3a & [23]Lk 11:10).

9:31 Verse 31 tells us <u>three</u> significant things that the Holy Spirit was doing, at this early stage, in the mission of the Church: **a)** First of all, he gave *"peace"* (v 31) to his mission after a very stressful time of persecution. Even though the persecution had caused the believers to scatter, so that they spread the Gospel on Levels 2 and 3, it would have been very dangerous for them to try to communicate with each other during that time. Therefore, a time of peace made it possible for love to flow freely between them and bring unity and mutual support ([24]M. M. Ro 5:1). **b)** Secondly, the Church *"was being built up"* and *"comfort[ed]"* or encouraged by the Holy Spirit. As they were depending on his grace by *"walking in the fear of the Lord"* through regular prayer and listening to his holy Word, he was, of course, always eager to do this gracious work in their hearts ([25]M. I. Lk 12:40). The regular worship of the Church should always be centered around the Scriptures, so that every worshiper stays focused on the <u>grace</u> of their Lord Jesus ([26]M. M. Jn 4:21). **c)** And finally, the Church was being *"multiplied"* (v 31) by the Holy Spirit through the same gracious means of his holy Word. The Holy Spirit was also busy creating faith in more and more hearts as the believers faithfully witnessed to the lost about their Lord Jesus ([27]M. I. Lk 8:11).

The Healing of Aeneas 9:32-35

9:32 *Now as Peter went here and there among them all, he came down also to the saints who lived at Lydda.*
9:33 *There he found a man named Aeneas, bedridden for eight years, who was paralyzed.*
9:34 *And Peter said to him, "Aeneas, Jesus Christ heals you; rise*

and make your bed." And immediately he rose.

9:35 *And all the residents of Lydda and Sharon saw him, and they turned to the Lord.*

9:32 Note that Luke seems to imply in verse 32 that Peter was continuing to go to various towns either as a missionary or as the most prominent leader of the early Church (M. M. Ac 4:28). (See the discussion at (8:14) that it was God who was in full control of the early Church.)

9:34 Once again, a miracle attracted people to hear the Gospel about Jesus, because Peter did not proudly heal Aeneas in his own name but in the powerful name of Jesus. He said very clearly, *"Aeneas, Jesus Christ heals you"* ([28]M. I. Ac 3:6).

Dorcas Restored to Life 9:36-43

9:36 *Now there was in Joppa a disciple named Tabitha, which, translated, means Dorcas. She was full of good works and acts of charity.*

9:37 *In those days she became ill and died, and when they had washed her, they laid her in an upper room.*

9:38 *Since Lydda was near Joppa, the disciples, hearing that Peter was there, sent two men to him, urging him, "Please come to us without delay."*

9:39 *So Peter rose and went with them. And when he arrived, they took him to the upper room. All the widows stood beside him weeping and showing tunics and other garments that Dorcas made while she was with them.*

9:40 *But Peter put them all outside, and knelt down and prayed; and turning to the body he said, "Tabitha, arise." And she opened her eyes, and when she saw Peter she sat up.*

9:41 *And he gave her his hand and raised her up. Then calling the saints and widows, he presented her alive.*

9:42 *And it became known throughout all Joppa, and many believed in the Lord.*

> 9:43 *And he stayed in Joppa for many days with one Simon, a tanner.*

9:40 Verse 40 says that Peter performed an even more spectacular miracle than healing a paralyzed man (v 34) when he raised Tabitha from the dead. He healed her in the holy name of Jesus; and the Holy Spirit added more miracles when *"many believed in the Lord"* (v 42; [29]M. M. Ac 4:12).

9:43 Verse 43 says that Simon was a leatherworker; and of course, Simon is a Jewish name. However, the Law of Moses says that a Jew who touches a dead animal is <u>unclean</u> until evening (Lev 17:15); therefore, his work would have made him perpetually unclean and an outcast in the local Jewish community. Thus, the question is: how could a pious Jew like Peter even consider going to his house, let alone stay with him *"for many days"* (v 43)? There may be two possible answers to this question. **a)** On the one hand, Peter may have been making a very bold move, because it would have been a clear example to the Jewish community that God had begun a new era. He had, no doubt, been publicly proclaiming that the Lord Jesus had fulfilled the whole Law; and therefore, those who trust in him are now free from the Laws of Moses. If Peter did, indeed, plan this as a bold move, it certainly would have dramatically reinforced what he had been saying. However, we must also add that this possibility is only implied in this one verse 43. **b)** Secondly, on the other hand, it seems doubtful that Peter had changed his way of thinking so radically. If he had changed so completely, then, why was it necessary for the Holy Spirit to use a vision in order to jar his thoughts so strongly, as we read in the next two chapters? Obviously, Peter had begun to change his thinking, but it's not completely clear in Luke's account just how much he had changed ([30]M. I. Ac 1:8).

---

[1] M. M. Ac 4:28: The heavenly Father is always in full control of his mission to all nations of the world.

[2] M. M. Lk 14:34: A Christian's faith relationship with Jesus is a precious <u>treasure</u> and a completely <u>unique</u> personal relationship, because no one deserves it and it will last forever.

[3] M. M. Ac 4:12: <u>Only</u> the power of Jesus' name can save a person from sin.

[4] M. I. Lk 4:15: Christians should seize <u>every</u> opportunity to proclaim the Gospel to lost people of all nations.

[5] M. I. Lk 9:23: Christians should deceive no one by <u>only</u> telling them the Gospel about Jesus, but rather they should <u>also</u> give them two warnings: a) that they may have to suffer for the sake of Jesus if they follow him, b) and that, on Judgment Day, Jesus will be ashamed of people who were ashamed of him.

[6] M. M. Ro 6:18: In his Baptism, Jesus graciously sets a new Christian free from his slavery to sin and gives him the power of his Spirit to gratefully obey his new Lord by doing good deeds.

[7] M. M. Mt 5:14: When the Holy Spirit creates faith in a person's heart, he also graciously gives him a new mission-heart that is eager to shine the light of the Gospel throughout the whole world.

[8] M. M. Ac 13:46: As he did with the old Israel, God <u>first of all</u> strengthens the faith of the new Israel, the Church with his Word and Sacraments, so that they can go and witness to the lost people of all nations.

[9] M. M. Heb 9:12: As the great High Priest, Jesus offered his <u>human</u> and <u>divine</u> blood as the one perfect sacrifice for <u>all</u> of the sins of <u>all</u> of his brothers and sisters.

[10] M. I. Ac 1:8: Christians should go and witness about Jesus to all who are lost from all languages and cultures by depending on the power of the Holy Spirit to help them bridge all of the language/cultural boundaries whether they are relatively easy, as in their own language, or extremely difficult.

[11] M. I. Lk 11:10: Christians should <u>continuously</u> pray to their heavenly Father and <u>always</u> depend on his grace, and not on their own feeble strength, because he <u>always</u> loves them.

[12] M. I. Mt 28:19: Christians should go and proclaim God's Law and Gospel to all nations; then, baptize all who repent and believe after teaching them the meaning of holy Baptism.

[13] M. M. Mt 5:14: When the Holy Spirit creates faith in a person's heart, he also graciously gives him a new mission-heart that is eager to shine the light of the Gospel throughout the whole world.

[14] M. I. Lk 4:17: Christians should always base their messages on the Bible, so that the Holy Spirit can use his holy Word to create and strengthen faith in their hearers.

[15] M. I. Lk 4:15: Christians should seize <u>every</u> opportunity to proclaim the Gospel to lost people of all nations.

[16] M. M. Ro 1:16b: The Gospel is so powerful because it contains the central truth that Jesus rose from the dead with a glorified body in order to save all of his brothers and sisters from sin and death.

[17] M. I. Eph 6:10: Christians should always be ready to fight against the devil and stand firm against all of his evil schemes by prayerfully putting on the whole armor of the Holy Spirit.

[18] M. M. Lk 4:21: <u>Every</u> verse in the entire Bible points in some way to Jesus and his mission to seek and save the lost.

[19] M. I. Lk 12:40: Christians should "eat" God's Word every day in order to keep their faith strong, so that they are always ready for their Lord's return.

[20] M. I. Lk 16:17: Christians should wield the sword of the Spirit with confidence as they go and tell the Gospel because his Word can never fail.

²¹ When Christians baptize people the same Holy Spirit graciously gives each one faith in Jesus plus a unique set of spiritual gifts so that he can use them in order to expand the Lord's mission.

²² M. I. Lk 3:3a: Christians should, in love, warn lost people who do not repent.

²³ M. I. Lk 11:10: Christians should <u>continuously</u> pray to their heavenly Father and <u>always</u> depend on his grace, and not on their own feeble strength, because he <u>always</u> loves them.

²⁴ M. M. Ro 5:1: On the cross, Jesus earned <u>peace</u> with God for <u>all</u> of his brothers and sisters from every nation on earth.

²⁵ M. I. Lk 12:40: Christians should "eat" God's Word every day in order to keep their faith strong, so that they are always ready for their Lord's return.

²⁶ M. M. Jn 4:21: <u>All</u> people from <u>all</u> nations are equally free to worship God everywhere on earth because he is their heavenly Father who made the people of all nations.

²⁷ M. I. Lk 8:11: Christians should faithfully do their job of preaching and leave the <u>results</u> to the Holy Spirit.

²⁸ M. I. Ac 3:6: Christians should heal a person's physical problem by speaking the <u>name</u> of Jesus, so that everyone knows that it was the divine power of Jesus that healed him.

²⁹ M. M. Ac 4:12: <u>Only</u> the power of Jesus' name can save a person from sin.

³⁰ M. I. Ac 1:8: Christians should go and witness about Jesus to all who are lost from all languages and cultures by depending on the power of the Holy Spirit to help them bridge all of the language/cultural boundaries whether they are relatively easy, as in their own language, or extremely difficult.

Chapter 10

Peter and Cornelius 10:1-8

10:1 *At Caesarea there was a man named Cornelius, a centurion of what was known as the Italian Cohort,*
10:2 *a devout man who feared God with all his household, gave alms generously to the people, and prayed continually to God.*
10:3 *About the ninth hour of the day he saw clearly in a vision an angel of God come in and say to him, "Cornelius."*
10:4 *And he stared at him in terror and said, "What is it, Lord?" And he said to him, "Your prayers and your alms have ascended as a memorial before God.*
10:5 *And now send men to Joppa and bring one Simon who is called Peter.*
10:6 *He is lodging with one Simon, a tanner, whose house is by the seaside."*
   10:7 *When the angel who spoke to him had departed, he called two of his servants and a devout soldier from among those who attended him,*
   10:8 *and having related everything to them, he sent them to Joppa.*

10:1-2 (1) Did God send this Gentile, Cornelius a vision because he <u>deserved</u> to hear about the name of Jesus? Certainly not, but God had seen that he was *"a devout man who feared"* him (v 2). This phrase is significant because it was a phrase that Luke uses here in verse 2 and in (v 22; 13:16, 26) to refer to a Gentile who had accepted certain aspects of the Jewish religion, such as the ones Luke mentions in verse 2: he *"gave alms generously, and prayed continually to God."* However, he was not a full proselyte because he was not circumcised. (Note that the phrase *"devout men"* in (2:5) is different in the original Greek.) But most importantly, God had seen that he was open to hearing the Gospel ([1]M. I. Ac 2:4). **2)** Even though Peter and John had gone on a Level 2 mission trip to the hated Samaritans, in order to inspect the work of the mission there (8:14); and even though Peter had shown some change in his thinking by going to stay with "unclean" Simon in Joppa (9:43), God knew that Peter was still harboring some racial prejudice in his heart. He was still harboring the proud idea that <u>only</u> the Jews <u>deserved</u> to hear the Gospel and did not yet truly believe that the Church should go out on its mission to <u>all</u> nations. Therefore, God <u>also</u> chose to give this vision to Cornelius because he was a <u>Gentile</u> (v 1), since he wanted Peter to <u>fully</u> understand that his mission-heart *"shows no partiality"* (v 34); and he longed to completely transform Peter's heart to be like his own (2 Cor 5:17; [2]M. M. Ac 13:46).

Peter's Vision 10:9-33

10:9 *The next day, as they were on their journey and approaching the city, Peter went up on the housetop about the sixth hour to pray.*

10:10 *And he became hungry and wanted something to eat, but while they were preparing it, he fell into a trance*

10:11 *and saw the heavens opened and something like a great sheet descending, being let down by its four corners upon the earth.*

10:12 *In it were all kinds of animals and reptiles and birds of the air.*

10:13 *And there came a voice to him: "Rise, Peter; kill and eat."*

10:14 *But Peter said, "By no means, Lord; for I have never eaten anything that is common or unclean."*

10:15 *And the voice came to him again a second time, "What God has made clean, do not call common."*

10:16 *This happened three times, and the thing was taken up at once to heaven.*

10:17 *Now while Peter was inwardly perplexed as to what the vision that he had seen might mean, behold, the men who were sent by Cornelius, having made inquiry for Simon's house, stood at the gate*

10:18 *and called out to ask whether Simon who was called Peter was lodging there.*

10:19 *And while Peter was pondering the vision, the Spirit said to him, "Behold, three men are looking for you.*
10:20 *Rise and go down and accompany them without hesitation, for I have sent them."*
10:21 *And Peter went down to the men and said, "I am the one you are looking for. What is the reason for your coming?"*
10:22 *And they said, "Cornelius, a centurion, an upright and God-fearing man, who is well spoken of by the whole Jewish nation, was directed by a holy angel to send for you to come to his house and to hear what you have to say."*
10:23 *So he invited them in to be his guests. The next day he rose and went away with them, and some of the brothers from Joppa accompanied him.*
10:24 *And on the following day they entered Caesarea. Cornelius was expecting them and had called together his relatives and close friends.*
10:25 *When Peter entered, Cornelius met him and fell down at his feet and worshiped him.*
10:26 *But Peter lifted him up, saying, "Stand up; I too am a man."*
10:27 *And as he talked with him, he went in and found many persons gathered.*
10:28 *And he said to them, "You yourselves know how unlawful it is for a Jew to associate with or to visit anyone of another nation, but God has shown me that I should not call any person common or unclean.*
10:29 *So when I was sent for, I came without objection. I ask then why you sent for me."*
10:30 *And Cornelius said, "Four days ago, about this hour, I was praying in my house at the ninth hour, and behold, a man stood before me in bright clothing*
10:31 *and said, 'Cornelius, your prayer has been heard and your alms have been remembered before God.*
10:32 *Send therefore to Joppa and ask for Simon who is called Peter. He is lodging in the house of Simon, a tanner, by the sea.'*
10:33 *So I sent for you at once, and you have been kind enough to come. Now therefore we are all here in the presence of God to*

hear all that you have been commanded by the Lord."

10:11-16 (1) Obviously, Peter still did not fully understand that the Jewish people did not deserve to hear and believe the Gospel any more than any other nation does; all of mankind is sinful and deserves nothing from God but eternal condemnation. Yet God's mission-heart is full of love for everyone, and he wants all to live with him forever (1 Tim 2:3; [3]M. M. Ro 3:24 & [4]Ro 3:26). Peter had heard his Lord Jesus teach these truths and seen him practice them every day, but he still didn't fully understand God's rich grace for everyone; and his recent experiences with Gentiles hadn't quite convinced him either. Therefore, beginning with verse 10, God gave him a series of severe, jolting illustrations in order to finally open his spiritual eyes. Two times, he gave him direct, concrete commands to actually eat <u>unclean animals,</u> and then he gave him a direct command to go to the unclean house of a Gentile and physically walk through his door. Both the visions and the actual visit to a Gentile home were <u>concrete,</u> culturally relevant illustrations that God used in order to teach him the <u>new abstract</u>, spiritual truth ([5]M. I. Lk 5:36).

10:24 Even before Cornelius knew the full Gospel himself, his devotion to God had already moved him to share the Gospel with *"his relatives and close friends"* (v 24). He was not a fully informed missionary, but a missionary nevertheless (Lk 8:9; [6]M. M. Mt 5:14)!

10:25-26 Cornelius spontaneously attempted to worship Peter (v 25); therefore, it's very obvious that he knew nothing about the first commandment, that it's a sin to worship anyone but the true God himself. As noted at verse 2, he had accepted certain aspects of the Jewish religion, but he was not a full proselyte because he was not circumcised. He may have been worshipping in a synagogue but had not yet learned very much from the Jewish Scriptures. Nevertheless, his eagerness to learn more about God is obvious; and it may explain why God chose him as a living example, a concrete, culturally relevant illustration, in order to teach Peter and the other apostles the powerful lesson that their racial prejudice against Gentiles was sinful (M. I. Lk 5:36).

10:28 No doubt all of the Gentiles present had sensed Peter's initial reluctance to associate with them; therefore, this opening statement in verse 28 that *"God has shown me that I should not call any person common or unclean"* cleared the air for them and made them even more eager to listen to him ([7]M. M. 1 Tim 2:3). Peter had finally learned that he should extend the lesson of his visions from food to <u>people</u>, to the Gentiles (Mt 15:14). This truth was, of course, vital for the mission of the Church; and Peter soon expanded this statement in verse 34.

10:31 When the angel said to Cornelius in verse 31, *"Cornelius, your prayer has been heard and your alms have been remembered before God,"* was he saying that God chose Cornelius because he deserved it? Definitely not! Such an interpretation would obviously be totally wrong in this context, where God was teaching Peter the very opposite truth that no one deserves God's grace! Rather, the angel was merely acknowledging that Cornelius was very devout and eager to learn more about worshipping the true God ([8]M. I. Ac 1:8).

Gentiles Hear the Good News 10:34-43

10:34 *So Peter opened his mouth and said: "Truly I understand that God shows no partiality,*

10:35 *but in every nation anyone who fears him and does what is right is acceptable to him.*

10:36 *As for the word that he sent to Israel, preaching good news of peace through Jesus Christ (he is Lord of all),*

10:37 *you yourselves know what happened throughout all Judea, beginning from Galilee after the baptism that John proclaimed:*

10:38 *how God anointed Jesus of Nazareth with the Holy Spirit and with power. He went about doing good and healing all who were oppressed by the devil, for God was with him.*

10:39 *And we are witnesses of all that he did both in the country of the Jews and in Jerusalem. They put him to death by hanging him on a tree,*

10:40 *but God raised him on the third day and made him to appear,*

10:41 *not to all the people but to us who had been chosen by God as*

> *witnesses, who ate and drank with him after he rose from the dead.*
> 10:42 *And he commanded us to preach to the people and to testify that he is the one appointed by God to be judge of the living and the dead.*
> 10:43 *To him all the prophets bear witness that everyone who believes in him receives forgiveness of sins through his name."*

10:34-35 (1) What a day this was for this family of Gentiles and their friends! Peter told them in verses 34-35, *"Truly I understand that God shows no partiality, but in every nation anyone who fears him and does what is right is acceptable to him."* They had never heard that the true God's heart was a mission-heart—that he has always loved them and planned to save them! He accepts anyone who turns to him in fear and faithfully obeys him. And the fact that God had sent a Jew to tell this Gospel to them must have been astounding. It's a new mission message. M. M. Ac 10:34: God shows no partiality to any person from any nation on earth, but accepts anyone who fears and obeys him. **2)** Obviously, no one can do anything to make himself *"acceptable"* to God (v 35), because only the Lord Jesus was able to obey him perfectly on behalf of all of his brothers and sisters ([9]M. M. Ro 3:24). Rather, Peter is saying here that anyone in any nation who has repented in *"fear"* and awe of God (v 35), and received God's gracious gift of faith (v 43) is *"accepted"* by God because they do *"what is right"* in faith (v 35). They are depending on God's grace, not their own strength, to serve him (Heb 11:6; Eph 2:8-10; [10]M. M. Eph 2:10). And Peter clarifies this truth by saying in verse 43 that *"everyone who believes in him receives forgiveness of sins through his name"* ([11]M. M. Ro 1:5). **3)** Furthermore, this was, of course, likewise an extremely significant occasion for the entire Church and its mission to the world. God had finally completely changed Peter's heart, one of the leaders of the Church in Jerusalem, so that he finally, fully understood the full extent of God's grace: that the deepest desire of his mission-heart is that every single person he has ever made would live forever under the power of his grace ([12]M. M. Ro 1:16b). Therefore, it was Peter who, some years later, helped the Church understand this truth as they met in Jerusalem to discuss the vital issue of whether Gentile believers should be circumcised or not (Ch. 15). They decided to advise the Gentile believers that they did not need to be circumcised (15:19), in order to be *"accepted"* by God (v 35); like every other believer, they should only depend on his rich grace. And hence, in chapter 13, Luke changed the focus of his narrative from Peter's mission to the Jews to Paul's mission to the Gentiles; and he does not even mention Peter's name after chapter 15. The Lord's mission turned a corner that day, in order to begin focusing on the Gentiles ([13]M. M. Ac 10:34).

10:36 In verse 36, Peter continued to explain how God first began to reveal his gracious plan of salvation to mankind; his mission-heart moved him to choose the nation of Israel by calling Abraham (Gen 12:1-3), so that he could first reveal his *"good news of peace"* (v 36) to them. But that was only the first part of his plan, because, in doing so, he gave them the awesome responsibility to pass this *"good news"* on to all other nations. And the heart of this *"good news"* is that Jesus Christ *"is Lord of all;"* and he brought *"peace"* to all nations (v 36; [14]M. M. Ac 13:46). But how miserably the nation of Israel had failed to carry out this responsibility for many generations! And of course, Peter himself had also implied in verse 28 that he too had failed to carry out this responsibility because of his sinful prejudice against his Gentile hearers. And, since his hearers were certainly sensitive to any prejudice against them by the Jews, they had, no doubt, appreciated his admission ([15]M. I. Jn 4:7).

10:41 Peter expresses his awe and a deep sense of responsibility in verse 41 that his resurrected Lord Jesus had appeared *"not to all the people but to us [twelve apostles] who had been chosen by God as [eye] witnesses, who ate and drank with him after he rose from the dead"* (Lk 24:42-43; Jn 21:12-15; [16]M. I. Ac 4:20). Then, some years later, Peter wrote in his first letter that even the Old Testament prophets and the angels had longed to be eye witnesses of the fulfillment of what God had promised to do in history, in order to save all mankind through his Son, Jesus (v 43; 1 Pet 1:10, 12; [17]M. M. Ac 2:24). Therefore, we can only imagine how eager Peter now was to witness to the name of Jesus on a much broader level on Level 3 (along with Saul) to his new Gentile friends at every opportunity he had ([18]M. I. Ac 2:4). (It's true that, sometime later, Peter himself did briefly fail to live according to his new understanding, until Paul had to rebuke him (Gal 2:11-14); however, he quickly repented and was forgiven.)

10:43 When Peter says in verse 43 *"that everyone who believes in him receives forgiveness of sins through his name,"* he clarifies his statement in verse 35 that *"anyone who fears him [God] and does what is right is acceptable to him."* The holy sacrifice of Jesus rescued <u>all</u> people from all nations from sin; however, on the last Day, when God will judge all of mankind (v 42), he will <u>only</u> accept those who have received his gracious <u>gift</u> of faith in his Son Jesus, and depended on his <u>grace</u>, and not on their own strength, to serve him (Heb 11:6; Eph 2:8-10; [19]M. M. Eph 2:10).

The Holy Spirit Falls on the Gentiles 10:44-48

10:44 *While Peter was still saying these things, the Holy Spirit fell on all who heard the word.*
10:45 *And the believers from among the circumcised who had come with Peter were amazed, because the gift of the Holy Spirit was poured out even on the Gentiles.*
10:46 *For they were hearing them speaking in tongues and extolling God. Then Peter declared,*
10:47 *"Can anyone withhold water for baptizing these people, who have received the Holy Spirit just as we have?"*
10:48 *And he commanded them to be baptized in the name of Jesus Christ. Then they asked him to remain for some days.*

10:44-46 (1) When verse 44 says that *"the Holy Spirit fell on all [of the Gentiles] who heard the word,"* we see that God, in fact, graciously gave them <u>four</u> gifts: **a)** First, he used the Gospel to create <u>faith</u> in his Son, Jesus in all of their hearts (2 Cor 4:6). **b)** Secondly, he also gave them his <u>Holy Spirit</u> to live in their hearts (v 45). **c)** Third, he also gave them totally new hearts, <u>mission-hearts</u> (Mt 5:14). **d)** Fourth, he also immediately gave them another spectacular gift that he normally does not give to a new believer so quickly ([20]M. I. 1 Cor 14: 2). The Jewish believers who were there were surprised when they saw the Gentiles *"speaking in tongues and extolling God"* (v 46). Under normal circumstances, a new Christian's faith is, of course, invisible (such as when a baby is baptized)—until his new faith moves him to do a good deed. However, this was a very unique Level 3 occasion in the mission of the new Church, because that day, the first group of Gentiles believed. Therefore, God used this spectacular gift, in order to immediately show Peter and the Jewish believers that he had also graciously given them the other three gifts, so that Peter would go back to Jerusalem and report to the Jewish believers there about what God had done (11:1-17). And thus, the Jewish believers in Jerusalem also glorified God by saying, *"Then to the Gentiles also God has granted repentance that leads to life"* (11:18). A new day had dawned in the new mission of the Church ([21]M. I. Lk 15:7)! **2)** When verse 45 says that *"the gift of the Holy Spirit was poured out even on the Gentiles,"* it teaches a very significant new truth, because it is another wonderful Gospel for the new Church and for its new mission to people of all nations. Verse 45 says that when God graciously gives a person the gift of faith, he also gives him the gift of his Holy Spirit, who is now dwelling in his new mission-heart. What wonderful Gospel for people from every nation on earth! And what wonderful Gospel it likewise was for the new Church, especially since the believers in Jerusalem recognized the significance of this important event (11:1-17)! It's a new mission message. M. M. Ac 10:45: When God graciously gives the gift of faith in his Son, Jesus to a person from any nation on earth, he also graciously gives him his Holy Spirit who now lives in his new mission-heart.

10:47-48 When Peter *"commanded them [the Gentiles] to be baptized"* (v 48), it's clear that he had seen exactly what the Holy Spirit wanted him to see: that the Gentiles had received four gracious gifts from God: faith in Jesus, and his Holy Spirit (v 45), who was now dwelling in their new mission-hearts (Mt 5:14), and obviously, the spectacular gift of speaking in tongues. And Peter obviously also knew that the fourth spectacular gift that they had received had nothing to do with a person's eternal salvation, because it is only a fruit of saving faith in Jesus that believers only use to praise God. On the other hand, the gift of faith is, of course, a believer's vital personal connection to Jesus ([22]M. M. Lk 13:24); therefore, Peter gave this command to baptize them, because they now had faith; and holy Baptism had already replaced circumcision as the outward sign of membership in the Church (2:38; [23]M. I. Mt 28:19 & [24]M. M. Ac 13:46).

10:48 Note that Peter *"commanded them to be baptized in the name of Jesus Christ,"* and he did not say: "in the name of the holy Trinity," as Jesus had commanded in (Mt 28:19). This new Trinitarian Baptism focused on Jesus as the God/man who had earned the forgiveness that a person receives as a gracious gift in holy Baptism (2:38; 8:16; 10:48; M. I. Mt 28:19).

---

[1] M. I. Ac 2:4: In cross-cultural situations, Christians should always focus on all of the needs of the target group by learning their heart-language and culture as deeply as possible, so that they can tell them the Gospel clearly in their own language and also help them with the true needs of their society.

[2] M. M. Ac 13:46: As he did with the old Israel, God first of all strengthens the faith of the new Israel, the Church with his Word and Sacraments, so that they can go and witness to the lost people of all nations.

[3] M. M. Ro 3:24: Jesus lived a life of perfect obedience and shed his precious blood on the cross, in order to graciously set all nations free from sin, which a person only receives by faith in him.

[4] M. M. Ro 3:26: God is just and fair to everyone, both when he condemns all people of all nations because all have sinned, and also when he only declares those people righteous who have faith in Jesus.

[5] M. I. Lk 5:36: Christians should use various kinds of illustrations that are culturally relevant in order to teach the Gospel, because illustrations begin with what their hearers already know about a concrete idea or a physical object in order to teach them a new abstract, spiritual truth.

[6] M. M. Mt 5:14: When the Holy Spirit creates faith in a person's heart, he also graciously gives him a new mission-heart that is eager to shine the light of the Gospel throughout the whole world.

[7] M. M. 1 Tim 2:3: It pleases God their Savior when Christians pray for all people because he desires all people to be saved and to come to the knowledge of the truth about Jesus.

[8] M. I. Ac 1:8: Christians should go and witness about Jesus to all who are lost from all languages and cultures by depending on the power of the Holy Spirit to help them bridge all of the language/cultural boundaries whether they are relatively easy, as in their own language, or extremely difficult.

[9] M. M. Ro 3:24: Jesus lived a life of perfect obedience and shed his precious blood on the cross, in order to graciously set all nations free from sin, which a person only receives by faith in him.

[10] M. M. Eph 2:10: God first prepares all of the good deeds that Christians will do in order to please him, and then he unites them with Jesus Christ, and then his Spirit helps them do them.

[11] M. M. Ro 1:5: The same Holy Spirit who creates <u>faith</u> and a new missionary <u>nature</u> in a person's heart also graciously empowers him to gratefully respond to his Lord's love by <u>obeying</u> him.

[12] M. M. Ro 1:16b: The Gospel is so powerful because it contains the central truth that Jesus rose from the dead with a glorified body in order to save all of his brothers and sisters from sin and death.

[13] M. M. Ac 10:34: God shows no partiality to any person from any nation on earth, but accepts anyone who fears and obeys him.

[14] M. M. Ac 13:46: As he did with the old Israel, God <u>first of all</u> strengthens the faith of the new Israel, the Church with his Word and Sacraments, so that they can go and witness to the lost people of all nations.

[15] M. I. Jn 4:7: Christians should begin witnessing to a person from a different language/culture by showing through their words and actions that they love him and are not prejudiced against him.

[16] M. I. Ac 4:20: Christians should boldly witness to the name of Jesus and allow nothing to stop their witness because it is the Holy Spirit's own message.

[17] M. M. Ac 2:24: Our Lord Jesus loosed the pangs of death for us mortal human beings when God raised him from the dead, because it was not possible for him to be held by death.

[18] M. I. Ac 2:4: In cross-cultural situations, Christians should always focus on all of the needs of the target group by learning <u>their</u> heart-language and culture as deeply as possible, so that they can tell them the Gospel clearly in their own language and also help them with the true needs of their society.

[19] M. M. Eph 2:10: God first prepares all of the good deeds that Christians will do in order to please him, and then he unites them with Jesus Christ, and then his Spirit helps them do them.

[20] M. I. 1 Cor 14:2: Christians should not use the Holy Spirit's gift of speaking in a strange language in a worship service when no one is present to interpret his message for other members, because obviously he is only speaking to God, and he is not using this gift to build up the members who cannot understand him.

[21] M. I. Lk 15:7: Christians should rejoice together with the heavenly Father and his angels when just <u>one</u> lost person hears the Law and Gospel and then receives the gracious gifts of a repentant heart and faith in Jesus.

[22] M. M. Lk 13:24: The <u>only</u> way to enter the Kingdom of God is to have <u>faith</u> in Jesus as one's Savior.

[23] M. I. Mt 28:19: Christians should go and proclaim God's Law and Gospel to all nations; then, baptize all who repent and believe after teaching them the meaning of holy Baptism.

[24] M. M. Ac 13:46: As he did with the old Israel, God <u>first of all</u> strengthens the faith of the new Israel, the Church with his Word and Sacraments, so that they can go and witness to the lost people of all nations.

Chapter 11

Peter Reports to the Church 11:1-18

11:1 *Now the apostles and the brothers who were throughout Judea heard that the Gentiles also had received the word of God.*

11:2 *So when Peter went up to Jerusalem, the circumcision party criticized him, saying,*

11:3 *"You went to uncircumcised men and ate with them."*

11:4 *But Peter began and explained it to them in order:*

11:5 *"I was in the city of Joppa praying, and in a trance I saw a vision, something like a great sheet descending, being let down from heaven by its four corners, and it came down to me.*

11:6 *Looking at it closely, I observed animals and beasts of prey and reptiles and birds of the air.*

11:7 *And I heard a voice saying to me, 'Rise, Peter; kill and eat.'*

11:8 *But I said, 'By no means, Lord; for nothing common or unclean has ever entered my mouth.'*

11:9 *But the voice answered a second time from heaven, 'What God has made clean, do not call common.'*

11:10 *This happened three times, and all was drawn up again into heaven.*

11:11 *And behold, at that very moment three men arrived at the house in which we were, sent to me from Caesarea.*

11:12 *And the Spirit told me to go with them, making no distinction. These six brothers also accompanied me, and we entered the man's house.*

11:13 *And he told us how he had seen the angel stand in his house and say, 'Send to Joppa and bring Simon who is called Peter;*

11:14 *he will declare to you a message by which you will be saved, you and all your household.'*

11:15 *As I began to speak, the Holy Spirit fell on them just as on us at the beginning.*

11:16 *And I remembered the word of the Lord, how he said, 'John baptized with water, but you will be baptized with the Holy*

>
> *Spirit.'*
>
> 11:17 *If then God gave the same gift to them as he gave to us when we believed in the Lord Jesus Christ, who was I that I could stand in God's way?"*
>
> 11:18 *When they heard these things they fell silent. And they glorified God, saying, "Then to the Gentiles also God has granted repentance that leads to life."*

11:1-4 Verse 2 says, *"So when Peter went up to Jerusalem, the circumcision party criticized him."* This is the first time in Luke's account that the issue of circumcision arose in the new Church; and sadly, Satan used it to plague them off and on for several years. Peter quickly answered it this first time in verses 4-17; however, it became a much more serious issue in (15:5), where it will be discussed at greater length. It became such a serious issue because the circumcision ceremony was a physical sign of membership in the Old Testament Jewish religion; until Jesus himself commanded the Church to baptize new believers, which replaced circumcision as the outward sign of membership in the Church (Mt 28:19). And he did this partly so that holy Baptism would become the public sign that, through him, the Church, as the new Israel has fulfilled the religion of the Old Israel; it is intimately connected to the old religion; and it is not a new sect ([1]M. M. Ro 3:31). However, it's rather obvious why this change was easily misunderstood by many believers and unbelievers; and the devil is very clever at using misunderstanding and confusion to cause division in the Church. And ultimately, his evil work led to the need for the crucial meeting in (15:5; [2]M. I. Lk 3:8 & [3]Lk 4:4).

11:5-18 Verse 3 is the first time in Luke's account that the issue about whether *circumcision* was still necessary first arose in the church in Jerusalem; therefore, Peter quickly defended his actions, since he obviously had learned God's will on the issue from his own experience. And, by quoting God's Word, he taught them two things in a very convincing way in verses 5-17: **a)** First, he assured them that he went to the house of a Gentile and ate with them because God had given him a clear command to do so in (v 9), *"What God has made clean, do not call* *common"* (Mt 15:11). Therefore, God himself clearly says that it is wrong to be racially prejudiced against anyone ([4]M. I. Jn 4:7). **b)** Secondly, Peter also told them that he had immediately ordered the believers who had gone with him to baptize the Gentiles because he had *"remembered the <u>word</u> of the Lord, how he said, 'John baptized with water, but you will be baptized with the Holy Spirit'"* (v 16). It was obvious to Peter that the Holy Spirit had gracious given the Gentiles faith in Jesus, because he also gave them the spectacular gift of speaking in tongues (10:46). Therefore, it was God's holy <u>Word</u> that easily convinced the believers in Jerusalem; and they *"glorified God"* in verse 18, saying, *"Then to the Gentiles also God has granted repentance that leads to life"* (16:9; [5]M. I. Lk 4:17).

The Church in Antioch 11:19-30

11:19 *Now those who were scattered because of the persecution that arose over Stephen traveled as far as Phoenicia and Cyprus and Antioch, speaking the word to no one except Jews.*
11:20 *But there were some of them, men of Cyprus and Cyrene, who on coming to Antioch spoke to the Hellenists also, preaching the Lord Jesus.*
11:21 *And the hand of the Lord was with them, and a great number who believed turned to the Lord.*
11:22 *The report of this came to the ears of the church in Jerusalem, and they sent Barnabas to Antioch.*
11:23 *When he came and saw the grace of God, he was glad, and he exhorted them all to remain faithful to the Lord with steadfast purpose,*
11:24 *for he was a good man, full of the Holy Spirit and of faith. And a great many people were added to the Lord.*
11:25 *So Barnabas went to Tarsus to look for Saul,*
11:26 *and when he had found him, he brought him to Antioch. For a whole year they met with the church and taught a great many people. And in Antioch the disciples were first called Christians.*

> 11:27 *Now in these days prophets came down from Jerusalem to Antioch.*
> 11:28 *And one of them named Agabus stood up and foretold by the Spirit that there would be a great famine over all the world (this took place in the days of Claudius).*
> 11:29 *So the disciples determined, everyone according to his ability, to send relief to the brothers living in Judea.*
> 11:30 *And they did so, sending it to the elders by the hand of Barnabas and Saul.*

11:19-20 Since verse 19 says that *"those who were scattered"* spoke *"the word to no one except Jews,"* it's obvious that the believers were confused about who should hear "the Word" (v 19). However, verse 20 adds that *"there were some of them"* who *"spoke to the Hellenists also, preaching the Lord Jesus."* Some believers must have been still following the biased way of thinking that they had grown up with that the Gentiles didn't deserve to hear the Gospel (vs 2-3). But others were eager to share such tremendous Gospel with both Jews and Gentile Greeks. Perhaps there was so much confusion over this issue because they suddenly were refugees, driven out of their homes in Jerusalem by persecution (8:1-4). And in such a chaotic situation, the believers were of course, also not able to communicate with each other about how they should be proclaiming the Gospel ([6]M. I. Ac 1:8).

11:22 Luke says in (8:14) that *"when the apostles at Jerusalem heard that Samaria had received the word of God, they sent to them Peter and John."* However, verse 22 is perhaps significant because it says that it was the church in Jerusalem that sent Barnabas to Antioch in Syria. It appears that, at least in Jerusalem, the church was more organized and felt responsible for sending out missionaries. Furthermore, the Christians in Antioch were Gentiles, so this was part of a Level 3 mission to all nations (M. I. Ac 1:8).

11:23-26 Next, the church in Jerusalem sent Barnabas to Antioch. And verse 23 says that Barnabas *"exhorted them all to remain faithful to the Lord with steadfast purpose."* And verse 24 adds that *"he was a good man, full of the Holy Spirit and of faith. And a great many people were added to the Lord."* But Barnabas must have also seen that there were still many more opportunities to spread the Gospel in Antioch; therefore, he went to find another missionary to help him. So Barnabas went to Tarsus to look for Saul ([7]M. I. Ac 6:3); and *"for a whole year they met with the church and taught a great many people. And in Antioch the disciples were first called Christians"* (v 26; [8]M. M. Ac 4:28). How wonderfully they advanced the Level 3 mission of the Church to many Gentiles in this one city! But Luke's account in chapters 13-28 reveals that the Lord of the mission had much more in mind for this strong group of Christians in Antioch in Syria. His Spirit was also building them up to become a <u>base</u> of operations for his great missionary, Saul, on <u>three</u> of his four missionary journeys (13:2-3; 15:40; 18:23; [9]M. I. Ro 15:20).

11:27-28 Verse 27 is the first time that Luke mentions *"prophets"* in the Church. (Other references are: 13:1; 15:32; 19:6; 21:9.) The fact that these prophets traveled together from Jerusalem to Antioch in Syria is reminiscent of the groups of prophets who went about together in some periods of the Old Testament (1 Sam 10; 1 Kng 18; 2 Kng 2). However, Luke gives no hint of why they went to Antioch; and they must not have stayed in Antioch because in (13:1), Agabus is not in the list of five prophets who were there at that time. Therefore, it's important to ask what <u>functions</u> prophets had in the mission of the early Church. **a)** First of all, here in verse 28 and in (21:11), Agabus was guided by the Holy Spirit to <u>predict</u> the future. Obviously, this must have been helpful to the Church; however, a message that predicts the future does not contain the Gospel, and therefore, it cannot create faith ([10]M. M. Ro 10:17a). **b)** Secondly however, (15:32) says that other prophets and prophetesses *"encouraged and <u>strengthened</u>"* the Christians; and a message that strengthened them would certainly contain the Gospel which does create and strengthen faith; therefore, the latter function was much more important for the mission of the Church (M. M. Ro 10:17a). Nevertheless, Luke says very little about prophets in his account; and in his letter, Paul mentions Christian prophets only once in (1 Cor 14:37).

11:29 Verse 29 adds that this group of Christians in Antioch *"determined, everyone according to his ability, to send <u>relief</u> to the brothers living in Judea."* In addition to their later important work of being a base of operations for Saul and his missionary teams, the Holy Spirit now also moved them to contribute to the <u>physical</u> needs of the Church. They sent help to the Christians living in Judea who were suffering from a famine ([11]M. I. Ac 4:34).

---

[1] M. M. Ro 3:31: Christianity <u>fulfills</u> the Jewish religion because the Holy Spirit empowers Christians to <u>obey</u> God's Law and thus also obey Jesus who fulfilled all of God's Laws for them.

[2] M. I. Lk 3:8: Christians should always be prepared to boldly and publicly refute false teaching, so that Satan cannot easily deceive people.

[3] M. I. Lk 4:4: When Satan attacks Christians on their mission they should wield the sword of God's Word by quoting from it, and not depend on their own strength.

[4] M. I. Jn 4:7: Christians should begin witnessing to a person from a different language/culture by showing through their words and actions that they love him and are not prejudiced against him.

[5] M. I. Lk 4:17: Christians should always base their messages on the Bible, so that the Holy Spirit can use his holy Word to create and strengthen faith in their hearers.

[6] M. I. Ac 1:8: Christians should go and witness about Jesus to all who are lost from all languages and cultures by depending on the power of the Holy Spirit to help them bridge all of the language/cultural boundaries whether they are relatively easy, as in their own language, or extremely difficult.

[7] M. I. Ac 6:3: The local group of Christians should choose men who will lead them; and then those in authority should publicly commission them before they begin their work.

[8] M. M. Ac 4:12: <u>Only</u> the power of Jesus' name can save a person from sin.

[9] M. I. Ro 15:20: As Christians go on their mission to the world, they should maximize their efforts by establishing mission bases, in order to be able to spread the Gospel in areas where no other missionaries have worked.

[10] M. M. Ro 10:17a: The Holy Spirit <u>only</u> creates and preserves faith by using the message of God's grace in his holy Word.

[11] M. I. Ac 4:34: Christians should care for needy people, so that they can not only help them, but the public would also see their love for them, which could also create opportunities for them to tell them the Gospel.

Chapter 12

James Killed and Peter Imprisoned 12:1-5

12:1   *About that time Herod the king laid violent hands on some who belonged to the church.*
12:2   *He killed James the brother of John with the sword,*
12:3   *and when he saw that it pleased the Jews, he proceeded to arrest Peter also. This was during the days of Unleavened Bread.*
12:4   *And when he had seized him, he put him in prison, delivering him over to four squads of soldiers to guard him, intending after the Passover to bring him out to the people.*
12:5   *So Peter was kept in prison, but earnest prayer for him was made to God by the church.*

12:1-5 (1) Satan was becoming more and more angry with the fact that many people on all three levels of the mission, both Jews and Gentiles, were starting to follow *"the Way,"* so he, once again, found another human instrument to use against the proclamation of the Gospel. This time it was King Herod Agrippa. It was the king's enormous pride that made him a useful tool for Satan, because he even went to the extent of claiming to be a god (v 22). King Herod's attack was against the leaders of the church because he was eager to gain the favor of the Jewish religious leaders. He had James the brother of John killed (v 2); and this pleased the Jews so much that he went after their main leader, Peter (v 3). However Peter's death at this time would probably have been devastating to the Church's mission; but it was neither Satan nor the king who were in control. It was, of course, the Lord of the mission who was in full control ([1]M. M. Ac 4:28). **2)** Verse 5 says that *"earnest prayer for him [Peter] was made to God by the church."* Prayer was, and of course, still is powerful for Christians because prayer shows that they are depending on God's grace, and not on their own strength ([2]M. I. Lk 11:10).

Peter is Rescued 12:6-19

12:6   *Now when Herod was about to bring him out, on that very night, Peter was sleeping between two soldiers, bound with two chains, and sentries before the door were guarding the prison.*
12:7   *And behold, an angel of the Lord stood next to him, and a light shone in the cell. He struck Peter on the side and woke him, saying, "Get up quickly." And the chains fell off his hands.*
12:8   *And the angel said to him, "Dress yourself and put on your sandals." And he did so. And he said to him, "Wrap your cloak around you and follow me."*
12:9   *And he went out and followed him. He did not know that what was being done by the angel was real, but thought he was seeing a vision.*
12:10 *When they had passed the first and the second guard, they came to the iron gate leading into the city. It opened for them of its own accord, and they went out and went along one street, and immediately the angel left him.*
12:11 *When Peter came to himself, he said, "Now I am sure that the Lord has sent his angel and rescued me from the hand of Herod and from all that the Jewish people were expecting."*
12:12 *When he realized this, he went to the house of Mary, the mother of John whose other name was Mark, where many were gathered together and were praying.*
12:13 *And when he knocked at the door of the gateway, a servant girl named Rhoda came to answer.*
12:14 *Recognizing Peter's voice, in her joy she did not open the gate but ran in and reported that Peter was standing at the gate.*
12:15 *They said to her, "You are out of your mind." But she kept insisting that it was so, and they kept saying, "It is his angel!"*
12:16 *But Peter continued knocking, and when they opened, they saw him and were amazed.*
12:17 *But motioning to them with his hand to be silent, he described to them how the Lord had brought him out of the prison. And he said, "Tell these things to James and to the brothers." Then he*

> *departed and went to another place.*
> 12:18 *Now when day came, there was no little disturbance among the soldiers over what had become of Peter.*
> 12:19 *And after Herod searched for him and did not find him, he examined the sentries and ordered that they should be put to death. Then he went down from Judea to Caesarea and spent time there.*

12:7 The Lord of the mission intervened a second time, as he did in (5:19), by sending an angel to rescue Peter from prison (v 7). The Holy Spirit still had many ways that he could use Peter's *"apostolic ministry to the circumcised [the Jews]"* (Gal 2:8) on Level 1 of the mission (^{3}M. M. Ac 4:28).

12:17 Verse 17, is Luke's first reference in the book of Acts to James, a half-brother of Jesus. Obviously, when Peter says in this verse that they should *"tell these things to James"* he is implying that James was already a leader in the church Jerusalem; and we do, in fact, see him later filling that role in (15:13; 21:18; 1 Cor 15:7; Gal 1:19; Gal 2:9). The holy Words of Jesus had eventually touched his heart and created faith there (Gal 1:19; ^{4}M. M. Ro 10:17a).

The Death of Herod 12:20-25

> 12:20 *Now Herod was angry with the people of Tyre and Sidon, and they came to him with one accord, and having persuaded Blastus, the king's chamberlain, they asked for peace, because their country depended on the king's country for food.*
> 12:21 *On an appointed day Herod put on his royal robes, took his seat upon the throne, and delivered an oration to them.*
> 12:22 *And the people were shouting, "The voice of a god, and not of a man!"*
> 12:23 *Immediately an angel of the Lord struck him down, because he did not give God the glory, and he was eaten by worms and breathed his last.*
> 12:24 *But the word of God increased and multiplied.*

> 12:25 *And Barnabas and Saul returned from Jerusalem when they had completed their service, bringing with them John, whose other name was Mark.*

12:20-23 King Herod failed to stop the mission of the Church (v 24); however, his arrogance just increased more and more until God himself destroyed him, so that Satan could no longer use him against God's mission. He must have been incredibly evil because Scripture records very few times when God himself killed someone evil (1 Sam 2:34, 25:38; M. M. Ac 4:28).

12:24-5 After King Herod was dead, the Church had peace again and *"the word of God increased and multiplied"* (v 24; [5]M. I. Lk 11:10 & [6]M. M. Ro 5:1). It was, of course, the Holy Spirit who used the sharp sword of his holy Word to win many followers of *"the Way."* This is Luke's third summary of progress of the Lord's mission (6:7; 9:31; [7]M. M. Ro 10:17a & [8]Lk 13:24).

---

[1] M. M. Ac 4:28: The heavenly Father is always in full control of his mission to all nations of the world.

[2] M. I. Lk 11:10: Christians should <u>continuously</u> pray to their heavenly Father and <u>always</u> depend on his grace, and not on their own feeble strength, because he <u>always</u> loves them.

[3] M. M. Ac 4:28: The heavenly Father is always in full control of his mission to all nations of the world.

[4] M. M. Ro 10:17a: The Holy Spirit <u>only</u> creates and preserves faith by using the message of God's grace in his holy Word.

[5] M. I. Lk 11:10: Christians should <u>continuously</u> pray to their heavenly Father and <u>always</u> depend on his grace, and not on their own feeble strength, because he <u>always</u> loves them.

[6] M. M. Ro 5:1: On the cross, Jesus earned <u>peace</u> with God for <u>all</u> of his brothers and sisters from every nation on earth.

[7] M. M. Ro 10:17a: The Holy Spirit <u>only</u> creates and preserves faith by using the message of God's grace in his holy Word.

[8] M. M. Lk 13:24: The <u>only</u> way to enter the Kingdom of God is to have <u>faith</u> in Jesus as one's Savior.

Chapter 13

Barnabas and Saul Sent Off 13:1-3

13:1 *Now there were in the church at Antioch prophets and teachers, Barnabas, Simeon who was called Niger, Lucius of Cyrene, Manaen a member of the court of Herod the tetrarch, and Saul.*
13:2 *While they were worshiping the Lord and fasting, the Holy Spirit said, "Set apart for me Barnabas and Saul for the work to which I have called them."*
13:3 *Then after fasting and praying they laid their hands on them and sent them off.*

13:1 The strength of the group of Christians in Antioch in Syria was also apparent in the fact that there were five prophets and teachers among them—including Barnabas and Saul. Because Luke calls them both *"prophets and teachers,"* their main function apparently was to *"encourage[d] and strengthen[ed]"* the Christians, as in (15:32), and not to predict the future (11:28). Just as Jesus himself was both a prophet (Lk 4:24) and a teacher (Lk 6:40), there were apparently few distinctions in the early Church between the functions of prophets and teachers (v 1, (2 Tim 1:11). The main mission of the Church was then, and will always be, to create and strengthen faith through proclaiming and teaching the Gospel (6:4; [1]M. I. Ac 6:1).
13:2-3 (1) Four things are very significant in verses 2-3 for the new Christian Church and for the Lord's mission: **a)** First, these verses mark a major shift in Luke's account from focusing on Peter's mission to the Jews on Level 1 to focusing on Saul's missionary journeys to the Gentiles on Level 3 throughout the remainder of his book ([2]M. M. Ac 1:8). It's the beginning of the first of Saul's four missionary journeys. **b)** And secondly, it's likewise very significant that verse 2 says that it was the Holy Spirit who chose Barnabas and Saul to leave their work in Antioch as prophets and teachers, in order to go out as his first missionaries to Gentile territories (v 4; [3]M. M. Ac 4:28). **c)** And thirdly,

we see that the Holy Spirit had indeed made the church in Antioch strong enough to became Saul's base of operations for three of his four missionary journeys (11:25). They showed their dependence on the guidance of the Holy Spirit by *"worshiping the Lord"* and by *"fasting and praying"* before they *"sent them off"* (v 2). It's a new mission imperative. M. I. Ac 13:3: Christians should prayerfully seek the will of the Lord of the mission as they decide how they are going to deploy their missionaries. **d)** And finally, also note that the Holy Spirit deliberately sent out his missionaries two-by-two, just as Jesus had done in (Lk 10:1), so that their testimony would be confirmed by two witnesses ([4]M. I. Lk 10:1). It's true that John Mark did accompany them at times (v 5); however, that only demonstrates that the number two was a minimal number of witnesses that were important ([5]M. I. Lk 6:13).

Barnabas and Saul on Cyprus 13:4-12

13:4 *So, being sent out by the Holy Spirit, they went down to Seleucia, and from there they sailed to Cyprus.*

13:5 *When they arrived at Salamis, they proclaimed the word of God in the synagogues of the Jews. And they had John to assist them.*

13:6 *When they had gone through the whole island as far as Paphos, they came upon a certain magician, a Jewish false prophet named Bar-Jesus.*

13:7 *He was with the proconsul, Sergius Paulus, a man of intelligence, who summoned Barnabas and Saul and sought to hear the word of God.*

13:8 *But Elymas the magician (for that is the meaning of his name) opposed them, seeking to turn the proconsul away from the faith.*

13:9 *But Saul, who was also called Paul, filled with the Holy Spirit, looked intently at him*

13:10 *and said, "You son of the devil, you enemy of all righteousness, full of all deceit and villainy, will you not stop making crooked the straight paths of the Lord?*

13:11 *And now, behold, the hand of the Lord is upon you, and you will be blind and unable to see the sun for a time." Immediately mist and darkness fell upon him, and he went about seeking people to lead him by the hand.*

13:12 *Then the proconsul believed, when he saw what had occurred, for he was astonished at the teaching of the Lord.*

13:4 (1) Luke emphasizes again in verse 4 that it was the Spirit of Jesus who sent Saul, Barnabas (Luke adds John Mark in v 5) on this mission because he was, of course, in charge of the mission ([6]M. M. Ac 4:28). **2)** No doubt, Barnabas and Saul started their missionary journey on the island of Cyprus (v 4) because it was the home of Barnabas. He would have known many people there who would have welcomed them in their homes; and they may also have been open to hearing the Gospel ([7]M. I. Ac 2:4).

13:5 Note that verse 5 says that *"they proclaimed the word of God in the synagogues of the Jews."* As Saul began his first missionary journey, we note that he chose the synagogue as his first venue to proclaim the Gospel. Many, many times throughout his first three missionary journeys, when Saul first arrived in a new town, he consistently first went to the synagogue. But why did he do so? He had perhaps as many as *six* good reasons for this: **a)** First of all, nearly every Gentile town that Saul visited had a synagogue where Jews and Gentiles gathered to worship; and this, of course, created ready opportunities to speak to a group. Furthermore, apparently there were only a few towns, such as Philippi (16:13), that had no synagogue ([8]M. I. Lk 4:15). **b)** Secondly, the synagogues were the only places, except for the temple in Jerusalem, where copies of the Scriptures were kept. And two Scripture readings were important parts of every worship service; and, of course, Saul wanted to base his messages on God's holy Word ([9]M. I. Lk 4:17). **c)** Thirdly, in every worship service that a visiting teacher was present, it was common practice for the leader of the synagogue to invite him to read one passage from the Law and one from the prophets and then expound on their meanings. This obviously created an open opportunity for visitors to speak, which Jesus himself, of course, also exploited (Lk

4:16; M. I. Lk 4:15). **d)** Fourthly, both <u>Jews</u> and also <u>Gentile</u> converts to Judaism, as well as both men and women, were regular worshippers in the synagogues (vs 16, 26, 43). It provided opportunities for Saul to witness to devout Gentiles, and then to also meet them, so that he could also meet their family and friends ([10]M. M. Ac 5:1). **e)** Fifthly, all of these worshippers would also have been <u>ready</u> to listen to how Saul would interpret the readings since they all devoutly (2:5) believed that the Scriptures are God's <u>inspired</u> Word ([11]M. M. Ro 10:17a). **f)** And finally, Saul made every effort to tell the Gospel to his fellow Jews <u>first</u> ([12]M. M. Ac 13:46). The Jews who were devout would have been the ones who worshiped regularly in their synagogues (2:5), and therefore, they also would have been most open to hearing the Gospel ([13]M. I. Ac 1:8). And Saul apparently first witnessed to Jews in spite of the fact that, on his very first missionary journey, he had his first major confrontation with some radical Jews in Antioch in Pisidia (13:46; M. M. Ac 13:46).

13:6-9 Why did the Roman governor send for Barnabas and Saul? Since he was *"a man of intelligence"* (v 7), he was no doubt alert to any new ideas; and some people who heard Barnabas and Saul preaching in the synagogues must have eagerly shared the Gospel with him. However, Satan had other plans to try to stop the proclamation of the Gospel. He possessed and inspired a false prophet, Barjesus, who was close to the governor, so that he could use him to try to prevent the governor from hearing the Gospel. (In Luke's account, it may appear that Barjesus (an Aramaic name) and Elymas (a Greek name) are two different people, but the one man had two names.) However, Saul was *"filled with"* a more powerful Spirit, *"the Holy Spirit"* (v 9), who gave him the power to strike Barjesus blind. This miracle was a public refutation of his evil lies; and it attracted the governor to the Gospel even more. And the Holy Spirit, then, used *"the teaching of the Lord"* so that *"he believed"* (v 12; [14]M. I. Ac 3:6 & [15]Lk 3:8).

13:9 Verse 9 is the first time that Luke began using Saul's Greek name, <u>Paul</u> in his account. Saul was his Hebrew name, which means: "asked [of God];" and Paul was his Greek name, which means: "little." Some scholars speculate that he did so because, from this point on, he had now fully entered into his mission to the Gentiles. However, another explanation may be that Luke was acknowledging in this way that Paul was exceptionally qualified to be a cross-cultural missionary ([16]M. I. Ac 1:8). In any case, Luke consistently calls him Paul from this point on.

Paul and Barnabas in Antioch of Pisidia 13:13-52

13:13 *Now Paul and his companions set sail from Paphos and came to Perga in Pamphylia. And John left them and returned to Jerusalem,*
13:14 *but they went on from Perga and came to Antioch in Pisidia. And on the Sabbath day they went into the synagogue and sat down.*
13:15 *After the reading from the Law and the Prophets, the rulers of the synagogue sent a message to them, saying, "Brothers, if you have any word of exhortation for the people, say it."*
13:16 *So Paul stood up, and motioning with his hand said: "Men of Israel and you who fear God, listen.*
13:17 *The God of this people Israel chose our fathers and made the people great during their stay in the land of Egypt, and with uplifted arm he led them out of it.*
13:18 *And for about forty years he put up with them in the wilderness.*
13:19 *And after destroying seven nations in the land of Canaan, he gave them their land as an inheritance.*
13:20 *All this took about 450 years. And after that he gave them judges until Samuel the prophet.*
13:21 *Then they asked for a king, and God gave them Saul the son of Kish, a man of the tribe of Benjamin, for forty years.*
13:22 *And when he had removed him, he raised up David to be their king, of whom he testified and said, 'I have found in David the son of Jesse a man after my heart, who will do all my will.'*
13:23 *Of this man's offspring God has brought to Israel a Savior, Jesus, as he promised.*
13:24 *Before his coming, John had proclaimed a baptism of repentance to all the people of Israel.*
13:25 *And as John was finishing his course, he said, 'What do you*

suppose that I am? I am not he. No, but behold, after me one is coming, the sandals of whose feet I am not worthy to untie.'

13:26 *"Brothers, sons of the family of Abraham, and those among you who fear God, to us has been sent the message of this salvation.*

13:27 *For those who live in Jerusalem and their rulers, because they did not recognize him nor understand the utterances of the prophets, which are read every Sabbath, fulfilled them by condemning him.*

13:28 *And though they found in him no guilt worthy of death, they asked Pilate to have him executed.*

13:29 *And when they had carried out all that was written of him, they took him down from the tree and laid him in a tomb.*

13:30 *But God raised him from the dead,*

13:31 *and for many days he appeared to those who had come up with him from Galilee to Jerusalem, who are now his witnesses to the people.*

13:32 *And we bring you the good news that what God promised to the fathers,*

13:33 *this he has fulfilled to us their children by raising Jesus, as also it is written in the second Psalm, "'You are my Son, today I have begotten you.'*

13:34 *And as for the fact that he raised him from the dead, no more to return to corruption, he has spoken in this way, "'I will give you the holy and sure blessings of David.'*

13:35 *Therefore he says also in another psalm, "'You will not let your Holy One see corruption.'*

13:36 *For David, after he had served the purpose of God in his own generation, fell asleep and was laid with his fathers and saw corruption,*

13:37 *but he whom God raised up did not see corruption.*

13:38 *Let it be known to you therefore, brothers, that through this man forgiveness of sins is proclaimed to you, and by him everyone who believes is freed from everything*

13:39 *from which you could not be freed by the Law of Moses.*

13:40 *Beware, therefore, lest what is said in the Prophets should come about:*

13:41 *"'Look, you scoffers, be astounded and perish; for I am doing a work in your days, a work that you will not believe, even if one tells it to you.'"*

13:42 *As they went out, the people begged that these things might be told them the next Sabbath.*

13:43 *And after the meeting of the synagogue broke up, many Jews and devout converts to Judaism followed Paul and Barnabas, who, as they spoke with them, urged them to continue in the grace of God.*

13:44 *The next Sabbath almost the whole city gathered to hear the word of the Lord.*

13:45 *But when the Jews saw the crowds, they were filled with jealousy and began to contradict what was spoken by Paul, reviling him.*

13:46 *And Paul and Barnabas spoke out boldly, saying, "It was necessary that the word of God be spoken first to you. Since you thrust it aside and judge yourselves unworthy of eternal life, behold, we are turning to the Gentiles.*

13:47 *For so the Lord has commanded us, saying, "'I have made you a light for the Gentiles, that you may bring salvation to the ends of the earth.'"*

13:48 *And when the Gentiles heard this, they began rejoicing and glorifying the word of the Lord, and as many as were appointed to eternal life believed.*

13:49 *And the word of the Lord was spreading throughout the whole region.*

13:50 *But the Jews incited the devout women of high standing and the leading men of the city, stirred up persecution against Paul and Barnabas, and drove them out of their district.*

13:51 *But they shook off the dust from their feet against them and went to Iconium.*

13:52 *And the disciples were filled with joy and with the Holy Spirit.*

13:13 (1) John Mark's desertion did not seem to have any immediate consequences for the missionary journey of Paul and Barnabas; however, it did have a dramatic effect later on because it <u>separated</u> this dynamic team of two men (15:36-40). Nevertheless, they did at that time then form two missionary teams instead of one, because Barnabas then took John Mark on his second missionary journey; and Paul took Silas on his second missionary journey. There is no doubt that Satan was behind this disagreement; however, it's equally obvious that it was the Holy Spirit who was in full control; and he turned it into an expansion of his mission rather than its demise ([17]M. M. Ac 4:28). **2)** Paul did, however, reconcile with John Mark some years later. In fact he was so eager to have him with him in his imprisonment in Rome that he said, *"Only Luke is with me. Get Mark and bring him with you. He is useful to me in my work"* (2 Tim 4:11).

13:14-15 These verses explicitly express two main reasons (that are included in the list above at verses 4-5) why synagogues were such an excellent venue for proclaiming the Gospel. **a)** The rulers of the synagogue said in verse 15, *"Brothers, if you have any word of exhortation for the people, say it."* It was such a wonderfully wide open door that it could only have been the Lord of the mission himself who created it in almost every city and town in the entire Roman Empire. **b)** Equally important, this was an open door to expound the meaning of the Scriptures to both Jews and also Gentile converts to Judaism who believed them to be God's inspired Word. The fact that such wide open doors were scattered throughout the Empire demonstrates at least two things: that the Lord Jesus truly was in control of his mission, and that he was, of course, still truly eager to *"seek the lost"* (Lk 19:10; 15:20; [18]M. I. Lk 4:15 & [19]Ac 4:20).

13:16 In his very brief introduction in verse 16, Paul addressed both the *"men of Israel and you who fear God [Gentiles]."* He was obviously saying that the Gospel was meant for all of them; however, this must have been especially good news for his Gentile hearers to hear ([20]M. M. Ro 3:24). The fact that these Gentiles were worshipping in the synagogue showed that God had already graciously given them faith in him; but now they were about to hear even better Gospel: that Jesus had fulfilled all of God's promises in Scripture for them as well. And then Paul confirmed that the Gospel was also meant for them in verse 26 when he said, *"Brothers, sons of the family of Abraham, and those* *among you who fear God, to us has been sent the message of this salvation."* What tremendous Gospel this was for these Gentiles ([21]M. I. Ac 2:4)!

13:17-37 In verses 17-37, Paul recounted the life of Jesus in order to demonstrate to his hearers how Jesus had completely fulfilled God's promises in their Scriptures. He said in verses 32-33, *"we bring you the good news that what God promised to the fathers, this he has fulfilled to us their children by raising Jesus."* He made it very clear to them that the death and resurrection of Jesus are the final proof that he had fulfilled every promise that his heavenly Father had ever made to his people (2 Cor 1:20; [22]M. M. Ac 2:24 & [23]M. I. Ac 4:20).

13:38-41 Paul begins his conclusion in verses 38-39 by briefly summarizing the Gospel once again; however, he ends his message in verse 40-41 with the Law, a severe warning to not reject the Gospel. The situation in Antioch in Pisidia may have been similar to the angry audience of Jews that Stephen faced in chapter 7. On that occasion, Stephen had waited until the end of his message to convict his fellow Jews of their sins. Here in Paul's case, the initial reaction of the Jews seemed to be very positive; however, in a few short days, some of the Jews in the town turned against the mission team. Therefore, it appears that the Holy Spirit gave Paul the wisdom to sense their true mood before he began to speak to them, so that he first told them the Gospel before he convicted them of their sin ([24]M. I. Lk 3:3b & [25]Lk 12:12).

13:42-43 The Holy Spirit used Paul's Law and Gospel message to work in the hearts of many of his hearers, so that on this first day *"the people begged that these things might be told them the next Sabbath"* (v 42). Furthermore, many of them followed Paul and Barnabas in order to eagerly hear more. They did not reject it as some other Jews did one week later. In fact, their faith is so obvious that it's possible that Paul may have baptized them immediately, but Luke is silent on this point ([26]M. I. Mt 28:19).

13:44-45 The Jews who became jealous because Paul and Barnabas had become so popular were evidently a vocal few, but they were perhaps wealthy and powerful because verse 50 says that they were able to incite *"the devout women of high standing and the leading men of the city."*

Luke does not say whether these Jews also heard Paul speak; but even if they did, their hearts were obviously already hardened and resistant to the Holy Spirit ([27]M. M. Ro 11:7).

13:46 (1) In God's gracious mission-plan, he called Abraham, gave him faith and blessed him and his descendants first, so that they would be able to share the Gospel with the Gentile nations (Gen 12:1-3). However, two sad things happened in this Old Testament era: **a)** Scripture reveals that this nation of Israel seldom shared the Gospel with the Gentile nations. **b)** And furthermore, some of the Israelites stubbornly and persistently rejected God. And Paul's words in verse 46, *"Since you reject the word and consider yourselves unworthy of everlasting life,"* indicate that some Jews were still doing so (M. M. 2 Cor 2:16). Furthermore, much later Paul wrote about this in (Rom 11:25-26) *"a partial hardening has come upon Israel, until the fullness of the Gentiles has come in. And in this way all Israel will be saved"* (Rom 11:11-24; [28]M. M. Ro 3:26 & [29]Ro 11:26). **2)** Also note in verse 46 that Paul said, *"It was necessary that the word of God be spoken first to you."* **a)** God had first blessed the nation of Israel in the Old Testament era, in order to strengthen their faith in him, so that they would be able to bless all other nations with the Gospel. **b)** In the same way, after Jesus' ascension (1:9; Mt 28:20), in this new era, God first of all strengthens the faith of the new Israel, the Church with his Word and Sacraments, so that we can bless the lost people of all nations with the Gospel. God's mission-heart, of course, has never changed because he continues to use his same perfect mission plan. He is still busy creating a new world-wide spiritual nation of Israel, the Church. It's a new mission message. M. M. Ac 13:46: As he did with the old Israel, God first of all strengthens the faith of the new Israel, the Church with his Word and Sacraments, so that they can go and witness to the lost people of all nations.

13:48 The Gentiles who hear Paul's bold reply in verse 46, on the other hand, rejoiced to hear the very good news that the Gospel was also meant for them (Lk 20:16; [30]M. M. 1 Tim 2:3). Verse 48 says that they *"were pleased with what they heard and praised the Lord's word. Everyone who had been prepared for everlasting life believed."* In contrast to the Jews, they did not have the same problem of assuming that they were already God's people, and therefore, deserved God's rescue from sin. Verse 48 teaches God's rich grace for <u>all</u> people of <u>all</u> nations because from eternity he chose those who would be his own eternally (Eph 1:3-14; [31]M. M. Ro 4:11), and he graciously gives them the gift of faith (Eph 2:8-9). But those who stubbornly reject his grace choose for themselves eternal condemnation. These conflicting truths are so difficult to understand that our feeble human minds cannot grasp the <u>divine</u> "logic" of our gracious God. It may sound like God discriminates against some people; but nothing could be further from the truth ([32]M. I. Jn 4:7).

13:49 The statement in verse 49 is another in a long series of "progress reports" (12:24), but this one is the first report concerning growth on Level 3 of the mission among the Gentiles. And like some of the earlier reports, many Gentiles in Antioch in Pisidia believed the Gospel, in spite of the fact that some Jews started persecuting Paul and Barnabas (vs 50-51). It is also obvious here that it was the Lord of the mission who was in control in spite of all of the opposition from a few Jews ([33]M. M. Ac 4:28).

13:50-52 People who reject God's grace in Jesus have made a terrible decision that may mean that if they persist in rejecting him, God may, after great patience, condemn them forever. However, as long as there is still a possibility that they may on another occasion hear the Gospel, they could still repent and believe. Therefore, in love and concern for them, Paul and Barnabas gave them a warning that was very graphic in their own culture; they *"shook off the dust from their feet"* (v 51; [34]M. I. Lk 3:8). It was a severe warning that Paul and Barnabas were not responsible for God's punishment on them, since they had faithfully proclaimed the Gospel to them ([35]M. M. Lk 8:11).

---

[1] M. I. Ac 6:1: Christians should always remember that the main aspect of the mission is to proclaim the Law and Gospel message and should not allow any other aspect of the work to hinder this main work.

[2] M. I. Ac 1:8: Christians should go and witness about Jesus to all who are lost from all

languages and cultures by depending on the power of the Holy Spirit to help them bridge all of the language/cultural boundaries whether they are relatively easy, as in their own language, or extremely difficult.

³ M. M. Ac 4:28: The heavenly Father is always in full control of his mission to all nations of the world.

⁴ M. I. Lk 10:1: Christians should go on their mission to all nations two by two in order to affirm each other's witness.

⁵ M. I. Lk 6:13: Christians should choose new leaders and train them in order to multiply the work.

⁶ M. M. Ac 4:28: The heavenly Father is always in full control of his mission to all nations of the world.

⁷ M. I. Ac 2:4: In cross-cultural situations, Christians should always focus on all of the needs of the target group by learning their heart-language and culture as deeply as possible, so that they can tell them the Gospel clearly in their own language and also help them with the true needs of their society.

⁸ M. I. Lk 4:15: Christians should seize every opportunity to proclaim the Gospel to lost people of all nations.

⁹ M. I. Lk 4:17: Christians should always base their messages on the Bible, so that the Holy Spirit can use his holy Word to create and strengthen faith in their hearers.

¹⁰ M. M. Ac 5:1: The Holy Spirit often uses personal relationships in order to strengthen the unity of the family of the Church.

¹¹ M. M. Ro 10:17a: The Holy Spirit only creates and preserves faith by using the message of God's grace in his holy Word.

¹² M. M. Ac 13:46: As he did with the old Israel, God first of all strengthens the faith of the new Israel, the Church with his Word and Sacraments, so that they can go and witness to the lost people of all nations.

¹³ M. I. Ac 1:8: Christians should go and witness about Jesus to all who are lost from all languages and cultures by depending on the power of the Holy Spirit to help them bridge all of the language/cultural boundaries whether they are relatively easy, as in their own language, or extremely difficult.

¹⁴ M. I. Ac 3:6: Christians should heal a person's physical problem by speaking the name of Jesus, so that everyone knows that it was the divine power of Jesus that healed him.

¹⁵ M. I. Lk 3:8: Christians should always be prepared to boldly and publicly refute false teaching, so that Satan cannot easily deceive people.

¹⁶ M. I. Ac 1:8: Christians should go and witness about Jesus to all who are lost from all languages and cultures by depending on the power of the Holy Spirit to help them bridge all of the language/cultural boundaries whether they are relatively easy, as in their own language, or extremely difficult.

¹⁷ M. M. Ac 4:28: The heavenly Father is always in full control of his mission to all nations of the world.

¹⁸ M. I. Lk 4:15: Christians should seize every opportunity to proclaim the Gospel to lost people of all nations.

¹⁹ M. I. Ac 4:20: Christians should boldly witness to the name of Jesus and allow nothing to stop

their witness because it is the Holy Spirit's own message.

[20] M. M. Ro 3:24: Jesus lived a life of perfect obedience and shed his precious blood on the cross, in order to graciously set all nations free from sin, which a person only receives by faith in him.

[21] M. I. Ac 2:4: In cross-cultural situations, Christians should always focus on all of the needs of the target group by learning their heart-language and culture as deeply as possible, so that they can tell them the Gospel clearly in their own language and also help them with the true needs of their society.

[22] M. M. Ac 2:24: Our Lord Jesus loosed the pangs of death for us mortal human beings when God raised him from the dead, because it was not possible for him to be held by death.

[23] M. I. Ac 4:20: Christians should boldly witness to the name of Jesus and allow nothing to stop their witness because it is the Holy Spirit's own message.

[24] M. I. Lk 3:3b: Christians should always depend on the Holy Spirit's guidance for whether they should emphasize God's Law or the Gospel about Jesus, and which one to apply first.

[25] M. I. Lk 12:12: Christians should go and tell the Gospel depending on the Holy Spirit to teach them what they should say.

[26] M. I. Mt 28:19: Christians should go and proclaim God's Law and Gospel to all nations; then, baptize all who repent and believe after teaching them the meaning of holy Baptism.

[27] M. M. Ro 11:7: After patiently waiting for a person to repent, God may ultimately eternally condemn him by hardening his heart and closing his ears to hear and understand his holy Word.

[28] M. M. Ro 3:26: God is just and fair to everyone, both when he condemns all people of all nations because all have sinned, and also when he *only* declares those people righteous who have faith in Jesus.

[29] M. M. Ro 11:26: God graciously continues to graft Jews and Gentiles into the new Israel through the proclamation of the Gospel, until the remnant of Israel and the fullness of the Gentiles form one, holy Nation and are saved.

[30] M. M. 1 Tim 2:3: It pleases God their Savior when Christians pray for all people because he desires all people to be saved and to come to the knowledge of the truth about Jesus.

[31] M. M. Ro 4:11: All Christians from every nation on earth belong to the spiritual family of Abraham, the Church because they share the same faith in Jesus that their father had.

[32] M. I. Jn 4:7: Christians should begin witnessing to a person from a different language/culture by showing through their words and actions that they love him and are not prejudiced against him.

[33] M. M. Ac 4:28: The heavenly Father is always in full control of his mission to all nations of the world.

[34] M. I. Lk 3:8: Christians should always be prepared to boldly and publicly refute false teaching, so that Satan cannot easily deceive people.

[35] M. I. Lk 8:11: Christians should faithfully do their job of preaching and leave the results to the Holy Spirit.

Chapter 14

Paul and Barnabas at Iconium 14:1-7

14:1 *Now at Iconium they entered together into the Jewish synagogue and spoke in such a way that a great number of both Jews and Greeks believed.*
14:2 *But the unbelieving Jews stirred up the Gentiles and poisoned their minds against the brothers.*
14:3 *So they remained for a long time, speaking boldly for the Lord, who bore witness to the word of his grace, granting signs and wonders to be done by their hands.*
14:4 *But the people of the city were divided; some sided with the Jews and some with the apostles.*
14:5 *When an attempt was made by both Gentiles and Jews, with their rulers, to mistreat them and to stone them,*
14:6 *they learned of it and fled to Lystra and Derbe, cities of Lycaonia, and to the surrounding country,*
14:7 *and there they continued to preach the Gospel.*

14:1-7 Paul and Barnabas remained on their missionary journey in Iconium for a long time, and both their mission methods and the responses to their messages remained the same. **1)** Their methods were the same: **a)** They <u>first</u> went to the local synagogue (v 1), **b)** they spoke *"boldly for the Lord"* (v 3) with a Law and Gospel message (vs 1, 3, 7), **c)** and they healed some people of physical problems in Jesus' name to attract people to the Gospel, because the miracles confirmed that it was God's own message (v 3; [1]M. I. Ac 3:6). **2)** And the response to their messages was the same because the people were divided in their response: **a)** *"A great number of both Jews and Greeks believed"* (v 1), **b)** but *"the unbelieving Jews stirred up the Gentiles and poisoned their minds against the brothers"* (v 2), so the situation became so dangerous that Paul and Barnabas had to flee (v 6; [2]M. I. Lk 8:11). **3)** In such a situation where people are divided and don't know what to believe, it's extremely important for the mission of the Church to do what Paul and

Barnabas did and boldly and publicly proclaim the whole truth about Jesus, so that Satan's lies are openly refuted ([3]M. I. Lk 3:8). **4)** It should not be completely surprising that, in verses 4 and 14, Luke refers to both Paul and Barnabas as *"apostles,"* since this word literally means "sent ones;" and it's used in three different ways in the New Testament: **a)** First of all, it is most often used as a more technical term in the Gospels for *"the twelve"* men whom Jesus himself chose as his disciples (Mk 3:14); and it is later used in this same sense to refer to Paul (Gal 1:19; 1 Cor 15:9). **b)** And secondly, it is also used to refer to persons whom Christians have sent out as missionaries, as the church in Antioch in Syria publicly sent Paul and Barnabas out as missionaries to the Gentiles in the Roman Empire (13:2-3; Rom 16:7). **c)** And finally, in its most generic sense, Jesus himself tells us that all Christians are "sent ones" or missionaries whom he has sent out as "lights" in order to proclaim the Gospel to the lost, dark world ([4]M. M. Mt 5:14).

Paul and Barnabas at Lystra 14:8-18

14:8 *Now at Lystra there was a man sitting who could not use his feet. He was crippled from birth and had never walked.*

14:9 *He listened to Paul speaking. And Paul, looking intently at him and seeing that he had faith to be made well,*

14:10 *said in a loud voice, "Stand upright on your feet." And he sprang up and began walking.*

14:11 *And when the crowds saw what Paul had done, they lifted up their voices, saying in Lycaonian, "The gods have come down to us in the likeness of men!"*

14:12 *Barnabas they called Zeus, and Paul, Hermes, because he was the chief speaker.*

14:13 *And the priest of Zeus, whose temple was at the entrance to the city, brought oxen and garlands to the gates and wanted to offer sacrifice with the crowds.*

14:14 *But when the apostles Barnabas and Paul heard of it, they tore their garments and rushed out into the crowd, crying out,*

14:15 *"Men, why are you doing these things? We also are men, of like*

14:16 *In past generations he allowed all the nations to walk in their own ways.*
14:17 *Yet he did not leave himself without witness, for he did good by giving you rains from heaven and fruitful seasons, satisfying your hearts with food and gladness."*
14:18 *Even with these words they scarcely restrained the people from offering sacrifice to them.*

14:8-13 Perhaps there was no synagogue in Lystra; and therefore, Paul and Barnabas decided to begin their work there by performing a miracle in order to attract attention to Jesus ([5]M. I. Ac 3:6). However, when Paul healed the lame man (v 10), he attracted so much attention that it was difficult to proclaim the Gospel. Jesus had, at times, experienced the same problem, but, a few times, he was able to slip away from the crowd (Lk 5:14; 7:14); Paul and Barnabas, however, could only make the best of a difficult situation by trying to teach them who the true God is by describing him as the creator God (v 15; [6]M. I. Ac 6:1).

14:14-18 (1) Paul and Barnabas tried to prevent this crowd of Animistic idol worshippers from offering sacrifices to them by proclaiming a different <u>type</u> of message. They said in verse 17, *"Yet he [God] did not leave himself without witness, for he did good by giving you rains from heaven and fruitful seasons, satisfying your hearts with food and gladness."* They knew that their audience believed that it was God who created the world and continues to control it; therefore, they began by referring to these true beliefs that they shared with them. Some years later, Paul did the same thing when he spoke to another audience of idol worshippers in Athens (17:22-31); he also began his message there by referring to the creator God. It's a new mission imperative. M. I. Ac 14:15: They should teach people who the true God is by using what they know about the natural world because God made them and uses nature to care for them. **2)** Furthermore, it's very significant that Paul and Barnabas did <u>not</u> quote from the Scriptures, since they knew that these people had <u>not</u> been converted to Judaism and had <u>not</u> come to know and accept the Scriptures as God's Word. Rather, they emphasized God's goodness to them through the world he made; and they only hinted at the truth that God had not yet punished them even though they all <u>deserved</u> it, by saying in verse 16, *"In past generations he [God] allowed all the nations to walk in their own ways"* (17:30; Rom 3:25; [7]M. I. Lk 3:3a). And of course, in their message, Paul and Barnabas also boldly refuted the <u>lie</u> (v 11) that they were gods ([8]M. I. Lk 3:8).

Paul Stoned at Lystra 14:19-23

14:19 *But Jews came from Antioch and Iconium, and having persuaded the crowds, they stoned Paul and dragged him out of the city, supposing that he was dead.*
14:20 *But when the disciples gathered about him, he rose up and entered the city, and on the next day he went on with Barnabas to Derbe.*
14:21 *When they had preached the Gospel to that city and had made many disciples, they returned to Lystra and to Iconium and to Antioch,*
14:22 *strengthening the souls of the disciples, encouraging them to continue in the faith, and saying that through many tribulations we must enter the kingdom of God.*
14:23 *And when they had appointed elders for them in every church, with prayer and fasting they committed them to the Lord in whom they had believed.*

14:19 Verse 19 is only the first time in his missionary journeys that angry enemies very nearly killed Paul because he proclaimed the name of Jesus so boldly (2 Cor 11:23-29). In this case, the devil obviously moved them to be so angry at him that they pursued him all the way from Antioch in Pisidia and Iconium to Lystra ([9]M. I. Lk 11:10). Satan hates the mission work of proclaiming the Gospel, and therefore, he drives people who worship him to attack missionaries who do so; and, of course, he will continue this evil work until the Last Day, when he will finally be totally destroyed ([10]M. I. 2 Cor 10:4)

14:21-22 Paul and Barnabas did not end their first missionary journey in Derbe by going east from there and straight home to Antioch in Syria; rather, they turned around and *"returned"* (v 21) west to the cities from which they had been forced to flee. They knew that the Christians there were probably still very much afraid of the Jews there who were their violent enemies. Thus, Paul and Barnabas returned, *"strengthening the souls of the disciples, encouraging them to continue in the faith"* (v 22). How did they do this? They encouraged them in at least four ways: **a)** First, by building them up with the rich food of the Gospel, of course ([11]M. M. Ro 10:17a). **b)** Secondly, by leaving some members of their team behind or by sending them back to these cities (v 23; 17:14-15). **c)** Thirdly, by also training more local leaders (v 23), although this training is seldom mentioned in Luke's account ([12]M. I. Lk 6:13). **d)** And finally, and most importantly, by entrusting the Christians into the gracious care of Jesus, the Lord of the mission. He would remain with them through his indwelling Spirit to give them all the strength that they would need for every circumstance. Thus, to *"continue in the faith"* (v 22) is to remain in God's rich grace, depending on him for everything, and depending on no mere human being ([13]M. I. Jn 14:13).

14:22 Because Satan hates Jesus so much, he also hates anyone who confesses faith in him and proclaims the Gospel; therefore, he attacks them bitterly, cleverly and relentlessly. Therefore, Paul and Barnabas also added in verse 22, *"through many tribulations we must enter the kingdom of God."* Just as Jesus did not try to deceive the people who heard his Gospel by hiding the truth that, if they follow him, they will have to share in his suffering (Lk 14:25-33; [14]M. M. Lk 6:22); so likewise, Paul and Barnabas told the whole truth to their hearers ([15]M. I. Lk 9:23).

14:23 (1) One of the main reasons why Paul and Barnabas returned to these cities was to urge the Christians to choose leaders that they would begin to train, especially because so many enemies surrounded them. Paul and Barnabas knew that without leaders they would probably lose all sense of direction and scatter (Jn 10:12; [16]M. I. Ac 6:3 & [17]Lk 6:13). **2)**

Most likely the Greek word *"appointed"* in verse 23 indicates that Paul and Barnabas urged the <u>local churches</u> to choose leaders and did not appoint them for the churches, even though the meaning of this word is ambiguous in this context. In two other similar contexts, (6:3 & 2 Cor 8:19), a different Greek verb is used, but both clearly mean that <u>the whole group</u> appointed new leaders. They were certainly guided by the Holy Spirit, because it was obviously the local Christians (and not visitors like Paul and Barnabas) who knew which men have the right abilities to lead people in their own language and culture ([18]M. I. Ac 6:5). **3)** Luke then continues in verse 23, *"with prayer and fasting they committed them to the Lord in whom they had believed."* By entrusting the new leaders into the hands of the Lord of the mission they acknowledged that he alone was in control and that his Spirit alone was able to use the unique abilities that he had given these men in order to rapidly advance his mission in their area ([19]M. I. Ac 6:3).

Paul and Barnabas Return to Antioch in Syria 14:24-28

14:24 *Then they passed through Pisidia and came to Pamphylia.*
14:25 *And when they had spoken the word in Perga, they went down to Attalia,*
14:26 *and from there they sailed to Antioch, where they had been commended to the grace of God for the work that they had fulfilled.*
14:27 *And when they arrived and gathered the church together, they declared all that God had done with them, and how he had opened a door of faith to the Gentiles.*
14:28 *And they remained no little time with the disciples.*

14:26 Paul and Barnabas ended their first missionary journey by returning to their home *base*, the church in Antioch in Syria, who had sent them out under the direct guidance of the Holy Spirit (13:2-4; [20]M. M. Ac 4:28).

14:27 Paul and Barnabas reported back to the church in Antioch: *"all that God had done with them, and how he had opened a door of faith to* *the Gentiles"* (v 27). The best news was that Holy Spirit had made the first missionary journey on Level 3 very successful in reaching many Gentiles (11:18; [21]M. M. Ro 11:26). Although some Jews also heard the Gospel and now believed in Jesus, it was mainly some other Jews, whom Satan had used to create bitter opposition, in order to try to stop the work. They stubbornly refused to believe that Jesus was indeed the Son of God and their Messiah ([22]M. I. Ac 2:4 & [23]Ac 4:20).

14:28 Note that in verse 28, *"And they remained no little time"* means that "they stayed a long time," so that they had a long time to teach and encourage their fellow Christians. And of course, they also needed time to rest and prepare for the next mission trip.

---

[1] M. I. Ac 3:6: Christians should heal a person's physical problem by speaking the name of Jesus, so that everyone knows that it was the divine power of Jesus that healed him.

[2] M. I. Lk 8:11: Christians should faithfully do their job of preaching and leave the results to the Holy Spirit.

[3] M. I. Lk 3:8: Christians should always be prepared to boldly and publicly refute false teaching, so that Satan cannot easily deceive people.

[4] M. M. Mt 5:14: When the Holy Spirit creates faith in a person's heart, he also graciously gives him a new mission-heart that is eager to shine the light of the Gospel throughout the whole world.

[5] M. I. Ac 3:6: Christians should heal a person's physical problem by speaking the name of Jesus, so that everyone knows that it was the divine power of Jesus that healed him.

[6] M. I. Ac 6:1: Christians should always remember that the main aspect of the mission is to proclaim the Law and Gospel message and should not allow any other aspect of the work to hinder this main work.

[7] M. I. Lk 3:3a: Christians should, in love, warn lost people who do not repent.

[8] M. I. Lk 3:8: Christians should always be prepared to boldly and publicly refute false teaching, so that Satan cannot easily deceive people.

[9] M. I. Lk 11:10: Christians should continuously pray to their heavenly Father and always depend on his grace, and not on their own feeble strength, because he *always* loves them.

[10] M. I. 2 Cor 10:4: Christians should use the powerful weapons that God gives them, in order to fight against Satan's defensive weapons and to destroy all of the proud and evil arguments that his false teachers use.

[11] M. M. Ro 10:17a: The Holy Spirit only creates and preserves faith by using the message of God's grace in his holy Word.

[12] M. I. Lk 6:13: Christians should choose new leaders and train them in order to multiply the work.

[13] M. I. Jn 14:13: Christians should ask their heavenly Father for everything that they need in Jesus' name and he will do it; and then, everyone who sees God's grace will praise him in Jesus' name.

[14] M. M. Lk 6:22: The Lord Jesus will surely bless a Christian in the midst of suffering for his sake; and he will also bless him with eternal life if he remains faithful to him.

[15] M. I. Lk 9:23: Christians should deceive no one by only telling them the Gospel about Jesus, but rather they should also give them two warnings: a) that they may have to suffer for the sake of Jesus if they follow him, b) and that, on Judgment Day, Jesus will be ashamed of people who were ashamed of him.

[16] M. I. Ac 6:3: The local group of Christians should choose men who will lead them; and then those in authority should publicly commission them before they begin their work.

[17] M. I. Lk 6:13: Christians should choose new leaders and train them in order to multiply the work.

[18] M. I. Ac 6:5: Christians should choose spiritually wise leaders who know the language and culture of both the target language group and the source language group to deal with cross-cultural problems.

[19] M. I. Ac 6:3: The local group of Christians should choose men who will lead them; and then those in authority should publicly commission them before they begin their work.

[20] M. M. Ac 4:28: The heavenly Father is always in full control of his mission to all nations of the world.

[21] M. M. Ro 11:26: God graciously continues to graft Jews and Gentiles into the new Israel through the proclamation of the Gospel, until the remnant of Israel and the fullness of the Gentiles form one, holy Nation and are saved.

[22] M. I. Ac 2:4: In cross-cultural situations, Christians should always focus on all of the needs of the target group by learning their heart-language and culture as deeply as possible, so that they can tell them the Gospel clearly in their own language and also help them with the true needs of their society.

[23] M. I. Ac 4:20: Christians should boldly witness to the name of Jesus and allow nothing to stop their witness because it is the Holy Spirit's own message.

Chapter 15

The Jerusalem Council 15:1-21

15:1 *But some men came down from Judea and were teaching the brothers, "Unless you are circumcised according to the custom of Moses, you cannot be saved."*

15:2 *And after Paul and Barnabas had no small dissension and debate with them, Paul and Barnabas and some of the others were appointed to go up to Jerusalem to the apostles and the elders about this question.*

15:3 *So, being sent on their way by the church, they passed through both Phoenicia and Samaria, describing in detail the conversion of the Gentiles, and brought great joy to all the brothers.*

15:4 *When they came to Jerusalem, they were welcomed by the church and the apostles and the elders, and they declared all that God had done with them.*

15:5 *But some believers who belonged to the party of the Pharisees rose up and said, "It is necessary to circumcise them and to order them to keep the Law of Moses."*

15:6 *The apostles and the elders were gathered together to consider this matter.*

15:7 *And after there had been much debate, Peter stood up and said to them, "Brothers, you know that in the early days God made a choice among you, that by my mouth the Gentiles should hear the word of the Gospel and believe.*

15:8 *And God, who knows the heart, bore witness to them, by giving them the Holy Spirit just as he did to us,*

15:9 *and he made no distinction between us and them, having cleansed their hearts by faith.*

15:10 *Now, therefore, why are you putting God to the test by placing a yoke on the neck of the disciples that neither our fathers nor we have been able to bear?*

15:11 *But we believe that we will be saved through the grace of the*

15:12 *And all the assembly fell silent, and they listened to Barnabas and Paul as they related what signs and wonders God had done through them among the Gentiles.*
15:13 *After they finished speaking, James replied, "Brothers, listen to me.*
15:14 *Simeon has related how God first visited the Gentiles, to take from them a people for his name.*
15:15 *And with this the words of the prophets agree, just as it is written,*
15:16 *"'After this I will return, and I will rebuild the tent of David that has fallen; I will rebuild its ruins, and I will restore it,*
15:17 *that the remnant of mankind may seek the Lord, and all the Gentiles who are called by my name, says the Lord, who makes these things*
15:18 *known from of old.'*
15:19 *Therefore my judgment is that we should not trouble those of the Gentiles who turn to God,*
15:20 *but should write to them to abstain from the things polluted by idols, and from sexual immorality, and from what has been strangled, and from blood.*
15:21 *For from ancient generations Moses has had in every city those who proclaim him, for he is read every Sabbath in the synagogues."*

15:1-2 (1) The men from Judea that Luke refers to in verse 1 were Jewish Christians, but, as verse 24 indicates, they went to Antioch without the knowledge of the apostles and elders in Jerusalem. If the church had sent them there with a message, there perhaps would have been no conflict in the Church; however, their secret action was a serious threat to the *unity* of the Church. The Jews said in verse 1, *"Unless you are circumcised according to the custom of Moses, you cannot be saved."* Thus, the issue was whether Gentile Christians should live under the Law of Moses, which was marked by physical circumcision, or if they should live under God's grace. Therefore, it's very easy to see Satan's hand in this threat, since he always tempts people to live under the law—any law—and not under God's grace (^{1}M. I. Lk 11:4b). Nevertheless, the Lord of the mission, once again, showed that he was in full control, since his Spirit gave Paul and Barnabas the wisdom to see the gravity of this threat. And therefore, they immediately *"had no small dissension and debate with them [these Jews from Judea],"* which means that their disagreement was very serious (v 2; ^{2}M. M. Ac 4:28). **2)** Furthermore, it's also significant that Paul and Barnabas did not decide on their own to go to Jerusalem; rather, it was the Christians in Antioch who sent them and some other men *"to Jerusalem to [ask] the apostles and the elders about this question"* (v 2). Unlike the Jews from Judea, these men were representatives from the church in Antioch and were not acting on their own. This was very significant, since, if they had also acted on their own, the whole issue could have been complicated even further and caused even more division. It's a new mission imperative. M. I. Ac 15:2: For the sake of unity in the Church, Christians should act as one unit in order to settle internal disputes, and not allow small groups to act on their own.

15:3 The representatives from Antioch, however, did not just travel to Jerusalem to deliver their message; Paul and Barnabas also took this opportunity to strengthen and encourage Christians in cities along the way by telling them about how much the Holy Spirit had done among the Gentiles on their first missionary journey. They encouraged them in their faith by giving them a good report, so that they too could live under God's grace just as they were (^{3}M. I. Gal 6:2).

15:4 It's significant to note that, even though these men had been sent to Jerusalem to seek help in settling a major *dispute* in the Church (vs 1-2), this problem was obviously not the first matter that they share with the church in Jerusalem. Rather, they continued to focus on what God had done through their missionary efforts. They *"declared all that God had done with them"* (v 4). As they had done in Phoenicia and Samaria, Paul and Barnabas reported to the church in Jerusalem the same good news that many Gentiles were now living under God's rich grace and in the power of the Holy Spirit (^{4}M. I. Lk 11:4b).

15:5 It seems very likely that these *"believers from the party of the Pharisees"* (v 5) were some of the same Jews who went to Antioch to stir up this trouble concerning circumcision, although Luke doesn't explicitly say so. Even though they may have had faith in Jesus, they themselves were still living under the Law of Moses and not totally under God's grace. Furthermore, they wrongfully assumed that they deserved his grace since they were physical sons of Abraham; and therefore, they believed that it was obvious that Gentiles did not deserve his grace, since they were not his physical sons. Thus, they also believed that if the Gentiles wanted to be true Christians, they had to obey the Laws of Moses and become sons of Abraham by submitting to circumcision in order to earn it. They did not yet understand that everyone becomes *true* spiritual sons of Abraham by God's grace alone through receiving the free gift of faith in Jesus (Gal 3:7; [5]M. M. Gal 3:10 & [6]Ga 4:31). Satan still controlled part of their hearts with legalism and prejudice; therefore, this was clearly false teaching that needed to be publicly refuted ([7]M. I. Lk 3:8).

15:5-35 In verses 5-35, the very important Council at Jerusalem discussed the important issue of male circumcision. However, it's obvious that Gentile women were also becoming Christians, even though (for cultural reasons) the text does not mention them or female circumcision (which is often called female mutilation). Therefore, there were a number of issues in this section that concern men and women separately. **1)** First of all, consider the issues concerning the men. **a)** Because many Jews in this period of history grew up and lived in a society in which a basic assumption of their worldview was that they alone were God's chosen people, many of them sinfully assumed that only Jews deserved to hear the Gospel (v 2). Yes, some Jews did actively try to convert Gentiles to their religion, and they did have some measure of success because the New Testament refers to proselytes several times (8:27); but they also insisted that any male converts must submit to circumcision. And some did submit to this painful ceremony, but others did not and were content to remain on the fringe of the Jewish religion (10:2). Within this social context, then, some Jewish Christians considered it very "normal" to look **askance** at any Gentile who might convert to their new religion, Christianity and they likewise assumed that these Gentiles would have to submit to circumcision (vs 2, 5). **b)**

However, in God's eyes, there should have been no Jew who was prejudiced against the Gentiles (v 2); and all Jews should have made every effort to share the blessings that the Jews had graciously received from God with all nations since God explicitly gave this responsibility to the nation of Israel when he called Abraham (Gen 12:1-3; [8]M. M. Ac 13:46). Thus, Peter and all of the Christians in Jerusalem should have started witnessing to Gentiles without giving it any more thought, as their Lord had commanded them in (1:8); and the entire lesson that God had to teach to Peter by sending him to the Gentile, Cornelius should not have been necessary at all, since he had already received a mission-heart along with his faith in his Lord Jesus ([9]M. M. Mt 5:14). **2)** Secondly, consider the issues concern the women. **a)** In all of the cultures in that period of history—Jews and Gentiles alike—the men sinfully considered the women inferior and insignificant. Furthermore, in the Old Testament, God did not command the Jews to practice female circumcision; therefore, any Gentile woman who converted to Judaism was merely absorbed into Judaism, almost invisibly, on the fringes of their religion and society together with the Jewish women. And of course, the women who converted to Christianity were also absorbed without much notice. Luke does, however, refer to two ladies in Acts who were outstanding Christians: Lydia (16:14) and Priscilla (18:2; M. M. Mt 5:14). **b)** Nevertheless, the fact of the matter is, throughout the known history of the world, it has always been, and continues to be, it is women who seem to respond to the Gospel much more quickly and actively than men. (And no one has ever been able to explain this phenomenon, at least not to my satisfaction.) Therefore, as these issues concerning the relationships between the sexes within and outside the Church continue impact its mission, all Christians have the responsibility to study all of Scripture very carefully and prayerfully before they speak and take any action on these issues. No one should do so without solid evidence from Scripture ([10]M. I. Lk 4:17).

15:6-11 (1) Peter's speech in verses 6-11 shows that he was still one of the main leaders in the Church in Jerusalem, although, already in chapter 13, Luke had stopped focusing on Peter's mission to the Jews and had begun to focus on Paul's mission to the Gentiles. And after this meeting of the Church, Luke no longer even mentions Peter. **2)** When Peter says in verse 7, *"God made a choice among you, that by my mouth the Gentiles should hear the word of the Gospel and believe,"* he is not saying that God had chosen him to be his apostle to the Gentiles, because that was Paul's assignment (9:15; Gal 2:8). However, in chapter 10, God did single Peter out, in order to teach him a special object lesson through the Gentile, Cornelius that he saves <u>all</u> people by his grace <u>alone</u>. And Peter's speech here shows that he had finally learned this important lesson, so that he could also teach it to all of the Church in this meeting. He made three significant Gospel points: **a)** He said in verse 8, *"God, who knows the heart, bore witness to them [the Gentiles], by giving them the Holy Spirit just as he did to us."* This is, of course, wonderful Gospel for <u>all</u> nations ([11]M. M. Ac 10:45). **b)** And Peter added in verse 9, *"He [God] made no distinction between us and them [the Gentiles], having cleansed their hearts by faith."* From before creation, God has *"made no distinction between"* any of the human beings he has ever made ([12]M. M. 1 Tim 2:3). **c)** Then, Peter said in verse 11, *"But we believe that we will be saved through the <u>grace</u> of the Lord Jesus, just as they will."* God's rich <u>grace</u> in the cross and resurrection has made everyone equally dependent on his love and mercy for us ([13]M. M. Ro 3:26). **3)** However, Peter also had a stern warning in verse 10 for the Jews who had raised this divisive issue. He said, *"Why are you putting God to the test by placing a yoke on the neck of the disciples that neither our fathers nor we have been able to bear?"* He warned them that it's not even <u>possible</u> for anyone to obey the whole Law to please God, since <u>only</u> Jesus could and did do that as true man and true God ([14]M. M. Ro 3:24). And anyone who tries to do this is, in fact, despising God's grace by trying to please him with his own good deeds. He is only earning condemnation for himself ([15]M. M. Gal 3:10 & [16]Lk 13:24).

15:12 The crowd was deeply moved by Peter's speech; and then, Barnabas and Paul added more evidence of God's <u>gracious</u> acceptance of the Gentiles by describing the amazing miracles that they did among them in Jesus' name. Not only did the Holy Spirit give the Gentiles faith and fill them with his power, he also showed his power among them by

healing their sick, just as Jesus himself had also healed both Jews and Gentiles on more than one occasion (Lk 7:9-10; 17:17; [17]M. I. Ac 3:6).
15:13-18 (1) James (v 13), who was another leader of the church in Jerusalem and was a half-brother of Jesus, then, used a quotation from (Amos 9:11-12) in (vs 16-18) in order to reinforce what Peter, Barnabas and Paul had said. He reminded, especially his fellow Jews, that, in his mission-heart, God has always planned that his chosen nation, Israel would first receive his Gospel, so that they would share it with all nations (Lk 4:25-27). The number of Old Testament passages that say that God wants all nations to hear the Gospel and be saved is a very long list indeed; and especially James' Jewish hearers would have been very familiar with them. However, the New Testament record clearly indicates that many of them had chosen to forget them and proudly assume that they deserved to be God's people ([18]M. M. Ac 13:46). **2)** However, after the ascension of Jesus (1:9), in the new era of the Christian Church (Rom 11:26), God has given his mission-plan a fresh application. He has given all Christians his gracious call to use his holy Word and Sacraments in order to first of all strengthen each other ([19]M. M. Mt 5:14), so that they are able to go out as his missionaries to proclaim the Gospel to the lost from all nations on earth (Mat 28:19-20; [20]M. M. Ro 8:15).
15:19-21 (1) It must have been obvious to everyone in the meeting that the Gentiles had to make a clean break from sacrificing to their evil pagan gods. That is why the first two rules in verse 20 said that. However, it may appear that James' advice was very legalistic, that he was urging the Council to add more laws (besides circumcision) that the Gentiles should obey in order to become Christians, instead of allowing them the freedom to live under God's grace (v 28). However, note that he began in verse 19 by saying that *"we should not trouble those of the Gentiles who turn to God;"* therefore, we can see that this was *not* legalistic advice at all. Rather, he was saying that the Gentile Christians should live freely under God's grace, just as their fellow Jewish Christians were, but he had the wisdom to realize that they were living in a cross-cultural situation that was now further complicated by their new faith in Jesus. **a)** On one side of the cultural boundary, the Jewish

Christians undoubtedly still obeyed some of the Laws of Moses, even though they may have known that they no longer had to obey them; and they were still, no doubt, very sensitive about their Gentile brothers in Christ who didn't obey them and lived as they pleased without worrying about what their Jewish brothers in Christ thought. **b)** And on the other side of the boundary, before the Gentiles were Christians, some of their behavior, of course, frequently offended their Jewish neighbors, but at that time, they weren't concerned about that in the least. Now however, they were living in a new family in Christ together with Jewish Christians, and they could no longer ignore the fact that some of their behavior offended the Jews. Therefore, these few rules that James was recommending were very practical advice to them. If they kept these few rules in love and for the sake of the unity of the Church, they would be living under God's rich grace, and it would help to avoid at least some of the more serious personal relationship problems between them and their Jewish brothers in Christ. Therefore, James advised them *"to abstain from the things polluted by idols, and from sexual immorality, and from what has been strangled, and from blood"* (v 20). By avoiding these few things, it would go a long way toward keeping the *unity* of the faith ([21]M. I. 1 Cor 9:21). **2)** Nevertheless, there was yet another aspect to this cross-cultural problem that the new Gentile Christians needed to consider. They not only had a new Christian family to live in, their Lord Jesus had also called them to share the Gospel with everyone they met: both Gentiles and Jews who were not Christians (Mt 5:14). Therefore, the new Gentile Christians had a responsibility to try to avoid offending these unbelieving Jews as well, so that they would see their new behavior and be open to hear about how Jesus had changed their lives. Therefore, obeying these few new rules could also be a mission tool for reaching out to unbelieving Jews, and perhaps to Gentiles as well (M. I. 1 Cor 9:21).

The Council's Letter to Gentile Believers 15:22-35

15:22 Then it seemed good to the apostles and the elders, with the whole church, to choose men from among them and send them

> *to Antioch with Paul and Barnabas. They sent Judas called Barsabbas, and Silas, leading men among the brothers,*
> 15:23 *with the following letter: "The brothers, both the apostles and the elders, to the brothers who are of the Gentiles in Antioch and Syria and Cilicia, greetings.*
> 15:24 *Since we have heard that some persons have gone out from us and troubled you with words, unsettling your minds, although we gave them no instructions,*
> 15:25 *it has seemed good to us, having come to one accord, to choose men and send them to you with our beloved Barnabas and Paul,*
> 15:26 *men who have risked their lives for the sake of our Lord Jesus Christ.*
> 15:27 *We have therefore sent Judas and Silas, who themselves will tell you the same things by word of mouth.*
> 15:28 *For it has seemed good to the Holy Spirit and to us to lay on you no greater burden than these requirements:*
> 15:29 *that you abstain from what has been sacrificed to idols, and from blood, and from what has been strangled, and from sexual immorality. If you keep yourselves from these, you will do well. Farewell."*
> 15:30 *So when they were sent off, they went down to Antioch, and having gathered the congregation together, they delivered the letter.*
> 15:31 *And when they had read it, they rejoiced because of its encouragement.*
> 15:32 *And Judas and Silas, who were themselves prophets, encouraged and strengthened the brothers with many words.*
> 15:33 *And after they had spent some time, they were sent off in peace by the brothers to those who had sent them.*
> 15:34 *[But it seemed good to Silas to remain there.]*
> 15:35 *But Paul and Barnabas remained in Antioch, teaching and preaching the word of the Lord, with many others also.*

15:22-23 (1) The decision of this meeting to send a letter to the Gentile Christians in Antioch in Syria not only conveyed their message in a completely unambiguous manner, but it also clearly told them that it was

a decision of the whole group, in contrast with the small group of men who had threatened the unity of the Church by going to Antioch, *"although we gave them no instructions"* (v 24; 15:1; [22]M. I. Ac 15:2).
2) Furthermore, since this was such a widespread concern in the Church, when the Council accepted James' advice and decided to write a letter to the Gentile Christians who were living in *"Antioch and Syria and Cilicia"* (v 23) and beyond to other parts of the Roman Empire, this wise advice eventually had a profound effect on the entire mission of the Church wherever Jews and Gentiles lived and worshipped together (16:4-5). This is the reason why Paul later discussed this issue at length in two of his letters (Rom 14:1-23) and (1 Cor 8:1-13).
15:25-26 It's very significant to note that the Council in Jerusalem, who represented the entire Christian Church showed deep love for their missionaries by calling them, *"our beloved Barnabas and Paul, men who have risked their lives for the sake of our Lord Jesus Christ"* (vs 25-26). It was the church in Antioch who had chosen them and sent them out on their first mission trip (13:2-3); however, we see here that the entire Church clearly recognized that they had done so under the guidance of the Holy Spirit. And their missionaries had *"risked their lives for the sake of"* their dear Lord, and therefore, they loved them dearly and felt that they represented *all* of them ([23]M. I. Ac 1:8).
15:28-31 When the meeting advised the Christian Gentiles in verse 28 to obey these few rules, they were placing on them *"no greater burden than these requirements."* Clearly they were urging them to act in love, and not because they were compelled by these rules; rather, they were bits of wise advice to follow in a very complicated social situation (vs 19-20). Verse 31 says that *"they rejoiced because of its [the letter's] encouragement;"* and if they had understood them to be legalistic demands that the Church was making on them, it would have been impossible to feel encouraged because the Law always kills (2 Cor 3:6). Obviously these rules were matters of "adiaphora" or optional, but nevertheless, they would be wise to follow them and they would also be showing love by doing so. Thus, this advice gave the Gentile Christians the opportunity to live freely under God's grace because they did not obey them under compulsion but under the law of love ([24]M. I. 1 Cor

9:21).

15:35 Verse 35 says, *"Paul and Barnabas remained in Antioch, teaching and preaching the word of the Lord, with many others also."* The new freedom from living under the Laws of Moses had added new life to the mission of the church in Antioch. It must have been a joyous time with the Holy Spirit freely working among them through his holy Word ([25]M. M. Ro 10:17a).

Paul and Barnabas Separate 15:36-41

> 15:36 *And after some days Paul said to Barnabas, "Let us return and visit the brothers in every city where we proclaimed the word of the Lord, and see how they are."*
> 15:37 *Now Barnabas wanted to take with them John called Mark.*
> 15:38 *But Paul thought best not to take with them one who had withdrawn from them in Pamphylia and had not gone with them to the work.*
> 15:39 *And there arose a sharp disagreement, so that they separated from each other. Barnabas took Mark with him and sailed away to Cyprus,*
> 15:40 *but Paul chose Silas and departed, having been commended by the brothers to the grace of the Lord.*
> 15:41 *And he went through Syria and Cilicia, strengthening the churches.*

15:36-39 (1) From one point of view, this was obviously a sad dispute between Paul and Barnabas since all such disagreements have their source in human pride and are, therefore, inspired by Satan. It was another one of his evil attacks on the <u>unity</u> of the Church. Nevertheless, from another point of view, the Holy Spirit changed the end result of this dispute into something good in that a single team of missionaries became <u>two</u> teams. And, following Jesus' command, both teams went out two by two ([26]M. I. Lk 10:1). **2)** Barnabas took John Mark back to Cyprus to visit the churches they had started there; however, note that the church in Antioch did not send this team off; and we also hear no more about any other mission journeys that these two men may have made. Nevertheless, it is also very significant for the future mission of the Church that the personal relationships between these three men were only <u>temporarily</u> broken, since Paul later commended Barnabas in (1 Cor 9:6), and he enjoyed John Mark's companionship in Rome in (Col 4:10).

15:40 Paul, in the meantime, started his <u>second</u> missionary journey accompanied by Silas, who became his constant companion for two more mission trips. And verse 40 says that they left *"having been commended by the brothers to the grace of the Lord."* Therefore, it was once again the church in Antioch in Syria who sent them out under the Holy Spirit's gracious guidance (13:2-3; [27]M. I. Ac 1:8).

15:41 Verse 41 says that Paul *"went through Syria and Cilicia, strengthening the churches."* Since he was a missionary who seldom stayed in one place very long, he surely encouraged and *"strengthened"* them by preaching and teaching God's holy Word (M. M. Ro 10:17a), and by entrusting them into the loving and gracious care of the Lord of the mission ([28]M. M. Ac 4:28).

---

[1] M. I. Lk 11:4b: Christians should ask their heavenly Father that he would not allow Satan to tempt them so severely that they lose their faith, and also that he would give them his strength to depend on his grace in all of their trials.

[2] M. M. Ac 4:28: The heavenly Father is always in full control of his mission to all nations of the world.

[3] M. I. Gal 6:2: Strong Christians should be in mission to weak Christians by helping them to resist the temptations of work-righteousness, and lovingly urging them to continue to live under God's grace alone.

[4] M. I. Lk 11:4b: Christians should ask their heavenly Father that he would not allow Satan to tempt them so severely that they lose their faith, and also that he would give them his strength to depend on his grace in all of their trials.

[5] M. M. Gal 3:10: All people who try to please God by their own good deeds are under God's curse because only Jesus, God's Son was able to obey God perfectly for the sake of all of his fellow human beings.

[6] M. M. Gal 4:31: People who trust in Jesus as their dear Lord live under his grace as freeborn children of God, because God has set them free from slavery to Satan as his children.

[7] M. I. Lk 3:8: Christians should always be prepared to boldly and publicly refute false teaching, so that Satan cannot easily deceive people.

[8] M. M. Ac 13:46: As he did with the old Israel, God first of all strengthens the faith of the new Israel, the Church with his Word and Sacraments, so that they can go and witness to the lost people of all nations.

[9] M. M. Mt 5:14: When the Holy Spirit creates faith in a person's heart, he also graciously gives him a new mission-heart that is eager to shine the light of the Gospel throughout the whole world.

[10] M. I. Lk 4:17: Christians should always base their messages on the Bible, so that the Holy Spirit can use his holy Word to create and strengthen faith in their hearers.

[11] M. M. Ac 10:45: When God graciously gives the gift of faith in his Son, Jesus to a person from any nation on earth, he also graciously gives him his Holy Spirit who now lives in his new mission-heart.

[12] M. M. 1 Tim 2:3: It pleases God their Savior when Christians pray for all people because he desires all people to be saved and to come to the knowledge of the truth about Jesus.

[13] M. M. Ro 3:26: God is just and fair to everyone, both when he condemns all people of all nations because all have sinned, and also when he *only* declares those people righteous who have faith in Jesus.

[14] M. M. Ro 3:24: Jesus lived a life of perfect obedience and shed his precious blood on the cross, in order to graciously set all nations free from sin, which a person only receives by faith in him.

[15] M. M. Gal 3:10: All people who try to please God by their own good deeds are under God's curse because only Jesus, God's Son was able to obey God perfectly for the sake of all of his fellow human beings.

[16] M. M. Lk 13:24: The only way to enter the Kingdom of God is to have faith in Jesus as one's Savior.

[17] M. I. Ac 3:6: Christians should heal a person's physical problem by speaking the name of Jesus, so that everyone knows that it was the divine power of Jesus that healed him.

[18] M. M. Ac 13:46: As he did with the old Israel, God first of all strengthens the faith of the new Israel, the Church with his Word and Sacraments, so that they can go and witness to the lost people of all nations.

[19] M. M. Mt 5:14: When the Holy Spirit creates faith in a person's heart, he also graciously gives him a new mission-heart that is eager to shine the light of the Gospel throughout the whole world.

[20] M. M. Ro 8:15: God the Father has adopted all people from all nations, who trust in Jesus, as his own dear children.

[21] M. I. 1 Cor 9:21: Especially when Christians are trying to communicate the Gospel in cross-cultural situations, they should focus on the needs of their hearers and avoid offending them. Thus, they should by obey the rules of the hearers' culture, in order to use every possible means to save some of them; however, if a man-made rule violates Christ's Law of love, they should obey God (and explain their action to their hearers if possible).

[22] M. I. Ac 15:2: For the sake of unity in the Church, Christians should act as one unit in order to settle internal disputes, and not allow small groups to act on their own.

[23] M. I. Ac 1:8: Christians should go and witness about Jesus to all who are lost from all languages and cultures by depending on the power of the Holy Spirit to help them bridge all of the language/cultural boundaries whether they are relatively easy, as in their own language, or

extremely difficult.

[24] M. I. 1 Cor 9:21: Especially when Christians are trying to communicate the Gospel in cross-cultural situations, they should focus on the needs of their hearers and avoid offending them. Thus, they should by obey the rules of the hearers' culture, in order to use every possible means to save some of them; however, if a man-made rule violates Christ's Law of love, they should obey God (and explain their action to their hearers if possible).

[25] M. M. Ro 10:17a: The Holy Spirit <u>only</u> creates and preserves faith by using the message of God's grace in his holy Word.

[26] M. I. Lk 10:1: Christians should go on their mission to all nations two by two in order to affirm each other's witness.

[27] M. I. Ac 1:8: Christians should go and witness about Jesus to all who are lost from all languages and cultures by depending on the power of the Holy Spirit to help them bridge all of the language/cultural boundaries whether they are relatively easy, as in their own language, or extremely difficult.

[28] M. M. Ac 4:28: The heavenly Father is always in full control of his mission to all nations of the world.

Chapter 16

Timothy Joins Paul and Silas 16:1-5

> 16:1 *Paul came also to Derbe and to Lystra. A disciple was there, named Timothy, the son of a Jewish woman who was a believer, but his father was a Greek.*
> 16:2 *He was well spoken of by the brothers at Lystra and Iconium.*
> 16:3 *Paul wanted Timothy to accompany him, and he took him and circumcised him because of the Jews who were in those places, for they all knew that his father was a Greek.*
> 16:4 *As they went on their way through the cities, they delivered to them for observance the decisions that had been reached by the apostles and elders who were in Jerusalem.*
> 16:5 *So the churches were strengthened in the faith, and they increased in numbers daily.*

16:3 (1) When Paul circumcised Timothy (v 3), it may appear that he was contradicting the decision that the meeting in Jerusalem had just made that the Gentiles did <u>not</u> have to obey the Laws of Moses in order to become Christians. However, upon closer examination, we can see that he was very sensitive to the cross-cultural situation and his action was thoroughly consistent with the decision that he made some years later in a similar situation ([1]M. I. 1 Cor 9:21). He decided that by choosing to obey the Law of Moses and circumcise him (v 3) he would avoid any <u>unnecessary</u> offense, and it would, therefore, be the best way that he could show <u>love</u> to any Jews that he and Timothy might meet on their mission journey, whether they were Christians or not. He didn't <u>have</u> to do so, as a free Christian under God's grace, but he did so in <u>love</u> in order to avoid any offense. And the fact that Luke never again refers to Paul's action in his account demonstrates that he had made both the most God-pleasing decision and also the right cross-cultural decision, since his action must have caused no negative reactions on either side of the cultural barrier—either on the part of Jews or the Gentiles ([2]M. I. Ac 1:8). **2)** Some years later, in very different circumstances, however, Paul demonstrated that he was free from the Law and was living in God's grace because he made the opposite decision at that time (Gal 3:3). In this case, some Galatians demanded that he circumcise Titus, so Paul decided that it would convey the wrong message that he had to obey the Laws of Moses if he gave in to them; thus, he did not circumcise Titus (M. I. 1 Cor 9:21).

16:4-5 Just as the Gentile Christians in Antioch in Syria had rejoiced because the decision of the meeting in Jerusalem gave them the freedom to live under God's grace (15:31), so likewise, the Gentile Christians in many other cities rejoiced when they heard this wise advice wherever Paul went. Whenever God's people live in the power of God's grace, the Holy Spirit freely displays his power in their hearts and lives, *"so the churches were strengthened in the faith, and they increased in numbers daily"* (v 5). Paul and his missionary team were obviously using God's holy Word to *"strengthen"* their faith (v 5; [3]M. M. Ro 10:17a).

The Macedonian Call 16:6-10

16:6 *And they went through the region of Phrygia and Galatia, having been forbidden by the Holy Spirit to speak the word in Asia.*

16:7 *And when they had come up to Mysia, they attempted to go into Bithynia, but the Spirit of Jesus did not allow them.*

16:8 *So, passing by Mysia, they went down to Troas.*

16:9 *And a vision appeared to Paul in the night: a man of Macedonia was standing there, urging him and saying, "Come over to Macedonia and help us."*

16:10 *And when Paul had seen the vision, immediately we sought to go on into Macedonia, concluding that God had called us to preach the Gospel to them.*

16:6-10 (1) Verses 6-10 are without a doubt Luke's clearest expression of the truth that God's mission-heart never changes, and he and his Holy Spirit are always in full control of their mission to the lost world ([4]M. M. Ac 4:28). **a)** First, the Holy Spirit had given the Council in Jerusalem clear cross-cultural directions to the Level 3 mission of the Church when they wrote a letter to Gentile Christians all over the Empire (15:20, 30). This wise advice guided them as they lived as Christian brothers together with Jewish Christians in many cross-cultural situations. **b)** Secondly, Paul and his team of missionaries had their own ideas of where they should go in order to most effectively spread the Gospel (vs 6-7); however, the Holy Spirit obviously knew better. He now gave the team new geographical directions, by giving them three unambiguous messages in a short period of time (vs 6, 7 & 9) about which directions they should go. And thus, the Holy Spirit took firm control of the future of the mission team with unambiguous directions to them (M. M. Ac 4:28). **2)** However, the key word here is unambiguous messages, since some churches, missionaries and pastors alike continue to say, yet today, that they have seen visions or heard specific instructions from the Lord of the mission about where they should go or what they should do. Therefore, the questions for the Lord's mission today are: Does the Holy Spirit give his churches and missionaries specific directions yet today? Did he ever promise to do so? The prophet Joel answers the latter question in the affirmative when he says in (Joel 2:28), *"And it shall come to pass afterward, that I will pour out my Spirit on all flesh; your sons and your daughters shall prophesy, your old men shall dream dreams, and your young men shall see visions."* However, this passage is certainly not nearly as specific as some Christians may wish it were, since God has given several different kinds of visions and dreams to people in the past, especially in the Old Testament. Therefore, we Christians should be very cautious about saying that God specifically told us to go somewhere or to do something on his mission. We would be much wiser to humbly and prayerfully seek his will for the direction that he wants his mission to go through careful examination of his holy Word. And if what we read in his Word is not completely clear to us, we should also prayerfully consider any thoughtful advice that we may receive from fellow Christians. It's a new mission imperative. M. I. Ac 16:6: Christians should start planning all mission efforts and continue to evaluate them based on both prayerful study of God's Word and also on thoughtful advice from fellow Christians; and they should not base their plans entirely on any visions or dreams.

The Conversion of Lydia 16:11-15

16:11 *So, setting sail from Troas, we made a direct voyage to Samothrace, and the following day to Neapolis,*
16:12 *and from there to Philippi, which is a leading city of the district of Macedonia and a Roman colony. We remained in this city some days.*
16:13 *And on the Sabbath day we went outside the gate to the riverside, where we supposed there was a place of prayer, and we sat down and spoke to the women who had come together.*
16:14 *One who heard us was a woman named Lydia, from the city of Thyatira, a seller of purple goods, who was a worshiper of God. The Lord opened her heart to pay attention to what was said by Paul.*
16:15 *And after she was baptized, and her household as well, she urged us, saying, "If you have judged me to be faithful to the Lord, come to my house and stay." And she prevailed upon us.*

16:11-15 (1) Obviously Paul must have asked where the synagogue was in Philippi, since he most frequently began his mission work in a synagogue (13:14; [5]M. I. Ac 2:4). However, there evidently were not enough Jews living in Philippi in order to be able to build a synagogue, so the devout Jews and Gentile converts to Judaism chose to worship on the bank of a river. And three further points concerning this worship site may be significant: **a)** First of all, since there apparently was no synagogue in the town, it's also very likely that they also had no copies of the Scripture with them out in the open air and by a river. Furthermore, it was two readings from Scripture that were the main focus of worship in a synagogue, but this was *"a place of prayer"* (v 13). **b)** Secondly, it was apparently only women who gathered there (v 13), which meant that, even if they did have copies of the Scripture, there would have been no man there to read the Scripture and apply it to them. Their worship apparently only consisted of prayer, but they were *"faithful to the Lord"* (v 15), and praying to the true, Triune God of the

Jewish Scriptures (vs 14-15). **c)** Thirdly, Lydia is the only person whom Luke names; and she was a <u>Gentile</u> who had <u>converted</u> to the Jewish religion (v 14). And some of the other women there may also have been Gentiles. The fact that she was a convert is very significant, since the Holy Spirit had already created faith in her heart through hearing his Word; and he also made her eager to hear about Jesus (v 14). **2)** Thus, Paul seized this wonderful opportunity and obviously told Lydia that Jesus had fulfilled all of the promises that she was already clinging to, because he baptized her and her family immediately (v 15; [6]M. I. Mt 28:19). And thus, by water and the Word of God, the Holy Spirit gave birth to the first Christians from the continent of <u>Europe</u>! This was, of course, extremely significant! The Level 3 mission to the Gentiles had taken a dramatically new and very significant <u>geographical</u> direction, because the Holy Spirit had specifically guided them with three visions (vs 6, 7 & 9; M. I. Mt 28:19 & [7]Lk 12:12).

16:15 Verse 15 says that *"she [Lydia] was baptized, and her household as well,"* which, of course, raises some questions: **a)** Did Paul also baptize her <u>children</u>? Yes, seems to be the most logical answer, although this question is still hotly debated yet today. **b)** Did it also include her husband? Yes, would again seem to be the most logical answer, if she had a husband, especially since she invited Paul's team to stay in her home (v 15). **c)** Does the term *"household"* in verse 15 refer only to her <u>immediate</u> family (her husband and children) or to her extended family, which could include many people? Most likely it referred to her immediate family; however, this is unclear, since Luke used a different Greek word for *"household"* in a similar context in verse 33 ([8]M. I. Mt 28:19). (Also see the discussion about holy Baptism at (2:37-38).)

Paul and Silas in Prison 16:16-24

> 16:16 *As we were going to the place of prayer, we were met by a slave girl who had a spirit of divination and brought her owners much gain by fortune-telling.*
> 16:17 *She followed Paul and us, crying out, "These men are servants of the Most High God, who proclaim to you the way of*

salvation."

16:18 *And this she kept doing for many days. Paul, having become greatly annoyed, turned and said to the spirit, "I command you in the name of Jesus Christ to come out of her." And it came out that very hour.*

16:19 *But when her owners saw that their hope of gain was gone, they seized Paul and Silas and dragged them into the marketplace before the rulers.*

16:20 *And when they had brought them to the magistrates, they said, "These men are Jews, and they are disturbing our city.*

16:21 *They advocate customs that are not lawful for us as Romans to accept or practice."*

16:22 *The crowd joined in attacking them, and the magistrates tore the garments off them and gave orders to beat them with rods.*

16:23 *And when they had inflicted many blows upon them, they threw them into prison, ordering the jailer to keep them safely.*

16:24 *Having received this order, he put them into the inner prison and fastened their feet in the stocks.*

16:16-18 (1) This story in verses 16-18 illustrates once again how much Satan hates it when the Gospel is being proclaimed freely and the Holy Spirit is able to use this proclamation to create and strengthen faith. Satan so fully controlled this slave girl that he could use her to cause serious distractions for Paul's preaching and teaching (vs 16-20; [9]M. I. 2 Cor 11:14). **2)** Satan has always used (and of course, continues to use) primarily two types of sins in order to try to deceive people and hinder or destroy the mission of the Church: the love of money and power, and the love of sinful physical pleasures—especially sex. Therefore, the fact that the owners of this slave girl obviously loved money was another sure sign that Satan was controlling both her and her owners (v 16; [10]M. I. Eph 6:10). **3)** Why Satan would give a "free" advertisement, so-to-speak, to the truth of what Paul's mission team was doing by saying that they *"proclaim to you the way of salvation"* (v 17) is somewhat of a mystery. The most logical explanation is that this demon was in fact expressing deep frustration that was similar to the frustration of the demons who shouted to Jesus in despair in (Lk 4:34), *"Have you come to destroy us? I know who you are-the Holy One of God!"* Satan and his demons must <u>always</u> despair of trying to defeat the vastly superior power of the Holy Spirit, because Satan knows that he can't stop the Holy Spirit if someone is proclaiming the Gospel. The only thing he can try to do is stop the <u>missionary</u>. Thus, in this instance in Acts, Satan first tried to slow down the Spirit's work through verbal harassment; and when that didn't have much effect, he used the <u>greed</u> of the owners of the slave girl in order to stir up trouble in the city to try to stop the public proclamation of the Gospel completely (vs 19-20; [11]M. I. Lk 3:8). **4)** Note that Jesus also continued to display tremendous power through the use of his holy <u>name</u>. It was Paul's mere mention of Jesus' <u>name</u> that drove this demon out of the girl; he was not drawing attention to himself, but was glorifying the <u>name</u> of Jesus ([12]M. I. Ac 8:12).

16:19-24 (1) We see in verses 19-24 how Satan used <u>two</u> lies in order to temporarily stop the mission team from proclaiming the Gospel. **a)** First of all, he used the love of money in order to create all kinds of other evil; and his *lie* is that money and power give true happiness. Verse 19 says that the owners of the girl *"saw that their hope of gain was gone."* This lie blinded them to the truth of the Gospel; and as a result of their unbelief, many other people in the city were also blinded to the truth ([13]M. I. 2 Cor 11:14). **b)** Secondly, Satan used the <u>lie</u> that the Christian Church was <u>illegal</u> because it was a new religious <u>sect</u> and a <u>threat</u> to the peace of the Empire, and not a <u>true</u> fulfillment of the ancient Jewish religion, which had <u>legal recognition</u> by the Roman government ([14]M. M. Mt 1:22). The owners of the girl said that *"they advocate customs that are <u>not lawful</u> for us as Romans to accept or practice"* (v 21). And they must have said this in an emotionally charged manner because the officials obviously didn't stop to consider whether anyone on the mission team might be a Roman citizen (v 37; [15]M. M. Jn 14:6). **2)** Thus, we see how clever Satan is; therefore, yet today, the Church should still constantly be alert to the fact that Satan will continue to use his lies. He is always trying to counter the truths of the Holy Spirit's Law and Gospel message in order to slow down or stop its proclamation and deceive people. It will always be his <u>lies</u> versus the <u>truth</u> about God and Jesus; and the gravest danger is that his lies so often <u>seem</u> to be true or resemble the truth (M. I. 2 Cor 11:14).

The Philippian Jailer Converted 16:25-40

16:25 *About midnight Paul and Silas were praying and singing hymns to God, and the prisoners were listening to them,*
16:26 *and suddenly there was a great earthquake, so that the foundations of the prison were shaken. And immediately all the doors were opened, and everyone's bonds were unfastened.*
16:27 *When the jailer woke and saw that the prison doors were open, he drew his sword and was about to kill himself, supposing that the prisoners had escaped.*
16:28 *But Paul cried with a loud voice, "Do not harm yourself, for we are all here."*
16:29 *And the jailer called for lights and rushed in, and trembling with fear he fell down before Paul and Silas.*
16:30 *Then he brought them out and said, "Sirs, what must I do to be saved?"*
16:31 *And they said, "Believe in the Lord Jesus, and you will be saved, you and your household."*
16:32 *And they spoke the word of the Lord to him and to all who were in his house.*
16:33 *And he took them the same hour of the night and washed their wounds; and he was baptized at once, he and all his family.*
16:34 *Then he brought them up into his house and set food before them. And he rejoiced along with his entire household that he had believed in God.*
16:35 *But when it was day, the magistrates sent the police, saying, "Let those men go."*
16:36 *And the jailer reported these words to Paul, saying, "The magistrates have sent to let you go. Therefore come out now and go in peace."*
16:37 *But Paul said to them, "They have beaten us publicly, uncondemned, men who are Roman citizens, and have thrown*

> *us into prison; and do they now throw us out secretly? No! Let them come themselves and take us out."*
> 16:38 *The police reported these words to the magistrates, and they were afraid when they heard that they were Roman citizens.*
> 16:39 *So they came and apologized to them. And they took them out and asked them to leave the city.*
> 16:40 *So they went out of the prison and visited Lydia. And when they had seen the brothers, they encouraged them and departed.*

16:25 In spite of severe, unjustified punishment, Paul and Silas <u>boldly</u> proclaimed the Gospel in prison by *"praying and singing hymns to God"* (v 25) loud enough that the other prisoners and also the jailer could hear their witness. Nothing could quell their great <u>joy</u> in their Lord Jesus, especially since they knew that it was an <u>honor</u> for them to share in his suffering (Phil 4:4). They also knew that <u>all</u> times and <u>all</u> places were <u>opportunities</u> for them to share their joy ([16]M. I. Ac 5:41 & [17]Lk 4:4).

16:26-34 The manner in which the jailer and his family came to faith and were baptized by Paul is strikingly similar to the case of Lydia and her family in verses 14-15. In this case, the powerful witness of Paul and Silas plus the dramatic earthquake moved the jailer to seek rescue. But it was the Holy Spirit's mighty Word that created faith in their hearts; and Paul baptized them <u>immediately</u> ([18]M. I. Mt 28:19 & [19]Lk 4:15).

16:37 In verse 37, Paul invoked his rights as a Roman citizen and forced the Roman officials to <u>publicly</u> apologize to Paul and Silas in the same way that they had <u>publicly</u> arrested them, beat them and put them in jail without a trial. But Paul was <u>not</u> mainly concerned about his personal reputation, although that was surely immensely important to him; rather he was very much concerned about two things: **a)** the reputation of the <u>name</u> <u>of Jesus</u> **b)** and about making sure that his team and the Christians in Philippi would be able to continue to <u>freely</u> proclaim the Gospel there in the <u>future</u>. Since Luke does not give a reason why the Roman officials changed their minds the next morning, it may be that it would not have been necessary for Paul to tell them that he was a Roman citizen; however, this was only the first time, that we know of, that Paul chose to use his high social status to defend and promote the Gospel. Satan had been able to bring public insult and shame on the name of Jesus and temporarily close the door of opportunity to publicly proclaim the Gospel in that town, but his power was very limited. It may appear that the Lord of the mission was no longer in control of this situation, but he was, of course, using the servant whom he himself had chosen and equipped with all of his abilities and social status to defend the Gospel (22:25; 25:11). It's a new mission imperative. M. I. Ac 16:37: All Christians, but especially Christian leaders should do everything in their power to promote the good reputation of the name of Jesus, in order to make it possible for them to freely and publicly proclaim the Gospel.

16:39 In verse 39, the Roman officials realized their mistake and were forced to publicly apologize to the missionaries; and this made it possible for the mission team to once again visit the Christians and encourage them; and then, they decided that it would be wise for them to leave. However, we should also note two things: **a)** first, that Paul and Silas had not yet had a chance to choose and train a local leader, as they normally did, so that they did not leave a church in confusion, **b)** and secondly, that Luke begins the next chapter with only Paul and Silas traveling on (17:4). (However, Luke seldom lists all of the movements of all of the members of the mission teams in his account.) Therefore, it's possible that both Luke and Timothy remained there in Philippi as their leaders for a time. In any case, there is no doubt that Paul and Silas, who were the leaders of the mission team, left the Christians in Philippi in the gracious hands of the Lord of the mission before they left ([20]M. M. Ac 4:28 & [21]M. I. Ac 6:3).

---

[1] M. I. 1 Cor 9:21: Especially when Christians are trying to communicate the Gospel in cross-cultural situations, they should focus on the needs of their hearers and avoid offending them. Thus, they should by obey the rules of the hearers' culture, in order to use every possible means to save some of them; however, if a man-made rule violates Christ's Law of love, they should obey God (and explain their action to their hearers if possible).

[2] M. I. Ac 1:8: Christians should go and witness about Jesus to all who are lost from all languages and cultures by depending on the power of the Holy Spirit to help them bridge all of the language/cultural boundaries whether they are relatively easy, as in their own language, or

extremely difficult.

³ M. M. Ro 10:17a: The Holy Spirit only creates and preserves faith by using the message of God's grace in his holy Word.

⁴ M. M. Ac 4:28: The heavenly Father is always in full control of his mission to all nations of the world.

⁵ M. I. Ac 2:4: In cross-cultural situations, Christians should always focus on all of the needs of the target group by learning their heart-language and culture as deeply as possible, so that they can tell them the Gospel clearly in their own language and also help them with the true needs of their society.

⁶ M. I. Mt 28:19: Christians should go and proclaim God's Law and Gospel to all nations; then, baptize all who repent and believe after teaching them the meaning of holy Baptism.

⁷ M. I. Lk 12:12: Christians should go and tell the Gospel depending on the Holy Spirit to teach them what they should say.

⁸ M. I. Mt 28:19: Christians should go and proclaim God's Law and Gospel to all nations; then, baptize all who repent and believe after teaching them the meaning of holy Baptism.

⁹ M. I. 2 Cor 11:14: Christians should beware of Satan because he not only disguises himself as an angel of light, but he also sends out false teachers who also disguise themselves as servants of the light, in order to deceive people by telling lies that appear to be the truth of the Gospel.

¹⁰ M. I. Eph 6:10: Christians should always be ready to fight against the devil and stand firm against all of his evil schemes by prayerfully putting on the whole armor of the Holy Spirit.

¹¹ M. I. Lk 3:8: Christians should always be prepared to boldly and publicly refute false teaching, so that Satan cannot easily deceive people.

¹² M. I. Ac 8:12: Christians should only use miracles of healing in order to point to Jesus, and beware of people who use Satan's power to do miracles in order to point to themselves.

¹³ M. I. 2 Cor 11:14: Christians should beware of Satan because he not only disguises himself as an angel of light, but he also sends out false teachers who also disguise themselves as servants of the light, in order to deceive people by telling lies that appear to be the truth of the Gospel.

¹⁴ M. M. Mt 1:22: God sent his only Son, Jesus to be born as a true human being, so that he could save all of his brothers and sisters of all nations by fulfilling all of God's promises in the Old Testament.

¹⁵ M. M. Jn 14:6: As the only Son of the heavenly Father, Jesus is the only Way to go to his Father, the only source of all Truth, and the only source of all Life.

¹⁶ M. I. Ac 5:41: Christians should consider it a great honor to be persecuted for proclaiming the name of Jesus.

¹⁷ M. I. Lk 4:4: When Satan attacks Christians on their mission they should wield the sword of God's Word by quoting from it, and not depend on their own strength.

¹⁸ M. I. Mt 28:19: Christians should go and proclaim God's Law and Gospel to all nations; then, baptize all who repent and believe after teaching them the meaning of holy Baptism.

¹⁹ M. I. Lk 4:15: Christians should seize every opportunity to proclaim the Gospel to lost people of all nations.

²⁰ M. M. Ac 4:28: The heavenly Father is always in full control of his mission to all nations of the world.

²¹ M. I. Ac 6:3: The local group of Christians should choose men who will lead them; and then

those in authority should publicly commission them before they begin their work.

Chapter 17

Paul and Silas in Thessalonica 17:1-9

17:1 *Now when they had passed through Amphipolis and Apollonia, they came to Thessalonica, where there was a synagogue of the Jews.*
17:2 *And Paul went in, as was his custom, and on three Sabbath days he reasoned with them from the Scriptures,*
17:3 *explaining and proving that it was necessary for the Christ to suffer and to rise from the dead, and saying, "This Jesus, whom I proclaim to you, is the Christ."*
17:4 *And some of them were persuaded and joined Paul and Silas, as did a great many of the devout Greeks and not a few of the leading women.*
17:5 *But the Jews were jealous, and taking some wicked men of the rabble, they formed a mob, set the city in an uproar, and attacked the house of Jason, seeking to bring them out to the crowd.*
17:6 *And when they could not find them, they dragged Jason and some of the brothers before the city authorities, shouting, "These men who have turned the world upside down have come here also,*
17:7 *and Jason has received them, and they are all acting against the decrees of Caesar, saying that there is another king, Jesus."*
17:8 *And the people and the city authorities were disturbed when they heard these things.*
17:9 *And when they had taken money as security from Jason and the rest, they let them go.*

17:1 Note that Paul continued to carry out his mission plan of first going to the synagogue in Thessalonica in order to witness to people who were open to the Gospel (^{1}M. I. Lk 4:15).

17:3 (1) Luke first reports in verse 3 that everywhere that Paul went he was *"explaining and proving that it was necessary for the Christ to*

suffer and to rise from the dead." Paul proclaimed to Jews and Gentiles alike that Jesus <u>fulfilled</u> all of Scripture for all people of all nations and that his resurrection <u>proves</u> this because it was his heavenly Father who raised him from the dead (2 Cor 1:20; [2]M. M. 2 Cor 1:20 & [3]Ro 8:35).
2) Then, Luke continues in verse 3 by quoting Paul directly, *"This Jesus, whom I proclaim to you, is <u>the</u> <u>Christ</u>."* This statement is, of course, very similar to what Paul declared in (1 Cor 2:2) *"For I decided to know <u>nothing</u> among you <u>except</u> Jesus Christ and him crucified."* The entire focus of Paul's mission work was on the person and work of Jesus, his dear Lord. To devout Jews and Gentiles who were faithfully studying their Scripture in order to learn when they might finally see *"the Christ"* or the Messiah, Paul clearly taught them from God's holy Word that this Jesus was the God/man whom they had long waited for. All of Scripture says that Jesus is *"the Christ"* (Lk 24:27, 44; [4]M. M. Lk 4:21 & [5]2 Tim 3:16).

17:4 Verse 4 says that *"some of them [Paul's hearers] were persuaded and joined Paul and Silas, as did a great many of the devout Greeks and not a few of the leading women."* Clearly, Paul's message in verse 3 was the beautifully sharp sword that the Holy Spirit was able to use in order to create faith in the hearts of *"many"* of his devout <u>Gentile</u> hearers, because Paul, of course, always based his messages on God's holy Word ([6]M. I. Lk 4:17 & [7]M. M. Ro 10:17a).

17:5 Note that when verse 5 says, that *"the Jews were <u>jealous</u>"* that so many people had become Christians, they were obviously prompted by the same devil who had possessed the evil Jews who were *"jealous"* of Jesus because he was so popular (Mt 27:18; Lk 20:19). Just as they had hounded his gracious Lord until they finally killed him, they also constantly hounded Paul (13:45, 50; 20:3; 21:27; 24:9; [8]M. I. Lk 4:4). And evil people will always hound Christians who faithfully proclaim their Lord Jesus, because Satan hates Jesus and his holy Word. It was Jesus who totally defeated him on the cross; and he knows that the time is very short that he has left in which to deceive those who trust in Jesus as their Lord ([9]M. I. Lk 12:40).

17:7 (1) And just like Satan's attack against Paul and Silas in Philippi (16:21), the devil tried to use these Jews (v 5) in order to make this into a political problem by claiming in verse 7 that *"all of them oppose the emperor's decrees by saying that there is another king, whose name is Jesus."* Obviously, this was, indeed, a very serious political charge that they brought against the Church and its dear Lord. However, it was, of course a lie from Satan, *"the father of lies"* (Jn 8:44) that Jesus was a political, earthly king. And just like many of the devil's lies, it was partly true, because Jesus is indeed a King; but the *whole* truth is that he is the King over all kings (Lk 1:32-33; Mt 2:2; [10]M. M. Lk 1:27). **2)** Therefore, the good news is that the devil was only temporarily able to use this lie in order to stop the proclamation of the Gospel in Thessalonica. We read in Paul's two letters to the Christians in Thessalonica that, some years later, there was, indeed, a church in Thessalonica. The Lord of the mission had, of course, not lost control of his work; and the King of kings was ruling in the mission-hearts of his chosen people in Thessalonica ([11]M. M. Ac 4:28 & [12]M. I. Ac 5:41).

Paul and Silas in Berea 17:10-15

17:10 *The brothers immediately sent Paul and Silas away by night to Berea, and when they arrived they went into the Jewish synagogue.*
17:11 *Now these Jews were more noble than those in Thessalonica; they received the word with all eagerness, examining the Scriptures daily to see if these things were so.*
17:12 *Many of them therefore believed, with not a few Greek women of high standing as well as men.*
17:13 *But when the Jews from Thessalonica learned that the word of God was proclaimed by Paul at Berea also, they came there too, agitating and stirring up the crowds.*
17:14 *Then the brothers immediately sent Paul off on his way to the sea, but Silas and Timothy remained there.*
17:15 *Those who conducted Paul brought him as far as Athens, and after receiving a command for Silas and Timothy to come to him as soon as possible, they departed.*

17:10-12 (1) Once again, the mission team first went to the synagogue in Berea, and the Holy Spirit had three opportunities to work mightily in the hearts of many people there. **a)** First of all, verse 11 says that *"they received the word with all eagerness."* Obviously, they had been studying the Scripture because they knew that it was God's inspired, holy Word ([13]M. M. 2 Tim 3:16). The Holy Spirit had already prepared their hearts to hear the Gospel about Jesus. **b)** Secondly, we can also be certain that, as Paul proclaimed the Gospel in their synagogue, he based his message on Scripture ([14]M. I. Lk 4:17). **c)** And thirdly, verse 11 continues by saying that the people were also *"examining the Scriptures daily to see if these things were so"* (v 11; [15]M. M. Lk 4:21). They had to go to the synagogue to hear and study God's Word, since, at that time, no one had personal copies of the Scriptures—and now, after hearing Paul, they did so very eagerly and *"daily."* Obviously, these new Christians were finding more and more proof in the Old Testament that Jesus was, indeed, *"the Christ"* (v 3), because he had, indeed, fulfilled everything that God had promised that his Messiah would do to rescue his people. Obviously, Paul had used the Scriptures this way in his preaching to them (M. M. Lk 4:21); and, in their joy, they now began to search for more and more of the same kind of rich Gospel. It's a new mission message. M. M. Ac 17:11: When a person learns from the Bible how Jesus graciously fulfilled everything that God has promised him in the Bible, Jesus' grace fills him with eagerness to daily search for more proof in the Bible that Jesus did it for him. **2)** This new mission message highlights how urgently Bible translation is needed all over the world! It's impossible to overemphasize how important it is that each person should have the opportunity to privately confirm for himself (or perhaps not confirm) that the message that a preacher is telling him is indeed God's own truth and the whole truth (Lk 16:29, 31; Jn 5:39). If a preacher says in public, "Thus says the Lord," and his hearers can privately confirm for themselves in their own Bibles that this is indeed God's truth, the Holy Spirit can mightily create faith in one person's heart or strengthen the faith in another hearer's heart. But if a hearer can say, "Wait a minute preacher! I can't find what you are saying in my Bible," he is able to hold the preacher accountable for what he has said.

Therefore, the tremendous importance of <u>Bible translation</u> is obvious, since billions of people in the world yet today do not have even a portion of the Bible in their heart-language, and therefore, they cannot hold a missionary or a preacher <u>accountable</u> in this manner. And all over the world, it's <u>Satan</u> who is having a good time, since he's sure to fill these gaps with his lies! It is a sad situation in thousands of languages yet today; and therefore, it is also a very urgent situation. Why has it taken the Christian Church nearly 2,000 years to realize that it's time to get busy translating the Bible? People in nearly 4,000 languages still do not have even a portion of the Bible translated in their heart-language. And only a handful of Christian organizations are doing so ([16]M. M. Ac 17:11).

17:12-13 Verse 12 says that *"many of them [the Bereans] therefore believed, with not a few Greek women of high standing as well as men."* Therefore, this very fertile ground in Berea, where the Spirit of Jesus could work so well with the written <u>Scriptures</u>, of course, filled Satan with <u>hatred</u>. Thus, verse 13 continues by saying that *"when the Jews from Thessalonica learned that the word of God was proclaimed by Paul at Berea also, they came there too, agitating and stirring up the crowds."* The Jews in Thessalonica were so angry that they pursued the mission team all of the way to Berea (v 13; [17]M. I. Lk 11:10). How bitterly the devil hates the proclamation of God's holy Word! And how easily he stirs up people who are already in his evil kingdom ([18]M. M. Ac 17:11)!

Paul in Athens 17:16-21

> 17:16 *Now while Paul was waiting for them at Athens, his spirit was provoked within him as he saw that the city was full of idols.*
> 17:17 *So he reasoned in the synagogue with the Jews and the devout persons, and in the marketplace every day with those who happened to be there.*
> 17:18 *Some of the Epicurean and Stoic philosophers also conversed with him. And some said, "What does this babbler wish to say?" Others said, "He seems to be a preacher of foreign divinities"--*

because he was preaching Jesus and the resurrection.
17:19 And they took hold of him and brought him to the Areopagus, saying, "May we know what this new teaching is that you are presenting?
17:20 For you bring some strange things to our ears. We wish to know therefore what these things mean."
17:21 *Now all the Athenians and the foreigners who lived there would spend their time in nothing except telling or hearing something new.*

17:16 Verse 16 says, *"Now while Paul was waiting for them [his missionary team] at Athens, his spirit was provoked within him as he saw that the city was full of idols."* Paul now found himself in a new city and in a completely *new* cultural/social situation. But why did Luke write that Paul's *"spirit was provoked within him?"* Paul had wisely learned from his past encounters with the Animistic religion that it was incredibly evil, since idolatry is the worship of Satan. The devil hates everyone and provokes everyone who worships him to kill others with witchcraft. Therefore, this city was full of spiritual danger; and it's no wonder that Paul was deeply provoked ([19]M. I. Lk 11:4b). However, the Holy Spirit also gave him both the time and the wisdom to visit all parts of the city and carefully plan the mission methods that his team should use here ([20]M. I. Ac 16:6).

17:17-21 And, as Paul carefully studied the situation, he would have taken careful note of the fact that, while the society was full of spiritual danger, there were at least three good venues available for them to proclaim the Gospel ([21]M. I. Lk 4:15). **a)** *First* of all, Paul saw that there was a synagogue in Athens; therefore, he *"reasoned in the synagogue with the Jews and the devout persons [Gentiles]"* (v 17), as he had done in so many other cities ([22]M. I. Lk 4:17). **b)** The second venue was the public square or market place where Stoic and Epicurean philosophers had daily discussions. Therefore, verse 17 continues by saying that Paul *"reasoned… in the marketplace every day with those who happened to be there."* And because Paul *"was preaching Jesus and the resurrection to them"* (v 18), which was a totally new teaching to them, *"they took* *him and brought him to the Areopagus"* (v 19) so that they could hear more. He had used the public square as such an effective venue to proclaim the Gospel that the philosophers offered him the third venue ([23]M. I. 1 Cor 1:17). **c)** And the third venue was a type of <u>religious court</u> called the Areopagus (v 19), although Paul may have spoken to them on the "hill of Ares" near there. Therefore, we see that, while the city of Athens was a new and unique cultural/social situation, Paul (His team had not yet joined him.) had at least <u>three</u> wide open doors of opportunity to proclaim the name of *"Jesus and the resurrection to them"* (v 18); and, as he always did, he wisely made full use of them (M. I. Lk 4:15).

Paul Addresses the Areopagus 17:22-34

17:22 *So Paul, standing in the midst of the Areopagus, said: "Men of Athens, I perceive that in every way you are very religious.*
17:23 *For as I passed along and observed the objects of your worship, I found also an altar with this inscription, 'To the unknown god.' What therefore you worship as unknown, this I proclaim to you.*
17:24 *The God who made the world and everything in it, being Lord of heaven and earth, does not live in temples made by man,*
17:25 *nor is he served by human hands, as though he needed anything, since he himself gives to all mankind life and breath and everything.*
17:26 *And he made from one man every nation of mankind to live on all the face of the earth, having determined allotted periods and the boundaries of their dwelling place,*
17:27 *that they should seek God, in the hope that they might feel their way toward him and find him. Yet he is actually not far from each one of us,*
17:28 *for "'In him we live and move and have our being'; as even some of your own poets have said, "'For we are indeed his offspring.'*
17:29 *Being then God's offspring, we ought not to think that the*

> *divine being is like gold or silver or stone, an image formed by the art and imagination of man.*
17:30 *The times of ignorance God overlooked, but now he commands all people everywhere to repent,*
17:31 *because he has fixed a day on which he will judge the world in righteousness by a man whom he has appointed; and of this he has given assurance to all by raising him from the dead."*
17:32 *Now when they heard of the resurrection of the dead, some mocked. But others said, "We will hear you again about this."*
17:33 *So Paul went out from their midst.*
17:34 *But some men joined him and believed, among whom also were Dionysius the Areopagite and a woman named Damaris and others with them.*

17:22-31 (1) Paul's audience in Athens was completely different from any other one that he had ever faced; nevertheless, the Holy Spirit had taught him at least three things as a missionary of the Gospel: **a)** First of all, he knew that he had to take time to study his unique audience in order to learn what opportunities there were to touch their hearts with the Gospel ([24]M. I. Col 4:5). **b)** Secondly, he knew that the Holy Spirit produces the results and not human efforts, but that does not excuse the missionary from failing to carefully prepare his message ([25]M. I. Lk 8:11). **c)** Thirdly, he knew that he could not depend on his own wisdom to plan his message, but he could depend on the guidance of the Holy Spirit ([26]M. I. Lk 3:3b). **2)** Careful examination of Paul's message reveals the wisdom that the Holy Spirit gave him to shape it to this unique audience in <u>six</u> different ways: **a)** First of all, Paul obviously knew how evil their Animistic religion was, but instead of making them angry by immediately condemning it, he made the positive statement in verse 22: *"I perceive that in every way you are very <u>religious</u>."* **b)** Secondly, since Paul's hearers loved to come to the Areopagus to discuss the <u>false</u> ideas about God and the <u>false</u> gods that the Stoic and Epicurean philosophers had invented, Paul briefly described, in verses 23-27, the <u>truth</u> that the Bible teaches about who the true God is and the world and the people whom he has made. Most importantly, Paul taught them in verses 25-26 that God made and controls all human beings, so that *"they should <u>seek</u> God… and find him. Yet he is actually <u>not far from each one of us</u>"* (v 27; 1 Cor 1:20-25). **c)** Thirdly, Paul attempted to apply this bit of Gospel directly to all of their hard hearts by *quoting* from their own poets in verse 28 by saying, *"for 'In him we live and move and have our being;' as even some of your own poets have said, 'For we are indeed his offspring.'"* Obviously, Paul was familiar with the writings of these philosophers and he also understood his audience very well; and the Holy Spirit was clearly guiding him to use this knowledge to touch their hearts **d)** Fourthly, Paul then added some severe warnings from God's <u>Law</u> close to the end of his message. As he spoke verse 29 he, no doubt gestured to the many idols all around them, and warned them that they were, in fact, *"<u>ignorant</u>"* (v 30) of the truth, because, *"being then God's offspring, we ought <u>not</u> to think that the divine being is…an image formed by the art and imagination of man."* But he add a bit of comfort in verse 30, *"The times of ignorance God overlooked, but now he commands all people everywhere to repent."* But he warned them again in verse 31, that a *Judgment* Day is coming by adding that God *"has fixed a day on which he will judge the world in righteousness by a man whom he has appointed."* **e)** Fifthly, note that Paul did *not* proclaim two truths in his *conclusion*, which was very unusual for him. First, he did not mention Jesus' <u>name</u>, but he referred to him in verse 31 as *"a man whom he has appointed."* Secondly, he did not refer to the apparent weakness of God in the *cross* of Jesus (1 Cor 1:25). **f)** Finally, Paul also knew the custom of the Greek philosophers of leaving their most significant point to the <u>end</u> of their message. Therefore he concluded in verse 31 with the richest <u>Gospel</u> in the history of the world, *"and of this he [God] has given assurance to all by <u>raising</u> him from the dead."* The <u>resurrection</u> of Jesus is the richest Gospel, because it is the final, sure proof that God has always kept all of his promises, and he always will do so (2 Cor 1:20; [27]M. I. Ac 4:20 & Lk 3:3b).

17:32-34 (1) After such careful preparation, and after proclaiming such rich, rich Gospel in the resurrection of Jesus in verse 31, <u>all</u> of the hard hearts in this audience should have melted. But most of their hearts were clearly not much different from the hard hearts of some of Jesus' listeners, such as the scribes and Pharisees (Lk 13:34; 20:19). Nevertheless, the Holy Spirit did create faith in the hearts of a few of them, as verse 34 says, *"But some men joined him and believed...and a woman named Damaris and others with them."* Obviously, these philosophers were full of pride in their <u>own</u> "wisdom," Satan was able to keep them under his firm, evil control (1 Cor 1:20-25; [28]M. M. 2 Cor 4:4 & [29]M. I. Lk 8:11). **2)** Furthermore, we today are left wondering what happened to the few new Christians in Athens, because: **a)** Luke says nothing about whether Paul trained any leaders there or left any of his team there for a time. Luke simply says in (18:1), *"After this Paul <u>left</u> Athens and went to Corinth."* **b)** And the remainder of the New Testament is silent about any church in Athens after Paul left. Obviously, we cannot argue anything from silence; however, this silence is very unusual, especially since Athens was a capital city of the region. Paul could only leave the new Christians and all of the results of his work there in his Lord's gracious hands (M. I. Lk 8:11 & [30]M. M. Ac 4:28).

---

[1] M. I. Lk 4:15: Christians should seize <u>every</u> opportunity to proclaim the Gospel to lost people of all nations.

[2] M. M. 2 Cor 1:20: It is Jesus who graciously died and rose from the dead in order to fulfill all of the promises that God made to his people in the Old Testament; therefore, everyone should confess that Jesus is their dear Lord and give God all of their praise.

[3] M. M. Ro 8:35: God has proven the depth of his love for *all* whom he has chosen, who trust in Jesus, by sending his Son, Jesus to die for them; therefore, <u>nothing</u> in all creation can separate them from his love.

[4] M. M. Lk 4:21: <u>Every</u> verse in the entire Bible points in some way to Jesus and his mission to seek and save the lost.

[5] M. M. 2 Tim 3:16: The Holy Spirit inspired the entire Bible; and therefore, the whole Bible is useful for teaching people the truth, for teaching them how to live a life that pleases God, for rebuking their errors, and for correcting their faults.

[6] M. I. Lk 4:17: Christians should always base their messages on the Bible, so that the Holy Spirit can use his holy Word to create and strengthen faith in their hearers.

[7] M. M. Ro 10:17a: The Holy Spirit <u>only</u> creates and preserves faith by using the message of God's grace in his holy Word.

[8] M. I. Lk 4:4: When Satan attacks Christians on their mission they should wield the sword of

God's Word by quoting from it, and not depend on their own strength.

[9] M. I. Lk 12:40: Christians should "eat" God's Word every day in order to keep their faith strong, so that they are always ready for their Lord's return.

[10] M. M. Lk 1:27: Jesus had to be born as a true human being and as a true Jew in order to become the King of kings in his heavenly kingdom forever.

[11] M. M. Ac 4:28: The heavenly Father is always in full control of his mission to all nations of the world.

[12] M. I. Ac 5:41: Christians should consider it a great honor to be persecuted for proclaiming the name of Jesus.

[13] M. M. 2 Tim 3:16: The Holy Spirit inspired the entire Bible; and therefore, the whole Bible is useful for teaching people the truth, for teaching them how to live a life that pleases God, for rebuking their errors, and for correcting their faults.

[14] M. I. Lk 4:17: Christians should always base their messages on the Bible, so that the Holy Spirit can use his holy Word to create and strengthen faith in their hearers.

[15] M. M. Lk 4:21: <u>Every</u> verse in the entire Bible points in some way to Jesus and his mission to seek and save the lost.

[16] M. M. Ac 17:11: When a person learns from the Bible how Jesus graciously fulfilled everything that God has promised him in the Bible, Jesus' grace fills him with eagerness to daily search for more proof in the Bible that Jesus did it for him.

[17] M. I. Lk 11:10: Christians should <u>continuously</u> pray to their heavenly Father and *always* depend on his grace, and not on their own feeble strength, because he <u>always</u> loves them.

[18] M. M. Ac 17:11: When a person learns from the Bible how Jesus graciously fulfilled everything that God has promised him in the Bible, Jesus' grace fills him with eagerness to daily search for more proof in the Bible that Jesus did it for him.

[19] M. I. Lk 11:4b: Christians should ask their heavenly Father that he would not allow Satan to tempt them so severely that they lose their faith, and also that he would give them his strength to depend on his grace in all of their trials.

[20] M. I. Ac 16:6: Christians should start planning all mission efforts and continue to evaluate them based on both <u>prayerful</u> study of God's Word and also on thoughtful advice from fellow Christians; and they should *not* base their plans entirely on any supposed visions or dreams.

[21] M. I. Lk 4:15: Christians should seize <u>every</u> opportunity to proclaim the Gospel to lost people of all nations.

[22] M. I. Lk 4:17: Christians should always base their messages on the Bible, so that the Holy Spirit can use his holy Word to create and strengthen faith in their hearers.

[23] M. I. 1 Cor 1:17: Christians should always proclaim the Gospel by focusing very clearly on the gracious power of the <u>cross</u> of Jesus, so that the faith of their hearers is based on its power; and they should not try to persuade people by using clever arguments, which would rob his cross of its power because the faith of their hearers would then be based on human wisdom.

[24] M. I. Col 4:5: Christians should always be ready to use the opportunities that God gives them to witness by depending on the Holy Spirit to a) guide them in their conduct toward unbelievers and b) give them wise answers to the questions that they may ask.

[25] M. I. Lk 8:11: Christians should faithfully do their job of preaching and leave the <u>results</u> to the Holy Spirit.

[26] M. I. Lk 3:3b: Christians should always depend on the Holy Spirit's guidance for whether they should emphasize God's Law or the Gospel about Jesus, and which one to apply <u>first</u>.

[27] M. I. Ac 4:20: Christians should boldly witness to the name of Jesus and allow nothing to stop their witness because it is the Holy Spirit's own message.

[28] M. M. 2 Cor 4:4: Jesus is the Light of the world and the perfect image of God; and Christians have proclaimed this Gospel message to the lost world; however, Satan, the evil god of this world, has blinded the minds of their hearers so that they do not believe in Jesus.

[29] M. I. Lk 8:11: Christians should faithfully do their job of preaching and leave the <u>results</u> to the Holy Spirit.

[30] M. M. Ac 4:28: The heavenly Father is always in full control of his mission to all nations of the world.

Chapter 18

Paul in Corinth 18:1-17

18:1 *After this Paul left Athens and went to Corinth.*
18:2 *And he found a Jew named Aquila, a native of Pontus, recently come from Italy with his wife Priscilla, because Claudius had commanded all the Jews to leave Rome. And he went to see them,*
18:3 *and because he was of the same trade he stayed with them and worked, for they were tentmakers by trade.*
18:4 *And he reasoned in the synagogue every Sabbath, and tried to persuade Jews and Greeks.*
18:5 *When Silas and Timothy arrived from Macedonia, Paul was occupied with the word, testifying to the Jews that the Christ was Jesus.*
18:6 *And when they opposed and reviled him, he shook out his garments and said to them, "Your blood be on your own heads! I am innocent. From now on I will go to the Gentiles."*
18:7 *And he left there and went to the house of a man named Titius Justus, a worshiper of God. His house was next door to the synagogue.*
18:8 *Crispus, the ruler of the synagogue, believed in the Lord, together with his entire household. And many of the Corinthians hearing Paul believed and were baptized.*
18:9 *And the Lord said to Paul one night in a vision, "Do not be afraid, but go on speaking and do not be silent,*
18:10 *for I am with you, and no one will attack you to harm you, for I have many in this city who are my people."*
18:11 *And he stayed a year and six months, teaching the word of God among them.*
18:12 *But when Gallio was proconsul of Achaia, the Jews made a united attack on Paul and brought him before the tribunal,*
18:13 *saying, "This man is persuading people to worship God contrary to the Law."*

18:14 *But when Paul was about to open his mouth, Gallio said to the Jews, "If it were a matter of wrongdoing or vicious crime, O Jews, I would have reason to accept your complaint.*

18:15 *But since it is a matter of questions about words and names and your own Law, see to it yourselves. I refuse to be a judge of these things."*

18:16 *And he drove them from the tribunal.*

18:17 *And they all seized Sosthenes, the ruler of the synagogue, and beat him in front of the tribunal. But Gallio paid no attention to any of this.*

18:2 In Corinth, the Holy Spirit led Paul to meet a Jewish married couple, Aquila and Priscilla (v 2); and they quickly became close companions of Paul, no doubt, partly because all three of them were tentmakers (v 3). This couple played a very important *supporting* role on Paul's mission team. From this time on, it appears that his mission team was at times six people: Paul, Silas, Timothy, Luke, Aquila and Priscilla, although they were not always working together in the same city on their mission; and neither Luke or Paul recorded all of their movements in their accounts of their travels ([1]M. M. Ac 4:28).

18:3, 5 (1) Paul and his mission team knew that those who hear the Gospel should be responsible for supporting the preacher ([2]M. M. 1 Cor 9:4 & [3]M. I. Lk 8:11); however, when they first arrived in Corinth we first read about two different kinds of external support that they needed and received, because there were no new Christians there who could support them. **a)** In verse 3, we learn that Paul made and sold tents; and this income was one of the main ways in which he supported his team on his second and third mission trips. **b)** And we also learn from verse 5 and from (2 Cor 11:9) that, at about this time, the Christians in Philippi sent monetary support to Paul's team in Corinth through Silas and Timothy. This support was especially important to the team, since it enabled Paul to be fully *"occupied with the word"* (v 5), because that was, obviously, the main work of the mission ([4]M. I. Ac 6:1). **2)** Furthermore, we also read in (Phil 4:15-16) that *"no church entered into partnership with me in giving and receiving, except you [Philippians]* *only. Even in Thessalonica you sent me help for my needs once and again."* How extremely grateful Paul was for this *external* support that he continued to receive from this one church in Philippi. How generous they were because the grace of their Lord Jesus had filled their mission-hearts with gratitude to him ([5]M. M. Lk 18:29)! And furthermore, this generous support also, in some situations, allowed Paul's mission team to focus on the main part of their work of proclaiming the Gospel (M. I. Ac 6:1).

18:6 (1) Paul continued to proclaim the Gospel to his fellow Jews; however, this time, some of them (not the family of Crispus (v 8)) sinned grievously *"when they opposed and reviled him [Paul]"* (v 6). Obviously, these Jews assumed that they *deserved* God's grace because they were Abraham's physical descendants, and in their hard hearts, they rejected the Gospel. Therefore, their own tragic choice made their eternal spiritual death their own responsibility ([6]M. M. Lk 14:34 & [7]Ro 4:11). And this is the reason why Paul decided to try to warn them that it was Satan who was controlling them by using the strongest possible warning against grave spiritual danger in the Jewish culture (13:51). Verse 6 continues by saying that Paul *"shook out his garments and said to them, 'Your blood be on your own heads! I am innocent. From now on I will go to the Gentiles'"* This severe warning should have shocked them into repenting of their grave sin. However, we do not read that they did so (13:46; [8]M. I. Lk 3:8 & [9]Ac 4:20). **2)** The Gentiles who heard Paul say, *"from now on I will go to the Gentiles"* (v 6), on the other hand, must have been filled with joy to hear Paul say that the Gospel was also meant for them. They would now eagerly look forward to hearing it again ([10]M. M. Lk 1:1 & [11]Ro 3:26).

18:7 Although some Jews rejected the Gospel, verse 7 says that a Gentile man named, Titius Justus welcomed Paul, and presumably his whole team, into his home. And verse 7 adds that he was *"a worshiper of God,"* which means that he was an uncircumcised Gentile who was worshipping in the synagogue, like Cornelius in (10:2). Thus, his home became the mission-base for the team's work for a whole year and a half, as verse 11 says. Therefore, Titius not only housed them, but his home also gave the team an opening into the Roman/Greek society in

Corinth (v 6; [12]M. I. Lk 10:7a & [13]Lk 10:7b).

18:8 Then, verse 8 adds three significant details concerning the 18 month mission in Corinth: **a)** First of all, some Jews such as Crispus *"believed in the Lord."* **b)** Secondly, *"his entire household"* also believed, which would imply that Paul baptized his children, since his *"entire household"* would certainly have included children (16:33; [14]M. I. Mt 28:19). **c)** Thirdly, verse 8 also adds that "many of the Corinthians hearing Paul believed and were baptized. And the grammatical forms of the Greek verbs *"believed"* and *"baptized"* indicate repeated action. During the time that they were there, every day some people repented and believed; and they baptized them. The Holy Spirit was using his holy Word powerfully among them, as the team faithfully proclaimed the Gospel ([15]M. M. Ro 10:17a).

18:9-17 (1) However, verses 9-17 indicate that the situation in Corinth must have been just as dangerous as it had been in other cities where angry Jews drove Paul out of town. It was so dangerous that the Lord of the mission appeared to Paul one night in a vision and said, *"Do not be afraid, but go on speaking and do not be silent, for I am with you"* (vs 9-10). Paul must have, once again, been praying for guidance from his Lord, but also seriously thinking about fleeing ([16]M. I. Lk 11:10). However, this direct communication from the Lord of the mission gave him the courage that he needed to stay in Corinth, not just a short time, but even a whole year and a half ([17]M. M. Ac 4:28). **2)** The specific legal charge, in verse 13, that the Jews brought against Paul was that *"this man is persuading people to worship God contrary to the law."* They tried to take advantage of the fact that the Jewish religion was a legal religion in the Roman Empire while Christianity was illegal (16:21). This was, of course, a lie from Satan, since the truth was that Christianity is the beautiful fulfilment of the Jewish religion of the Old Testament. God's mission-heart had planned this fulfilment in his Son, Jesus from before he created the world. Therefore, it was he who was in full control of his mission and, once again, did not allow the devil to stop his Church from expanding among the Gentiles (vs 16-17; Rom 11:25-26; M. M. Ac 4:28). **3)** There are two pieces of evidence that suggest that Paul's mission team did not remain in the city of Corinth itself but traveled to other areas around Corinth during those eighteen months. **a)** First of all, note that when verse 27 says that, sometime later, Apollos *"wished to cross to Achaia;"* it probably refers to the whole province of Achaia including its capital city of Corinth. Obviously, he was eager to help strengthen all of the churches in that region. **b)** Secondly, note that Paul addressed his second letter to Corinth in (2 Cor 1:1), *"To the church of God that is at Corinth, with all the saints who are in the whole of Achaia [Greece]."* It's quite clear that Paul's team was very busy spreading the Gospel far and wide and establishing churches in several towns (1 Thess 5:27; [18]M. I. Ac 1:8).

Paul Returns to Antioch 18:18-23

18:18 *After this, Paul stayed many days longer and then took leave of the brothers and set sail for Syria, and with him Priscilla and Aquila. At Cenchreae he had cut his hair, for he was under a vow.*
18:19 *And they came to Ephesus, and he left them there, but he himself went into the synagogue and reasoned with the Jews.*
18:20 *When they asked him to stay for a longer period, he declined.*
18:21 *But on taking leave of them he said, "I will return to you if God wills," and he set sail from Ephesus.*
18:22 *When he had landed at Caesarea, he went up and greeted the church, and then went down to Antioch.*
18:23 *After spending some time there, he departed and went from one place to the next through the region of Galatia and Phrygia, strengthening all the disciples.*

18:18 Verse 18 mentions *"a vow;"* however, the details are not clear. Apparently Paul had survived some grave danger and took a vow to thank God for delivering him. And he marked the end of his vow by cutting his hair, since this act ended Old Testament vows (Nu 6:2; 5:18). **18:18-19** On his way back to Jerusalem, Paul now returned to Asia Minor and went to Ephesus (v 19), which was a new city on their mission. He had at least two reasons for going to Ephesus: **a)** First of all, it was a capital city of the region and it was also a geographically strategic city for a mission base. **b)** Secondly, his fellow missionaries, Aquila and Priscilla evidently wanted to settle there, since they remained there and did not continue on with Paul (v 19). And this faithful couple proved to be very important leaders of the church in Ephesus, especially since they later gave further training to another missionary, who was named Apollos (vs 24-26; [19]M. I. Ac 13:3).

18:20-21 However, Paul did not remain in Ephesus very long on this trip. Verse 20 says that *"when they asked him to stay for a longer period, he declined,"* but he did promise to *"return to you if God wills"* (V 20). He may have been in a hurry because winter weather would soon shut down all travel on the Mediterranean Sea, and he was eager to first go greet *"the church (probably in Jerusalem), and then went down to Antioch [in Syria]"* (v 22). This marked the end of his second missionary journey, because he was returning to his mission base. It was the Christians in Antioch who had sent Paul and his mission team out on this trip ([20]M. I. Ro 15:20).

18:23 *"After spending some time"* (v 23) at his mission-base in Antioch, verse 23 then marks the beginning of Paul's third missionary journey. Obviously the church in Antioch sent Paul's team off with their blessing; and *"he departed and went from one place to the next through the region of Galatia and Phrygia."* The team traveled by land once again, *"strengthening all the disciples"* in the churches that they had established on their second journey, especially since they had not been able to stay in some towns long enough to train leaders. And of course, it was the Holy Spirit who was giving them the *"strength"* that they needed through his holy Word ([21]M. M. Ac 4:28 & [22]M. I. Ac 13:3).

Apollos Speaks Boldly in Ephesus 18:24-28

18:24 *Now a Jew named Apollos, a native of Alexandria, came to Ephesus. He was an eloquent man, competent in the Scriptures.*
18:25 *He had been instructed in the way of the Lord. And being fervent in spirit, he spoke and taught accurately the things concerning Jesus, though he knew only the baptism of John.*

18:26 *He began to speak boldly in the synagogue, but when Priscilla and Aquila heard him, they took him and explained to him the way of God more accurately.*

18:27 *And when he wished to cross to Achaia, the brothers encouraged him and wrote to the disciples to welcome him. When he arrived, he greatly helped those who through grace had believed,*

18:28 *for he powerfully refuted the Jews in public, showing by the Scriptures that the Christ was Jesus.*

18:24-26 (1) The appearance of Apollos in Ephesus demonstrates how important it was that the Lord of the mission had sent Priscilla and Aquila there because, according to verse 26, they were able to explain *"to him the way of God more accurately."* Where he first came to faith in Jesus and why his knowledge of Jesus was incomplete are mysteries (8:16). However, Apollos was clearly a very gifted person who could contribute a great deal to Paul's mission team, mainly because, as verse 24 says, he was *"competent in the Scriptures."* Note the striking similarities between the abilities of Apollos and those of Stephen in chapter 7 ([23]M. I. Lk 6:13).

18:25 (1) Verse 25 says that Apollos *"knew only the baptism of John."* John the Baptist was the last Old Testament prophet; therefore, he baptized people who had repented and believed in a Messiah who was still coming (Lk 1:17). However, Jesus commanded his disciples to baptize people who had repented and now believed in him, because he had fulfilled everything that his heavenly Father had sent him to do (Mt 28:19-20). Nevertheless, it's not clear in verses 24-25 why Apollos did not yet know the whole truth about Jesus. **2)** It's unfortunate for the world mission of the Church, yet today, that verse 25 (or any other verse) offers no explanation as to which method the early Church used to baptize people. The verb "baptize" refers to different types of actions in different contexts in the New Testament; it may refer to immersion, pouring or sprinkling. Therefore, it's important that Christians today should apply water in some manner in the name of the Triune God; however, the method that they apply it is not important. Nevertheless, Bible translation teams must choose the words for translating the word "baptize" very carefully, so that all of the local church denominations can happily accept it and use it. If, for example, they use a word or phrase that implies immersion, this one-sided choice obviously would cause a very painful and divisive discussion, which makes Satan very happy. And in this case, some of these Christians may reject the entire Bible translation. Therefore, all translation teams need our constant and urgent prayers as they make these types of vital word choices every single day ([24]M. I. Lk 11:10 & [25]Jn 14:13).

18:27-28 Verse 27 says that when Apollos *"wished to cross to Achaia, the brothers encouraged him and wrote to the disciples to welcome him."* It's obvious that Priscilla and Aquila not only *"explained the way of God more accurately"* to Apollos (v 26), they also saw that he had a zealous mission-heart to go as a missionary to people who had not yet heard the Gospel. And they also knew that the young churches in Achaia needed strengthening with God's Word; therefore, they must have encouraged him to go there. Furthermore, sometime later, Paul wrote at least three letters to the Christians in Corinth and Achaia, and in all of his letters he struggled to help them overcome one problem after another. Wherever missionaries proclaim the Gospel, Satan hates it; and he especially has many opportunities to cause misunderstanding and confusion in cross-cultural situations like Achaia ([26]M. I. Ac 2:4 & [27]Ac 19:10).

---

[1] M. M. Ac 4:28: The heavenly Father is always in full control of his mission to all nations of the world.

[2] M. M. 1 Cor 9:4: God gives those who proclaim the Gospel the right to receive enough support from their hearers to make a living.

[3] M. I. Lk 8:11: Christians should faithfully do their job of preaching and leave the <u>results</u> to the Holy Spirit.

[4] M. I. Ac 6:1: Christians should always remember that the main aspect of the mission is to proclaim the Law and Gospel message and should not allow any other aspect of the work to hinder this main work.

[5] M. M. Lk 18:29: All Christians will certainly receive rewards in heaven as gracious gifts, but not because they earned them by going into the lost world to proclaim the Gospel; rather, they went because they also received <u>grateful</u> mission-hearts from their Lord.

[6] M. M. Lk 14:34: A Christian's faith relationship with Jesus is a precious <u>treasure</u> and a

completely <u>unique</u> personal relationship, because no one deserves it and it will last forever.

[7] M. M. Ro 4:11: All Christians from every nation on earth belong to the <u>spiritual family</u> of Abraham, the Church because they share the same faith in Jesus that their father had.

[8] M. I. Lk 3:8: Christians should always be prepared to boldly and publicly refute false teaching, so that Satan cannot easily deceive people.

[9] M. I. Ac 4:20: Christians should boldly witness to the name of Jesus and allow nothing to stop their witness because it is the Holy Spirit's own message.

[10] M. M. Lk 1:1: Jesus earned salvation for <u>all</u> lost people from <u>every</u> nation on earth.

[11] M. M. Ro 3:26: God is just and fair to <u>everyone</u>, both when he condemns <u>all</u> people of all nations because all have sinned, and also when he <u>only</u> declares those people righteous who have faith in Jesus.

[12] M. I. Lk 10:7a: When Christians go to a strange town on their mission, they should search for a family that welcomes them and their Gospel and stay with them, because that home may be an <u>open</u> door into the <u>entire</u> community.

[13] M. I. Lk 10:7b: Church leaders deserve to be paid for their work of preaching and teaching the Gospel.

[14] M. I. Mt 28:19: Christians should go and proclaim God's Law and Gospel to all nations; then, baptize all who repent and believe after teaching them the meaning of holy Baptism.

[15] M. M. Ro 10:17a: The Holy Spirit *only* creates and preserves faith by using the message of God's grace in his holy Word.

[16] M. I. Lk 11:10: Christians should <u>continuously</u> pray to their heavenly Father and <u>always</u> depend on his grace, and not on their own feeble strength, because he <u>always</u> loves them.

[17] M. M. Ac 4:28: The heavenly Father is always in full control of his mission to all nations of the world.

[18] M. I. Ac 1:8: Christians should go and witness about Jesus to all who are lost from all languages and cultures by depending on the power of the Holy Spirit to help them bridge all of the language/cultural boundaries whether they are relatively easy, as in their own language, or extremely difficult.

[19] M. I. Ac 13:3: Christians should prayerfully seek the will of the Lord of the mission as they decide how they are going to deploy their missionaries.

[20] M. I. Ro 15:20: As Christians go on their mission to the world, they should maximize their efforts by establishing mission bases, in order to be able to spread the Gospel in areas where no other missionaries have worked.

[21] M. M. Ac 4:28: The heavenly Father is always in full control of his mission to all nations of the world.

[22] M. I. Ac 13:3: Christians should prayerfully seek the will of the Lord of the mission as they decide how they are going to deploy their missionaries.

[23] M. I. Lk 6:13: Christians should choose new leaders and train them in order to multiply the work.

[24] M. I. Lk 11:10: Christians should <u>continuously</u> pray to their heavenly Father and <u>always</u> depend on his grace, and not on their own feeble strength, because he <u>always</u> loves them.

[25] M. I. Jn 14:13: Christians should ask their heavenly Father for everything that they need in Jesus' name and he will do it; and then, everyone who sees God's grace will praise him in Jesus'

name.

[26] M. I. Ac 2:4: In cross-cultural situations, Christians should always focus on all of the needs of the target group by learning <u>their</u> heart-language and culture as deeply as possible, so that they can tell them the Gospel clearly in their own language and also help them with the true needs of their society.

[27] M. I. Ac 19:10: Christians should try to plant churches in strategic social/cultural centers, in order to be able to use them as mission-bases from which the mission can expand to the whole region.

Chapter 19

Paul in Ephesus 19:1-10

19:1 *And it happened that while Apollos was at Corinth, Paul passed through the inland country and came to Ephesus. There he found some disciples.*

19:2 *And he said to them, "Did you receive the Holy Spirit when you believed?" And they said, "No, we have not even heard that there is a Holy Spirit."*

19:3 *And he said, "Into what then were you baptized?" They said, "Into John's baptism."*

19:4 *And Paul said, "John baptized with the baptism of repentance, telling the people to believe in the one who was to come after him, that is, Jesus."*

19:5 *On hearing this, they were baptized in the name of the Lord Jesus.*

19:6 *And when Paul had laid his hands on them, the Holy Spirit came on them, and they began speaking in tongues and prophesying.*

19:7 *There were about twelve men in all.*

19:8 *And he entered the synagogue and for three months spoke boldly, reasoning and persuading them about the kingdom of God.*

19:9 *But when some became stubborn and continued in unbelief, speaking evil of the Way before the congregation, he withdrew from them and took the disciples with him, reasoning daily in the hall of Tyrannus.*

19:10 *This continued for two years, so that all the residents of Asia heard the word of the Lord, both Jews and Greeks.*

19:1-7 Verses 1-7 leave several questions unanswered about how these twelve Gentiles in Ephesus came to faith in Jesus. The confusion in the minds of these men seems to be quite similar to that of Apollos (18:25) and of the Samaritans in Samaria in (8:16-17). Why these twelve men were so poorly informed about Jesus and his Baptism is difficult for us to understand today. Some suggest that Apollos may have been their teacher before Priscilla and Aquila taught him more fully (18:24-26). But, since (18:19) says that *"he [Paul] left them there"* in Ephesus, why Priscilla and Aquila didn't also explain *"the way of God more accurately"* (18:26) to these twelve men is a mystery. Nevertheless, verses 1-7 tell us that Paul helped these twelve Gentiles in three ways: **a)** He <u>taught</u> them the full truth about Jesus and his Baptism (vs 2-4). **b)** Then, he <u>baptized</u> them *"in the name of the Lord Jesus"* (v 5), so that they received three <u>gifts</u>: the Holy Spirit, faith in Jesus and a new mission-heart ([1]M. M. Tit 3:5 & [2]Mt 5:14). Note that Luke does <u>not</u> say that Paul baptized them in the name of the Trinity. This new Trinitarian Baptism focused on <u>Jesus</u> as the God/man who earned the forgiveness that these Gentiles had now received as a gracious gift (Mt 28:19-20; 2:38; 8:16; 10:48). **c)** And then, he placed his hands on them (v 6), so that they also received some <u>spectacular</u> gifts of the Holy Spirit, *"and they began speaking in tongues and prophesying."* Paul did this so that everyone present would see that they had already received the three <u>hidden</u> spiritual gifts (2:4; 10:44, 46; [3]M. I. 1 Cor 14:1 & [4]1 Cor 14:2).

19:8-9 Once again here in Ephesus, verse 8 says that Paul <u>first</u> proclaimed the Gospel boldly to the <u>Jews</u> in their synagogue ([5]M. M. Ac 13:46). But when they stubbornly refused to repent and believe in Jesus (18:6), he left them and began witnessing to the <u>Gentiles</u> about Jesus in a new venue, *"the hall of Tyrannus"* (v 9; [6]M. I. Lk 4:15). This excellent opportunity to proclaim the Gospel was probably a <u>school</u> where a philosopher named Tyrannus often taught. This venue sounds quite similar to the public square in Athens where Paul made good use of an open forum of philosophers (17:17). Paul was also well versed in Greek philosophy (17:18, 28), so that he could no doubt also use this venue effectively (M. I. Lk 4:15).

19:10 Verse 10 then explains why Paul chose to proclaim the Gospel in Ephesus for such a long period of time when it says that *"this continued for two years, so that <u>all</u> the residents of Asia heard the word of the Lord, both Jews and Greeks."* Paul understood that Ephesus was a very important religious and social/cultural <u>center</u>; therefore, the church that he established there could become a new mission-base and his mission would be able to easily spread throughout the whole region. As a matter of fact, in addition to his main mission-base in Antioch in Syria (13:1-2), Paul very consistently tried to establish churches as new mission-bases in strategic social/cultural locations such as: Paphos on the island of Cyprus (13:4-6), Antioch in Pisidia (13:14), Philippi (16:12), Thessalonica (17:1), Athens (17:15), Corinth (18:1), and eventually Rome itself (28:24). It's a new mission imperative. M. I. Ac 19:10: Christians should try to plant churches in strategic social/cultural centers, in order to be able to use them as mission-bases from which the mission can expand to the whole region.

The Sons of Sceva 19:11-20

19:11 *And God was doing extraordinary miracles by the hands of Paul,*
19:12 *so that even handkerchiefs or aprons that had touched his skin were carried away to the sick, and their diseases left them and the evil spirits came out of them.*
19:13 *Then some of the itinerant Jewish exorcists undertook to invoke the name of the Lord Jesus over those who had evil spirits, saying, "I adjure you by the Jesus, whom Paul proclaims."*
19:14 *Seven sons of a Jewish high priest named Sceva were doing this.*
19:15 *But the evil spirit answered them, "Jesus I know, and Paul I recognize, but who are you?"*
19:16 *And the man in whom was the evil spirit leaped on them, mastered all of them and overpowered them, so that they fled out of that house naked and wounded.*
19:17 *And this became known to all the residents of Ephesus, both Jews and Greeks. And fear fell upon them all, and the name of the Lord Jesus was extolled.*
19:18 *Also many of those who were now Christians came, confessing and divulging their practices.*
19:19 *And a number of those who had practiced magic arts brought*

their books together and burned them in the sight of all. And they counted the value of them and found it came to fifty thousand pieces of silver.
19:20 *So the word of the Lord continued to increase and prevail mightily.*

19:11 Verse11 is the most important verse in verses 11-16 because it says that Paul performed miracles in *"the name of the Lord Jesus,"* in order to point to him. He always wanted many more people to hear the Gospel about Jesus' cross and resurrection. Only this greatest of all miracles can create saving faith in Jesus, because he rose from the dead for all people ([7]M. I. Ac 8:12 & [8]M. M. Ro 1:16b).

19:15-16 Verse15 is also very significant in this section because it says that *"the evil spirit answered them, 'Jesus I know, and Paul I recognize, but who are you?'"* Of course, the evil spirit knew that these men were lying when they used the name of Jesus to heal, because it knew that they were, in fact, using the evil power of its own master, the devil. And it also knew that Jesus had sent Paul to do miracles because he had faith in him and he was his missionary. Therefore, the evil spirit attacked these men and exposed them as impostors (v 16; [9]M. I. Ac 3:6 & [10]M. M. Ro 10:17a).

19:17-20 When the demon beat the seven men (v 16), there were three very important results for everyone from every language and culture in Ephesus and in the entire region: **a)** First of all, verse 17 says that *"fear fell upon them all, and the name of the Lord Jesus was extolled"* ([11]M. I. Ac 3:6 & [12]Ac 19:10). **b)** Secondly, verses 18-19 tell about how the Holy Spirit cleansed the church in Ephesus by exposing the Christians who had had two hearts because they trusted in Jesus, but they were still very much afraid of the evil power of Satan that he displayed in the magical books. However, this beating by the demon taught them that Jesus was even more powerful than Satan's feeble magic. But they also knew that Satan and all of his demons would, of course, be extremely angry if they were bold enough to try escape from his evil grasp. Furthermore, most of their family and friends who were still bound by Satan would also become their enemies. And all of their spiritual and human enemies would now try to use Satan's evil power in these books to harm them. Therefore, it would take great <u>courage</u> and faith in Jesus for them to <u>publicly</u> confess their faith in Jesus and burn their books. But through Paul's preaching about the much greater, almighty power of Jesus, the Holy Spirit gave them the faith and the <u>courage</u> that they needed to publicly burn the books. They finally saw that Jesus <u>alone</u> could free them from Satan's bondage and be able to serve their dear Lord by living in his <u>grace</u> ([13]M. I. Lk 12:51 & [14]Ac 4:20). **c)** And thirdly, verse 20 concludes this section, *"So the word of the Lord continued to increase and prevail mightily."* His almighty Word will never fail (Is 55:10; Mt 16:18; [15]M. I. Lk 16:17).

A Riot at Ephesus 19:21-41

19:21 *Now after these events Paul resolved in the Spirit to pass through Macedonia and Achaia and go to Jerusalem, saying, "After I have been there, I must also see Rome."*
19:22 *And having sent into Macedonia two of his helpers, Timothy and Erastus, he himself stayed in Asia for a while.*
19:23 *About that time there arose no little disturbance concerning the Way.*
19:24 *For a man named Demetrius, a silversmith, who made silver shrines of Artemis, brought no little business to the craftsmen.*
19:25 *These he gathered together, with the workmen in similar trades, and said, "Men, you know that from this business we have our wealth.*
19:26 *And you see and hear that not only in Ephesus but in almost all of Asia this Paul has persuaded and turned away a great many people, saying that gods made with hands are not gods.*
19:27 *And there is danger not only that this trade of ours may come into disrepute but also that the temple of the great goddess Artemis may be counted as nothing, and that she may even be deposed from her magnificence, she whom all Asia and the world worship."*
19:28 *When they heard this they were enraged and were crying out,*

"Great is Artemis of the Ephesians!"

19:29 *So the city was filled with the confusion, and they rushed together into the theater, dragging with them Gaius and Aristarchus, Macedonians who were Paul's companions in travel.*

19:30 *But when Paul wished to go in among the crowd, the disciples would not let him.*

19:31 *And even some of the Asiarchs, who were friends of his, sent to him and were urging him not to venture into the theater.*

19:32 *Now some cried out one thing, some another, for the assembly was in confusion, and most of them did not know why they had come together.*

19:33 *Some of the crowd prompted Alexander, whom the Jews had put forward. And Alexander, motioning with his hand, wanted to make a defense to the crowd.*

19:34 *But when they recognized that he was a Jew, for about two hours they all cried out with one voice, "Great is Artemis of the Ephesians!"*

19:35 *And when the town clerk had quieted the crowd, he said, "Men of Ephesus, who is there who does not know that the city of the Ephesians is temple keeper of the great Artemis, and of the sacred stone that fell from the sky?*

19:36 *Seeing then that these things cannot be denied, you ought to be quiet and do nothing rash.*

19:37 *For you have brought these men here who are neither sacrilegious nor blasphemers of our goddess.*

19:38 *If therefore Demetrius and the craftsmen with him have a complaint against anyone, the courts are open, and there are proconsuls. Let them bring charges against one another.*

19:39 *But if you seek anything further, it shall be settled in the regular assembly.*

19:40 *For we really are in danger of being charged with rioting today, since there is no cause that we can give to justify this commotion."*

19:41 *And when he had said these things, he dismissed the assembly.*

19:21 In verse 21, Paul sets out two objectives for himself and his mission team: **a)** First of all he wanted to go to Jerusalem. Some speculate that his intention was to carry the donation from the Macedonian Christians to the Christians in Jerusalem who were suffering in a famine (1 Cor 16:1-4; 2 Cor 8:16), but that is somewhat uncertain, because he next went to Macedonia, in order to strengthen the churches there (20:1-2). **b)** But secondly, that was not his main objective, because he continues *"After I have been there [Jerusalem], I must also see Rome."* Paul still longed to proclaim the Gospel in Rome, the capital of the Roman Empire. However, we soon see in chapter 21 that it was his Lord's gracious plan that Paul should reach his goal in Rome, not as a free missionary but as a missionary who was a prisoner of both his Lord and of the Roman Empire ([16]M. M. Ac 4:28 & [17]M. I. Ac 19:10).

19:22 Then, in verse 22, we meet yet another new member of Paul's mission team, a Gentile named Erastus, who was from Corinth (Rom 16:23). The Lord of the mission was still controlling and guiding his mission by deploying his workers to places where he could most effectively use the abilities that he had given them ([18]M. I. Lk 6:13).

19:23-41 This huge riot in Ephesus, in verses 23-41, shows clearly that Satan was indeed angry that the Holy Spirit was taking more and more people away from his evil grasp; therefore, he used people whom he controlled through their love of money and their love of the fertility goddess, Artemis to attack the mission. Obviously he still controlled not only the majority of the people in Ephesus but the most influential people as well since the crowd that Luke describes here must have been huge. Nevertheless, it's equally obvious that it was the Lord of the mission who was truly in control since, first the Christians prevented Paul from going into the crowd, and then the city clerk prevented the crowd from actually harming Paul and his mission team (M. M. Ac 4:28).

19:37 The city clerk's statement in verse 37 that *"you have brought these men here who are neither sacrilegious nor blasphemers of our goddess"* is significant, since he told the crowd the essential truth about Paul's mission team: that they were proclaiming a Gospel about the only true God, their Lord Jesus. Because everyone in Ephesus heard this truth, the Christians there could continue to proclaim the name of Jesus without further persecution. Some years later, the church in Ephesus did suffer, once again, when Satan stirred up false teachers among them (v 30; Rev 2:2); however, we read nowhere that they suffered more persecution from the public ([19]M. M. Ac 4:28 & [20]Lk 6:22).

---

[1] M. M. Tit 3:5: When a person is baptized, God graciously saves him and gives him the gift of a new birth from his indwelling Holy Spirit; and he does this because his mercy is so great, and not because of any good deeds that that person has done.

[2] M. M. Mt 5:14: When the Holy Spirit creates faith in a person's heart, he also graciously gives him a new mission-heart that is eager to shine the light of the Gospel throughout the whole world.

[3] M. I. 1 Cor 14:1: Christians should always try to show love and also earnestly ask the Holy Spirit for all of his gifts; but especially ask him for his greatest gift, which is the ability to proclaim the Gospel.

[4] M. I. 1 Cor 14:2: Christians should not use the Holy Spirit's gift of speaking in a strange language in a worship service when no one is present to interpret his message for other members, because obviously he is only speaking to God, and he is not using this gift to build up the members who cannot understand him.

[5] M. M. Ac 13:46: As he did with the old Israel, God first of all strengthens the faith of the new Israel, the Church with his Word and Sacraments, so that they can go and witness to the lost people of all nations.

[6] M. I. Lk 4:15: Christians should seize *every* opportunity to proclaim the Gospel to lost people of all nations.

[7] M. I. Ac 8:12: Christians should only use miracles of healing in order to point to Jesus, and beware of people who use Satan's power to do miracles in order to point to themselves.

[8] M. M. Ro 1:16b: The Gospel is so powerful because it contains the central truth that Jesus rose from the dead with a glorified body in order to save all of his brothers and sisters from sin and death.

[9] M. I. Ac 3:6: Christians should heal a person's physical problem by speaking the name of Jesus, so that everyone knows that it was the divine power of Jesus that healed him.

[10] M. M. Ro 10:17a: The Holy Spirit only creates and preserves faith by using the message of God's grace in his holy Word.

[11] M. I. Ac 3:6: Christians should heal a person's physical problem by speaking the name of Jesus, so that everyone knows that it was the divine power of Jesus that healed him.

[12] M. I. Ac 19:10: Christians should try to plant churches in strategic social/cultural centers, in order to be able to use them as mission-bases from which the mission can expand to the whole region.

[13] M. I. Lk 12:51: Christians should cling to their faith relationship with Jesus at all costs, even if

it means suffering the pain of breaking their loving, but temporary family relationships, so that they can live with him in heaven forever.

[14] M. I. Ac 4:20: Christians should boldly witness to the name of Jesus and allow nothing to stop their witness because it is the Holy Spirit's own message.

[15] M. I. Lk 16:17: Christians should wield the sword of the Spirit with confidence as they go and tell the Gospel because his Word can never fail.

[16] M. M. Ac 4:28: The heavenly Father is always in full control of his mission to all nations of the world.

[17] M. I. Ac 19:10: Christians should try to plant churches in strategic social/cultural centers, in order to be able to use them as mission-bases from which the mission can expand to the whole region.

[18] M. I. Lk 6:13: Christians should choose new leaders and train them in order to multiply the work.

[19] M. M. Ac 4:28: The heavenly Father is always in full control of his mission to all nations of the world.

[20] M. M. Lk 6:22: The Lord Jesus will surely bless a Christian in the midst of suffering for his sake; and he will also bless him with eternal life if he remains faithful to him.

Chapter 20

Paul in Macedonia and Greece 20:1-6

20:1 *After the uproar ceased, Paul sent for the disciples, and after encouraging them, he said farewell and departed for Macedonia.*
20:2 *When he had gone through those regions and had given them much encouragement, he came to Greece.*
20:3 *There he spent three months, and when a plot was made against him by the Jews as he was about to set sail for Syria, he decided to return through Macedonia.*
20:4 *Sopater of Berea, the son of Pyrrhus from Berea, accompanied him; and of the Thessalonians, Aristarchus and Secundus; and Gaius of Derbe, and Timothy; and the Asians, Tychicus and Trophimus.*
20:5 *These went on ahead and were waiting for us at Troas,*
20:6 *but we sailed away from Philippi after the days of Unleavened Bread, and in five days we came to them at Troas, where we stayed for seven days.*

20:1 After such a huge riot, it was, of course, very important for Paul to visit the Christians in Ephesus one more time before leaving because they would have been afraid of the authorities and very discouraged if he had not done so. But, even though Paul was leaving, the Spirit of their Lord was still in their hearts; and his almighty and gracious presence was all that they needed because he was in control of his mission ([1]M. M. Ac 4:28 & [2]M. I. Lk 12:40).

20:3 Verse 3 reports that it was, once again, <u>Jews</u> whom Satan used to attack the Lord's mission. At every turn on all three of his missionary journeys, Paul and his team met opposition, and many times it was groups of <u>Jews</u> who were angry and jealous of the number of people who came to faith in Jesus. But of course, the Lord of the mission was likewise always with the team; and his mighty angels were protecting them (Heb 1:14), because he, and not Satan, was in full control of his mission. Furthermore, the Lord Jesus had a very special plan for Paul that he would soon send him on his <u>fourth</u> and final missionary journey to Rome (23:11; Chs 21-28; ³M. M. Heb 1:14).

Eutychus Raised from the Dead 20:7-16

20:7 *On the first day of the week, when we were gathered together to break bread, Paul talked with them, intending to depart on the next day, and he prolonged his speech until midnight.*
20:8 *There were many lamps in the upper room where we were gathered.*
20:9 *And a young man named Eutychus, sitting at the window, sank into a deep sleep as Paul talked still longer. And being overcome by sleep, he fell down from the third story and was taken up dead.*
20:10 *But Paul went down and bent over him, and taking him in his arms, said, "Do not be alarmed, for his life is in him."*
20:11 *And when Paul had gone up and had broken bread and eaten, he conversed with them a long while, until daybreak, and so departed.*
20:12 *And they took the youth away alive, and were not a little comforted.*
20:13 *But going ahead to the ship, we set sail for Assos, intending to take Paul aboard there, for so he had arranged, intending himself to go by land.*
20:14 *And when he met us at Assos, we took him on board and went to Mitylene.*
20:15 *And sailing from there we came the following day opposite Chios; the next day we touched at Samos; and the day after that we went to Miletus.*
20:16 *For Paul had decided to sail past Ephesus, so that he might not have to spend time in Asia, for he was hastening to be at Jerusalem, if possible, on the day of Pentecost.*

20:7, 11 Many scholars agree that the words in verse 7 *"when we were* *gathered together to break bread"* refer to Holy Communion, even though the word *"bread"* in verse 11 obviously refers to ordinary bread. However, verse 7 is only the second time in Luke's account after (2:42) that he referred to the fact that the early Church obeyed their Lord and partook of Holy Communion. Nevertheless, we can, of course, assume that they celebrated this holy meal much, much more frequently than the number of these references might indicate, since we know that they all firmly believed that their dear Lord was present with them in the bread and wine, in order to give them the forgiveness that they all needed (Lk 22:19; 1 Cor 11:24-26; [4]M. M. Lk 22:19a & [5]M. I. Ac 2:42).

20:9-12 Verse 10 says that Paul performed an amazing miracle by raising a boy from the dead, which, of course, glorified the holy name of Jesus in the entire city, because we can be certain that Paul used his name to do so (3:6). And equally important, it was likewise very encouraging for the Christians in Troas, because verse 12 says that they *"were not a little comforted."* And they needed this comfort, because Paul and his mission team decided to leave them almost immediately (V 11; [6]M. I. Ac 3:6).

20:13-16 Since verse 16 says that Paul *"was hastening to be at Jerusalem, if possible, on the day of Pentecost,"* Luke gives us very few details verses 13-16 about what Paul and his team did on this last part of their third missionary journey. In any case, we can be sure that the Christians in all of these towns were very happy to see them one last time, even though it may have been very brief ([7]M. I. Lk 12:40).

Paul Speaks to the Ephesian Elders 20:17-38

20:17 *Now from Miletus he sent to Ephesus and called the elders of the church to come to him.*
20:18 *And when they came to him, he said to them: "You yourselves know how I lived among you the whole time from the first day that I set foot in Asia,*
20:19 *serving the Lord with all humility and with tears and with trials that happened to me through the plots of the Jews;*
20:20 *how I did not shrink from declaring to you anything that was*

20:21 *profitable, and teaching you in public and from house to house, testifying both to Jews and to Greeks of repentance toward God and of faith in our Lord Jesus Christ.*
20:22 *And now, behold, I am going to Jerusalem, constrained by the Spirit, not knowing what will happen to me there,*
20:23 *except that the Holy Spirit testifies to me in every city that imprisonment and afflictions await me.*
20:24 *But I do not account my life of any value nor as precious to myself, if only I may finish my course and the ministry that I received from the Lord Jesus, to testify to the Gospel of the grace of God.*
20:25 *And now, behold, I know that none of you among whom I have gone about proclaiming the kingdom will see my face again.*
20:26 *Therefore I testify to you this day that I am innocent of the blood of all of you,*
20:27 *for I did not shrink from declaring to you the whole counsel of God.*
20:28 *Pay careful attention to yourselves and to all the flock, in which the Holy Spirit has made you overseers, to care for the church of God, which he obtained with his own blood.*
20:29 *I know that after my departure fierce wolves will come in among you, not sparing the flock;*
20:30 *and from among your own selves will arise men speaking twisted things, to draw away the disciples after them.*
20:31 *Therefore be alert, remembering that for three years I did not cease night or day to admonish everyone with tears.*
20:32 *And now I commend you to God and to the word of his grace, which is able to build you up and to give you the inheritance among all those who are sanctified.*
20:33 *I coveted no one's silver or gold or apparel.*
20:34 *You yourselves know that these hands ministered to my necessities and to those who were with me.*
20:35 *In all things I have shown you that by working hard in this way we must help the weak and remember the words of the Lord Jesus, how he himself said, 'It is more blessed to give than to receive.'"*

20:36 *And when he had said these things, he knelt down and prayed with them all.*
20:37 *And there was much weeping on the part of all; they embraced Paul and kissed him,*
20:38 *being sorrowful most of all because of the word he had spoken, that they would not see his face again. And they accompanied him to the ship.*

20:17-35 Luke obviously recognized how significant Paul's final message to the leaders of the church at Ephesus was, since he recorded so many details in verses 17-35. Paul explicitly told them the sad truth in verse 22 that they would never see him again, although, no doubt, all of them had already sensed it (vs 37-38). Nevertheless, cross-cultural missionaries have always known that they must at some point leave the dear Christians who have come to faith through their preaching ([8]M. I. Ac 26:12).

20:18 Paul said in his farewell message in verse 18, *"You yourselves know how I lived among you the whole time from the first day that I set foot in Asia."* His first point was clearly his most important point because he repeated it several times in (vs 18, 20-21, 25-27 and 31. He emphasized to the leaders at Ephesus that he always faithfully and sincerely told them the whole plan of God (v 20). His relationship with them was based on mutual trust; they knew that he was completely sincere in everything he said and did for two reasons: his life always matched what he said ([9]M. I. Mt 10:42; & [10]1 Cor 3:13), and he always used the Scriptures to prove to them that it's God's truth ([11]M. I. Lk 4:17). Paul's sincerity was absolutely vital to their relationship, so that, after he was gone, they would continue to believe what Paul had told them even when false teachers came (v 30) and tried to deceive them with Satan's lies ([12]M. I. Lk 3:8).

20:19 As verse 19 says, Paul was *"serving the Lord with all humility and with tears and with trials."* Everything that Paul did and said among the Christians in Ephesus he did as a humble servant of them and of their Lord Jesus (2 Cor 10:1). He never tried to lord it over them. This too would be very important for them in the future, because he warned them in verse 30 that *"from among your own selves will arise men speaking twisted things, to draw away the disciples after them."* How <u>proud</u> false teachers always are as they serve Satan and try to deceive and control people! It's another new mission imperative. M. I. Ac 20:19 Christians should humbly serve their hearers and their Lord Jesus because he first humbly served all of them.

20:20-21 Paul's reference in verse 20 to teaching them *"from house to house"* is only the second time in Acts (5:42) that Luke mentions this mission method. However, this may not give any indication as to how frequently he and his mission teams used this method of going to the homes of people who were lost ([13]M. I. Ac 1:8).

20:22-23 Once again, we see in verses 22 and 23 that the <u>Holy Spirit</u> directly revealed to Paul where he wanted him to go (16:9); he told him to go to Jerusalem and that he would suffer there for the name of Jesus once again. What his Lord had not yet revealed to him was that this imprisonment would make it possible for him to carry out his <u>final</u>, fourth missionary journey that ended in Rome (23:11; Chs 21-28). The Holy Spirit had at this point already graciously given him the faith and courage that he would continue to need to complete his service to his Lord on his last journey ([14]M. I. Lk 11:10).

20:24 In verse 24, Paul uses the illustration of a person who is running a race; and he says that he is running this race, so that *"I may finish my course [race NIV] and the ministry that I received from the Lord Jesus, to testify to the gospel of the grace of God"* (v 24d). Thus, the race and *"the ministry"* that Paul was running was proclaiming the Gospel to the Gentiles (Gal 2:7). And his race was not yet finished, because (even though he himself did not yet know it) he was about to begin his fourth and last missionary journey to Gentile kings (Ac 23:11; [15]M. I. Ac 1:8). What wonderful opportunities to witness to Jesus he had on his last journey, but he likewise had to endure many troubles as he finished his race (Ch. 27).

20:28 Verse 28 is a final, beautiful exhortation that Paul gives to the leaders of the church in Ephesus: *"Pay careful attention to yourselves and to all the flock, in which the Holy Spirit has made you overseers."* It is always one of the main tasks of a cross-cultural missionary to train church leaders, so that he can pass on to them his responsibility as an under-shepherd of *"the great shepherd of the sheep"* (Heb 13:20), who is the Lord of the mission ([16]M. I. Lk 6:13 & [17]M. M. Heb 8:1).

20:30 Verse 30 says that the Holy Spirit also had revealed to Paul the very sad truth that perhaps some of these same church leaders whom he was talking to and whom he had diligently trained would become <u>false</u> teachers (v 30). Therefore, Paul had to warn all of them to be alert for these internal vicious attacks by the devil. How painful this warning must have been for both him and them to hear ([18]M. I. Lk 3:8 & [19]Lk 11:10)!

20:33-35 And Paul's final point in verses 33-35 was that he had always worked at his tent making trade in order to support himself and had never asked them for support (18:3; 2 Thess 3:8-9). Although Paul is referring to Jesus' mission imperative that a worker in the church deserves his pay from the people he serves ([20]M. I. Lk 10:7b), he is making a different point here. His point is that these leaders should do honest labor so that they will be able to be <u>generous</u> to others. Therefore, in verse 35 Paul adds that *"it is more blessed to give than to receive."* (Although he is quoting from Jesus himself, this quotation is unique since it is not recorded in any of the Gospels.) Paul is urging them to be generous to others because their gracious Lord Jesus has been so gracious and generous to them by giving them so many physical and spiritual gifts ([21]M. M. Ro 6:18 & [22]M. I. 2 Cor 8:2).

---

[1] M. M. Ac 4:28: The heavenly Father is always in full control of his mission to all nations of the world.

[2] M. I. Lk 12:40: Christians should "eat" God's Word every day in order to keep their faith strong, so that they are always ready for their Lord's return.

[3] M. M. Heb 1:14: Christians will inherit salvation, and God sends out his holy angels to be with them and protect them; therefore, they should not be afraid of their spiritual enemies as they go on their mission.

[4] M. M. Lk 22:19a: The Lord Jesus graciously offers full forgiveness for all of his sins to a person who repents of his sin and knows that he does not deserve to partake of his Lord's true body and true blood in Holy Communion.

[5] M. I. Ac 2:42: Christians should celebrate Holy Communion frequently in order to receive

forgiveness and strength from their Lord's grace in order to continue on his mission.

⁶ M. I. Ac 3:6: Christians should heal a person's physical problem by speaking the <u>name</u> of Jesus, so that everyone knows that it was the divine power of Jesus that healed him.

⁷ M. I. Lk 12:40: Christians should "eat" God's Word every day in order to keep their faith strong, so that they are always ready for their Lord's return.

⁸ M. I. Ac 26:12: Christians should use their own personal experience of coming to faith in Jesus by the almighty power of his resurrection as a powerful example for their hearers to follow.

⁹ M. I. Mt 10:42: Christians should always be sure that their <u>actions</u> match their *verbal* witness to the name of Jesus, because if they do <u>not</u> match they will destroy their message.

¹⁰ M. I. 1 Cor 3:13: Christians should be sure that they build their mission work on Jesus, the foundation of the Church because God will test their work on Judgment Day with the fire of judgment, and God will base their rewards on the quality of their work.

¹¹ M. I. Lk 4:17: Christians should always base their messages on the Bible, so that the Holy Spirit can use his holy Word to create and strengthen faith in their hearers.

¹² M. I. Lk 3:8: Christians should always be prepared to boldly and publicly refute false teaching, so that Satan cannot easily deceive people.

¹³ M. I. Ac 1:8: Christians should go and witness about Jesus to all who are lost from all languages and cultures by depending on the power of the Holy Spirit to help them bridge all of the language/cultural boundaries whether they are relatively easy, as in their own language, or extremely difficult.

¹⁴ M. I. Lk 11:10: Christians should <u>continuously</u> pray to their heavenly Father and <u>always</u> depend on his grace, and not on their own feeble strength, because he <u>always</u> loves them.

¹⁵ M. I. Ac 1:8: The Christian Church should go and witness about Jesus to all who are lost from all languages and cultures by depending on the power of the Holy Spirit to help them bridge all of the language/cultural boundaries whether they are relatively easy, as in their own language, or extremely difficult.

¹⁶ M. I. Lk 6:13: Christians should choose new leaders and train them in order to multiply the work.

¹⁷ M. M. Heb 8:1: As our Royal High Priest, Jesus sits at the right hand of the throne in the <u>heavenly</u> temple ruling over and praying for his mission on earth.

¹⁸ M. I. Lk 3:8: Christians should always be prepared to boldly and publicly refute false teaching, so that Satan cannot easily deceive people.

¹⁹ M. I. Lk 11:10: Christians should <u>continuously</u> pray to their heavenly Father and <u>always</u> depend on his grace, and not on their own feeble strength, because he <u>always</u> loves them.

²⁰ M. I. Lk 10:7b: Church leaders deserve to be paid for their work of preaching and teaching the Gospel.

²¹ M. M. Ro 6:18: In his Baptism, Jesus graciously sets a new Christian free from his slavery to sin and gives him the power of his Spirit to gratefully obey his new Lord by doing good deeds.

²² M. I. 2 Cor 8:2: Since God's rich grace has overflowed in their hearts, Christians should first of all give themselves to the Lord, so that the Holy Spirit will then also enable them (even though they may be extremely poor) to give very joyously and generously toward the physical relief of their fellow Christians.

Chapter 21

Paul Goes to Jerusalem 21:1-16

21:1 *And when we had parted from them and set sail, we came by a straight course to Cos, and the next day to Rhodes, and from there to Patara.*

21:2 *And having found a ship crossing to Phoenicia, we went aboard and set sail.*

21:3 *When we had come in sight of Cyprus, leaving it on the left we sailed to Syria and landed at Tyre, for there the ship was to unload its cargo.*

21:4 *And having sought out the disciples, we stayed there for seven days. And through the Spirit they were telling Paul not to go on to Jerusalem.*

21:5 *When our days there were ended, we departed and went on our journey, and they all, with wives and children, accompanied us until we were outside the city. And kneeling down on the beach, we prayed*

21:6 *and said farewell to one another. Then we went on board the ship, and they returned home.*

21:7 *When we had finished the voyage from Tyre, we arrived at Ptolemais, and we greeted the brothers and stayed with them for one day.*

21:8 *On the next day we departed and came to Caesarea, and we entered the house of Philip the evangelist, who was one of the seven, and stayed with him.*

21:9 *He had four unmarried daughters, who prophesied.*

21:10 *While we were staying for many days, a prophet named Agabus came down from Judea.*

21:11 *And coming to us, he took Paul's belt and bound his own feet and hands and said, "Thus says the Holy Spirit, 'This is how the Jews at Jerusalem will bind the man who owns this belt and deliver him into the hands of the Gentiles.'"*

21:12 *When we heard this, we and the people there urged him not to*

> *go up to Jerusalem.*
> 21:13 *Then Paul answered, "What are you doing, weeping and breaking my heart? For I am ready not only to be imprisoned but even to die in Jerusalem for the name of the Lord Jesus."*
> 21:14 *And since he would not be persuaded, we ceased and said, "Let the will of the Lord be done."*
> 21:15 *After these days we got ready and went up to Jerusalem.*
> 21:16 *And some of the disciples from Caesarea went with us, bringing us to the house of Mnason of Cyprus, an early disciple, with whom we should lodge.*

21:4 The week-long visit to the church in Tyre (v 4) must have been very encouraging for the whole mission team; however, verse 4 adds that *"through the Spirit they [the Christians in Tyre] were telling Paul not to go on to Jerusalem."* The Holy Spirit was repeating two earlier warnings that he would have to suffer in Jerusalem (20:23; 21:10-11). Nevertheless, the same Spirit was also filling Paul with courage and determination to obey him and gladly continue on his journey, because his imprisonment there would, in fact, be the beginning of his fourth and final mission journey (23:11; [1]M. M. Ac 4:28 & [2]M. I. Ac 5:41).

21:5-6 Once again the mission team had to leave a group of Christians (vs 5-6); but the future of the mission in that place did not depend on their human presence but on the presence of the Lord of the mission who was always with them as their Immanuel (M. M. Ac 4:28).

21:8-9 We once again meet Philip in verse 8; he had now settled down to raise a family in Caesarea (8:40). And we, of course, are not surprised to see that he was still busy as an *"evangelist"* (v 8) or missionary in this Gentile city. Furthermore, his four daughters were likewise missionaries, since they *"prophesied"* in the power of the Holy Spirit (v 9). Luke does not add any details about when and where they prophesied; nevertheless, although this is a topic that is still hotly debated in the Church yet today, there are, in fact, two other references in the New Testament to women who prophesied by proclaiming the Gospel (Lk 2:36; 1 Cor 11:5; [3]M. I. Ac 1:8).

21:10-14 We likewise once again (11:28) meet the prophet Agabus in verse 10. This time, in verse 11, the Holy Spirit gave him a very dramatic warning that Paul would be imprisoned in Jerusalem by the Gentiles. However, the Holy Spirit obviously also continued to fill Paul with more and more <u>courage</u> along with each warning that he gave him. When the Christians started weeping in verse 13, Paul responded, *"I am ready not only to be imprisoned but even to die in Jerusalem for the name of the Lord Jesus."* Therefore, he was giving them a powerful <u>example</u> of faith and courage in the face of persecution and death. Thus, as Paul and his mission team traveled to Jerusalem, his powerful example was teaching the Christians in each town that, by also depending on the rich <u>grace</u> of their Lord Jesus, they would be able to face suffering for his sake with the same faith and courage (M. M. Ac 4:28 & [4]M. I. Lk 11:10).

Paul Visits James 21:17-26

21:17 *When we had come to Jerusalem, the brothers received us gladly.*
21:18 *On the following day Paul went in with us to James, and all the elders were present.*
21:19 *After greeting them, he related one by one the things that God had done among the Gentiles through his ministry.*
21:20 *And when they heard it, they glorified God. And they said to him, "You see, brother, how many thousands there are among the Jews of those who have believed. They are all zealous for the Law,*
21:21 *and they have been told about you that you teach all the Jews who are among the Gentiles to forsake Moses, telling them not to circumcise their children or walk according to our customs.*
21:22 *What then is to be done? They will certainly hear that you have come.*
21:23 *Do therefore what we tell you. We have four men who are under a vow;*
21:24 *take these men and purify yourself along with them and pay their expenses, so that they may shave their heads. Thus all will*

> know that there is nothing in what they have been told about you, but that you yourself also live in observance of the Law.
> 21:25 But as for the Gentiles who have believed, we have sent a letter with our judgment that they should abstain from what has been sacrificed to idols, and from blood, and from what has been strangled, and from sexual immorality."
> 21:26 Then Paul took the men, and the next day he purified himself along with them and went into the temple, giving notice when the days of purification would be fulfilled and the offering presented for each one of them.

21:15-19 Verse 17 says that *"the brothers [in Jerusalem] received us [the mission team] gladly."* And this included James, who was a half-brother of Jesus and the leader of the church in Jerusalem, and all of the elders (v 18). However, note that there is no indication here that these leaders were in charge of the mission of the Church who were receiving a report from missionaries whom they had sent out (v 19; 12:17); rather, they did so as fellow Christians. It's significant that, on all three of Paul's first missionary journeys, it was not the church in Jerusalem that sent them out; rather, all three times they left from Antioch of Syria (13:2-4; 15:40; 18:23). And even though Luke only explicitly says the first time, in (13:4), *"So, being sent out by the Holy Spirit, they went,"* it was obviously the Lord of the mission who was directly in control; and there was no formal church structure of any kind at that time ([5]M. M. Ac 4:28).

21:20-26 (1) In verses 20-25, we see the beginning of the trouble in Jerusalem that soon led to Paul being arrested. The same question of whether Gentile Christians need to be circumcised and obey the Laws of Moses raised its ugly head once again; even though the Church had already settled the matter in the Council in Jerusalem in (15:20, 29). In this case, some Jewish Christians who were from the province of Asia (v 27; 24:19) were the ones whom Satan used to stir it up, once again, by spreading rumors about what Paul had been teaching Gentile Christians about obeying the Laws of Moses. However, the leaders of the church in Jerusalem suggested that Paul should join four men who had sworn a vow to perform some sacrifices (vs 23-24), in order to publicly show that he had the free choice to obey or to not obey Moses' Laws ([6]M. I. Ac 2:4 & [7]Ac 15:20). **2)** But Satan had other plans. He tried to do two things: <u>divide</u> the Church—Jews against Gentiles, and to stop the <u>proclamation</u> of the Gospel by Paul's mission team among the Gentiles. However, he was not successful on either account, since it was the almighty Jesus who was, of course, in control of his mission, not Satan. The Lord of the mission was busy using this arrest of Paul to send him off on his <u>fourth</u> and final missionary journey to Gentile kings and rulers (23:11; [8]M. M. Ac 4:28).

Paul Arrested in the Temple 21:27-36

21:27 *When the seven days were almost completed, the Jews from Asia, seeing him in the temple, stirred up the whole crowd and laid hands on him,*
21:28 *crying out, "Men of Israel, help! This is the man who is teaching everyone everywhere against the people and the Law and this place. Moreover, he even brought Greeks into the temple and has defiled this holy place."*
21:29 *For they had previously seen Trophimus the Ephesian with him in the city, and they supposed that Paul had brought him into the temple.*
21:30 *Then all the city was stirred up, and the people ran together. They seized Paul and dragged him out of the temple, and at once the gates were shut.*
21:31 *And as they were seeking to kill him, word came to the tribune of the cohort that all Jerusalem was in confusion.*
21:32 *He at once took soldiers and centurions and ran down to them. And when they saw the tribune and the soldiers, they stopped beating Paul.*
21:33 *Then the tribune came up and arrested him and ordered him to be bound with two chains. He inquired who he was and what he had done.*
21:34 *Some in the crowd were shouting one thing, some another. And as he could not learn the facts because of the uproar, he*

>   *ordered him to be brought into the barracks.*
> 21:35 *And when he came to the steps, he was actually carried by the soldiers because of the violence of the crowd,*
> 21:36 *for the mob of the people followed, crying out, "Away with him!"*

21:26 Paul once again exercised his freedom under his Lord's <u>grace</u> by taking the recommendation of the church leaders and *choosing* to obey the Laws of Moses; and he, of course, did <u>not</u> violate any of the Laws of Moses by bringing Gentiles into forbidden areas of the temple as they accused him of doing (v 28; [9]M. I. Ac 2:4 & [10]Ac 15:20). This should have satisfied the Jews from the province of Asia (21:27), but Satan was obviously using them; and they were just looking for any excuse to get him in trouble. Thus, the devil was successful in ending Paul's freedom by using the misdirected passion of the Jewish mob. However, what Satan didn't know was that this was exactly what the Lord Jesus had planned, in order to launch Paul on his new mission journey on Level 3 to Gentile <u>rulers</u> in the Roman Empire: military officers, kings, queens, governors, and perhaps the emperor himself, as his Lord had told him he would (9:15; 27:24; Lk 21:12-13; M. M. Ac 4:28).

21:33 (1) Verse 33 says, *"Then the tribune came up and <u>arrested</u> him [Paul] and ordered him to be bound with two chains."* The Lord's missionary was *"bound with two chains!"* What a launching that was! Not as a free man, but as a <u>prisoner</u> of both the emperor and of his Lord Jesus! Such a missionary journey would have been impossible if Paul had remained a free man; yet in this way his Lord gave him <u>opportunities</u> to have audiences before some of the most powerful people in the Empire, while such types of opportunities were rare during his first three trips ([11]M. I. Lk 4:15). In his all-surpassing wisdom, the Lord had prepared Paul in at least the following <u>five</u> ways to be his <u>unique</u> person, in order to do this <u>unique</u> task: **a)** a very perceptive student of the Scriptures, **b)** highly skilled in communicating the Gospel in cross-cultural situations, **c)** a Roman citizen, **d)** faithful and courageous in the face of suffering and death, **e)** and his Lord's humble servant ([12]M. M. 1 Cor 12:11 & [13]M. I. Ac 2:4). **2)** Furthermore, there is little evidence that, after Paul proclaimed the Gospel to these Gentile leaders, even one of them came to faith in Jesus. Nevertheless, their responses to the Gospel may have been positive in a different and very significant way. Some of these leaders had powerful authority over many, many people; therefore, we can only imagine the significance of the <u>positive</u> <u>influence</u> that some of them may have had on the people who were under their authority. At the very least, their clearer vision of who <u>Jesus</u> is may have contributed to a more positive reception of the Gospel by many people. It's a new mission imperative. M. I. Ac 21:26: Christians should seek opportunities to witness to Jesus' name to people who are influential leaders in the target society, so that they can influence others to trust in Jesus. **3)** Finally, even though Paul was a <u>prisoner</u> of the Empire and not a free man throughout his final mission assignment, he did not allow any shame that might have been associated with his chains to have any <u>negative</u> impact on his witness to the name of Jesus. He knew that it was much more important that he was a humble, yet also a <u>bold</u> prisoner of his *victorious* Lord Jesus. He was *"<u>not</u> ashamed of the Gospel"* (Rom 1:16) nor ashamed of his chains (2 Tim 1:16) because he wore them for the <u>sake</u> of his dear Lord Jesus. To him, neither he nor his chains were important; but his Lord and his mission were all important ([14]M. I. Ac 4:20 & [15]Lk 12:51). As a matter of fact, on at least on one occasion, he boldly <u>pointed out</u> his chains as part of his witness before King Agrippa (26:29; M. I. Ac 4:20).

Paul Speaks to the People 21:37-22:21

21:37 *As Paul was about to be brought into the barracks, he said to the tribune, "May I say something to you?" And he said, "Do you know Greek?*

21:38 *Are you not the Egyptian, then, who recently stirred up a revolt and led the four thousand men of the Assassins out into the wilderness?"*

21:39 *Paul replied, "I am a Jew, from Tarsus in Cilicia, a citizen of no obscure city. I beg you, permit me to speak to the people."*

21:40 *And when he had given him permission, Paul, standing on the steps, motioned with his hand to the people. And when there was a great hush, he addressed them in the Hebrew language, saying:*

21:37-40 Verse 37 says that Paul now tried to escape from this very dangerous situation by appealing to the officer who was arresting him to allow him to speak to the mob. He convinced him to listen to his appeal by speaking <u>Greek</u> (v 37), the lingua franca of the Roman Empire, and by telling him that he was a <u>Roman citizen</u> (v 39). And he obviously impressed the officer, so that he was able to speak in his defense; and obviously, the mob also did not kill him that day and end his final mission journey before it began. Therefore, we already see how important it was that Paul was a <u>Roman citizen</u>. The Lord of the mission had chosen very wisely, and he also clearly continued to be in full control of his mission ([16]M. M. Ac 4:28).

---

[1] M. M. Ac 4:28: The heavenly Father is always in full control of his mission to all nations of the world.

[2] M. I. Ac 5:41: Christians should consider it a great honor to be persecuted for proclaiming the name of Jesus.

[3] M. I. Ac 1:8: Christians should go and witness about Jesus to all who are lost from all languages and cultures by depending on the power of the Holy Spirit to help them bridge all of the language/cultural boundaries whether they are relatively easy, as in their own language, or extremely difficult.

[4] M. I. Lk 11:10: Christians should <u>continuously</u> pray to their heavenly Father and <u>always</u> depend on his grace, and not on their own feeble strength, because he <u>always</u> loves them.

[5] M. M. Ac 4:28: The heavenly Father is always in full control of his mission to all nations of the world.

[6] M. I. Ac 2:4: In cross-cultural situations, Christians should always focus on all of the needs of the target group by learning <u>their</u> heart-language and culture as deeply as possible, so that they can tell them the Gospel clearly in their own language and also help them with the true needs of their society.

[7] M. I. Ac 15:20: To preserve the unity of the Church and to make it possible to reach out to unbelievers from all cultural backgrounds, they should show love to their fellow Christians and to all people of all cultures by refraining from actions that would easily offend them.

[8] M. M. Ac 4:28: The heavenly Father is always in full control of his mission to all nations of the world.

[9] M. I. Ac 2:4: In cross-cultural situations, Christians should always focus on all of the needs of

the target group by learning their heart-language and culture as deeply as possible, so that they can tell them the Gospel clearly in their own language and also help them with the true needs of their society.

[10] M. I. Ac 15:20: To preserve the unity of the Church and to make it possible to reach out to unbelievers from all cultural backgrounds, they should show love to their fellow Christians and to all people of all cultures by refraining from actions that would easily offend them.

[11] M. I. Lk 4:15: Christians should seize every opportunity to proclaim the Gospel to lost people of all nations.

[12] M. M. 1 Cor 12:11: When Christians baptize people the same Holy Spirit graciously gives each one faith in Jesus plus a unique set of spiritual gifts so that he can use them in order to expand the Lord's mission.

[13] M. I. Ac 2:4: In cross-cultural situations, Christians should always focus on all of the needs of the target group by learning their heart-language and culture as deeply as possible, so that they can tell them the Gospel clearly in their own language and also help them with the true needs of their society.

[14] M. I. Ac 4:20: Christians should boldly witness to the name of Jesus and allow nothing to stop their witness because it is the Holy Spirit's own message.

[15] M. I. Lk 12:51: Christians should cling to their faith relationship with Jesus at all costs, even if it means suffering the pain of breaking their loving, but temporary family relationships, so that they can live with him in heaven forever.

[16] M. M. Ac 4:28: The heavenly Father is always in full control of his mission to all nations of the world.

Chapter 22

22:1 *"Brothers and fathers, hear the defense that I now make before you."*

22:2 *And when they heard that he was addressing them in the Hebrew language, they became even more quiet. And he said:*

22:3 *"I am a Jew, born in Tarsus in Cilicia, but brought up in this city, educated at the feet of Gamaliel according to the strict manner of the Law of our fathers, being zealous for God as all of you are this day.*

22:4 *I persecuted this Way to the death, binding and delivering to prison both men and women,*

22:5 *as the high priest and the whole council of elders can bear me witness. From them I received letters to the brothers, and I journeyed toward Damascus to take those also who were there and bring them in bonds to Jerusalem to be punished.*

22:6 *"As I was on my way and drew near to Damascus, about noon a great light from heaven suddenly shone around me.*

22:7 *And I fell to the ground and heard a voice saying to me, 'Saul, Saul, why are you persecuting me?'*

22:8 *And I answered, 'Who are you, Lord?' And he said to me, 'I am Jesus of Nazareth, whom you are persecuting.'*

22:9 *Now those who were with me saw the light but did not understand the voice of the one who was speaking to me.*

22:10 *And I said, 'What shall I do, Lord?' And the Lord said to me, 'Rise, and go into Damascus, and there you will be told all that is appointed for you to do.'*

22:11 *And since I could not see because of the brightness of that light, I was led by the hand by those who were with me, and came into Damascus.*

22:12 *"And one Ananias, a devout man according to the Law, well spoken of by all the Jews who lived there,*

22:13 *came to me, and standing by me said to me, 'Brother Saul, receive your sight.' And at that very hour I received my sight and saw him.*

22:14 *And he said, 'The God of our fathers appointed you to know his will, to see the Righteous One and to hear a voice from his mouth;*

22:15 *for you will be a witness for him to everyone of what you have seen and heard.*

22:16 *And now why do you wait? Rise and be baptized and wash away your sins, calling on his name.'*

22:17 *"When I had returned to Jerusalem and was praying in the temple, I fell into a trance*

22:18 *and saw him saying to me, 'Make haste and get out of Jerusalem quickly, because they will not accept your testimony about me.'*

22:19 *And I said, 'Lord, they themselves know that in one synagogue after another I imprisoned and beat those who believed in you.*

22:20 *And when the blood of Stephen your witness was being shed, I myself was standing by and approving and watching over the garments of those who killed him.'*

22:21 *'Go, for I will send you far away to the Gentiles.'"*

22:2 Paul had extensive cross-cultural experience; therefore, he wisely chose to speak to the mob in Hebrew which was their mother-tongue. And *"they became even more quiet"* (v 2; [1]M. I. Ac 2:4).

22: 6-16 In verses 6-16, Paul now described his conversion on the road to Damascus, even though he was now ashamed of going there in order to persecute the Church (1 Cor 15:9). He wanted them to see that their zeal was just as misdirected as his zeal was at that time, so that he could call them to repentance and faith in the name of Jesus. He told them in verses 14-15 that his Lord Jesus told him: *"The God of our fathers appointed you to know his will, to see the Righteous One and to hear a voice from his mouth; for you will be a witness for him to everyone of what you have seen and heard."* Therefore, in this way, Paul turned his most shameful experience into a powerful witness to the power of the name of Jesus ([2]M. I. Ac 4:20 & [3]Ac 1:8).

21:21-22 Evidently it was when Paul said in verse 21, *"And he [the Lord Jesus] said to me, 'Go, for I will send you far away to the*

Gentiles'" that the mob got angry all over again. Verse 22 continues, *"Up to this word they listened to him. Then they raised their voices and said, 'Away with such a fellow from the earth! For he should not be allowed to live.'"* Obviously, these Jews sinfully assumed that they alone <u>deserved</u> to be God's chosen people because they were <u>physical</u> descendants of Abraham, and the Gentiles should not even hear the Gospel that Jesus had fulfilled the whole Law for the sake of <u>all</u> people from all nations on earth (Gen 12:1-3; [4]M. M. Mt 1:22 & [5]Ac 13:46). To their own condemnation, they depended on their physical relationship to Abraham and on their self-righteous <u>obedience</u> to the Law of Moses (7:51-53; [6]M. I. Lk 3:8 & [7]Lk 4:15).

Paul and the Roman Tribune 22:22-29

22:22 *Up to this word they listened to him. Then they raised their voices and said, "Away with such a fellow from the earth! For he should not be allowed to live."*
22:23 *And as they were shouting and throwing off their cloaks and flinging dust into the air,*
22:24 *the tribune ordered him to be brought into the barracks, saying that he should be examined by flogging, to find out why they were shouting against him like this.*
22:25 *But when they had stretched him out for the whips, Paul said to the centurion who was standing by, "Is it lawful for you to flog a man who is a Roman citizen and uncondemned?"*
22:26 *When the centurion heard this, he went to the tribune and said to him, "What are you about to do? For this man is a Roman citizen."*
22:27 *So the tribune came and said to him, "Tell me, are you a Roman citizen?" And he said, "Yes."*
22:28 *The tribune answered, "I bought this citizenship for a large sum." Paul said, "But I am a citizen by birth."*
22:29 *So those who were about to examine him withdrew from him immediately, and the tribune also was afraid, for he realized that Paul was a Roman citizen and that he had bound him.*

22:22 When the Jews shouted in verse 22 that Paul *"should not be allowed to live,"* they were, of course, mimicking a similar crowd who did murder Paul's dear Lord (Lk 23:18-23). The mob showed that they were fully under Satan's control; neither the warning of the Law nor God's grace for them in the Gospel in Paul's message were able to penetrate their hard hearts (Lk 3:8; [8]M. M. Lk 6:22). But Paul's heart, on the other hand, was probably full of joy because he was willing to *"share his [Lord's] sufferings"* and also die (Phil 3:10; [9]M. I. Ro 5:3b), since he did not yet know anything about his Lord's plan for his new mission trip to Rome as a prisoner ([10]M. M. Ac 4:28).

22:25 Paul invoked his Roman citizenship in verse 25 by asking, *"Is it lawful for you to flog a man who is a Roman citizen and uncondemned?"* They were about to beat an innocent man without a trial; therefore, public shame would not only dishonor the name of *Jesus* but it would also prevent Paul from freely proclaiming the Gospel ([11]M. I. Ac 16:37). And furthermore, Paul only invoked his Roman citizenship three times on all four of his missionary journeys (16:37; 22:25; 25:11); therefore, we see that he did not do so lightly. The gracious Lord Jesus had made him to be the person that he needed for his mission to the Gentiles; and the Holy Spirit was also empowering Paul to depend on his grace in order to honor the name of Jesus in every situation ([12]M. I. Ro 5:3a).

---

[1] M. I. Ac 2:4: In cross-cultural situations, they should always focus on all of the needs of the target group by learning their heart-language and culture as deeply as possible, so that they can tell them the Gospel clearly in their own language and also help them with the true needs of their society.

[2] M. I. Ac 4:20: Christians should boldly witness to the name of Jesus and allow nothing to stop their witness because it is the Holy Spirit's own message.

[3] M. I. Ac 1:8: Christians should go and witness about Jesus to all who are lost from all languages and cultures by depending on the power of the Holy Spirit to help them bridge all of the language/cultural boundaries whether they are relatively easy, as in their own language, or extremely difficult.

[4] M. M. Mt 1:22: God sent his only Son, Jesus to be born as a true human being, so that he could save all of his brothers and sisters of all nations by fulfilling all of God's promises in the Old Testament.

⁵ M. M. Ac 13:46: As he did with the old Israel, God <u>first of all</u> strengthens the faith of the new Israel, the Church with his Word and Sacraments, so that they can go and witness to the lost people of all nations.

⁶ M. I. Lk 3:8: Christians should always be prepared to boldly and publicly refute false teaching, so that Satan cannot easily deceive people.

⁷ M. I. Lk 4:15: Christians should seize <u>every</u> opportunity to proclaim the Gospel to lost people of all nations.

⁸ M. M. Lk 6:22: The Lord Jesus will surely bless a Christian in the midst of suffering for his sake; and he will also bless him with eternal life if he remains faithful to him.

⁹ M. I. Ro 5:3b: Christians should <u>rejoice</u> in the midst of <u>suffering</u> for Jesus' sake because unbelievers may see their joy, which may create opportunities to witness to Jesus.

¹⁰ M. M. Ac 4:28: The heavenly Father is always in full control of his mission to all nations of the world.

¹¹ M. I. Ac 16:37: All Christians, but especially Christian leaders should do everything in their power to promote the good reputation of the name of Jesus, in order to make it possible for them to freely and publicly proclaim the Gospel.

¹² M. I. Ro 5:3a: Christians should <u>rejoice</u> in the midst of <u>suffering</u> for Jesus' sake because suffering teaches them to depend on their Lord's rich grace, and thus continue to grow in more spiritual gifts.

Chapter 23

Paul Before the Council 22:30-23:11

22:30 But on the next day, desiring to know the real reason why he was being accused by the Jews, he unbound him and commanded the chief priests and all the council to meet, and he brought Paul down and set him before them.

23:1 And looking intently at the council, Paul said, "Brothers, I have lived my life before God in all good conscience up to this day."

23:2 And the high priest Ananias commanded those who stood by him to strike him on the mouth.

23:3 Then Paul said to him, "God is going to strike you, you whitewashed wall! Are you sitting to judge me according to the Law, and yet contrary to the Law you order me to be struck?"

23:4 Those who stood by said, "Would you revile God's high priest?"

23:5 And Paul said, "I did not know, brothers, that he was the high priest, for it is written, 'You shall not speak evil of a ruler of your people.'"

23:6 Now when Paul perceived that one part were Sadducees and the other Pharisees, he cried out in the council, "Brothers, I am a Pharisee, a son of Pharisees. It is with respect to the hope and the resurrection of the dead that I am on trial."

23:7 And when he had said this, a dissension arose between the Pharisees and the Sadducees, and the assembly was divided.

23:8 For the Sadducees say that there is no resurrection, nor angel, nor spirit, but the Pharisees acknowledge them all.

23:9 Then a great clamor arose, and some of the scribes of the Pharisees' party stood up and contended sharply, "We find nothing wrong in this man. What if a spirit or an angel spoke to him?"

23:10 And when the dissension became violent, the tribune, afraid that Paul would be torn to pieces by them, commanded the soldiers to go down and take him away from among them by

force and bring him into the barracks.
23:11 *The following night the Lord stood by him and said, "Take courage, for as you have testified to the facts about me in Jerusalem, so you must testify also in Rome."*

23:1 Paul first defended himself before the Council by saying in verse 1, *"Brothers, I have lived my life before God in all good conscience up to this day."* He talked about his right relationship with God because he was standing before a Jewish court and not a Roman court. Here we once again see Paul's concern, not for his own reputation, but for the honor of the name of Jesus and of his Gospel. He could say that his conscience was clear, since he had always proclaimed God's own truth in the cross and empty tomb of Jesus. His words were not his own words or the words of a religious fanatic who was trying to start a new religion that opposed their Jewish religion. In fact, he had always taught that the Way of Jesus was the complete fulfillment of their religion. This court, or any other court, could do with him as they wished, but he knew that the reputation of Jesus' name was at stake ([1]M. I. Ac 16:37).
23:3 In verse 3, Paul apparently unknowingly abused the high priest by saying to him, *"God is going to strike you, you whitewashed wall!"* Scholars have, of course, hotly debated the reason or reasons why Paul said this; however, what we do know is that Paul would never do or say anything that would bring shame on right authority or on the holy name of Jesus (M. I. Ac 16:37).
23:6 (1) Obviously Paul very deliberately caused confusion in the Council by saying in verse 6, *"It is with respect to the hope and the resurrection of the dead that I am on trial."* He knew that he had no chance at all for a fair trial before this fanatical court. Their mentality had not changed from a few years earlier when they prejudged and condemned his Lord Jesus to death. Nor were these men any more reasonable than the mob in the temple who Paul had just escaped from (22:29). Therefore, his true statement about the bodily resurrection from the dead did *two* things: **a)** Paul faithfully witnessed to his Lord's death and resurrection even in a hostile environment ([2]M. M. Ac 2:24 & [3]M. I. Lk 4:15). **b)** And secondly, Paul also very wisely slipped from their

grasp because he knew that some of them passionately believed in the resurrection of the dead and others bitterly denied it (v 8), and his statement would do exactly what it did (v 9). **2)** The real irony here is that the resurrection of Jesus is, of course, the very heart of the Gospel that Paul proclaimed. And it was, therefore, the mighty sword that the Holy Spirit had been using so effectively in order to create faith in the hearts of thousands of Gentiles, whom these men despised so much. In their self-righteousness, these Jews thought that they deserved God's grace, but Gentiles did not ([4]M. I. 1 Cor 15:3a).

23:11 If Paul had had any doubts that his Lord was now sending him on his fourth missionary journey, his Lord now dispelled all of these doubts by this vision in verse 11; he now made his assignment very clear and explicit. And his Lord likewise once again dispelled any of his doubts that he was in full control of his mission. It would be a very long and perilous journey from Jerusalem to Rome, but Jesus already knew all about every one of these dangers, and Satan could do nothing to stop his mission no matter how hard he tried ([5]M. M. Ac 4:28).

A Plot to Kill Paul 23:12-22

> 23:12 *When it was day, the Jews made a plot and bound themselves by an oath neither to eat nor drink till they had killed Paul.*
> 23:13 *There were more than forty who made this conspiracy.*
> 23:14 *They went to the chief priests and elders and said, "We have strictly bound ourselves by an oath to taste no food till we have killed Paul.*
> 23:15 *Now therefore you, along with the council, give notice to the tribune to bring him down to you, as though you were going to determine his case more exactly. And we are ready to kill him before he comes near."*
> 23:16 *Now the son of Paul's sister heard of their ambush, so he went and entered the barracks and told Paul.*
> 23:17 *Paul called one of the centurions and said, "Take this young man to the tribune, for he has something to tell him."*
> 23:18 *So he took him and brought him to the tribune and said, "Paul*

23:19 *The tribune took him by the hand, and going aside asked him privately, "What is it that you have to tell me?"*
23:20 *And he said, "The Jews have agreed to ask you to bring Paul down to the council tomorrow, as though they were going to inquire somewhat more closely about him.*
23:21 *But do not be persuaded by them, for more than forty of their men are lying in ambush for him, who have bound themselves by an oath neither to eat nor drink till they have killed him. And now they are ready, waiting for your consent."*
23:22 *So the tribune dismissed the young man, charging him, "Tell no one that you have informed me of these things."*

23:12-22 Satan had so thoroughly possessed this group of Jews from the province of Asia that they conspired together with the equally evil men in the Jewish Council to plot in order to kill Paul. They even made a very evil <u>vow</u> to do so or be cursed by God. But of course, the Lord of the mission, once again, easily defeated Satan's plot because he had just given Paul a very important assignment and nothing could stop his almighty mission plan ([6]M. M. Ac 4:28).

Paul Sent to Felix the Governor 23:23-35

23:23 *Then he called two of the centurions and said, "Get ready two hundred soldiers, with seventy horsemen and two hundred spearmen to go as far as Caesarea at the third hour of the night.*
23:24 *Also provide mounts for Paul to ride and bring him safely to Felix the governor."*
23:25 *And he wrote a letter to this effect:*
23:26 *"Claudius Lysias, to his Excellency the governor Felix, greetings.*
23:27 *This man was seized by the Jews and was about to be killed by them when I came upon them with the soldiers and rescued him,*

having learned that he was a Roman citizen.
23:28 *And desiring to know the charge for which they were accusing him, I brought him down to their council.*
23:29 *I found that he was being accused about questions of their Law, but charged with nothing deserving death or imprisonment.*
23:30 *And when it was disclosed to me that there would be a plot against the man, I sent him to you at once, ordering his accusers also to state before you what they have against him."*
23:31 *So the soldiers, according to their instructions, took Paul and brought him by night to Antipatris.*
23:32 *And on the next day they returned to the barracks, letting the horsemen go on with him.*
23:33 *When they had come to Caesarea and delivered the letter to the governor, they presented Paul also before him.*
23:34 *On reading the letter, he asked what province he was from. And when he learned that he was from Cilicia,*
23:35 *he said, "I will give you a hearing when your accusers arrive." And he commanded him to be guarded in Herod's praetorium.*

23:23-35 There are two significant things to note in verses 23-35 concerning the Lord's mission: **a)** First of all, the Lord of the mission continued to protect Paul through the fact that he was a Roman citizen. Since the Lord Jesus likewise establishes all human governments (Rom 13:1-4), it was he himself who was using the highly disciplined Roman army to provide the protection that the evil Jews could not overcome (M. M. Ac 4:28). **b)** Secondly, verse 25 says that the tribune wrote a letter to explain to Governor Felix why he was sending this prisoner, Paul to him. And he wrote in his letter in verse 29 that *"I found that he was being accused about questions of their law, but charged with nothing deserving death or imprisonment."* This means that everyone who was in charge of Paul knew that he was innocent. The integrity of the Gospel was being preserved, so that the name of Jesus was still being honored. In this way, neither the officer nor his men nor the governor would have been antagonistic to Paul and all of these men would have been open to his witness to the name of Jesus. Therefore, we can be sure that Paul took many opportunities to talk about Jesus to his captors ([7]M. M. Mt

5:14 & [8]M. I. Lk 4:15).

---

[1] M. I. Ac 16:37: All Christians, but especially Christian leaders should do everything in their power to promote the good reputation of the name of Jesus, in order to make it possible for them to freely and publicly proclaim the Gospel.

[2] M. M. Ac 2:24: Our Lord Jesus loosed the pangs of death for us mortal human beings when God raised him from the dead, because it was not possible for him to be held by death.

[3] M. I. Lk 4:15: Christians should seize <u>every</u> opportunity to proclaim the Gospel to lost people of all nations.

[4] M. I. 1 Cor 15:3a: The most important Gospel message that Christians should proclaim is the truth that Jesus died and rose again to save all people from their sins.

[5] M. M. Ac 4:28: The heavenly Father is always in full control of his mission to all nations of the world.

[6] M. M. Ac 4:28: The heavenly Father is always in full control of his mission to all nations of the world.

[7] M. M. Mt 5:14: When the Holy Spirit creates faith in a person's heart, he also graciously gives him a new mission-heart that is eager to shine the light of the Gospel throughout the whole world.

[8] M. I. Lk 4:15: Christians should seize <u>every</u> opportunity to proclaim the Gospel to lost people of all nations.

Chapter 24

Paul Before Felix at Caesarea 24:1-21

24:1 *And after five days the high priest Ananias came down with some elders and a spokesman, one Tertullus. They laid before the governor their case against Paul.*

24:2 *And when he had been summoned, Tertullus began to accuse him, saying: "Since through you we enjoy much peace, and since by your foresight, most excellent Felix, reforms are being made for this nation,*

24:3 *in every way and everywhere we accept this with all gratitude.*

24:4 *But, to detain you no further, I beg you in your kindness to hear us briefly.*

24:5 *For we have found this man a plague, one who stirs up riots among all the Jews throughout the world and is a ringleader of the sect of the Nazarenes.*

24:6 *He even tried to profane the temple, but we seized him. [and we would have judged him according to our law.]*

24:7 *[But the chief captain Lysias came and with great violence took him out of our hands,]*

24:8 *[commanding his accusers to come before you.] By examining him yourself you will be able to find out from him about everything of which we accuse him."*

24:9 *The Jews also joined in the charge, affirming that all these things were so.*

24:10 *And when the governor had nodded to him to speak, Paul replied: "Knowing that for many years you have been a judge over this nation, I cheerfully make my defense.*

24:11 *You can verify that it is not more than twelve days since I went up to worship in Jerusalem,*

24:12 *and they did not find me disputing with anyone or stirring up a crowd, either in the temple or in the synagogues or in the city.*

24:13 *Neither can they prove to you what they now bring up against*

> *me.*
>
> *24:14 But this I confess to you, that according to the Way, which they call a sect, I worship the God of our fathers, believing everything laid down by the Law and written in the Prophets,*
>
> *24:15 having a hope in God, which these men themselves accept, that there will be a resurrection of both the just and the unjust.*
>
> *24:16 So I always take pains to have a clear conscience toward both God and man.*
>
> *24:17 Now after several years I came to bring alms to my nation and to present offerings.*
>
> *24:18 While I was doing this, they found me purified in the temple, without any crowd or tumult. But some Jews from Asia--*
>
> *24:19 they ought to be here before you and to make an accusation, should they have anything against me.*
>
> *24:20 Or else let these men themselves say what wrongdoing they found when I stood before the council,*
>
> *24:21 other than this one thing that I cried out while standing among them: 'It is with respect to the resurrection of the dead that I am on trial before you this day.'"*

24:1-9 (1) The Jewish Council knew very well that all of their accusations against Paul were false; therefore, they needed every advantage that they could find. They desperately needed a lawyer who was very clever and who spoke the Roman governor's language, Greek. So they were forced to choose a Gentile lawyer whom they hated named Tertullus. **2)** And Tertullus showed in four ways that he was very clever: **a)** He first of all praised the governor in verses 2-3 for all of the wonderful things that he had done for them, which was mere flattery, since he was, in fact, cruel and oppressive. **b)** He then emphasized in verse 4 how quick and easy this case would be—before he brought three bogus charges against Paul. **c)** The first two charges that he mentioned in verse 5 were offenses against the Roman government. (Two things were illegal here: Paul *"stirs up riots among all the Jews throughout the world,"* and he *"is a ringleader of the sect of the Nazarenes."* He was supposedly stirring up political trouble and was promoting a new, illegal religion.) **d)** Then finally in verse 6, he mentioned the charge that the

Jews were most concerned about, but which would not interest the governor in the least. He said, *"He even tried to profane the temple."* **3)** Nevertheless, Paul was, of course, very proud of being *"a ringleader of the sect of the Nazarenes"* (v 5); and in fact, that was the very reason why he was standing before them, in order to witness to the holy name of this man from Nazareth. However, it's also significant to note in verse 22 that the governor did, in fact, already have *"a rather accurate knowledge of the Way."* Perhaps he knew even more about Jesus than these Jews did. They should have been waiting for this *"Nazarene"* to fulfill all of God's promises in their Scriptures; and therefore, his *"Way"* was not *"a sect"* at all, but the beautiful fulfilment of their religion ([1]M. M. Mt 1:22). And here standing before them all was a missionary of this *"Nazarene"* who longed to tell all of these secular and religious leaders about what Jesus had done for all of them ([2]M. I. Ac 1:8 & [3]Lk 12:12).

24:10 Paul was also wise because, like the lawyer Tertullus, he greeted the governor in verse 10 with praise for the sound judgment that he had been giving his people. Not only did Paul say this because he himself obviously needed a fair trial at that time, but also because fair trials without corruption are essential for any stable government. And a stable government was, of course, very important for the free spread of the Gospel of Jesus throughout the Roman Empire, and so that Paul and all Christians could effectively proclaim the Gospel (M. I. Ac 1:8). (As a matter of fact, this freedom for Christians to spread *"the Way"* far and wide in the Roman Empire did end a few years later when Emperor Nero began to persecute Christians in many horrible ways.)

24:11-13 Paul then defended himself in verses 11-13 against the first charge made against him that he was a troublemaker. He tried to make it clear in verse 18 that all of the evidence pointed to the fact that it was *"some Jews from Asia"* who had stirred up the trouble in the temple courtyard, and not he who had done so; therefore, they should be the ones on trial and not himself. This was, of course, completely true; but Paul couldn't point to any witnesses who could verify his claims. Nevertheless, we know that Paul was not actually concerned first of all about his own reputation, but rather about the holy name of Jesus ([4]M. I. Ac 16:37).

24:14-15 (1) Then, Paul <u>boldly</u> witnessed to <u>three</u> important truths in verses 14-15. He said: **a)** that, *"according to the Way, which they call a sect, I worship the <u>God</u> of our fathers"* (v 14), **b)** and that I believe *"everything laid down by the Law and written in the Prophets [the entire <u>Scriptures</u>], having a hope in God"* (v 14), **c)** and that I have *"a hope in God, which these men themselves accept, that there will be a <u>resurrection</u> of both the just and the unjust"* (v 15). He boldly made it very clear that he and all Christians believe these essential truths in exactly the same way that these accusing Jews did. Christians are <u>not</u> following a mere <u>sect</u> because they have *not*, in fact, left Judaism (5:17-18). And Jesus did not reject their religion either; rather, he <u>fulfilled</u> all of God's promises in their own Scriptures. Therefore, Christianity is <u>not a new</u> religion; and there is no reason for the government to ban it or to persecute those who follow it. It's a new mission imperative. M. I. Ac 24:14: Christians should always be bold to make it clear to government authorities in lands where they are proclaiming the Gospel that Christianity is a legitimate religion. **2)** These truths should have touched the hearts of the Jews who were accusing Paul, especially since they already believed them; but their hearts were harder than stone (Lk 3:8). Nevertheless, Paul was especially witnessing these bold truths to the governor, since, even though he had *"a rather accurate knowledge of the Way"* (v 22), such an important government official needed to hear these main truths. Can there be any doubt that it was his gracious Lord Jesus who had placed Paul before the governor? But it clearly was not his Lord's plan for his missionary journey to end there, since this was only the <u>first</u> official whom he would witness to ([5]M. M. Ac 4:28).
24:15-16, 21 Paul then boldly witnessed in verses 15-16 and 21, once again, to the death and <u>resurrection</u> of Jesus, as well as to the hope that all who trust in him will also rise from the dead. He concluded in verse 21, *"It is with respect to the <u>resurrection</u> of the dead that I am on trial before you this day."* And it's possible that no one in the room knew or had heard this vital truth, which was, of course, another very important reason why the Lord of the mission had sent Paul to be standing just where he was. And Paul did not miss his chance! He faithfully and boldly did his job ([6]M. I. Ac 4:20 & [7]M. M. Jn 20:8).

24:20 In verse 20, Paul made only a vague reference to the third charge against him that he had brought Gentiles into the temple courtyard (v 6). He knew that the governor probably could not have cared less about this charge; but it was the main charge in the eyes of his accusers. Thus, Paul showed no fear of them or of the governor, since the Holy Spirit had given him the boldness that he needed in the face of their religious and secular power ([8]M. I. Ac 4:20).

Paul Kept in Custody 24:22-27

24:22 But Felix, having a rather accurate knowledge of the Way, put them off, saying, "When Lysias the tribune comes down, I will decide your case."
24:23 Then he gave orders to the centurion that he should be kept in custody but have some liberty, and that none of his friends should be prevented from attending to his needs.
24:24 After some days Felix came with his wife Drusilla, who was Jewish, and he sent for Paul and heard him speak about faith in Christ Jesus.
24:25 And as he reasoned about righteousness and self-control and the coming judgment, Felix was alarmed and said, "Go away for the present. When I get an opportunity I will summon you."
24:26 At the same time he hoped that money would be given him by Paul. So he sent for him often and conversed with him.
24:27 When two years had elapsed, Felix was succeeded by Porcius Festus. And desiring to do the Jews a favor, Felix left Paul in prison.

24:22-27 (1) Obviously, the Lord of the mission had made sure that the governor had heard about *"the Way"* before Paul stood before him. But who had witnessed to him? This emphasizes the truth that we should never underestimate the importance of witnessing to the name of Jesus at every opportunity, since it is the Holy Spirit who is in control of the result of our witness. It doesn't matter who told the governor heard about Jesus, but the Holy Spirit used that witness mightily ([9]M. I. Lk

8:11). **2)** Because the governor already knew about Jesus, he helped to advance the Lord's mission in the following ways: **a)** He acquitted Paul of all charges by adjourning the trial (v 22). **b)** He thereby frustrated Paul's Jewish enemies (v 22). **c)** He also *"gave orders to the centurion that he should be kept in custody but have some liberty and none of his friends should be prevented from attending to his needs"* (v 23). **d)** He also wanted to hear more about Jesus from Paul, thus Paul had many more opportunities to witness to him for two years (vs 24, 26). **e)** He likewise invited his Jewish wife to hear more about Jesus (v 24). What wonderful, surprising results! This was exactly what the Lord of the mission had had in mind—that his missionary should have these many wonderful opportunities to confess him before a powerful Gentile ruler who was open to the Gospel. **3)** But the two facts—that the governor did not repent when Paul proclaimed the Law to him (v 25), and that not all of his motives for wanting to talk to Paul were good (v 26)—do nothing to mitigate the importance of Paul's repeated witness to him. Paul had done his job and left the results to his Lord's Spirit. Furthermore, we do not know whether he or his wife repented and believed in Jesus some time later; nor do we know how Paul's witness effected how he governed his people. These potential results were entirely in the gracious hands of the Holy Spirit (M. I. Lk 8:11).

---

[1] M. M. Mt 1:22: God sent his only Son, Jesus to be born as a true human being, so that he could save all of his brothers and sisters of all nations by fulfilling all of God's promises in the Old Testament.

[2] M. I. Ac 1:8: Christians should go and witness about Jesus to all who are lost from all languages and cultures by depending on the power of the Holy Spirit to help them bridge all of the language/cultural boundaries whether they are relatively easy, as in their own language, or extremely difficult.

[3] M. I. Lk 12:12: Christians should go and tell the Gospel depending on the Holy Spirit to teach them what they should say.

[4] M. I. Ac 16:37: All Christians, but especially Christian leaders should do everything in their power to promote the good reputation of the name of Jesus, in order to make it possible for them to freely and publicly proclaim the Gospel.

[5] M. M. Ac 4:28: The heavenly Father is always in full control of his mission to all nations of the world.

⁶ M. I. Ac 4:20: Christians should boldly witness to the name of Jesus and allow nothing to stop their witness because it is the Holy Spirit's own message.

⁷ M. M. Jn 20:8: God gave faith in Jesus to people who personally saw that the tomb of Jesus was empty, because it proved that he was alive.

⁸ M. I. Ac 4:20: Christians should boldly witness to the name of Jesus and allow nothing to stop their witness because it is the Holy Spirit's own message.

⁹ M. I. Lk 8:11: Christians should faithfully do their job of preaching and leave the <u>results</u> to the Holy Spirit.

Chapter 25

Paul Appeals to Caesar 25:1-12

25:1 *Now three days after Festus had arrived in the province, he went up to Jerusalem from Caesarea.*

25:2 *And the chief priests and the principal men of the Jews laid out their case against Paul, and they urged him,*

25:3 *asking as a favor against Paul that he summon him to Jerusalem--because they were planning an ambush to kill him on the way.*

25:4 *Festus replied that Paul was being kept at Caesarea and that he himself intended to go there shortly.*

25:5 *"So," said he, "let the men of authority among you go down with me, and if there is anything wrong about the man, let them bring charges against him."*

25:6 *After he stayed among them not more than eight or ten days, he went down to Caesarea. And the next day he took his seat on the tribunal and ordered Paul to be brought.*

25:7 *When he had arrived, the Jews who had come down from Jerusalem stood around him, bringing many and serious charges against him that they could not prove.*

25:8 *Paul argued in his defense, "Neither against the Law of the Jews, nor against the temple, nor against Caesar have I committed any offense."*

25:9 *But Festus, wishing to do the Jews a favor, said to Paul, "Do you wish to go up to Jerusalem and there be tried on these charges before me?"*

25:10 *But Paul said, "I am standing before Caesar's tribunal, where I ought to be tried. To the Jews I have done no wrong, as you yourselves know very well.*

25:11 *If then I am a wrongdoer and have committed anything for which I deserve to die, I do not seek to escape death. But if there is nothing to their charges against me, no one can give me up to them. I appeal to Caesar."*

> 25:12 *Then Festus, when he had conferred with his council, answered, "To Caesar you have appealed; to Caesar you shall go."*

25:1-7 Through Festus, the new governor, the Lord of the mission continued to keep his servant, Paul in prison where he was safe and could continue to proclaim the Gospel to influential people. Even though the new governor did not have a personal interest in hearing what Paul had to say as governor Felix had—and therefore, Paul apparently had no private audience with the governor—we can be sure that Paul took every opportunity he had to tell others around him about Jesus (¹M. I. Lk 4:15).

25:3 However, when Governor Festus went to Jerusalem, and the Jewish leaders plotted to urge him to bring Paul to Jerusalem in order to kill him on the way (v 3), the governor may have seen through their plot. Therefore, he ordered the Jewish leaders to go to Caesarea where he would hear their accusations against Paul; and in this way, he did two things to help Paul: **a)** he protected Paul's rights as a Roman citizen to stand trial, **b)** and he kept him safe in prison in Caesarea. But of course, it was the Lord of the mission who was busy carrying out his perfect plan in order to keep Paul on his final missionary journey; and the governor was actually not the one who was in control of the situation (²M. M. Ac 4:28).

25:11 Verse 11 is a crucial juncture in Paul's final missionary journey, because he said in verse 11, *"I do not seek to escape death. But if there is nothing to their charges against me, no one can give me up to them. I appeal to Caesar."* At issue was who was in both spiritual and physical control? Obviously, it was Jesus himself who is both the Lord of the mission and also the King of all kings. **a)** It's true that Satan continued to control the Jewish leaders from Jerusalem, but Jesus had severely limited his evil spiritual power on the cross (Jn 19:30). Therefore, it was Jesus who now used these evil men to force Paul to exercise his most important right as a Roman citizen: to appeal to Caesar (v 11). **b)** And Caesar controlled the entire Roman Empire, but, as God, it was Jesus himself who had placed him in power (Rom 13:1). Therefore, the emperor was under a much higher authority. And by appealing to Caesar's governmental power, it was vital that Paul remain <u>under</u> the protection of the enormous power of Roman rule—and <u>not</u> running from it. The Lord of the mission was keeping Paul exactly where he wanted him to be on his last missionary journey, so that he could safely proclaim the Gospel to men in governmental power (M. M. Ac 4:28).

Paul Before Agrippa and Bernice 25:13-27

25:13 *Now when some days had passed, Agrippa the king and Bernice arrived at Caesarea and greeted Festus.*
25:14 *And as they stayed there many days, Festus laid Paul's case before the king, saying, "There is a man left prisoner by Felix,*
25:15 *and when I was at Jerusalem, the chief priests and the elders of the Jews laid out their case against him, asking for a sentence of condemnation against him.*
25:16 *I answered them that it was not the custom of the Romans to give up anyone before the accused met the accusers face to face and had opportunity to make his defense concerning the charge laid against him.*
25:17 *So when they came together here, I made no delay, but on the next day took my seat on the tribunal and ordered the man to be brought.*
25:18 *When the accusers stood up, they brought no charge in his case of such evils as I supposed.*
25:19 *Rather they had certain points of dispute with him about their own religion and about a certain Jesus, who was dead, but whom Paul asserted to be alive.*
25:20 *Being at a loss how to investigate these questions, I asked whether he wanted to go to Jerusalem and be tried there regarding them.*
25:21 *But when Paul had appealed to be kept in custody for the decision of the emperor, I ordered him to be held until I could send him to Caesar."*
25:22 *Then Agrippa said to Festus, "I would like to hear the man*

myself." "Tomorrow," said he, "you will hear him."

25:23 *So on the next day Agrippa and Bernice came with great pomp, and they entered the audience hall with the military tribunes and the prominent men of the city. Then, at the command of Festus, Paul was brought in.*

25:24 *And Festus said, "King Agrippa and all who are present with us, you see this man about whom the whole Jewish people petitioned me, both in Jerusalem and here, shouting that he ought not to live any longer.*

25:25 *But I found that he had done nothing deserving death. And as he himself appealed to the emperor, I decided to go ahead and send him.*

25:26 *But I have nothing definite to write to my lord about him. Therefore I have brought him before you all, and especially before you, King Agrippa, so that, after we have examined him, I may have something to write.*

25:27 *For it seems to me unreasonable, in sending a prisoner, not to indicate the charges against him."*

25:13-21 (1) Note that, at Paul's trial before the governor in verses 1-12, Luke does not tell us that Paul boldly witnessed to King Agrippa and Queen Bernice about the resurrection of Jesus. But when Governor Festus summarized the events of that day in verses 14-22, we read in verse 19 that Paul had told them, *"about a certain Jesus, who was dead, but whom Paul asserted to be alive."* Two points are significant. **a)** First of all, it's significant to note that the governor himself must have taken special note of this vital truth of Jesus' resurrection that day, perhaps because Paul boldly emphasized it so clearly. He never missed a chance to share this life-changing truth about the death and resurrection of Jesus (³M. I. Ro 1:16a). **b)** Secondly, it's also interesting to note that—even before Paul stood before them—when the king and queen heard the governor's summary, they also heard about Jesus' resurrection. Therefore, whether the king and queen and the Jews from Jerusalem liked it or not, they all heard Paul's clear witness to the death and resurrection of Jesus. And how many times had these same Jews already heard it from Paul? Yet their hearts were still like stones (Lk 3:8)! The governor, on the other hand, had very quickly mentioned Paul to King Agrippa; therefore, it's very possible that he was showing so much interest in this unique prisoner of his because he had now also faith in Jesus as his Lord and Savior ([4]M. I. Ac 4:20). **2)** Furthermore, Governor Festus also sought the assistance of King Agrippa concerning Paul's case because Paul had appealed to the emperor. Therefore, he was required to send an explicit report on his case to the emperor; and he recognized that the real charges against Paul had nothing to do with Roman law; rather they were religious matters among the Jews that he knew nothing about. King Agrippa, on the other hand, was in charge of the temple treasury and could even appoint the high priest; therefore, he was very familiar with Jewish religious affairs (26:3). But then, after Paul's long defense before them, the king told the governor in (26:32), *"This man could have been set free if he had not appealed to Caesar."* He was fair and honest enough to recognize the truth that the leaders of the Jews simply hated Paul and were willing to do anything to kill him. Therefore, once again, we, of course, see that it was not these mere men, as powerful as they were who were in control of the situation. The Lord of the mission was still the King over <u>all</u> kings. And he continued to keep Paul in a safe place—just where he wanted him to be, standing before human kings and rulers who had not yet heard the Gospel (23:11). If Paul had been set free, since he was innocent (v 25), these Jews would probably have been able to kill him ([5]M. M. Ac 4:28).

25:22-23 Verse 23 says, *"So on the next day Agrippa and Bernice came with great pomp."* What pomp and fanfare! This <u>venue</u> was precisely what the Lord of the mission had had in mind for Paul (23:11)! How many very powerful people were there to be an <u>audience</u> for the Lord's missionary, even though he was a <u>prisoner</u>? What a golden <u>opportunity</u> Paul had here! And he would never have had this opportunity as a free man. Yet, on the other hand, it was also because he was a Roman citizen that they were willing to listen to him. Thus, King Agrippa said in verse 22, *"I would like to hear the man myself."* Of course, it's no surprise that the gracious plan of the King of kings to create these kinds of venues for his missionary could not have been more perfect (v 23; M. M. Ac 4:28 & [6]M. I. Ac 1:8).

[1] M. I. Lk 4:15: Christians should seize every opportunity to proclaim the Gospel to lost people of all nations.

[2] M. M. Ac 4:28: The heavenly Father is always in full control of his mission to all nations of the world.

[3] M. I. Ro 1:16a: Christians should not be ashamed to proclaim the Gospel, even though it may appear to be weak and foolish; rather, they should be proud to proclaim it because it is the almighty power that the Holy Spirit uses to create faith in Jesus.

[4] M. I. Ac 4:20: Christians should boldly witness to the name of Jesus and allow nothing to stop their witness because it is the Holy Spirit's own message.

[5] M. M. Ac 4:28: The heavenly Father is always in full control of his mission to all nations of the world.

[6] M. I. Ac 1:8: Christians should go and witness about Jesus to all who are lost from all languages and cultures by depending on the power of the Holy Spirit to help them bridge all of the language/cultural boundaries whether they are relatively easy, as in their own language, or extremely difficult.

Chapter 26

Paul's Defense Before Agrippa 26:1-11

26:1 *So Agrippa said to Paul, "You have permission to speak for yourself." Then Paul stretched out his hand and made his defense:*

26:2 *"I consider myself fortunate that it is before you, King Agrippa, I am going to make my defense today against all the accusations of the Jews,*

26:3 *especially because you are familiar with all the customs and controversies of the Jews. Therefore I beg you to listen to me patiently.*

26:4 *"My manner of life from my youth, spent from the beginning among my own nation and in Jerusalem, is known by all the Jews.*

26:5 *They have known for a long time, if they are willing to testify, that according to the strictest party of our religion I have lived as a Pharisee.*

26:6 *And now I stand here on trial because of my hope in the promise made by God to our fathers,*

26:7 *to which our twelve tribes hope to attain, as they earnestly worship night and day. And for this hope I am accused by Jews, O king!*

26:8 *Why is it thought incredible by any of you that God raises the dead?*

26:9 *"I myself was convinced that I ought to do many things in opposing the name of Jesus of Nazareth.*

26:10 *And I did so in Jerusalem. I not only locked up many of the saints in prison after receiving authority from the chief priests, but when they were put to death I cast my vote against them.*

26:11 *And I punished them often in all the synagogues and tried to make them blaspheme, and in raging fury against them I persecuted them even to foreign cities.*

26:1-3 It's very significant that King Agrippa began Paul's hearing by telling Paul in verse 1, *"You have permission to speak for yourself"* since Paul was a prisoner who was accused of some very serious crimes. Of course, it's also true that Paul was a Roman citizen, which may have influenced the king's attitude toward him. Nevertheless, it was the Lord of the mission who had graciously prepared this venue so that these powerful people would hear his Gospel. How did he do so? **a)** First of all, he planned the political situation so that this king was a Jew who, according to verse 3, was *"especially…familiar with all the customs and controversies of the Jews."* **b)** Secondly, verse 3 implies that the king also knew that the accusations of the leaders of the Jewish council against Paul were politically motivated and completely bogus. Therefore, he would have been even more open to giving Paul a serious hearing. **c)** Thirdly, he made the Roman Empire peaceful with a just court system. **d)** And finally, he had made Paul to be who he was—a Roman citizen, whom they would respect, in spite of the fact that he was a prisoner (22:25). He did all of this so that his missionary and servant would be *"free to speak for himself"* (v 1). Nevertheless, Paul, of course, did not speak for himself; rather he seized this golden opportunity to speak for his dear Lord ([1]M. I. Lk 4:15 & [2]M. I. Ac 1:8).
26:2 (1) Paul defended himself before King Agrippa by addressing him personally in verse 2. And the content of his message reveals that he did so as a Jew talking to a Jew with the intent of calling him, as well as his entire audience, of course, to repentance and faith in Jesus. Paul was, of course, very conscious of his current assignment to witness to kings and to other leaders (23:11; [3]M. I. Ac 21:26). **2)** However, it would not be reasonable to assume that Paul's message was so personal that he spoke in Hebrew or Aramaic. Rather, he almost certainly spoke in Greek because the king certainly spoke Greek; and the majority of his audience must have been Gentiles who also spoke Greek (M. I. Ac 1:8).
26:4-29 Paul appealed to this Jewish king and especially the other Jews in his audience in three different ways in order to try to convince them that the zeal that they had for their Old Testament religion was misdirected. **a)** First, Paul made a direct connection with them by referring, in verses 6-7 and 22-23, to their zeal for their Jewish religion

which he shared with them. **b)** Secondly, Paul also witnessed to the power of the resurrection of Jesus in verses 8 and 23 that could change their hearts. **c)** And finally, Paul also used his own personal example, in verses 4, 12-23 and 29, in order to urge them to repent and believe in Jesus as he now did. Paul's risen Lord Jesus had, of course, placed him there before this audience very purposely so that he would be his bold missionary and witness to his almighty resurrection power ([4]M. M. Ac 4:28).

26:6-7, 22-23 Two different times in his message, Paul appealed to his fellow Jews based on the ancient Jewish religion which they shared. **a)** In verses 6-7, Paul said to his fellow Jews that he still had the same *"hope in the promise made by God to our fathers to which our twelve tribes hope to attain."* This should have made it clear to the Jews in his audience that the Church or *"the Way"* (9:2) was in fact the same Jewish religion that was now beautifully fulfilled in God's Son, Jesus. It was not an illegal sect or a totally new religion ([5]M. M. Mt 1:22). **b)** Then, what turned out to be Paul's final appeal in verses 22-23 (because Governor Festus interrupted him) was another appeal to King Agrippa's religious roots in the Old Testament. He said that *"the prophets and Moses said that the Christ must suffer and that, by being the first to rise from the dead, he would proclaim light both to our people and to the Gentiles."* These two direct connections with their shared Jewish religion should have been any easy opening into the hearts of Paul's audience, although Luke does not record any responses to his appeals ([6]M. I. Lk 8:11).

26:8, 23 (1) Secondly, and most importantly, Paul boldly witnessed to the resurrection of Jesus two times. **a)** He asked his accusers in verse 8, *"Why is it thought incredible by any of you that God raises the dead?"* This was both a bold and a loving appeal to his fellow Jews to trust in the resurrection of Jesus because he knew that their zeal was just as misdirected as his had been (v 11). **b)** Secondly, Paul said in verse 23, *"the Messiah must suffer and be the first one to rise from death."* His fellow Jews would all have immediately recognized his reference to a *"suffering Messiah"* from (Is 53:1-11), but a risen Messiah may have been a new teaching to them. And Paul emphasized the resurrection of

Jesus these two times for at least two reasons. It is the final <u>proof</u> that Jesus had fulfilled their Jewish religion (2 Cor 1:20; [7]M. M. Ro 3:31). And Jesus' resurrection was also the almighty power that had dramatically changed his entire life and could change theirs as well ([8]M. M. Ro 1:16b). **2)** It's not clear why the king suddenly interrupted Paul when Paul referred to the resurrection of Jesus a second time in verse 23. Whether the king was offended or not, we don't know. And the remainder of Luke's account also does not give us much hope that the Holy Spirit was able to change any stony hearts that day. Paul's many arguments should have been very persuasive to the king and to all present; and especially his repeated witness to Jesus' <u>resurrection</u> should have moved them. Nevertheless, Paul had carried out his Lord's assignment and planted the seed of God's holy Word in their hearts; and of course, the Holy Spirit is always eager to continue to work in the hearts of unbelievers to make it sprout and grow (M. I. Lk 8:11).

Paul Tells of his Conversion 26:12-32

26:12 *"In this connection I journeyed to Damascus with the authority and commission of the chief priests.*
26:13 *At midday, O king, I saw on the way a light from heaven, brighter than the sun, that shone around me and those who journeyed with me.*
26:14 *And when we had all fallen to the ground, I heard a voice saying to me in the Hebrew language, 'Saul, Saul, why are you persecuting me? It is hard for you to kick against the goads.'*
26:15 *And I said, 'Who are you, Lord?' And the Lord said, 'I am Jesus whom you are persecuting.*
26:16 *But rise and stand upon your feet, for I have appeared to you for this purpose, to appoint you as a servant and witness to the things in which you have seen me and to those in which I will appear to you,*
26:17 *delivering you from your people and from the Gentiles--to whom I am sending you*
26:18 *to open their eyes, so that they may turn from darkness to light*

and from the power of Satan to God, that they may receive forgiveness of sins and a place among those who are sanctified by faith in me.'

26:19 *"Therefore, O King Agrippa, I was not disobedient to the heavenly vision,*

26:20 *but declared first to those in Damascus, then in Jerusalem and throughout all the region of Judea, and also to the Gentiles, that they should repent and turn to God, performing deeds in keeping with their repentance.*

26:21 *For this reason the Jews seized me in the temple and tried to kill me.*

26:22 *To this day I have had the help that comes from God, and so I stand here testifying both to small and great, saying nothing but what the prophets and Moses said would come to pass:*

26:23 *that the Christ must suffer and that, by being the first to rise from the dead, he would proclaim light both to our people and to the Gentiles."*

26:24 *And as he was saying these things in his defense, Festus said with a loud voice, "Paul, you are out of your mind; your great learning is driving you out of your mind."*

26:25 *But Paul said, "I am not out of my mind, most excellent Festus, but I am speaking true and rational words.*

26:26 *For the king knows about these things, and to him I speak boldly. For I am persuaded that none of these things has escaped his notice, for this has not been done in a corner.*

26:27 *King Agrippa, do you believe the prophets? I know that you believe."*

26:28 *And Agrippa said to Paul, "In a short time would you persuade me to be a Christian?"*

26:29 *And Paul said, "Whether short or long, I would to God that not only you but also all who hear me this day might become such as I am--except for these chains."*

26:30 *Then the king rose, and the governor and Bernice and those who were sitting with them.*

26:31 *And when they had withdrawn, they said to one another, "This man is doing nothing to deserve death or imprisonment."*

> 26:32 *And Agrippa said to Festus, "This man could have been set free if he had not appealed to Caesar."*

26:4, 12-23, 29 (1) The third thing that Paul used to urge his Jewish audience to repent was his own personal example, in verses 4, 12-23 and 29. **a)** He said in verse 4, *"My manner of life from my youth…is known by all the Jews."* They all knew that he had had great zeal for the Jewish religion as a strict Pharisee because he even persecuted the Church (v 9-11; 22:4). He hoped to persuade them to follow his example by repenting and allowing the Holy Spirit to redirect their former zeal from legalistic Judaism toward trusting in Jesus ([9]M. I. Ac 26:12). **b)** Then, in verse 12-23, he went into great detail in order to describe his own conversion experience as an example for his audience to follow. He told them how the Lord Jesus himself had appeared to him as his risen Lord, called him to faith in him, and also called him to be his missionary to the Gentiles (v 17). In this very dramatic way Jesus had harnessed Paul's zeal as a Pharisee in order to use it for his own mission. What a dramatic example this was for them to hear about (M. I. Ac 26:12)! **c)** And Paul perhaps used his final personal example for its shock value. He very boldly pointed to his chains in verse 29 in order to turn the *shame* of being a prisoner into a positive impact on his hearers (2 Cor 12:9). He said, *"I would to God that not only you but also all who hear me this day might become such as I am—except for these chains"* The Lord's missionary was very bold because he was a servant of his risen Lord who was no longer dead but very much alive and longed to change their hearts as well by his almighty power ([10]M. M. Ro 1:16b). **2)** Thus, we see that in these three ways Paul was using his own personal example in order to try to persuade the king and his fellow Jews that they should also repent. As his risen Lord had dramatically changed him, the almighty power of his resurrection could also change them and redirect their former zeal from legalistic Judaism toward trusting in Jesus as their true Lord and King (Rom 1:16; Eph 1:18-19; Phil 3:10). It's a new mission imperative. M. I. Ac 26:12: Christians should use their own personal experience of coming to faith in Jesus by the almighty power of his resurrection as a powerful example for their hearers to follow.

26:17-23 Three times in verses 17-23, Paul also indirectly addressed the *Gentiles* who were in the room, in order to tell them that the risen Lord Jesus had sent him to all Gentile nations. **a)** First, Paul said in verses 17-18 that his Lord Jesus promised him that he would be, *"delivering you from your people and from the Gentiles—to whom I am sending you to open their eyes, so that they may turn from darkness to light and from the power of Satan to God, that they may receive forgiveness of sins and a place among those who are sanctified by faith in me."* No doubt, when Paul's Gentile hearers heard that Paul had been sent to them (9:15; Gal 2:7), they must have started listening to him much more eagerly (Jms 1:22). **b)** Secondly, Paul added in verse 20 that he proclaimed the Gospel *"also to the Gentiles, that they should repent and turn to God, performing deeds in keeping with their repentance."* **c)** And thirdly, in verse 23, Paul said that the risen Lord Jesus Christ *"would proclaim light both to our people [the Jews] and to the Gentiles."* Obviously, there also were many Gentiles who were listening to Paul that day; and this very good news that the risen Lord Jesus had sent Paul to be his missionary to the Gentiles must have touched their hearts ([11]M. M. Ac 10:45 & [12]Ro 11:26).

26:24-26 When Paul saw King Agrippa's strong reaction in verse 24, he asserted in verses 25-26, *"I am not out of my mind, most excellent Festus, but I am speaking true and rational words…and this has not been done in a corner."* Thus, Paul was pleading with the governor to give more thought to what he had just said, since what he said was based on historical facts that everyone *knew* because *"this has not been done in a corner"* (v 26). It's very significant that Luke, who was the author of this book of Acts began his Gospel with this very same thought that everyone *knew* what Jesus had done for all mankind. Luke had traveled with Paul many, many miles and therefore had many opportunities to learn about the Lord Jesus from him. Thus, Luke began his Gospel by saying in (Lk 1:1) that he was writing *"a narrative of the things that have been accomplished among us."* Both Paul and Luke emphasized that everyone saw what Jesus did. He was a real person, both true man and true God; and he died and rose again in the public, therefore, they were not hidden secrets. It was all nations—not only the Jews, but Jews and Gentiles <u>alike</u>, who saw everything that Jesus did in order to rescue everyone from sin. He loves every human being he has made and longs for every one of them to <u>see</u> and <u>hear</u> what he has done for them and believe in him (Jn 3:16-17; Jn 18:20; [13]M. M. Lk 1:1). It's a new mission message. M. M. Ac 26:26: Everything that Jesus did in his life, and especially his death and resurrection, he graciously did in the <u>public</u> for everyone from every nation on earth to see, so that everyone would believe in him.

26:27-28 Paul then challenged the king to make a public confession by asking him in verse 27, *"Do you believe the prophets? I know that you believe."* This put the king in a dilemma because, if he said "Yes," Paul could make another affirmation that Jesus had fulfilled all the prophets; but if he said "No," he would have to defend his answer before his fellow Jews who were present. Therefore, the king avoided answering his question by asking his own question in verse 28, *"In a short time would you persuade me to be a Christian?"* Clearly, the king was perceptive enough to see that Paul was trying to convert him by his appeals to the Old Testament, by his references to the resurrection of Jesus, and by recounting his own personal example. But the king was too stubborn to yield to the Holy Spirit—at least in front of his colleagues ([14]M. I. Lk 8:11).

26:30-32 Even though the king, the governor and Bernice left the room talking about the fact that there was no rightful case against Paul (v 31-32), their hearts must have, in fact, been full of Paul's message to them. God's Word had struck home, and the Holy Spirit was very busy using his mighty two-edged sword (M. I. Lk 8:11). Then, the king concluded the matter in verse 32, *"This man could have been set free if he had not appealed to Caesar."* Although this may have, once again, appeared to be very unfortunate for Paul, we know that this was <u>precisely</u> what his gracious Lord had planned for him (23:11). It meant that <u>his</u> plan was going forward perfectly, since Paul would not only remain <u>protected</u> by the might of Rome but would also continue to have <u>opportunities</u> to witness to powerful people ([15]M. M. Ac 4:28).

[1] M. I. Lk 4:15: Christians should seize every opportunity to proclaim the Gospel to lost people of all nations.

[2] M. I. Ac 1:8: Christians should go and witness about Jesus to all who are lost from all languages and cultures by depending on the power of the Holy Spirit to help them bridge all of the language/cultural boundaries whether they are relatively easy, as in their own language, or extremely difficult.

[3] M. I. Ac 21:26: Christians should seek opportunities to witness to Jesus' name to people who are influential leaders in the target society, so that they can influence others to trust in Jesus.

[4] M. M. Ac 4:28: The heavenly Father is always in full control of his mission to all nations of the world.

[5] M. M. Mt 1:22: God sent his only Son, Jesus to be born as a true human being, so that he could save all of his brothers and sisters of all nations by fulfilling all of God's promises in the Old Testament.

[6] M. I. Lk 8:11: Christians should faithfully do their job of preaching and leave the results to the Holy Spirit.

[7] M. M. Ro 3:31: Christianity fulfills the Jewish religion because the Holy Spirit empowers Christians to *obey* God's Law and thus also obey Jesus who fulfilled all of God's Laws for them.

[8] M. M. Ro 1:16b: The Gospel is so powerful because it contains the central truth that Jesus rose from the dead with a glorified body in order to save all of his brothers and sisters from sin and death.

[9] M. I. Ac 26:12: Christians should use their own personal experience of coming to faith in Jesus by the almighty power of his resurrection as a powerful example for their hearers to follow.

[10] M. M. Ro 1:16b: The Gospel is so powerful because it contains the central truth that Jesus rose from the dead with a glorified body in order to save all of his brothers and sisters from sin and death.

[11] M. M. Ac 10:45: When God graciously gives the gift of faith in his Son, Jesus to a person from any nation on earth, he also graciously gives him his Holy Spirit who now lives in his new mission-heart.

[12] M. M. Ro 11:26: God graciously continues to graft Jews and Gentiles into the new Israel through the proclamation of the Gospel, until the remnant of Israel and the fullness of the Gentiles form one, holy Nation and are saved.

[13] M. M. Lk 1:1: Jesus earned salvation for all lost people from every nation on earth.

[14] M. I. Lk 8:11: Christians should faithfully do their job of preaching and leave the results to the Holy Spirit.

[15] M. M. Ac 4:28: The heavenly Father is always in full control of his mission to all nations of the world.

Chapter 27

Paul Sails for Rome 27:1-12

27:1 *And when it was decided that we should sail for Italy, they delivered Paul and some other prisoners to a centurion of the Augustan Cohort named Julius.*

27:2 *And embarking in a ship of Adramyttium, which was about to sail to the ports along the coast of Asia, we put to sea, accompanied by Aristarchus, a Macedonian from Thessalonica.*

27:3 *The next day we put in at Sidon. And Julius treated Paul kindly and gave him leave to go to his friends and be cared for.*

27:4 *And putting out to sea from there we sailed under the lee of Cyprus, because the winds were against us.*

27:5 *And when we had sailed across the open sea along the coast of Cilicia and Pamphylia, we came to Myra in Lycia.*

27:6 *There the centurion found a ship of Alexandria sailing for Italy and put us on board.*

27:7 *We sailed slowly for a number of days and arrived with difficulty off Cnidus, and as the wind did not allow us to go farther, we sailed under the lee of Crete off Salmone.*

27:8 *Coasting along it with difficulty, we came to a place called Fair Havens, near which was the city of Lasea.*

27:9 *Since much time had passed, and the voyage was now dangerous because even the Fast was already over, Paul advised them,*

27:10 *saying, "Sirs, I perceive that the voyage will be with injury and much loss, not only of the cargo and the ship, but also of our lives."*

27:11 *But the centurion paid more attention to the pilot and to the owner of the ship than to what Paul said.*

27:12 *And because the harbor was not suitable to spend the winter in, the majority decided to put out to sea from there, on the chance that somehow they could reach Phoenix, a harbor of Crete, facing both southwest and northwest, and spend the winter there.*

27:1 Paul's Jewish enemies certainly must have been very angry at the result of Paul's hearing before the king and the governor; therefore, the fact that *"they delivered Paul and some other prisoners to a centurion"* (v 1) was very important for his safety. A centurion led 100 men; therefore, Paul was still under the protection of his Lord Jesus through the might of the Roman Empire as its prisoner, but was also still on assignment as a *prisoner* of his Lord Jesus (23:11; [1]M. M. Ac 4:28).

27:1-3 (1) In verses 1-3, we see that Julius, the centurion did two kind things in order to help Paul: **a)** First of all, in verse 1, Luke very subtly informs us that he was with Paul on his journey to Rome by saying, *"it was decided that we should sail for Italy."* This means that Julius very kindly allowed Luke to accompany Paul, even though Paul was his prisoner; therefore, he certainly could have forced Paul to go on board the ship alone. Therefore, it must have been very encouraging to Paul to have his dear brother in the faith with him to give him courage and support. And it was certainly once again the Lord of the mission who made this possible, so that Paul would not become discouraged ([2]M. M. Ac 5:1). **b)** And secondly, verse 3 says that *"Julius treated Paul kindly and gave him leave to go to his friends and be cared for."* This suggests that there must have been a church in Sidon, which was a Gentile, coastal town of Phoenicia; and Julius kindly allowed Paul and Luke to go ashore so that the Christians there to also *"care for"* and encourage them ([3]M. I. 1 Cor 12:26). **2)** Nevertheless, Julius was, of course, a tough, disciplined soldier; so why was he so kind to Paul and Luke? We can hope that, perhaps, Julius had been listening very carefully to the seed of God's Word that Paul had scattered so liberally before the king and governor. And then this powerful seed had sprouted and grown in his heart (Lk 8:5-7; [4]M. I. Lk 8:11).

27:11 Luke reports in verse 11, *"But the centurion paid more attention to the pilot and to the owner of the ship than to what Paul said."* Even though this decision eventually led to the total loss of the ship, the Lord of the mission must have had some reason why he wanted his missionary to get to Rome as soon as possible, since Paul's more cautious advice would have led to a delay of many months. Neither the army officer nor the owner of the ship was actually in control of the situation; the Lord Jesus was in full control of them as well as the mighty wind and waves. He would carry out his perfect plan, in spite of all odds (M. M. Ac 4:28).

The Storm at Sea 27:13-38

27:13 *Now when the south wind blew gently, supposing that they had obtained their purpose, they weighed anchor and sailed along Crete, close to the shore.*
27:14 *But soon a tempestuous wind, called the northeaster, struck down from the land.*
27:15 *And when the ship was caught and could not face the wind, we gave way to it and were driven along.*
27:16 *Running under the lee of a small island called Cauda, we managed with difficulty to secure the ship's boat.*
27:17 *After hoisting it up, they used supports to undergird the ship. Then, fearing that they would run aground on the Syrtis, they lowered the gear, and thus they were driven along.*
27:18 *Since we were violently storm-tossed, they began the next day to jettison the cargo.*
27:19 *And on the third day they threw the ship's tackle overboard with their own hands.*
27:20 *When neither sun nor stars appeared for many days, and no small tempest lay on us, all hope of our being saved was at last abandoned.*
27:21 *Since they had been without food for a long time, Paul stood up among them and said, "Men, you should have listened to me and not have set sail from Crete and incurred this injury and loss.*
27:22 *Yet now I urge you to take heart, for there will be no loss of life among you, but only of the ship.*
27:23 *For this very night there stood before me an angel of the God to whom I belong and whom I worship,*

27:24 *and he said, 'Do not be afraid, Paul; you must stand before Caesar. And behold, God has granted you all those who sail with you.'*
27:25 *So take heart, men, for I have faith in God that it will be exactly as I have been told.*
27:26 *But we must run aground on some island."*
27:27 *When the fourteenth night had come, as we were being driven across the Adriatic Sea, about midnight the sailors suspected that they were nearing land.*
27:28 *So they took a sounding and found twenty fathoms. A little farther on they took a sounding again and found fifteen fathoms.*
27:29 *And fearing that we might run on the rocks, they let down four anchors from the stern and prayed for day to come.*
27:30 *And as the sailors were seeking to escape from the ship, and had lowered the ship's boat into the sea under pretense of laying out anchors from the bow,*
27:31 *Paul said to the centurion and the soldiers, "Unless these men stay in the ship, you cannot be saved."*
27:32 *Then the soldiers cut away the ropes of the ship's boat and let it go.*
27:33 *As day was about to dawn, Paul urged them all to take some food, saying, "Today is the fourteenth day that you have continued in suspense and without food, having taken nothing.*
27:34 *Therefore I urge you to take some food. It will give you strength, for not a hair is to perish from the head of any of you."*
27:35 *And when he had said these things, he took bread, and giving thanks to God in the presence of all he broke it and began to eat.*
27:36 *Then they all were encouraged and ate some food themselves.*
27:37 *(We were in all 276 persons in the ship.)*
27:38 *And when they had eaten enough, they lightened the ship, throwing out the wheat into the sea.*

27:24-25 As the storm raged, Paul certainly must have been remembering his Lord's Words of encouragement in (23:11), *"Take* *courage, for as you have testified to the facts about me in Jerusalem, so you must testify also in Rome."* Therefore, he knew that they must somehow reach Rome. However, since they were now in such a desperate situation, they all needed further Words of encouragement. Thus, an angel repeated the same encouraging Words to him in verse 24, *"Do not be afraid, Paul; you must stand before Caesar. And behold, God has granted you all those who sail with you."* Not only did his Words fill everyone with courage, but they also confirmed for everyone else on the ship that Paul was indeed a messenger of God. Paul, no doubt, had told them as much; but many of them may not have believed him. Thus, the encouraging Words from the angel also "watered" the seeds that Paul had planted in their hearts with his witness to Jesus and they trusted his advice in verse 25 to *"take heart, men"* ([5]M. M. Ac 4:28).

27:31 As their situation became more and more desperate, the sailors tried to selfishly save themselves and leave the passengers helpless without anyone who knew how to sail the ship. This would certainly have been fatal for all of them; therefore, Paul took charge of the situation (as a servant of his Lord) and talked to the officer and soldiers and said in verse 31, *"Unless these men stay in the ship, you cannot be saved."* And, even though Paul was a prisoner, they listened to him because they believed the Words of the angel and knew that Paul was a servant of God. He certainly had no authority in their eyes apart from that. Thus the control of the Lord Jesus over their lives was very obvious throughout this entire episode (M. M. Ac 4:28).

The Shipwreck 27:39-44

> 27:39 *Now when it was day, they did not recognize the land, but they noticed a bay with a beach, on which they planned if possible to run the ship ashore.*
> 27:40 *So they cast off the anchors and left them in the sea, at the same time loosening the ropes that tied the rudders. Then hoisting the foresail to the wind they made for the beach.*
> 27:41 *But striking a reef, they ran the vessel aground. The bow stuck*

> *and remained immovable, and the stern was being broken up by the surf.*
> 27:42 *The soldiers' plan was to kill the prisoners, lest any should swim away and escape.*
> 27:43 *But the centurion, wishing to save Paul, kept them from carrying out their plan. He ordered those who could swim to jump overboard first and make for the land,*
> 27:44 *and the rest on planks or on pieces of the ship. And so it was that all were brought safely to land.*

27:43 The soldiers wanted to kill the prisoners to save their own lives, because, if any of them had escaped, the soldiers would have been killed. But once again, the centurion showed that, even if he didn't already have faith in Jesus, he was at the very least very kind to the Lord Jesus' missionaries. He intervened and prevented his soldiers from killing the prisoners (M. M. Ac 4:28).

---

[1] M. M. Ac 4:28: The heavenly Father is always in full control of his mission to all nations of the world.

[2] M. M. Ac 5:1: The Holy Spirit often uses personal relationships in order to strengthen the unity of the family of the Church.

[3] M. I. 1 Cor 12:26: In the one Body of Christ there should be no divisions, but instead each member should care for the other members, so that if one member suffers, all should suffer together; and if one member is honored, all should rejoice together.

[4] M. I. Lk 8:11: Christians should faithfully do their job of preaching and leave the <u>results</u> to the Holy Spirit.

[5] M. M. Ac 4:28: The heavenly Father is always in full control of his mission to all nations of the world.

Chapter 28

Paul on Malta 28:1-10

28:1 *After we were brought safely through, we then learned that the island was called Malta.*
28:2 *The native people showed us unusual kindness, for they kindled a fire and welcomed us all, because it had begun to rain and was cold.*
28:3 *When Paul had gathered a bundle of sticks and put them on the fire, a viper came out because of the heat and fastened on his hand.*
28:4 *When the native people saw the creature hanging from his hand, they said to one another, "No doubt this man is a murderer. Though he has escaped from the sea, Justice has not allowed him to live."*
28:5 *He, however, shook off the creature into the fire and suffered no harm.*
28:6 *They were waiting for him to swell up or suddenly fall down dead. But when they had waited a long time and saw no misfortune come to him, they changed their minds and said that he was a god.*
28:7 *Now in the neighborhood of that place were lands belonging to the chief man of the island, named Publius, who received us and entertained us hospitably for three days.*
28:8 *It happened that the father of Publius lay sick with fever and dysentery. And Paul visited him and prayed, and putting his hands on him healed him.*
28:9 *And when this had taken place, the rest of the people on the island who had diseases also came and were cured.*
28:10 *They also honored us greatly, and when we were about to sail, they put on board whatever we needed.*

28:2 It was, of course, not merely an "accident" that they landed on the small island of Malta because it would have been much more likely that their ship would have run aground on the much larger island of Sicily. And we also know that it was not merely the storm that was directing the ship; rather it was, of course, the Lord of the mission who was still in control ([1255]M. M. Ac 4:28). Furthermore, the Lord had also prepared the hearts of the people on Malta, who were Gentiles, because Luke says, in verse 2, that *"the native people showed us unusual kindness"* ([1256]M. M. Ac 4:34).

28:3, 8 Nor was it merely an "accident," of course, that the snake bit Paul and no one else (v 3). Furthermore, Paul did more miracles of healing on the island, including the fact that he healed the father of Governor Publius (v 8). All of these miracles, therefore, were very effective in <u>attracting</u> the local people to listen to the Gospel from Paul; and, more importantly, the governor was also <u>attracted</u> to hearing Paul. And this was obviously the main reason why the Lord Jesus had brought Paul to this small island, so that he could preach the Gospel to yet another Gentile in a high position ([1257]M. I. Ac 3:6 & [1258]Ac 21:26).

Paul Arrives at Rome 28:11-16

> 28:11 *After three months we set sail in a ship that had wintered in the island, a ship of Alexandria, with the twin gods as a figurehead.*
> 28:12 *Putting in at Syracuse, we stayed there for three days.*
> 28:13 *And from there we made a circuit and arrived at Rhegium. And after one day a south wind sprang up, and on the second day we came to Puteoli.*
> 28:14 *There we found brothers and were invited to stay with them for seven days. And so we came to Rome.*
> 28:15 *And the brothers there, when they heard about us, came as far as the Forum of Appius and Three Taverns to meet us. On seeing them, Paul thanked God and took courage.*
> 28:16 *And when we came into Rome, Paul was allowed to stay by himself, with the soldier that guarded him.*

28:14-15 The first contact that the mission team of Paul and Luke had with other Christians was in Puteoli. Verse 14 says that *"there we found brothers and were invited to stay with them for seven days."* How happy they must have been! And what a welcome rest! Then, since there must have been many people who were constantly traveling between Rome and its port city, Puteoli, it's no surprise that verse 15 says that the Christians in Rome *"heard about us;"* and, *"on seeing them, Paul thanked God and took courage."* And what a joyous reunion that must have been, since Paul's final greetings in his letter to the Christians in Rome (Rom 16:3-16) indicate that he already knew many of them! How encouraging, indeed, after all that the mission team had been through! More than once they were very near to death, yet their dear Lord had brought them safely through it all to their final destination ([1259]M. M. Ac 4:28 & [1260]Lk 6:22).

28:14, 16 (1) The fact that the centurion was apparently willing to keep his whole contingent of 100 men in Puteoli for a whole week (v 14), so that Paul could visit the Christians there, is another strong indication that he also had faith in Jesus. Then, the final kindness that he showed to Paul was that he must have given a very good report about Paul to the garrison commander. According to verse 16, *"Paul was allowed to stay by himself, with the soldier that guarded him."* Therefore, this was, as far as we know, how Paul lived the rest of his life. He was a prisoner and still protected by the might of Rome, but at the same time he was free to welcome fellow Christians, so that they could build each other up in the faith ([1261]M. I. Lk 4:17). **2)** However, some scholars see some hints of two things in Paul's Pastoral Letters: **a)** that he was eventually freed after a second imprisonment, since he was, of course, not guilty of any crime against the Empire. **b)** And that he may even have gone on the mission trip to Spain which he had long dreamed of doing (Rom 15:24, 28).

Paul in Rome 28:17-31

> 28:17 *After three days he called together the local leaders of the Jews, and when they had gathered, he said to them, "Brothers, though I had done nothing against our people or the customs of our*

fathers, yet I was delivered as a prisoner from Jerusalem into the hands of the Romans.

28:18 *When they had examined me, they wished to set me at liberty, because there was no reason for the death penalty in my case.*

28:19 *But because the Jews objected, I was compelled to appeal to Caesar--though I had no charge to bring against my nation.*

28:20 *For this reason, therefore, I have asked to see you and speak with you, since it is because of the hope of Israel that I am wearing this chain."*

28:21 *And they said to him, "We have received no letters from Judea about you, and none of the brothers coming here has reported or spoken any evil about you.*

28:22 *But we desire to hear from you what your views are, for with regard to this sect we know that everywhere it is spoken against."*

28:23 *When they had appointed a day for him, they came to him at his lodging in greater numbers. From morning till evening he expounded to them, testifying to the kingdom of God and trying to convince them about Jesus both from the Law of Moses and from the Prophets.*

28:24 *And some were convinced by what he said, but others disbelieved.*

28:25 *And disagreeing among themselves, they departed after Paul had made one statement: "The Holy Spirit was right in saying to your fathers through Isaiah the prophet:*

28:26 *"'Go to this people, and say, You will indeed hear but never understand, and you will indeed see but never perceive.*

28:27 *For this people's heart has grown dull, and with their ears they can barely hear, and their eyes they have closed; lest they should see with their eyes and hear with their ears and understand with their heart and turn, and I would heal them.'*

28:28 *Therefore let it be known to you that this salvation of God has been sent to the Gentiles; they will listen."*

28:30 *He lived there two whole years at his own expense, and welcomed all who came to him,*

28:31 *proclaiming the kingdom of God and teaching about the Lord*

Jesus Christ with all boldness and without hindrance.

28:17-20 In verses 17-20, we see how eager Paul was to establish a good relationship with the Jewish community in Rome, since, after only three days, he *"called together the local leaders of the Jews"* (v 17). He obviously assumed that they had heard from the Jews in Jerusalem about why he was a prisoner; and if that were the case, they would perhaps not only be trying to find ways to kill him, but more importantly they would be offended by his Gospel message. Thus, Paul was eager to tell them the truth about three things: **a)** First of all, he said in verse 17, *"Brothers, though I had done nothing against our people or the customs of our fathers, yet I was delivered as a prisoner from Jerusalem into the hands of the Romans."* The initial charge against him that he had violated a Jewish custom or a Law of God was completely false. **b)** Then, Paul continued in verse 18, *"When they had examined me, they wished to set me at liberty, because there was no reason for the death penalty in my case."* He was also not guilty of any crime against the Empire, but the Jews forced him to appeal to Caesar (v 19). **c)** And most importantly, Paul started to introduce them to his Lord Jesus in verse 20 by saying that *"it is because of the hope of Israel that I am wearing this chain."* He reminded them of their shared hope for a Messiah, so that he could teach them that Jesus had fulfilled all of their hopes (26:6). Furthermore, note that Paul once again boldly referred to his shameful chains in order to positively add more impact to his message about Jesus. He was *"not ashamed of the Gospel"* (Rom 1:16) nor of his chains, because he wore them for the sake of the Gospel ([1262]M. I. Ac 4:20 & [1263]M. M. Lk 6:22).

28:21-24 However, rather surprisingly, the Jews in Rome had not heard about the case against Paul, as verse 21 says, *"none of the brothers coming here has reported or spoken any evil about you."* However, they had heard bad reports about the Church; verse 22 continues, *"But we desire to hear from you what your views are, for with regard to this sect we know that everywhere it is spoken against."* They needed to hear the truth that the Lord Jesus had, in fact, fulfilled every promise in their Scripture (2 Cor 1:20); therefore his Church was not a separate, new sect at all. Rather, Jesus truly was their Messiah and everything that they had *"hoped"* for for so many years ([1264]M. M. Mt 1:22). Therefore, Paul witnessed to them a few days later about *"the kingdom of God…both from the Law of Moses and from the Prophets"* (v 23). And their own Scriptures did convince some of them that Jesus was indeed their Messiah (v 24), but not all of them believed ([1265]M. I. Lk 8:11).

28:25-27 (1) Since some of the Jews refused to believe their own Scriptures (v 24), Paul was compelled to send them away with a severe warning from the prophet Isaiah. He told them that "the Holy Spirit was right in saying" (v 25), *"Go to this people, and say, You will indeed hear but never understand, and you will indeed see but never perceive. For this people's heart has grown dull…"* (vs 26-27). While it's true that God's gracious mission-heart patiently waits for <u>all</u> of lost people to repent and return to him, he does not force his will on anyone (1 Tim 2:4; [1266]M. M. Lk 1:1 & [1267]M. I. Lk 3:3a).

28:28 Then, Paul emphasizes one of Luke's main themes in both of his books in verse 28 when he concluded, *"Therefore let it be known to you that this salvation of God has been sent to the Gentiles; they will listen."* The glorious Gospel about the cross and resurrection of Jesus is for *all* people from <u>all</u> nations on earth because God made all of them and loves each one dearly ([1268]M. M. Ro 1:16b).

28:30 As verse 30 says, Paul then *"lived there [in Rome] two whole years at his own expense, and welcomed all who came to him."* He had finally reached the final goal that his Lord had set for him—to proclaim the Gospel in Rome, the capital of the Empire (23:11; [1269]M. M. Mt 5:14). However, it's quite unlikely that any of the people who came to see him were Gentile leaders, which was still Paul's main target audience on his final fourth mission trip (23:11). Some scholars feel that he may have actually stood before the emperor himself, but that does not seem to be likely. And the speculation that he was eventually freed and even went to Spain on another mission trip is likewise uncertain (v 16; [1270]M. I. Ac 1:8).

28:31 According to verse 31, Paul had lost none of his <u>boldness</u> because he knew that he was still serving his Lord just as he had called him to do (9:15-16; 23:11; [1271]M. I. Ac 4:20). Furthermore, the fact that the final verse 31 also says that Paul taught *"without hindrance"* gives one final affirmation that the Lord of the mission, of course, continued to be in full control of his mission as the King of kings ([1272]M. M. Ac 4:28).

[1255] M. M. Ac 4:28: The heavenly Father is always in full control of his mission to all nations of the world.

[1256] M. I. Ac 4:34: Christians should care for needy people, so that they can not only help them, but the public would also see their love for them, which could also create opportunities for them to tell them the Gospel.

[1257] M. I. Ac 3:6: Christians should heal a person's physical problem by speaking the name of Jesus, so that everyone knows that it was the divine power of Jesus that healed him.

[1258] M. I. Ac 21:26: Christians should seek opportunities to witness to Jesus' name to people who are influential leaders in the target society, so that they can influence others to trust in Jesus.

[1259] M. M. Ac 4:28: The heavenly Father is always in full control of his mission to all nations of the world.

[1260] M. M. Lk 6:22: The Lord Jesus will surely bless a Christian in the midst of suffering for his sake; and he will also bless him with eternal life if he remains faithful to him.

[1261] M. I. Lk 4:17: Christians should always base their messages on the Bible, so that the Holy Spirit can use his holy Word to create and strengthen faith in their hearers.

[1262] M. I. Ac 4:20: Christians should boldly witness to the name of Jesus and allow nothing to stop their witness because it is the Holy Spirit's own message.

[1263] M. M. Lk 6:22: The Lord Jesus will surely bless a Christian in the midst of suffering for his sake; and he will also bless him with eternal life if he remains faithful to him.

[1264] M. M. Mt 1:22: God sent his only Son, Jesus to be born as a true human being, so that he could save all of his brothers and sisters of all nations by fulfilling all of God's promises in the Old Testament.

[1265] M. I. Lk 8:11: Christians should faithfully do their job of preaching and leave the results to the Holy Spirit.

[1266] M. M. Lk 1:1: Jesus earned salvation for all lost people from every nation on earth.

[1267] M. I. Lk 3:3a: Christians should, in love, warn lost people who do not repent.

[1268] M. M. Ro 1:16b: The Gospel is so powerful because it contains the central truth that Jesus rose from the dead with a glorified body in order to save all of his brothers and sisters from sin and death.

[1269] M. M. Mt 5:14: When the Holy Spirit creates faith in a person's heart, he also graciously gives him a new mission-heart that is eager to shine the light of the Gospel throughout the whole world.

[1270] M. I. Ac 1:8: Christians should go and witness about Jesus to all who are lost from all languages and cultures by depending on the power of the Holy Spirit to help them bridge all of the language/cultural boundaries whether they are relatively easy, as in their own language, or extremely difficult.

[1271] M. I. Ac 4:20: Christians should boldly witness to the name of Jesus and allow nothing to stop their witness because it is the Holy Spirit's own message.

[1272] M. M. Ac 4:28: The heavenly Father is always in full control of his mission to all nations of the world.

www.ingramcontent.com/pod-product-compliance
Lightning Source LLC
Chambersburg PA
CBHW081212170426
43198CB00017B/2594